D0116889

Shaping the College Curriculum

Related Titles of Interest

Faculty Work and Public Trust: Restoring the Value of Teaching and Public Service in American Academic Life
James S. Fairweather
ISBN: 0-205-17948-7

College Teaching Abroad: A Handbook of Strategies for Successful Cross-Cultural Exchanges
Pamela Gale George
ISBN: 0-205-15767-X

The Art of Writing for Publication
Kenneth T. Henson
ISBN: 0-205-15769-6

Multicultural Course Transformation in Higher Education: A Broader Truth
Ann Intili Morey and Margie K. Kitano
ISBN: 0-205-16068-9

Sexual Harassment on Campus: A Guide for Administrators, Faculty, and Students
Bernice R. Sandler and Robert J. Shoop
ISBN: 0-205-16712-8

Shaping the College Curriculum
Academic Plans in Action

JOAN S. STARK
and
LISA R. LATTUCA
The University of Michigan

ALLYN AND BACON
Boston   London   Toronto   Sydney   Tokyo   Singapore

Associate Publisher: Stephen D. Dragin
Editorial Assistant: Susan Hutchinson

Copyright © 1997 by Allyn & Bacon
A Simon & Schuster Company
Needham Heights, Massachusetts 02194

Library of Congress Cataloging-in-Publication Data

Stark, Joan S.
    Shaping the college curriculum : academic plans in action / Joan
S. Stark and Lisa R. Lattuca.
        p.   cm.
    Includes bibliographical references and index.
    ISBN 0-205-16706-3
    1. Education, Higher—United States—Curricula.   2. Curriculum
planning—United States.   3. Curriculum change—United States.
    I. Lattuca, Lisa R.   II. Title.
LB2361.5S73   1996
378.1′99′0973—dc20   95-44529
                                                          CIP

Printed in the United States of America

10 9 8 7 6 5 4 3 2 1   00 99 98 97 96

Contents

Preface   *xiii*

Need for a Curriculum Book   xiii

Audiences   xiv

Research Base   xv

Supplementary Materials   xv

Acknowledgments   xv

**PART I
DEFINING CURRICULUM**

Chapter 1
*From Influences and Assumptions
to Actions*   *1*

Purpose   1

Perspective and Organization   2

Chapter 2
*Defining Curriculum: An Academic
Plan*   *7*

Defining Curriculum   7

   Common Definitions of Curriculum   *7*

   *The Need for a Definitional
      Framework*   *8*

The Academic Plan as a Useful
   Definition   9

   Elements of Academic Plans   *10*

      Purpose: Knowledge, Skills, and
         Attitudes to Be Learned   11

Content: Subject Matter for
   Learning   12

Sequence: A Curricular
   Arrangement   13

Learners   13

Instructional Process: The Learning
   Activities   13

Instructional Resources: Materials and
   Settings   14

Evaluation   14

Adjustment: Improving the Plan   14

   *Advantages of Defining Curriculum as
      an Academic Plan*   *14*

Constructing Plans: Curriculum
   Development   15

   *Influences on Curriculum
      Planning*   *16*

      External Influences   18

      Organizational Influences   18

      Internal Influences   19

      Interaction of Influences   19

Academic Plans in Environmental
   Context   19

Chapter 3
*Curriculum Perspectives and
Frameworks*   *22*

Curricular Frameworks   22

Single Element Curricular Perspectives   24

   *Perspectives on Educational
      Purpose*   *24*

Perspectives on Content Selection   *26*

Perspectives on Learners   *27*

Curriculum Sequence Perspectives   *29*

Instructional Process Perspectives   *30*

*Perspectives on Evaluation and
Adjustment*   *30*

General Curriculum Frameworks   31

*Precollegiate Curriculum
Frameworks*   *31*

*Frameworks from Higher
Education*   *33*

Curriculum Planning and Design   37

Linking the Elements: Toward a Theory of
Curriculum   40

Chapter 4
**Recurring Debates about the College
Curriculum   42**

Influences Create a Complex Educational
Environment   42

Patterns of Curriculum Debate   44

*The Educational Purpose Issue:
Debating the Balance of General and
Specialized Studies*   *45*

Three Missions Solidify   46

The Twentieth Century   48

Current Diversity   49

Approaching the Twenty-first
Century   53

The Debate Continues   56

*Learners: Periods of Emphasis on
Access*   *56*

Opportunity Increases   57

Improved Preparation Fuels Rapid
Growth   58

The "Typical" Student Disappears   58

Entitlement for Learners   60

Maintaining Access in the Twenty-
first Century   60

*Content Debates: Prescription
versus Choice in Courses and
Programs*   *63*

Pressure for Choice Increases   63

Students Advocate Greater
Choice   65

Choice as the Century Turns   66

*Instructional Process: Occasional
Innovation*   *70*

Early Educational Experiments   70

Student Activists Encourage
Relevance and Freedom   70

Instructional Change: A Muted Debate
Gains in Volume   73

*Evaluation Debates: Emphasis on
Quality Control*   *73*

Government Funding and Quality
Control   74

Current Pressure for Evaluation   75

Influences and Potential Reforms   79

Chapter 5
Calls for Curriculum Reform   80

The Reform Era of the Late 1900s   80

Critical Reports   *80*

Constructive Proposals   *83*

Curriculum Reform and Academic
Plans   84

Purpose and Content   *84*

Sequence and Structure   *87*

Learners   *91*

Instructional Process   *94*

Instructional Resources   *95*

Evaluation and Adjustment   *96*

Summary   *97*

Impact of the Reform Proposals   97

External Influences   *98*

Organizational Influences   *101*

Internal Influences   *101*

The Pace of Change   102

A Doubting Voice   103

Relation to Earlier Debates   105

   *General versus Specialized
     Education   105*

   Prescription versus Choice   106

   Instructional Process   107

   Emphasis on Access   107

   Evaluation and Quality Control   108

New Approaches to Old Debates   109

**PART II
DEVELOPING CURRICULUM**

Chapter 6
Creating Academic Plans   **113**

Curriculum Planning: Realities and
   Prospects   113

Course Planning: A Faculty Role   113

   The Course Planning Process   114

   Influences on Planning Courses   115

      Content   116

      Context   118

      Form   119

      Evaluating and Adjusting   121

   *Patterns of Involvement in Course
     Planning   122*

Program Planning: A Group Endeavor   124

   Program Planners   124

   The Program Planning Process   125

   Influences on Program Planning   126

      Content   126

      Context   126

      Form   127

      Evaluating and Adjusting   129

   Patterns of Involvement in Program

Planning   129

College Planning: A Matter of
   Mission   129

   The Collegewide Planners   130

   *The Collegewide Planning Process and
     Influences   130*

   Evaluating and Adjusting   133

Systematic Design Models   133

   Course Design   134

   Program Design   136

   College-level Design   139

From Plan to Design   140

Chapter 7
Influence of Academic Fields   **141**

Influences of Academic Fields on
   Planning   141

   *Defining and Characterizing Academic
     Fields   143*

   *Characteristics of Traditional Academic
     Disciplines   144*

   *Characteristics of Professional and
     Occupational Fields   148*

Academic Fields and Course Planning   150

   *Content and Background
     Considerations   151*

   *Four Illustrative Profiles of Course
     Planning   154*

      Profile 1: Synoptic and Substantive
        Aesthetic Fields (Illustrative Case:
        Literature)   154

      Profile 2: Substantive Empiric Fields
        (Illustrative Case: Biology)   155

      Profile 3: Symbolic Communication
        Fields (Illustrative Case: English
        Composition)   155

      Profile 4: An Enterprising/Production
        Career Field (Illustrative Case:
        Business)   156

Mapping the Fields on Content
Dimensions   156

Academic Fields and Program
Planning   158

*Disciplinary Major Programs in Arts
and Sciences   158*

Curricular Coherence   160

Critical Perspectives   160

Connecting Learning   162

*Undergraduate Professional Major
Programs   163*

Curricular Dimensions of
Undergraduate Professional
Programs   164

Coherence, Connectedness, Critical
Perspectives, and Academic
Time   167

Occupational Major Programs   168

Designing Balanced Courses and
Programs   169

*Using Influence Well: Achieving
Balance   169*

Balancing Attention to Characteristics
of Academic Fields   171

Balancing Purpose and Content   172

Balancing Coherence and Critical
Perspectives   172

Balancing Discourse
Communities   174

Balancing Scholarship and Its
Application   175

*Negotiating Linkages among Academic
Fields   176*

Building on the Strength of Academic
Fields   178

Chapter 8
Influence of Learners   179

Learners' Influences on Academic
Plans   179

*Learners' Influence on Course
Planning   181*

Learners' Backgrounds   181

Learners' Preparation and
Ability   182

Learners' Goals   183

Learners' Effort and
Involvement   184

Program Plans   185

Collegewide Plans   187

Contemporary Views of Learning and
Learners   187

What Is Cognition?   188

Cognitive Influences   188

Intelligence/Ability   189

Cognitive Styles   190

Learning Strategies   192

Motivational Influences   193

Motivation   194

Goals   195

Interest and Involvement   196

Considering Learners in Course and
Program Design   196

*Building on Student Goals and
Enhancing Motivation   197*

*Improving Learning through
Involvement   199*

*Encouraging Integration, Coherence,
and Connectedness   201*

*Fostering Intellectual
Development   202*

*Academic Plans for Diverse
Learners   206*

*Enhancing Students' Learning
Strategies   207*

Developing Intentional Learners   208

Establishing Two-way Communication with
Learners   209

Chapter 9
Selecting Instructional Processes   212

Translating Content to Instructional
    Form   212

Selecting Instructional Processes for
    Courses   214

   *Educational Objectives: Product of
      Purpose and Content   214*

   *Teaching Style: Product of Content and
      Faculty Background   216*

   *Choosing Forms for
      Implementation   217*

   *Instructional Variations for
      Courses   220*

   *Influence of Educational Context and
      Environment   222*

      College and Program Goals   224

      Faculty Time and Incentives   226

      Learners' Goals   226

      Available Resources   227

      Organizational Structures and
         Traditions   229

Selecting Instructional Processes for
    Programs and Colleges   230

   *Contextual Influences on General
      Education Programs   231*

   *Contextual Influences on Major
      Fields   232*

      Accreditors and Professional
         Associations   232

      Employers, Articulation, and Practical
         Matters   233

   *Organizational Structures, Traditions,
      and Adaptations   233*

Expanding Choice among Instructional
    Processes   235

   *Fostering Intellectual
      Development   236*

      Developing Study Skills and Learning
         Strategies   237

      Promoting Reflection and
         Metacognition   238

      Cultivating Effective Thinking   239

      Encouraging Research and
         Inquiry   244

      Fostering Intentional Learning   245

   *Increasing Motivation, Encouraging
      Involvement, and Achieving
      Integration   248*

      Modifying Lectures   249

      Using Discussions as Active
         Processes   251

      Case Studies and Their
         Variations   252

      Collaborative and Cooperative
         Learning   253

      Peer Teaching   255

      Learning Communities   255

      Extending Classrooms   256

   *Creating Learner-Centered Academic
      Plans   257*

      Establishing Classroom and Program
         Environment   257

      Establishing and Communicating
         Expectations   259

      Individualizing Instructional
         Processes   263

Reflecting on Planning and Teaching   264

Chapter 10
*Evaluating and Adjusting Academic
Plans   266*

Evaluating Courses and Programs   266

How Faculty Evaluate and Adjust Academic
    Plans   268

   Course Plans   269

      Professional Judgment   269

      Student Opinion   270

      Other Opinions   271

      Making Adjustments   272

Program Plans   274

    Evaluating Programs   274

    Making Adjustments   276

Collegewide Plans   278

    Internal Evaluations   279

    External Evaluations   280

    Making Adjustments   281

Evaluation Models: An Overview   282

Expanding the Range of Useful Evaluation
Models   287

Informal Assessment   287

    Classroom/Course Assessment   287

    Program Evaluation   289

    Collegewide Evaluation   290

Student-Centered Evaluation   291

    Course Level   291

    Program Level   293

    College Level   294

Goal-Free Evaluation   295

    Course Level   295

    Program Level   295

    College Level   295

Goal-Focused Evaluation   296

    Course Level   296

    Program Level   300

    College Level   303

Evaluating Evaluation   308

PART III
ENHANCING CURRICULUM

Chapter 11
Administering Academic Plans and
Guiding Change   310

Who Administers Academic Plans?   310

Curriculum Leadership and Administrative
Roles   314

*Establishing the Educational
Environment (Managerial Roles:
Mentor; Facilitator)   315*

    Shared Responsibility and Freedom to
Experiment   316

    Open Communications and High
Expectations   318

*Developing Academic Plans
(Managerial Roles: Producer;
Director)   319*

    Choosing Faculty Who Value
Teaching   320

    Stressing the Centrality of
Learners   320

    Promoting Goal Congruence   321

*Coordinating Academic
Planning (Managerial Role:
Coordinator)   322*

    Providing Linkages and Encouraging
Articulation   322

    Examining Administrative
Functions, Structures, Policies,
and Processes   323

*Implementing Academic Plans
(Managerial Roles: Broker;
Coordinator)   325*

    Facilitating Instructional
Choices   325

    Providing Resources   325

    Providing Central Services and
Facilities   326

*Encouraging Evaluation (Managerial
Role: Monitor)   326*

    Establishing Evaluation Plans and
Expectations   327

    Developing Faculty Skills   327

    Maintaining Evaluation
Standards   328

    Using Evaluation Results
Internally   328

    Interpreting Evaluation Results
Externally   329

Adjusting Academic Plans (Managerial Roles: Monitor; Facilitator) 330

Administering Curriculum Adjustments 331

Selecting and Using Effective Change Strategies 332

Recognizing Change Decisions 333

External Influences, Adaptive Development, and Change 335

The Influence Process and Stages of Internalization 337

Leadership for Adaptive Development 340

Curriculum Change and Leadership: Past and Future 341

Chapter 12
Curriculum Changes in Progress   **343**

Curricular Challenges Colleges Face 343

Incorporating Diverse Perspectives 344

Multicultural Studies: Adoption Stage 346

Ethnic Studies 346

Women's Studies 347

Pluralist Voices and New Paradigms: Screening Stage 348

Globalization: Awareness Stage 349

Increasing Coherence 352

The Continuing Core Curriculum Debate: Adoption Stage 353

Interdisciplinary Approaches: Screening Stage 355

Connecting with Life and Work: Awareness Stage 357

Meeting Conflicting Expectations for Quality Education 360

Learning to Think Effectively: Adoption Stage 361

Assessing and Adjusting Quality: Screening Stage 362

Using Technology Effectively: Awareness Stage 363

Technology in Classrooms 364

Distance Learning 366

Implications of Changes for Academic Planning 367

Purpose and Content 367

Sequence 368

Resources 369

Instructional Process 370

Learners 370

Evaluation and Adjustment 371

Educational Environments 371

The Dynamic Curriculum 372

Chapter 13
Shaping Curriculum Research and Practice   **374**

The Academic Plan Theory as a Guide for Research 374

What Is Curriculum Theory? 375

Testing and Extending the Theory 378

Exploring Relationships among the Plan's Elements 379

Exploring Environmental Influences on Academic Plans 381

Connecting with Emerging Curriculum Research 381

The Academic Plan Theory as a Guide for Shaping Practice 385

Assumptions and Advantages 385

Intent and Its Development 386

Implementation 387

Reflective Evaluation and Adjustment 387

The Academic Plan Theory as a Guide for
Leaders in Enhancing Curriculum   387

    Asking the Right Questions   388

    *Asking the Questions in the Right
Way   389*

Guiding Responsiveness to Society   392

    Anticipating Important Influences   392

    Basing Decisions on Analysis   392

Shaping Academic Plans for the
Future   394

Bibliography   395

*Appendix: Timeline of Trends in
United States Curriculum:
1600s to 1994   424*

Index   439

Preface

NEED FOR A CURRICULUM BOOK

The nation's educational requirements are increasingly complex. College students face the contradictory demands of gaining more specialized knowledge and learning how to retrieve and interpret a broader knowledge base that extends beyond their own expertise. These students are of all ages and backgrounds, and some find the learning task easier and more comfortable than others. They receive their education in a wide array of institutions with different missions and standards in a country where freedom to teach and learn according to one's interests has traditionally been valued over centralized planning of advanced education.

Faculty, administrators, and scholars need new ways of thinking about curriculum so that they can respond to current challenges and future demands for excellence in higher education. A new view should recognize and accommodate wide variation among colleges, disciplines, and students. It should allow new ideas about the curriculum to be heard, honored, and examined as easily as traditional ones. It should highlight the utility of existing knowledge about curriculum planning and place the curriculum in its historical and social context. At the same time, it should present new and more systematic approaches that will help educators make effective decisions about all aspects of teaching and learning. This book, *Shaping the College Curriculum: Academic Plans in Action,* presents a

synthesis of previous knowledge and a new conceptualization of curriculum that will meet these criteria.

Ironically, as a period of agitation for curricular reform commenced in the 1980s, several important books about the college curriculum went out of print or became outdated. A standard reference work, Levine's *Handbook on the Undergraduate Curriculum* (1978), was not updated. Notable scholars with an enduring interest in the curriculum, such as Paul Dressel, passed away. Three important books by Dressel, *College and University Curriculum* (1968; 2nd ed., 1971), *Improving Degree Programs* (1980), and *On Teaching and Learning in College* (with Dora Marcus, 1982) had provided material for discussion among higher education administrators, scholars, and students for many years. The gap has only partially been filled by *Curriculum in Transition,* edited by Clifton Conrad and Jennifer Grant Haworth (1990), *Curriculum: A History of the American Undergraduate Course of Study Since 1636* by Frederick Rudolph (1977); and *Undergraduate Education: Goals and Means* by Rudolph Weingartner (1993).

Recently a few authors have written treatises on various curriculum topics or literature reviews summarizing curriculum studies and trends. These brief volumes include *Designing the Learning Plan* (Stark & Lowther, 1986), "Research on Academic Programs: An Inquiry into an Emerging Field" (Conrad & Pratt in J. C. Smart, ed. *Higher Education:*

Handbook of Theory and Research, Volume II, 1986); *Developing Academic Programs: The Climate for Innovation* (Seymour, 1988); *Meeting the Mandate: Renewing the College Departmental Curriculum* (Toombs & Tierney, 1991); and *New Life for the College Curriculum* (Gaff, 1991). Of course, many new books relevant to the field of curriculum have appeared that deal with teaching and learning in college or that cover special curriculum topics such as writing across the curriculum, freshman seminars, outcome assessment, general education, and interdisciplinarity. The result of this proliferation of short reviews and special-topic books is that one must read a great many books, articles, and critiques to acquire a broad sense of the history, status, and future of the undergraduate curriculum. No one author has recently provided the carefully selected summary my colleague and I are now attempting.

AUDIENCES

This book is intended for everyone concerned with planning, implementing, and evaluating college curricula. Many people share this responsibility, including faculty members, college administrators, trustees, and state and federal policy analysts and scholars. Many academic deans, department chairs, and curriculum committee chairs are eager for information relevant to their curriculum leadership roles. Task forces and curriculum committees who spend many hours trying to synthesize literature from a vast array of sources have called me seeking bibliographic suggestions. Their queries often begin "Has anything been written about . . . ?" The amount that has actually been written is daunting, but no comprehensive and coherent summary has been available. Various universities and associations have invited me to speak about the implications of curriculum research and have ordered materials my colleagues and I prepared about curriculum during five years of study in

the National Center for Research to Improve Postsecondary Teaching and Learning.

Many universities offer workshops or faculty development programs on curriculum and teaching. Their audiences, often teaching assistants, faculty members, and department chairs, will find that this book provokes thoughtful discussion. Discussions of curriculum are also included in both formal and ad hoc programs operated by scholarly and professional associations. For example, the American Council on Education provides workshops to help department chairs acquire needed academic leadership skills, while the Association for Institutional Research has created a professional development institute for new entrants to the field. We hope that this book will be useful for all of these varied persons, programs, and associations in workshops and everyday decision making.

Nearly one hundred doctoral programs in higher education throughout the country prepare a select number of administrators, scholars, policy analysts, and faculty for scholar/leader positions at various levels. Universities offering such formal programs almost always expect students to take a curriculum course. Their rationale is that no matter how far an administrator's daily activities may seem from the classroom, he or she should understand the academic program as the central reason for the administrative function. In our particular program at the University of Michigan, many students are experienced faculty and administrators who come to earn advanced degrees. Others are visiting scholars who simply wish to study a particular higher education topic. These colleagues typically appreciate systematic attention to the college curriculum. Although the book has evolved to meet needs of a broader audience, the needs of these doctoral students for a comprehensive book about curriculum were the original stimulus for this volume.

My colleagues teaching in higher education programs around the country have shared their frustration about the lack of a single current book focused on curriculum and curriculum reform. The popularity of a pamphlet on building a course syllabus based on the academic plan concept reinforced my view that I could inform these varied audiences—administrators, faculty members, higher education students, and researchers—by preparing this book. Because the book broadly covers the history and nature of the college curriculum, curriculum development, administration, organization, and evaluation, as well as emerging curriculum research and challenges, it forms a conceptual introduction to the topic that some will wish to expand by reading more detailed literature. I hope that most readers will read the entire book, because our discussion of the curriculum as an integrated plan is itself a seamless presentation. Some will read alone, but I suggest that the book forms an excellent basis for informal or structured discussion with colleagues.

RESEARCH BASE

The book draws on a great deal of research I have conducted with various colleagues from 1986 to 1994. Only a part of this work has been readily accessible to those working in the everyday task of curriculum development. Because we refer to these studies so often in the text, we have summarized them briefly here.

We conducted several studies of course planning among college faculty, including interviews of nearly 100 faculty members and some of their students in varied types of colleges, and a nationally representative survey of over 2,500 full- and part-time instructors teaching introductory and advanced courses. We also interviewed faculty members in some very different colleges about their perceptions of how curriculum development occurs at the program level in the major field.

During the same period, we conducted a second nationally representative study of edu-

cational goals and processes endorsed by faculty teaching in twelve different professionally directed programs at over 700 colleges. Again, we interviewed many professors and followed up to discuss by phone their written comments about how they try to achieve specific outcomes characteristic of their particular type of professional education.

Over a period of eighteen months, working with a group of curriculum leaders from eight professional fields and their institutional colleagues from the liberal arts, we grappled with the ways in which the two types of curricula are similar and different in their goals and educational processes. Finally, we have gained a great deal of knowledge through consultation with various colleges around the country which enabled us to observe first-hand their efforts to develop effective academic plans.

SUPPLEMENTARY MATERIALS

Readers of this book have different information needs. Some leaders of formal workshops or classes may desire auxiliary materials to help group members focus their thinking and launch discussions concerning the material in the book. To assist in these efforts, I have prepared a separate instructional guide with learning objectives, active learning exercises, and suggested additional readings for each chapter.

ACKNOWLEDGMENTS

Many individuals and groups have contributed to the development of ideas in this book. My colleague and husband, Malcolm A. Lowther, contributed many of the early ideas during our work together between 1984 and 1991. During those years a number of sources of funding assisted our research and, thus, the development of ideas in the book. I thank the Center for the Study of Higher and Postsecondary Education, as well as the

Offices of Research and Academic Affairs at the University of Michigan, the Spencer Foundation, the Fund for the Improvement of Postsecondary Education, and the Office of Educational Research and Improvement, U.S. Department of Education.

Lisa Lattuca was my valued intellectual companion during the three years that I worked on the book. She completed extensive literature searches, wrote first drafts of many difficult sections, and helped to make the entire conceptual development flow smoothly. Marlene Francis commenced this project with me in 1991 by listening to and analyzing the progress of my curriculum class. From this experience she contributed many essential ideas about the organization of the book and made contributions to specific chapters. Karen Zaruba and Ann Killenbeck assisted with the research on the history and current status of the curriculum, commented on various drafts and performed many other essential tasks. Lavina Fielding Anderson wisely and conscientiously edited the penultimate draft and prepared the index. My longtime secretary and friend Linda Stiles helped in numerous ways, not only with the book but by keeping my life free of distracting tasks and my office cheerfully quiet.

Several classes of students in the Center for the Study of Higher and Postsecondary Education at the University of Michigan tried out these ideas in fledgling and more mature forms. Other students became research assistants participating in studies that informed the development of this book, especially on undergraduate professional education, the role of the disciplines, course planning, program planning, and program review. I also wish to thank William Toombs of Pennsylvania State University for his helpful review of the manuscript. Finally, I owe a great debt to the giants who provided inspiration and background for my work and whose own work is no longer available in print.

Joan S. Stark
Ann Arbor, Michigan

Shaping the College Curriculum

CHAPTER 1

From Influences and Assumptions to Actions

PURPOSE

As we approach the year 2000, many American educators and public leaders are calling for new thinking and change in the college curriculum. Organizational, financial, political, and governance issues dominated meetings of higher education leaders and scholars during the 1960s and 1970s, with little direct attention to the educational program. However, during the 1980s, national attention refocused on teaching and learning at all levels, including colleges. Leaders of higher education began to appraise directly what is taught, how it is taught, and what is learned. In 1989 the governors of all fifty states and the U.S. president jointly established goals for educational reform, targeting the year 2000 as the time to see results.

The goal of this book is to contribute to the reform effort and discussion by offering some perspectives on the college curriculum, by analyzing the forces that shape it, and by suggesting routes to improvement. Historically and currently, the college course of study is determined by a complex network of assumptions, background factors, and purposes.

Because of this complexity, improvement requires that educators define what they mean when they talk about curriculum. Earlier writers arrived at no general definition of curriculum. Consequently, discussions of curriculum have focused variously on the set of courses a college offers, the particular courses students take, or the goals and objectives of a course or academic program. The discussions may also include the teaching methods used to achieve the objectives, the extent to which students achieve them, or both of these.

As the pace of campus discussion about curriculum reform has increased, these purpose and process dimensions have become muddier instead of clearer. Faculty engaging in curriculum discussions often fail to communicate because they define curriculum in different ways or focus on different aspects. Similarly, college curriculum committees and academic administrators find themselves uncertain about the scope of their responsibilities; they are in charge of a territory with ambiguous boundaries. These communication failures and territorial uncertainties hinder both analysis of curriculum influences and proposals for change, rendering efforts to

1

improve more time consuming and less productive than need be. To avoid these difficulties, we expand a definition of curriculum
as an *academic plan* that we have proposed
elsewhere (Stark & Lowther, 1986) and link
this definition with a broad curricular influence framework previously developed (Stark,
Lowther, Hagerty, & Orczyk, 1986). We believe this definition has great potential to improve curriculum development by reducing
confusion about the scope of the curriculum
and its components.

Briefly put, the *academic plan* includes
decisions about what, why, and how a specific group of students are expected to learn,
as well as a way of knowing what they have
or have not learned, and of using this information to improve the plan. Described in a
different way, the plan is set in a *context,* including not only the institution, program, or
course mission but also the goals and characteristics of a specific group of learners. The
plan also includes a set of process strategies,
as well as an evaluation and feedback component. Defining curriculum as an academic
plan with these dimensions has helped to
focus our analysis. It helps us separate assumptions and background influences acting
on the plan from the plan itself and from the
conscious or unconscious decisions made
when developing it. That is, our definition
clarifies that neither those things that influence the plan, nor the planning process, are
synonymous with the plan itself.

Separating purposes and processes,
often confused in curriculum discussions,
broadly defines curriculum yet clearly de-
marcates its territory so that specific areas for
improvement can be identified. Our definition suggests that what needs improvement
are the skills involved in constructing a plan.
For example, during program review or
teaching evaluation, the definition suggests
improving faculty members' planning skills
rather than isolating their classroom demeanor for criticism. Such distinctions can
help educators avoid confusing curricular
purpose with process, teaching with learning,
and evaluations of teaching with evaluations
of student achievement.

Our focus on constructing the academic
plan as the central task in curriculum development in no way implies that either societal
influences on the plan or students' educational
goals are unimportant. Indeed, focusing on
the plan encourages us to recognize and analyze many separate influences on it from
sources within and outside of the university.
External influences (such as public views,
employer needs, and adequacy of funding) interact with organizational factors (like program linkages), and internal forces (such as
student characteristics and goals) to create an
environment strongly influencing the academic plan (Stark, Lowther, Hagerty, & Orczyk,
1986). We view the immediate context in
which curriculum is developed as a micro-en-
vironment, influenced by a broader contextual
environment.

PERSPECTIVE AND ORGANIZATION

Early in the book we introduce the idea of
defining curriculum as an academic plan and
discuss more fully the advantages of doing
so. One important advantage is that curriculum becomes a concept more amenable to
parallel examination at several levels of college organization. The idea of an academic
plan is viable for a single lesson, for a course,
a program, or an entire college curriculum. At
each of these levels within the college organization, there is a micro-plan, subject to the
broader influences on the plan exerted by
forces within the academic unit, within the
larger college or university organization and
from the outside community. The book
speaks to both the micro and macro views.

In Part I, we discuss a variety of perspectives that educators use to talk about curriculum, and we place these perspectives and
current demands for reform in the broad his-

torical context of society's influences on curriculum. In Part II, we develop the idea of the academic plan in some detail, considering separately the elements of an academic plan at each organizational level: course, program, and institution. This analytical approach, which deliberately (if somewhat artificially) separates the elements of a plan for examination, concludes with a discussion of an important but frequently overlooked element, evaluation. In Part III, we discuss the roles of faculty leaders and administrators as planners when supporting and enhancing modest adjustments in the curriculum as well as when guiding substantial change. Here we describe some curriculum changes that reflect current responses to the demands of today's world but challenge the plan itself. The examples we have chosen illustrate how diverse and competing influences determine the context in which academic plans are developed. We conclude by elaborating on the comprehensive theory of curriculum which has guided the book's organization. We summarize our argument that this theoretical framework is immediately useful as a way of thinking clearly about curriculum development. Simultaneously, it is also open to refinement and embellishment through research that extends knowledge about the relationships it describes and further increases its usefulness.

In Part I, "Defining Curriculum," (Chapters 1–5) the use of the academic plan as an organizing scheme for the book reveals our bias for careful attention to influences, purposes, and processes. While use of the scheme represents a specific perspective on the *process* of curriculum analysis, we do not intend to espouse any strong point of view about the nature of any specific academic plan. We do not try to convince readers that any specific topic or content area should be taught, that any particular teaching method is superior to another, nor that any specific method of evaluating academic results should be required. Rather, we emphasize that a plan should be intentionally constructed, that the developers should give conscious attention to choosing among alternatives, and that they should recognize the influences that affect these choices. To use a common illustration, every professor makes a choice of how to sequence subject content. For example, a history professor may arrange material chronologically, according to themes important in today's world, or according to the views of classic historical thinkers, or perhaps to coincide with recent lines of historical inquiry. The choice may be influenced by a view of how students learn best, by personal preference, or by such pragmatic constraints as the length and timing of scheduled classes. Whether a given reader, even an expert history teacher, would agree with how the material is arranged does not change the fact that a decision was made contributing to the total academic plan.

We view college faculty and administrators as concerned and creative professionals, willing to examine alternatives and to make curriculum planning decisions carefully and conscientiously. Educators make these decisions constantly. But we think that too many of them find themselves responsible for curriculum decisions without background about how academic plans have evolved historically and with little encouragement to consider the influence of both global and local influences on their own academic planning process. A "how to do it" book on curriculum development would be inappropriate for faculty from disciplines with disparate perspectives. Nor would such a book be useful for administrators and faculty leaders who are trying to stimulate faculty discussion and collaboration. Rather than providing prescriptions, we hope to present multiple viewpoints that help readers formulate their own positions on curriculum development and encourage them to share their differing views, using the rubric of curriculum as an academic plan to organize these varied ideas.

We define curriculum as an academic plan in Chapter 2. Then, in Chapter 3, we examine several perspectives from which others have analyzed curriculum plans, explicitly or implicitly. Reviewing the most comprehensive frameworks helps to highlight some of the assumptions that guide policy-level curriculum critics as well as faculty and administrators in their daily work.

After our review of perspectives and frameworks about curriculum, we examine the history of curriculum change in the United States in Chapter 4. In a necessarily brief summary, we identify some recurring debates about academic plans that have persisted over time and still face colleges today. We explore the underlying assumptions of some recurring themes in curriculum development, discussing trends in the history of curriculum that can inform future decisions.

To conclude Part I, in Chapter 5 we examine some criticisms of college curricula in the current period of reform. We explore some reasons that government leaders and others are discontent with the way academic plans are designed, implemented, and evaluated. We consider what assumptions undergird these criticisms, what specific aspects are of concern, and what general propositions for improvement have been made. We ask: What elements of academic plans are most severely criticized and why? Finally, we consider the influences that these critiques exert on colleges and place the recent criticisms in the perspective of the recurring curriculum debates.

In Part II, "Developing Curriculum," each of the chapters (Chapters 6–10) addresses three questions: In what ways are academic plans currently made? What are the influences that shape these plans and how strong are they? In what ways might the plans be improved? Each chapter is developed in two parts. The first section draws primarily on our own research to describe the ways in which faculty and groups of faculty actually plan, and the second suggests alternative ideas and strategies that might be used. We have taken this approach to encourage faculty members to examine their own practice and entertain new ideas but to avoid giving them prescriptions. When we do provide suggestions—for example, when we discuss how learners and instructional processes might be revised in light of new knowledge about learning—we submit our ideas as "postulates," encouraging faculty to accept them tentatively and adapt them in their own situation.

Our focus on planning, then on more intentional development, or design, begins with the course as the basic building block of college curriculum. In Chapter 6, we review curriculum planning and design, distinguishing between planning as it occurs in most colleges and design as a more theoretical and idealized process. We begin by describing our extensive research about how faculty members construct course plans and what, according to their own reports, they believe influences them. Then, moving to the program level for both general education and varied major fields, we ask what new influences affect the curriculum plan and the planning process, a group activity. Next, we examine collegewide curriculum planning and note the gaps in systematic attention to curriculum at this level. Finally, we review various strategies experts have developed for effective course and program design.

The influence of discipline in course and program design in higher education is so important that we devote a separate chapter (Chapter 7) to what is known about disciplinary differences and how these differences affect academic plans. Our analyses of faculty responses to curricular reform efforts bring new perspectives to this discussion. Another unique aspect of our discussion is an elaboration of how undergraduate professional fields differ from the traditional liberal arts disciplines and from each other.

The college professor creates the academic plan, but the learner creates meaningful learning from it. It is not sensible to talk about the "integrity" of the plan until the learner "integrates" new learning with old. With this caveat in mind, in Chapter 8 we discuss the influence of learners on the development of academic plans, emphasizing the diversity of learner backgrounds and cognitive styles. We ask: How and to what degree should learners be considered as the curriculum plan is constructed? How is the plan communicated to students? In Chapter 9, we review the decisions professors must make as they select learning resources and instructional activities to help accomplish their curricular goals. As contextual factors, we consider perennial organizational arrangements that constrain the selection of instructional alternatives and the limited opportunity professors typically have to expand their instructional skills and resources. We then summarize the rapidly emerging literature on active learning that can help faculty members increase the range of instructional alternatives. We note the strong possibility that rapidly advancing electronic technology will substantially change how instructional processes are selected and used. We make suggestions for improved syllabi at the course level and improved articulation of curricular goals at the program level.

In Chapter 10 we complete our discussion of the elements of an academic plan by discussing how evaluation is and might be carried out in courses and programs. Currently, college curriculum evaluation tends to be informal and non-systematic. We demonstrate the wide range of evaluation strategies available for different questions and different contexts by describing varied options such as client-centered evaluation, goal-free evaluation, and more structured goal-focused assessment. Viewing academic plans as dynamic rather than static entities, we emphasize how the results of evaluation and assessment can be used for improvement.

In Part III, "Enhancing Curriculum," (Chapters 11–13) we focus on the people and processes that keep the curriculum vital and responsive. Who is responsible for ensuring quality and for helping professors improve curriculum planning and teaching? What methods and what people are and should be involved to create a supportive environment that is regularly maintained and strengthened? How can strong curricular leadership in colleges and universities maximize encouragement to faculty and reduce hindrances to creativity?

We judge that both faculty members and administrators have important roles but the administrative support role becomes more prominent as one moves from the course to the program, and then to the college level. In Chapter 11 we discuss the variety of managerial and leadership roles administrators must play in curriculum development. Like the responsibility for creating, supporting, and administering the curriculum, evaluation of the plan is considered a responsibility faculty and administrators share. As we discussed some of the ideas in this chapter with administrators, they encouraged us to be more direct with suggestions for curriculum administration. Department chairpersons, in particular, feel the need for clear guidelines to help them define their role and suggested that we set forth principles that they might use as checklists. So our approach in Chapter 11 is more direct than in earlier chapters; it provides "guidelines" to support good course and program planning, rather than "postulates."

In Chapter 11, we also review processes of change and innovation as they apply to leadership for the college curriculum. From this review, we identify three major stages of change: awareness, screening and adoption. We develop the thesis that selected strong influences from society gradually become part of the internal agenda of colleges and universities. The stage of curriculum change, we hypothesize, is related to the degree of internalization of the demands made by external voices calling for change. Using this framework, we return in Chapter 12 to the broader view of influences that act on the educational environment and influence the construction of academic plans. We discuss three broad themes of curriculum change now in progress: incorporating diverse perspectives, increasing coherence, and meeting conflicting expectations for quality and access. Within each, we select and focus on three specific changes, one at each of the three stages of the change process.

In Chapter 13, the concluding chapter of the book, we return to the question of how our emerging theory of curriculum assists in meeting varied challenges. We outline our current state of knowledge of the relationships delineated by theory and suggest additional research that is needed to improve understanding of how curriculum is developed, evaluated, and enhanced. What do we need to know about the influences on the academic plan, about the relationships of elements in the plan itself, and about how systematic evaluation process and improved leadership can help us promote improvement? Educational research is another form of evaluation and feedback. What is curricular research today? What could it become? In this last chapter we also summarize how the academic plan theory guides curriculum practice for faculty and for administrators. And we share some challenging questions with which academic leaders continue to grapple.

In summary, the book proceeds from examining current and historical assumptions about the academic plan, to suggestions for improving its planning and design. Throughout, we examine the multiple influences on the college curriculum and its development. We consider ways in which the plans can be improved, examining supportive roles for college leaders as well as design and implementation roles for faculty. Finally, we suggest that both society's leaders and careful educational thinkers have roles in helping to understand and improve curriculum as well as to refine the definitions set forth here.

CHAPTER 2

Defining Curriculum: An Academic Plan

DEFINING CURRICULUM

Common Definitions of Curriculum

Ask any college student or graduate "What is the college curriculum?" and you will get a ready answer. Almost everyone thinks of the curriculum as a set of courses or experiences needed to complete a college degree. Probe more deeply, however, and you will find that these ready answers differ. Some respondents will refer to the total set of courses a college offers, others will mean the set of courses a specific student took, while still others will include informal experiences in college that are not listed in the catalog of courses. Some may include the ways teaching and learning took place as part of their definition, while others will not. At a superficial level, the public assumes it knows what the college curriculum is. Surely the news media commonly discuss the curriculum at this level of generality. But when we get down to specifics, we often focus on quite different phenomena. Even among those closely involved with the curriculum, a consistent definition is lacking. Knowledgeable respondents may point out

that the college curriculum cannot be defined unless one knows which college is under discussion since the mission, clients, and programs of colleges vary widely.

Over the years, as we solicited definitions from students, faculty, and others, we noted a certain consistency in the elements included in the definition. Most definitions include at least one and usually more of the following elements:

1. A college's or program's mission, purpose, or collective expression of what is important for students to learn
2. A set of experiences that some authorities believe all students should have
3. The set of courses offered to students
4. The set of courses students actually elect from those available
5. The content of a specific discipline
6. The time and credit frame in which the college provides education (Stark & Lowther, 1986)

Whichever of these elements provides the *primary* basis for an educator's definition of curriculum, an individual often mentions other elements, including the learner, the society, a personal view of the purpose of education, an opinion about how people learn, or some valued techniques for teaching and learning. Faculty members with broad curriculum development responsibilities typically will mention a greater number of elements in their curriculum definitions than persons without such duties. Yet they may be more definite about which elements should be included or excluded. We can infer that operational definitions of curriculum have evolved locally despite lack of formal agreement.

We have noticed, too, that faculty members seldom link the elements they mention into an integrated definition of the curriculum that suggests how it is developed. Rather, they tend to think of separate educational tasks or processes, such as establishing the credit value of courses, selecting the specific disciplines to be taught or studied, teaching their subject, dealing with student learning problems, and, less frequently, specifying objectives for student achievement or evaluating the curriculum. Probably the most common linkage that faculty do address is the structural connection between the set of courses offered and the related time and credit framework. These "structural" elements, based on the Carnegie credit unit, are relatively recent additions to the curriculum and tend to be emphasized primarily in American colleges (Toombs & Tierney, 1991).

Because college faculty members may feel uncomfortable discussing content in disciplines other than their own, it is not surprising that their efforts at curriculum change focus on curriculum structure, an aspect common to all fields. In fact, some observers have indicated that the most common curriculum change is "tinkering" with the structure (see Bergquist, Gould, & Greenberg, 1981; Toombs & Tierney, 1991). Even among knowledgeable individuals, this common usage of the term *tinkering* leads to an interpretation of "curricular change" as meaning a change in the course listings, college calendar, number of credits required of students, or other dimensions of the framework in which learning typically is arranged and often, by implication, in its cost.

One of the very important consequences of the lack of consensus on a definition of curriculum is that when the American public talks broadly about "improving curriculum," it means not only improving student learning at little or no increased cost, but also demonstrating the improvement. Meanwhile, faculty discussions of curricular change continue to focus on the structural framework rather than on the overall plan for learning envisioned for specific students.

The Need for a Definitional Framework

Since the mid-1980s the extensive literature urging educational reform has focused on the ambiguous term *curriculum.* This use of *curriculum* has been frequently modified by several equally ambiguous adjectives such as *coherent* and *rigorous* or undefined processes such as *integration.* The curriculum is said to "lack integrity" or to be in "disarray," but the meaning of these terms remains subject to the interpretation of the speaker and listener. Is it the mission or purpose of colleges that lacks integrity? the set of courses offered to implement the mission? the choice of courses made by the students? the actual experiences students take away from the courses? the teaching styles and strategies chosen by the professors? or all of the above? Only when there is a working definition of curriculum to guide the discussion and to help us differentiate among the various aspects of education in need of change will we be able to discuss curriculum reform meaningfully.

Nevertheless, faculty members, curriculum committee chairs, deans, instructional development specialists, academic vice presidents, assessment researchers, and teaching assistants regularly make decisions about the curriculum. In doing so, they talk about "curriculum" with the untested assumption that it constitutes a shared language (Conrad & Pratt, 1986). Yet it is no secret that faculty sometimes find it difficult to work together for curriculum improvement. In fact, in many colleges there is little formal discussion of curriculum except under the greatest duress. And when discussions do occur, participants tend to argue from varied definitions and assumptions without spelling them out, particularly in working groups that include many disciplines. Such discussions frequently grow contentious. It is no wonder that curriculum development is not popular work among college faculty.

Yet society and policymakers are calling faculty and administrators to account for perceived failures of the curriculum. Powerful constituencies are urging administrators and faculty to establish clear expectations for students, improve teaching and advising, use new technology, and measure student outcomes. Some forces in society push for a common learning for all college students; other equally vocal groups advocate cultural pluralism in the course of study. To provide a framework for productive discussions and effective decisions, faculty and administrators must come to some agreement on what the curriculum is and what aspects are to be targeted for improvement. Does improving the curriculum mean improving what is offered, what is studied, or what outcomes are measured? A vague definition of curriculum may suffice for the general population, but faculty and administrators have more specialized needs that require more precise definition.

To talk effectively about curriculum change in either an abstract or a technical sense, we must define curricular terms in useful ways. Most current definitions do not provide a framework that helps us understand the assumptions that undergird curriculum devel-

opment. And because they are general and nonspecific, most are not helpful in strengthening administrative support for the curriculum, in evaluating it, or in communicating its intentions to students. Choosing a definition for curriculum does not mean that everyone must agree about what content should be studied, how it should be studied, or who should study it. It certainly does not mean that everyone must agree on the specific skills or outcomes students must achieve. Our higher education system is characterized—indeed, distinguished—by diversity of students, programs, and institutions. It is unlikely that the college curriculum can, or should be, the same for all Americans.

Yet to see beyond the mechanistic structure of college programs, we need a framework. We must explicitly reject the common but incomplete definition of curriculum as a set of course offerings written down in a bulletin or catalog. Such a definition would require us to confine curricular change to swapping courses, as in a game of checkers, or, at best, deciding that some courses have more power or value than others, as in a game of chess. We must also reject that definition which construes curriculum as the set of courses a student has taken. If, using such a definition, the student has not acquired the desired outcomes, the primary implied adjustment to improve learning is that a different set should have been studied. An appropriate definition of curriculum should allow a wider range of corrective actions.

THE ACADEMIC PLAN AS A USEFUL DEFINITION

To remedy the lack of a comprehensive definition of curriculum, we suggest defining the curriculum as an "academic plan." A plan for any endeavor incorporates a total blueprint for action, including purposes, activities, and ways of measuring success. A plan implies both intentions and rational choices among alternatives to achieve the intentions. We define curriculum as an *academic* plan because its intention is to foster students' academic development. It is devised with a given group of students in mind and within the confines of objectives for those students. An important result of this focus is that it causes planners to put students' education—the primary reason for the existence of the college curriculum—first.

Viewing curriculum as a plan implies a deliberate planning process that focuses attention on important educational considerations which can vary by field, student body, institutional goals, instructor, and others. Despite these variations, the notion of a plan provides a template—a checklist, if you wish—that encourages a careful process of decision making. Every curriculum includes each element of the plan described below, whether conscious attention has been given to it or not, whether a deliberate decision has been made, or whether a default has been accepted. The plan exists whether or not it is (in someone's view) a "correct" plan. Thinking of curriculum as a plan encourages planners to consider major elements, rather than to advocate inclusion of specific content or use of particular instructional strategies.

We are not the first to use *plan* as a synonym for curriculum (see, e.g., Eisner, 1979, and Taba, 1962) or to argue that building a plan involves *decisions* (see Leithwood, 1985). Some have also argued for use of *design* (see Toombs, 1977–1978; Toombs & Tierney, 1991, 1993). We prefer *plan* because it communicates in familiar terms the kind of informal process that a broad range of faculty members shared with us in our extensive research on course and program planning (Stark, Lowther, et al., 1988, 1990). We typically use *plan* to describe the current state of affairs and introduce *design* when we wish to convey a revised and more intentional process that faculty members in any discipline might pursue after considering alternatives we discuss in this book.

Specifically, we propose that the academic plan should include at least the following elements:

1. *Purpose:* The general goals that guide the knowledge, skills and attitudes to be learned
2. *Content:* The subject matter or content within which the learning experiences are embedded
3. *Sequence:* An arrangement of the subject matter intended to lead to specific outcomes for learners
4. *Learners:* Information about the learners for whom the plan is devised
5. *Instructional Processes:* The instructional activities by which learning may be achieved
6. *Instructional Resources:* The materials and settings to be used in the learning process
7. *Evaluation:* The strategies used to determine if skills, knowledge, attitudes, and behavior change as a result of the learning process
8. *Adjustment:* Changes in the plan to increase learning, based on experience and evaluation.

Elements of Academic Plans

In this section we will introduce briefly each of the eight elements of the academic plan mentioned above and displayed in Figure 2-1. We view them as the core of an emerging theory of curriculum, although all the relationships among them have not yet been explored. Thus, in this chapter, we state the theory in its entirety. In later chapters, we will trace its roots, elaborate on it, and discuss its full implications.

One relationship among plan elements is well understood. From our interviews with faculty members, we have learned that purpose and content are nearly always closely re-

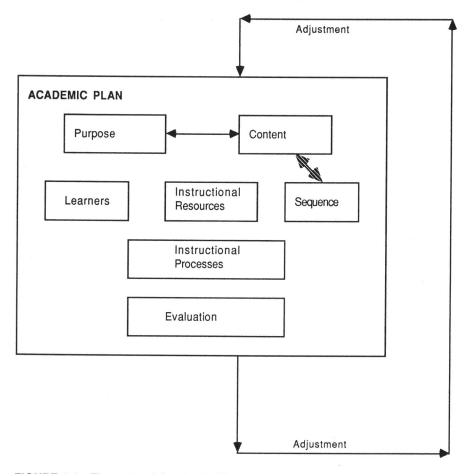

FIGURE 2-1   Elements of Academic Plans

lated elements of academic plans. Thus, we have shown their reciprocity with a double arrow in Figure 2-1. Frequently, faculty members link content and sequence as they plan but not consistently. Thus, we have shown the relationship between content and sequence with a dotted double arrow. We have arranged the other elements in the approximate order of their mention in many reports of faculty planning. For example, we know that faculty consider learners, resources, and sequence simultaneously, but after purpose and content. Despite our hunches about such relationships among other elements of the plan, we have avoided inserting more arrows because we do not wish to imply that these elements constitute a flow chart or that all curriculum planners do or must carry out their planning activities in a particular sequence. In fact, faculty reasonably pursue their planning steps in many different orders.

Purpose: *Knowledge, Skills, and Attitudes to Be Learned*

Discussions about curriculum typically grow out of strong convictions. Thus, we have placed the intended outcomes of education as the first element in the plan. The selection of knowledge, skills, and attitudes to be acquired reflects one's views about the purpose of collegiate education. Thus, in discussions of educational quality, it is not unusual to find that educators, policymakers, and the public express specific views about purposes and cite as support for their own views the opinions of prestigious others with congruent convictions about the curriculum.

In interviews and surveys with college faculty members in different fields, we have found them to hold varying beliefs about educational purpose (Stark, Lowther, Ryan, et al., 1988). Table 2-1 shows several broad statements describing some of these views. Purpose B, which we call "learning to think effectively," is the most commonly espoused purpose, but in any faculty group there are likely to be strong proponents for each of the other statements as well. Some of these statements will be strongly endorsed at one type of college and flatly denied as educational purposes at another type. Considering curriculum as an academic plan can direct attention to these differences in basic purposes of the plan, help to augment this list as necessary for a specific college, and launch discussion of curriculum development with some understanding of the underlying assumptions appropriate to the local setting.

Content: Subject Matter for Learning

Intended educational purposes can be achieved by studying many different topics. Despite the allegiance of most faculty mem-

---

TABLE 2-1   Statements of Educational Purpose Common among College Faculty

A. In general, the purpose of education is to make the world a better place for all of us. Students must be taught to understand that they play a key role in attaining this goal. To do this, I organize my course to relate its content to contemporary social issues. By studying content that reflects real life situations, students learn to adapt to a changing society and to intervene where necessary.

B. The main purpose of education is to teach students how to think effectively. As they interact with course content, students must learn general intellectual skills, such as observing, classifying, analyzing, and synthesizing. Such skills, once acquired, can transfer to other situations. In this way, students gain intellectual autonomy.

C. Education should provide students with knowledge and skills that enable them to earn a living and contribute to society's production. I believe a fundamental role for me as an instructor is to help students achieve their vocational goals.

D. Education should involve students in a series of personally enriching experiences. To meet this broad objective, I select content that allows students to discover themselves as unique individuals and thus acquire personal autonomy. I discuss appropriate activities and content with students in an effort to individualize the course.

E. In my judgment, education should emphasize the great products and discoveries of the human mind. Thus, I select content from my field to cover the major ideas and concepts that important thinkers in the discipline have illuminated. I consider my teaching successful if students are able to demonstrate both breadth and depth of knowledge in my field.

F. Whatever the curriculum, it should help students clarify their beliefs and values and thus achieve commitment and dedication to guide their lives. For me, the development of values is an educational outcome as important as acquisition of subject knowledge in the field I teach.

Source: From *Planning Introductory College Courses* by Stark, Lowther, Bentley, et al. (1990). Reprinted by permission of the National Center for Research to Improve Postsecondary Teaching and Learning, The University of Michigan.

bers to their specific disciplines, it would be difficult to argue that any field has a monopoly on encouraging students' intellectual or value development or ability to think effectively. And of course our society demands that students learn concepts and principles in many subjects. Thus, in our definition of the second element of the academic plan, we indicate that some subject matter typically must be selected to serve as the vehicle for learning. The separation of the first and second elements of the plan emphasizes that the purpose (or desired learning outcomes) and the subject matter are not synonymous.

Although not the same, subject matter goals and educational goals are surely interdependent. Faculty teaching in specific fields are more likely to endorse certain educational beliefs than others and to view their disciplines in ways related to these beliefs. For example, professors in social science fields are more likely than those in physical sciences to endorse Purpose A, "making the world a better place for us all." Furthermore, faculty from different fields may define desirable educational outcomes such as "thinking effectively" in different ways. These disciplinary differences in both intent and meaning complicate discussions of the curriculum. Placing purposes and content in the academic plan as two different interacting elements allows us to emphasize the distinction and helps clarify discussion.

Sequence: A Curricular Arrangement

By curricular *sequence* we mean the ways in which the subject matter is arranged to facilitate the learner's contact with it. We emphasize here not the mechanical and bureaucratic devices by which colleges organize their relationships with students (such as credit hours) but, rather, the assumptions behind how knowledge is conveyed and learned. For example, is the material presented chronologically or thematically? Is there a practice

component to accompany theoretical presentations? Is the new material taught meaningful to students because it is connected with their previous experiences? Is it meaningful because it is conveyed in a way that demonstrates its relevance to their future lives? Is the structure arranged so that students will see a broad picture, such as how inquiry is connected in a particular field of study, or how two fields are interrelated? To be sure, the use of resources, such as the existence of internships or laboratories may be related to these rationales for subject matter structure. The point is that the recognized pedagogical reasons should drive the sequencing of content and the choice of resources rather than the reverse.

Learners

The sequence of the academic plan, like other elements, must be related to the ability, previous preparation, and goals of the learner. Although there is little danger that professors will forget the sequencing typical of their discipline, some may overlook the specific students for whom the curriculum is intended. Yet whether the curriculum actually "works" may depend on whether the plan is reasonably congruent with student goals and needs. Stated another way, educators and students each have purpose, objectives, and a plan to reach those objectives. The interaction among all three elements for both—particularly the relation between the two plans—requires advance attention.

Instructional Process: The Learning Activities

Learning processes (and accompanying teaching processes) are often discussed separately from the curriculum, but, realistically, the choice of teaching and learning mode may dictate the learning outcomes. Some learning processes are more often used within certain disciplines than others. But by default, much college teaching is done by the lecture method, while at the same time faculty desire to teach students to think effectively—a process more easily achieved through active learning techniques. Although specific teaching strategies such as self-paced plans, collaborative learning, interdisciplinary seminars, or technological aids should not be viewed as panaceas, we have observed that separating such concepts of teaching from curriculum often results in their easier acceptance. We believe that faculty members will expand their repertoire of teaching strategies if pedagogical choices are consciously recognized as part of curriculum development.

Instructional Resources: Materials and Settings

Curriculum discussions seldom include considerations of learning materials, such as textbooks and media, or availability of settings, including classrooms, laboratories, and practicum sites. Yet the actual educational program is often structured by these items, and sometimes they are the primary source of an academic plan. Many faculty members observe that they arrange their teaching according to the organization of the selected textbook or the configuration of the classroom. This possibility is increasing with the sale of "complete learning packages" by publishers. If for no other reason than to encourage faculty members to examine and weigh varied alternatives to traditional materials, the plan should include these considerations.

Evaluation

Evaluation of the curriculum, through both program review and assessment of student outcomes for specific courses, is strongly emphasized today. Typically, however, curriculum review is viewed as a separate process from curriculum planning. In our view, the best time to devise an evaluation is when the

goals and objectives of the program are being clarified and the program designed. We suggest too that the list of elements we have defined in the academic plan helps to draw attention to the students' perspective. Most evaluation plans emphasize educators' goals as measured by student achievement rather than including students' goals.

Adjustment: Improving the Plan

Although some college curriculum development efforts include evaluation plans, we believe that our definition is unique in specifying the use of evaluation results to improve the plan and the planning process. Our scheme calls attention to this important step during the curriculum development process. Careful specification of the steps in the academic planning process can help to identify the particular strategy that needs improvement when the curriculum plan is revised.

Advantages of Defining Curriculum as an Academic Plan

We have pointed out some reasons that we view the idea of a plan as a useful template. Taking a very broad view, several additional advantages of defining curriculum as an academic plan are also apparent. We will discuss them briefly. We will return to them and add other advantages when we have more fully developed each element in our theory of curriculum.

Advantage 1. Promotes clarity about curriculum influences. Although curriculum discussions frequently focus on constraints to change, a variety of factors may influence the development of any plan; only some are constraints. When the curriculum is viewed as a plan, the potential influences on planning can be readily identified, assessed, and even purposefully varied, so that faculty and administrators can recognize both facilitators and constraints. The plan also helps curriculum planners recognize both facilitators and constraints for what they are, rather than confusing them with basic assumptions. This recognition is particularly useful in separating decisions based on constraints due to materials, settings, and structure from the important decisions about desired educational outcomes. We will discuss the importance of recognizing internal, external, and organizational curriculum influences shortly, and often.

Advantage 2. Applicable at lesson, course, program, and college levels. The definition of curriculum as an academic plan is applicable to all levels of curriculum. A plan can be constructed for a single lesson, for a single course, for aggregations of courses (usually called programs or majors), for broader organizational groupings of majors (such as a school or college), and for a college or university as whole (Stark & Lowther, 1988a). Defining curriculum as a plan allows plans at these several organizational levels to be examined for integrity and consistency.

Advantage 3. Encourages explicit attention to student learning. The definition of curriculum as an academic plan can facilitate and make concrete certain concepts that are now widely seen as essential in improving collegiate learning: clarifying expectations for students, encouraging student involvement, and assessing student achievement (National Institute of Education, 1984). The attempt to consider potentially fruitful new curricular approaches such as coherence, active learning processes, and consideration of student goals as part of the plan also builds on recent psychological understandings about how learners reconstruct their knowledge by meshing new information with old.

Advantage 4. Encourages faculty to share views as they plan. By examining their differing beliefs as they construct academic plans, faculty members in diverse fields can better recognize their commonalities, under-

stand how to bridge disciplinary gaps, and gain from each other's pedagogical skills. The recognition of different planning assumptions fosters respect for curricular pluralism and avoids acrimonious debates. Such sharing is especially useful in reducing tension during collegewide curriculum development, in constructing core curricula, or developing interdisciplinary themes.

Advantage 5. Encourages a dynamic view of curriculum development. The assumption of a built-in adjustment mechanism encourages iterative change by making it an expected part of regular practice. Evaluation becomes more closely tied to the curriculum because it is viewed as a normal adjustment in the plan, subject to consideration at every iteration of the planning process. Unlike the static definition of curriculum as a set of courses, a plan implies vigorous strategic adjustment as conditions change because the process of creating the plan can also be examined and influenced.

CONSTRUCTING PLANS: CURRICULUM DEVELOPMENT

To make the most of the opportunity supplied by our definition of curriculum, we distinguish the academic plan itself (curriculum) from the iterative process of planning (curriculum development). Defining curriculum as a plan not only calls attention to the necessity for a planning process but also helps to identify parts of the plan that are subject to specific influences and to identify intervention points for productive curriculum change. Each of the seven elements of the plan implies an associated planning step as follows:

1. *Purpose:* Setting educational goals and objectives
2. *Content:* Selecting subject matter
3. *Sequence:* Organizing content appropriately

4. *Learners:* Considering characteristics, goals, and abilities of learners

5. *Instructional Resources:* Selecting learning materials

6. *Instructional Processes:* Selecting learning and teaching activities

7. *Evaluation:* Assessing student outcomes, and appraising learner and teacher satisfaction with the plan

8. *Adjustment:* Making improvements in both the plan and the planning process

Breaking down the planning process in this way enables us to ask questions about the process itself. We can determine decisions about each element of the plan as well as who influences the decision makers and who bears responsibility for change. For example, we might ask such questions as these:

- Who constructs the plan? Who are the curriculum decision makers operating at each curriculum level?

- How is the plan constructed? What knowledge of curriculum planning do faculty bring to the task? What level of knowledge do they need? What training is needed?

- What premises or purposes undergird the plan? Are these purposes representative of faculty views generally or of those in specific disciplines?

- What stakeholders are included in the plan? Are students included? To what degree are specifications of accreditors, employers, and other external agents congruent with college purposes?

- How is the plan described or represented both formally and informally? How is it articulated to students?

- What educational outcomes do various types of students achieve under the plan?

- How will we know how various types of students experience the plan?

- Who decides when changes in the plan are needed?

- What provisions are made so that changes in the plan can be made promptly?

Some of the questions we pose generate considerable disagreement today. Indeed, some groups may question the legitimacy of the questions themselves or even challenge the notion that any plan should reflect purposes of educational experts or society, rather than those of individual learners. The mere suggestion of such potential questions about the plan and the planning process leads us to a brief consideration of the many influences on curriculum development and thus on the curriculum itself. For us, each question about the planning process suggests an analysis of influences on a step in that process. For example, the plan may be strongly influenced by lack of available information on learner goals or characteristics. Or faculty may need to consider contacts with local employers who could provide important information for planning a vocational program. Or it may become readily apparent that faculty planners are not knowledgeable about changing pedagogical trends. Finally, various interest groups may be trying to change how educational plans are created and implemented. We turn now to a scheme for recognizing and classifying such influences.

Influences on Curriculum Planning

Some years ago the Carnegie Foundation for the Advancement of Teaching (1977) discussed influences on the college curriculum. Elaborating on the scheme they used, we divided the influences into three sets—external influences, organizational influences, and internal influences—to characterize the educational environment for varied professional preparation programs (Stark, Lowther, Hagerty & Orczyk, 1986). In Figure 2-2 we

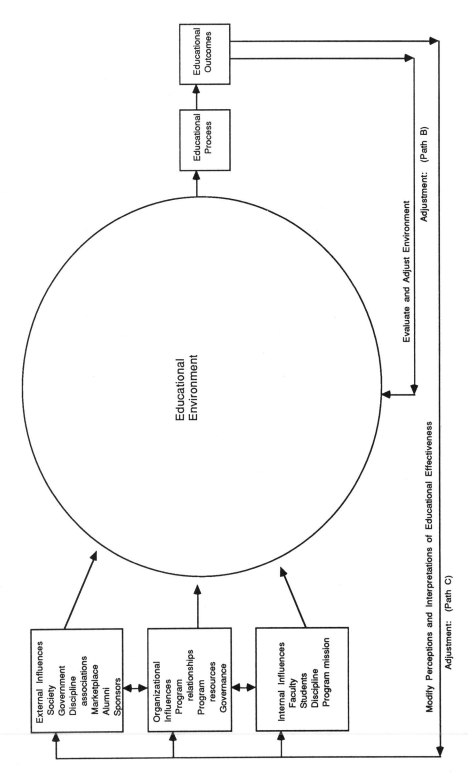

FIGURE 2-2 Influences on the College Educational Environment

17

show a simplified version of these three sets of influences acting on the educational environment. External influences stem from society and its agents outside the college or university. Internal and organizational influences both originate within the institution. However, internal influences stem from characteristics, views, and demands of those closest to the decision process, such as faculty and students, whereas organizational influences, for example central administrative officers, are farther removed from the immediate level of planning. We believe that this scheme continues to have broad utility and can be fruitfully applied to influences on curriculum in general. Thus, we suggest here that the interaction of these three sets of influences determines an educational environment for curriculum planning that helps to structure the planning decisions. In turn, curriculum decisions affect educational processes and outcomes.

External Influences

Historically, society's influence on educational planning has resulted in very gradual adaptation of the curriculum to a changing world. In most colleges and universities, curriculum content traditionally has been considered the business of the faculty experts (Toombs & Tierney, 1991) and somewhat insulated from non-student constituencies. Yet other interests do exist and do make themselves heard. Curriculum planning is often subject to strong external influences from disciplinary associations (e.g., the Modern Language Association), publications (like a recent book on cultural literacy by E. D. Hirsch), and accrediting agencies that review both entire colleges and specialized programs. The current era of demand for curriculum reform is an example of a time when the voices of the stakeholders are particularly clear and when change is occurring at a faster pace than usual.

Toombs and Tierney (1991) correctly point out that faculty members often work alone in designing courses without being sufficiently concerned about the various external interest groups. We assert, however, that faculty members in most programs are more attentive to these groups than may be apparent or more than even they may recognize. Influences such as the concerns of employers, the job market, and the society may simply seem muted because they often are filtered through such groups as accreditors, professional associations, and the media. Especially for community colleges, a relatively new type of institution, external groups may exert very strong and direct influence on the curriculum today.

The consideration of curriculum development as a planning process helps us identify the steps that are particularly sensitive to external forces. For example, Purpose, Content, Learners, and Instructional Resources in the planning process outlined earlier are more often subject to pressure from external constituencies. Planning decisions closer to the actual implementation of the plan, such as Instructional Process and Evaluation, are more likely to involve educators as internal forces. Because of their greater susceptibility to external influences, pressures for changes in Purpose, Content, Learners, and Instructional Resources are more politically explosive and, for some types of colleges, result in major curriculum debates.

Organizational Influences

Most academic programs we will discuss exist as part of a larger college context, supported by an organizational infrastructure. Aspects of this infrastructure, particularly college mission, financial stability, and governance arrangements, can have a strong influence on curriculum. The infrastructure provides support for the academic plan to be devised and carried out. But depending on the centrality of the specific course or program to the college or university, resource availability, advising systems, opportunity for faculty renewal, and so on may either be supportive—or not so supportive—influences on curriculum planning. For example, some courses and programs are connected to a wide variety of departments and programs and are influenced strongly by this interdependence; others are more isolated. It is important to distinguish between organizational influences in the college but outside the specific setting where planning occurs, and internal influences closer to the selection of content and teaching process.

Internal Influences

Internal influences are very strong in curriculum planning because faculty are the actual planners. These influences include faculty backgrounds, educational beliefs, and disciplines, as well as student characteristics and goals when they are recognized. These influences vary in salience and intensity at various levels of curriculum development. When the faculty member works alone in planning a course, some influences may be more influential than when a group of colleagues plans an entire program.

Interaction of Influences

In thinking about the curricular planning process, we need to consider simultaneously all three types of influences since they do not operate independently. For simplicity's sake, we say that their interaction produces an environment in which curriculum plans are developed. Here are four of the many potential interactions that might affect the academic plan:

- Society's educational needs interact with faculty members' educational beliefs, views of how people learn, values, and

sensitivities to learner needs to produce educational objectives.

- Subject matter, the vehicle for learning, is influenced by society, culture, technological advances, and ways of knowing as well as by institutional mission.

- Instructional processes are influenced by knowledge of pedagogical techniques, technology, and available materials, as well as by discipline preferences.

- Evaluation of academic plans is influenced by the amount of leadership available internally for improvement, by the allocation of organizational resources for data collectors, and by public policies such as state mandates for accountability.

These few selected examples illustrate that the academic plan is not the product of totally rational and context-free deliberations by faculty members. Rather, curriculum development is a complicated process embedded in a larger context that is complex and unpredictable.

ACADEMIC PLANS IN ENVIRONMENTAL CONTEXT

To provide a total view of curriculum, we must be aware not only of the desired elements of an academic plan and the steps in the planning process but also of the influences on the plan (and on planning) from within and outside the university. Although our analytical approach will be to consider the academic plan elements separately or in related pairs, we must reunite them in recognition of their interdependence. Thus, in Figure 2-3 we link the two frameworks we have just discussed, showing that the interaction of the three sets of influences on curriculum planning produce an environment in which the academic plan is created—an environment that influences the plan's development

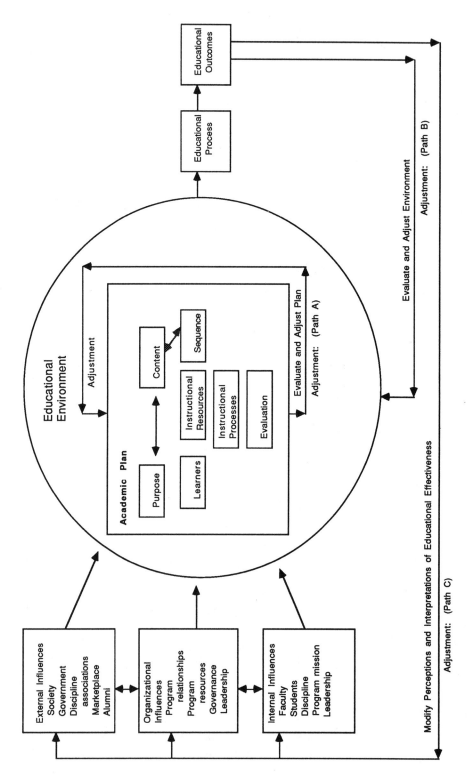

FIGURE 2-3   Academic Plans in Environmental Context

and eventual shape. The considerable diversity of academic plans in our colleges results from planning processes that cannot escape these three types of influence. Curriculum development can be adequately discussed only when the actual academic plan, its development, and its evaluation are seen as embedded in the environment created by these influences.

We have drawn Figure 2-3 to show that the educational process itself results from the plan but emerges from inside the environment. Just as there is an evaluation and adjustment process for a plan (Path A), there is an evaluation and adjustment process for the educational environment (Path B). Finally, external and internal audiences form perceptions and interpretations of the educational outcomes which cause them to modify the influences they exert (Path C). In proposing this comprehensive framework, which we call "Academic Plans in Environmental Context," we have begun to develop a curriculum theory.

Historically and currently, debate concerning the purposes of college education and the manner in which these purposes should be achieved has engendered much rhetoric but little real understanding. Multiple definitions of *curriculum* are both cause and effect for this rhetorical focus and have hindered the consideration of curriculum planning as a process. Our definition of the curriculum as an academic plan includes the major variables that regularly surface in discussions of the planning, implementation, evaluation, or improvement of teaching and learning. Without prescribing specific curricula, the idea of the academic plan provides a conceptual umbrella that can incorporate the plans constructed for such diverse fields as liberal arts disciplines, undergraduate professional fields, and vocational programs taught in community colleges. The plan may be constructed for a course, a program of courses, or an entire institution, but in each case the template calls attention to the importance of the context and the learners served.

Is there only one process of constructing an academic plan? Not at all. In keeping with the diversity of collegiate institutions and learners in U.S. higher education, there are many process models. They vary in their underlying purposes, in their implementation, and in how their success might be evaluated. Some of these variations are associated with disciplines, with institutional or program missions, and with prior student preparation. But we have distinguished the plan from the process of planning to focus attention on the important decisions being made.

The diversity within the broad concept of curriculum exists in part because, as the academic plan is developed, the planners are subjected to influences from society and its various agents. Thus, both planning and implementing the plan occur in a specific context of influences from inside and outside the institution. Once this context is recognized, the influences can be acknowledged and their interaction with other influences assessed. As we shall show, awareness of this environment is important if meaningful plans are to be constructed and enhanced.

Although our definition of curriculum synthesizes the research literature and was enhanced by our own interviews and surveys of faculty, it departs from the usual daily terminology used in higher education. The definition is considerably more detailed than any of those in common use and has not yet entered the everyday discourse of faculty members. Thus, we intend to state the definition frequently and develop it carefully in future chapters. In the next chapter, we will consider some related perspectives on the curriculum developed by other educators and show how our ideas benefit from many of them as we continue to develop our framework.

CHAPTER 3

Curriculum Perspectives and Frameworks

CURRICULAR FRAMEWORKS

We have stressed that the vaguely-defined concept called *curriculum* can be viewed more concretely when discussed as a *plan* for students' academic development. Because this academic plan includes several elements, from purpose to evaluation and adjustment, nearly all literature written about topics such as college mission, teaching and learning, or educational evaluation is in some way relevant to our definition of curriculum. In this chapter we selectively review ideas that focus on one or more of the eight elements we have included in our definition of the academic plan. We hope to show how we came to think of the curriculum as an academic plan and to compare and contrast this comprehensive approach with those of others who have taken more limited approaches. Finally, we will discuss more fully why we believe curricular theory is a useful guide for faculty in constructing and analyzing curriculum plans.

Our view of curriculum as an academic plan builds on the thinking of earlier scholars. Perhaps it is because higher education is so complex and diverse that few scholars have

attempted to develop comprehensive frameworks concerning what is taught and why. Much college curriculum literature focuses on specific disciplines and is published in specialty journals, making it difficult for generalists to access and synthesize. Relatively few higher education scholars have outlined frameworks that assist faculty and administrators in classifying, developing, or evaluating the ideas about curriculum from varied sources. In contrast, among those interested in elementary and secondary school curriculum, where it is assumed most practitioners are familiar with the subject matter to be taught, educational psychologists and teacher educators have generated a large body of expository literature about curriculum, curriculum development, and curriculum theory (see, e.g., Jackson, 1992; Posner, 1992; Walker, 1990). We have found some of this literature useful in developing systematic ways to view the college curriculum as well.

In this chapter, therefore, we review work of influential scholars from all levels of education, including those few who have tried to bring order to a limited but increasing set of curricular studies in higher education (see, e.g., Conrad & Pratt, 1983, 1986; Dressel, 1971, 1979b, 1980; Dressel & Marcus, 1982; Levine 1978; Stark & Lowther, 1986; Toombs, 1977–1978).

An ideal framework for thinking about college curriculum would allow us to identify the elements of an academic plan and the relationships among them, as well as to examine how various types of influence interact to affect the elements and the entire plan. The elements and influences specified should be sufficiently general to fit diverse disciplines and diverse types of colleges and students. We should avoid value judgments about what should be taught, to whom, or how, if the framework is to be generally applicable. To the extent that some value judgments or assumptions cannot be avoided, we should recognize them and make them explicit.

We find that existing approaches to studying curricula generally are either not value-neutral or not comprehensive. Indeed, some scholars believe all curricular decisions are implicitly value-laden (Walker, 1990). Surely, much current discourse about the college curriculum is undertaken to persuade, rather than to analyze. Even ostensibly neutral perspectives often conceal tacit assumptions about what should be taught or how it should be taught; for example, some writers incorporate support for either culturally pluralistic content or a common core of knowledge for all students. They may extol education based on special instructional strategies or urge the involvement of specific interest groups in curriculum planning. The influence of constituencies is important, as we shall show, but tends to obscure attention to basic educational assumptions that should undergird curriculum development.

Many considerations of curriculum by educational leaders seem less than comprehensive because they avoid any substantive definition or discussion of important curriculum elements. They may merely defer to the presumed wisdom of the faculty in developing the curriculum, report how many students are studying in what types of colleges or majors, or even suggest that curriculum does not exist because each student experiences education in his or her own way. Another typical approach involves the construction of lists, histories, or typologies of "innovative" programs and attempts at curricular change, such as those occurring periodically in general education or specific academic majors. Because such typologies usually are based on only one or two elements of curriculum, they may provide little information that helps in curriculum planning, generally.

Many educators try to describe the curriculum as they see it in their institutions or to highlight innovative approaches as they emerge, rather than advocating a specific content or educational process. Their conceptual schemes frequently represent attempts to classify their observations. Among the diverse conceptions, we will review only those we have found most useful and relevant to developing our emerging theory. In our discussion, we note what we believe are the underlying assumptions of the perspectives we review. We will organize our review by discussing the simplest curriculum perspectives first, then the more complex. Most writers focus on only one or two elements of the academic plan, so "single-element" perspectives are very common. We first summarize these single-element approaches, beginning with discussions of educational purpose and ending with those primarily concerned with evaluation and adjustment. Next, we discuss perspectives that consider several elements. Only a few writers in higher education have tried to view several elements of curriculum simultaneously or examine how the elements are interrelated—that is, how each element is influenced, implemented, and enhanced by the others. These come closer to representing general curricular frameworks because they propose relationships to connect some elements of the academic plan. Finally, we show

how our own thinking about curriculum as a plan builds on the work of these others and extends it.

None of the literature we have reviewed purports to constitute a theory—that is, a framework that encourages analysis or prediction of relationships between the various curriculum elements or guides practice. Indeed, some previous theorists (Dressel, 1980; Toombs, 1977–1978) have doubted that it was possible to build such a theory for postsecondary curriculum. We agree that the diversity of collegiate educational settings, programs, and learners certainly makes it very difficult to generate a simple framework with wide applicability. We believe, however, that this difficulty may stem from the tendency of scholars to take normative approaches. In viewing curriculum as an academic plan, we deliberately maintain an analytical stance. As we identify and hypothesize relationships among elements of the plan and between the plan elements and the varied influences, we will approach a general theory of college curriculum.

Because most other writers have separated the academic plan from the influences upon it, we will only occasionally mention influences on the plan in this review of the work of others. Later, we will turn our attention to influences and outline how our framework emerges in the context of changes in society.

SINGLE-ELEMENT CURRICULAR PERSPECTIVES

Analysts and advocates alike have focused, not on all elements of the curriculum plan but, rather, on one or two key elements or on the processes and politics of curriculum change. Some elements of the academic plan have received more attention than others. The most commonly discussed elements, those that most people consider the foundation of curriculum, are the elements we call purposes, content, and sequence. Discussions of purpose and content are often intricately linked by academic writers, whereas considerations of sequence usually take the form of "structural" curriculum discussions, emphasizing student progression through an entire college program or the formal listing and sequencing of courses. In these structural discussions, writers typically state obvious relationships among the curriculum elements, then proceed to disregard these linkages in their analysis. For example, although studies of postsecondary students have a long tradition and are clearly relevant to the structural view of curriculum, authors seldom relate discussions of students to the proposed sequences. Similarly, discussions of instructional processes often focus on the activities or development of faculty members but seldom consider the relation of these concerns to subject content and the learner. Although it is important to understand the actors in higher education, the focused interests of scholars in studying *either* learners *or* teachers have led to research that artificially separates who teaches and who learns from the context of what is taught, how, and in what order.

Perspectives on Educational Purpose

Many curricular perspectives involve a single element of the academic plan, namely educational purpose. The literature advocating specific missions and objectives is especially extensive. Often these speakers are college presidents, scholars, and educational statespersons, and thus they may represent one of at least four different sets of stakeholders who hold varying purposes: society, colleges, faculty members, and students. Some writers fail to specify which stakeholder group is represented, leaving the implicit and erroneous assumption that the purposes of these groups are congruent. Such congruence can usually be achieved only if the statements of purpose are very broad indeed.

College presidents frequently write and talk about educational purposes and missions, and their words, in speeches and college catalogs, have enjoyed strong credibility and provoked useful discussions. Howard Bowen (1977), a university president and scholar of higher education, collected and classified many such college goal statements. Other illustrations of this genre are the writings of Derek Bok (1974), former president of Harvard University, Donald Kennedy of Stanford University (1991), and community college presidents Robert McCabe (1988) and Judith Eaton (1988). Usually such statements emphasize broad principles but lack the specificity needed to translate them into functional curriculum objectives. Often, too, they relate to specific societal and institutional contexts.

Usually college presidents advocate that students should acquire information and knowledge, skills and habits of thought, judgment, and values (Bok, 1974) that will prepare them for participation in society as citizens, workers, technocrats, businesspersons, scholars, or a combination of such roles. Or they may advocate developing various types of literacy for civic and occupational purposes (Eaton, 1988). Often they avoid grappling with the important questions of *which* "information and knowledge," *which* "skills and habits of thought," and *which* "values" should be taught or how these learnings should be achieved. The pronouncements of college presidents tend to reflect their interpretation of what society demands of their colleges and what is suitable for their students. But minefields of unacknowledged dissent and disagreement lie ahead of the college that seeks to use only the broad and neutral presidential view of purpose to achieve a curriculum plan in its own environmental context or to assess its success as the other elements of the academic plan come into play.

Arthur Levine (1978), in a report for the Carnegie Commission, saw faculty members as the primary architects of curriculum and summarized a typology of purposes that he believed illustrated faculty views on U.S. campuses. Levine identified four general educational purposes or "philosophies" that potentially underlie curriculum decisions.

1. *Perennialism*—training the rational faculties of the mind

2. *Essentialism*—learning a prescribed knowledge, cultural heritage

3. *Progressivism*—building on life experience—student-centered, problem-oriented

4. *Reconstructionism*—reconstructing society

Levine left out such purposes as vocational preparation and value development, which we have found to be especially important to faculty members in community colleges and denominational colleges, respectively. But the typology is useful in reminding us that an appropriate model for curriculum planning must provide for multiple faculty viewpoints of educational purpose. Although presidential views may be too broad to guide curriculum development, faculty may express educational goals too narrowly, based on their discipline and the type of college where they teach.

Students' voices are often expressed through the voices of researchers who have queried them. Based on surveys of entering college students over many years, researchers have reported that educational goals of students have become increasingly vocational (Dey, Astin, & Korn, 1991). Our own studies, asking enrolled students to answer surveys about college and course goals, confirm this strong vocational purpose, but find that it usually coexists with broader purposes such as those expressed by presidents and faculty.

During the 1960s and early 1970s, students asked that education be made relevant to their lives and interests. In the 1980s and

1990s, some have been asking for greater consideration of diversity in higher education. Today's spokespersons for students feel that a list of educational purposes must include the goal of granting legitimacy and higher status to those with diverse lifestyles, particularly underrepresented ethnic groups and gay students. As yet, few educational theorists have incorporated these student views into their expressions of educational purpose.

Traditionally, society sought college graduates with well-developed cultural tastes, the habit of continuing to learn, and the ability to think critically (Kaysen, 1974, p. 180). Recently, a more technologically complex society has preferred a view of the educated person as a specialized and professionally competent worker, able to make rational decisions in "the application of organized knowledge" (p. 184). Yet, as debate about the purpose of an undergraduate college education emerged again in the 1980s, varied blue-ribbon commissions and educational statespersons wrote opinions that returned to traditional purposes.

There are many views of collegiate purposes, ranging from transmission of a shared culture to the position that no shared culture exists, and ranging from the view that cultural development is the primary purpose of education to the view that students must achieve scientific-rational decision-making capabilities to serve the economy or achieve full employment. At any single point in time, great diversity exists even within primary groups of higher education constituents because of the wide diversity of missions that college and disciplines define for themselves. In our view, therefore, the extensive rhetoric that expounds on the "appropriate" college mission nonetheless fails to resolve the "correct" purposes of the curriculum in any specific context. A general framework for careful discussion of curriculum will help decision makers in a specific context recognize how essential it is to achieve agreement on their plan's pur-

pose. But purpose does not automatically help decision makers select content, process, or sequence. Rather, attention to these other elements of the academic plan must follow and extend discussions of purpose to make them more concrete. We turn next to frameworks that focus on the selection of content.

Perspectives on Content Selection

The general goals that educators or society's spokespersons advocate could be achieved by selecting many different types of content to teach. However, general and specific educational purposes are typically embedded in some content area of learning. Thus, selecting subject matter to help students achieve educational objectives is crucial in shaping accepted views of educational purposes into the actual academic plan. In this process, faculty purposes become very important since content is traditionally selected according to faculty interests and scholarly preparation in specific disciplines or professional fields.

Embedding educational objectives in the disciplines is based on the assumption that these divisions of knowledge are appropriate vehicles by which to simultaneously develop specific knowledge and general learned abilities, such as thinking skills. For example, among those whose educational goals include transmitting the cultural heritage (described by Levine as "essentialism"), certain disciplines and classic reading materials are assumed to promote such general abilities as effective thinking and the ability to make value judgments. For those who view the development of problem-solving abilities as a key educational purpose, other types of study, including philosophy, the logical structure of mathematics, and language, are often cited as essential vehicles. In fact, most colleges try to ensure students' exposure to the varied disciplines, rather than focusing on other objectives such as general abilities.

Conceivably, however, educators who view the learner's intellectual development as the most important goal of the academic plan may successfully challenge the monopoly of the traditional disciplines. Currently, some are urging attention to different purposes and other bases for selecting content to be learned in college. One such purpose is to develop generic skills or "general learned abilities" that cross disciplines. Another is to embed the achievement of educational objectives in the study of societal problems from the perspective of several disciplines. Faculty members teaching in area studies, ethnic studies, or women's studies programs frequently challenge traditional views and propose other rationales for content selection. They claim, for example, that both the great books and the traditional disciplines of knowledge have excluded important segments of our population. Thus, while educators debate not only what Americans should know to participate meaningfully in a common culture and also what content should be used as the teaching vehicle, other educators challenge the idea that such a "common" culture even exists. In short, the question is not only *which* cultural heritage is to be learned but *how* and *why*. To solve the problem of exclusiveness, these groups advocate departure from the traditional disciplines as the appropriate content to teach.

Even those who agree that reading classic works of literature, philosophy, and history should be the primary way to learn the cultural heritage disagree on important issues. This debate especially centers on the best ways to achieve the educational purpose Levine called "perennialism"—that is, cultivation of the ability to think effectively. According to one view, reading the great works is assumed inherently to promote effective thinking. But, a second view holds that important outcomes like effective thinking are generic; the content chosen is distinctly secondary to the end itself. In still a third view,

no content promotes effective thinking unless it is linked with explicit pedagogical attention to developing this ability. The following types of questions characterize this discussion: What topics should a student be able to think effectively about? Which academic subjects best develop critical thinking? What ways of learning will most likely strengthen effective thinking, regardless of topic? How do we evaluate whether the desired ways of thinking have been achieved? In these arguments, adversaries make clear their positions but tend to make some connections among curricular purpose, content, and educational process on faith.

The connection between educational purpose and the content chosen is a key issue as we think of the curriculum as an academic plan. While some might try to separate these two elements, we believe that their linkage is so well entrenched in our culture that it is not possible at present to do so.

Perspectives on Learners

In addition to mirroring educators' interpretations of society's goals, college goals may reflect the goals of the students who attend. These sets of goals may be out of phase. The educators' curriculum may not quite match the students' curriculum. The separation between students' and faculty's goals especially persists when one examines the relative importance of vocational goals to the two groups. In studies of both faculty and students in all types of colleges, vocational goals are very important for enrolled students but quite unimportant to most of their teachers, particularly in introductory courses (Stark, Lowther, Ryan, et al., 1988). Whether one agrees that colleges should be responsive to students' vocational orientation, the fact remains that enrolled students may have different educational purposes from those of the college and its faculty. In the vocational realm, student demands for specific career majors tend to reflect society's demand more quickly than the college's response; thus, colleges frequently seem to lag in changing curricula to meet student interests.

Educators expect that the curriculum plans they construct will guide students' learning activities. They also traditionally evaluate the success of the curriculum by looking at operational aspects of the faculty members' plan (syllabus, reading list, activities, and exam questions) and whether students achieve goals specified in the plan. As we have argued elsewhere (Stark, Shaw, & Lowther, 1989), it is also necessary to examine the learners' abilities, goals, and effort to predict how appropriate and successful an academic plan may be for them. Scholars such as Thomas F. Green, Alexander W. Astin, K. Patricia Cross, Arthur W. Chickering, and William G. Perry have focused attention on learners as a key element of the academic plan and, to some extent, have linked them with other elements of academic plans such as purposes and educational processes.

Thomas Green described learner development in terms of broad processes like "developing competence" that lead learners to both maturational and intellectual goals of service and judgment. He asserted that acquired information, skills, habits, qualities of mind and understanding, judgments, and values should interact and operate to structure the attitudes and behavior of the educated person (Green in Chickering & Associates, 1981, pp. 543–555). Green used the idea of professional "competence" to illustrate the ideal interaction of processes and outcomes, showing that competence is self-reinforcing. That is, the person who experiences a sense of developing competence in any field is encouraged to continue learning. Humanistic frameworks such as that proposed by Green are useful in creating an appropriate academic plan because they link purpose and process with notions of continuing learner development. The stance is neutral, but there

is clear emphasis on the learner as an important entity.

K. Patricia Cross has directed educators' attention to the diversity of learners whose goals and talents academic plans must accommodate. She has been concerned with "new students"—that is, adult, underprepared, and members of underrepresented groups of learners who began to enter higher education in the 1970s (Cross, 1976a, 1976b, 1981)—and has reinforced the importance of considering students' talents and capabilities when constructing a curricular plan.

In Alexander Astin's scheme, which he calls the "talent development model," the purpose of the curriculum is to move the student toward acquiring specified improved qualities (Astin, 1985, 1988, 1993). To Astin, the specific absolute standard of "quality of mind" is less important than how far the student progresses toward this quality during college. Yet his work has become more closely linked with evaluation than with learners.

William Perry studied the intellectual development of Harvard students over a lengthy period and developed a scheme showing how students progress in cognitive and ethical development. Perry's work helps to illuminate the interaction between the student's level of thinking and the types of content and instructional activities that are likely to be successful curriculum components. Although there is much discussion of Perry's "scheme" among college educators, examples of its successful use in curriculum planning are not abundant.

These few scholarly frameworks focusing on learners amply illustrate the diversity of such emphases. Both Cross and Astin have been concerned with fostering development of individual learner talents. Without being specific about desired outcomes, Astin has developed a model that local educators can use to think of how learners develop in ways that they desire. Perry, in contrast, merely described learner intellectual development and, by his own report, did not intend his description to be a model (Perry in Chickering and Associates, 1981, pp. 76–116). Each of these scholars would make learners a central element in constructing an academic plan. Their contribution to our thinking is to show the impossibility of constructing an effective academic plan without considering the learners who will pursue it. Our awareness of student development processes makes it impossible for us to continue to define curriculum as a set of courses or structures that exist in a catalog or policy book, independent of the learner.

Curriculum Sequence Perspectives

Sequences and structures result from decisions about arranging content in the academic plan. Curriculum sequences occur at all levels. At the course level, making such decisions is usually called "arranging content," or "sequencing." At the program level, making functional decisions about sequence is often called "creating curriculum structure." Teachers make deliberate decisions to sequence course content in certain ways—for example, from simplest to most complex or chronologically (Posner & Strike, 1976). At the college program level, the type and extent of structure created may depend on how much consensus exists on a discipline paradigm (Lattuca & Stark, 1994). Unfortunately, when taken alone, decisions about sequencing and structure do not always include attention to the learner and may be based on unwarranted assumptions about relations of content, its sequencing, and desired outcomes.

Curricular structures at the college level may be policies or rules intended to ensure that students are exposed to a variety of educational beliefs, a variety of learning processes, and varied critical perspectives, as well as varied subject matter. In fact, the sequencing structures that college educators have created to guide student progress have typically been so prominent that many think of college curriculum at the program or college level primarily in terms of credit hour structure, perhaps because such structure comes to be a surrogate for educational philosophy. This definition has led to research studies that gather information manually from catalogs or transcripts or electronically from student data files to describe the structural aspects of the curriculum and the presumed educational results (see, e.g., studies by Blackburn et al., 1976; Dressel & DeLisle, 1970; Ratcliff, 1992b; Zemsky, 1989).

A useful analysis of the influence of curriculum structure directed at the program level, rather than at specific courses, was completed by Bergquist, Gould, and Greenberg, who proposed six generic dimensions of all college curricula and attempted to show how they can be used in curricular design:

1. *Time:* Duration and schedule of instructional units
2. *Space:* Use of instructional and non-instructional areas both on and off the college campus
3. *Resources:* Instructional use of people, situations, and materials, both on and off campus, from instructional and non-instructional areas
4. *Organization:* Arrangement and sequencing of instructional units and arrangement of academic administrative units
5. *Procedures:* Planning, implementing, evaluating, and crediting instructional units
6. *Outcomes:* Defining the intended desired results of a particular instructional unit or academic program (1981, p. 5; emphasis in original)

The authors propose that these dimensions are arranged in a hierarchy of importance, from lower order (time) to higher order (outcomes) and that their importance is inversely proportional to the ease with which changes can be made. That is, it is relatively easy to change the time dimensions of the academic program but relatively difficult to change the intended outcomes. The three lower level dimensions (time, space, and resources) require only structural changes, whereas the three higher level dimensions (organization, procedure, and outcomes) require increasingly greater changes in processes and attitudes as well as structure (pp. 6–7). This framework is extremely useful because it exposes the erroneous assumption that curriculum reform consists of changing relatively unimportant structural dimensions. Viewing curriculum as an academic plan requires that all dimensions be examined and potentially changed, but the emphasis is directed to the top three levels: arrangements, procedures, and especially intended outcomes.

Instructional Process Perspectives

The common definition of curriculum as a set of courses or structural dimensions artificially separates instructional processes from curriculum. However, by viewing curriculum as an academic plan, we necessarily ally instructional process to other elements of the plan. Faculty base decisions about instructional processes on expectations that certain strategies will help students achieve the desired purposes better than others. Often we think of instructional processes as concerned only with decisions made when curriculum is planned at the course level, but similar decisions are made at the program and college level. For example, a course-level decision would be to use lecture or seminar presentations. The suitability of the process depends on whether the purpose is to transmit information to students (lecture) or to engage students in active problem-solving behavior (discussion). At the program level, a parallel example is the use of the "freshman seminar."

Not only may the content of the seminar be carefully chosen to involve students, capture their interests, and build on their goals and backgrounds, but the seminar instructional process may be deliberately chosen to augment and enhance students' problem-solving abilities. (Upcraft, Gardner & Associates, 1989). Such links between process and the goal of effective thinking have been advocated by many who discuss active learning or "learning to learn" (see, e.g., Bonwell & Eison, 1991; McKeachie et al., 1986; Weimer, 1990).

Perspectives on Evaluation and Adjustment

Traditionally, broad mission statements have received more attention and publicity in higher education than have lists of specific intended learner outcomes. Examination of student achievement has typically been a semiprivate interaction between an instructor and a group of students; the instructor's expert judgment of student learning is rarely questioned. In colleges, all instructors evaluate students, but few talk much about the process except when several instructors teach multiple-section courses with common syllabi and examinations.

The assumption that learning can be measured and attributed to specific courses has not been popular among college faculty; they frequently assert that, as learning objectives become more complex, learning is intangible or "ineffable" (Ewell, 1991b). In the 1980s, however, interest in evaluating college student learning more broadly than course-specific achievement increased because of a crisis in public confidence, pressures from government leaders for accountability, and responses of voluntary accreditors. Advocates of this recent assessment movement believe that "general learned abilities" and broad college outcomes can be measured or documented along with course-specific outcomes.

A well-established evaluation framework is based on "the Tyler rationale," named after Ralph Tyler, known to elementary and secondary educators as the father of educational evaluation (see Madaus & Stufflebeam, 1989). Steps in this framework include: establishing goals, objectives, and desired outcomes; identifying the learning processes intended to teach them; choosing measures to see if the learners have achieved them; collecting performance data; and finally comparing the data with the original goals and objectives. The assumption underlying these steps is that what is learned can be measured and also can be reasonably attributed to the instructional process. Depending on which step is in progress, curriculum development under the Tyler rationale can variously be viewed as goal setting, instructional planning, or evaluation.

In the higher education assessment movement, Alexander Astin's "input, environment, and outcome" framework (sometimes known as "value-added assessment") is the counterpart to the Tyler rationale (Astin, 1991a). Whereas Tyler defines excellence as the achieving the stated objectives at a predetermined level, in Astin's broader scheme educational effectiveness is documented by observing appropriate changes in the students after considering pretests to account for their initial level of knowledge, development, and other relevant characteristics. As with the Tyler rationale, Astin's ideas about assessment are popular but not wholly accepted among college faculty and educational researchers (for a contrary view, see Warren, 1984).

Like the notion of an academic plan, value-added assessment can be used to assess outcomes at several levels: for individual students, courses, programs, and whole colleges (Ewell, 1991b). Although the value-added perspective leaves the specific objectives and related content unspecified, it comes close to a general framework because it helps to specify desired outcomes, focuses attention on both the learner and the instructional environment, and encourages feedback that can be used to revise the curriculum plan.

A different perspective on evaluation is called "classroom assessment" (Angelo & Cross, 1993; Cross & Angelo, 1988), a scheme to gather evaluation information informally and regularly in the classroom and use it to improve teaching and planning. This idea, capturing what many good teachers may always have done, has become popular among college teachers, who typically guard autonomy and privacy in the classroom (Angelo, 1991). Recent evaluation perspectives like those developed by Angelo and Cross and by Astin seem likely to concentrate on more elements of the academic plan and their relationships. Noting this possible trend, we move to consider more general curriculum frameworks.

GENERAL CURRICULUM FRAMEWORKS

A general framework for viewing curriculum should consider all or most of the elements that constitute an academic plan and, ideally, should show that these elements are frequently interdependent. This is because decisions about educational purpose, selection of content, and choice of instructional processes are often based on related assumptions about learning and the learner. The elementary and secondary school literature recognizing these links is more fully developed than that in higher education, and we have found some of it particularly useful. Therefore, as our first general curriculum framework we will review a set of models from the precollege literature.

Precollegiate Curriculum Frameworks

The four-model curricular framework set forth by Geneva Gay (1980) is worth discussing in detail because it illustrates the tensions or conflicts between several strong sets of beliefs that cause dissent among faculty members as they plan curriculum. Ideas similar to Gay's have been discussed by other educational theorists; Eisner and Vallance (1974) aptly called them "conflicting conceptions" of the curriculum. We chose Gay's models from among the many possible configurations because they capture dimensions familiar to college educators.

Although focusing strongly on educational purposes, Gay's four models link purposes with instructional processes, indicating a tendency for educators to adopt purpose and process concomitantly. Indeed, as we shall show shortly, we also found this temporal and conceptual link between purpose and process in the college literature (Chickering, 1969; Dressel, 1980) and demonstrated it empirically among college faculty in studies of course planning (Stark, Lowther, Ryan, et al., 1988). The expression of the link may indicate the planner's assessment of the relative importance of learners in the discipline. Several such links among at least three elements of the academic plan in each of Gay's hypothetical models, summarized below, render them reasonably close to being a full curriculum framework.

The *academic-rational model,* a "systematic" view of curriculum, assumes that choices of curriculum content are based on scholarly logic and a clear view of what knowledge is worth knowing. In this model, the curriculum planners strive for a balance among five tensions: the learner, the society, the subject matter and disciplines, philosophy of education, and psychology of learning. They also seek a balanced emphasis on physical, psychological, intellectual, and moral dimensions of learning. The academic-rational design assumes that curriculum development is a linear process in which decisions are made sequentially about objectives, content, learning activities, teaching techniques, and evaluation processes.

The *experiential model* is more subjective and learner-centered than the academic-rational model. In this model, the planner engages students in planning their own active, self-directed learning experiences. Because of student involvement, the planning steps for this model cannot be specified in advance. The desired outcomes include intellectual, emotional, social, physical, aesthetic, and spiritual development; self-control; and a sense of personal efficacy.

The *technical model,* derived from systems management and production, assumes that education is a rational process. If the process is carefully controlled, the nature of the products can be predicted and determined. Like the Tyler model, the technical curriculum development process requires specifying desired objectives in advance, constructing activities to achieve these objectives, and evaluating their success, primarily as observed changes in learner behavior. Frequently, the purposes are linked with preparing the learner for life's functions.

The *pragmatic model* is neither systematic nor rational; rather, it is a dynamic political and social interaction model, reacting to events and stakeholders who wield power in determining both the purpose and process of curriculum. In this model, curriculum development is often localized and pluralistic. Planning is a consensual process, responsive to constituencies and seeking to distribute influence and resources and to exert pressure on various sources to develop and sustain the negotiated curriculum.

Faculty always espouse a philosophy of education (purpose) and a related view of the psychology of learning and teaching, each of which is related to their discipline. Often, however, they do not recognize or make explicit these concepts. Evidence indicates that faculty in different disciplines generally support different purposes, thus choosing related views of learning and planning according to different models among those mentioned by

Gay. For example, science faculty tend to espouse the academic-rational model, while faculty in English and some other humanities are likely to espouse the experiential model. Generally, only faculty who teach career-directed courses endorse the technical model; this model is congruent in some respects with the emphasis on skill development in the new assessment movement.

College faculty acknowledge but do not endorse the pragmatic model. Yet they often report the types of influences in curriculum development suggested by the pragmatic model, including graduate schools, the media, suppliers of instructional materials, federal aid programs that support specific curricula, the courts, lobbies, unions, scholarly societies, and accreditors. Observation of curriculum development at the department level leads us to believe that, depending on the discipline(s) involved, each of the other planning models may be combined with the pragmatic model. This phenomenon is consistent with Gay's observation that the models do not exist in pure form. The process of college curriculum development may begin with one of the first three models but, as diverse views are considered, pragmatic concerns influence the final results. At the public school level, where Gay's models originated, political tension and value conflicts occur in the local community. In the college or university community, these same tensions affect curriculum development, resulting in political compromise within and between curriculum committees or departmental groups, or among the entire faculty. Just as faculty do not recognize other assumptions that direct their curriculum thinking, we believe they often fail to recognize the political aspects of curriculum planning and development. The pragmatic model helps us to recognize that the framework of the academic plan is incomplete without considering the internal and external influences on it.

Frameworks from Higher Education

Chickering has helped scholars develop an effective understanding of the learner through his work on vectors of student growth and maturation (Chickering, 1969; Chickering & Reisser, 1993). Consideration of the changes that traditional-age college students undergo in seven areas—competency, emotions, autonomy, identity, personal relationships, purpose, and integrity—clarifies the multidimensional nature of student development in college. Chickering believed that connections could be made between these dimensions of student change and the educational policies and practices in both formal instruction and less formal learning situations such as residential life. Linking learner development with instructional processes is an appropriate step toward a more complete model of an academic plan that includes student maturation. To use Chickering's words, "Curriculum arrangements, teaching practices, and evaluational procedures are systematically linked. To consider one element in isolation from the others is unwise; to modify one part without threatening the others is impossible" (1969, p. 196). Chickering tried to relate several curriculum models much like those Gay described to all seven dimensions of student development. In the end, however, only some of the models could be closely connected to some of the student development dimensions (1969, pp. 196–219).

In considering curriculum from multiple perspectives over a career of sixty-five years, Paul Dressel seems to have moved steadily toward a conceptualization of curriculum as a comprehensive academic plan (1971/1968, 1976, 1980; Dressel & DeLisle, 1970; Dressel & Marcus, 1982). Dressel created numerous frameworks within which to examine curriculum, but he regularly took normative positions on most of the plan's elements, making his work more of a prescriptive treatise on curriculum than an open framework to guide thinking.

Dressel addressed the "purpose" element of curriculum plans directly. While acknowledging affective development as an important correlate, he argued that the primary purpose of college instruction is to promote students' *cognitive* growth. Further, the primary objective of emphasis on cognitive growth is to make learners self-sufficient thinkers and continuing learners.

Dressel also addressed the "content" element. He believed that attention to the structure of the disciplines is essential in achieving appropriate educational outcomes and, therefore, in devising instructional plans. In his view, the disciplines, artifacts of human intellectual development, have emerged as organizers of human history and experience. Consequently, they represent useful and essential classifications for organizing teaching and learning. Since disciplines and their methods are seen as tools for achieving understanding and gaining meaning in relation to one's environment, the educated person must know about the objectives, methods, concepts, and structures of disciplines and their interrelationship.

With respect to "learners," Dressel believed that individuals are unlikely to acquire knowledge, values or abilities, unless they attach some importance to them (although the term *active learner* had not yet become fashionable in his lifetime). He hoped therefore that students would read classical works because they got satisfaction from them, not only because someone viewed them as "good for you." In a nutshell, his framework called for education to be simultaneously useful, individualized, eclectic, and beneficial to the student. Dressel did not say, however, how he would entice to the fount of knowledge a student who found little satisfaction in learning or who did not see its benefits.

Dressel also discussed educational structures and "processes." Structure, in his view,

is intrinsic either to the learning process or the content. Although his writing took place before recent developments in cognitive psychology, Dressel clearly presaged the need for the learner to associate new experiences with prior experiences. He felt the college must provide structures and arrangements for learning that help the learner integrate the topics of a course and relate them to other courses and experiences. The process of studying a discipline must therefore involve assimilating previous learning and may involve the creation of new concepts, relationships, and organizational patterns of knowledge.

Dressel also addressed the instructional process element of the academic plan. His view of the psychology of learning, however, seemed to contain an unresolved tension between the development of the individual and the development of society. In their book *On Teaching and Learning in College* (1982), Dressel and co-author Dora Marcus departed from the disciplines and leaned more toward individual student development, outlining a model they called "humanizing education." Humanizing education transcends the disciplines and suggests six humanizing competences directed toward achieving the common interests of the community (pp. 62–63). The model focuses on educational purpose but the use of the verbs *humanizing*, *socializing*, and *individualizing* imply a process to which the learner is to be subjected or led.

Dressel devoted much attention to the evaluation of students, teachers, and programs. In *Improving Degree Programs,* he observed,

> An ongoing program evaluation that transcends courses should attempt to find out what students have gained from a course or program, what elements of the program have been successful or unsuccessful in promoting this development, and what aspects of the course, content, resource materials, and experiences need to be revised to maintain vigor and enthusiasm. This form of evalua-

tion produces information that tends to modify instructional materials and processes and also the manner in which they are conjoined into courses. In an integrated, cumulative curricular experience, evaluation must be a major structural component, but it cannot be the sole instrument for developing or maintaining such a program. (1980, p. 57)

Carrying this thought further, Dressel added that "Ultimately, evaluation becomes a review of the actual outcomes and a reflection upon the processes, content, and instructional patterns used to determine whether alteration is needed," and he portrayed the relationships among these academic plan elements in a pyramid with objectives as the apex and content, instruction, evaluation, and procedures as the base (1980, p.146). He also constructed a flow model of steps in course and program development and evaluation (1980, pp. 145–146). This flow model incorporates most fully Gay's academic-rational model, which Dressel believed most popular among faculty, but it also includes some attention to internal, organizational, and external influences on the college curriculum. Finally, Dressel noted that not only intended objectives should be examined in evaluation but also that information about unintended outcomes of curriculum programs should enter into the adjustment process.

Clearly, as we try to conceptualize curriculum and build models to guide research and practice, our debt to Dressel is great, as was his to theorists from other educational levels. While some theorists, like Chickering, have developed the association between two or three elements of the academic plan, Dressel discussed almost all of the eight elements in detail, as well as acknowledging some of the important influences on curriculum development.

We also acknowledge the achievement of Clifton Conrad and Anne Pratt (1983), who attempted to develop a nonprescriptive model of curriculum just before we began to outline the academic plan. After an extensive search of the literature on college curriculum, Conrad and Pratt (1986) identified a few conceptual frameworks that refine terminology or suggest potential avenues for organizing future research about the curriculum. They emphasized the lack of a comprehensive view of curriculum in any of the sources they examined. Indeed, lack of agreement on basic terms describing the relationship between the arrangements for learning and the substance of learning constricts vision of the dimensions along which variations may be introduced. Specifically, they noted that the curriculum was frequently viewed as a structure, but they failed to find views of the curriculum that also included consideration of educational outcomes for which the structure was devised.

Like us, Conrad and Pratt saw curriculum as a series of decisions or "options." Some options they called "curricular design variables" and, following Toombs, divided these variables into content and form. Context, presumably, was subsumed under the internal and external influences on curriculum and produced an effect they called "input variables." Finally, Conrad and Pratt described two types of outcome variables—curriculum design outcomes and educational outcomes. In our terms, curriculum design outcomes designate the plan itself and the shape it takes after the decisions are made; educational outcomes are linked to purpose (see Figure 3-1).

Conrad and Pratt, noting that decisions depend on professors' behavior, recognized the importance of the disciplines and the fact that college professors do not plan in a linear way. Our primary concern with this model is that we believe it may be overly specific, thus limiting its potential external validity for the wide range of curriculum-decision situations. Thus, we have tried to simplify our own emerging theory for greater utility in guiding practice.

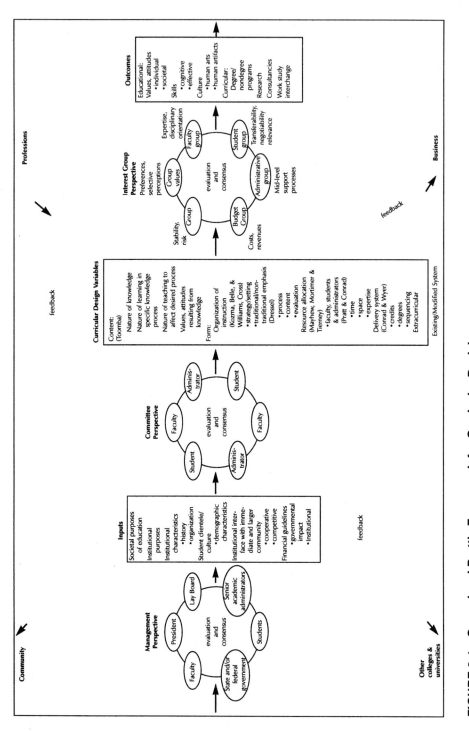

FIGURE 3-1 Conrad and Pratt's Framework for Curricular Decisions

Source: Figure 2 from "Making Decisions about Curriculum" by Clifton F. Conrad and Anne M. Pratt, *Journal of Higher Education*, Vol. 54, No. 1 (January–February 1983) is reprinted by permission. Copyright 1983 by the Ohio State University Press. All rights reserved.

CURRICULUM PLANNING AND DESIGN

As they discuss the process of developing curriculum, most higher education writers (except for Dressel and Conrad & Pratt) have used frameworks quite different from that which we are developing in this book. According to Conrad and Pratt (1986), who exhaustively reviewed curriculum literature, many curriculum studies are case study reports of programs or colleges deemed innovative by the writer. This genre, best illustrated by reports of new colleges or those that adopted experimental programs during periods of educational reform (Levine, 1978; Cardozier, 1993), continues to attract researchers' interest and attention. As a result, several planning frameworks have stressed the political nature of curriculum development or have been based on theories of change, innovation, and diffusion (Lindquist, 1974) or the administrative climate within a college (Seymour, 1988). In emphasizing innovations, writers seem to focus on change for change's sake rather than seek to understand how academic plans are continually evaluated and the evaluations used to improve the original plan. Such approaches bring a few colleges that have made broad changes into the limelight and foster a "bandwagon effect" as change diffuses to other colleges. We believe that studies of innovation, rather than continual and systematic curriculum adjustment, are appropriate primarily when researchers study change at the program and collegewide levels, where the pragmatic model of conflicting ideas (as outlined by Gay) becomes visible. These approaches do not, however, provide much assistance to colleges with established programs that wish to improve or respond with less radical restructuring.

Political frameworks decrease in usefulness—and analytical frameworks increase in usefulness—as one moves to individual courses. Toombs contended (and our studies confirmed) that while courses are meaningful to faculty, programs are typically courses "strung together"—and are not easily comprehended or defended (1977–1978, p. 19). At the course level of curriculum development, faculty make regular small adjustments and occasional drastic overhauls of their academic plans and usually can state their rationale for doing so very clearly (Lowther & Stark, 1990). Because faculty are directly involved, improving the way courses are incrementally adjusted may have greater impact on students than the dramatic changes at the program and college level so frequently heralded in case studies and touted in conference presentations.

Because of these very different levels of faculty involvement, we believe an appropriate curriculum development framework should include a perspective in which to view both extensive and incremental change at several levels: course, program, and the college. The framework can then equally well serve to analyze and guide the broad-scale changes of reform eras when external influences are strong and the smaller scale changes of more "normal" times as faculty intermittently respond to both internal and external influences on the curriculum. To some extent, writers who view construction of academic plans as a systematic design process already take such dual perspectives.

By definition, both *design* and *plan* imply deliberate decisions incorporating some desired relationship among setting and students, purpose, and process or, using Toombs's terminology, context, content, and form (Toombs, 1977–1978). Curriculum designs or plans are far more complex than simple statements of goals or descriptions of instructional processes. Accordingly, the process of creating the design is more elaborate than getting a few people with different views to compromise. A few frameworks exist that serve as lenses through which to examine both the current attempts at systematic curriculum design and critiques of them.

Toombs (1977–1978) and Toombs and Tierney (1993) used the idea of design to discuss both curriculum planning and curriculum analysis. They argued that *design* is a process that involves deliberate decisions about curriculum and can be understood by faculty members in diverse fields ranging from art to engineering. By curriculum *analysis,* Toombs (1977–1978) meant design in reverse—that is, the process of analyzing the curriculum plan to determine whether it contains the assumptions, structures, and activities necessary to meet the objectives.

Although directed primarily at elementary and secondary education, George Posner's (1992) recent work on analyzing curricula complements his earlier work on sequencing (more recently, he calls it "organization") and on course design. At least for illustrative purposes, Posner's work on course design portrays the development of a course as a linear process. Even so, it allows the developer to iterate portions of the process when fine-tuning the academic course plan as faculty typically do in practice. When Posner speaks of curriculum analysis, he means the close examination of academic plans—their origins, their ideological basis, the way the components fit together, and their implications (1992, p. 12).

Robert Diamond (1989), a long-time college-level instructional developer, sees curriculum development as a dynamic process but emphasizes systematic design. In Diamond's process, a discipline-neutral consultant leads a faculty member or group of faculty through the development process, making the process explicit, questioning their assumptions and helping them associate educational objectives with instructional strategies. Typically, Diamond's development process emphasizes student learning gains over content transmission. Curriculum devel-

opers like Posner and instructional developers like Diamond come relatively close to implementing in practice a view of curriculum as an academic plan. In these frameworks, faculty are planners and the focus is on their activities as planners rather than on the plan itself. The extent to which they carry out the process systematically depends on the guide they follow.

David Halliburton (1977a, 1977b) also focused on curricular design and developed another useful framework for viewing curriculum planning in higher education. Halliburton pointed out that curricula need adjustment because (1) the role of education changes with respect to broad historical and social needs, (2) new trends occur within the higher education system itself, and (3) the disciplines undergo paradigmatic shifts (or changes in accepted assumptions (1977a, p. 37). He categorized curricular change as typically occurring according to one or more of three processes of curriculum planning: (1) mechanism or statics (a process of tinkering or curriculum maintenance rather than overhaul); (2) dualism (curriculum change that swings from one popular trend or focus to another), and (3) knowledge-ism (a focus on changes in disciplinary content). Each of these processes, according to Halliburton, is associated with a different assumption about education. Mechanism (tinkering) assumes that the student is an empty vessel to be filled; the question is how to organize the filling process. Dualism assumes that teaching is separate from learning. Knowledge-ism is based on content acquisition rather than learner development. Halliburton emphasized that the disciplines, which reflect the assumptions, values, and habits of their practitioners, play a large part in determining which process is used. We concur. Like Halliburton, we have found that curriculum change processes vary at several levels of the academic plan and among the disciplines. But there is also reason to believe that the local context acts as a "filter" for the disciplinary frameworks in the curriculum development process at both the course level and the program level (Stark, Lowther, Ryan, et al., 1988). At the program level, resource allocations, structures, and leadership may constitute the contextual filters. (Posner, 1992; Seymour, 1988). Finally, at broader levels, such as that of an entire college, this contextual filtering may translate into competing societal and political interests. Thus, it is possible that the discipline orientations are potent at all levels of curriculum planning but manifest themselves differently and with different visibilities at different levels of the academic plan.

Drawing on the work of others, Halliburton (1977a, p. 47) saw that systematic curriculum planning needs a built-in process for change, should be articulated across levels, and should include evaluation. He stated that current curriculum development processes, bound as they are to assumptions about teaching and learning, limit our ability to create effective academic plans. Escape from these assumptions "will depend upon our learning to see the curriculum as a process that is subject to change, and our discovery of how to bring about change" (1977a, p. 45). Conrad and Pratt apparently endeavored to use these same ideas in their framework incorporating influences from inside and outside the collegiate institution.

These ideas about planning bring us full cycle in our process of considering curriculum itself as an academic plan based on unwritten and often unrecognized assumptions. At every turn we see that observers have noted the important associations between educational purpose, instructional processes, and change processes. They have also noted the strong impact of the disciplines on each of these, not separately but interdependently. In considerations of planning, the influences of forces both external and internal to the university become more visible than when curriculum is considered a static entity. How, then, can these ideas, repeated throughout the literature on curriculum, be tied together meaningfully? We believe that planning, however haphazard, occurs in all cases. A theory is essential to encourage faculty members and leaders to carry out curriculum planning as an intentional and informed design process.

In addition to varying in comprehensiveness, the frameworks we have examined vary in other ways. For example, they vary in origin—that is, the phenomena that have been observed to create them and the perspective of the educators who wrote about curriculum. Some are primarily descriptive, telling the story of what has been observed in colleges; others not only report these stories but attempt to interpret them through classifying and categorizing elements and processes. Still other frameworks are normative, taking a strong point of view about what should be taught, how it should be taught, or how curriculum change should be engineered. In such normative frameworks, how the theorists views linkages among the parts of the curriculum definition and the importance they give to each constitute a philosophy of education. Such frameworks cannot accommodate views stemming from contrary philosophies.

Each of the frameworks we have described has helped us to identify important elements that enter into academic plans and important influences on the plans educators make. The greatest number of prescriptive frameworks focus on questions like: "How will we define an educated person?" "How much is it necessary to study the established disciplines?" "How many great books must students read to appreciate our heritage?" Frameworks that include similar questions about the learner, the structure, and the types of activities to be used helped us to broaden these questions and recognize that the questions of purpose do not stand alone.

We believe that Dressel was closer to a theory of curriculum than he realized; his progress was limited, however, because he took a prescriptive position on many elements of the academic plan. A theory must be complex enough to accommodate uniqueness and diversity; it cannot take a normative stance. Conrad and Pratt's framework was also close to a theory but lacked a parsimonious set of curriculum elements and influences. Now, given our definition of curriculum as an academic plan, we are attempting to derive a coherent, linked framework for analyzing curriculum. There could be many ways of developing such a framework, and our choices reflect both our own perspectives and those of others whose work we have reviewed.

LINKING THE ELEMENTS: TOWARD A THEORY OF CURRICULUM

Why is a theory of the college curriculum important to such educational practitioners as faculty members and administrators? A curriculum theory permits the "careful systematic use of a well-defined set of ideas" and "provides an intellectual foundation or grounding for practice" (Walker, 1990, p. 133). Thus, a theory is first and foremost important in identifying curriculum elements and providing a way for faculty groups to systematically analyze curricular questions. For college faculty members, a theory may be particularly useful in eliminating pointless ideological debates that ensue when elements and assumptions are not distinguished. Theory can help ensure that systematic thinking replaces common sense, folklore, and disciplinary biases in developing the curriculum.

Second, we need theory to recognize and explore the interdependence of the elements within the complex phenomenon we call curriculum. Theory helps us appreciate that changes in one element of the plan are not independent from changes in other elements. Dressel indicated that we also needed a theory of curriculum to guide us in generating a set of interrelated and testable hypotheses (see also Kerlinger, 1973, p. 9).

Third, we need theory to help develop methods of detecting changes in the societal environment, cultivating a supportive institutional climate, and developing appropriate planning processes for curriculum at different levels. In particular, theory can help us to recognize the varied influences on curriculum planning and to estimate their influence on particular elements of the academic plan at specific levels.

Fourth, we need theory to help us understand how information about various elements of the curriculum plan is diffused among faculty within and between colleges and departments. This knowledge can help decision makers develop meaningful faculty development programs for improving all aspects of the curriculum.

Fifth, we need theory to recognize and assess the recursiveness of curriculum planning and its relation to society. The curriculum is shaped by the forces of society, true, but the curriculum also shapes society by shaping the knowledge, attitudes, and skills of the educated populace.

Making the best use of theory requires identifying and defining as many important elements (variables) related to curriculum as possible. It further requires that theorists speculate or hypothesize about relationships among elements that are sufficiently general to apply to a wide variety of cases and that can be observed or otherwise subjected to empirical test. Ultimately, we need theory to help us answer the most important question about curriculum: What is the relationship between desired educational outcomes and curriculum elements, alone and in combination? This question and others like it have only begun to be explored. We will present evidence for some of the connections within our emerging theory and point to others about which little is known. Later, we will return to the proposed theory to discuss its extension, testing, and limitations. The usefulness of our attempt to generate theory will be determined as we further specify the relationships between the steps, writing the propositions for each step, and verifying that the relationships hold. The ultimate test of usefulness will be in how well the theory of the academic plan can guide practice.

CHAPTER 4

Recurring Debates about the College Curriculum

INFLUENCES CREATE A COMPLEX EDUCATIONAL ENVIRONMENT

Curricular planning in American higher education has been characterized by periodically recurring debates about key issues, superimposed on a long-term trend toward diversification of institutions, educational missions, students, and programs. The debates have been created by influences acting on the educational environment from outside colleges as well as within them. These influences have modified the educational environment substantially during the relatively short history of American higher education; consequently, the perspectives of educators and the academic plans they create have also evolved. Educators have responded to external influences somewhat more frequently than they have initiated change.

Current and historical influences that shape the educational environment can be categorized into external, organizational, and internal influences. To illustrate, external influence may be felt from changes in the nation's economy and from state governing board mandates. Organizational influences

may come from missions assigned to an academic program by a higher level of authority in a college or from a change in the program's resource allocation. Internal influences stem from changes in faculty expertise or faculty decisions about teaching newly emerging knowledge. These are just a few examples of the many influences that affect the educational environment today. Because academic plans are constructed within an educational environment, it is important to acknowledge the complex set of influences that causes the environment to change (see Figure 4-1).

To place today's influences in historical perspective, we have identified recurring debates about persistent issues, and have interpreted the debates in terms of the elements of an academic plan. We have also provided timelines showing our estimates of periods of intense debate for each issue discussed. The key debates since the Civil War period that have shaped today's courses of study inform our understanding of the current college curriculum and of recent reform efforts. Some of today's proposals seem aimed, in the short run at least, at increasing the homogeneity of higher education rather than sustaining the

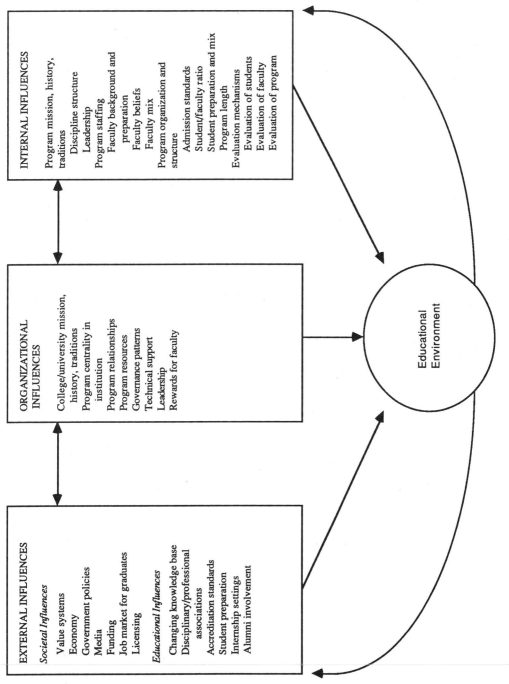

FIGURE 4-1   Influences on Educational Environments

long-term trend toward diversification. Historical perspective helps us to recognize that this may be but a short-term event within the greater trend toward diversity. Our discussion of the historical background of each periodic debate is necessarily brief. (See Appendix A for a comprehensive timeline of American curriculum history, and for a complete development see Stark, Zaruba, Francis, & Lattuca, 1994.)

The trend toward diversification—of institutional missions, of students, of academic programs, and of financial support and accountability—is reflected in changes that have occurred over time to specific elements of the academic plan (purpose, content, sequence, learners, instructional resources, instructional process, and evaluation). Thus, while most issues related to developing academic plans have surfaced at several periods, the discussions are not the same each time. Some have likened curriculum at all levels of American education to a swinging pendulum because of apparently recurring patterns (see, for example, Cuban, 1990; Hansen & Stampen, 1993; SREB, 1979). Like a pendulum, history may repeat itself, but never exactly.

The three types of influences on the curriculum—internal, organizational, and external—are not, of course, independent of each other. For example, we have classified accrediting agencies as an influence external to a given academic program and faculty influences as internal. Yet both regional and specialized accrediting agencies comprise groups of colleges and programs that voluntarily conform to particular standards, and most examiners are faculty. Thus, accrediting is strongly influenced by faculty expertise; and while the accrediting process is usually viewed as external, it is not entirely so. When we speak of accreditation we are speaking of the interaction of external and internal influences. We also focus on a single direction of influence—from society (external) to higher education (internal and organizational), rather than the reverse. Yet colleges do help to shape society just as society shapes the academic plans developed by colleges. Such a discussion would exceed our scope here since our primary interest is the development and improvement of academic plans, not societal change.

Although our attempt to categorize influences simplifies discussion and helps to keep us aware of the varied influences acting on curriculum and their importance, it also highlights the complexity, interrelatedness, and countercurrents of the influences as they ebb and flow. Such complexity constantly reminds us that developing or analyzing academic plans in the American educational environment is not a simple task.

PATTERNS OF CURRICULUM DEBATE

In the foreword to Rudolph's *Curriculum: A History of the American Course of Study since 1636,* Clark Kerr (1977, p. x) observed that curriculum is the battleground on which society debates education. Because we focused our attention on topics closely allied with elements of the academic plan, the five debates we have identified for discussion are similar to, but not identical with, Kerr's list of key battles.

Our first discussion focuses on educational *purpose* and includes debates about whether education should be general or vocationally-oriented, whether undergraduates should pursue only broad education or should specialize, and whether education should transmit a common view of culture or one adapted to include students' varied cultural backgrounds and interests. Kerr subsumed most of these discussions under the rubric of "general education versus specialized study." These debates have coincided with a trend toward increasing diversity in institutions and educational missions.

Our second discussion focuses on a series of external influences that have fostered increasing diversity of *learners.* This discussion encompasses the debates Kerr labeled "elitism versus egalitarianism" and "mass versus individualized education." Although it is difficult to document and attribute deliberate periods of elitism, we have identified alternating periods of relatively stronger and weaker emphasis on access and, perhaps, periodic neglect of the expanding pool of students. Debates about access, however, must be viewed in the context of a long-term trend toward broadened access.

Third, we discuss *content* by examining the debate Kerr called "prescription versus choice." With the rapid proliferation of knowledge, academic programs and courses have also changed, but not without considerable debate about the necessity and desirability of those changes. This debate, of course, also involves questions of institutional mission as well as the balance between general and specialized education.

Our fourth topic, *instructional process,* describes relatively few periods of modest educational experimentation at the course, program, and college level. We address experiments with instructional processes and structural arrangements, of which the one Kerr singled out ("subject-based versus competency-based education") is but one example. However, after only modest change thus far, the pace of change in instructional process is escalating as the information revolution continues.

Finally, we discuss the relation of these four sets of debates to periods of emphasis on *evaluation and adjustment.* Society has emphasized accountability—whether for funds or "quality control"—many times in the past. Often this emphasis has been intended to change the direction or pace of change. De-

spite these occasional periods of emphasis, higher education evaluation and adjustment mechanisms have remained idiosyncratic and unsystematic.

Although Kerr's analogy of the curriculum as a battleground for society's debates is appealing, the analogy of navigating a ship may better portray how changes in curriculum have occurred over time. Diversification has been the long-term direction, but along the way society and educators have suggested periodic adjustments and corrections. Sometimes the demand for adjustment has been intense and urgent, possibly resulting in overcorrections. At other times change has been a gradual veering. The most significant undulations in the intensity of debate about change have been produced by external influences; intensity has increased with societal turbulence related to financial developments (such as economic depression), technological developments (the industrial and information revolutions), international economic competition, and international or domestic conflicts (wars or police actions). Relatively speaking, the debates produced by internal influences within colleges have been mere flutters and the changes less dramatic, sometimes intensifying and sometimes retarding corrections sought by society. Meanwhile, overall, the course toward greater diversity in curriculum has continued.

The Educational Purpose Issue: Debating the Balance of General and Specialized Studies

Periodic debate has accompanied the gradual change from education designed with a common purpose—to prepare young men for gentlemanly status—to education to prepare today's students of all ages for useful life and work. The debate was initially inspired by changing societal needs, but it also reflected the tension between students' backgrounds, interests, and precollege preparation, on the one hand, and professors' judgments about the preservation, transmission, and creation of knowledge on the other. Figure 4-2 shows some of the periods when general and specialized education have been emphasized during American higher education history.

The debate over educational purposes has been accompanied (and perhaps encouraged) by the evolution of distinctly different types of higher education institutions, including technical schools, liberal arts colleges, state universities, private two-year colleges, community colleges, and research universities. In fall 1993, 3,632 four-year and two-year collegiate institutions existed in the fifty United States, each slightly different from the others in its educational purpose or mission (*Chronicle of Higher Education Almanac,* 1995, p. 17). Postsecondary education also includes from 5,000 to 7,000 career or specialized schools, enrolling over 5.5 million students, which we will not include in our discussion. ("Characteristics of the Nation's," 1993, p. 11, Table 2).

Three Missions Solidify

Discussion of general versus specialized educational purposes became polarized at the end of the nineteenth century, when three types of college missions could be clearly distinguished. The first was a utilitarian mission, based on the belief that colleges should train citizens to participate in the nation's economic and commercial life. Institutions espousing this type of mission offered programs characterized by career-oriented programs, particularly studies like business and science, buttressed by general education electives. The Morrill Land-Grant Act of 1862 provided the framework for large numbers of state institutions, particularly those stressing agriculture, to follow this model. By the 1920s, teacher education and other occupationally useful fields, like business and engineering (of inter-

est primarily to male students) and social work and nursing (demanded primarily by women), began to move into four-year colleges and universities, particularly in state-sponsored institutions. Today, many state colleges still emphasize a mission of practical education and social improvement through economic growth and upward mobility. These colleges attempt to meet the practical educational needs of their regional constituencies, providing relatively open access to training in the skilled professions and service in matters of civic concern, including the education of teachers. State colleges have now been joined in this mission by some "comprehensive" private colleges with varied programs. While the state colleges accepted liberal arts education to buttress career programs, many private comprehensives added preprofessional and occupational majors to supplement liberal arts programs. In search of varied funding sources and clienteles, some of these new comprehensives, both public and private, have developed large "extension" programs serving students far from their home campuses.

The research university, patterned after the German model and dedicated to the production of new knowledge, espoused another type of mission. In its purest form, the research mission had little place or need for undergraduates. However, financial concerns and faculty sentiment convinced most universities to retain their undergraduate programs rather than become exclusively research institutes serving only graduate students. This group of institutions now includes not only the universities that have historically pursued new knowledge, but also an increasing number of doctorate-granting universities, including some that evolved from state colleges. The research universities, both public and private, continue to devote large segments of their resources to the discovery of new knowledge, both in the arts and sciences and in the many professional fields that now make up separate colleges within the universities. Although un-

FIGURE 4-2   Periods of Emphasis on General and Specialized Education

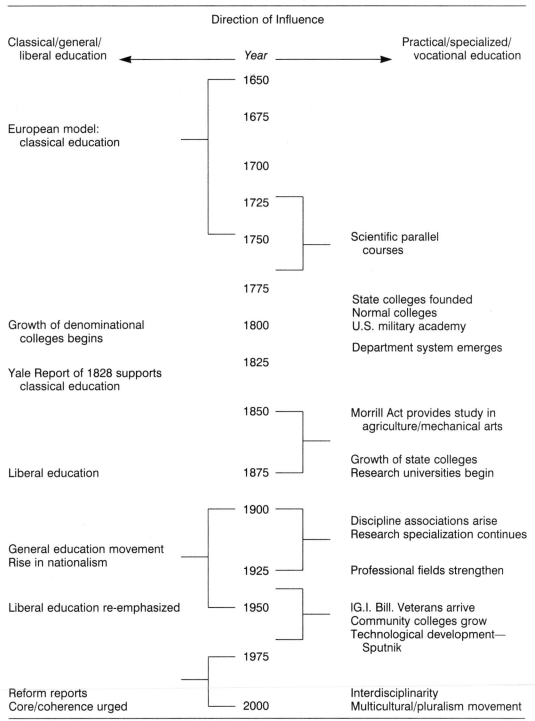

Direction of Influence

| Classical/general/
liberal education | ← Year → | Practical/specialized/
vocational education |

dergraduate students typically constitute less than half of their enrollment, the prestige of research activities and advanced degrees often draws students interested in specialized study with research-oriented professors. The tension between general and specialized study is exacerbated when some faculty groups try to stem early undergraduate specialization, while other groups advocate it.

A third mission, especially prominent just before the turn of the century, grew from the previous classical model of education and evolved into today's liberal arts model. This mission, and the resulting curriculum, stressed understanding and improving society more than the "classic" education offered earlier. Above all else, however, the liberal arts movement sustained the faculty belief in classical education. Today, the belief remains strong that studying the liberal arts, including classic authors, improves students' ability to think, to appreciate knowledge, and to serve. These abilities, in turn, are believed to transfer to other tasks and settings, allowing graduates to serve society. Thus, many of these colleges specifically prepare students for entrance into professional schools, such as law and medicine. Prototypic liberal arts colleges maintain their mission of educating students to think critically about many subjects and ideas thereby producing broadly educated citizens, some of whom will seek more advanced specialized study. Most of these colleges discourage early specialization, particularly in vocational fields.

As knowledge expanded rapidly, faculty members in all three types of institutions became more interested in advancing new specializations and less concerned with defending the existing classical course with its emphasis on rhetoric, ancient languages and moral philosophy. Departments emerged to organize the curriculum, and close associations of scholars in similar fields motivated faculty members to stay on the forefront of knowledge. (Harvard and the University of Virginia are both said to have created the first academic departments around 1825.) Thereafter, it became possible for students, too, to specialize, expanding their broad education to include concentration in a single field. The last half of the nineteenth century saw an increase in the number of subjects being taught, the emergence of new fields like science and psychology, and increasingly more social and technological needs to be filled. The development of majors in these new subjects helped focus students' academic programs. The major field is said to have been created partly to stem the rising tide of student free choice of courses in the late 1800s and has become an important component of education in nearly all four-year colleges.

Despite the early introduction of Harvard Law School in 1817, most colleges did not include professional schools as we know them today until early in the twentieth century when the prestigious professions of medicine, dentistry, and law joined the university. These fields and their foundation disciplines in the sciences and social sciences gained stronger footholds in the college curriculum as the knowledge base for such professions expanded.

The Twentieth Century

After 1900, the pendulum swung back, again emphasizing general education. Faculty groups reacted to the threat of overspecialization by launching a period of general education reform in the first thirty years of the 1900s (Bell, 1966). Between 1915 and 1935 the number of courses in social ethics increased, reminiscent of the eighteenth century's emphasis on moral philosophy. The rise of international communism and World War I increased awareness of political ferment abroad. Ideological discussions again joined technical discussions in college classrooms. During the Great Depression of

1929–1932, students, faced with a dismal job market, wanted career flexibility, and also began to reduce specialization by majoring in more general fields.

In 1945, Harvard University produced *General Education in a Free Society,* popularly called the Harvard "Redbook," which focused on citizens' need for general education. It came just when World War II had pressed the curriculum again toward specialization. The President's Commission on Higher Education in 1947 called for balance: "Colleges must find the right relationship between specialized training on the one hand, aiming at a thousand different careers, and the transmission of a common cultural heritage toward a common citizenship on the other" (Zook, 1948, p. 49).

From the 1950s to the 1970s, specialization was again in vogue, fueled by the enormous needs during World War II for technological development, the practical outlook of the career-oriented returning veterans, and the fear of obsolescence generated by the Russian launching of Sputnik in October 1957. Even private colleges formerly devoted to the liberal arts introduced new career-oriented majors in an attempt to keep up with technology and to maintain their share of the student market.

A new type of institution, the two-year community college, began before 1910 but developed most rapidly after 1940, offering occupational studies and diversifying college missions even further. The community colleges, originally designed to provide academic foundations for students planning to transfer to four-year institutions, began to provide short-term and long-term vocational training of types previously provided by employers. These colleges meet the needs of local communities and employers for vocational programs as distinctive as horticulture, welding, refrigeration technology, or animal training. Local influences, which once encouraged denominational colleges to focus on the classics, now encourage specialized occupational programs for community colleges.

Finally, like comprehensive colleges, community colleges also defined service to their communities as part of their mission, offering leisure-time pursuits for senior citizens. Increasingly, they have contracted with local businesses to offer professional development courses tailored to employees specific needs. Some offer programs for adult members of the community with special needs who are beyond the age of eligibility for secondary school services. The missions of community colleges overlaps somewhat with those of other undergraduate institutions. Two-year and four-year colleges compete in many areas, particularly for students who wish to specialize in occupational programs.

Current Diversity

The Carnegie classification, developed in the mid–1970s and revised in 1987 and again in 1994, provides a snapshot of existing colleges and universities that is relevant to discussing curriculum because it is based on the major missions we have described: the types of academic degrees granted, the numbers of professional programs offered, and the amounts of external research funds obtained and spent. Within the subpopulation of liberal arts colleges, the college's selectivity in choosing its student body is also a criterion for classification. After these variables have formed the basic categories, the Carnegie classification further subdivides colleges by private and public sponsorship as shown in Table 4-1.

The types of available specializations, like the types of colleges, have diversified and proliferated. In 1991–1992, 1,136,553 bachelor's degrees were granted (*Chronicle of Higher Education Almanac,* 1994, p. 31) (In addition to the commonly known Bachelor of Arts and Bachelor of Science degrees, there are many additional types of bachelor's

TABLE 4-1 Carnegie Classification of Colleges: Numbers of Institutions and Students, 1994

Type of Institution	Enrollment (Thousands)			Percentage		Number of Institutions			Percentage	
	Total	Public	Private	Public	of Total	Total	Public	Private	Public	of Total
Total	15,263	12,072	3,191	79.1	100.0	3,595	1,576	2,019	43.8	100.0
Doctorate-granting institutions:	3,981	3,111	869	78.2	26.1	236	151	85	64.0	6.6
Research universities I	2,030	1,652	379	81.3	13.3	88	59	29	67.0	2.5
Research universities II	641	488	153	76.2	4.2	37	26	11	70.3	1.0
Doctoral universities I	658	467	191	70.9	4.3	51	28	23	54.9	1.4
Doctoral universities II	651	505	147	77.5	4.3	60	38	22	63.3	1.7
Master's colleges and universities**:	3,139	2,291	848	73.0	20.6	529	275	254	52.0	14.7
Master's colleges and universities I	2,896	2,177	719	75.2	19.0	435	249	186	57.2	12.1
Master's colleges and universities II	243	114	129	46.9	1.6	94	26	68	27.7	2.6
Baccalaureate colleges***:	1,053	275	777	26.2	6.9	637	86	551	13.5	17.7
Baccalaureate colleges I	268	20	248	7.5	1.8	166	7	159	4.2	4.6
Baccalaureate colleges II	784	255	529	32.5	5.1	471	79	392	16.8	13.1
Associate of arts colleges	6,527	6,234	292	95.5	42.8	1,471	963	508	65.5	40.9
Specialized institutions	548	145	404	26.4	3.6	693	72	621	10.4	19.3
Tribal colleges and universities*	15	15	0	100.0	0.1	29	29	0	100.0	0.8

Source: From *A Classification of Institutions of Higher Education.* Princeton, NJ: The Carnegie Foundation for the Advancement of Teaching, 1994, p. xiv. Enrollment figures are adapted from U.S. National Center for Education Statistics data. Copyright 1994, The Carnegie Foundation for the Advancement of Teaching. Reprinted with permission.

Note: Enrollments are rounded to the nearest 1,000.

*Figure excludes institutions with unavailable enrollment figures.

**Formerly called "comprehensive colleges" and universities.

***Formerly called "liberal arts colleges."

degrees, ranging from the B.Mus. (music) to the B.B.A. (business administration) and the B.S.W. (social work). Table 4-2 describes the percentage of all undergraduate degrees con-ferred in various specializations in 1989–1990.

The wide scope of content subjects taught in two-year and four-year institutions

TABLE 4-2 Undergraduate Degrees Conferred in 1989–1990, by Major Specialization

	Associate Degrees N=429,946	(percent)	Bachelors Degrees N=1,015,239
Agriculture and natural resources	1.1		1.3
Architecture and environmental design	0.4		0.9
Area and ethnic studies	—*		0.4
Business and management	24.8		24.3
Communications	0.9		4.8
Computer and information science	1.8		3.0
Education	1.7		9.6
Engineering	13.0		0.4
Fine and applied arts	3.0		3.7
Foreign languages	—		1.1
Health professions	13.8		5.8
Home economics	2.4		1.4
Law	0.9		0.1
Letters	.01		4.9
Library science	—		—
Life sciences	0.2		3.6
Mathematics	0.2		1.5
Military science	—		—
Physical sciences	0.5		1.7
Psychology	0.3		4.8
Public affairs and services	3.9		3.4
Social sciences	0.6		10.6
Theology	0.1		0.5
Interdisciplinary studies	30.2		4.1
Total	99.8		99.9

Source: From *Race/Ethnicity Trends in Degrees Conferred by Institutions of Higher Education: 1978–79 through 1988–89,* National Center for Education Statistics, Table 8.

Notes:

*<.01

Types of degrees under a category may differ at the two degree levels. *Example:* An associate degree in education may connote preparation to be a teacher's aide or a plan to major in teacher education upon transfer; a bachelor's degree recipient may become a certified teacher. Some categories, such as letters, include several disciplines or subdisciplines such as general English, literature, speech, creative writing and so on. Public affairs includes social work.

can be grasped by reviewing the U.S. Office of Education coding system that colleges use to report their majors, courses taught and degrees granted. This comprehensive system, the Integrated Postsecondary Education Data System (IPEDS), classifies and describes courses and programs currently offered in postsecondary schools of all types. The main categories of this system are shown in Table 4-3.

In four-year college programs, academic specializations within the arts and sciences are of four types: an academic discipline major (typically intended to prepare students for graduate school in academic or prestigious professional fields), a general education or liberal studies major, an interdisciplinary major, and a planned preprofessional major. Four-year public and private comprehensive colleges (and, increasingly, nonselective lib-

TABLE 4-3   Major Categories of Academic Programs, According to the Integrated Postsecondary Education Data System

01 Agricultural Business and Production	31 Parks, Recreation, Leisure and Fitness Studies
02 Agricultural Sciences	32 Personal Improvement and Leisure Programs
03 Conservation and Renewable Natural Resources	33 Citizenship Activities
04 Architecture and Related Programs	34 Health-related Knowledges and Skills
05 Area, Ethnic and Cultural Studies	36 Leisure and Recreational Activities
08 Marketing Operations, Marketing and Distribution	37 Personal Awareness and Self-Improvement
09 Communications	38 Philosophy and Religion
10 Communications Technologies	39 Theological Studies and Religious Vocations
11 Computer and Information Sciences	40 Physical Sciences
12 Personal and Miscellaneous Services	41 Science Technologies
13 Education	42 Psychology
14 Engineering	43 Protective Services
15 Engineering-Related Technologies	44 Public Administration and Services
16 Foreign Languages and Literatures	45 Social Sciences and History
19 Home Economics	46 Construction Trades
20 Vocational Home Economics	47 Mechanics and Repairers
21 Technical Education/Industrial Arts Programs	48 Precision Production Trades
22 Law and Legal Studies	49 Transportation and Materials-Moving Workers
23 English Language and Literature/Letters	50 Visual and Performing Arts
24 Liberal Arts and Sciences, General Studies, and Humanities	51 Health Professions and Related Sciences
25 Library Science	52 Business, Management and Administrative Services
26 Biological Sciences/Life Sciences	53 High School, Secondary Diplomas/Certificates
27 Mathematics	
28 Reserve Officers Training Corps	
29 Military Technologies	
30 Multi/Interdisciplinary Studies	

eral arts colleges) also offer undergraduate career studies (professional) majors that prepare students for entry-level positions in diverse occupations, and two-year colleges offer more technical occupational concentrations.

The proliferation of career-oriented undergraduate majors in nonselective four-year colleges, both public and private, has provided programs attractive to students. The most common career majors in recent years have been business and management, education, engineering, and combined health professions. These choices are influenced by many factors, of which the job market is the most prominent. For example, the choice of education as a major by young women students declined drastically as opportunities for new entrants to teaching jobs decreased in the 1970s and, simultaneously, opportunities for women in formerly male-dominated fields like business and engineering increased. Some specialized programs that require more than four years of undergraduate study, such as architecture and pharmacy, are found in larger universities.

About 34% of students who attend a two-year college study arts and sciences; 20% study technological fields; 20% study business; and the remaining 25% study health, trades, and other services (*Condition of Education,* 1994, p. 84). Like the four-year program, the two-year college curriculum may also include a general education segment, a major specialization, and some electives. But this distribution takes place in a total of 60 credits or fewer (two years if pursued full time), rather than in 120 credits or four years of work.

The proportions of various types of content students include in academic programs has been well documented over the years (Blackburn et al., 1976; Dressel & DeLisle, 1970; Toombs, Amey, & Fairweather, 1989). Studies of college requirements for students' coursework showed a trend between 1970 and the mid–1980s toward an increase in the portion of students' programs devoted to specialization or supporting coursework.

Approaching the Twenty-first Century

Many students at research, doctoral, or comprehensive universities begin their studies in the arts and sciences colleges in their universities. Even those who least often follow this pattern (engineering and fine arts students), usually must take some arts and science courses. Thus, the typical four-year college degree consists of about 120 credits divided into three parts: 33%–40% general education in arts and sciences, and the remaining 60%–66% divided between the major or specialization and other courses—usually electives or specific collegewide requirements. Because of the persistence of the debate about the balance of general and specialized study, considerable effort is being undertaken to document actual student course patterns (see, e.g., the studies by Adelman, 1990, 1992b; Ratcliff, 1992b; Zemsky, 1989).

General Study. According to the American Council on Education (El-Khawas, 1990), 86% of colleges and universities currently require all students to complete a certain amount of general education coursework. Many colleges use distribution requirements, requiring students to take a specified number of courses in varied areas to achieve breadth of knowledge and a course in English to demonstrate competence in writing and/or other communication skills. Forty-five percent of all colleges and universities require students to take courses focused on Western civilization and/or world civilization (El-Khawas, 1990). According to an analysis of the high school graduating class of 1972, students who attended college typically took more of these types of courses than the minimum their college required (Adelman, 1990). In 1967, 43% of the average student's course work was reported to be in general education

(Dressel & DeLisle, 1970), decreasing to 33.4% in 1974 (Blackburn et al., 1976), but increasing again to 38% in 1988 (Toombs, Amey, & Fairweather, 1989; Locke 1989). In addition to increasing the proportion of credits allocated to general education in total, colleges were beginning to require at least one course in mathematics by the late 1980s. According to Lawrence Locke (1989), only 33% of colleges required mathematics as part of general education in 1967, decreasing to 20% in 1974 but rising to 65% in 1988. In 1992, half of the nation's four-year colleges were engaged in general education reform (El-Khawas, 1993).

Specialization. The important concepts of a major field and the methods of inquiry to be taught are determined by the society of scholars in that field. This group interprets the discipline; adapts it to society's needs; and typically is responsible for including new material, new questions, and new ways of thinking in the curriculum. The disciplinary major may be defined specifically and tightly as an academic plan if there is consensus of scholars in a field; it is usually more loosely structured if the discipline is in transition or lacks consensus on the questions of interest or the ways of studying them. Especially in colleges and universities where faculty participate externally in the scholarship of their field, the major plan also may reflect ferment due to recent advances.

Typically, the broad academic plan for the undergraduate disciplinary major follows a sequence in which the student gains increasingly more depth of knowledge in the field. It has an introductory course (which may double as a general education requirement), a set of intermediate courses, and some advanced courses. It may require a thesis, a senior paper, or some other "synthesizing" experience such as a seminar or comprehensive examination. Some students who major in an academic discipline plan to continue study in the field at the graduate level, but a much greater number finish college and seek work in varied occupations, some related to the major, some not.

An interdisciplinary major (or a double major) may combine two or even three fields of the student's choice; or, if there is sufficient student interest, a college may formalize an interdisciplinary major by drawing courses from several academic departments. Often an interdisciplinary major brings the methods and questions of several disciplines to bear on a particular problem or genre of problems. Examples are urban studies, Near Eastern cultures, or international relations.

Some colleges offer general education or liberal studies majors, which may involve greater flexibility and wider choice of courses than do majors in specific disciplines. The liberal studies major generally lacks the structure of the formal discipline or interdisciplinary major and is intended for students who wish to learn in many fields but resist specialization. In some colleges, it is viewed as a catch-all category for students who are undecided about which specific field to pursue in depth, or as an "escape hatch" for unmotivated students. Such negative reaction to the liberal studies major in some colleges provides evidence of how far higher education has moved from a general core curriculum toward one centered around a specialized major program of study.

A preprofessional major is usually a recommended set of courses qualifying a student to apply to a graduate-level professional school such as law, medicine, veterinary medicine, or dentistry. Frequently, a special advisor is assigned to preprofessional aspirants to help them choose the necessary courses and apply to the graduate school. But advanced professional schools typically do not require a specific major, so students who take a collection of relevant subjects often can present themselves as appropriately prepared. In many colleges, students are advised to study an appropriate disciplinary major in depth, rather than pursue a preprofessional major.

Students who pursue professional majors often practice their future occupation in fieldwork settings as undergraduates. In these fields, the major conveys a knowledge base of skills, attitudes, and behaviors needed for entry to a specific occupation on receipt of the bachelor's degree. Educators have long debated what to call these undergraduate majors. Some theorists have referred to them as preparation for the "semiprofessions" to distinguish them from the study of the "learned" or "prestigious" professions such as law, medicine, and dentistry. In comparison to occupational training for the laboring or blue-collar occupations, these fields seem to be professional because they require four to six years of college training. Some of the fields we include among the undergraduate professions are architecture, business, education, engineering, journalism, library science, nursing, occupational therapy, physical therapy, pharmacy, public administration, and social work. Today, more than 50% of U.S. college students enroll in these types of programs that, we suggest, appropriately may be called collegiate career studies.

Collegiate career studies often are viewed more favorably by students and groups external to the university than by some faculty members in the collegiate organization who accuse them of deflecting students from academic discipline majors they traditionally see as more appropriate higher learning. In fact, professional education concentrates on preparing students for ambiguous situations calling for informed, complex judgment. Students in such professional programs also consider questions of how the knowledge was gained, what usefulness it has to society, and how it can continue to be advanced, as well as what specific career uses it has for the aspiring professional. Collegiate career education that asks these questions differs from education that teaches students to perform specific well-defined tasks in an occupation.

Occupational majors, as typically offered in two-year colleges and some four-year colleges, help students to apply knowledge in specific and usually predictable situations. Although they may enjoy their work and be committed to it, graduates in these fields are not expected to be concerned about advancing knowledge in their occupation or about continuing to be independent learners. Occupational educators tend to be clear about the specific skills they are teaching and how to measure when they have been mastered. Performance-oriented subjects lend themselves to instructional processes based on diagnosis, grading, and prescription of additional practice to achieve competence. Cohen (1979, pp. 57–58) suggests that community college occupational programs may be conveniently grouped into three sets: (1) production—manufacturing, construction, mining, skilled trades, design, processing, and engineering fields; (2) commerce and general business—banking and finance, sales, advertising, marketing, communications, hospitality and tourism, retail and wholesale distribution; (3) services—allied health, education, law, criminal justice, public safety, and civil service.

Preparation for occupational positions may require less than two years and may take place on a year-round basis rather than in the traditional academic semesters. This preparation often addresses specific community manpower needs, and the college accepts additional job placement obligations as well as other support and guidance obligations for students. Still, colleges expect occupational majors to develop basic literacy and mathematical skills. These general education components may be an unpopular part of the program if students lack intellectual motivation.

Despite favorable federal and state funding of occupational programs to meet hiring needs, these programs suffer from some disrespect when placed in colleges. Students who pursue occupational majors in community colleges and later attempt to continue their education in four-year colleges without similar offerings, may have difficulty in obtaining transferable college credit, partly because occupational programs often are not offered in parallel form at four-year colleges. Indeed, some occupational programs require that faculty members with practical experience in trade fields but nonstandard credentials (by college standards) be hired. Yet a large portion of the student population in the mid–1990s attends college to obtain occupational training in many fields, from health services to industrial trades and office systems. These enrollments are continuing to grow. In some areas of the country, community colleges have replaced vocational high schools in serving area hiring needs.

The Debate Continues

Today, increased specialized knowledge promotes continued segmentation of occupational fields into subspecialties like nuclear engineering or pediatric social work. Sometimes such disciplinary splintering is encouraged by federal and state government to address social needs. Over 350 years, the move toward program diversification has included several cycles of diminished and renewed emphasis on specialization. In the 1990s, once again, increased rhetoric supports general studies, especially concern for preserving the cultural heritage and helping students broaden their outlooks. However, faculty cite expanding knowledge bases and increasingly demanding disciplinary accrediting agencies as unrelenting pressures toward specialized study. The specialization and diversification of academic programs surely are closely related, and both are opposed by advocates of breadth rather than depth.

The three missions, utilitarian, research, and liberal arts, still form the primary basis for the diversity among colleges, but now the debate over general and specialized study sometimes occurs within a single complex institution. For example, the concept of liberal arts as a foundation for life or further study for all college students dominates the undergraduate programs in many large universities or, as Clark Kerr called them "multiversities." Here the colleges of arts and sciences typically provide a core liberal arts curriculum before students branch out into more specialized studies. Clearly, they endorse a general form of education for all, in preference to specialization in either an academic discipline or a professional field. Yet professional schools within the same universities offer career-oriented education, and some prefer to enroll their students as freshmen. In large universities, organizational influences enter the debate, and competition for resources may be strong. As program is pitted against program and college against college in the budget process, the historical debate on the relative merits of general versus specialized study is often revisited in very pragmatic terms.

Learners: Periods of Emphasis on Access

The issue of access focuses on learners and grows from the debate Kerr called "elitism versus egalitarianism." A steady long-term trend toward increased access for learners has been marked by periods when strong advocacy faltered or attention turned to other issues. Calls for "quality control" sometimes camouflage stereotypes and prejudices about the capabilities or efforts of nontraditional learners. Pockets of restricted access are hardly ancient history; Princeton University first admitted Blacks after World War II, and Harvard did not abolish its admissions quota for undergraduate women until 1975.

The increased diversity of college students is strikingly illustrated by examining statistics over the last 120 years of American higher education. In 1850 it is estimated that only 1% of the population actually finished college. The rapid rise in bachelor's degrees granted after records were begun in 1870 is shown in Figure 4-3.

Opportunity Increases

The Industrial Revolution and the spread of settlement across the continent inspired change. The needs of the country—and thus its potential students—now included expertise in areas such as surveying and agriculture. An education encompassing these more practical subjects appealed to a broader spectrum of the population, and public pressure led to passage of the 1862 Morrill Land-Grant Act so that "every American citizen is entitled to receive some form of higher education" (Brubacher & Rudy, 1976, p. 66). America was producing a growing number of families willing to finance a son's education if it fitted him for entry into a world of greater opportunity. During the Civil War, some colleges also filled classes by admitting women, a trend that continued as a

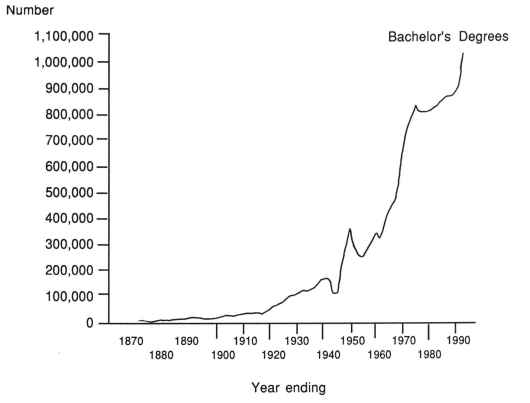

FIGURE 4-3   Bachelors' Degrees Conferred by U.S. Institutions of Higher Education: 1869–1870 to 1989–1990

Source: Adapted from Thomas Snyder (Ed.), *120 Years of American Education: A Statistical Portrait.* Washington, DC: Department of Education, National Center for Education Statistics.

result of reformist ideals. The post–Civil War period and the passage of a second Morrill Act in 1890 made college education available for Black Americans, primarily by creating segregated colleges.

During the rest of the nineteenth century, access increased but assumptions of educational elitism remained, especially for women and Blacks. While more White men from outside the upper classes sought the education provided by the new and more practical institutions, Black Americans did not have full access to the types of education provided to White students until well after World War II. Figure 4-4 shows the periods of emphasis on access.

Improved Preparation Fuels Rapid Growth

In 1870 less than 2% of the 18- to 24-year-old population was enrolled in college (Snyder, 1993). In the same year, most of the nation's existing colleges offered preparatory programs because many students were not ready for college-level study (Rudolph, 1977, p. 160). Thus, the next period of increased access awaited expansion and improvements in public high school education. After 1870, high school attendance grew rapidly (Rudolph, 1977, p. 158). The University of Michigan developed the first articulation agreements with secondary schools during the 1870s, and thereafter the increasing standardization of the high school curriculum meant that college preparation did not require private schooling or expensive tutoring.

The influx of Jewish immigrants from Europe around the turn of the century brought a new immigrant group greatly interested in the intellectual life (Wechsler, 1977). This group swelled enrollments at colleges and universities in eastern cities and challenged them to help prepare a new professional class of doctors, lawyers, businessmen, professors, and scientists. However, in the period immediately following World War I, many eastern colleges began to limit entering class size in a possible return to elitism. They selected the best and the brightest students by using newly developed standardized admissions tests intended to assure adequate preparation. While in many ways raising admission standards was a positive step, at some universities the action represented scarcely veiled anti-Semitism. Some eastern urban institutions, eager to reduce what they considered detrimentally large concentrations of Jewish students on campus, claimed a strong concern for students' "character" and thus freed themselves to make decisions based on criteria other than academic preparation and potential.

The "Typical" Student Disappears

Although most smaller liberal arts colleges encouraged primarily full-time residential students until well after World War II, many urban institutions in the areas heavily populated by immigrants became commuter schools and established large evening divisions in the early twentieth century. World War II was, however, the most significant catalyst in diversifying college student attendance nationwide. The Servicemen's Readjustment Act of 1944, popularly known as the G.I. Bill, was stimulated by worries about the possible effects of mass unemployment when large numbers of service personnel were demobilized. Although the government assumed that only a small number would take advantage of the offer to finance their education, about 2.2 million veterans returned to college. Their attendance challenged existing visions of the typical student, required massive expansion of higher education, and paved the way for further enrollment growth and increasing student diversity in following decades.

When the President's Commission on Higher Education published its 1947 report entitled *Higher Education for Democracy*, it

FIGURE 4-4   Periods of Emphasis on Access

Direction of Influence

Selective Limited access ⟵	Year ⟶	Open Broadened access
	1650	
	1675	
Limited access		
	1700	
	1725	
	1750	
	1775	
	1800	
		Jacksonian era/broadened access
	1825	
		Lowered admissions standards
	1850	
		Morrill Act broadens access
	1875	Women and Black students admitted
	1900	
		High schools improve and standardize Jewish enrollments rise
	1925	Part-time students increase
Elitist quotas at eastern colleges	1950	Truman Commission report G.I. Bill. Veterans attend college Community colleges increase local access
	1975	Federal financial aid External degree programs Segregation ends
Quality control movement		
	2000	Distance learning feasible

affirmed the usefulness of a college or university education and asserted that citizens were "entitled" to higher education whether or not they could personally afford it. Further, the report declared that the nation would benefit when postsecondary education, appropriate to student needs and talents, had been made available to all who had the requisite ability (then estimated at 50% of the population).

After the Supreme Court declared segregation illegal in the 1960s, Black Americans gained entry to colleges previously closed to them. During the 1960s, women also began to enter college in larger numbers. In the late 1960s, "external degree" colleges, or "universities without walls," sprang up to serve adult learners unable to attend formal classes on campuses. This small but distinctive group of colleges, which often award some degree credit for life experiences outside of formal education, often station faculty in locations convenient to clusters of students. An ever-increasing portion of the U.S. population has attended college. A recent study of the high school graduating class of 1980 found that 66% had entered some form of postsecondary education by 1986 (Ottinger, 1989, p. 46). Today the "typical" college student may be a U.S. citizen of any age or background.

Entitlement for Learners

Notions of entitlement and access strengthened throughout the 1950s. The report of the President's Commission laid the foundation for the Higher Education Act of 1972, which created grant and loan programs based on the principle that college attendance should not be precluded for capable students because of inability to pay. In 1972, this legislation to supply college financial aid to all needy and deserving students bolstered college attendance once more and increased student choice among existing colleges. It also led to strong federal influence on higher education.

The public two-year sector began to expand in the mid-1900s. Today, most states join with local governmental units to sponsor community-oriented colleges that account for 37% of all undergraduate enrollments and 46% of all public college enrollments. In 1992–1993, these colleges (and a few four-year colleges that also grant two-year degrees) awarded 514,756 associate degrees (*Chronicle of Higher Education Almanac,* 1995, p. 20). Citizens feel entitled to attend a community college near their home regardless of their financial resources or previous record of academic success.

Maintaining Access in the Twenty-first Century

With entitlement and antidiscrimination laws firmly in place, the final thirty years of the twentieth century are characterized by most observers as a period of strong continuing emphasis on access. This period witnessed a continued increase in numbers and diversity of students pursuing postsecondary study. In fall 1993, 14.3 million students, of whom 86% were undergraduates, were enrolled in American collegiate education, the highest enrollment in history (*Chronicle of Higher Education Almanac,* 1995, p. 8). Of the total number of students, 11,190,000 were in public colleges and 3,117,000 were in private colleges. Four-year colleges enrolled 8,740,000, while two-year colleges enrolled 5,566,000 students (*Chronicle of Higher Education Almanac*, 1995, p. 8).

Whereas only about 5% of the U.S. population had completed college in 1940; in 1989, 21% of the adult population (25 years and older) had completed four or more years of college. By 1993, 53% of individuals in the 35–39-year-old age group (born right after World War II) had attended some college, 25% had bachelor's degrees, and 8% had advanced degrees (National Center for Education Statistics, 1994b, pp. 68–69).

A higher percentage of our adult population attends college than in any other nation in the world, and adult enrollment is still rising. Approximately 56% of all college en-rollees are over 24 years old; many attend on a part-time basis and live with their own nu-clear families or parental families instead of same-age roommates. Part-time students re-cently have made up 43% of the undergradu-ate population in two- and four-year colleges combined.

Women made up 54.8% of college en-rollments in 1991–1992. They received 58% of associate degrees and 54% of the 1,105,000 bachelor's degrees. International students also contribute to diversity. In 1991–1992, 419,585 international students enrolled in U.S. colleges; nearly half of them were un-dergraduates.

Yet, not all agree that full access has been achieved. Educational levels remain considerably higher for White adults than for Blacks or Hispanics. In the 35- to 39-year-old age group, only 43% of Blacks and 31% of Hispanics have attended some college, 15% of Black and 11% of Hispanic citizens have bachelor's degrees, and less than 4% of each of these minority groups has advanced de-grees (*Condition of Education*, 1994, pp. 68–69). Table 4-4 gives the percentage of various ethnic groups that received under-graduate degrees in 1991–92. Although the number enrolled has reached record highs since 1990, Black and Hispanic students, who are disproportionately enrolled in two-year colleges, have also received a relatively lower proportion of bachelor's degrees than white students.

Furthermore, composite figures obscure very different student bodies at different col-leges. Table 4-5 gives a summary view from 1989–1990 for students with selected charac-teristics by type and control of the college in which they are enrolled (*Condition of Educa-tion*, 1994, p. 140). Clearly, older part-time students who live off campus and are finan-cially independent more commonly attend public two-year colleges.

The community colleges are the largest and fastest growing single segment of higher education (*Community and Junior Colleges: A Recent Profile*, 1990). They will continue to experience substantial enrollment gains (El-Khawas, 1992) since technical support and related jobs—those often prepared for at community colleges—are expected to grow over 30% between 1988 and 2000, more rapidly than any other occupational group. ("College Graduates in the Labor Market," 1990).

A common target for continued attack by advocates of greater access is student "track-ing." Although it is alleged to take place at all

TABLE 4-4. Percentage of Earned Undergraduate Degrees Conferred on Students by Ethnic Group (1991–1992)

	Associate's Degrees (N = 504,231)	Bachelor's Degrees (N = 1,136,553)
	(percent)	
American Indian/Alaskan Native	0.8	0.5
Asian/Pacific Islander	3.1	4.1
Black non-Hispanic	7.8	6.4
Hispanic	5.3	3.6
White	79.4	82.4
Nonresident alien	1.6	2.5
Race unknown	1.9	0.6

Source: From *The Chronicle of Higher Education Almanac,* 1994, p. 31.

TABLE 4-5 Percentage of Undergraduate Students with Selected Characteristics, by Type and Control of Postsecondary Institution, 1989–1990

Characteristic	Public			Private, Nonprofit		
		Four-year			Four-year	
	Two-year	Non-Ph.D.-granting	Ph.D.-granting	Two-year	Non-Ph.D.-granting	Ph.D.-granting
Attended part-time	70.1	30.8	24.1	28.5	26.9	17.2
Lived off campus	98.7	78.4	73.9	72.4	57.6	57.2
24 years of age or older	56.2	32.6	25.0	34.2	31.7	21.2
Married	34.8	19.6	14.5	19.9	20.0	11.4
Financially independent	65.6	41.0	32.5	45.1	38.1	27.7
Family income (dependent students)						
Low	19.8	19.3	14.6	21.7	20.9	15.3
Lower middle	23.8	20.3	17.8	21.7	17.6	14.3
Middle	19.3	21.5	20.6	22.5	18.5	14.8
Upper middle	21.3	21.5	23.0	14.2	19.3	19.1
Upper	15.7	17.4	24.0	19.9	23.6	36.6
Parents' highest education level						
High school graduate or less	47.9	38.4	29.0	44.3	36.0	22.7
Bachelor's degree or higher	28.4	37.4	48.7	33.2	43.1	62.2

Source: From The Condition of Education by the National Center for Education Statistics, 1994, p. 140.

levels of education, some argue that community colleges—which were supposed to equalize access to higher education—are particularly guilty of legitimizing inequality by keeping minority students in the least prestigious types of institutions (Brint & Karabel, 1989). One writer notes, "The democratic American system is still dogged by the ghost of Plato and the ancient superstition of fundamental inequality" (Featherstone, 1989, p. 343).

Many educators proudly labeled the U.S. system "mass higher education" and saw open access as an attained goal. Others, however, believe a period of reduced emphasis on access occurred under Republican federal and state administrations in the 1980s and 1990s, when officials questioned affirmative action policies and sought to reduce funding to support students. The critics of these actions, typically of Democratic leanings, urge renewed emphasis to ensure that all deserving students have access not only to postsecondary education but to postsecondary education of equal quality.

The sheer numbers of students have caused many to characterize the U.S. system of higher education as "universal." This term is exaggerated in that many Americans still do not attend college, but the nation has moved far from the elitist concepts of education. External influences, including several important wars, waves of immigration, desegregation, and the shift from an agrarian to a postindustrial society, have caused colleges to accept a dramatically diverse population. The nation has moved steadily from a view of education as the privilege for a few to an entitlement for citizens of all ages, races, and interests. Though more slowly, the colleges have followed.

Today, with the information society in full swing, many states are attempting to reach the last bastion of learners who cannot easily commute to campuses by developing advanced technological systems for "distance education." We may expect to see continued discussion of lifelong entitlements to support such learners, particularly for job retraining. In this sense, concerns for access and for vocational preparation are not separable.

Content Debates: Prescription versus Choice in Courses and Programs

New college missions and broader access for students have been accompanied by an increase in the variety of courses and programs colleges and universities offer. This variety has led to periodic debates about whether students should choose their own courses of study or whether institutions should prescribe requirements for all. The variations in intensity of the debate provide a very clear illustration of another recurring pattern in American curriculum history. Despite this debate's obvious periodicity, however, it is difficult to separate it from discussions of the relative virtues of general versus specialized education.

The debate between advocates of choice and prescription dates from at least 1820 (see Figure 4-5). Each recurrence of the debate includes a temporary victory for one side or the other but never a lasting truce. Each sector of higher education has sometimes settled the issue of content requirements temporarily, while another sector is just beginning its discussion. Even during periods when the debate about elective studies has been overshadowed by other topics, individual proponents and opponents of student choice have been vocal. Yet it is possible to identify broad patterns in this debate for higher education as a whole.

Pressure for Choice Increases

Several mid-nineteenth-century events fostered efforts for increased student choice in their studies. The Morrill Act encouraged elective choice as the land-grant institutions

FIGURE 4-5   Debates about Content: Choice and Prescription

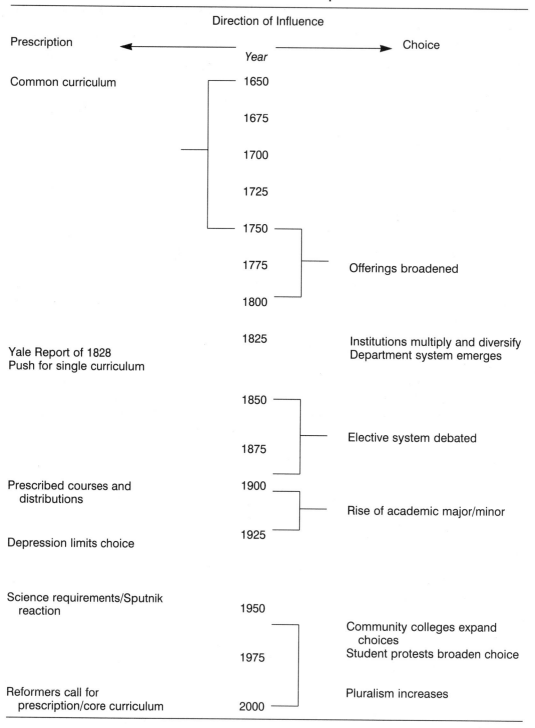

"fostered the emancipation of American higher education from the purely classical and formalistic tradition" (Brubacher & Rudy, 1976, p. 66). The Civil War era initiated new choices of studies geared to the needs of women and Black Americans.

The forty-year campaign for the elective system waged between 1869 and 1909 by Charles William Eliot, president of Harvard University, is legendary. Through Eliot's efforts, Harvard had abolished all requirements by 1898. Yet detractors claimed that the new elective system failed to guide students toward clear and coherent educational programs. With insufficient guidance, some students studied an array of subjects at an introductory level while avoiding pursuit of any subject in depth. Between 1885 and 1905, educators responded by shaping the system of general education and major/minor concentrations that is still common today. The major system, first introduced in 1885 at Indiana University and put in place at Harvard by 1910, coincided with the rise of specializations, retreated from the ideology of total choice, and, as some saw it, remedied the lack of structure and coherence that resulted when colleges abandoned all or most requirements (Rudolph, 1977, p. 227). The system of the major and general education distribution requirements was widely established by 1920.

Under this system, colleges allowed students to choose an area of specialization but required a general education program covering "distribution requirements" in subjects the faculty believed supplied important common knowledge. Departments specified basic foundation courses and other specific requirements for the majors, and then allowed students latitude to fill other credit hour requirements. The majors, therefore, could be nearly as structured as the total college requirements that had preceded them prior to the elective system. Minors were more freely chosen.

As the twentieth century continued, however, the new majors in academic fields such as language, history, and chemistry were supplemented by newer choices in career studies, such as business and education. Additional new majors like sociology and psychology grew out of disciplines like philosophy. The number of choices among fields in which to specialize continued to grow. As options increased, more educators became concerned that students share a common knowledge of Western culture and values. This view, fostered by World War I's nationalism, led to reintroduction of humanities and social science core courses and renewed emphasis on general education requirements.

Then, in 1957, when the Russian launching of the satellite Sputnik challenged notions of U.S. competitiveness and scientific preparedness, the scientific specialists had their day. Educators created more serious scientific requirements for students in high school and college, a different type of victory for advocates of a prescribed curriculum. They strengthened and expanded the distribution requirements that required students to sample each of several fields of knowledge, including laboratory science. This method of preventing students' escape from the laboratory became the norm in most colleges.

Students Advocate Greater Choice

It was not long before the tighter distribution requirements were eliminated, modified, or evaded by students. In the 1960s and 1970s, students became the strongest advocates of greater choice. Students facing the Vietnam War but denied adult choices on campuses protested curricular restrictions. With an increasingly diverse set of students entering college and a strong social-reform agenda sweeping the country, they labeled requirements as "establishment"—poisonous to individual development and freedom. Conrad and Wyer (1980) described this period as a "virtual free-for-all of the distribution approach" (p. 17). The height of student choice may have been in 1971; in this year Amherst College eliminated all general education requirements. At about the same time, experimental institutions like Hampshire College were allowing students to design completely individualized programs.

Despite many concessions to student demands during this turbulent period, most colleges retained, even if they did not fully enforce, programs in general education (required or distributed in groups of courses), a major field of study or combined related studies, and limited electives. As the job market tightened in the 1970s and 1980s, students themselves selected more structured and practical programs to enhance their employment options. In some colleges, academic credit is given for life experience, for remedial study, and for career exploration.

Choice as the Century Turns

Although checks and balances exist in most colleges, student choice today is unquestionably broad—among institutions, among majors, and among elective courses. Many students complete their education in a different college than where they began, a trend that is still increasing. But some states have acted to coordinate and systematize student movement. California, for example, has evolved a three-tier system of higher education (University of California system, California State University system, and California Community College system) and arranged these three tiers in a hierarchical master plan. Students who are best prepared academically may attend the University of California system as beginning undergraduates. Others must attend the community or state colleges and transfer for upper-division work.

About 20% of community college students transfer to four-year colleges. The transferability of courses they took may determine whether their course choices were well advised. What is called a major specialization in a transfer curriculum at a two-year college may be the approximate equivalent of the introductory and beginning specialization (intermediate level) courses for the same field at a four-year college and directly credited there. But what is called a major specialization in an occupational program at a two-year college is not often offered at a four-year college and, thus, may not be transferable.

A related constraint on flexibility of course choice is the amount of articulation between two- and four-year colleges. Faculty and administrators increasingly work out agreements about the linkages. But faculty in upper-division fields, such as accounting, and advisors in some preprofessional fields such as medicine and other health-related professions (31% of all organic chemistry courses are taken at community colleges), sometimes express concern about the rigor of community college courses and refuse to accept them. In some states this concern may be valid. Increasingly, however, syllabi are coordinated between the two levels of colleges to reduce variation in course content and level. This promotion of student access also has the effect of limiting student choice of colleges and courses.

Major fields of study also have control over courses students choose. Different demands result in different ratios of general education courses to major courses for students and also may determine the number of courses students are free to chose as electives. According to the Office of Educational Research and Improvement ("Curricular Content of Bachelor's Degrees," 1986) students majoring in both quantitative fields and the humanities traditionally have tended to take 60% of their work in their majors, social science majors about 50%, and business and education majors less than 35%. However, students often use their electives to support and enhance the major. Some majors, such as teacher education and engineering, may require a more extensive number of course credits for a degree than some others. Thus, in reality, up to three-quarters of a student's coursework may be taken in the major and closely related fields, with only a third or less in general education. Many educators lament the fact that students manage to avoid studying some fields, especially sciences and mathematics. Some are particularly concerned about the foreclosure of opportunities for some ethnic groups because, while choices may theoretically exist, students are poorly prepared to choose and succeed in courses in these fields. Some ethnic and gender-related patterns are illustrated in Table 4-6.

More often than educators would like, students' choices are limited by their previous preparation and academic success. Because most community colleges have open-door admissions policies, they are somewhat more likely than four-year colleges to offer compensatory programs for students who need to develop basic skills before or concurrent with college work. Ninety percent of two-year colleges offer at least one remedial course ("College-Level Remedial Education," 1989). In most colleges, enrollment in these developmental or remedial programs is voluntary, but a few well-known colleges like Miami-Dade Community College require students to acquire basic skills before taking courses that require their use.

Although only 2% of U.S. colleges have a totally prescribed academic program (Dey, Astin, & Hurtado, 1989), "core curricula" based on the belief that all students should have a common experience or be exposed to particular knowledge are on the increase. According to the American Council on Education, eight of ten American colleges expect all students to complete a "core amount" of course work in general education (El-Khawas, 1988). Most of these requirements allow students choice among sets of courses

in several disciplinary domains but the "core" may also be:

- A set of courses (perhaps six to eight) required for all students
- A single common course required of all students, perhaps one that spans disciplines
- Two or three required and linked courses in each of several disciplinary domains

Required core courses at the upper-division level are increasing as well. About 52% of baccalaureate and comprehensive colleges now have such requirements at the upper-division level as well as in the lower division (El-Khawas, 1992, p. 38).

In earlier days educators' prescription of content often stemmed from internal and organizational influences within the college or university, including strong beliefs about student needs. Traditionally, the periodic debate about the relative merits of student choice was limited to higher education leaders and faculty advocates of the various positions. Recently, with increases of public funding, however, government officials have frequently entered the debate on the grounds of both quality maintenance and cost containment. What was once an internal debate continues to develop external dimensions.

Figure 4-6 provides a graphic representation of the relation (and overlap) of academic programs in the various types of U.S. postsecondary study as well as how it may build on the foundation of precollege preparation. The diagram shows that there are many choices and options within the universe of postsecondary education. One cost-related concern is that the abundance of choices and options is costly and duplicative. Belief is strong in some quarters that flexibility for students to stop out, repeat previous education, and move among colleges freely is sapping public resources. Still, an alternative

TABLE 4-6 Percent of Bachelor's Degree Recipients Who Took One or More Courses in Selected Subjects, by Sex and Race/Ethnicity, 1985–1986

Subject	Total	Sex		Race/Ethnicity				
		Men	Women	White	Black	Hispanic	Asian	American Indian
Arts	63.1	59.0	67.4	63.6	63.3	59.0	59.1	64.1
English literature/letters	86.8	87.2	86.7	87.1	85.5	89.4	83.9	78.5
Foreign language	36.1	31.9	40.2	35.6	34.3	49.8	39.2	32.4
Philosophy and religion	52.6	53.0	52.5	53.1	53.6	46.6	50.4	57.6
Area and ethnic studies	9.0	6.7	10.2	8.0	13.5	8.2	19.3	6.1
Psychology	65.3	60.3	71.5	66.3	72.3	60.6	55.9	63.6
Economics	52.8	59.9	45.7	52.9	54.1	49.7	48.1	47.6
Geography	14.2	14.6	14.3	14.8	9.7	10.9	17.7	19.3
Political science	40.6	43.1	37.4	40.3	41.8	42.8	30.5	45.0
Sociology/anthropology	61.0	55.6	65.9	61.4	61.8	57.4	47.5	53.5
History	63.2	64.7	62.8	64.2	64.6	63.3	49.2	55.5
Life sciences	52.9	46.6	59.9	53.9	55.7	49.1	43.8	45.5
Physical sciences	66.9	72.4	62.4	68.2	55.3	56.5	76.8	62.8
Mathematics	78.1	82.8	74.0	78.4	78.1	77.3	78.5	76.2
Computer and information sciences	42.1	48.1	37.6	42.9	40.2	40.3	46.3	35.5
Engineering	17.7	27.0	8.6	17.4	14.7	16.5	32.2	18.7
Education	36.3	29.5	43.6	36.8	44.2	36.5	24.1	30.2
Business/management	53.7	58.1	49.6	53.8	60.8	51.4	43.7	56.0

Source: From *The Condition of Education* by the National Center for Education Statistics, 1994, p. 82.

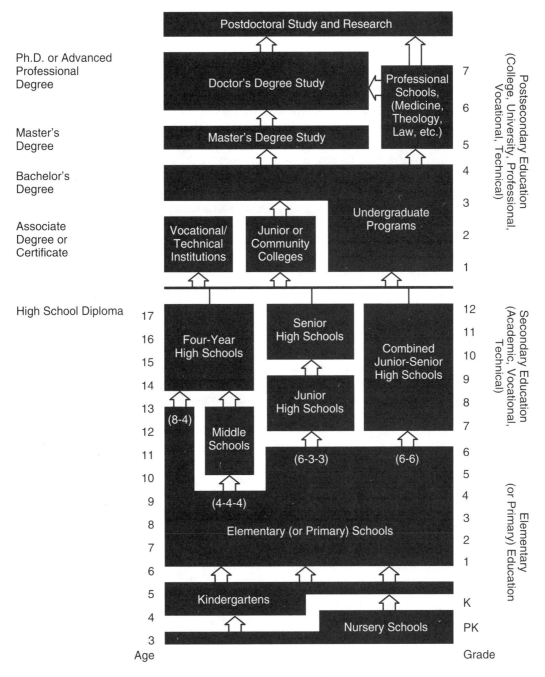

FIGURE 4-6   The Structure of Education in the United States

Source: From *Mini-Digest of Education Statistics* by National Center for Educational Statistics, November 1994, pp. 5–6.

view persists that citizens are entitled to make their own educational choices and to learn throughout their lifetime.

Instructional Process: Occasional Innovation

Changes in instructional process have frequently accompanied temporary victories in the debate about content choice and prescription. Prior to Civil War times, faculty typically thought that students' minds would be disciplined and improved by memorizing and reciting moral prescriptions and by logical disputation. These instructional processes were based on beliefs that ways of thinking transfer from topic to topic and that educators and clergymen knew best what students should learn.

Instructional processes began to change in the mid-1800s as land-grant colleges focused instruction on improving agricultural and business production. Learning by demonstration and by laboratory practice were necessary in these more practical fields. The extension movement, intended to bring new techniques to farmers, also reinforced changes in instructional methods by serving adult farmers with distinctly individual and pragmatic goals. Possibly because few records were kept, there is little evidence that this gradually changing emphasis on instructional process (outlined in Figure 4-7) actually involved much debate among educators.

Early Educational Experiments

Debated or not, distinct periods of educational experimentation occurred in the history of higher education, notably in the 1920s, 1930s, 1960s, and 1990s. Experimentation with teaching methods was first stimulated by scientific studies in the psychology of learning, which Thorndike began at Columbia University in the early 1900s. By 1914 his idea of disciplining the mind had lost credibility (Bigge & Shermis, 1992, p. 28). Also in the early 1900s, John Dewey and his followers urged that learning be based on learner experiences, and successfully promoted course instruction based on discussions, projects, and fieldwork rather than memorization and recitation. At the same time, particularly from 1925 to 1935, experimental colleges such as "The College" founded by Robert Maynard Hutchins at Chicago and The Experimental College by Alexander Meiklejohn at Wisconsin emphasized coherence and connection within the classical tradition of general education.

The emphasis on social values during the 1920s led to further emphasis on classroom discussion. This movement toward learner involvement was readily accepted in the lower schools; but lecturing and demonstration remained primary among college teachers. The discussion method's influence was again checked by rapid enrollment increases following World War II and, in some universities, by professors' interest in better research rather than better teaching. Individualized education became the victim of mass education as the need to process large numbers of students encouraged lecturing as the dominant instructional mode and the use of graduate assistants to teach undergraduate courses.

Student Activists Encourage Relevance and Freedom

Several alternatives to large lecture classes were tried again in the 1960s as students protested the impersonality of many college procedures. Many small colleges experimented with competency-based learning and mastery learning programs like the Keller plan of self-paced instruction (Keller, 1968). Competency-based education adapted the "behavioral objective" movement in elementary and secondary schools that encouraged teachers to specify precisely each behavior

FIGURE 4-7 Periods of Change in Instructional Processes

Direction of Influence

Passive learning ⟵————————   ————————⟶ Active learning

Year

Recitation prevails

Year	
1650	
1675	
1700	
1725	
1750	
1775	
1800	
1825	
1850	Land-grant institutions increase Use of laboratories and demonstrations
1875	
1900	
1925	Increase of discussion and seminars
1950	Experimental colleges
1975	Self-paced instruction Experimental colleges and curricula
2000	Active learning/involvement Computer-assisted instruction

students were expected to demonstrate. In colleges, proponents of self-paced instructional systems were seldom so specific; instead they believed that students should understand the learning objectives, engage a subject intensively at their own pace, and take examinations when they felt prepared to demonstrate competence. During this same period, demands for "relevance" prompted some colleges to create study arrangements that required immersion in one subject at a time (such as the one-month intensive term, typically scheduled in January in the 4-1-4 calendar system), living and learning experiences in dormitories, and more flexible grading systems that allowed students to experiment with new topics without threat of failure. While educationally exciting, many of these experiments were short lived because they consumed large amounts of faculty time and often limited students' chances for transfer or graduate school admission. Many changes in term structures or grading practices were never fully accepted, even among faculty in the colleges that experimented with them; thus, reversion to more traditional instructional processes was rapid during the 1980s. This era of emphasis on student needs did, however, succeed in making discussion of instructional processes acceptable, if not fashionable, among some college professors.

Some of the innovations, notably pass/fail grading, independent study, and student-created majors, have endured. Some instructional reforms from this era, originally tried in nonselective colleges of tenuous financial circumstances, are now found in the most stable and selective institutions. Most of the changes are structural, however, rather than broad-scale changes in philosophy of teaching. Faculty attitudes toward some of the procedural changes reluctantly adopted in the 1960s and 1970s resembled attitudes their predecessors had held in resisting earlier changes. For example, introduction of pass/fail grading involved lengthy debates on many campuses; the final result was that students were allowed only a limited number of such grading options per term. This was a compromise that pacified students while retaining the traditional grading structure, just as earlier faculties had allowed the granting of a second-class scientific degree while retaining the classical curriculum.

Levine (1978) traced some of the sources and results of specific curricular reforms. His reports indicate periodic change in the predominant view of educational purpose and related instructional processes. We have summarized his ideas about curricular reform in 1960s and 1970s and added our own summary of the decade of the 1980s.

1960s Dominant educational philosophies were education for life (relevance) and education for personal development. Characteristic experiments included new interdisciplinary studies (ethnic studies, environmental studies) and reduced requirements including independent study, student-created majors, pass/fail grading, and experimental colleges.

1970s The U.S. college became committed to social justice and universal access. New groups of nontraditional students were admitted and, to accommodate them, variable scheduling, alternatives to courses, off-campus study, credit for experience, and compensatory education were introduced. Eventually, a strong concern for education and work emerged.

1980s This decade saw a revival of the 1940s reforms—a trend away from electives and toward greater structure. More prescribed distribution requirements emerged except in two-year colleges, where requirements continued to be reduced. Observers began expressing concern for quality and its measurement and about general rather than specialized education. Experimental colleges and free universities had almost disappeared.

Instructional Change: A Muted Debate Gains in Volume

Among educational debates, debate about instructional processes has been muted, a lifted eyebrow compared to the raised voices generated by purpose, access, and choice. Most discussions about instructional process have remained internal until recently. In the 1980s and 1990s, however, several developments have focused increased attention on instruction. One influence, largely from internal sources, was increasing support from psychologists for more active student involvement in learning activities. This view, stemming from credible faculty colleagues but encouraged by external groups such as higher education associations, is encouraging professors to reduce their dependence on lectures in favor of group processes, discovery activities, simulations, and fieldwork. Critical thinking skills, endorsed as educationally important by most faculty members, are now believed to develop less as a result of the specific course content than as a result of appropriate instructional processes for engaging the content.

The most dramatic advances in instruction, however, are likely to come from external sources, especially technology. As computers become more and more common, colleges have had little choice but to embrace them. Instructional processes will continue to change, perhaps substantially, within a few years as new skills and ways of thinking emerge in response to electronic media. Unlike earlier media, computers have initiated new forms of instruction centered on the learner as an independent agent, often pursuing learning alone except for the help of a computer program. These new instructional media seem especially likely to increase both access and student choice as well. Unparalleled changes and educational expansions, due to both development of computers and new advances in cognitive psychology, are likely to affect all of the other debates we have discussed.

Evaluation Debates: Emphasis on Quality Control

The recurring emphasis on evaluation may be viewed as a pattern of continuing discussion in its own right. Alternatively, since the appeal for curriculum corrections in each of the other debates is often made in the name of quality control or its financial counterpart, accountability, evaluation may be seen as part of each other debates we have described. When repeated debates focus on purpose, access, and choice, calls for evaluation to assure quality may be the mechanism for refocusing the curriculum. To cite the frequently used pendulum analogy, calls for quality control or accountability are often effective in slowing the pendulum or act to change its direction.

The sources of demand for quality-control mechanisms are varied. They emanate from society at some times, from educators or students at other times, but most frequently from funders of higher education. At various times during U.S. history, these funders have been churches, philanthropic foundations, business and industry, and state and federal governments. Examples of demands for accountability to these varied sponsors have always been abundant. Today, more frequently than in the past, the demands focus on the curriculum.

Calls for evaluation and adjustment can be linked to the debate about general and specialized education. For example, when educators and government officials believe that educational purpose has veered too far toward specialized vocationalism, they may initiate discussions about the neglect of general education, using quality-control rhetoric to "correct" the course of colleges. Conversely, if educational purpose seems too general to serve the country's civic and commercial needs, educators and statespersons raise issues of economic accountability and technological competitiveness in an effort to increase the specialized capability of students and colleges.

Evaluation debates have obvious connections to debates on increased access that have caused higher education to adjust academic standards. When educators and the public perceive access as too open, they blame it for decline in standards and tighten admissions or financial aid mechanisms. Implicitly, if not explicitly, the question becomes: In what ways is quality sacrificed when almost everyone can enter college? Each of these events—lowering entrance standards in early colleges seeking to extend access or increase enrollments, the development of agricultural and mechanic arts in the land-grant movement, the development of open-access community colleges, and finally financial programs to help new groups of students—has produced a backlash of concern about quality. Fear of decreased quality has followed most periods of increased diversity. In some cases, institutions developed remedial programs to improve student quality; in others, they chose to restrict access and enrollments.

The debate about choice is also related to evaluation. When educators or the public perceive that student freedom to make content choices within the academic program has become too great and that students are choosing unwisely, they see a greater number of required courses as the way to restore quality and academic rigor. Cycles of relaxed curricular requirements to provide more choice for students give way to cycles of tightened requirements to increase "rigor." The 1920s and the 1980s illustrate the content/prescription versus quality debate. In the 1920s elitism

under the guise of quality control countered what some perceived as excessively open access. Subsequently, in the 1980s, calls for quality control in the form of increased prescription indirectly countered both access and specialization. It is perhaps most appropriate, then, to define our present stage in curriculum history as one in which colleges and universities are pressed toward greater prescription in deference to strong and continuing external demands for both accountability and quality control.

Government Funding and Quality Control

Throughout U.S. history the funding of all types of colleges has become more heterogeneous. As states began to provide some funds for independent colleges and financial assistance to their students, and as public colleges have successfully competed for private donations, institutions that had been private have become quasi-public, while some that had been public have become quasi-private. Indeed, interested parties in states with large state-supported universities as far flung as Michigan and Oregon, sometimes talk about becoming privatized by necessity when states support lags. In contrast, within the last fifty years, formerly private universities like the University of Pennsylvania have become "state-related" or "state-assisted." For all colleges, however, governmental control has strengthened with increases in student support and subsidies for academic research. Today, colleges face demands for evaluation and quality control from many sources, although accountability to the federal and state governments is key.

Federal support for higher education originally was very small, and, despite a few proposals, no "national" university or ministry of education was ever founded. But federal funds were channeled to higher education through special-purpose legislation such as the Morrill Land-Grant Act (1862), the Hatch Act, and the second Morrill Act (1890). With each new federal initiative, record-keeping and evaluation processes developed to ensure that funds were properly spent. These factors created the first period of emphasis on quality control in the final decade of the nineteenth century.

The second period of increasing accountability ensued when World War II helped forge ties between universities and the federal government. Because the nation needed defense research and because it was efficient to use talent and resources already in place, the federal government directly funded research at major universities, an arrangement that continued after the war. The Servicemen's Readjustment Act of 1944 (G.I. Bill) enlisted accrediting agencies (voluntary associations of colleges) to assure the government that colleges were of appropriate quality to teach returning G.I.s with federal entitlements. While the accreditors did not exactly welcome this responsibility, they accepted it because it firmly entrenched their role by leaving quality control in the hands of educators. (For a more thorough discussion, see Stark and Associates, 1977.) Recently, the ability of accreditors to monitor quality has been seriously questioned. They remain the official evaluators, but many additional government mechanisms now coexist.

The National Defense Education Act (1958), and the Higher Education Act (1965) and its subsequent amendments (1968 and 1972) spurred the development of bookkeeping and accountability requirements. Especially after 1972, when new types of students began using tuition funds from public coffers, the federal government felt an increased responsibility to monitor many aspects of college activity and responsiveness. Research universities and colleges that accept students with federal grants and loans are regularly subject to new quality-control initiatives. Community colleges are subject to local (usually county or school district) control as well. In many states, articulation agreements between the community colleges and the four-year state colleges increase uniformity in the curriculum.

In this complex system of higher education, who can call for evaluation and adjustment in college missions, programs, and access policies? Nearly everyone, it seems—all government levels as well as private agencies—takes part in the shaping and reshaping of college missions and thus of their academic programs. As a consequence, some institutions shift their missions, their funding sources, their academic plans, and even their names in response to societal influences and financial pressures.

Current Pressure for Evaluation

The nation periodically reacts to exposure of student deficiencies with reform movements intended to tighten requirements, access, or both. An emphasis on quality often has alternated with an emphasis on equity. The 1980s witnessed a search for both quality and equity of access. Figure 4-8 shows the historical periods of emphasis on evaluation, accountability, and quality control.

Academic aptitude and achievement test data show that students attending college now have a broad range of preparation. College admissions test scores declined substantially beginning about 1968, and the decline continued through the 1970s, raising concern about preparation. Scholastic Aptitude Test scores reached their lowest point in the early 1980s. Since 1983, scores have been fairly stable (verbal ability) or rising (mathematical ability), despite 8% more students taking the tests (*Condition of Education,* 1994, pp. 64–65). There are varying interpretations of how well prepared students really are for college in the 1990s, partly depending on the data source and the period used for comparison. (For example, student self-report data from the

FIGURE 4-8   Periods of Emphasis on Evaluation, Accountability, and Quality Control

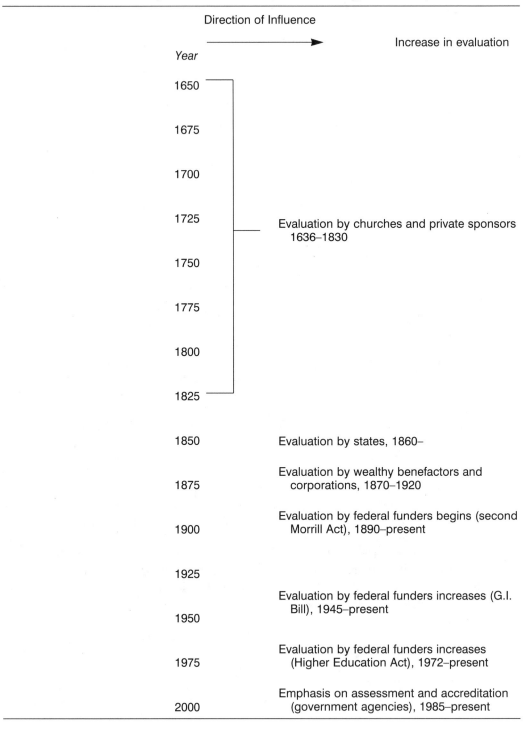

Direction of Influence

Increase in evaluation

Year

1650

1675

1700

1725   Evaluation by churches and private sponsors
            1636–1830

1750

1775

1800

1825

1850   Evaluation by states, 1860–

1875   Evaluation by wealthy benefactors and
            corporations, 1870–1920

1900   Evaluation by federal funders begins (second
            Morrill Act), 1890–present

1925

1950   Evaluation by federal funders increases (G.I.
            Bill), 1945–present

1975   Evaluation by federal funders increases
            (Higher Education Act), 1972–present

2000   Emphasis on assessment and accreditation
            (government agencies), 1985–present

UCLA/ACE Cooperative Institutional Research Program often conflict with test scores from Advanced Placement Tests and data from high school records.)

In response to questionable preparation, one of the 1980s reform initiatives has been to strengthen high school requirements and extend the school year; some states have reported improved student learning as a result. Nevertheless, many college students still require compensatory education, even in basic skill areas, to proceed with college work. Today's "compensatory" or "developmental" programs provide remediation that is similar to the college preparatory divisions in the mid–1800s prior to the full development of secondary schools.

The distinction between compensatory education and college-level general education is not clear even to those sponsoring such programs. In Table 4-7 we illustrate on the left the skills and knowledge that the College Board

identified in 1983 as essential preparation for college. On the right are the "experiences" that the Association of American Colleges identified in 1985 as necessary for a liberal education. Because the types of experiences, understandings or skills are so similar, the difference between secondary school and college must be one of depth or focus. But the level of proficiency is ambiguous and subject to interpretation, possibly deliberately so, to accommodate the wide diversity of American students and colleges.

Although the public is currently concerned about the value of a college degree, both educators and the public feel obliged to meet the special needs of students whose pre-college opportunities have been limited. Since at least 1960, increasing numbers of students are arriving on campus with nontraditional preparation. One in seven high school diplomas recently awarded (1991) was earned through the General Equivalent

TABLE 4-7   Expected Understandings for High School and College

Academic Preparation for College (College Board, 1983)	*Experiences Appropriate for a Liberal Education* (Association of American Colleges, 1985)
Basic competencies	
Reading	Literacy (reading, writing, speaking, listening)
Writing	
Speaking and listening	
Mathematics	Understanding numerical data
Reasoning	Inquiry/critical analysis/logical thinking
Studying	
Computer competence	
Basic academic subjects	
English	Literacy
Arts	The arts
Mathematics	Understanding numerical data
Science	Scientific understanding
Social studies	Historical consciousness
Foreign languages	International/multicultural experience
	Values
	Study in depth

Diploma (GED), and increasing numbers of these students—an all-time high of 60% in 1993—indicated plans to continue their education ("Participation in GED Program," 1994). But of the high school seniors who took the 1992 American College Testing Program entrance tests (ACT), almost half reported that they had not completed a core program in high school. This is true even though the ACT assessment is generally taken by those who consider themselves college-bound. ("1992 ACT Scores Remain Stable," 1993, p. 2). Like those mentioned earlier, these figures about student preparation conflict. Possibly, secondary school course enrollment is not a good indicator of subject mastery.

Whatever the correct interpretation of these conflicting data, in 1989, 90% of two-year public colleges and 64% of four-year public colleges offered remedial courses, and most offered college credits for taking them. ("College-level Remedial Education," 1989). Thirty percent of all college freshmen in the United States took at least one remedial course (in mathematics, writing, or reading). Roueche (1977) has mentioned a number of important characteristics of compensatory education programs and has urged that students who need them should be identified and more actively recruited for them.

Some representatives of the public argue that compensatory education at the college level should not be funded because the same education is paid for twice. Others indicate that the increased diversity and access of college education to the population is sufficient justification for serving these special student needs. According to its strongest advocates, students should be offered the opportunity but should not be compelled to take compensatory education courses.

Although the public has increasingly sought quality control, colleges have only begun to develop procedures for evaluating whether the academic plans they devise fully

support excellence, Public agencies are asking such questions as: How will the government know if "developing institutions," particularly historically Black colleges and universities (HBCUs), are maintaining their mission and thus their eligibility for funding? How will states know if the special missions they have assigned to specific institutions are being fulfilled? How will federal officials know that students receiving financial aid funds are getting high-quality education in the colleges they attend? Increasingly, as planners and policymakers at high levels of government bureaucracies continue to ask these questions, colleges must respond with appropriate systems for evaluation and adjustment. The debate about quality control and accountability shows no sign of abating. Indeed, this debate sparked a widespread discussion about the quality of higher education in the 1980s and 1990s.

As the extensive curricular diversity that we have described has led to public uncertainty about who is studying (and learning) what in various types of colleges, government agencies have sponsored researchers in developing new techniques to evaluate the outcomes of education. Studies of academic plans and their results, sadly neglected by colleges in the past, now are receiving considerable attention. To illustrate the range of activity in examining academic plans, we mention five types of increasingly complex and sophisticated studies.

1. Student self-reports about their academic behavior and learning progress

2. Surveys of institutional curricula

3. Studies that count what courses colleges offer (catalog studies) and what courses students select from these offerings (transcript studies)

4. Studies that not only count what courses students take but examine patterns and sequences of course taking

5. Studies that count courses, examine patterns and sequences, and relate the patterns to measures of academic achievement

INFLUENCES AND POTENTIAL REFORMS

Historian Frederick Rudolph characterized the curriculum as a battleground for society, a locus and transmitter of values, a social artifact, a reproduction of the national ideology, a reflection of faculty research interests and student desires, a mixture of the cultural and the utilitarian, and sometimes a creature of convenience. Surely, it has been all of these things. The main thesis of Rudolph's history, and ours, is that curriculum history is American history because of the continual interaction between curriculum and society. Social change, Rudolph held, often has been more rapid than the colleges' capacity to respond. College response has, by and large, been developed according to a pragmatic model, responding to various external and internal influences.

All in all, we believe that the relationship between academic plans and influences on the educational environment reflects a heavy societal influence toward access and toward a balance between general and specialized education. Debates about student choices among academic programs and the design of instructional processes more clearly reflect influences internal to colleges and universities. We have suggested, however, that this balance of internal and external forces may be changing as a result of new calls for quality control through external evaluation. As more perspectives are taken into account, even the design of academic plans may move farther from educators' models and more toward the pragmatic models of curriculum change.

The theoretical model we introduced in Chapter 1 is potentially very helpful in describing influences on the educational environment and enhancing understanding of how they relate to academic plan elements. The model places the development of the academic plan in the context of an educational environment responsive to society, as well as to educators. In future chapters, we will suggest that certain types of influences act more directly on certain elements of academic plans than on others. In other words, some parts of the academic plan are open to direct societal influences, while others are sheltered by internal influences.

Our examination of these trends and recurring debates in curriculum history will help us to keep in mind the current set of influences as we discuss demands for reform in today's college curriculum and responses of educators. Now that societal influences have increased access and choice, academic decisions are more subject to public debate and potentially more volatile. Colleges are increasingly are aware of the ideas of interested factions that debate matters once left to university presidents and faculties. Over time, curriculum planning in colleges has become more political and less "rational." Yet, it is also more responsive to U.S. society and, consequently, more vulnerable to demands for accountability and quality control from many sources. For these reasons, our theoretical framework recognizes both a rational component in developing and evaluating academic plans within colleges and universities, and the more political set of influences from both inside and outside institutions that affect the planning process directly and indirectly. The rational component and the political component meet in the reform initiatives of the final decades of the twentieth century, which we will consider next.

CHAPTER 5

Calls for Curriculum Reform

THE REFORM ERA OF THE LATE 1900s

Agitation for reform of higher education curricula has been extremely strong during the last decades of the twentieth century. Reformers accuse colleges of abandoning their primary purposes, neglecting undergraduate education, and preparing students poorly for today's world. Critics advocate narrowing educational purpose and limiting content, tightening the prescription and sequencing of courses, enhancing instructional quality, and evaluating the effects of education on students more fully. Governmental agencies, higher education associations, and the media carry reform messages to a public whose confidence in colleges has reportedly declined. As colleges respond to these criticisms and proposals, the pace of change appears uncharacteristically rapid.

In this chapter we will discuss the various reform proposals as they relate to eight elements of academic plans; discuss external, organizational, and internal influences that interact to create the critiques and shape college response; and place the critiques in historical perspective relative to the recurring debates about curriculum. Finally, we speculate about how the reform movement may modify curriculum debates in the future.

Critical Reports

Several national reports and proposals on undergraduate education were published in the mid-1980s, and reports and proposals continued to appear in the mid-1990s. For reference, we have provided a chronological list of major critical reports in Table 5-1 and a similar list of some ensuing proposals for action in Table 5-2.

The earliest reports during this period, published about fifteen years after many colleges began loosening requirements in response to student activism, uniformly expressed the belief that the college curriculum needed tightening. The critiques included *To Reclaim a Legacy: A Report on the Humanities in Higher Education* (Bennett, 1984), *Involvement in Learning: Realizing the Potential of American Higher Education* (National Institute of Education, 1984) and *Integrity in the College Curriculum: A Report to the Academic Community* (Association of American

TABLE 5-1   A Chronology of Reports Critical of Higher Education, 1984–1994

1984   (November) *To Reclaim a Legacy: A Report on the Humanities in Higher Education.* William Bennett, National Endowment for the Humanities. (NEH)

1984   (October) *Involvement in Learning: Realizing the Potential of American Higher Education.* Study Group on the Condition of Excellence in American Higher Education, National Institute of Education. (NIE)

1985   *Integrity in the College Curriculum: A Report to the Academic Community.* Task Force of the Association of American Colleges. (AAC)

1985   *Higher Education and the American Resurgence.* Frank Newman. The Carnegie Foundation for the Advancement of Teaching.

1986   (November) *To Secure the Blessings of Liberty.* Report of the National Commission on the Role and Future of State Colleges and Universities. American Association of State Colleges and Universities. (AASCU)

1986   (July) *Transforming the State Role in Higher Education.* Education Commission of the States. (ECS)

1986   (August) *Time for Results: The Governors' 1991 Report on Education.* National Governors' Association. Center for Policy Research and Analysis.

1987   (November) *College: The Undergraduate Experience in America.* Ernest L. Boyer. The Carnegie Foundation for the Advancement of Teaching.

1988   (September) *Humanities in America: A Report to the President, the Congress, and the American People.* Lynne V. Cheney. National Endowment for the Humanities. (NEH)

1989   "Moral Messages of the University." Alexander Astin. *Educational Record*, 70 (2).

1989   (October) *50 Hours: A Core Curriculum for College Students.* Lynne V. Cheney. National Endowment for the Humanities. (NEH)

1993   (December) *An American Imperative: Higher Expectations for Higher Education.* Wingspread Group on Higher Education. The Johnson Foundation and others.

TABLE 5-2   A Chronology of Recent Proposals for Reform, 1984–1994

1988   *A New Vitality in General Education.* Task Group on General Education. Association of American Colleges. (AAC)

1988   (March) *Strengthening the Ties That Bind: Integrating Undergraduate Liberal and Professional Study.* Joan S. Stark and Malcolm A. Lowther. Professional Preparation Network, University of Michigan. (PPP)

1988   *Unfinished Design: The Humanities and Social Sciences in Undergraduate Engineering Education.* Joseph S. Johnston, Jr., Susan Shaman and Robert Zemsky.

1990   *Scholarship Reconsidered: Priorities of the Professoriate.* Ernest L. Boyer. The Carnegie Foundation for the Advancement of Teaching.

1991   *The Challenge of Connecting Learning.* Project on Liberal Learning, Study- in-Depth, and the Arts and Sciences Major. Association of American Colleges. (AAC)

1991   *Reports from the Fields.* Project on Liberal Learning, Study-in-Depth, and the Arts and Sciences Major. Association of American Colleges. (AAC)

1992   *Program Review and Educational Quality in the Major.* Project on Liberal Learning, Study-in-Depth, and the Arts and Sciences Major. Association of American Colleges. (AAC)

1994   (January) *Sustaining Vitality in General Education.* Project on Strong Foundations for General Education. Association of American Colleges. (AAC)

Colleges, 1985). These three reports were sponsored, respectively, by two government agencies—the National Endowment for the Humanities and the National Institute of Education—and by the Association of American Colleges, a Washington-based association of colleges with a history of interest in the liberal arts tradition.

While celebrating the diversity of American higher education and praising broad access to college, the reports urged colleges and universities to place more emphasis on common learning for all students. The curriculum, variously viewed as skills to be learned, courses to be pursued, and subject matter to be transmitted, was the central concern of all three reports. Although key foci differed, each report espoused liberal (or general) education and associated goals as the most important course of study during the undergraduate years. Furthermore, all suggested that liberal education had been seriously eroded by increasing specialization of course content and encroachment of a vocational mentality. Each report presented a plea for a redefinition of the undergraduate experience—a clarification of what "going to college" should mean. While choosing different words to describe their goals—for example, *coherence, connectedness, community, seamlessness, integrity,* and *integration*—all urged more deliberate unity and linkages within the college experience.

In different ways, the reports blamed the perceived failures of higher education on colleges and universities. All criticized the colleges for excessive specialization in current academic programs; more specifically, they chided educators for an inability to agree—and insist on—what students should know to be granted a college degree. They were critical of the autonomy of academic departments which fostered increased specialization to the detriment of liberal learning. All called for renewed emphasis on excellence in teaching and on greater faculty responsibility for planning the curriculum. The reports reflected a widespread concern that political, social, and economic pressures of the 1960s and 1970s, including student activism, an increasingly diverse student body, and predictions of falling enrollments, had distorted the mission of higher education and had led to a loss of educational purpose.

These reports presented a call for corrective action in the name of quality control. They urged that colleges reconsider the balance of general versus specialized education and return the pendulum to greater emphasis on general study. They indicated a need to move away from elective educational experiences and toward more prescribed course patterns restoring faculty control in the matter of what students should learn. While formally lauding wide access to college for all Americans, some critiques and proposals hinted broadly that quality would be higher and college costs lower if collegiate institutions with open access missions were monitored more closely, if students with inadequate preparation received no college credit until their deficits were remedied, and if expectations for students were declared and enforced. Several of the reports particularly emphasized the importance of evaluation, especially assessment of what students are learning. Critics perceived the ship of higher education to be headed off course and called for educators to turn the wheel.

The belief that change was needed was echoed with slight variations as reports sponsored by other nationally representative groups followed. These "second-wave" reports often came from those representing states or state higher education systems. For example, the Education Commission of the States (1986) reiterated many key points of earlier reports but focused its comments in *Transforming the State Role in Higher Education* on public undergraduate education and stressed the role of state leaders in encouraging and supporting reform. In its 1986 report, *To Secure the Blessings of Liberty,* the American Association of State Colleges and Universities took a different approach. The AASCU report, admitting to being unabashedly political, stressed the economic benefits of state colleges to individuals and society, defended the colleges' role in providing increased access, and urged policymakers to provide sufficient funding for the important functions these colleges serve. While elaborating on the important role state colleges play in teacher training and the eventual efficacy of higher education, AASCU suggested few specific curriculum reforms that others had not already mentioned. Also in 1986, the nation's governors published *Time for Results: The Governors' 1991 Report on Education* (National Governors' Association, 1986). While devoting primary attention to the condition of the nation's elementary and secondary schools, the governors commented briefly on higher education, emphasizing the importance of assessing what students are learning and of sharing these assessments with the public.

In 1987, Carnegie Foundation President Ernest Boyer published another analysis of the status of undergraduate education in *College: The Undergraduate Experience in America.* This report was based on visits to selected campuses and talks with students and faculty. The Carnegie study identified and made recommendations to deal with eight points of tension in undergraduate programs. Five of the tensions are clearly relevant to the curriculum. These include the transition from school to college, the goals and curriculum of education, the condition of teaching and learning, measuring educational outcomes, and connecting the campus and the larger world. (The other three points of tension, less relevant to our discussion of curriculum, were priorities of faculty, quality of campus life, and governance of colleges.)

Constructive Proposals

As the reform movement gathered momentum, a variety of specific proposals for curriculum change were developed and publicized. The Association of American Colleges (now the Association of American Colleges and Universities) was particularly active, following up its 1985 criticisms with concrete proposals for change in general education (*A New Vitality in General Education,* 1988; *Strong Foundations: Twelve Principles for Effective General Education Programs,* 1994) and in undergraduate majors (*The Challenge of Connecting Learning,* 1991a; *and Reports from the Fields,* 1991b). AAC also published a series of projects focused on increasing breadth in collegiate career studies programs such as business (Johnston & Associates, 1987), teacher education (Johnston & Associates, 1989), and engineering (Johnston, Shaman, & Zemsky, 1988), and proposed how programs might be appropriately evaluated in *Program Review and Educational Quality in the Major* (AAC, 1992).

At the National Endowment for the Humanities (NEH), Director Lynne V. Cheney, following the example of her predecessor, William Bennett, insisted that colleges should devote more attention to what all students should study. In a 1988 report, *Humanities in America,* she wrote, "Deciding what it is that undergraduates should study is not only the most important task that a faculty undertakes as a group, it may also be the hardest; and the newly politicized nature of debate in the humanities has made it more difficult" (p. 14). Subsequently, in 1989, Cheney issued *50 Hours: A Core Curriculum for College Students*, suggesting in detail what a program taken by all college students might include. This proposal placed NEH in the position of suggesting a nationally acceptable curriculum more directly than federal agencies had previously done. *50 Hours* itself was seen as politicized and added fuel to the debate about whether a "canon" or common study should be required of all college students.

CURRICULUM REFORM AND ACADEMIC PLANS

Writers of the various critiques and reform proposals used varied definitions of curriculum to guide their thinking. In fact, *Integrity in the College Curriculum,* explicitly or implicitly, used more than ten different definitions of curriculum (ranging from course requirements to student experiences to faculty judgments) in a relatively short document. Nevertheless, it is useful to examine key reports and proposals written from 1984 to 1994 from the perspective of the curriculum as an academic plan, to determine more precisely which aspects of the plan were targeted for improvement and which aspects received little or no attention.

Purpose and Content

In describing the elements of the academic plan, we expressly separated purpose and content because both broad aims and specific objectives of education can usually be achieved with different types of content as a vehicle. Only when the learning objectives are to assimilate concept knowledge, principles, or laws within a specific discipline is a single type of content the exclusive vehicle for learning.

Analysis of the reports shows clearly, however, that both policymakers and educators link the achievement of certain objectives with the study of certain subject matter, rather than associating objectives with appropriately varied types of content. In reviewing the recommendations of these reports, any attempt to separate content from objectives would be artificial and distorting, so we will discuss them together.

To Reclaim a Legacy was unequivocal in its recommendations about the purpose of education. The primary goal is that students learn about culture and civilization (Bennett, 1984, p. 1). To achieve this goal, one must select the right content; that is, educators must establish a core undergraduate curriculum in which the study of humanities and Western civilization is the central, unifying purpose. Mastering this curriculum will allow students to understand how people through the ages have addressed fundamental questions. The essential elements of the curriculum as Bennett saw them are studying the history of Western civilization; reading several master works of English, American, and European literature; acquiring an understanding of the most significant ideas and debates in the history of philosophy; becoming familiar with the history, literature, religion, and philosophy of at least one non-Western culture; and understanding the history of science and technology. While specifying a list of authors and great works all students should read, *To Reclaim a Legacy* indicates that the common curriculum for students at a college should be finally determined by each institution.

A definitive, but more limited, position on a single type of content was taken by a report sponsored by a college association. While not prescribing content for college curricula generally, the AASCU report, *To Secure the Blessings of Liberty* (American Association of State Colleges and Universities, 1986) took an international view and asserted that all students should learn a foreign language to function in a multilingual, global, and technological society.

Integrity in the College Curriculum, sponsored by another group of colleges (the AAC), illustrates another set of assumptions—the tripartite linkage between desired outcomes, educational processes and subject matter content. By choosing the word *experience* to exemplify the desired form of education, thus leaving the instructional process unspecified, *Integrity* used either content or process—one may choose—as a mediator between the other two elements. According to this report, the desired product of education is the achievement of general knowledge, behaviors, and attitudes characteristic of the "alert and inquiring citizen and worker." The authors believe these outcomes will most likely be accomplished if students (whether seeking liberal arts degrees or professional baccalaureate degrees) participate in nine content-related "experiences." The essential experiences (in brief) are "1) Inquiry: abstract logical thinking, critical analysis; 2) Literacy: writing, reading, speaking, listening; 3) Understanding numerical data; 4) Historical consciousness; 5) Science; 6) Values; 7) Art; 8) International and multicultural experiences; and 9) Study in depth" (Association of American Colleges, 1985, pp. 15-24). The aim is to guide students in a philosophical and moral inquiry that produces a "vision of the good life, a life of responsible citizenship and human decency" (p. 6). Thus, the curriculum should emphasize wisdom in the truest sense, not just the sheer accumulation of facts and not just classical wisdom. The emphasis is on "methods and processes, modes of access to understanding and judgment, that should inform all study" (p. 15). One can infer from this complex relationship that many types of instructional processes or types of experiences are equally appropriate. On the other hand, the nature of the content specified makes reasonably clear the nature of the experience—for example, the experiences that produce literacy are reading and writing, but the experiences that produce historical consciousness include the reading of (and possibly writing about) history.

According to NIE's *Involvement in Learning* (National Institute of Education, 1984), restoring excellence to higher education requires that colleges produce demonstrable improvements in students' knowledge, capacities, skills, and attitudes between entrance and graduation. These demonstrable improvements should be guided by clearly expressed, publicly announced, and consistently maintained standards of performance for awarding degrees—standards that are based on societal and institutional definitions of college-level academic learning. The goals will best be achieved if colleges find ways to involve students in their own learning and to measure the outcomes. This position, of course, captured the essence of the talent development (value-added) model proposed by Alexander Astin (1991a), who, like Zelda Gamson, was a member of the study group that produced the report.

Five of the twenty-four explicit recommendations of *Involvement in Learning* focused directly on the knowledge, skills, and attitudes to be learned. Two emphasized institutional responsibility/autonomy for establishing purposes and objectives or measuring their achievement. Taken together, these two objectives came close to incorporating all elements of the academic plan. First, "Faculties and chief academic officers in each institution should agree upon and disseminate a statement of the knowledge, capacities, and skills that students must develop prior to graduation" (p. 39), and second, "Accrediting agencies should hold colleges accountable for clear statements of expectations for student learning, appropriate assessment programs to determine whether those expectations are being met, and systematic efforts to improve learning as a result of those assessments" (p. 69).

Three of the NIE recommendations linked purpose and content or purpose and instructional process. They called on undergraduate colleges to expand liberal education requirements and emphasize the development of students capacities to analyze, solve problems, communicate, synthesize, and integrate knowledge from various disciplines (p. 43), for each college to examine and adjust its programs to match the knowledge capacities and skills it expects students to achieve (p. 45). To stress the same issue from another leverage point, NIE also urged graduate schools to require that applicants have a broad undergraduate education to balance their specialized training (p. 64).

These three recommendations, all indicating that an undergraduate education should be both broad and integrated, are among the strongest content prescriptions contained in *Involvement in Learning.* Like most of the government-sponsored reports, the NIE Study Group deferred to groups such as educators, accreditors, employers, and professional associations as more appropriate selectors of specific purposes and content. Taking an even more neutral stance, the National Governors' Association report, *Time for Results* (1986), indicated simply that the purpose of education is the acquisition of knowledge and development of the ability to organize and use it.

Using a more normative approach, Ernest Boyer's *College: The Undergraduate Experience in America* (1987) asserted that colleges must ensure that learners acquire proficiency in reading, writing, and composition to be prepared for social and civic obligations. Boyer indicated that conflicting priorities and lack of definitive goals currently create tension—for example, the tension between careerism and the liberal arts that has existed for nearly two centuries. Boyer also laid out a set of general education objectives in the form of seven areas of inquiry that touch on the disciplines and relate knowledge to experiences common to all people: Language: The Crucial Connection; Art: The Esthetic Experience; Heritage: The Living Past; The Social Web; Nature: Ecology of the Planet; Work: The Value of Vocation; and Identity: The Search for Meaning. The topics Boyer listed are broad but stress the integrative task of the core of learning more strongly than do some of the other reports. Boyer hoped that the core would introduce students to essential knowledge, the connections across disciplines, and the application of knowledge to life beyond college. He commented on the major specialization as well. For him, the merit of the major must be judged by whether the field has intellectual content of its own and the capacity to enlarge rather than narrow the students' vision.

We move now to even more specific proposals for translating the reform ideas into action that focus on the first elements of the academic plan, purpose and content. In her treatise *50 Hours: A Core Curriculum for College Students,* Lynne Cheney (1989) used the core curriculum as a device for organizing material so that the student would "know the literature, philosophy, institutions and art of our own and other cultures" (p. 11). Extending Bennett's reasoning, Cheney believed that the study of this core (or one like it) will expand choices and enrich possibilities for individuals. Using the traditional structure of the semester hour, she proposed a set of courses to be taken over three years: 18 semester hours in the study of Cultures and Civilizations, 12 in a foreign language, 6 hours in Concepts of Mathematics, 8 hours in Foundations of the Natural Sciences, and 6 hours in The Social Sciences and the Modern World. Within the largest segment, Cultures and Civilizations, she proposed four three-credit segments: Origins of Civilizations, Western Civilization: Pericles to the Reformation; Western Civilization: Reformation to the Twentieth Century; American Civilization: Colonial Times to the present; and a six-credit segment on Other Civilizations (Africa, East Asia, Islam, Latin America, etc.) Cheney allowed other prototypes but insisted that studying a common core would bring order and coherence to education and encourage a community of learners on a campus. "History, literature, philosophy, and art are at the heart of this curriculum because life lived in their company is richer and fuller than life spent in their absence" (p. 21).

In *A New Vitality in General Education,* the Association of American Colleges (1992) also proposed definite ways of reaching the desired ends in a general program intended for all students. With respect to purpose and content, this report built on AAC's 1985 report, *Integrity in the College Curriculum.* It further defined general education as the cultivation of knowledge, skills, and attitudes that all of us use and live by during most of our lives, as parents, citizens, travelers, participants in the arts, leaders, volunteers, or good Samaritans. Students could benefit in these endeavors, the authors of *New Vitality* felt, from a common text and a common learning program that might, but need not, be a "great books" approach focusing on classical readings.

Strengthening the Ties That Bind: Integrating Liberal and Professional Study was a report produced by the Professional Preparation Network, a volunteer national task force of faculty teaching in varied liberal and professional education fields. The group was convened with FIPSE sponsorship to discuss common purposes (Stark & Lowther, 1988; Armour & Fuhrmann, 1989). Based on literature searches, a national survey of educators in professional programs, and extensive discussion, members of the Network concurred that liberal studies and seemingly diverse collegiate career studies programs have many more common objectives than is often realized. The report, circulated to most chairs of professional programs in American colleges and universities, stressed that educators can construct different academic plans and use different content to achieve similar purposes, whether the content material is viewed as liberal or professional. The report identified ten outcomes that are important in both types of education, ranging from communication skills to ethics. Table 5-3 lists and defines the ten outcomes educators considered important *in addition to* the specific outcomes unique to either liberal or professional education, re-

spectively, such as education for citizenship or technical competence. Members of the Professional Preparation Network felt that recognizing these common purposes provided opportunities to develop concrete proposals for integration that could reduce tension in the continuing debate about balance between general and specialized education.

Sequence and Structure

We have described *sequence* as the arrangement of subject matter to facilitate the learner's contact with it. Sequence includes, but is not limited to, the established structures in which colleges arrange their relationships with students. The authors of the various reform reports placed heavy emphasis on structural changes that they believed were optimum arrangements for college learning.

The authors of *Integrity in the College Curriculum* (Association of American Colleges, 1985) devoted a great deal of attention to sequence. They defined higher education's primary problem as a collapse of structure in the curriculum caused by uncontrolled indulgence of individual faculty and student choices. The tone of the criticism was acerbic:

> As for what passes as a college curriculum, almost anything goes. We have reached a point at which we are more confident about the length of a college education than its content and purpose . . . The curriculum has given way to a marketplace philosophy: it is a supermarket where students are shoppers and professors are merchants of learning . . . It is as if no one cared, so long as the store stays open. (pp. 2–3)

The report specified nine "experiences," selected by faculty, and a reduction in student choice to offset a perceived loss of quality control. We consider the nine experiences, which includes one for study in depth, to be concerned with sequence (or curricular structure) as well as purpose because the AAC task

TABLE 5-3   Outcomes Important to Educators in Both Liberal Arts and Undergraduate Professional Programs

Communication Competence:

The graduate can read, write, speak, and listen and use these processes effectively to acquire, develop, and convey ideas and information.

Comment:
Reading, writing, speaking, and listening are skills essential to professional practice and to continued professional growth as well as to informed citizenry and continued personal growth.

Critical Thinking:

The graduate examines issues rationally, logically, and coherently.

Comment:
Although critical thinking is a universally desired educational outcome, professionals particularly need a repertoire of thinking strategies that will enable them to acquire, evaluate, and synthesize information and knowledge. Since much professional practice is problematical, students need to develop analytical skills to make decisions in both familiar and unfamiliar circumstances.

Contextual Competence:

The graduate has an understanding of the societal context (environment) in which the profession is practiced.

Comment:
The capability to adopt multiple perspectives allows the graduate to comprehend the complex interdependence between the profession and society. An enlarged understanding of the world and the ability to make judgments in light of historical, social, economic, scientific, and political realities is demanded of the professional as well as the citizen.

Aesthetic Sensibility:

The graduate will have an enhanced aesthetic awareness of arts and human behavior for both personal enrichment and application in enhancement of the profession.

Comment:
Sensitivity to relationships among the arts, the natural environment, and human concerns epitomizes aesthetic awareness. Through learning to approach life as an aesthetic experience and by viewing work as an act of aesthetic judgment, professionals can more effectively assess and understand the world and their roles within it.

Professional Identity:

The graduate acknowledges and is concerned for improving the knowledge, skills, and values of the profession.

Comment:
Professional identity both parallels and supplements the liberal education goal of developing a sense of personal identity. The sense of personal worth and self-confidence that develops from experiencing success in professional practice, often including a contributing or altruistic relationship with clients, is an effective vehicle for gaining a sense of one's place in the world as an individual and citizen.

TABLE 5-3 *Continued*

Professional Ethics:

The graduate understands and accepts the ethics of the profession as standards that guide professional behavior.

Comment:
Liberally educated individuals are expected to have developed value systems and ethical standards that guide their behavior. Since in every field professionals face choice and responsibility in the profess of making decisions with full understanding of their consequences, the student of ethics provides a context for development of professional ethics.

Adaptive Competence:

The graduate anticipates, adapts to, and promotes changes important to the profession's societal purpose and the professional's role.

Comment:
A liberally educated person has an enhanced capacity to adapt to and anticipate changes in society. Since professional practice is not static, adaptability can be fostered by promoting the need to detect and respond to changes and make innovations in professional practice.

Leadership Capacity:

The graduate exhibits the capacity to contribute as a productive member of the profession and to assume leadership roles as appropriate in the profession and society.

Comment:
All education carries with it the responsibility of developing leadership capacity. This is particularly true for professional education where the problem-decision-action cycle may have broad environmental, social, and individual ramifications. Not only does leadership imply both functional and status obligations, it requires the intelligent humane application of knowledge and skills.

Scholarly Concern for Improvement:

The graduate recognizes the need to increase knowledge and advance the profession through systematic, cumulative research on problems of theory and practice.

Comment:
The heart of the intellectual process is attention to a spirit of inquiry, critical analysis of logical thinking. Although many critical analysis skills are developed as theory and practice are integrated, the professional curriculum can be specifically designed to foster among graduates an obligation to participate in inquiry, research, and improvement of the profession.

Motivation for Continued Learning:

The graduate continues to explore and expand personal, civic, and professional knowledge and skills throughout a lifetime.

Comment:
A truly educated person will wish to continue learning throughout life. In professional education, substantial emphasis can be placed on fostering individual responsibility for continued professional growth.

force specified that these experiences should be distributed across subject matter domains. *Integrity* (Association of American Colleges, 1985) came out strongly for "connectedness" (used as a synonym for integration) but left specific definitions to be worked out by local faculty groups. As the Association of American Colleges made additional concrete proposals for improvement, it first addressed sequence in general education, then in liberal arts majors. In *New Vitality in General Education,* the AAC Task Group on General Education (1988) devoted considerable time to sequence. It stated: "We should look at courses in their sequences and interrelations to see that they build up to coherent competencies over the four years and to allow students opportunities to practice and demonstrate the competencies" (p. 23). The Task Group acknowledged the importance of reinforcement in learning and suggested also that "faculty might plan to reintroduce certain topics or concepts with differing emphases or applications, at different times and in different contexts, over the four-year undergraduate cycle" (p. 24). Finally, they suggested that sequencing ought to include "connectedness." This implies not only conscious attention to the connectedness of courses within fields, but to the connections between fields of study, and also among study, life, and work.

Integrity also stressed that various aspects of knowledge should be integrated into a cumulative, coherent whole:

> We *do not* believe that the road to a coherent undergraduate education can be constructed from a set of required subjects or academic disciplines. We *do* believe that there are methods and processes, modes of access to understanding and judgment, that should inform all study. While learning cannot of course take place devoid of subject matter, how that subject matter is experienced is what concerns us here. . . . (p. 15; emphasis in original).

With the exception of emphasis on modes of inquiry that have informed human knowledge of the world, *Integrity* left undeveloped any specific recommendations for achieving the desired integration. The clear implication, however, is that faculty members themselves possess integrated knowledge, know what needs to be done, and need only to accept the responsibility of achieving this goal.

New Vitality introduced the notion that students also should be fully aware of the intellectual debate among faculty regarding course sequence and become more aware of "the underlying philosophies that lead us to establish their sequence of courses" (p. 21). Although the AAC linked sequence with learners, it did not retreat from its earlier stance of less student choice among courses and more faculty prescription.

The AAC's effort to stimulate change in liberal arts majors was initially set forth in *Integrity.* This first AAC report asserted that study-in-depth should include "sequential learning, building on blocks of knowledge that lead to more sophisticated understanding and encourage leaps of imagination and synthesis" (p. 24). Focusing its attention specifically on the major, the Association of American Colleges issued four challenges to the disciplines within the traditional liberal arts fields. In a brief document entitled *The Challenge of Connecting Learning* (1991a), AAC indicated that, unlike general education, major programs are devised by organized groups within the faculty. These groups of faculty are the appropriate source of specific purpose and content requirements for the major, but they should choose them with attention to their connection to the student's entire education. Thus, the broad challenges to which the AAC sought a response from faculty in the major fields dealt largely with sequence and structure of the academic plan. They defined coherence in the major as a course of study with an organization that is clear to both faculty and students (pp. 8, 11). Such an organization is essentially sequential in structure, with a beginning, a middle, and an end.

Involvement in Learning addressed sequence only briefly by stating that all college students should study two years of general education; the appropriate time for such study was left open. The report also suggested "integrative mechanisms" that would require students to reflect on the knowledge gained over several years of college.

In *To Reclaim a Legacy,* Bennett (1984) asserted that a foundation in general education should precede studying a major. He suggested reassigning key faculty to cover the introductory humanities courses to improve education offered to freshman and sophomore students. Interestingly, while encouraging study of the humanities throughout the four years, Bennett did not question whether the freshman year is the best time to study these ideas. Nor did he say much about the ideal sequence, if any, in which the great works should be read.

Building on *To Reclaim a Legacy,* Cheney's proposal, *50 Hours* (1989), gave a specified number of credit hours of core studies to be taken over three years and also specified a particular sequence. In proposing the sequence for the study of civilizations Cheney suggested that students first study the most familiar civilizations, American and Western cultures, then move to the unfamiliar. Cheney also felt that repeating the study of themes in a spiral pattern could increase coherence. Her rationale was:

> a core program should have a sequence that most students follow. When professors know what students have studied, they can assume a base of knowledge and build upon it. They can reach across courses with references, adding depth, richness, and coherence to general education. (p.18)

Boyer's book *College: The Undergraduate Experience in America* (1987) proposed that education become a "seamless web" with integration between school and college levels, integration of studies, clearly articulated goals, and assessment that supports academic advising and curriculum development at all levels. Boyer claimed that colleges should become "learning communities" where discussion of varied points of view about all subjects, including education, would take place. More specifically, Boyer suggested that college work should integrate liberal arts and professional study over the entire four-year program, that the major should be "enriched" or put into perspective by other courses, and that the college experience culminate with a senior capstone thesis and related seminar.

The Professional Preparation Network convened by Stark and Lowther opposed grouping all the general education courses into the first two years, followed by study in a professional major. Rather, the network asserted that students with strong inclination toward professional study might develop increased interest in the liberal arts if connections between the two were made explicit early. Once made, these linkages should continue to be emphasized for students throughout the academic program as the major is continually placed in the context of the larger society through the liberal arts. Such a position would simultaneously capitalize on student interests and relate collegiate career studies to needs of society. But it would require new relations between faculty in specific liberal arts programs and their colleagues in professional fields.

Learners

Whether the material taught in the academic plan is learned depends on whether it interests and motivates learners, whether it is material that connects with their previous learning and current lives, and whether they see its potential for future use. Because of this knowledge about what makes learning effective, we might expect reform reports to strongly emphasize the needs and characteristics of learners in today's colleges. In our examination, we saw, rather, that direct expressions of student needs received minimal attention; the varied task forces and report writers reported or interpreted student opinions from sources that were not always clear.

In *To Reclaim a Legacy,* Bennett paid little attention to learners except to indicate that current students have deficiencies in their knowledge of subject matter due to lack of exposure. For example, "few [students] can be said to receive an adequate education in the culture and civilization of which they are members" (p. 1). The report decried the fact that "a student can obtain a bachelor's degree from 75 percent of all American colleges and universities without studying European history; from 72 percent without studying American literature or history, and from 86 percent without having studied the civilization of classical Greece and Rome" (p. 1).

The task force that approved *Integrity in the College Curriculum* decided to emphasize "learning to learn." However, the assumption that seemed to underlie this report is that professors know what students need to achieve the desired learning and should create structures to encourage students to learn this material. This assumption translated into heavy student advising responsibility for faculty. Consequently, the authors of *Integrity* argued that more reliable information on who students are and a more accurate sense of their progress in the mastery of skills and capacities defined by the proposed minimum curriculum is needed. Advising students at the program level can be considered the parallel of making expectations clear at the course level. The AAC consistently emphasized faculty responsibility to make expectations clear and understand student progress more fully.

The idea of making expectations clear to students was emphasized even more strongly in *Involvement in Learning.* While *Integrity* and *To Reclaim a Legacy* focused primarily on improving programs of study and how they are taught, *Involvement* concentrated to a greater degree on learners and the learning process. Of all the reports, this one from the National Institute of Education is the only one that seemed to recognize the wide diversity of students in today's colleges; it discussed adult students, commuter students in community colleges, students with family obligations, and the average 50% attrition rate for entering students who intend to earn a bachelor's degree. Like *Integrity*, it placed strong emphasis on faculty roles in advising and making expectations clear to students. Its primary emphasis, however, was on ensuring the involvement of learners in the educational process. It even included a set of recommendations directly addressed to learners.

Four recommendations especially emphasized learners' needs. Three of these have already been mentioned in the previous section because their primary focus was on educational purpose and content. The fourth recommendation suggested that remedial courses would enable students to perform well in subsequent college-level study (p. 48). This recommendation recognized the need for a balance between quality control and broad access to college.

Reports of the states and the state colleges seemed to be in agreement about learners. In *To Secure the Blessings of Liberty,* the American Association of State Colleges and Universities (1986) took the position that education is an investment in human capital. The authors called for more attention to minorities, multiculturalism, and remedial education and asserted that the state colleges and universities are places where anyone who wants to earn a bachelor's degree should have an opportunity to do so. Adult and continuing education should be restructured, making it accessible to individuals in all regions of the country. Tuition in public colleges should be kept low, and the colleges should work with the high schools to improve student preparation. Similarly, in *Transforming the State Role*, the Education Commission of the States (1986) welcomed the learner (and taxpayer) to the public college and called for improved preparation to reduce attrition, especially of minority students.

In *50 Hours* Cheney described the explorations learners must undertake and the insights they should gain in the core curriculum. She acknowledged that there are different types of learners by including special sections on core curricula for two-year colleges and for honors programs. This distinction was interpreted by some as suggesting that some students (and some colleges) are more likely to meet traditional college standards than others. While seeming to recognize individual differences among students, the recommendation for different educational tracks sounded something like parallel scientific courses in the early 1800s and seemed directly opposed to the open-access position that AASCU took in *To Secure the Blessings*.

In *A New Vitality in General Education*, the AAC Task Group recognized that learners differ in capabilities, preparation, lifestyle, and interests. A chapter entitled "Reorienting Teaching" could as well have been titled "Reorienting Learning." It proposed actively involving students in jointly setting learning goals with faculty, in collaborative learning with peers, and in inquiry and research during the undergraduate years. The AAC discussion assumes a close relationship between the learner and the choice of instructional processes as faculty members develop academic plans.

The Challenge of Connecting Learning (Association of American Colleges, 1991a) contained a charge to academic departments unique among these reports and proposals by stressing increased access to specialized study. The AAC challenged academic major programs to work for more "inclusiveness" by reducing barriers for underrepresented students. The report states: "Faculty members in each program must explore what obstacles their fields present to the participation of discrete groups of underrepresented students and make a strong commitment to eliminating those obstacles" (p. 17). This approach is consistent with other parts of the report that described the process by which students become members of the community of the major. As members of this community, students have a right to expect that the major field recognizes, reflects, and values their goals, perspectives, and experiences. They have a right to expect that teachers and colleges will help them inquire, understand, and connect their knowledge, and that introductory courses will not be used as screening devices to filter out particular groups of students. While specifically opposing separate remedial tracks, *The Challenge* acknowledged that learners who attend college intermittently and at varying periods of their lives may need different sequences of courses than more traditional learners (pp. 17–18). They also urged "periodic faculty-student dialogue about what is supposed to be accomplished through the common parts of the program" (p. 11).

In similar fashion, *Strengthening the Ties That Bind* (Stark & Lowther, 1988) encouraged students who are emerging professionals to enter into the discussion of their education. In *College,* Boyer (1987) mentioned community (along with individuality) as a tradition in college education that helps to define the undergraduate experience. In his view, community will be better achieved if colleges take seriously their obligation to offer students a more coherent view of knowledge. Overall, the proposals that considered learners argued clearly that students be included in the dialogue about their education.

Instructional Process

Instructional processes are chosen either consciously or by default, and the choices are increasingly recognized as crucial to effective learning. Compared to purpose, content, and sequence, only gradual change has characterized instructional process over the past 350 years of collegiate education in the United States. Attention to instruction, however, has increased dramatically during the last two decades of the twentieth century.

The primary focus of *Involvement in Learning* was on learning; how it might take place, how it is achieved, and how it might be measured. Although this report was less prescriptive than others regarding course content, it emphatically expressed the belief that education would be significantly improved if American colleges would find ways to involve students more fully in their education, while at the same time clarifying and stating high expectations for them to meet. Thus, *Involvement* paid attention both to integrating knowledge and to individualizing education. Several recommendations directly addressed the teaching/learning process. The NIE Task Force urged faculty to make greater use of active modes of teaching and require that students take greater responsibility for their learning (p. 27). They urged colleges to resist substituting learning technologies for personal teacher–student interaction (p. 29), suggested that all colleges create learning communities organized around intellectual themes and tasks (p. 33), and asserted that all bachelor's degree recipients should complete at least two full years of liberal education (p. 41).

The attention Bennett (1984) paid to the learning process in *To Reclaim a Legacy* is clear, direct, and simple: Learners should read and discuss the recommended great works, and excellent teachers should be reassigned to the undergraduate courses to ensure that this process is well done. Similarly, in *50 Hours,* Cheney (1989) recommended having the "most distinguished faculty" teach core courses and emphasized the participation that is possible when engaging ideas in small classes. Boyer's (1987) book, *College*, was quite specific about the need for active learning and for small seminar opportunities with vigorous intellectual exchange that may foster student creativity, rather than conformity.

The concern for good teaching was echoed in varied ways in all of the other reports and proposals. It was the general consensus of the reformers that college professors have neglected teaching in favor of research, have neglected undergraduates in favor of graduate students, have neglected teaching duties by assigning them to poorly prepared teaching assistants who sometimes do not speak English as their first language, and above all, have neglected curriculum development. To deal with these charges, each report gave different types of remedies.

As we have noted, *Integrity in the College Curriculum* focused on nine educational "experiences." In contrast to the focus on "good teachers" advocated by Bennett, Cheney, and Boyer, a focus on "experiences" implies that students learn in many ways, perhaps even without deliberate "teaching" by faculty. Later in *New Vitality*, the AAC Task Group asserted that what is taught is probably less important than how it is taught. The report gave specific suggestions for how to encourage active learning in general education, including collaborative projects, out-of-class study groups, electronic media, undergraduate research, and identification of major concepts to stimulate active comprehension.

The Challenge of Connecting Learning was unique in its extensive attention to faculty responsibility for helping students develop "critical perspective" in the major. Critical perspective is seen as the capacity to ask sophisticated questions and compare and connect proposals of the discipline community with those of other discipline communities. The report stresses that faculty will need to serve as guides and models of inquiry in the discipline to support this type of student development.

Instructional Resources

At the course and program levels, we think of resources as books and other teaching materials used in class, as well as settings for laboratories, field placements, and the like. At the college level, our attention might turn to libraries, well-prepared and committed faculties, a supportive college infrastructure, and overall financial stability. The reports issued by state groups and associations of public colleges were especially attentive to these matters, despite their silence or deference to faculty on issues of purpose, content, and instructional process.

To Secure the Blessings of Liberty strongly urged that states and federal legislators supply ample funds, maintain student financial assistance, encourage higher education's participation in economic goals, and assist higher education in playing an important role internationally. State fiscal policies, as well as institutional policies, should be modified to ensure faculty vitality and excellence in teaching, and new ways of cooperating should be found to reduce competition among colleges and universities for limited state resources. As the authors made clear, this report was intended for policymakers rather than for educators. It spent little time on issues typically thought of as curriculum. Yet its presence reminds us that curriculum development requires attention to resources of varying types.

Faculty are the primary resources in developing academic plans. But several proposals do not consider professors competent "planners" so much as those whose planning activities must be guided and monitored by some more responsible group of leaders. According to some reports, the leadership group that must ultimately take responsibility is college administrators. Authors urged administrators to ensure the careful selection of faculty, provide experience for faculty in how to develop syllabi and instructional plans, promote more effective use of student evaluations of teaching, refocus reward systems to focus on teaching, issue strong statements of commitment to the undergraduate program, and improve faculty salaries.

Focusing more directly on academic plans, we note that today the growth of complex and rapid ways to transmit information implies new uses of resources. The recommendations of Bennett and Cheney for reading original texts call for the simplest and most traditional of instructional resources and materials. Surprisingly, these reports made no mention of enhancing the humanities by making history, culture, and literature more vivid through videodisc or CD-ROM technology. *Involvement in Learning* opposed the use of technology that might decrease student interaction with faculty on intellectual issues.

In contrast, Boyer considered technology a resource to be exploited today. He recommended linking new technology to the library and classroom. He also suggested that colleges need comprehensive plans and resources for technological development, including training for faculty in how to use new strategies to best advantage.

To Secure the Blessings of Liberty recommended that field settings be considered a resource and emphasized the increasingly popular idea of student public service as an educational experience. Public service was seen as an antidote to alleged narrowness and self-centeredness for both students and programs. In the early 1990s, the Clinton administration initiated a community service program for college students that builds on this idea.

Evaluation and Adjustment

Our definition of curriculum as an academic plan intentionally includes evaluation and the use of evaluative information to adjust the curriculum. Curriculum evaluation and adjustment are certainly not new ideas, but they have not been given strong emphasis in colleges. Historically, as we have shown, curriculum correctives have been unsystematic and, as in our current discussion, have often resulted from strong external influences during eras of educational reform. It seems to us, however, that a distinguishing feature of the most recent reform era was its heavy emphasis on developing more systematic evaluation plans. If appropriately constructed and used, such plans should make higher education more self-correcting in the future. A few of the reports devoted attention to new ways of evaluating college effectiveness, particularly student achievement.

To Reclaim a Legacy and *50 Hours* did not emphasize evaluation or assessment of student learning. The implicit assumption of these reports is that reading and discussing the great works will produce the desired outcomes in students. Similarly, *Integrity in the College Curriculum* also paid only modest attention to assessment, indicating in general terms that students, programs, and faculty should all be evaluated. Presumably, the measurement of what students achieve as a result of the nine experiences should be conducted in existing and traditional ways, perhaps with course examinations and, occasionally, a senior thesis.

In contrast, *Involvement in Learning* placed heavy emphasis on evaluation, specifically on assessing student outcomes. It also advocated that faculty be directly involved in developing and using assessment programs,

thereby suggesting an adjustment process. The recommendations on assessment called for faculty and academic deans to "design and implement a systematic program to assess the knowledge, capacities and skills developed by students in academic and co-curricular programs" (p. 55). Faculty should receive appropriate training to "participate in the development, adoption, administration and scoring of instruments and methods appropriate for 1) the knowledge capacities and skills addressed and 2) the stated objectives of undergraduate education at their institutions" (pp. 57, 58). The report urged that faculty learn to use assessment as a teaching tool (p. 58) and that regular student assessments of the learning environment be widely disseminated and discussed (p. 61). *Involvement in Learning* assigned to accrediting agencies the responsibility to hold all types of colleges "accountable for clear statements of expectations for students learning, appropriate assessment programs to determine whether those expectations are being met, and systematic efforts to improve learning" based on the results (p. 69).

State policymakers also see assessment as a facet of accountability that has strong potential to promote positive change. In *Transforming the State Role,* the Education Commission of the States (1986) indicated that assessment should be improved at all levels and include widespread testing of student achievement. Following suit, *Time for Results* (National Governors' Association, 1986) posed the rhetorical question, "Does a degree tell us what the student learned?" and made assessment a key concept in its higher education recommendations. The report recommended that assessment programs be developed, used for improvement, and shared with the public. In contrast, *To Secure the Blessings of Liberty,* sponsored by an association of state-funded institutions, spoke somewhat more conservatively, indicating that assessment should be seen as a way of enhancing programs, not just demonstrating quality. But it advised colleges to establish minimum academic skill levels that all students should attain by the end of their sophomore year.

Boyer (1987) emphasized the importance of outcome assessment that transcends courses, is adaptable, and demonstrates that students can integrate knowledge. He urged frequent evaluation of student intellectual and linguistic development, as well as development of a good assessment tool for general education. For collegewide assessment, Boyer favored senior theses and senior colloquia. He did not favor standardized tests as assessment tools and definitely opposed direct involvement of public agencies in outcomes assessment. A similar emphasis on flexibility and local autonomy was strong in *A New Vitality.* The authors urged the development of creative assessment tools that can adequately reflect development in general education and facilitate comparisons with appropriately similar colleges. They also emphasized student involvement in assessment as students reflect on their own learning, develop portfolios, and contribute their perspectives in classes.

Summary

As we analyze the critiques and proposals for reform, we note that the reformers heavily emphasized educational purpose and content. They emphasized sequence and instructional resources more modestly and learners even less. These patterns of varied attention to the elements of academic plans are similar to those we have detected in previous reform discussions in the history of American higher education. We noted some new emphases, however, that hold promise for the future. We will return to these emphases following a discussion of external, organizational, and internal influences and the related impact of the reforms on campuses.

IMPACT OF THE REFORM PROPOSALS

In a decentralized system of higher education, blue-ribbon reports generally are considered successful if they stimulate modest discussion before fading into oblivion. The traditionally slow pace of change in college curricula predicts that the impact of recommendations may be delayed. Recent reform reports, however, have stimulated more discussion than is typical. Despite initial faculty (and sometimes administrator) resistance to the reports and their recommendations, external, organizational, and internal influences have converged to create a climate for change in campus educational environments.

Viewed in the context of the historically recurring debates we have described, the recent reform era was predictable. Student activism during the late 1960s caused curriculum requirements to be loosened or abolished; such periods of loosening nearly always are followed by calls for tightened quality control and more prescriptive requirements. External forces converged in the 1980s to produce corrective changes to restore balance in other aspects of higher education as well. The general conditions influencing the debates included the following:

- *International competition:* Competition among nations frequently stimulates educational reform and specific types of curriculum change. Like the influence of Sputnik in the 1950s, the perceived decline of U.S. economic competitiveness in the 1980s, accompanied by embarrassing comparisons of test results for Japanese and American children, brought new calls for higher educational standards.

- *Economic recession:* During periods of unemployment, adult students often return to college to gain new work skills. Ironically, in the 1980s, employers also complained that college graduates lacked basic skills, causing the public to question the effectiveness of college.

- *Changes in student profiles:* A long-term decline in college admissions scores (from 1968 to 1983) was fresh in the American mind. In the mid–1980s, entering college students were reported to be most interested in vocational goals and financial affluence, caring little about traditional college goals such as "developing a meaningful philosophy of life."

- *Accountability:* Financially, the nation struggled with a heavy public debt and burdensome financial commitment to ensure broad student access to postsecondary education. Cost-effective legislators scrutinized higher education when seeking places to cut the federal budget.

- *Changes in funding policies:* Republican administrations from 1981 through 1992 sought to decentralize higher education, passing both expenditures and responsibility to the states. One strategy for decentralization was to question college effectiveness and to hold the states more fully accountable for improvement.

These are only some of the general conditions that led to strong external reform influences on the educational environment in the 1980s. We turn now to more specific external influences that pushed colleges toward change.

External Influences

Reformers translated general influences, such as those we just described, into specific criticisms and proposals to encourage colleges to change. Our examination of recent occurrences verifies familiar patterns of debate.

In 1983, the first educational report to jar the public attention, *A Nation at Risk* (National Commission on Excellence, 1983)

focused on precollegiate education, not on colleges. This scathing critique attracted widespread attention, causing citizens who perceived high school preparation as deficient to wonder if and how colleges were dealing with the deficiencies. A federal administration intent on shifting both financial responsibility and accountability for colleges to the states quickly seized the opportunity for a parallel critical examination of higher education. Two successive Secretaries of Education, Terrell H. Bell and William Bennett (formerly chairman of the National Endowment for the Humanities), pursued strategies to encourage public scrutiny. The critical view of colleges coincided with diminished federal emphasis on increased access and refocused the nation's attention on educational quality. Reduced access and greater prescription of content may be the actual goals of reformers, but quality control and accountability are the rubrics under which they often propose change.

To state leaders also trying to cope with budget shortages, asking colleges and universities to demonstrate effectiveness seemed an appropriate route to improve education while cutting costs. Calls for accountability in higher education at the state level quickly followed Secretary Bell's controversial decision to use standardized test scores to compare and contrast public schools within and between states. Groups representing states could not afford to be silent on these issues; thus, each published its own report.

Various higher education associations began to exercise strong leadership to motivate colleges and universities to action. They urged colleges to respond quickly to criticism, lest government regulation be expanded, seriously limiting college autonomy. Members of Congress needed to be convinced that students were, in fact, learning something in college. Although it issued no reports of its own, the American Council on Education (ACE), located in Washington,

D.C., and representing most colleges and universities, exercised its important mediator role by gathering information about campus responses to reform suggestions and publishing them in an annual report called *Campus Trends* to show that colleges were responding to calls for change. In addition, the voluntary accrediting agencies that have traditionally certified quality of programs and institutions defended their role against direct attack by Secretary Bennett who asked them to document what students were learning in college. ACE helped the Council on Postsecondary Accreditation and its constituent accrediting agencies assert the integrity and efficacy of traditional collaborative mechanisms for quality control. Careful study reveals, however, that some association efforts were not independent of the federal government's influence. For example, ACE seemed eager to document change to bolster its efforts to maintain federal funding of higher education.

As the reform era reached the late 1980s, the American Association for Higher Education launched an important series of conferences beginning in 1985, encouraging student assessment and helping college personnel develop skill at this unfamiliar type of evaluation. Participating faculty and administrators viewed the conferences as helpful and interesting, and attendance swelled each year. Eventually, additional conferences were launched during the early 1990s to include related emphases on collaborative learning; reconsideration of the roles, responsibilities, and preparation of college professors; and the improvement of college administration through new management techniques ("Continuous Quality Improvement"). The AAHE and other agencies emphasizing assessment did not have sufficient financing for such initiatives; rather, they obtained funds from private foundations and from government agencies.

Rather than taking direct stands as Bennett and Cheney did, government agencies frequently foster curriculum change indirectly through various funded grants, projects, or regulations. Many reform projects have been sponsored by the federal Fund for the Improvement of Postsecondary Education (FIPSE), founded in 1972. This agency was created (and originally based on a private philanthropic model) in response to economic and social pressures resulting from civil rights, the women's movement, and other economic and social movements of the late 1960s; its authorizing legislation states its purpose as "encouraging the reform, innovation, and improvement of postsecondary education and providing equal opportunity for all" (Fund for the Improvement of Postsecondary Education, 1990).

With grants from FIPSE, various higher education scholars and college administrators executed specific proposals for changes or tried out innovative ideas and studied the effects even before the reform efforts of the 1980s. Based on one early study of innovative colleges, Gerald Grant and David Riesmann (1978) helped to expand the way scholars think about curriculum change in higher education. Another collaborative project of several colleges under FIPSE sponsorship, produced *Liberating Education* (Gamson & Associates, 1984). This book helped define the concept of liberal education used in some subsequent critiques and reports. Gamson and her associates described their conviction that undergraduate education should consist largely of general/liberal education and should involve students in an active learning community with their professors. The college curriculum, according to Gamson, should be diverse, integrative, experiential, critical, and pluralistic. Members of Gamson's project group advocated this position initially and buttressed it by including extensive observations and case studies of successful liberal/general education programs. Ideas from this work influenced the 1984 report *Involvement in Learning,* produced by the National

Institute of Education task force of which Gamson was a member (Study Group on the Condition, 1984).

Federal agencies also funded many important demonstration projects on assessing student outcomes. These included such diverse activities as a cooperative experimental assessment effort led by Alexander Astin at UCLA, a clearinghouse to develop and share assessment techniques headquartered at the University of Tennessee, and the series of annual conferences on assessment led by the American Association for Higher Education. Another FIPSE project, which we have discussed in detail, produced a proposal for integrating undergraduate liberal and professional study (Stark & Lowther, 1988; Armour & Fuhrmann, 1989).

Among other federal agencies, the National Institute of Education (NIE) was also interested in improving college instruction. During the period 1986–1991, NIE funded a national research center (the National Center for Research to Improve Postsecondary Teaching and Learning—NCRIPTAL) to study teaching and learning issues in higher education. The research and dissemination agenda, including many facets of college teaching and learning, ranging from student motivation to instructional use of computer technology, was developed by researchers located at the University of Michigan and approved by NIE. Shortly after the center began, the new Republican administration in Washington replaced NIE with the Office of Educational Research and Improvement (OERI). Under Assistant Secretary for Postsecondary Education Chester Finn, OERI played a much stronger role in deciding what changes were needed in higher education. In keeping with its interest in quality control, specifically assessment of student achievement, OERI rewrote the agenda for a second five-year research center grant to focus more strongly on quality control commencing in 1991. The grant was awarded to The Pennsylvania State

University, which founded the National Center for Teaching, Learning and Assessment (NCTLA), involving a consortium of researchers from several universities. Meanwhile, federal offices were attempting to document curriculum effects on various types of students by analyzing various data bases. OERI funded numerous smaller projects to analyze transcripts of college students and develop indicators of student learning. OERI published several detailed analyses of the data base of the National Longitudinal Study of 13,000 members of the high school class of 1972 and their college transcripts (Adelman, 1990, 1991, 1992a, 1992b, 1995).

As this partial listing of activities demonstrates, the reform efforts of the 1980s and 1990s were multifaceted. They included not only blue-ribbon reports that frequently received national headlines but less visible research and action projects that experimented with change—fostering goals and educational processes that might be more closely monitored. In addition to activities directly sponsored by federal agencies, some were undertaken by Washington-based higher education associations, a source faculty find more acceptable than direct federal initiatives. Overall, however, the primary impetus for reform came from forces external to colleges and universities rather than from their own initiatives.

A careful review of the events during the 1980s leaves no doubt that curriculum reform was not the idea of the colleges, of students or perhaps even of the general public. Rather, varied spokespersons perceived deficiencies and repeatedly brought them to the attention of the public through various media. Eventually the idea that colleges needed to institute quality control had become well accepted. The calls for reform were not much different than they were in earlier periods of tightening the curriculum. Although the criticism was largely external to colleges and universities, its acceptance was fostered by some preexisting organizational influences and some that developed in response.

Organizational Influences

The influences that operate in an era of curriculum reform are so intricately connected with the organization of each college or university that they are hard to identify out of context. Usually one must specify the type of institution, or even a specific academic program, to discuss influences accurately.

Generally, however, during the 1980s and early 1990s, competition within and between public colleges resulted from budgetary shortfalls as states cut back appropriations to public colleges, often in midyear. In times of shrinking and uncertain budgets, colleges frequently begin program reviews to reallocate resources to highest priorities. Such efforts provided administrators an opportunity to sharpen institutional mission and weed out programs that they viewed as poor in quality or less central to their mission. Program reviews also helped to eliminate duplication and promote collaboration in and across academic departments. Thus, in many cases, pending budget cuts and accompanying organizational tensions provided impetus in the 1980s and 1990s for administrators to focus missions and search for solutions to long-standing inefficiencies through program review. The organizational tensions within colleges as the 1980s commenced were less focused on educational enhancement than on budget improvement. On the one hand, this condition fostered receptivity to reform; on the other hand, it deflected colleges' attention from educational matters.

Internal Influences

Changes in academic plans at the course and program level most often stem from internal influences that compel faculty action. In many cases, the reports raised faculty awareness of problems they had overlooked; in other cases, they reinforced internal influences already operating on campuses. Thus, as critiques from external sources were discussed and translated into internal critiques, faculty examined their educational programs and devised solutions tailored to local settings.

At least two of the reports, *To Reclaim a Legacy* and *Integrity in the College Curriculum,* laid the responsibility for curriculum "decay" squarely at the door of educators and assigned the task of devising remedies there as well. Although a political appointee, NEH Director Bennett, himself a college professor and later Secretary of Education, spoke from the academic perspective as he prodded the professoriate to define the need for reform as an internal problem:

> The fault lies principally with those of us whose business it is to educate these students. We have blamed others, but the responsibility is ours. Not by our words but by our actions, by our indifference, and by our intellectual diffidence we have brought about this condition. It is we the educators—not scientists, business people, or the general public—who too often have given up the great task of transmitting a culture to its rightful heirs. Thus, what we have on many of our campuses is an unclaimed legacy, a course of studies in which the humanities have been siphoned off, diluted, or so adulterated that students graduate knowing little of their heritage. (p. 1)

Integrity in the College Curriculum, also blamed the "profound crisis" in American higher education on faculty members, whom it charged with developing and protecting their disciplinary interests at the expense of common standards and expectations for undergraduate education. The report strongly asserted that the "responsibility of the faculty *as a whole* for the curriculum *as a whole"* be revived (p. 9, emphasis in original).

When we interviewed faculty members in diverse colleges during 1986 and 1987, we found that they had heard little about the reports issued in the previous two years. Those who had heard about them were more familiar with *Involvement in Learning* than with the other reports, but their information usually came from newspapers not original documents. In many colleges we visited, it was business as usual. By late 1987, we found that humanities professors who had discussed Bennett's views did not agree that humanities should be emphasized by reading classical works, especially to the exclusion of other fields. They were more receptive to the report of the AAC Task Force report (*Integrity in the College Curriculum*), which they viewed as stemming from a legitimate source—other faculty—than to the NIE report (*Involvement in Learning*) written largely by higher education researchers. This was true even though the AAC faculty task force that approved *Integrity in the College Curriculum* transmitted a harsh message to their colleagues, accusing them of abandoning their responsibility.

Some faculty were angry about such accusations, asserting that they had been unfairly blamed. They lamented that poor student preparation and lack of student motivation, sometimes linked with increasing numbers of nontraditional students, precluded the levels of academic achievement desired by some spokespersons for college reform. In general, too, faculty members opposed initiatives to assess student learning, claiming that the desirable purposes and objectives of truly "higher" learning could not be measured by instruments typically devised by educators and educational psychologists.

Faculty reported that internal initiatives for change were generally weak within individual academic programs, but attributed examples of progress to special initiative of individual faculty leaders or administrators. Thus, they indicated that both administrative interest and new reward systems were needed to bolster their own efforts in curriculum change.

As in the past, internal influences directed at curriculum change seem to have arisen primarily in response to external prodding. Then, once the seeds of change had been planted, organizational leadership and supportive conditions cultivated them. From a historical perspective, one could hear echoes of the Yale Report of 1828, the faculty resistance to the elective system when President Charles W. Eliot attempted to introduce it at Harvard, and initial resistance to the return of veterans to college after World War II. In previous times, however, faculty were often defending a prescribed curriculum; now they are defending a more open curriculum based on pluralism and student choice.

The Pace of Change

Reports of changes in progress began to appear as early as 1985 in *Change: The Magazine of Higher Learning,* sponsored by the American Association for Higher Education (AAHE), and *Campus Trends,* published by the American Council on Education. Between 1984–1985 and 1985–1986, the number of cases in which colleges were said to have discussed the reports in faculty meetings increased from 45% to 61% of those responding to American Council on Education (ACE) campus trends surveys. The number of colleges reporting prompt changes in academic programs based on the reports increased from 28% to 36%. Possibly the large number of reports from diverse sponsors, coupled with modern communication systems, produced a synergism for change.

Perhaps because it spoke directly to faculty, *Integrity in the College Curriculum* fostered substantial reexamination of liberal arts programs and momentum to incorporate the nine recommended experiences. Considerable change between 1984 and 1994 can be documented, particularly at small colleges where curriculum change is easiest to achieve. In contrast, however, researchers at the New England Resource Center for Higher Education observed 48 comprehensive and doctoral colleges in New England seeking models for successful curricular change. They reported that limited resources hampered change in New England. In large universities, where individual departments and schools may have curricular autonomy as well as budgetary stringencies, the organizational influences opposing change are strong; changes may be slower and concentrated within specific colleges, such as the college of arts and science.

Anticipating opposing organizational influences in universities, some reports communicated to administrators and state policymakers the need for structural changes to support stronger curriculum development efforts. Speaking directly to administrators and policymakers who play a support role, *Involvement in Learning* devoted no less than 15 of its 24 recommendations to various types of structural or administrative considerations addressing needed improvements in the college or university environment for curriculum development. These recommendations focused on extremely diverse topics such as resource reallocations, student guidance and advisement, proficiency examinations, faculty salaries and personnel policies, and state funding for student assessment.

As the pace of change accelerated, scholars and other observers began to document it more closely and published numerous reports claiming progress. ACE based its reports on a survey of representative colleges (El-Khawas, 1986–1993). These sources indicated that most colleges were actively reviewing general education programs, many were adopting core programs, and some were developing assessment techniques. In *Campus Trends, 1992,* for example, El-Khawas reported:

- Most large universities have taken steps to strengthen undergraduate instruction and to consider expanded definitions of faculty scholarship.
- Linkages with foreign universities have grown, as have campus efforts to develop greater global awareness in course offerings and campus activities.
- New requirements in general education have been put in place, most often including coverage of multicultural subjects. (1992, p. vi)

The questions ACE asked colleges about curriculum change were very general, inviting positive responses. Possibly, too, positive reports that peer colleges were actively revising programs encouraged others to do so. Whatever the reasons, many observers felt that faculty and administrators seemed more receptive to examining educational programs by the decade of the 1990s than during the 1980s. They remained resistant, however, to implementing specific academic programs they perceived to be politically motivated such as those suggested by NEH leaders.

A Doubting Voice

Given the long time lag between calls for reform and widespread enactment of change in earlier eras, it is amazing that so much has been accomplished in ten years. But not all observers agree that change has taken place or is underway. Some have characterized the pace of reform as slow and criticized the "highly general nature of national discussions" (Cheney, 1989, p. 8).

Possibly the multiple criticisms—simultaneously attacking curriculum content, students' learning, instructional processes, and unsystematic evaluation mechanisms—were necessary to provide the wake-up calls heard in higher education by the beginning of the 1990s. But the alarms seem likely to continue; indeed, the term *wake-up call* was used by a belated report, *An American Imperative: Higher Expectations for Higher Education* (Wingspread Group, December 1993). In this document, an independent group of prominent college and university figures, sponsored by several foundations, asserted that the first alarms may not have been heard and fully comprehended.

An American Imperative relied on data reported in the prior critiques to reissue the warning, placing strong emphasis on increasing expectations and standards. The report asserted that too many college graduates are essentially illiterate and urged that colleges take immediate action. Calling for higher standards, *An American Imperative* charged that American colleges are expensive secondary schools:

> The harsh truth is that a significant minority of these graduates enter or reenter the world with little more than the knowledge, competence and skill we would have expected in a high school graduate scarcely a generation ago. (p. 2)

Following this charge, the report discussed three fundamental issues all colleges and universities should address: "taking values seriously; putting student learning first; and creating a nation of learners." Each of the three discussions was accompanied by a checklist of questions that colleges should ask about their programs.

The list of topics covered by the checklists in *An American Imperative* ranged far more broadly than the recommendations of most earlier reports. The questions colleges might ask themselves in the quest for self-improvement concern nearly every college function—from improving teaching to developing more truthful advertising; from creating statewide articulation compacts to governing the conduct of student organizations. Yet, the underlying curricular assumptions of this report were similar to those of its predecessors.

Quoting reports issued in the 1940s and 1970s, the authors focused primarily on educational purpose as they challenged colleges to develop a curriculum that would assure all graduates the benefits of a liberal education. They opined that the entry point for "taking values seriously" is to understand that "liberal education is central to living 'rightly and well in a free society.' " (p. 9). Thus, it provided little new thinking about curriculum, and its focus was diffused by attention to numerous issues. If its checklists have an impact, it may be because the change efforts were just reaching a crest when it appeared. Converging influences may have caused colleges to be ready to heed new calls for reform.

It is premature to determine the extent of change stimulated by the reports issued in the last two decades of the twentieth century. We anticipate, however, that the changes probably will not include some which reformers consider important. Colleges have concentrated their greatest efforts on general education reform, as advocated by various reports. As they have adapted general education recommendations to their local needs, they have primarily emphasized content to be included in courses and how it should be sequenced. The authors of *An American Imperative* were correct in finding little evidence that colleges have paid attention to the recommendation that they establish clear expectations for students.

In contrast to clear expectations, methods for assessing student achievement are developing rapidly. Many colleges have devised elaborate systems for comparing students' abilities as they enter and leave college. Usually, colleges have focused on general education outcomes; undergraduate professional programs, which enroll the vast majority of students, are less frequently included. In either type of program, little attention has been given to the connections between student outcomes and course and program plans.

From our perspective in discussing curriculum, another important recommendation for change in educational environments has been overlooked. The reformers sought to encourage greater faculty involvement in systematic curriculum development and evaluation, especially by increasing incentives and reducing disincentives for faculty to engage in these processes. Most reports also acknowledged that faculty and prospective faculty are not trained in curriculum development or teaching and urged colleges and universities to rethink this long tradition of neglect. Yet only modest attention has been given either to improved pedagogical preparation or to increased incentives for faculty to learn individually. Faculty incentive systems have received the greatest share of discussion, faculty development the least share. The potential for curriculum development as a collaborative process that can be exciting and intellectually revitalizing to faculty has not really been explored.

RELATION TO EARLIER DEBATES

During a reform era, it is useful to speculate on how the higher education enterprise may be permanently changed. Will old patterns of debate and change continue or have those challenges been resolved at last? Is there evidence that new debates, or newer long-term trends, will emerge from the discussions? Since the periodic nature of reform discussions makes it difficult to distinguish temporary from enduring emphases, speculation can be risky. Nevertheless, we believe that some barriers are being broken that will lead to new emphases, new definitions, and refocused old debates.

General versus Specialized Education

A revitalization of general education has definitely occurred. Many colleges attempted to redesign their general education programs to incorporate the general education experi-

ences outlined in *Integrity in the College Curriculum,* and the changes suggested in *A New Vitality in General Education.* To document progress, Gaff (1991) surveyed over 300 colleges that reported active programs of curriculum revision. He concluded that higher education was changing to make curricula more purposeful and more focused on learners and learning. As we noted earlier, a major change on some campuses was a recognition that the general education program needed clearer authority and responsibility.

Dissenting voices continued to be raised, particularly about the focus on humanities in general education. One dissenting voice, typical of the most severe critics, was that of Daniel Rossides (1987) who charged that behind the early reports' emphases on the liberal arts was a hidden agenda—that of legitimizing a society based on private property and self-interest, of keeping the elite in power, and of excluding the lower classes. Rossides claimed that the reports uniformly perpetuated the myth that liberal education serves valuable social functions, but provided no evidence that such education helps to improve society or that there is a positive relationship between what goes on inside and outside the classroom. The proposed common curriculum bears little relationship to the social world, and society has not defined what skills and values are really necessary for students to have. The humanities have disappeared, Rossides claimed, because the world they interpreted for us has disappeared. It is time for a new order, not for the "yoke of a dead humanities." In Rossides's view, we must ask what type of society we desire before we ask what type of education we need.

Others also questioned whether the right reforms were emphasized. For example, in 1986, J. Frederick Starr, then president of Oberlin College, criticized *College: The Undergraduate Experience in America* for failing to link education and research by ensuring that students learn about and engage in the processes of inquiry that have produced the knowledge we transmit. Like the authors of *Integrity in the College Curriculum*, Starr argued that it is important for students to learn *how* we come to know, as well as *what* we know.

As general education is changing, so is specialization. Traditional disciplinary major programs are in the early stages of revision. In the early 1990s, AAC surveyed 368 colleges and universities, or 55% of its institutional members. They reported that 45% of respondents were working to strengthen the major and another 13% had plans to begin. Colleges were reintroducing capstone experiences for integrating learning in the major, such as senior theses and senior seminars. Reportedly, change was slower and more difficult when colleges tried to link majors more effectively with general education programs.

Faculty in some undergraduate professional majors were receptive to calls for more liberally-educated graduates and discussed how to link liberal and professional education. Several fields, including social work, allied health, journalism, and accounting, began using concepts from the Professional Preparation Network's model (Armour & Fuhrmann, 1989; Blanchard & Christ, 1993; Curry, Wergin, & Associates, 1993; Reeves & McGovern, 1990; Williams, 1991). As part of their national change effort, accounting educators commissioned monographs on assessment and learning to learn. Additional projects funded by FIPSE, including extensive three-year curriculum development projects at Philadelphia College of Textiles and Science and Atlanta College of Art, focused on developing collegewide programs that produce "liberal-professional" graduates. The debate over the balance between general and specialized education may continue even after the current reform wave subsides. We believe, however, that the voices advocating a common humanities core will grow weaker;

and that educators may make renewed attempts to find integrative solutions.

Prescription versus Choice

The call to tighten requirements and introduce more common knowledge for all college students received a good deal of attention in the reform reports but also generated controversy. When instituting new general education programs, many colleges also reduced students' options among distribution requirements. The pendulum definitely swung back toward prescription, but educators did not completely abandon student choice.

The strong pleas by Bennett and Cheney for courses in Western Civilization, reinforced (and possibly contaminated) by the extreme position developed by Allan Bloom in *The Closing of the American Mind: How Higher Education Has Failed Democracy and Impoverished the Souls of Today's Students* (1987), may have created some backlash. Many read Cheney's proposal as a required single set of courses, despite her disclaimers that there would be many ways of achieving the desired ends of the core curriculum. Bloom strongly opposed "relativism," encouraging students to seek "the truth" rather than viewing any opinion as valid. In contrast, most educators agreed with Grant and Riesmann who have said "the multiversity is a pluralistic cathedral" (1978, p. 355). Thus, increased emphasis on humanities was tempered by incorporating considerably greater cultural pluralism (Gaff, 1991).

On the forefront of the pluralism debates, Stanford University publicly debated its required core program over a three-year period and finally adopted a broadened core called Culture, Ideas, and Values—roundly denounced by Secretary Bennett as a "dilution" of the Western Civilization requirement. Since then, most U.S. colleges have asserted that other cultural legacies also deserve study. Beyond a few vocal critics those who take the more limited view that only Western culture should be taught are hard to find in academe. The strong emphasis on pluralism has led some right-wing critics to declare that their freedom to speak their positions is violated since only liberal positions are "politically correct."

Some prominent educators criticized the proposals for core curricula on pluralistic grounds. Catherine Stimpson (1988), graduate dean at Rutgers University, for example, asked that we define what cultural literacy really means and that we consider whether any core is not, by nature, exclusionary. She worried whether we really do possess the central body of knowledge that a required core implies. James W. Reed (1990), also an administrator at Rutgers, argued that "the great traditions of scholarship rely upon large-scale intellectual combat rather than the bland consensus building that is suggested by common courses, common syllabi, and common readings" (p. 7). New subjects and new methodologies represent significant efforts to integrate the curriculum; a single canon may preclude these interdisciplinary activities and forestall new paradigms. Although the current reforms may increase colleges' attempts to develop agreement on what constitutes a coherent curriculum, it seems unlikely that a single canon will return. We will return to the discussion of this influence of pluralism, interdisciplinarity, and "political correctness" on educational environments.

Instructional Process

Instructional process received unprecedented attention in most of the reform reports, and many faculty have accepted the idea that active learning, student involvement, and intentional association of new ideas with old ones enhance learning. Student motivation is being given more credence as a factor in learning

and retention, although faculty vary in their willingness to accept responsibility for building motivation. During the last two decades of the century, new forms of instructional process have gained ground in widely dispersed readjustments such as "writing across the curriculum," collaborative learning groups in general education, problem solving by gathering information from large computerized databases, and participatory methods in teaching college mathematics. These newly accepted practices are also codified in a popular document entitled "Principles of Good Practice for Undergraduate Education" (Chickering & Gamson, 1987). Overall, however, the victory for active learning may be ephemeral—more evident in theory and advocacy than in practice. The AAC's survey showed such trends primarily in small colleges. Although several books have appeared to help faculty find new ideas for teaching large classes (Weimer, 1987, 1990), there is, as yet, only limited evidence that most traditional college lecturers have radically changed their ways of teaching. Adjustments in large research universities have not yet been well documented.

Emphasis on Access

The reform reports generally praised the achievement of wide access to college and supported its continuation. One important recommendation supporting increased access may have escaped wide notice because it was raised within the context of revising the college major. This challenge to improve "inclusiveness" was issued by the Association of American Colleges in *The Challenge of Connecting Learning* (1991a). As has been the case throughout history, even when access to collegiate institutions is very broad, restricted entry to certain prestigious programs may ultimately reduce access for specific groups. These effects are potent when major fields are closed to students who, through previous educational deficits or uninformed choices, have not developed certain prerequisite skills, such as in mathematics. The AAC report was alone in raising the issue of access as a responsibility of specific academic programs as well as a collegewide responsibility. Program concern directly affects development academic plans at the grass-roots level.

As in past times, access concerns were voiced under the rubric of quality control. A strong opinion about the relation of access and quality was published by Marc Tucker, president of the National Center on Education and the Economy in a *Chronicle of Higher Education* editorial (1991, p. A36). Citing varied types of evidence, Tucker reached the "inescapable conclusion" that "half of our 'colleges' are not colleges at all . . . [but] the highest cost secondary schools in the world." Based on the number of community college degree-seekers who fail to complete their programs, he also labeled our postsecondary system "among the least efficient secondary education systems in the world" in terms of costs. Finally, he reported that college faculty and administrators "said that if they were to limit enrollments to only those graduates who, in their judgment, could do college-level work, they would have to lay off professors and close down buildings and programs." Tucker advocated setting "a clear standard for college entrance that represents the level of achievement in high school that is needed to succeed at work that is college level by international standards."

Although few have argued for stringent admission standards as strongly as Tucker, standards have occasionally been raised to increase effectiveness and economy, thereby reducing access. One example is found in the more restrictive admissions policies adopted in the state colleges of Ohio. Perhaps the best example is Florida's "rising junior" exam which, since 1982, requires students to be cer-

tified as competent in basic skills before they enter the junior year in public colleges. Some Florida educators believe that students' motivation has increased with the clearer requirements and prerequisites and assert that rigorous standards can improve education for all, rather than restrict access. Simultaneously, reformers have been urging clearer and less capricious articulation agreements for transfer between two-year and four-year colleges.

Evaluation and Quality Control

Public and independent agencies pursued the recommendations of *Involvement in Learning* for assessing student achievement aggressively. Although many college administrators spoke out actively against assessment shortly after the publication of *Involvement* in 1984, support has now increased. This is true, at least in part, because assessment mandates, originally perceived as a significant threat by some educators, became a reality in many states over the last ten years. At early conferences about assessment, leaders and government officials predicted that the government would institute assessment requirements if institutions did not accept responsibility. This threat materialized during the late 1980s and early 1990s as more and more states adopted assessment requirements and the federal government required accrediting agencies to examine assessment plans. Reported assessment activity has increased; new mandates have added pressure and urgency.

Yet not all colleges began to study student learning because of external requirements. The movement to assess grew rapidly when several pioneering colleges sought and received considerable favorable publicity. Faculty and administrators from these colleges shared their work at numerous conferences, often claiming they had improved their educational programs by using assessment results. Since higher education association leaders provided special incentives for faculty teams to attend conferences to learn about these new efforts, word spread quickly. Resistance to assessment gradually dissipated, and assessment is gaining acceptance as a useful idea in its own right.

El-Khawas reported that in 1985–1986, between 60% and 85% of colleges considered various assessment techniques appropriate but only 15% to 40% were using them. In 1989, 70% of administrators said they were actually engaged in some assessment activity, but 40% said they were considering assessment only in response to mandates. In 1989, half of college administrators believed that assessment would significantly improve undergraduate education, but 70% still strongly feared misuse of data by public authorities and agencies (El-Khawas, 1989).

In 1992, El-Khawas reported:

- Methods of assessing student learning are being developed at 91 percent of colleges and universities; [compared with 45% in 1988]; 57 percent have made program or curriculum changes because of assessment results.
- Two-thirds of public institutions have state-mandated assessment procedures in place. (p. vi)

Neither assessment nor program evaluations are, as yet, fully internalized as regular college practices. If external attention turns elsewhere, fledgling attempts to document student outcomes may atrophy. Firm evidence of the links between assessment and curriculum improvement would help to institutionalize this reform as an internal college agenda. For the time being, it remains to be seen whether assessing student outcomes will help colleges better understand the relationships between the subjects currently taught in college and general outcomes that society deems meet its expectations for educated graduates.

NEW APPROACHES TO OLD DEBATES

The reform movement highlighted a historical dichotomy in thinking about the college curriculum. One group of reformers, interested primarily in a single purpose and in specific content to achieve these purposes, devoted very little attention to current societal conditions, to today's learners, or to how instructors might design successful learning processes to engage them. A second group, willing to accept multiple purposes and related content adjustments as times change, devoted substantial attention to how instructional processes might engage diverse learners in their education, encouraging them to be reflective about their learning. These two camps—opposing purposes and content to learners and instructional processes—are definitely not new, but their relationship is changing (for another view, see Carnochan, 1993).

The reform movement has brought the two camps into closer contact, primarily by elevating the importance of the discussion about learners and instruction. Compared to the active debate over content and purpose, discussions about learners and learning have been muted over the course of American educational history. In part, their new prominence results from the transition from education for a few to education for all. For many years, advocates for learners have worked for broader access. Now, their success forces educators to recognize the strong links among learners, their educational purposes, and the processes that will serve them. We suggest that the meaning of quality (or excellence) is being redefined in terms of the interaction of learners, purposes, content, and processes, rather than continuing to be defined in terms of any one or two of these elements.

In Figure 5-1 we provide a representation of these changing debates, emphasizing that

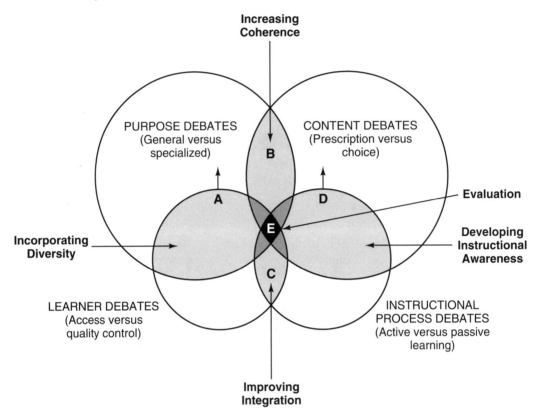

FIGURE 5-1   Old Debates Focus New Debates

our diagram is intended to be suggestive rather than precise. We show the traditional purpose–content debate as two overlapping circles—large because their combined influence is well established. The learner access–instructional process discussions also are represented by overlapping circles—smaller because attention to them is more recent and less well-documented. What we believe is new is that the newly debated learner–process pair substantially overlaps the purpose–content pair. The resulting intersection of four traditional debates and the evolution of more equal stature among them has potential to open more focused new discussions, and thus suggest new approaches to developing academic plans.

We believe it is feasible to argue that future debate can center on educational excellence, demarcated in our diagram by the petal-shaped central areas of overlap among the four debates. Discussions of various contributions to excellence will focus on more specific routes to achieving it. These discussions are portrayed by the overlap of two or more traditional debates. Some of the terminology developed in the reform era lends itself directly to characterizing the topics of the interdependent discussions. We have labeled them as follows:

A: Incorporating diversity (involving learners, purpose, and content)

B: Increasing coherence (involving purpose, content, and process)

C: Improving integration (involving content, learners, and purpose)

D: Developing instructional awareness (involving process, learners, and purpose)

Area E, where *all* of the discussions overlap, represents appropriate evaluation systems, successfully developed to represent the multiple perspectives and purposes that define academic plans. We define these admittedly speculative agendas for future discussions briefly here and return to them in Chapter 12.

Incorporating Diversity (Area A).
The calls for a return to a more singular educational purpose and common educational content reveal that diverse learners and diverse programs have not yet been fully incorporated into higher education. Because student enrollments continue to diversify, there seems little possibility that American higher education will restore the former prominence of uniform liberal learning for all. Rather, the debate will continue to explore *how* to incorporate diversity of both learners and content productivity, rather than *whether* to incorporate them.

Increasing Coherence and Improving Integration (Areas B and C).
An emphasis on coherence and integration (also variously called connectedness, integrity, or wholeness) of collegiate education has been a main theme of reform discussions of the 1990s. The web of coherence has many facets: connecting ideas within fields, between fields, between a field and how its

scholars explore questions, between teaching and research, and between college and career.

Both coherence (defined by faculty), and integration (achieved by the learner), must be considered in developing effective academic plans. Colleges and programs will develop their own definitions, but their conscious attempts to distinguish between coherence and integration will give renewed attention to the learner.

Developing Instructional Awareness (Area D).
Increased attention to instructional processes can help to improve acquisition of content. Yet the intersection of content and process is also related to learner needs as depicted by Area D. New attention to the relationship between process and the learner causes us to label the new discussion instructional "awareness." Advances in psychology, new communication technology, increased interdisciplinary collaboration, and attention to more balanced incentive systems suggest enhanced faculty awareness of improving instructional processes.

Evaluation (Area E).
A productive discussion of achieving expectations is likely to take place when colleges discard the ambiguous word *quality* and work to establish clear educational expectations that can be evaluated. Opportunities exist to move the new evaluation debates toward multiple strategies that accommodate several perspectives. Evaluation should become a central part of the debate, defined as intentional and directed at improvement.

Expectations for Excellence.
Conceivably, new discussions of educational excellence will and should encompass the entire area of overlap (Areas A–E) shown in Figure 5-1. A comprehensive definition of excellence incorporates the needs and purposes of

society, as well as the learner's growth. Such a definition incorporates diversity, seeks both coherence and integration, and increases instructional awareness by devoting conscious attention to each of these important and newly focused discussions. Carefully defined approaches to assessment and evaluation are at the center of the concern for excellence because they both help to define it and to recognize it when it occurs.

Our discussion of these issues leads us to conclude that periods of change and debate in higher education keep colleges responsive to changing times and societal needs. Each turn of a debate cycle causes us to reconsider not only the purposes of the academic plan but also all of its other elements, adjusting the plan to remain responsive to society. The recent era of reform, extensive in scope as it has been, should do no less. Several new discussions emerging from the reports—diversity, coherence, integration, instructional awareness, assessment, expectations, excellence— grow from old debates modified by new contexts. They hold potential for substantially changing the way academic plans are constructed in the future. Defining excellence is possible if we examine each element of the academic plan at each level and type of institution to clarify intended purposes and processes while recognizing that neither the elements nor the traditional debates about them are fully separable.

CHAPTER 6

Creating Academic Plans

CURRICULUM PLANNING: REALITIES AND PROSPECTS

In this chapter, we provide an overview of curriculum planning—that is, the creation of academic plans. We describe first what we know about curriculum planning as it currently occurs in colleges. Then we discuss varied design frameworks with potential to guide, and possibly improve, curriculum planning. These design frameworks tend to be more systematic than the methods college faculty and administrators actually use. Therefore, we refer to existing activities as *planning,* reserving the term *design* for a more deliberate scheme of choices and decision strategies, such as those suggested by the frameworks. This will help us to distinguish between the current state of college academic planning and more idealized processes. We take this approach because of our belief that faculty and administrators who thoughtfully examine their own patterns of behavior may then be receptive to thinking about alternative patterns.

As we have noted, academic plans may be created at several levels: course, program,

and college. The actors and processes, as well as the strength of internal and external influences, differ at each level. In describing how academic planning takes place, we will begin with courses as the structural building blocks of curriculum. Then, we broaden our discussion to include the creation of academic programs and collegewide curricula.

COURSE PLANNING: A FACULTY ROLE

Course planning in higher education is essentially a faculty role. Yet those who aspire to teach in colleges and universities receive little, if any, training in pedagogical planning. Over several years, we have studied how college professors plan, despite their lack of training for the task. Through interviews with faculty members, followed by a survey of a nationally-representative group of faculty, we studied faculty planning for a wide variety of introductory and advanced college courses (Stark, Lowther, Ryan, et al., 1988; Stark, Lowther, Bentley, et al., 1990; Stark & Shaw, 1990). We sought to discover what personal, disciplinary, and experiential factors these instructors believed strongly influenced their course planning. Because few similar studies exist, we largely draw on these studies and on our own experiences to describe, in general terms, how college teachers think about creating academic plans. In subsequent chapters we will discuss in greater depth the influence of academic fields, learners, and varied contextual factors on the planning process. (A refined version of our survey instrument and an accompanying manual is available for others who wish to examine their own views and behaviors in course planning; see Stark, Lowther, Sossen, & Shaw, 1991.)

The Course Planning Process

College professors spend relatively little time prior to teaching a existing course in systematic conceptual planning activities. For example, an early study showed that a college instructor spent only about two hours prior to the beginning date of the course considering content, intended outcomes, or the conceptual structure of the content to be taught in an existing course (Powell & Shanker, 1982). Rather, faculty members tend to plan courses almost continuously by fine-tuning or making adjustments, rather than concentrating on planning in advance of a course, as might be the case with a new course. In classifying various patterns of course planning, we characterized this dominant pattern for existing courses as "routine course planning" (Lowther & Stark, 1988). Faculty members less frequently plan new courses or conduct more extensive routine "reviews" or "major overhauls" of courses. But overhauls do occur when, for example, the instructor perceives the course to be unsatisfactory in some respect (Stark, Lowther, Ryan, et al., 1988, p. 68).

Course planning can "be characterized as decision making about the selection, organization, and sequencing of routines" and then the adjustment of contents of those routines (Yinger, 1979, p. 165). When no necessity for major change is perceived, routines tend to take over. College professors regularly told us that little change was required because students tended to be similar from semester to semester in age, ability, and interests. Structural factors, such as types of lecture halls and laboratory schedules, tended to reinforce routines and inhibit new course plans. Under these circumstances, we encountered a number of cases in which professors undertook radical changes in courses more to relieve their own boredom than to facilitate specific pedagogical decisions.

Although our understanding of planning processes used by college instructors is far from complete, we know that the linear "rational planning model" does not seem to describe their actual planning behavior. College instructors, who are usually well versed in and enthusiastic about the principles and concepts embodied in their fields, tend to start planning by considering content, rather than by stating explicit course objectives for students as design theorists might hope. Also, since they often take for granted the content they will teach, professors focus on selection of instructional activities quite early in the planning process. Although theoretical models of course planning often separate planning from choosing instructional activities, our evidence (and that of others) indicates that the two types of planning occur interactively. Plans for course structure and course implementation are closely related.

The fact that content and instructional process are not separate issues in planning for college professors is illustrated by research on instructional methods as well. For instance, when Thielens asked 81 faculty members why they lecture as opposed to using some other instructional technique, their answers revealed a strongly sensed need to cover content rather than an explicit choice of instructional process. They said, for example, that they (1) must select the correct material; (2) must organize complicated materials for students, even if the text has already done so;

(3) must digest material for students, performing a translation function; and (4) must correct student misconceptions, including those that can be obtained through reading the text (Thielens, 1987).

Some researchers studying the teaching and planning behavior of elementary and secondary teachers have posited a circular influence pattern between teachers' thoughts while interacting with a class and their theories, beliefs, and thoughts while doing preclass planning (Clark & Peterson, 1986). Most likely, a similar circular pattern for college professors causes changes in ongoing lectures as well as changes in plans for the next term the course is taught. We have surveyed many faculty about their course-planning thoughts and activities, and we can provide information like that in Table 6-1, which shows the "first steps" in planning faculty members report. However, we cannot yet explain the wide variations in how professors proceed and how they make the conceptual frameworks of their disciplines explicit to students.

Influences on Planning Courses

In the course planning studies, members of our NCRIPTAL research team found it useful to discuss our findings using the scheme originally devised by Toombs (1977–1978), which divides the influences on course planning into "content" and "context" and calls the results of these influences "form." In our studies, *content influences* encompassed both the faculty member's background and associated disciplinary and educational beliefs. *Contextual influences* referred to influences outside of the instructor's immediate control that cause adjustments in the course plans, such as student characteristics or instructional resources. Although we did not study the *form* of each course extensively, when we interviewed professors we observed that three aspects of form characterize all courses: the sequencing of course material, the choice of instructional activities and materials, and the way the course is described in a syllabus. Finally, consistent with our definition of the academic plan, we expanded Toombs's scheme by adding the categories of evaluation and adjustment as the final step in planning. In interviews, we asked faculty members how they evaluated and adjusted their courses.

It is important to recognize that we adopted these categories (content, context, form, and evaluation/adjustment) to organize our observations; they are not terms that faculty members used to discuss how they planned. Yet our discussions with faculty confirmed the notion that content and context interact and result in *form*—that is, the "shape" of the course results from specific choices or decisions. Thus we postulated the "contextual filters" model of course planning, the broad dimensions of which are shown in

TABLE 6-1 First Steps That Faculty Report When Planning Courses

Planning Step	Percentage of Faculty
Select course content	46
Draw on own background, experience	16
Think about student needs, characteristics	15
Choose activities to promote learning	9
Select textbooks, other resources	6
Set objectives, based on external standards	6
Examine student evaluations from previous courses	<1
Examine examinations from previous courses	<1

Source: From *Planning Introductory College Courses* by Stark, Lowther, Bentley, et al. (1990), p. 107. Reprinted by permission of the National Center for Research to Improve Postsecondary Teaching and Learning, The University of Michigan.

Figure 6-1. We continue to find this heuristic useful, because it emphasizes that course planning is nonlinear and, in part, nonrational. Based on our interviews and surveys, we will discuss each part of the model in more detail here and in subsequent chapters.

Content

Overwhelmingly, faculty members reported that their own background, scholarly preparation, teaching experience, beliefs about educational purpose (and, in special contexts

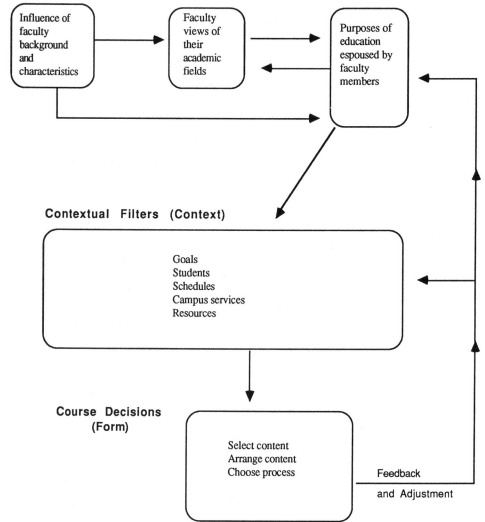

FIGURE 6-1   The Contextual Filters Model of Course Planning

Source: From *Planning Introductory College Courses* by Stark, Lowther, Bentley, et al., (1990), pp. 136–137. Reprinted by permission of the National Center for Research to Improve Postsecondary Teaching and Learning, The University of Michigan.

representing about 6% to 10% of the cases, their religious and political beliefs) influenced their course planning. These are their perceptions, of course, and perhaps real influences differ. However, we found in interviews that faculty could give sufficient concrete illustrations to convince us that they actually did feel the sources of influence they reported. Among the personal and background factors, discipline was such a strong and direct influence on course planning at all levels that we believe it deserves a important place in our discussions of academic plans. Thus, we mention this important influence briefly here but devote Chapter 7 to exploring it more thoroughly.

Instructors' beliefs about the purpose of education are also extremely important and, because they are so closely related to their views of discipline, we also consider them "content" influences. When we asked faculty members to choose their own beliefs among several statements of educational beliefs, they had little difficulty doing so, and most chose beliefs about education that were similar to those chosen by others in their discipline. Many of the statements of belief we posed for their consideration were broader in scope than learning the specific concepts or principles of an academic discipline.

We also asked instructors to tell us what goals they tried to communicate to students as important in a specific introductory course. In this case, we allowed the instructors to respond freely with their own course-level goals for students, rather than choose among categories we supplied. In most disciplines, over 50% of the objectives contributed were discipline-related goals of learning concepts, principles, or facts in the field. Thus, although faculty members define broad purposes of education, the goal of transmitting knowledge about a specific discipline tends to provide the initial framework for specifying learning outcomes that they use in course planning. To illustrate, a faculty member reading a prestructured list may respond that she believes the primary educational purpose is developing students' ability to think critically. Yet when asked about goals for her course, she may cite principles, concepts, or learning theories as the course goals she communicates to students.

In Table 6-2, we report the percentage of faculty in our studies who chose each of the various broad educational purposes in our study of planning introductory courses. Insofar as possible, we have categorized the specific course goals that faculty contributed spontaneously into these same purpose categories and these are also shown in Table 6-2. Note that, depending on discipline, from 23% to 69% of the faculty-generated statements of purpose focused on discipline-content goals, not broad developmental goals for students.

Generally, faculty members did not include knowledge of learning theory or pedagogical training among the types of scholarly preparation that strongly influenced their course planning. Only about 30% of the college instructors we talked with had any exposure to various educational and psychological theories through formal courses or workshops that might have created awareness of alternative planning strategies. Indeed, some who had formally taken education courses considered that experience a deterrent to consciously considering issues of student learning. The reasons faculty do not seek out this type of information from a vast available literature is an important topic for study.

We asked faculty members to indicate which of several reasons might support their choice of course content in introductory courses. The reasons we listed were drawn from learning theory and the faculty responses indicate that, whatever the source of this knowledge about pedagogy, faculty do include some ideas consistent with good practice as described by educational experts. Table 6-3 shows percentages of faculty choosing different reasons for selecting course content.

Recall that our emerging theory of curriculum includes three types of influences on

TABLE 6-2   Educational Purposes and Related Course Goals Reported by Faculty for Introductory Courses

	Range[a]	
	Percentage[b] Endorsing Educational Purpose	Percentage[c] Mentioning Specific Course Goal
Concepts or knowledge in the field	(not included)	23–69
Students' personal or social growth	11–51	7–22
Students' intellectual development (effective thinking, study habits, discerning relationships, etc.)	83–94	4–22
Students' ability to bring about social change	23–79	(not mentioned)
Students' skill development (such as development in mathematics, communication or an applied field such as nursing)	(not included)	2–38
Values development	35–81	0–3
Learning the great ideas of humanity	28–73	0–2
Preparing students for the future (a career, the major, graduate school, another course)	13–71	1–15
Aesthetic ("Appreciation of . . .") or creativity	(not included)	0–13
Goal area unclear	(not possible)	1–7

Source: From *Planning Introductory College Courses* by Stark, Lowther, Bentley, et al. (1990), p. 52; p. 114. Reprinted by permission of the National Center for Research to Improve Postsecondary Teaching and Learning, The University of Michigan.

Notes:
[a]The range of percentages given for specific course goals shows substantial variation by discipline.
[b]Percent who indicated that the goal was "Much like my belief."
[c]Percent who contributed goal in response to open-ended question.

academic plans: external, organizational, and internal. Influences on course-level planning are primarily internal to the academic program and often internal to the individual faculty planner. College instructors report that they typically select and interpret content for students based on their own beliefs, assumptions, experiences, and reasoning (valid or invalid). Of course, some organizational and even external forces affect how courses are planned, but they often do so indirectly—for example, by operating through program and college goals or student characteristics.

Context

We explored several contextual influences on course planning and found, not surprisingly, that internal influences (within the program) and selected organizational influences originating outside the program but within the college or university affect course planning most. For example, about two-thirds of faculty report that characteristics of learners in their courses and programs (particularly students' ability and preparation) are strong internal influences in their course planning. Because

TABLE 6-3   Reasons That Faculty Select Course Content in Introductory Courses

Reason for Content Choice	Percentage
Conveys fundamental concept	87
Is important concept or principle	88
Contributes to students' development	75
Relates field to other fields	74
Illustrates mode of inquiry of field	74
Helps acquire essential skills	71
Helps integrate ideas	70
Interrelates fundamental principles	68
Encourages investigation	67
Is important example of inquiry in field	65
Is useful in solving problems on job	53
Stimulates search for meaning	49
Links concepts to social problems	48
Examines diverse views	45
Assists in career search	28

Source: From *Planning Introductory College Courses* by Stark, Lowther, Bentley, et al. (1990), p. 36. Reprinted by permission of the National Center for Research to Improve Postsecondary Teaching and Learning, The University of Michigan.

learner characteristics and faculty perceptions of them are so important, we have devoted Chapter 8 to them. Program goals are also important but usually are more salient for courses in the major than for general education courses.

Among organizational influences, the strength of many contextual influences varied by discipline. For example, availability of fa-cilities influences science teachers more strongly than history teachers, while library resources are more important to history instructors than to mathematics instructors. These differences illustrate why we view the contextual influences as modifiers or "filters" on basic faculty assumptions. The closer the level of organizational influence to the course, the more influential it tends to be. For example, college goals generally tended to be weaker influences than disciplinary or program goals; only one-third of the faculty saw college goals as influential in their course planning. When the program had a collegewide focus, however, collegewide goals became more important—for example, for English composition instructors serving the entire school.

External influences (from outside the college) are important in course planning primarily in professional and occupational fields where scholarly or professional associations, employers, and accreditors set standards. External influences are also important in community colleges, where articulation agreements mandate course content or level for transfer to four-year colleges.

Form

In this section we turn our attention to how faculty arrange course content, how they select activities, and how they describe their course plans. As we have seen (Table 6-1) the strong influence of discipline on college course planning means that most instructors select the content first, treating specific goals as assumptions. Many then move quickly to arrange course material in ways that they believe achieve specific objectives.

Arranging Content. In the NCRIPTAL survey of course planning, we asked faculty members to rate a set of reasons for arranging the content of their introductory courses. The arrangements they described were modeled on the "sequencing" categories developed by Posner and Strike (1976), but we expanded and revised them following interviews with professors. The descriptions provided and the overall percentages of faculty preferring the different choices in our survey are given in Table 6-4. Course content is often arranged in ways characteristic of the discipline, and one or two sequencing patterns tend to predominate in each discipline.

While there was a great deal of commonality in the way faculty in a given discipline arranged course content, there were also variations within fields. Table 6-4 also shows the ranges for the fields that we studied. As we will see in Chapter 7, these variations in fields are linked with other discipline-related patterns.

Selecting Instructional Activities.

Most existing literature on planning instructional activities describes what instructors might (or should) do rather than describing current practices.Our studies have not specifically probed how and why faculty members chose particular instructional activities. Given

previous reports that over 90% of college classes are taught by the lecture method or lecture with laboratory (Thielens, 1987), we believed that such questions would not reveal many choices.

As we listened to faculty members describe course planning, we speculated that the extent to which they make choices among instructional activities may depend on whether they state course objectives explicitly or leave them implicit. For example, some faculty members try to choose activities that specifically improve students' ability to think critically or to relate and integrate content; others continue to teach concepts and principles rather than students. Similarly, we think the attention instructors give to course activities may depend on how seriously they take their responsibility to motivate students rather than just dispense information. Ways to engage students in the material, keep their attention, and encourage class discussion are worth considering only if the teacher sees student engagement as important. Finally, although most faculty recognize and lament current deficits in student preparation, the way they

---

TABLE 6-4   Ways Faculty Arrange Course Content for Introductory Courses

Preferred Way of Organizing	Percentage of Faculty	Percentage Range by Discipline
Way major concepts and relationships are organized	41	23–59
Way I know students learn	20	4–52
Way relationships occur in real world	15	3–47
Way knowledge has been created in my field	6	0–10
Way students will use knowledge in social, personal, or career setting	8	1–26
To help students clarify values and commitments	7	0–23
So that students prepare directly for careers	4*	0–19

Source: From *Planning Introductory College Courses* by Stark, Lowther, Bentley, et al. (1990), p. 118; p. 122; p. 119. Reprinted by permission of the National Center for Research to Improve Postsecondary Teaching and Learning, The University of Michigan.

Note: These were primarily general education courses, not professional or occupational courses, so career development may be understated.

choose instructional activities may depend on whether they accept these deficits as a challenge or a burden.

Describing the Plan. Half of faculty surveyed, regardless of field, develop syllabi that describe their courses to students. College professors may be more likely to write detailed syllabi when there is an administrative requirement to do so, when adult students expect a syllabus, or when discipline norms set precedents. In some fields, such as nursing, strong national norms seem to dictate very complete course syllabi or course manuals with objectives, rationale, and detailed organizing questions for each class session. In other fields, such as mathematics, the typical syllabus is likely to be very sketchy for at least half of the faculty, perhaps including only the name of the textbook and the chapters and problems or exercises assigned for each week (Stark, Lowther, Ryan, et al., 1988). The course planning studies demonstrated that, in contrast to syllabi, few instructors write detailed lesson plans; rather they may plan by constructing and retaining mental images of what they hope to teach. Like K–12 teachers, college professors appear to hold in mind comprehensive "lesson images" that encompass many of their planning assumptions (Clark & Peterson, 1986).

We found that faculty members depended far more on the spoken word for communicating course plans to students than on the written word. Many claim that they reiterate the goals and plan for the course to students at least once a week. Two-thirds of faculty members we surveyed said they reemphasized the goals of their course when giving specific assignments to students. This oral mode of communication about course purposes and plans may be preferred because the course plans are constantly evolving and changing in the faculty member's mind as he or she makes informal adjustments.

Evaluating and Adjusting

Evaluation plans are almost never included in descriptions of course plans, and few faculty we studied used any systematic means of course evaluation. Although student rating forms are almost universal, on average only 40% of faculty said they used these ratings when planning the next offering of the course. Instead, faculty members conduct their own ad hoc observations on which they base evaluations of how the course is going. Over 70% of faculty considered class attendance, observations of facial expression, and class participation their primary means of receiving information about student involvement and course progress. About half rely on examinations once a month, they assume that if students do well, the course is effective. On the basis of these sources, faculty members tend to speculate about the reasons for success or failure of their courses. Adjustment of the plan tends to be informal; in most cases, faculty try something new that may possibly work and abandon it if it appears not to help. Only when a major course restructuring occurs, and the academic plan to be created is viewed as unusual or risky, is a faculty member likely to use a systematic method for evaluating course success. The new work on classroom assessment techniques (Cross & Angelo, 1988; Angelo & Cross, 1993) probably appeals to faculty because it builds on this informal tradition of "sensing" how things are going in class.

In our survey, faculty reported using both tests and informal indicators such as personal observations to assess student involvement in their learning. In Table 6-5 we show the indicators faculty used most often and in which they felt most confidence. Most did not use the results of student evaluations in systematic ways to make adjustments in the course. Yet occasionally we found professors who employed elaborate procedures, including student committees, to give them feedback.

TABLE 6-5 Ways Faculty Observe Student Involvement in Learning

Indicator	Percentage of Faculty with 95% Confidence in Indicator
Examination results	62
Student papers	51
Observing discussions and student participation	50
Completion of assignments	47
Watching student faces	46
Class attendance	40
Observing after-class discussion	21
Student evaluations	21
Number of office visits	15
Student journals	8

Source: From *Planning Introductory College Courses* by Stark, Lowther, Bentley, et al. (1990), pp. 129–130. Reprinted by permission of the National Center for Research to Improve Postsecondary Teaching and Learning, The University of Michigan.

Patterns of Involvement in Course Planning

The results of our several studies of course planning cause us to question the folk wisdom that "college professors teach as their professors taught." Our evidence indicates that discipline is the strongest influence on course planning. This influence is, of course, linked with former mentors, but it may or may not include adopting their teaching styles. More commonly, professors adjust both content and pedagogy to deal with new knowledge and changing times rather than clinging to tradition. To make these adjustments, faculty require autonomy, flexibility to be creative, and colleagueship.

Autonomy is an important issue in course planning. Because curriculum planning at the course level is usually the task of a single individual, a high proportion (about two-thirds) of faculty members we interviewed or surveyed were highly autonomous and informal in their planning. We found that college teachers who had little or no input into the course plans they used (that is, they taught from pre-

fabricated courses or courses devised by others) were discontented with the courses they taught and dissatisfied with the teaching role.

Most faculty felt that developing a course was a creative act and were more satisfied with their course development role when they had flexibility to be creative. The faculty we talked with valued creativity, which sometimes, but not always, was linked with autonomy. We sensed that the course plan may be seen as a creative act of translating discipline norms into actual teaching processes. We encountered a fair number of cases, too, where instructors believed that interaction with colleagues enhanced creativity.

Colleagueship seems important in course planning, even when the faculty members essentially teach alone. When colleagues are congenial, they can stimulate new thoughts and provide support and reassurance. In cases where faculty members are not congenial, of course, enforced colleagueship can be detrimental. Some recent reform proposals emphasize linking and integrating courses in ways that may require increased colleagueship among faculty. It will be challenging to achieve these linkages without decreasing faculty autonomy and flexibility. Course planning that involves more than one person may take any of the forms listed next which imply different degrees of colleagueship:

1. A group of faculty members plans a course in which each will teach a different section.

2. A faculty member or group of faculty members plans a course in which they will team-teach or share responsibilities in some way. This pattern may include coordination and supervision of teaching assistants rather than other professors.

3. A faculty member makes minor adjustments on a course essentially planned by someone else, which must be taught largely as given.

4. A teaching assistant, lab assistant, or discussion leader gives input to the faculty member principally responsible for course planning, then implements that person's plans.

Another aspect of course planning closely related to autonomy is the locus of planning. Planning can take place close to the site and time where teaching takes place or courses can be developed externally in advance for use by many teachers. Traditionally, most college courses are developed on site. Currently, however, three influences are modifying this tradition and increasing the use of externally developed courses. First, textbook companies are supplying computerized materials, audio- and videotapes, and workbooks to provide entire courses that require little or no on-site teacher involvement in planning. Second, as software for instruction is becoming increasingly common, cost and expertise usually dictate its development apart from the local scene. Third, changing textbook and software resources make possible more distance learning so that centralized

course development can serve students who may never meet their instructor face to face. Our observations suggest at least the following possibilities, arranged by decreasing local involvement:

1. Plans are constructed autonomously and locally by instructors who will teach the course.

2. Plans are constructed by instructors in partnership with some other agency, for example, a professional association or accreditors.

3. Plans are constructed commercially or centrally but adapted for use by instructors locally.

4. Plans are constructed commercially or centrally and used with little instructor input.

In creating a climate for good planning, faculty hope their college will seek an appropriate balance among autonomy, colleagueship, and local responsibility. Although local autonomous development of courses by faculty is the norm and has advantages, the advantages of collaboration cannot be overlooked. For example, we found that faculty members who planned in groups (e.g., to teach a multisection course) gave more attention to student needs and varied pedagogical strategies than those who planned alone. Similarly, faculty members responsible for coordinating and supervising the work of laboratory or teaching assistants, as is often true in the sciences tend to be more systematic as course planners. Finally, some faculty have reported that working with others, once they have been accustomed to collaboration, is inspiring and reinforcing. As an exception to this general rule, we noticed that when unwilling faculty members were assigned to coordinate large service courses with little opportunity to teach their disciplinary specialty, they were likely to be unenthusiastic planners. Professors coordinating lower level mathematics courses were a prime example. The benefits of collaborative planning, then may be conditional: group activity may inspire more varied course planning activities than solitary activity if the group is engaged in a valued or exciting teaching endeavor rather than a routine teaching duty.

PROGRAM PLANNING: A GROUP ENDEAVOR

We define an academic *program* as a planned group of courses or experiences that faculty designate as appropriate for a specific group of students to pursue. Such a set of courses typically has a supporting rationale; a group of faculty members constructs the rationale, plans the sequence, and is responsible for implementing it. In addition to planning the educational experiences, these faculty members may also admit the students to the program, advise them, and evaluate their progress. A program is not necessarily congruent with a department or division; sometimes it may cross organizational lines. We have established this definition broadly to include not only majors in academic disciplines or professional fields, but also "general education" or "college studies" programs and formal interdisciplinary programs, as well as individualized programs that students construct with faculty advice and/or approval. If there is a specific academic plan and a specific group of faculty responsible for developing it, then we have called it a program. Thus, course sequences that are parts of a more general program, such as study abroad or cooperative education, could also fit the definition of a program.

Most frequently, when faculty think of programs, they think of majors in academic disciplines or collegiate career fields. The greatest faculty effort is devoted to program creation within these types of programs. Probably next most important are well-defined interdisciplinary fields such as Near Eastern studies or women's studies. Finally, the efforts of some faculty, often a special committee, are devoted to creating the academic plan for general education that all students pursue. As we have mentioned, increased emphasis on general education in the 1980s, sometimes including the appointment of special deans and associate deans to ensure continuing faculty concern, is resulting in greater faculty involvement at this level. Because new general education programs tend to be collegewide, we recognize that discussing them at the program level is somewhat arbitrary.

Studies of program planning tend to be historical or descriptive case studies of innovation (Conrad & Pratt, 1986). They may also be documentaries of initiatives of statewide coordinators, of program review efforts made either routinely or in times of budgetary crisis, or of leadership efforts that create new programs to respond to new demands (Keller, 1983; Seymour, 1988). Perhaps because considerable literature defines planning as administrative strategizing at high levels in the organization, faculty tend not to think of their own work as planning. Rather, they call it curriculum development; it is what they do collaboratively in their department settings. Our exploratory studies of program planning have focused at this level—on the thinking of faculty as they work together to devise plans they expect students to follow. Our studies are incomplete but, coupled with our personal experience in several types of colleges, have contributed to increased understanding. We will share what we know thus far in this section.

Program Planners

Subcommittees or committees of the whole in a department or division are usually responsible for academic planning at the program level. A primary difference between program planning and course planning is that the individual professor no longer has great discretion in decision making. Consequently, program planning often becomes a series of compromises between faculty members in the same discipline who have slightly different points of view, or between faculty members from different disciplines who have very different points of view. Some view these compromises as inherently political or even self-serving competitions for power, rather than academic choices. Although some power relationships are surely involved, our sense in talking with faculty is that the key stakes, and thus the key compromises, involve deeply held beliefs about what should be learned, what type of inquiry students should pursue, and what critical perspectives they should learn to employ.

What specific types of expertise do faculty members bring to this activity of compromise? Faculty bring primarily the same discipline expertise they bring to course planning. Faculty members are seldom experts on students' development or career needs, learning theory, or pedagogical alternatives. And although most campuses have experts in these areas in student affairs offices, instructional development offices, or media centers, for reasons we do not yet understand faculty do not always consult with them during program-level decisions about curricula. Thus, the pattern of program planning is dominated by scholars, not curriculum specialists or other campus contributors. The compromises that take place are primarily compromises of content and sequencing.

The Program Planning Process

Compared to the incremental adjustment that regularly takes place in course plans, academic program plans are created and revised only sporadically. Major adjustments often occur as a result of a strong organizational or external impetus. An external impetus for program adjustments often stems from shifts of thinking within the discipline, changes in job market opportunities or accreditation standards, or a systemwide process of program review. Organizationally, such an impetus may include the arrival of a new faculty member with special interests and expertise or a new high-level administrator who encourages reexamination and change. It may also be as complex as an institutional mandate to cut budgets. More rarely, major overhauls are due to decisions internal to the program.

Whatever the impetus, we have observed that faculty members have less personal interest and investment in program planning than they do in course planning. Time and again, when we asked faculty members to describe the process of program planning, they reverted instead to describing their own course or how their own efforts fit into the total development of a program plan. Faculty seem to take responsibility for program planning somewhat reluctantly and uneasily. We found, however, that they accepted the responsibility more readily and pursued it more systematically when there was strong leadership at the program or college level that established a climate for planning or a sense of the importance of the academic plans and their effects on students.

A research study that involved a large sample of academic vice presidents, presidents, department chairpersons, and faculty members in both community colleges and state colleges (Johnson et al., 1987) revealed that between 15% and 37% of respondents (differing by group) said there was never or seldom a systematic plan for program development. Between 18% and 65% of the respondents said there are never or seldom any experimental trials of new courses or programs. Significantly, faculty were considerably more likely to report these systematic processes as absent than were administrators.

It is difficult to talk about program planning processes unless one specifies whether the planning involves a single discipline, several disciplines, or an attempt to create an interdisciplinary plan. Each type of curriculum plan requires different assumptions and strategies. Each also may involve a different number of planners with diverse viewpoints. The more varied the backgrounds and disciplines of the planners, the more complex the process becomes and the more likely it is to be aborted before a satisfactory conclusion is reached.

Influences on Program Planning

In discussing influences on program planning, we follow our previous pattern, reporting influences on content, context, form, and evaluation/adjustment.

Content

As is true for course planning, the primary internal influences on program planning are the extent of faculty interest in teaching and their content expertise. Major shifts in the methods of teaching college disciplines occasionally involve broad change fostered and disseminated through disciplinary associations and accrediting agencies. Evidence of such curricular change can be found in the disciplinary journals and related literature. Examples include the introduction of qualitative research in social science fields to complement traditional quantitative approaches, new courses resulting from advances in genetic engineering, or the new emphasis in accounting education on training accountants as users (rather than producers) of information. In such cases, the disciplinary experts/instructors working together translate the views of broader discipline groups in their own terms. On each campus, what may seem like an internal process is really an adaptation of the field to the demands of the external world.

At the course level, we described how faculty members attempt to organize or sequence material in ways they find meaningful. At the program level, as well, sequencing is important. The program level parallel to the sequence of topics in a course is the sequence of courses in the program. An academic program ideally is not just a set of isolated courses but rather an intentional plan to help students achieve integration and a "coherent" view of the field or fields of study. Just as various conceptual links between topics hold courses together, so various types of "binding forces" hold courses together into a total plan or curriculum. These forces differ among academic fields. For example, the sciences are often linked hierarchically, each course building on the one before it; the social sciences in a relational way, and the humanities in a global or intricate web-like relationship. Other intellectually based forces which hold programs together are the development of specific intellectual skills such as problem solving, career preparation (for collegiate career fields), or themes (such as urban development). Faculty seldom discuss these academic forces that integrate programs as they create academic plans. The sense that this coherence is lacking for both general education and various major fields is one of the recent criticisms of higher education programs. Quite possibly, the diversity of faculty backgrounds and views brought to bear on general education precludes achieving coherence easily. In major fields, coherence may wax and wane, alternating with periods of turbulence as faculty members debate diverse perspectives.

Context

Among the many contextual influences on program planning, it is not surprising that faculty report program mission as strongest. Two-thirds of faculty in our studies rated program goals as important—fully twice the proportion who rated college goals as important. Often program goals are defined in terms of preparing majors, but the salient program goals may also be interdisciplinary, like the goals of groups of faculty planning African

American studies or environmental studies programs. In professional fields, the importance of program goals is probably highest; about 80% of faculty in some of these fields rate program goals as a strong influence.

In contrast to disciplinary or interdisciplinary missions, there are some organizational binding forces that faculty typically resist as unneeded bureaucratic mechanisms. Two examples of such forces are organizational divisions that persist as budgetary entities but are not congruent with programs. Often the service aspect of college mission enters strongly in the planning because it dictates part of the program mission, namely providing a range of service courses. But faculty view college goals that require experiences/courses for nonmajors as less influential than goals they set themselves in program groups.

We judge that the second most important internal influence in program planning is leadership. In contrast to course planning, where the impetus for a major overhaul of courses is usually the faculty member's own need for change, faculty often do not revise programs unless someone supplies initiative. We talked with faculty who complained that their programs had remained unchanged for years for lack of leadership, and we talked with faculty who could specifically identify the important stimulus a leader provided. Sometimes this stimulus was as simple as creating a feeling that program excellence or achieving the program mission was important. In other cases, it was clear that faculty workload was a strong inhibitor. One faculty member captured the situation in which program planning most likely takes place as "bottom up with support from the top."

Faculty judged a number of external influences that we explored to be weak influences on their planning. These included textbooks, alumni, turf battles, enrollment concerns, assessment initiatives, and accreditors (except in specific fields). In our discussions with faculty about program planning, we found that, although they purported to be strongly influenced by student characteristics, planners had little systematic data about learners. Groups of faculty working together as program planners tend to use anecdotal information about students rather than carefully collected data.

Form

Form incorporates the various decisions made in planning an academic program. It translates the interaction of content and context into actual events and implementation. Many dimensions of form could be discussed. We discuss here three dimensions that are parallel to the aspects of form that we discussed for course plans: arranging content, selecting instructional processes, and describing the plan.

Arranging Content. Controversies in program planning are often a function of discipline structure and the ways that discipline components are sequenced. Some disciplines insist on a systematic progression through increasingly difficult courses that build on each other; other disciplines eschew the idea of systematic planning or standard sequences altogether. For example, while faculty planning chemistry programs typically insist on a planned sequence of courses so that students may take foundational prerequisites in their field, faculty planning sociology courses prefer a broader latitude of choice and content for students. Yet, even in the sciences, there is often debate about course sequencing that parallels different views of the field. In our interviews, we talked with biologists who were convinced that best sequencing is to begin inside the cell as a microcosm of life and move toward the broader study of ecology, while others believed that learning would be more effective by starting at a macro level with ecology and progressing to the cell.

Like topics within courses, courses themselves can be arranged in various sequences. Some fields, like history, have traditionally sequenced courses in chronological order, but some historians now view thematic arrangements as more engaging for students. In a few fields, like sociology, faculty often prefer to allow students to explore topics in many different orders, depending on their interests. In professional fields, a sequence of courses may be largely dictated by the responsibilities students will undertake in scheduled field experiences. A nursing instructor in a community college described to us her frustration about teaching a large number of important topics, including not only content material but also personal hygiene, ethics, interpersonal skills, and professional demeanor, in the first six weeks of a program before students entered a hospital setting.

While sequencing is clear cut for some fields, an important debate about arranging programmatic content is inherent in the development of more focused general education programs. Thus, it appears that most colleges view the general education requirements as foundational to the upper-division specialized work in the major but do not judge any particular sequence within the general studies program itself as necessarily superior to any other. Yet considerable agreement in principle, if not in execution, seems to surround the idea of a capstone course to help students unite their learnings in any programmatic major. Of course, in the professional curricula an internship may, at least in part, serve this function. It is clear that according to discipline or other program, faculty answers to a question like "What are the concepts that unify your program?" will vary widely.

Selecting Instructional Activities.
At the program level, selection of instructional activities to carry out the academic plan may involve such decisions as establishing maximum class size, assuring the availability of seminar and laboratory opportunities, and requiring internships, capstone courses, or a senior thesis. Arguably, these activities parallel course level decisions such as deciding on classroom activities, examinations, and term papers. Frequently, the instructional activities included in the overall program plan are extracurricular, such as clubs, outside speakers, and other functions not assigned to particular classes. Conscious consideration of the academic plan at the program level often stops short of implementation through specific activities and is delegated instead to individual faculty members who are expected to create such activities within their courses or other assignments. Although there is vast variation by academic discipline, we found that faculty generally had given little thought to the potential of new technology for modifying their program sequence or delivery of courses.

Describing the Plan.
The parallel document to the course syllabus is a program description or general program curriculum plan. Most programs write statements of their general goals, requirements, course listings, and preferred sequence for the college catalog. These statements are written in general terms and only occasionally revised. It is less common for a program to develop a document with a full rationale for its academic plan. In small colleges where personal communication in advising is strong, students may not need such documents. In fact, the best use of these statements may be in causing faculty to think carefully about their plan. In larger institutions, we have found that departments of nursing are the most likely to have detailed program guidebooks for students that provide rationale as well as specific requirements and hints for success. As a consequence, nursing students are usually able to articulate their program's goals and thus can see faculty as role models in achieving them. The process of constructing these statements

guarantees faculty involvement in thinking about the academic plan. In contrast, we know of colleges that have developed entire new general education programs while making no effort to write down the plan or tell students of its purpose or structural dimensions. Under such circumstances, it is not surprising that students fail to appreciate the value of the course requirements and sequence they are obliged to pursue.

Evaluating and Adjusting

Many academic programs administer occasional graduate or enrolled student satisfaction questionnaires that are roughly parallel to student course rating instruments. Frequently, however, when we asked what information about learner experiences faculty used in planning academic programs, they provided only anecdotes about one or two outstanding or successful students, who typically had pursued advanced studies at prestigious institutions. When pressed, they indicated that their program collected and used very little information about the larger group of students who had disappeared into society and routine careers. Many campuses have institutional research offices that could help construct research questions and student surveys, ensure that data are correctly interpreted, and help faculty members use them for change. It appears that use of such services by faculty is infrequent.

Patterns of Involvement in Program Planning

Program planning (or curriculum development) is an activity faculty engage in sporadically and often reluctantly despite the opportunities it might provide for colleagueship and collaboration. Knowledge about program planning is sparse, and attempts to understand how faculty view the process are often seen as irrelevant by those who believe faculty efforts to defend existing budget and curricular turf preclude genuine efforts to improve. Yet with strong leadership, program planning may be orderly, collegial, and productive. Our observations lead us to believe that leaders need to recognize differences among fields; Biglan (1973a, 1973b) found that disciplines with well-accepted paradigms move to consensus on curriculum matters more quickly than those who lack such paradigms. This difference explains the impatience science faculty frequently exhibit as humanities and social sciences faculty engage in prolonged curriculum discussions. A second observation is that many professors feel insecure about discussing their views among peers because they lack training in curriculum development. More systematic models of planning might alleviate some of this hesitation.

COLLEGE PLANNING: A MATTER OF MISSION

The diversity of "colleges" is so great that it is almost impossible to generalize about how collegewide academic plans are constructed. A college can be a small free-standing unit that provides either very general (e.g., liberal arts) or very specialized (e.g., technical or religious) education. It can be a specialized entity, such as a professional school within a large complex university. It can be a public institution whose mission is to serve students from the local community of all ages and backgrounds, or a large private university whose mission is to serve a very selective group of traditional-age students. The meaning of *college* will determine what type of institutionwide academic plans are likely to be considered.

Although there are vice presidents whose main role is university planning, a Society for College and University Planning, and even a special journal entitled *College and University Planning*, the primary concerns of these persons and groups are with finance, enrollment, facilities, and strategic planning. A search of the planning literature in higher education turns up very little that fits our definition of an *academic* plan intended to guide student learning. In fact, few academic plans are created at the collegewide level. When the process does take place, it often attracts considerable attention and publicity.

To simplify our discussion as we consider academic plans created by and for colleges, we will focus on three convenient examples: the small liberal arts college, the large liberal arts college within a university (where some departments may be larger than the entire small liberal arts college), and the professional college also within a university.

The Collegewide Planners

In any of the three types of colleges we are considering as examples, a diverse group of faculty members, administrators, and students as well as other experts tend to be involved in collegewide curriculum planning. In the small liberal arts college, the entire faculty and administration typically debate changes in collegewide plans or mission in a committee of the whole, with the president or vice president chairing the meeting. In contrast, in the liberal arts unit within a large university, plans may be formulated by a blue-ribbon panel and presented to a representative governing body that acts on behalf of the faculty. Faculty meetings at large universities often are sparsely attended; the relevant points of view may be heard in other forums, including the campus newspaper and student debates. A professional school, depending on size and field, may be at either of these extremes, or somewhere in between. Judging from research on organizational style preferences of faculty in different fields (Biglan, 1973a, 1973b), enterprising fields with highly structured curricula (e.g., engineering, business) might delegate collegewide curriculum decisions to committees, while human-oriented fields with loosely structured paradigms (e.g., nursing, social work) might have much broader faculty involvement. Of course, size and college tradition will modify these speculative patterns.

The Collegewide Planning Process and Influences

Essentially, collegewide planning processes have four types of purposes: (1) adjusting academic programs to be more congruent with mission, (2) establishing (or adjusting) mission, (3) modifying academic programs to be more responsive to the changing external environment, and (4) joining the bandwagon of innovation. In each case except the first, the impetus for change is predominantly external, as are the facilitators of change. Of course, more than one of these purposes can exist at one time.

When collegewide discussions are held to adjust academic programs so that they complement existing missions, the impetus is often internal to the college but outside any specific program. The concern that motivates the planning effort may reflect one of the historical patterns of debate we have already described. For instance, the faculty or administration may feel that the college curriculum has evolved to include too many options. Or programs introduced to serve new clientele are judged too expensive to maintain. Finally, a new administrator may encourage a review of collegewide mission to call faculty attention to the mission or to reaffirm it. These adjustments are equally possible in each of the types of colleges we are considering. In the small or specialized college, the process is likely to include a broader range of campus stakeholders.

When a college undertakes a total overhaul of its program, makes a major change in its mission, or tries to achieve a more distinctive environment, the process tends to attract public and professional attention. Examples from the 1970s reform period are Mars Hill College in North Carolina and its competence-based curriculum; Alverno College in Wisconsin with its ongoing abilities-based curriculum and emphasis on student assessment; Evergreen State College of Washington, which abandoned grades; and the University of California, Santa Cruz, which was organized as a group of cluster colleges.

Such examples have received a good deal of study, often by those interested in leadership, as well as in curricular processes. Two recent books described a variety of innovative institutions (Cardozier, 1993; Townsend, Newell, & Wiese, 1992) and in *Academic Strategy* (1983), George Keller cited several major changes made by leaders attempting to position their colleges uniquely in the market. Quite often when administrators or faculty leaders create an innovative academic plan, the die is cast without full faculty involvement in curriculum development. In small colleges, academic plans developed in this way sometimes have a brief life. Still in other cases, the institution may stay alive by undertaking the visible change in academic plan.

In liberal arts units of large universities, sweeping changes of mission are often slow or difficult because of organizational complexity, faculty size, entrenched bureaucracy, and service obligations to other colleges within the institution. Within universities, relatively autonomous professional colleges often undertake extensive changes, usually in concert with similar colleges elsewhere. Striking recent examples are curriculum changes in accounting developed under the auspices of a prestigious national commission, and changes in pharmacy spearheaded by the national professional association (Boss & Lowther, 1993).

Most collegewide discussions about academic plans are responses to societal or organizational factors that urge consideration of adjustments. An external factor may be a national report or critique, a report from employers that students are not well prepared, a plan to gain publicity for distinctiveness by administration or trustees, or possibly the demands of pressure groups for recognition. An organizational factor may be a strong push from a women's group for gender-related requirements in the general education program or a successful grant proposal for change. With such external or organizational impetus, collegewide discussions have a stronger political tone than program-level discussions about academic plans. They are often riddled with political tension and characterized by concerns about budget and enrollment balance. Examples include the discussions at Harvard about the core curriculum (Harvard Committee, 1945; Keller, 1982) and the highly publicized revision of the Western Civilization requirement at Stanford University in the early 1990s (Carnochan, 1993). (For a related discussion of developmental planning versus adaptive planning that is sensitive to the environment, see Friedman, 1967.)

The "bandwagon effect" of diffusing innovations in higher education is probably a special case of adjustment to external factors. It appears to us that many of the changes at the college level proceed from the bandwagon effect rather than from a systematic assessment of the need for new academic plans. There are strong tendencies to adopt curriculum plans that a neighboring or peer institution or program has adopted. Some colleges make deliberate attempts to be leaders and innovators; conference sessions they lead are often filled with potential imitators, many hoping to attract outside funding for curriculum change. The bandwagon effect, however, is not necessarily bad. Ideas such as active learning, classroom research, and the use of technology in instruction have achieved popularity primarily because of national attention from a few colleges or other groups.

The type of collegewide planning process and the extent of involvement of the college community in developing academic plans as a whole probably depends on size, orientation toward teaching, the type of governance system in place, the existing sense of community, and, last but not least, college leadership. Small size, a strong sense of community, and governance systems that encourage involvement foster participation in curricular change in both liberal arts colleges and professional colleges. In contrast to liberal arts colleges which seem to hold frequent internal discussions of mission and curriculum, professional schools tend to respond rather quickly to new ideas that are consistent with their more external career-oriented focus. Either way, in small colleges a faculty forum frequently becomes an arena for the discussion of holistic curricular change.

In contrast, faculty in large research universities may be busy with their research, have a low sense of community, and a decentralized system of governance. In such cases, collegewide building of an academic plan is essentially laissez faire. In the 1980s, many large universities were slower to consider broad changes in general education requirements and initiation of assessment procedures than small colleges (Ory & Parker, 1989).

Because creating academic plans depends so heavily on disciplinary expertise shared by only a limited number of faculty, the end result is that curricular decisions are delegated ever downward, leaving only broad policy discussions at the college level. In college-level academic planning, there may be attention to broad statements of educational purpose or specific outcomes for students rather than attention to specific content. In observing this scene, some commentators have called this delegation "overspecialization" or lack of faculty responsibility for the curriculum; others have lamented a loss of community. Whatever the result, delegation is surely why many decisions are located at the program level. It is not clear that there is a basis for institutionwide attention to curriculum planning in large universities, however

suitable such planning is for a smaller and less diverse higher education institutions.

Even broad discussions, however, can become contentious. Recall that faculty who come together in college-level discussions hold varying beliefs about education (and accompanying views about course sequencing). Among those we explored in our studies, the primary belief that might seem to unite the faculty is the importance of teaching students to think effectively. But even in relation to this strongly held belief, there are considerable differences among fields about how to define, teach, and measure effective thinking. These differences alone are sufficient to explain the persistence of distribution requirements for general education.

Seldom are specific instructional activities chosen at broad levels of discussion. Instead, structural revisions, credit hour adjustments, and calendar revamping are examples of implementation that dominate the planning process at the college level. If we examine curricular change processes here, we cannot help agreeing with Bergquist, Gould, and Greenberg (1981) that most changes are structural.

At the collegewide level, the catalog, mission statement, or admissions viewbook becomes the vehicle for communicating the academic plan to various constituencies. At this level, communication is often replaced by salesmanship or by attempts to create a legal document to safeguard the college against student misunderstandings. In the past, with sponsorship from FIPSE, a group of colleges attempted "truth-in-advertising," trying to create viewbooks that more closely resembled an educational plan by describing actual students' educational outcomes (Stark, 1978; Stark & Marchese, 1979). In the face of intense competition for students such an effort was only modestly successful; the idea did not become popular. As colleges begin to consider stating goals and expectations for students more carefully, there could be a renewed effort at such descriptions, perhaps with greater success.

Evaluating and Adjusting

Although accrediting procedures increasingly require attention to student outcomes in self-study reports, most institutions do not follow regular schedules for evaluation and adjustment after a period of collegewide curriculum planning. Often the process leaves fatigue and dissension in its wake, and there is little incentive to revisit a new program soon after it has been painfully negotiated. In other cases, opponents of the adopted change immediately attempt to demolish the new program, sometimes achieving their goal before the plan has reached full potential. In fact, it may be this very reluctance to provide mechanisms for systematic adjustments at the institutional level that fuels the periodic process of curriculum ferment we have described in U.S. colleges.

SYSTEMATIC DESIGN MODELS

Traditionally, professors are believed to defend the privacy of the classroom vigorously, to plan and teach their courses as they were taught, and to oppose new ideas about curriculum or pedagogy. Based on this stereotype, curricular planning in higher education is seen as unequivocally "scholar-dominated" and irrevocably stagnant. During our varied curricular change and research projects, we have found this picture to be inaccurate. Many faculty members believe curriculum decisions are important and are reflective about creating academic plans. Many told us they seldom were asked to discuss their course planning thoughts and activities and they welcomed the opportunity. We observed that merely asking about goals and strategies for course and program planning provided an opportunity for faculty members to crystallize their thoughts and consider new alternatives.

Just as our interviews (and sometimes group discussions) stimulated thought among faculty, collaboration has strong potential to encourage improvement. Collaboration can increase faculty openness to acquiring new types of expertise by exposing them to plans used by colleagues. Collaborative discussions about course and program design may be an effective route for instructional development centers to improve teaching techniques indirectly. Faculty are less likely to feel that their personal style is at issue if they discuss curriculum, rather than teaching behavior.

Our studies have clearly shown that college faculty do not read much about the educational process. The abstract and technical nature of this literature may hamper their efforts to increase their knowledge about course and program design. They do, however, adopt educational ideas selectively. After considerable delay, new educational ideas may reach them, usually through the work of accepted "translators" (K. Patricia Cross and Wilbert J. McKeachie are examples). The ideas about teaching and learning are seldom accepted on their own terms; faculty may discuss and adapt them based on one of several reasons: they are grounded in disciplines—perhaps psychology—with greater prestige than education, they deal with intellectual development of students, or they are expressed in familiar language. For example, instructors have found useful Benjamin Bloom's taxonomy of educational objectives, William Perry's work on students' intellectual development, David Kolb's learning styles inventories, and K. Patricia Cross's development of classroom assessment techniques. With the exception of classroom assessment which received national attention quite quickly, all of these well-established ideas have been adapted for use by college faculty members somewhat belatedly. Recent emphasis on improving undergraduate teaching by national organizations may be accelerating the dissemination and acceptance of educational ideas and theories in colleges. Probably an even wider variety of mechanisms is needed to translate new ideas, to circulate them among faculty members, and to encourage their use.

Exposure to new ideas cannot help but expand instructors' capacities to think in new ways about curricular design and increase their options (Schubert, 1986, p. 299). However, relatively few works that are specifically intended for college faculty address course and program design. Even Wilbert McKeachie's well-known book, *Teaching Tips,* now in its ninth edition (1994), focuses on instructional techniques; its discussion of planning is limited to a timeline of course preparation steps.

Some excellent materials prepared for elementary and secondary educators need to be translated so that professors can readily understand and adapt them, while retaining their own course planning styles. We illustrate our point by noting that we are indebted to the several works of George Posner, who writes primarily for elementary and secondary teachers. In the next section and in subsequent chapters, we will continue to "translate" some of Posner's ideas we have found useful.

Course Design

Posner and Rudnitsky's sequence of steps in *Course Design* (1994) (see Table 6-6) has much in common with the elements we have included in the academic plan and with the decisions professors make in constructing such a plan. Content (what is to be learned) generally derives from an accepted body of knowledge (a discipline, disciplines, or the application of disciplinary knowledge to a problem). The framework assumes that the course planner, like most college instructors, has sufficient knowledge of the projected course content to construct the initial list of ideas to include in the course or solve the problem.

Posner and Rudnitsky's central message is to "teach with a purpose" (p. 183). The key

TABLE 6-6   Course Planning Steps, According to Posner and Rudnitsky

1. Jot down ideas.
2. Give course a title.
3. Make a tentative outline of what you want to include.
4. Make list of Intended Learning Outcomes (ILOs).
5. Categorize ILOs as either skills or understandings.
6. Develop central questions addressed by the ILOs.
7. Expand the ILOs based on consideration of student entry skills, prior knowledge, and background.
8. Identify needed new vocabulary.
9. Construct conceptual trees for the concepts embedded in the ILOs.
10. Construct flowcharts for the skills to be developed.
11. State and clarify the rationale for the course.
12. Cluster the ILOs into units of appropriate size (consider pragmatic factors).
13. Prioritize the ILOs.
14. Choose sequencing principles.
15. Choose teaching strategies.
16. Plan course evaluation.

Source: Summarized from *Course Design: A Guide to Curriculum Development for Teachers,* 4th ed., by Posner and Rudnitsky (1994).

components of *purpose* in this design scheme are *rationale,* which is broader than discipline concepts, and *intended learning outcomes* (ILOs), which convert discipline concepts into specific objectives. The learning outcomes desired in college may be cognitions (knowledge of principles, facts, concepts), cognitive strategies (ways of learning), affects (attitudes or emotions), or psychomotor skills. Simply put, rationale is the general problem or goal the curriculum is intended to address, and intended learning outcomes are what the student is to learn (the course objectives). Posner and Rudnitsky suggest that planners begin by listing ideas about content that should be covered in a course. But they encourage the process of stating intended learning outcomes as the ideas develop for three crucial reasons: (1) to guide instructional planning, (2) to communicate the learning goals to important others (e.g., students, the public), and (3) to provide a basis for developing indicators of success. Selecting content before learning objectives is comfortable for professors. And Posner and Rudnitsky acknowledge that course planning takes place most naturally in a cyclical or spiral mode, rather than a linear and rational one. Consequently, they suggest that planners reconsider and revise their intended outcomes as they rethink their rationale later in the planning. This suggestion accords with the iterative planning processes faculty reported that they use. These ideas are also consistent with McKeachie's suggestion (1994) that written course objectives be kept flexible and revisited frequently as planning proceeds.

Posner and Rudnitsky also divide planning into three decision areas: (1) deciding *what* is to be learned, (2) developing *why* it is to be learned, and (3) deciding *how to facilitate* the learning. Often, it seems, college faculty members skip the second step and assume that learning the discipline is justifiable on its own grounds. Professors may gain from being pressed to be explicit about their rationale for learning and about their governing beliefs about educational purpose. Thus, for many professors, following the Posner and Rudnitsky framework will be useful.

Posner and Rudnitsky separate curriculum development and instructional planning rather than subsuming instructional planning with curriculum development as we do. They define *instruction* as "all of the teacher's purposeful activities aimed at producing, stimulating, or facilitating learning by students" (p. 141). As they use this definition to discuss instructional planning, they also introduce their readers to important new advances in cognitive psychology (pp. 144–146). For example, they point out that course design may benefit from explicit conceptual maps which relate discipline ideas to one another and flowcharts which demonstrate the hierarchical or nonhierarchical relationships of skills and concepts necessary to learning. They consider it useful to cluster related outcomes and concepts into "chunks" of knowledge that can readily be connected with what the learner already knows. It is also useful to compare the student's notions of how concepts in the course are related with the instructor's notions.

Posner and Rudnitsky's ideas for evaluating success appear narrower than those we will describe in our academic plan framework. They suggest measuring achievement of the *actual learning outcomes* (ALOs) that correspond to the previously specified *intended learning outcomes* (ILOs). When interpreted broadly, however, their discussion of evaluation and adjustment permits a variety of measurement styles and also allows attention to unintended side effects of instruction.

The specific framework used to guide course design activities is less important than the process of engaging in reflection and analysis. Reflection by college teachers on the design of academic plans has many benefits. It helps, for example, to contrast active learning with passive learning as ways to help students construct meaning. It calls into question the appropriate instructional mode for a given rationale and set of intended outcomes. It can challenge the idea that learning is a solitary activity by revealing the benefits and viability of collaborative learning. Finally, it can promote attention to the relations between faculty planning decisions and the learning styles and strategies of students. A general design process leaves the specific rationale or content base up to the individual professor, safeguarding faculty autonomy and creativity. The steps in planning also can be varied; the idea is to establish a comfortable but systematic framework for course design.

Program Design

Perhaps the simplest framework for systematic program design is a checklist of questions that a group of faculty can ask as they create an academic plan. We propose four pressing questions faculty find hard to answer and thus tend to omit:

1. Have we specified the purpose/objectives of learning?
2. Have we explored the best sequence of arranging content?
3. Have we considered the relationship among the concepts taught and the relationship of concepts with the student's world?
4. Do we know how to evaluate success of the plan?

Of course, it is always important in systematic program design to consider the teaching/learning environment. In higher education, environmental factors might include student variables (age, ability, interests, goals, prior knowledge, cognitive capabilities), faculty variables (content preparation, goals, flexibility, motivation), organizational variables (cost, time, reward systems, climate, mission), and so on. The extent to which such factors will be considered in program-level design depends, in large part, on how the participants see the program mission. But we contend that these realities should not be the predominant considerations in program planning as they so often are. They should be dealt with only after the key questions about the purpose and ideal design of academic plan that we mentioned earlier are asked and answered.

A model in which instructional experts help faculty members focus on important questions and ideal designs, then adjust for the environment, has been developed by Robert Diamond and his colleagues at the Center for Instructional Development, Syracuse University (Diamond, 1989). Although it is potentially useful at both course and program levels, we classify Diamond's model under program design because it is an inclusive system to assist selected faculty and faculty groups in developing a complete academic plan. It may, however, lack appeal for faculty members in some disciplines because it uses terms like *managerial systems* to refer to instructional techniques.

Diamond's process is also unabashedly linear and requires a team approach, based on the assumption that the professor is the knowledge expert and the consultant from the instructional development center is the process expert. The instructional developer's role is to help the professor think in new ways about program structure, the process of setting objectives, and the simultaneous choice of evaluation strategies to assess success (p. 13). In this approach, the design process ends (rather than begins) with choice of instructional activities and production of instructional materials to facilitate learning.

Faculty using Diamond's model have successfully designed entire programs as well as individualized options and have produced detailed student manuals for students in large introductory courses. Those who complete the process successfully have included careful diagnosis of student needs and attitudes, have consciously assessed availability of needed resources and facilities, and have determined how much administrative support for new activities they can count on. They have considered future directions in their discipline, built-in diagnosis and remediation for students with inadequate background, and stated evaluation criteria.

The system intentionally incorporates feedback and adjustment. Diamond indicates that faculty either resent writing course objectives, or write far too many of them, including trivial ones. Therefore, in his process, they answer instead the question: "If I'm your student, what do I have to do to convince you that I'm where you want me to be at the end of this lesson (unit or course)?" The design of evaluation procedures begins at the beginning of the planning process, rather than being held until the end. Unlike Posner's scheme, Diamond's model doesn't necessarily encourage faculty members to address all important issues stemming from learning theory that may be important in program design. Rather, it concentrates on specific issues of design that are important independent of learning theory.

As faculty conceptualize academic designs, one idea that needs special emphasis at the program level is coherence. Just as the use of conceptual maps can help to show students how to integrate ideas *within* courses, models of program content can reveal the program faculty's view of coherence *among* courses. To state the parallel another way, the sequencing of ideas in courses should help students understand relationships among ideas in that course, and the sequencing of courses in programs should help students develop conceptual views of what coherence means among courses in a program.

When courses are arranged in a sequence to integrate material within a field appropriately, the result is a holistic view of the discipline. Of course, this rationale may be extended to include the sequence of the academic plan for an entire college. For programs involving more than one discipline, such as a general education core, the key agreement needed is how to define the holistic or coherent view and thus, the appropriate sequence. Interestingly, the recent discussions about core general education curricula have not achieved a clear method of promoting coherence. Schemes intended to ensure that students drink from the springs of the varied disciplinary perspectives may, in fact, have the opposite result. We translate part of another scheme by Posner (1974) that could provide a useful way to think about program

discussions and to develop core general education programs in particular.

In an attempt to create a parsimonious representation of curriculum structure, Posner classified curriculum content (units or courses) on two dimensions: (1) commonality and (2) temporality, roughly as follows.

Commonality refers to the similarity of curriculum units. Some pairs of topics are largely unrelated in purpose or content, such as studying Spanish grammar and studying geometric proofs. In contrast, some curriculum units involve a single purpose or content repeatedly, such as learning Spanish vocabulary or practicing a musical instrument. Between these two extremes are pairs of elements that are neither identical nor entirely unrelated; rather, they are related in some identifiable way, such as studying English history and studying English literature from the same period; or studying taxonomic classifications of plants and studying similar classifications in the animal kingdom. The closer the relationship, the higher the "commonality."

Temporality, in Posner's scheme, refers to the relationship of curricular units in time. For example, one may consecutively study U.S. history from 1800 to 1865, and then U.S. history from 1865–1900. These subjects also may be studied concurrently, or their sequence may be interrupted by other activities. The closer the time periods of study, the higher the "temporality."

Posner asserts that a curriculum in which units, courses, or programs are organized with both high commonality and high temporality is a curriculum with high structure. In contrast, in a low-structure curriculum, elements would both be unrelated in time and have little commonality. Colleges with fragmented general education programs allow students to take a series of unrelated courses according to their own time frame; no attempt is made to link these elements. Colleges with limited distribution requirements may make attempts to increase either commonality or temporality, or both, in the patterns of study students elect. Finally, colleges with deliberately designed core curricula have both high commonality and high temporality.

This scheme captures quite well the structural dimensions of the general education curriculum that are being debated today. The first question to be debated is the advantages of insisting that the courses students take (or other curriculum units) should have high commonality. A second question is whether they should be taken close in time, or specifically sequenced. Casting the debate in these terms can help faculty members focus on the process of design, rather than conducting an ideological debate about the nature and timing of the core program.

Recent examples of careful attention to commonality and temporality have also emerged as colleges try to integrate liberal arts disciplines and professional programs. In one case, such attempts are called clustered courses. An example is from Babson College of Boston, where a business student simultaneously takes courses in business law, history, and accounting that deal with overlapping ideas, time periods, or issues. In cluster course designs like Babson's, involved faculty may or may not integrate the content of the courses they teach.

One of the most common linking mechanisms connects content courses with skills courses in developmental education programs. Many institutions link general education courses with English composition courses. Links between courses to develop students' critical thinking skills, library research strategies, and understanding and use of mathematics may also be made in general education classes, and other combinations are also possible.

Other more fully coordinated course models, particularly those that create learning communities of students and faculty, often require the integration of content between or among courses. More radical learning community models—for example, the coordinated studies model—replace separate courses with a fully integrated program of courses for a term or an academic year. The coordinated studies model is the basis for the curriculum at Evergreen State College in Washington, an oft-cited example of a learning community. Faculty who participate in coordinated studies programs are responsible for redesigning the curriculum with an eye toward increased coherence and interdisciplinarity. Pedagogical changes often accompany content or topic changes, and faculty employ active learning strategies, cooperative learning, team teaching, and integration of skill and content teaching. Discussing curriculum sequencing in these terms moves the debate beyond the "choice versus prescription" concern, to provide a stronger rationale for arranging the academic plan in specific ways.

Another model that can be used for systematically thinking about programs, particularly when more than one organizational department or disciplinary unit is involved, is the set of outcomes common to liberal and professional study that we introduced in Chapter 5. The PLUSS Guide we constructed (Stark, Lowther, Hagerty, & Lokken, 1987) helps two groups of faculty—one from the liberal arts and another from a professional field or fields—to focus their discussion on the commonalities between them. It helps faculty answer such questions as, "What types of outcomes do both programs seek?" "What types of activities does each employ that may accomplish these objectives?" "What are the most appropriate types of cross-discipline integration to help students achieve specific important outcomes?" Successful use of the PLUSS requires more faculty time than some colleges are willing to commit for sufficient discussion of important common learning outcomes and the activities that might achieve them.

We have offered only a few examples of recent thinking about systematic program design that faculty could apply to replace ad hoc procedures now often in place. We don't wish to imply that faculty groups have been negligent in considering program design. In fact, some professional associations and accreditors have their own systematic design frameworks that are helpful. For example, in nursing, accreditors require all programs to have a model of "nursing process" that serves as the unifying force for program planning. We do wish to emphasize, however, that many useful schemes are available (see, e.g., the work of Toombs, 1977–1978, who used the concept of design and a mapping process to identify important curriculum changes at several institutions).

Evaluation techniques are abundant in the literature at the program level. Unfortunately, these program reviews are more often done by outside agencies and used for summative judgments about program continuance than for periodic adjustment of the academic plan (Barak & Breier, 1990).

College-level Design

Just as we found few studies that describe collegewide creation of academic plans, few frameworks are available to make collegewide design more systematic. Several related literatures may be mined for suggestions on setting mission, promoting change and innovation, establishing a sense of community, and measuring institutional effectiveness.

Since collegewide planning is often undertaken to adjust and confirm the institutional mission, some colleges use instruments like the Institutional Goals Inventory (Educational Testing Service) to strive for goal consensus. Such consensus building is usually only the first step because adjusting or refining the college mission provides a foundation for academic planning but is not synonymous with it. The broad mission statement is important primarily because it helps derive specific learning objectives (or intended out-

comes) for programs and groups of students. Curriculum development that proceeds from a clear mission is the process "of translating policy statements into an educational program, more a technical process than a governing or controlling activity" (Short, 1983, p. 44). The emphasis at the collegewide level is, rightfully, on policy, but the policy must guide specific academic plans—not always an easy task.

With modifications, some of the suggestions we provided to make program planning more systematic can be applied to collegewide curricula. The dimensions of commonality and temporality we drew from Posner's work are useful in thinking about sequence. Diamond's instructional process could be used to first develop an ideal scenario, then a more realistic one based on existing constraints. In this way, recognizing faulty thinking, choices, and decisions is stimulated by an outside instructional development consultant.

In this respect, the *Course Planning Exploration* (Stark, Lowther, Sossen, & Shaw, 1990) may be most useful in that it encourages faculty to discuss their most basic educational beliefs and how these are related to their disciplinary views. The various strategies from the PLUSS instrument can also be used to stimulate discussion on a collegewide basis. The Philadelphia College of Textiles and Science used the PLUSS to start discussion about achieving closer integration of liberal and professional curriculum segments. PLUSS helped to verify the agreement of many faculty about the importance of "liberal/professional outcomes." This agreement did not mean, however, that it has been easy to carry out the next steps to develop a working program satisfactory to all groups.

Probably one of the best documented collegewide processes of systematic curriculum design was conducted by Alverno College of Milwaukee, Wisconsin. Beginning in the 1970s and continuing to the present

Alverno faculty have struggled with collegewide curriculum design in quite a systematic way and have shared their process extensively with other colleges. As Alverno's experience illustrates, systematic curriculum design at the collegewide level both depends on and can help to build a positive institutional climate and focus attention on developing a sense of community.

Another type of new thinking about college-level planning is conveyed by the concept of *organizational learning.* Just as psychologists have visualized learners reshaping their knowledge structures to accommodate new knowledge, organizational theorists envision the organization as capable of "learning"—that is, developing the capacity to incorporate new information with old for improved functioning. Just as learners develop improved learning strategies that help them continue to learn more effectively, so organizations can develop strategies for continual improvement. If such a view persists and proves correct, collegewide planning could take on a more systematic appearance.

FROM PLAN TO DESIGN

In this chapter, we have reviewed what is known of the process of academic planning at three levels—course, program, and college. We have noted that, whether they work alone or in groups, college faculty members think first about their discipline when they create academic plans. As we move our analysis from the typical solitary level of planning to levels where large groups work together, group dynamics become more important, pragmatic concerns more potent, and leadership more necessary.

Despite these well-known difficulties, we accept the postulate put forth by Hewson and Posner (1984) that it is better for teachers to consider alternative ways of selecting and organizing content and to choose among them, than to remain unaware that alternatives exist. Thus, we have described a few of many possible schemes that could convert the process of ad hoc planning to one of systematic and deliberate design.

We believe a pattern of balanced participation of experts in course and program planning would also prove fruitful. Such a balanced pattern might include greater participation, for example, by individuals knowledgeable about the psychology of learning, the characteristics of students, the relation of education and work, and instructional design. Recognition of the contributions these experts have to offer would open the varied and extensive literature relevant to curriculum planning to curriculum decision makers. Next we will discuss differences among the academic fields that may limit attempts to generalize about course planning.

CHAPTER 7

Influence of Academic Fields

INFLUENCES OF ACADEMIC FIELDS ON PLANNING

The characteristics of an academic field strongly influence course planning. The beliefs of teacher/scholars as they select and arrange content in academic plans provide a strong internal influence on curriculum. Although we labeled them as two separate elements of the academic plan for analysis purposes, educational purpose and selection of course content are closely allied in action. Faculty specialties exert strong influence on academic plans because most faculty consider content first when they plan courses. Similarly, the field's organization provides a starting point for discussion when faculty collaborate in program development. At the same time, external influences on course planning may also be strong. Nearly all fields will respond to their respective associations and to any special field-related accrediting associations that may exist. In career-based programs, the job market and various credentialing agencies may exert another strong influence. Organizational influences may affect disciplinary programs either modestly or

strongly, depending on the program and its institutional setting. In particular, the distinctions among the fields and how they are viewed both within and outside of colleges also strongly affect how academic plans are constructed. We have sketched our perceptions of the relative strength of these three types of influences in Figure 7-1.

As we discuss the influence of the fields on academic planning, we will first explain why we use *academic fields* as an inclusive term to encompass disciplines, undergraduate professional study, and occupational study. Then we will discuss what we have observed as faculty draw on their academic fields to construct course and program plans. Finally, we will discuss how academic plans might change if curriculum development were viewed differently. In particular, after analyzing the differences in the disciplines and professional fields, we report various ideas that have been suggested for constructing curricula with more effective balances among them.

Faculty members, clustered in groups based on their specializations, have become more distinct in their interests and communication patterns. The resulting organizational

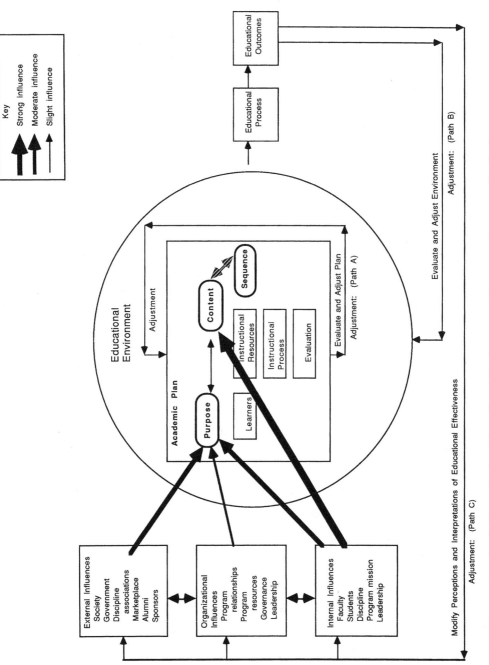

FIGURE 7-1   Academic Plans in the Educational Environment: Focus on Purpose, Content, and Sequence

units within colleges and universities have become more entrenched and isolated. The modern system of specialization and the separatism it has fostered have been sharply criticized for fragmenting teaching and learning in colleges and universities. A frequent basis of criticism is that specialities are based on the research interests of professors, not the learning needs of students.

Yet most educators would agree that some order must be imposed on both existing and new knowledge for students' benefit as well as for professors' research. Students especially need structure to relate ideas rather than learning them in isolation. As Dressel and Marcus (1982) put it:

> For effective learning, a student needs a framework made up of an appropriate set of clear stable concepts, principles or ideas at various levels of generality or inclusiveness. Such a structure provides the optimal possibility for correlating, anchoring, bridging or grouping new ideas in relation to those already known by inserting them in the existing framework. (pp. 164–165)

Educators feel a responsibility to help students establish structure, to relate new knowledge to old, and to link knowledge to problem solving in life or work. The specific structures that should guide learning and the nature of appropriate organizing schemes for undergraduate education, however, have been subjects of recurring debate. Traditionally, academic plans have been organized around the disciplines and occupational or professional fields.

Defining and Characterizing Academic Fields

Today's college programs are organized around an extensive variety of "fields," including subjects traditionally viewed as academic "disciplines," those that aim to prepare students for professional and occupational careers, and those that are interdisciplinary. To strive for clarity in our discussion, we will use *academic field* as the most inclusive term for all subjects taught and will reserve *discipline* primarily for fields traditionally taught in arts and science colleges, such as history, sociology, and physics. We will use the terms *applied, career-studies,* and *professional* for others, such as business, education, nursing, and agriculture, and reserve *occupational* for career-directed programs taught in two-year colleges.

These designations have a prestige hierarchy among faculty in some colleges, who do not view all of the fields now offered in colleges as equal in status or as essential to a complete education. Status distinctions among fields arose in the 1800s as faculty in early colleges attempted to limit scientific subjects in the curriculum. As higher education programs have expanded, new status distinctions have developed on other grounds. Some faculty members consider the arts and science fields to be "true higher learning," in contrast to applied or career-oriented fields. With the exception of the prestigious professions of law and medicine, education for its own sake is simply more highly valued in universities than education for an instrumental end such as career preparation. A corollary is that educational breadth for American undergraduates is often considered more prestigious than educational depth.

These status differentials among fields amplify curriculum debates. Some of the distinctions have an elitist tone and may have less to do with the subjects studied than with the fact that students from higher socioeconomic groups traditionally have studied the disciplines in liberal arts colleges, rather than the career-based programs in state colleges and universities. One scholar has developed the thesis that status differentials among and within professional fields are remnants of earlier status differentials based on class distinctions in British society (Haber, 1991). Another scholar found the emphasis on liberal arts "ironic and puzzling in a country that has probably the largest professionalized work force in the world" (Rhoades, 1991, p. 335).

Among the general public, the view that career preparation is an essential educational purpose is much stronger than among many groups of faculty members. The public values the arts and science disciplines but often sees them as complementary to professional and occupational study for students who must "learn to earn." Many educators, as well as students and parents, claim that these career fields provide an equally appropriate organizing framework that meets students' needs and interests. In fact, career-oriented fields such as business have captured the bulk of today's students, whereas more traditional subjects such as literature seem to have more tenuous connections to students' lives.

Although the distinctions among academic fields have multiple origins in our society, they have supported judgments of what is central in the missions of many colleges and universities. As we have seen, the conflict between general and specialized education, in particular, has been an enduring debate for at least two hundred years. Many of the distinctions rest on tradition. But traditions in U.S. higher education can have arisen quite recently. Many fields viewed as high in academic status have developed only since 1900, some older fields have declined in importance, and new fields continue to emerge as knowledge expands and differentiates. The distinctions are muddied further by recent complaints that the arts and science disciplines themselves have "professionalized" their majors, overemphasizing specialized training for jobs and graduate school to about the same degree as the career-based programs. We acknowledge these various types of distinctions based on career orientation, tradition, and prestige because they are organizational influences that bear on how academic plans are made.

Characteristics of Traditional Academic Disciplines

Scholars in several fields (history, philosophy, sociology, psychology, and education) have asked why colleagues in various academic disciplines have such different approaches. Several have studied the structure of disciplines and others have examined how faculty operate in their departmental groups. These scholars have looked for elements common to all fields, and for characteristics that differentiate the disciplines. They have created classifications in an attempt to clarify both epistemology and social norms within these discipline "cultures." We describe some of these classification schemes here because they help us understand the different orientations that faculty members bring to course and program development.

The simplest type of classification merely attempts to characterize groups of fields. In one description, Bell (1966) argued that the sciences are organized according to sequential paradigms, the social sciences according to linkages among concepts, and the humanities in a concentric way. Similarly, the Harvard Committee on General Education viewed the sciences as proceeding from a logical base, the social sciences from a relational base, and the humanities from an imaginative base (discussed in Halliburton, 1977a, pp. 46–47; 1977b, pp. 51–52). Toulmin (1972) described the sciences as "compact" disciplines, the social sciences as "diffuse" disciplines, and fields that are still in the developmental stages as "would-be" disciplines. These commentators consistently noticed similar distinctions; all describe the sciences as disciplines that are hierarchical and tightly knit, the social sciences are much more loosely linked by concepts and relationships, and the humanities are free in form and capable of expanding in any direction the human imagination leads. These orientations are associated with different beliefs about education and, thus, with different implications for developing curriculum. On the basis of observations that individuals with different learning styles are likely to study certain fields, Kolb (1981) created a parallel disciplinary classification based on two learning-style dimensions: abstract to concrete, and reflective to active.

Phenix (1964/1986) published an extensive study of the disciplines, describing six common elements which he called "realms of meaning." This work has been a foundation for many of the later classifications; several scholars have reproduced, expanded, and attempted to apply these realms of meaning in the disciplines. A more recent elaboration of Phenix's work is a useful classification by Dressel and Marcus (1982). According to this synthesis, all disciplines have five types of structures or components:

1. *Substantive structure:* Assumptions about the particular concepts of interest that control the questions asked and the inquiries undertaken. What are the types of problems with which the discipline deals?

2. *Symbolic structure:* A symbolic communication system (frequently linguistic or mathematical but sometimes nondiscursive). What is the symbol system that allows the expression of and communication about the unique aspects and relationships?

3. *Syntactical structure:* A system for collecting and organizing data, posing and testing hypotheses or assertions, and relating justified assertions to the broader generalizations and exploratory schemes of the discipline. What are the ways in which evidence is collected, organized, evaluated, and interpreted? In short, what is the mode of inquiry?

4. *Value structure:* A set of embedded values, orientations, or ways of viewing the world. What is worth studying and how should it be studied?

5. *Organizational structure:* The set of principles relating a discipline to other disciplines and dependent on the previous four structures, also called the *conjunctive* component (Dressel & Marcus, 1982, pp. 89–90, 108–133).

Phenix argued that the disciplines represent the natural order of knowledge and therefore provide an appropriate organizing scheme for curriculum. In his descriptive scheme, he even specified a group of disciplines (synoptics, including history, religion, philosophy) that help to bring coherence to the relationships of all the other disciplines. His view has been widely accepted by liberal arts educators who see these fields as the core of all college studies.

According to Dressel and Marcus, no teacher can fully understand or apply (or presumably teach) without some grasp of these five components, which markedly influence their discipline's nature and further development. Depending on the emphasis placed on each component, specific faculty members may teach their disciplinary fields in different ways. While reminding us that the disciplines are "artifacts of mankind's search for meaning," Dressel and Marcus classified the typical college disciplines into three groups as contributing mostly to student development in one or more of the major realms of meaning that Phenix outlined.

Dressel and Marcus include as the symbolic disciplines those that are concerned with symbols humans have constructed and emphasize the means of thought, understanding, and communication. These include language, mathematics, and other nondiscursive forms. The substantive disciplines are those that transmit the primary areas of knowledge and the means of attaining, testing, and organizing it. There are two subsets of this group: empiric disciplines that help us understand, explain, control, and predict phenomena (including physical, biological, psychological, and social sciences); and aesthetic disciplines that allow expression but transmit meaning through symbols that evoke emotion rather than cognitive meaning (including music, art, movement and dance, and literature). Finally, there are the synoptic disciplines that are concerned with the interpretation and integration of meaning. These include history, philosophy, and religion. Dressel and Marcus also mention a category called synnoetics, which, they judge, is not dealt with in a fully developed set of formal disciplines. By their definition, synnoetic questions deal with or describe interactions among humans or other highly subjective forms of awareness. Examples are some subjective questions considered within the study of religion, philosophy, psychology, and literature, including the areas of self-awareness, ethics, and morality.

When faculty within a field lack consensus about one or more of the dimensions that characterize their discipline, there is also less consensus on what should be taught and learned. This situation, which can produce both anxiety and lack of coordination among faculty about what to teach, may, as we shall see, characterize the humanities and some of the social sciences today. In contrast, because of strong agreement, faculty in sciences and mathematics may seem rigid or dogmatic in their views to observers outside their fields.

Internal differences among fields may affect academic plans. Other studies of differences have been based either on the work of Phenix (1964/1986) or Kuhn (1970), who theorized that disciplines employ different cognitive frameworks, specify different problems for study, use different methods for studying them, make different types of generalizations, and use different examples to illustrate them. These differences strongly influence academic plans in the disciplines, but Kuhn did not restrict his discussion to disciplines. His view that academic fields also solve problems using varied paradigms implies that collegiate career fields are also included. Like a discipline, Kuhn believed, a career field may be strongly influenced by a paradigm—one of its own or those borrowed from one or more disciplines. No less than those in the disciplines, faculty in professional programs are also subject to strong internal influences in their academic planning.

After interviewing faculty members in many fields, Becher (1989) interpreted the distinctions among academic fields somewhat differently from either Phenix or Kuhn, describing fields as constructed by human groups, rather than emerging from some natural order or inherent method of inquiry. Whereas Phenix believed that teachers and students try to understand their world in an objective way, uncontaminated by human considerations, Becher found disciplinary distinctions to be more subject to human interpretations and frailties. He spoke of the disciplines as communities, characterized by political and territorial disputes, status structures, and pecking orders. These power relationships join with order inherent in the disciplines themselves, he claimed, to help structure contemporary universities. The resulting organizational issues growing from the disciplinary distinctions clearly influence academic plans. In this regard, Becher's view is similar to that of Toulmin (1972), who asserted that a discipline has three aspects: a body of ideas and arguments, a community of scholars, and a system of institutions and proceedings (p. 308).

Researchers who focused more on the characteristics of the social action of scholars as they function within their organizational groups (usually departmental settings) in universities have produced the so-called Biglan classification (Biglan, 1973a, 1973b; Creswell & Roskens, 1981). Biglan concluded that the fields have different operational styles based on their degree of paradigm consensus (hard to soft), their degree of concern with application (pure to applied), and their degree of concern with life or nonlife systems.

Starting from Biglan's scheme but considering the realm of knowledge structures, Becher (1989, pp. 79–82) also divided the disciplines into hard/soft and pure/applied. When discussing how scholars in a field interact, however, he more fully used Kolb's scheme and divided them into convergent/divergent and rural/urban categories based on their discourse patterns and visibility. The most dominant learning styles for convergent disciplines are abstract conceptualization and active experimentation; for divergent disciplines they are concrete experience and reflective observation.

The rural/urban distinction centers on the density of scholarly work. A rural discipline, such as anthropology, pursues many topics, has high division of labor, is relatively noncompetitive and maintains a lower profile than the urban disciplines. Most of the "soft" fields and many applied sciences fit this description. An urban discipline, such as high energy physics, pursues a narrow area of study with discrete problems, studies only a few salient topics, and pursues problems with shorter-range solutions. Most disciplines that are considered "big science" fall in this category. Scholars in urban fields are more likely to communicate through indirect means and to write journal articles. Scholars in rural fields write more books and rely more on personal communication. Becher stressed that these labeled categories should not be considered to create dichotomies; rather the fields vary along continua on these dimensions.

Both Kuhn's idea that a discipline is a field of inquiry aimed at problem-solving and the social interactions explored by Becher, Toulmin, and Biglan are important in understanding how faculty construct academic

plans at the course and program level. The discipline as a problem-solving structure is relevant at the course level; the social interaction of scholars in the field, and with others, is particularly relevant at the program level.

Surely, to view the educated person as one who not only has a command of the six "realms of meaning" (Phenix) or the four groups of disciplines (Dressel and Marcus) but is able to relate one to another synoptically, is a valid, if ambitious, educational goal. Such a view greatly simplifies choices of what students should learn and how the material should be organized. But not all knowledgeable observers believe that current organization by academic fields results in the best academic plans. Alexander (1993) described the disciplines as organized to "support the creation, evaluation, and maintenance of new knowledge" rather than students' learning (p. B-3). He claimed that the organization of undergraduate study by discipline achieves neither the broad view (for the arts and sciences disciplines) nor the professional "point of view" (for collegiate career fields) at which it purportedly aims. As a substitute, he proposes *collegia,* which interrelate the disciplines and are taught by professors who wish to arrange their teaching around how students learn (p. B-3).

A similar point of view has been voiced with increasing frequency since the mid-1980s wave of educational reform began. This view is consistent with one of the goals faculty most commonly express for education— that is, learning to think effectively. It is inconsistent, however, with the choices faculty most often make as they plan courses, focusing on content from their own academic field. Observers have found that even when instructors believe they should organize learning to achieve the goal of critical thinking, in actuality, they tend to organize it around field-related content (Stark et al., 1990b; Angelo & Cross, 1993). The Association of American

Colleges' Project on Liberal Learning in the Major argued that that emphasis on discipline concepts is, to a large degree, appropriate and may, in fact, produce the desired critical thinking outcomes. The Project Task Force reasoned that students will find sufficient intellectual excitement to think critically primarily if they experience the intellectual excitement of joining faculty in the communities of scholarship that discover new knowledge (Association of American Colleges, 1992).

Characteristics of Professional and Occupational Fields

Sociologists have concentrated on defining professions and distinguishing education for the professions from education in the disciplines (see, e.g., Bucher & Stelling, 1977; Larson, 1977; Vollmer & Mills, 1966). Because they do not fit all aspects of accepted sociological definitions of a profession (such as controlling admission to their own ranks and serving society in an altruistic way), some feel that the major fields typically taught at the undergraduate level (such as teaching, engineering, nursing, and business) are not true professions. Our focus, however, is on the influences that affect programs, content, and sequence, not on entrance to elite professional groups. For our purposes in thinking about how academic fields influence curriculum development, it is preferable to define the professional fields according to everyday usage on four-year campuses. In our discussion, we will use collegiate career studies and undergraduate professional programs as synonyms for programs that prepare students for some reasonably well-defined career.

Although undergraduate professional specializations predominate in many colleges and universities today, scholars have not analyzed their characteristics carefully as Phenix and others have done for the disciplines (see Rhoades, 1991, for a review of the limited literature). In some studies, for example in those by Becher and most research using the Biglan model, collegiate career studies have been included as "disciplines," communicating the assumption that they are similar to the traditional academic fields. Such inclusions overlook important characteristics that these applied fields possess. Drawing from our earlier studies, we will make some relevant observations and suggest a scheme comparable to that may be useful in understanding academic planning in these fields.

First, we note that the collegiate career studies share some symbol systems and other characteristics with disciplines in which they have their roots. Scholars in these related disciplines are able to communicate reasonably well with college career study fields. In classifications using the Biglan model, for example, it is hardly surprising that electrical engineering is mapped close to physics and mathematics on the hard/soft dimension but is at the opposite end of the pure/applied dimension. The difference between the applied fields and their parent disciplines in Biglan's scheme lies in the degree of abstraction of the problems that are deemed appropriate for study. Physicists and mathematicians both would be interested in the discovery of knowledge in their field, regardless of whether they expected a practical use. But electrical engineers would be interested in the "craft" of using knowledge to solve problems at least as much as in the discovery of new knowledge. Each of the professional fields has a "craft" aspect, or technical competence, defined differently for each.

A second distinction for collegiate career studies is that the community of scholars extends outward from the collegiate setting to encompass practitioners who are using the knowledge in many other arenas. The practice settings or environments in which the knowledge is used help to define the professional field and separate it, not only from its pure antecedents, but also from other related career fields. For example, there are many types of engineering—aeronautical, electrical, mechanical, civil, electronic, structural, heating and ventilating, automotive, and transport, to name a few—each of which is useful in a somewhat different practice setting. The settings result in identifying different communities of individuals interested in the problem-solving activities of the professional field, and different settings may lead to specialized adaptations of methods of inquiry. Because the career fields tend to be eclectic in their choice of methods, one might argue that these types of engineering are really quite different fields. Demonstrably, chemical engineering is substantively different from mechanical engineering, Yet in a single practice setting, such as a chemical manufacturing operation, practitioners from several branches of engineering may work together, using closely related methods, and may have many more similarities than do members of the same field working in very different settings.

With these considerations of parent discipline, practice community, and adaptable, eclectic methods in mind as possible additional dimensions, we have developed a brief scheme describing the undergraduate fields that we intend to roughly parallel Phenix's dimensions (as adapted by Dressel and Marcus) that we listed earlier. The correspondences are not exact, but we believe that they serve to guide us in understanding the unique considerations of faulty teaching collegiate career studies as they construct academic plans. The Phenix-Dressel categories are in brackets.

1. *Type of service or technical role* [substantive structure]. This dimension defines the professional field in terms of the problems with which it deals and its type of "service" to society. Thus, it parallels the concept of interests or key questions for the disciplines. It also determines the conceptual foundations that professionals must acquire

and the kinds of technical skills that society expects practitioners to use when solving problems defined as within the profession's domain.

We propose that at least four different substantive service orientations to society's problems can be identified among the collegiate career fields: *human client service* (e.g., nursing or social work), *information service* (e.g., library science, journalism), *production/enterprise service* (e.g., business, engineering), and *creative service* (artistic professions). Fields may possess more or less of these attributes and may thus be hybrids that can be arrayed on a continuum; for example, education provides both client and information service; pharmacy is concerned with both client and production service, and architecture may involve both production and artistic service. [We are indebted to Anderson (1974) who used a twofold classification of service and production.]

2. *Symbolic systems and discourse communities* [symbolic]. On a continuum, the symbolic system specific to a professional field may be either relatively closed—that is, interpretable primarily by those with specialized education in the profession or who have been certified, such as in law and accounting. Or it may be relatively open to interpretation by anyone who spends a modest amount of reading time, such as in education and social work.

3. *Inquiry methods* [syntactical]. This dimension defines the methods used to answer questions or solve problems. It is distinctive only in the likelihood that a single method will not be as well accepted as multiple methods, drawn and adapted from other disciplines and professional fields.

4. *Values* [values]. The specific values linked to a collegiate career field involve attitudes about its relationship to society, to the client, to ethical problems, and to the improvement of the field itself. Earlier we have called these values professional *attitudes,* including professional identity, professional ethics, one's motivation to continue learning, and a scholarly concern for professional improvement (Stark et al., 1986). The value component and the service-technical component are closely linked, as are the value and substantive components for the disciplines, and we have clearly separated faculty members from three of the four types of service orientations on this dimension.

5. *Problems and linkages* [organizational/conjunctive]. This dimension describes the linkages with fields that teach the conceptual foundation professionals must acquire. The linkage system may be extensive because it includes both links with parent disciplines and with other fields. The roots of a collegiate career field may be in sciences, social sciences, or the arts, or in combinations of these. For example, nursing has roots in both sciences and social sciences, and architecture has roots in science, social science, humanities, and the arts. For most of these fields, we also note a third linkage dimension, that with other professions in similar service domains, as in relations between nursing and pharmacy, or between architecture and engineering.

Dressel and Marcus stated that teaching a discipline requires attention to all of the five discipline components but acknowledged that faculty may give them different emphases. Similarly, faculty in different collegiate career studies give different emphases in their educational plans to the five components above. The extent to which each dimension is incorporated depends on the specific orientation within the service and technical structure, just as the empiric and aesthetic disciplines relate differentially to Phenix's dimensions. Career fields that attend to all dimensions are likely to provide an extensive organizing structure or socialization process

to help students develop a picture of the academic plan.

Although we have not tested this thesis, we would argue that many occupational fields, such as those taught in the community colleges, may be seen as having similar components. In addition, the expanded colleague network leads to stronger influence from outside academe and greater responsiveness of the curriculum to societal needs. It leads faculty in these fields to be concerned with issues that are not characteristically the concerns of their disciplinary colleagues. For example, both occupational and professional educators worry about the balance of theory and practice and about providing experience for students in appropriate practice environments. As orientation to training (that is, emphasis on performing specific tasks rather than on solving unstructured problems) increases, the emphasis on other components may decrease. For example, the role of a nursing assistant requires less emphasis on professional ethics than that of a nurse because ethical decisions are less likely to be made independently; the role of an auto mechanic focuses less fully on foundations in mathematics and science than on the role of an engineer because tasks are more routine. Symbolic, syntactical, and value components might be minimal in occupational training programs, where emphasis is placed on performing existing tasks rather than on adapting them to new situations or inquiring about how they may be performed more effectively.

ACADEMIC FIELDS AND COURSE PLANNING

The contextual filters model of course planning we introduced earlier emphasizes the important role faculty attribute to their disciplines and career fields. Using this model, we found that assumptions underlying course planning and the influences on the process vary dramatically for different teaching fields. The importance of each influence also varies, but less dramatically, with the type of college. Thus, after describing the "content" part of the model, which captures these influences, we will focus on differences and similarities among academic fields.

In the general model, *content influences*—the field taught, the instructor's training in it, and the educational beliefs typically associated with it—most strongly influence how faculty members plan courses. Only after these field-specific influences have been taken into account does college context seem to influence a faculty member's planning significantly. Thus, we view *contextual considerations,* including the students and the specific college setting, as being mediators of the content influences on planning, rather than primary determiners of educational decisions. Later we will discuss more completely the contextual considerations, some external, some organizational, that cause faculty to modify their plans, especially as they translate them to instructional activities. Here we focus on content influences.

To illustrate these influences, we will describe perspectives of faculty members teaching in four clusters of fields that exhibit similar beliefs about the nature of the discipline and the purposes of education. Although faculty members teaching in a given discipline or group of related disciplines often report similar perspectives in course planning, not all faculty members within a discipline think just alike. Because of their particular backgrounds, prior teaching experiences, and other factors, as well as their teaching context, a few faculty members in each field will plan quite differently from their colleagues. Thus, there are some variations within fields, as well as the "typical" patterns we portray.

Content and Background Considerations

The three sets of influences in the "content and background" section of the contextual filters model are elaborated in Figure 7-2.

On the left side of Figure 7-2 we show important influences on course planning based on faculty's own characteristics and background, including training in an academic field. These influences stem from relatively stable values and beliefs about the world. For most faculty, scholarly training is the strongest influence, followed by teaching experience and educational beliefs. Religious and political beliefs influence faculty only in specific settings and disciplines. Only a few faculty report pedagogical training, thus, it influences only these few.

Moving to the right in Figure 7-2, we show three key faculty views of their academic fields. This simplified representation of several discipline orientations described by Dressel and Marcus seems to encompass the views of most faculty. Among faculty teaching introductory courses in several general education and collegiate career fields, we found the three views of the field to be about equally common: (1) as an organized body of knowledge, (2) as a group of scholars exploring the world or explaining phenomena, and (3) as a set of skills to be mastered and applied. The view chosen, however, depends heavily on one's field.

Social science and humanities instructors, in contrast to science instructors, more frequently view their disciplines as groups of individuals exploring common related interests, values, and phenomena, and as the methods of inquiry used by these groups rather than as organized bodies of knowledge. As shown by the direction of the arrows in Figure 7-2, faculty characteristics and disciplinary background influence their views of the teaching field more than the reverse.

The third "content" segment of the model includes seven different beliefs about the purposes of education. Faculty members may endorse more than one of these beliefs, but they seldom endorse all with equal fervor. Nearly all faculty endorsed "effective thinking" as an important purpose, yet "concept learning" and "students' personal and

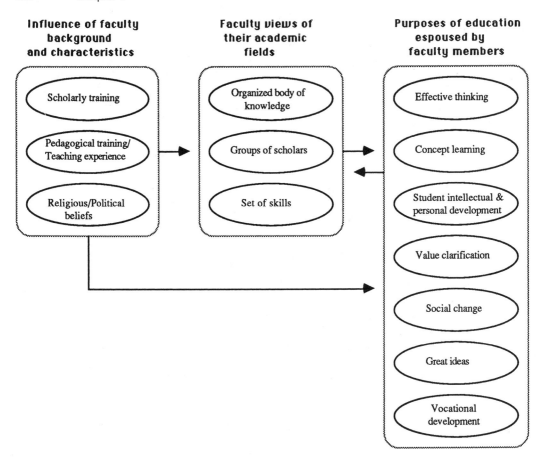

FIGURE 7-2   Content and Background Influences on Course Planning:
A General Framework

Source: Reprinted by permission of the National Center for Research to Improve Postsecondary
Teaching and Learning, The University of Michigan.

intellectual development" are the two beliefs
that seem to operate as they plan courses. In
fact, after early studies, we suspected that
faculty course planning styles were broadly
grouped into two discipline-related categories: (1) faculty whose decisions were discipline-identified and content-centered and
who viewed their roles as transmitting and
replicating knowledge for students, and (2)
faculty who were less discipline-identified,
who saw themselves as sharing interests and
perspectives with colleagues in their fields,

and who viewed their role as promoting student growth or skill acquisition (Stark,
Lowther, Bentley, & Martens, 1990).

To elaborate, "concept learning" usually
includes learning disciplinary and interdisciplinary concepts, understanding modes of inquiry, learning great ideas of the field, and
understanding the relations among ideas. In
part, this educational purpose is a composite
of responses that might be viewed as learning
a discipline for its own inherent interest or
value. "Student intellectual and personal de-

velopment" is also an umbrella concept we derived from faculty responses to a group of related objectives such as teaching students to search for meaning, integrate ideas, explore diverse viewpoints, and develop a desire to investigate further on their own. We elaborated several components of these two emphases and the extent to which a broad sample of faculty members endorsed them (see Chapter 6, Table 6-2). Emphasis on concept learning is consistent with the view of the academic field as an organized body of knowledge, whereas emphasis on the personal and intellectual development of students, value clarification, and social change are more consistent with views of one's field as a set of scholars pursuing related interests.

Figure 7-2 indicates a reciprocal relationship between faculty views of their academic fields and the purposes they espouse for education. Based on our conversations with faculty, the interaction between these elements is dynamic—that is, changing one's view of the discipline may change one's beliefs about educational purposes, or the reverse. Faculty background may also directly influence faculty beliefs about educational purpose, without being modified by a disciplinary view. A common example is the case of a faculty member teaching in a denominational college who adheres to the college's religiously defined purpose, regardless of the field taught.

Interviews with faculty suggested that only very small variations in academic plans could be attributed to an instructor's gender, academic rank, or the type of college in which he or she teaches; the absence of these personal and institutional characteristics from the model reflects their slight influence. In contrast, major differences seem to result from the different assumptions about educational purpose that faculty bring to the course planning process based on their disciplinary backgrounds and view of their academic field. Academic fields affect purpose, con-

tent, and sequence and also help determine which factors in the college environment will modify the instructor's desired plan. Furthermore, these relations are as strong or stronger for the same faculty members planning an advanced course. (Stark & Shaw, c. 1990).

K. Patricia Cross and Thomas Angelo, who constructed a Teaching Goals Inventory in conjunction with their efforts to help teachers assess classroom learning, came to a similar conclusion. Among teachers from community colleges and four-year colleges they found that faculty volunteered six general areas of educational goals: (1) higher order thinking skills, (2) basic academic skills, (3) discipline-specific knowledge and skills, (4) liberal education (a goal we believe merits further explanation), (5) academic values, and (6) personal development. Cross and Angelo concluded that "teacher priorities are related more to the teaching discipline than to any other factor we were able to identify. . . . Generally speaking, each disciplinary area identified different goals" (Cross, 1992).

Another reinforcing set of studies was done by Janet Donald who examined specific teaching concepts. Assuming that disciplines are the key organizing structures for education and that education should train future experts in these existing fields, Donald (1983) explored faculty selection of concepts for students in various fields, and later (1990) major characteristics of disciplines in such inquiry activities as validation processes and truth criteria. She found that the validation processes and truth criteria of a field govern "both how and what is learned" in the classroom. In the study of validation processes, Donald paired each of three disciplines from arts and sciences with a related applied field: physics and engineering, psychology and education, and English literature and English language. She found that empirical evidence was most often trusted in the sciences, and peer judgment review in the humanities; the social sciences fell closer to the natural sciences in their reliance on evidence. Furthermore, the use of conflicting evidence as a validation model was used more in pure fields than in applied fields. Donald concluded that the pure fields were clearer about their models, while the applied fields use eclectic models. She argued, however, that these criteria acknowledged by faculty need to be integrated more fully into the classroom as organizing schemes for students. In her view, the basic difference between an introductory course and an advanced course should be that advanced courses teach students more about conceptual analysis and modes of inquiry in the field, including validation processes and truth criteria. As in our own studies, Donald apparently found faculty concentrating more on facts and concepts than on the syntactical component (the methods of inquiry) of their fields.

Four Illustrative Profiles of Course Planning

To illustrate the influence of academic fields on course planning, we present four profiles: humanities, science and social science, language skills, and a career field. Each of the profiles (based on the "typical" cases of literature, biology, English composition, and business) provides a rough sketch of the general teaching orientation of a group of academic fields. Since the purpose of education strongly influences each profile, it is not surprising to find that the groups are related to Phenix's categories. The humanities group, illustrated by literature, jointly characterizes the synoptic disciplines and the aesthetic substantive disciplines. The science/social science group, illustrated by biology, portrays the empiric substantive disciplines, whereas the language skills group, illustrated by English composition, represents the symbolic disciplines. Because Phenix's scheme did not include career fields, we have chosen busi-

ness as a very common enterprising field. (In an earlier technical report, we provided graphic representations of each of the profiles that we describe here. For the technical and statistical detail, see Stark, Lowther, Bentley, et al., 1990a.)

Profile 1: Synoptic and Substantive Aesthetic Fields (Illustrative Case: Literature)

While the orientation of synoptic and substantive aesthetic fields is exemplified in our particular sample by literature instructors, with some variations it also describes many other humanities faculty such as those teaching fine arts appreciation courses and history. Faculty members teaching introductory literature courses attribute strong influence on course planning to their scholarly training but very little influence to pedagogical training. (Typically, these faculty members have had little formal training to teach.) Many of these instructors view their field of literature as a group of scholars who pursue related interests. Literature faculty stand out from others in the emphasis they place on values clarification and on students' intellectual and personal development as key educational purposes. They use exposure to literature, sometimes including "great ideas," as a way to achieve these outcomes. Often, but not always, clarifying values may be linked with concern for social causes. They tend to select content to maximize students' personal development, enjoyment, search for meaning in life, ability to solve problems, and ability to investigate independently.

For literature teachers, establishing course objectives seems less important than for faculty in many other fields; possibly the specific literature chosen for study and the activities based on this literature constitute both the medium and the message. That is, the materials chosen incorporate the objectives of the course within them; choosing and arranging materials are not easily separated from choosing learning activities.

Profile 2: Substantive Empiric Fields (Illustrative Case: Biology)

This orientation toward concept learning in an organized body of knowledge is exemplified by biology but also fits sociology and psychology quite well. Biology instructors attribute strong influence to their scholarly training; a view of biology as an organized body of knowledge predominates, including sets of principles, operations, and a mode of inquiry. While fostering effective thinking, biology instructors hope to teach the organized concepts and principles of their discipline to students. They are committed to concept learning as the primary educational purpose. Some biologists, however, are particularly interested in each of the other educational purposes; for example, some are interested in social causes such as environmental concerns, while others may be interested in the relation of biology and values clarification. Although they did not attach extremely high importance to vocational purposes, biology instructors were more sympathetic toward them than, say, literature instructors. Possibly this is because they are responsible for many introductory biology students who contemplate careers in the various health-related fields.

Biology instructors are more concerned with selecting and arranging content than are faculty in some other fields. The selection of content is related to their view that concepts are to be learned. Within the field, arrangement of material is a topic for consideration, or even debate, because the molecular biologists believe in starting with small life units and moving toward more comprehensive views, while the ecologists may take the reverse position.

Profile 3: Symbolic Communication Fields (Illustrative Case: English Composition)

The profile for symbolic fields is exemplified by English composition instructors, but to varying degrees it fits introductory mathematics and romance languages, each of which is similarly concerned with symbol systems. Some aspects of it may generalize to other courses that teach skills, rather than concepts.

English composition instructors stand out from others because they believe they are engaged in teaching students a body of skills to be learned and applied. To some extent, they may also be interested in selecting content to ensure the development of basic skills useful in problem solving, work, and career choice. Although they may belong to a community of scholars with respect to other courses they teach, such as in literature, they do not see the field of composition as either an organized body of knowledge or as a group of scholars. English composition teachers also attribute relatively strong influence to pedagogical training and teaching experience. This may be due to their background, which often includes pedagogical training and high school teaching. Alternatively, it may be due, in part, to heavy recent emphasis on pedagogy in various national associations of composition instructors. Perhaps linked with this background and emphasis, studies of teaching and learning are often a modestly important influence for composition teachers, whereas no other faculty group indicated attention to such studies. Beyond effective thinking, English composition instructors tend to espouse a variety of educational purposes for their students, and they try to achieve multiple purposes through the types of writing assignments students pursue.

English composition faculty members tend to see writing as an active, not passive, educational process. Thus, both student characteristics and student goals are important. Perhaps because composition instructors' roles are those of collegewide service, college and program mission are important contextual influences for them. Possibly because the skills to be learned are already well defined, composition faculty less often say they establish goals for the course or select subject matter. Rather, they emphasize selecting learning activities.

Profile 4: An Enterprising/Production Career Field (Illustrative Case: Business)

Of the four profiles illustrated here, instructors teaching business administration courses least often considered either their scholarly or pedagogical training as an extremely strong influence on course planning. They drew instead on work experience and employer needs outside academe. Business instructors did not strongly endorse a view of their field as a group of scholars; rather they characterized it as both an organized body of knowledge and a set of skills. Not surprisingly, among several educational purposes that are important to business instructors, an interest in the vocational development of students (including the search for an appropriate career) differentiates them from the other profiles we have discussed. In contrast, learning the "great ideas" is minimally important to business faculty. To business faculty, students' goals are more important than their characteristics, also a reversal from profiles based on the disciplinary fields.

In its emphasis on vocational purpose and the importance of student goals, this profile for business resembles that for the other collegiate career studies we examined, namely nursing and educational psychology. In other respects, however, the three professional fields we studied diverged, probably because they deal with different service sectors. Because schemes for classifying the pro-

fessional fields are still underdeveloped, we are not able to present a cluster. Experience leads us to speculate, however, that we might find identifiable clusters among the production service (enterprising) fields, like business; among the human client service fields (like nursing); among information service fields (like education and library science), and among the artistic fields of performing arts. We have noted, for example, that fields serving human clients tend to consciously foster personal development among students to prepare them for client interaction, including attention to appropriate service attitudes and professional commitment (including professional identity and professional ethics). Because many faculty members in some human service fields such as nursing are female, we remain unsure if this orientation is due to the service/technical component or to gender composition.

Mapping the Fields on Content Dimensions

Using the statistical procedure of discriminant analysis we graphically mapped the fields we studied according to the influences they assigned to content and background. The resulting map of fields in Figure 7-3 shows that we were able to separate the fields on two composite dimensions with fields nearest each other in the figure being similar on the dimensions that characterize the axes. In this case, based on their proximity along the horizontal axis, mathematics, nursing, and language instructors share an orientation related to vocational training and acknowledge the influence of pedagogy in their background. In this respect, they differ most from the orientation shared by history and literature instructors who are concerned with student development and more likely to acknowledge their own political and religious beliefs as entering their course planning. As displayed on the vertical dimension, however, mathe-

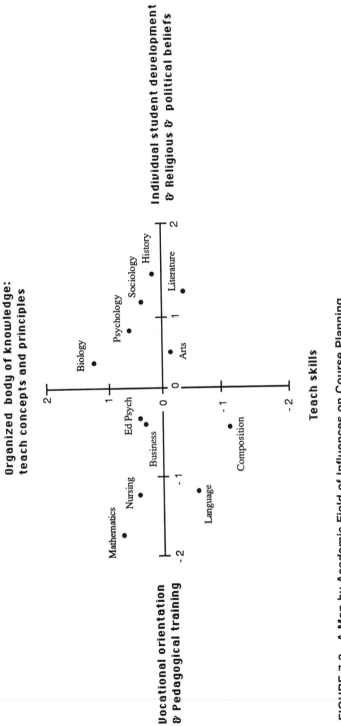

FIGURE 7-3 A Map by Academic Field of Influences on Course Planning

Source: From *Planning Introductory College Courses: A Synopsis of Findings* by Stark, Lowther, Bentley, et al. (1990), p. 6. Reprinted by permission of the National Center for Research to Improve Postsecondary Teaching and Learning, The University of Michigan.

matics and language instructors may be distinguished from each other in a different respect; the math instructors are more concerned with teaching concepts and the language instructors with teaching skills.

Although we have emphasized how the disciplines tend to differ on our model of course planning, we must not convey the idea that faculty in a particular field reported unanimous views or identical behavior. There was considerable variation within disciplines on certain aspects of content and background influences. Some of this lack of consensus may be due to variations in college type. A biologist teaching in a community college, for example, may attend to local mission seriously and espouse vocational orientation somewhat more strongly than a biologist teaching in a research university. These variations are small in comparison to the differences among disciplines. Our studies have led us to conclude that to understand influences on the development of academic plans in a very diverse higher education enterprise, we must first focus on a single academic field (or at most, some closely related fields) and then specify a particular type of college context.

ACADEMIC FIELDS AND PROGRAM PLANNING

Learning can be structured in many ways to help the learner achieve order, continuity, consistency, coherence and integration. One organizing structure in American higher education is the major field, a set of courses and experiences intended to give students a specialized base of knowledge in an academic or collegiate career study. This knowledge base may include a common vocabulary, an understanding of how scholars in this field approach problems, and the relation of this field to other fields and to society. The organization of the knowledge base is influenced strongly by the structure of the academic field—that is, by the influence of the disci-

pline or professional practice community. The term *major field* is often used synonymously with *program*. In the case of disciplines, a more specific definition of a major may be a "program of concentrated study that constitutes the *intellectual center* for students' undergraduate learning" (Association of American Colleges, 1992, p. 2). In professional programs, the concentration has a different aim—to provide graduates with *entry-level competence* in a reasonably well defined career field.

In this section, we will first discuss influences on program plans in disciplinary majors, then consider influences on collegiate career study programs that prepare students for entry to professions after four or five years of college study. In discussing program planning, we rely heavily on two studies. The first is our analysis of responses made by several academic fields (mostly disciplines) to the Association of American Colleges project which challenged them to redefine their major programs with greater coherence (Lattuca & Stark, 1994). The second is a comparative study of goals and processes in several undergraduate professional programs (Stark, Lowther, Hagerty, & Orczyk, 1988; Stark, Lowther, & Hagerty, 1986, 1987a, 1987b). We also mention the applicable work of researchers working on similar questions.

Disciplinary Major Programs in Arts and Sciences

Earlier we described several types of major programs that are offered under the rubric of liberal arts or arts and sciences. These include majors in a single academic discipline, double or interdisciplinary majors encompassing more than one discipline, general studies majors that may not have a "study in depth" component, and preprofessional majors that may be especially designed to meet entrance requirements to graduate professional schools such as law or medicine. Our primary focus here is on the most common major, pursued in a single academic discipline.

At the Association of American Colleges (AAC), the Liberal Learning and the Arts and Sciences Project was aimed at improving discipline majors. The work of this project provided us a unique opportunity to better understand how faculty think about majors. While acknowledging that education cannot occur apart from specific content, the AAC argued that students have the right to assume that their education will provide more than the simple coverage of unconnected subjects.

The challenge, outlined in *Liberal Learning and the Arts and Sciences Major: The Challenge of Connecting Learning* (Association of American Colleges, 1991a), urged faculty to participate actively in reinvigorating the college curriculum. To meet the challenge, the AAC asked faculty task forces in each of ten disciplines to grapple with what the content and structure of the major should be to achieve three goals: coherence, connectedness, and critical perspective, defined as shown in Table 7-1. The different ways in which the fields addressed this challenge—

TABLE 7-1   The Challenges Presented to Faculty in the Major Fields by the Association of American Colleges

Curricular Coherence

A shared understanding of what study in the field should accomplish. Must include a set of goals for student achievement, a curricular design that encourages attainment of these goals, a way of communicating them to students, and a way to assess the degree to which the aims are achieved.

Curricular coherence depends on the sequential organization of knowledge and techniques; thus, the major should have a beginning, a middle, and an end. A core set of courses should establish an intellectual agenda for the major. Students need to know how each course contributes to their overall educational experience.

Critical Perspectives

The development of a critical perspective requires that students become open to criticism, that they challenge their own views, and that they become willing to revise what they assumed was certain. Faculty must help students gain confidence in discourse of the field, subject it to sophisticated questions, and connect the proposals of their fields to those of other fields. Students must learn to discern when and for what instances an issue or argument is valid. Faculty must join disparate cross-disciplinary points of view to foster a critical perspective in students.

Connecting Learning

Making connections with other forms of knowledge: students must be introduced to unsuspected relationships often encountered at the boundaries of a field.

Applying learning to a wider world: students must be helped to see the connections between primary issues in their field and their own significant interests and concerns, including public issues and personal experience.

Inclusiveness

The field must be divested of barriers and obstacles to the participation of underrepresented students who may not fit traditional expectations. Multiple points of entry to study in depth should be created.

Source: Condensed from *The Challenge of Connecting Learning*, Association of American Colleges, 1991.

especially what they chose to describe and not to describe in the programs they recommended for students—give an informative picture of how faculty view their teaching in these particular disciplines.

Task forces, consisting of scholars appointed by their respective learned societies, were established in the fields of biology, economics, history, mathematics, philosophy, physics, political science, psychology, religion, and sociology. We analyzed and described the various approaches they took as revealed in *Liberal Learning and the Arts and Sciences: Reports from the Fields* (Association of American Colleges, 1991b). Content analysis allowed us to compare the separate disciplinary visions of a coherent curriculum.

We detected patterns that reflect the same enduring epistemological differences among the disciplines that we found in our studies of course planning; they reinforce patterns suggested by theorists such as Kuhn, Phenix, and Dressel and Marcus and researchers like Becher and Donald (1983) who explored conceptual structures actually used in college courses. We analyzed reports from each of the ten disciplines separately, but for simplicity we report our findings here in three broad traditional groupings of disciplines, the sciences, the social sciences, and the humanities. Our results are summarized in Table 7-2 (see Lattuca & Stark, 1994, 1995).

Curricular Coherence

In general, the science task forces had little difficulty describing curricular coherence in the major. As we have noted, mathematics and science fields typically view their disciplines as bodies of organized knowledge exhibiting high levels of interrelatedness among concepts, principles, and operations. Consequently, many of these faculty members viewed their programs, like their courses, as being tightly coordinated, highly interrelated,

and hierarchical, with a requisite order prescribed—by definition, coherent.

The concept of curricular coherence proved troublesome or alien, however, for most disciplines in social sciences and humanities. Although social science faculty (specifically sociology and psychology instructors) also viewed their disciplines as having high levels of interrelatedness among concepts and principles, they did not generally describe their courses or programs as either tightly coordinated, interrelated, or proceeding in any established sequence. Rather, particularly in sociology, the norm was to provide little curricular coordination, thus maintaining considerable autonomy and discretion for the instructor. History instructors saw even fewer relationships between concepts and principles in their fields, programs, and courses, than did instructors in sociology and psychology. The task force report brought to mind the words of a department head in history we once asked about coherence: "There's an assumption in your question that coherence is good," he said. "To the contrary, the best thing we can do for our students is to turn good teachers loose in the classroom to go in any direction they do best. Coherence is not one of our big goals."

Critical Perspectives

Science task forces gave little attention to critical perspective compared to the explicit, and sometimes expansive, discussions of this topic in the humanities and social sciences reports. The lack of emphasis on critical perspectives in the sciences is consistent with strong consensus on paradigms in these fields. In our earlier interviews with faculty about course planning, science faculty suggested that the need to spend time covering principles of the field and building a firm foundation for later courses prompted them to postpone introducing students to varying perspectives and controversies within the disci-

TABLE 7-2   Responses by Discipline to the Challenge of Connecting Learning in the Major

	Science and Mathematics	Social Studies	Humanities
Curricular coherence Coherent design	Integration of knowledge and skills readily addressed. Capstone courses and experiences advocated.	Problematic. Content is eclectic, but coherence can be enhanced.	Mixed response from fields. Some objected to or avoided idea. Some attempted to meet challenge.
Goals	Stressed need for local department variation and autonomy	Need for local department variation and autonomy.	Need for local department variation and autonomy.
Sequential learning	Possible to sequence. Some fields have natural sequence.	Sequential learning is unfamiliar, but potential.	Objections to prescribed sequences raised.
Critical perspectives	Unfamiliar. Fairly common belief in scientific method as primary perspective.	Addressed in varying ways. Important; diverse approaches acceptable.	Stressed; linked with cultural and humanistic sensitivity. Importance of context.
Connecting learning with other fields, life, and career	Critical of own efforts to help students connect.	Somewhat more confident that connections are made across disciplines. Few specifics.	Mixed response from fields. Assumed emphasis on connectedness.
Inclusiveness	Should be more open to students with diverse preparation. Emphasized pedagogy.	Suggested altering content, rather than pedagogy.	Stressed inclusiveness in terms of course content and learning environments.

pline until well into the major. Concern for building a foundation is not manifested as strongly among faculty in the humanities and social sciences, which thrive on argumentation and on the comparison of varied perspectives (Stark, Lowther, Ryan, et al., 1988). Donald's studies (1983, 1990) corroborate these results from a different perspective. She found that most science faculty accepted em-

pirical evidence as validation based on consensus about the value of empiricism, whereas faculty in humanities and social sciences relied on peer review, reflecting agreement to respect varied perspectives among scholars.

The results are also consistent with the reports of those who have used the Biglan model documenting that faculty in "hard" disciplines such as the sciences spend less time debating perspectives and methods than do those in the "soft" fields. Indeed, a glance at news media reports following any national conference of humanities scholars reveals the vastly different perspectives they bring to their fields and the extensive and lively debates that sometimes result. Science conferences, in contrast, while also reporting differences in views, are likely to depend on confirming empirical evidence for resolution of the issues.

Connecting Learning

Given their nature and content, one might expect that the humanities and social science fields could readily create major programs that provide opportunities for connecting learning. In fact, faculty in some of these fields do see their disciplines as linked to social problems. For example, some social science faculty, particularly in sociology, report that teaching students to work for important social causes to "make the world a better place" is an important educational purpose, thus connecting education with the world outside the college or university. In contrast, mathematics and biology faculty less often emphasize applications to world social or scientific problems in their fields (Lattuca & Stark, 1994; Stark, Lowther, Ryan, et al., 1988). This comparative lack of attention is reflected in the science task force reports, which make general, rather than specific, statements of the connections of the sciences with social problems.

While social science faculty mentioned numerous opportunities for connecting students' learning to the external world, they seldom mentioned the connections of their fields with other disciplines. Humanities task forces, in particular the history and religion groups, stressed linkages and the need for cross-disciplinary fertilization, reminding us of Phenix's view of them as the fields that provide a synoptic (or integrative) view.

In brief, we found that the academic disciplines that exhibited difficulty in defining and describing curricular coherence could readily describe critical perspectives. The reverse was also true: Those who easily defined coherence had little need for more than one perspective. These are the "two [academic] cultures" originally described by C. P. Snow (1959). Even in an era of widespread discussion about curricular reform, faculty members do not seem able to respond favorably to curricular conceptions held by the academic culture to which they do not belong. The consequences of these separate views are seen in every curriculum committee and faculty meeting.

Yet, when we probe the views of specific disciplines within the broad groupings of humanities, social science, and science, we find progressions of fields along various dimensions, and some disciplines with members in more than one of the cultures. For example, in different respects, sociology programs resemble both history programs and psychology programs. Psychology faculty resemble sociology faculty in their views of critical perspectives but biology programs in their orientation toward coherence. Indeed, perhaps because they share characteristics of two different groups of fields, colleges variously place psychology in either the natural science or the social science division; some place history with humanities and others with social sciences. We believe it is more useful to view disciplines as varying along these dimensions than as occupying discrete categories. The variations provide important foundations to build connectedness where appropriate among fields in curriculum planning.

With a few exceptions, faculty in academic disciplines spent little time describing the connectedness of their major programs to society. The influences on planning in these programs come from the discipline orientations of the faculty themselves. External influences act through the disciplinary and discourse communities of scholars as they develop their own internal views of coherence and connectedness.

Undergraduate Professional Major Programs

In contrast to the disciplines, majors in collegiate career studies are, by definition, "connected." They are linked to the foundational disciplines from which they draw their conceptual knowledge bases, to practice settings and communities, and sometimes to other professional fields with which they collaborate to solve problems and provide service and technical expertise in society. The occupations and professions are predominantly interdisciplinary, drawing from the base disciplines, from their relationships with society, and from professional communities. Researchers have only begun to explore the ideologies and paradigms that may influence educational strategies in various collegiate career studies. But we know that the idea of connecting learning with other subjects and with life's activities is an extremely familiar and important factor when faculty members in undergraduate career programs develop curricula (Stark, Lowther, & Hagerty, l986).

External influences, originating in society, operate on collegiate career study programs directly and strongly. Professional community influences include client orientations, professional certification requirements, accreditation standards, codes of professional ethics, job market fluctuations, and active alumni involvement. Coherence is provided by the ultimate goal of preparing a competent professional worker, who may have to meet external certification criteria to enter the practice field.

Organizational influences can act strongly on these career programs as well. Most undergraduate professional majors rely for conceptual foundation courses on discipline programs within the college or university,

making consultation, and often compromise, necessary. In these negotiations, there may be a "pecking order," dictating whether the program is sufficiently central to the university mission to be credible and receive support from the foundation group. For example, in colleges originating as normal schools that retain strong public missions, human service fields such as education, social work, and nursing may be large and highly valued programs with strong negotiating power. In research universities hoping to attract external funding and prestige, production/enterprising fields like engineering and business may appear more central than human services. Collegiate career study meets demands for relevant education that is supposed to return an investment to society. But forces within the colleges and universities may interpret that relevance in different ways.

In fact, we have found that a key characteristic differentiating the undergraduate professional programs is the extent to which their faculty perceive that they have support from society and prestige within their colleges and universities. Social work, nursing, and education perceive low support, whereas pharmacy, engineering, and business perceive strong societal support and higher prestige within the university. Architecture and journalism faculty see themselves as garnering moderate support. These perceptions of support may be based partly on the gender make-up of these fields and on the professional rewards and salaries to be anticipated (Stark, Lowther, & Hagerty,1987a).

Patterns of internal influence, parallel to the disciplinary paradigms, have not been fully clarified for the professional programs. New ideas seem more often to come through change in society and in practitioner roles than through changes in the thinking of scholars within the field. Of course, it may be unrealistic to try to separate internal influence from external influence for career fields where faculty members have often had (and continue to have) substantial experience as practitioners.

Curricular Dimensions of Undergraduate Professional Programs

On the basis of the fivefold typology of professional field characteristics we proposed earlier (and which parallels the work of Dressel and Marcus for disciplines), we have elaborated some patterns of curriculum influence

for the collegiate career study programs. We seek to better explain differences and similarities among several of the undergraduate programs based on the five dimensions: service role, connections with other fields, symbol systems and discourse communities, inquiry methods, and values. Like the disciplines, the professional fields may be arranged in order of their variations on several of these dimensions. A summary of our thinking is given in Table 7-3. In the development that follows,

TABLE 7-3   A Typology of Professional Fields on Postulated Curriculum Dimensions

Service and Technical Roles (Substance)	Problems and Connections (Conjunctions)	Symbol System (Symbolics)	Inquiry Methods (Syntactics)	Values for New Professionals (Values)
Human client service Nursing ( ) Social work Pharmacy	Sciences and social sciences Tight practice setting Limited settings	Technical (closed) and interpersonal (open)	Eclectic Empirical	High ethical emphasis High professional identity Commitment
Information service Education ( ) Library science Journalism	Social sciences Loose practice setting	Eclectic Nontechnical (open)	Eclectic Empirical and experiential	Mixed Varies by field
Production/enterprise service Business Engineering ( ) Architecture	Sciences, social sciences, humanities (field-specific) Broad practice setting	Mixed	Pragmatic	Low ethical emphasis Low professional identity
Artistic service Music Art ( ) Dance Drama	Humanities Loose and broad practice setting	Art forms (closed)	Experiential Peer review Aesthetic	Low ethical emphasis Individualized

Note: The typology was devised by Stark to parallel Dressel and Marcus's adaptation of Phenix's realms of meaning for the disciplines.

we will combine commentary on the fields themselves with related knowledge about how their characteristics are manifested in academic plans for the majors.

Service/Technical Role [Substantive Component].

In all professional programs, the faculty are concerned with *conceptual competence* and *technical competence.* These competences indicate that students have learned the knowledge base of the profession and the technical skills needed to practice. Of course, these concepts and skills are related to the type of service the profession provides, and each field may exhibit a different degree of certainty about what competence is essential. Societal values determine what is central for some of the service and technical sectors, whereas others have more autonomy. The conceptual and technical skills required of professionals in the human services fields are clearly prescribed and are often rigorously demanded of graduates, both by their professors and by society. Competence in the health services, for example, is controlled by external licensing. Entrance into the business field, on the other hand, is not dependent on a license or even a college degree; general skills may be as useful as strongly technical skills. Only selected business subspecialities, such as certified public accountancy, are publicly regulated.

We detect a pattern of gradual decrease in consensus on the conceptual and technical skills to be taught and learned as one proceeds from the human services toward the artistic services (from top to bottom in Table 7-3). This change is only partly due to the type of service provided. For example, the number of different settings in which a professional may practice gets broader as one moves down the table. Nurses and pharmacists practice in restricted settings, but a performing artist may exhibit her craft in an established theater or on a street corner. She needs no license to appear in either place.

Connections [Foundational/Conjunctive Component].

These variations in practice settings and in regulation of technical competence also lead to different types of linkages with the practice field. In general, fields that are strongly regulated have close connections with the practice community and supervise their students as they develop *integrative competence*—the ability to meld concepts and skills in practice. Not surprisingly, faculty in these fields also spend considerable time debating the balance of theory and practice and the type of integrating experience to be provided. This connection with the practice field is very tight for the human client fields, involving careful supervision and socialization. It becomes looser as one proceeds downward in Table 7-3. Relatively few programs in journalism or business require supervised practica or internships, although they may encourage students to obtain externships and gain experience on their own. This speculative pattern changes its dimensions, however, when one reaches the artistic service sector. In architecture, which shares some characteristics with the creative arts, students complete practical design projects which are publicly critiqued and obtain formal externships following graduation and before licensure. Such relationships involving creative endeavors are more individualized than the formally structured programmatic capstone field experience in clinical settings such as in nursing, social work, and education. Students in formal creative arts programs may be "apprenticed" to a master teacher, subsequently presenting a recital or other demonstration of their progress. The relationship between teacher and student in the apprentice setting is more flexible, since it may not involve an established segment of the practice community as does work in clinical settings.

Discourse Communities [Symbolic Systems].

All collegiate career fields are

concerned with developing standard communication competence in reading, writing, and speaking. In contrast to the disciplines, most career fields also emphasize interpersonal skills for client relations. We speculate that the progression of symbolic systems from closed to open presents a pattern somewhat reversed from that of the conjunctive component we have just discussed. That is, the weaker the linkages with external professional communities, the more closed the symbol system. For example, the creative professions have symbolic systems that are mostly closed to the lay public; although nonperformers may appreciate the arts, they cannot use or talk about art, music, and dance in the same way professionals do without considerable practice and education. In contrast, the production/enterprise services (such as business) and the information services have vocabularies and symbol systems reasonably available to those without much specialized training. Human services employ both a closed symbol system (technical language in the vocabulary of nurses and pharmacists) and an open symbolic system in the important interpersonal skills.

Methods of Inquiry [Syntactical Component].

The methods of inquiry used by faculty in collegiate career fields are often eclectic. This is true partly because they are borrowed from one or more root disciplines. Another reason is that the range of questions to be addressed in applied fields depends on the diversity of settings to be studied. The broader the field, the greater the diversity of methods of inquiry needed. For example, in business the same methods cannot serve both accounting and organizational behavior. Likewise, in nursing and teaching, the methods of study to address problems of student learning differ from those to address administration or policy relationships with government.

In general, inquiry paradigms are weaker when the collegiate career study is based in "soft" parent disciplines, as is true for education and social work whose root disciplines are typically sociology and psychology. Paralleling its root fields of mathematics, physics and chemistry, engineering has a strong paradigm; in journalism, ambivalent about whether it is a professional field or one of the arts and sciences, faculty report no identifiable research paradigm that characterizes the field as a whole.

For the career fields, methods of inquiry are often slow to change because controversies about them often depend on events in the parent discipline. A current example is the debate over the value and appropriateness of quantitative and qualitative research paradigms that began in sociology and psychology but which now affects education, social work, and nursing as well.

Value Component.

On the basis of our studies, the clearest distinction among the collegiate career studies is based on the value component and divides undergraduate professional programs into two groups. The human service fields, particularly nursing, social work, and education, strongly emphasize the development of professional identity and ethics among students. In contrast, engineering and business not only fail to stress this aspect of professional education, but do not agree on what ethical standards exist (Stark, Lowther, & Hagerty, 1987a). A third group of collegiate career fields, such as journalism, pharmacy, and architecture, are ambivalent about devoting attention to this aspect of professional development. The ambivalent fields tend to belong to more than one service sector (for example, they espouse orientations toward human services and enterprising services simultaneously) and recently have been debating their relation to society and the practice communities and settings.

A related issue is the emphasis placed by these professional programs on *contextual competence*. This term refers to the extent to which the field values the student's understanding of the social, economic, and political context in which the profession is practiced. In general, the stronger the value orientation, the stronger the emphasis placed on providing students with a contextual orientation to practice in society, and the stronger the emphasis on technical competence to provide the service. We have no information on the arts in this regard. Were we to speculate, we believe that the creative arts have a weak value component except as they value freedom of individual expression and oppose control by societal norms.

Coherence, Connectedness, Critical Perspectives, and Academic Time

How might the faculty teaching in collegiate career study programs have addressed the issues of coherence, connectedness, and critical perspectives in the major, if they, like the disciplines discussed earlier, had been asked to do so? First, just as is true for the disciplines, the views of professional program faculty within a field tend to be similar, even in different types of colleges. So we assume that the response would be strongly influenced by the three factors we have discussed as components of the professional fields: the nature of the foundation disciplines, the strength of connection with the practice community, and the extent of agreement on both the conceptual knowledge base and the inquiry method.

We believe that the responses of undergraduate professional program faculty as they grappled with challenges such as those posed by the Association of American Colleges would show that those fields citing strong coherence in their programs would also demonstrate connectedness. But encouraging students to develop critical perspectives would be linked with the value component for professional fields—that is, with the development of professional identity. To select a few illustrations, engineering programs would describe themselves as strongly coherent because they draw consensus about concepts and methods to be learned from their parent fields in the sciences. But they might give short shrift to critical perspectives (as they do to professional identity) and might cite few examples of connectedness beyond their links with the scientific disciplines. Although lacking full consensus about inquiry methods, nursing programs would see their programs as coherent largely because of the strong connection with the practice community and the human service orientation. They would also emphasize critical perspectives as they urge their students to pursue the contextual background in which practice is undertaken and the ethical standards to deal with dilemmas. In contrast, the professional community for business is heterogeneous and loosely connected with educational programs. Thus, we expect, business professors would describe their programs as exhibiting some coherent structure but placing little emphasis on connectedness, and, lacking strong emphasis on professional identity or ethics, giving little mention to critical perspectives.

Another important influence collegiate career study fields would undoubtedly address as they considered any curricular challenge is the allocation of "curricular time." This is the question of how crowded the program is with requirements for students. What can be done to provide room for breadth and reflection, while still developing conceptual and technical competence? Such discussions are frequent and urgent in fields such as teacher education and architecture with structured knowledge bases, strong connections to practice communities, and commitment to supervising an integrative experience—or some combination of two of these characteristics.

Teacher education, facing certification requirements in most states for proficiency in a broad range of subjects in a major field and in pedagogy, as well as a lengthy internship experience, has become a five-year program in credit hour requirements, if not in name. Architecture, which generally involves students in some creative activity early in the college career, is typically a five-year program. Pharmacy, recently embroiled in a national discussion about time frames for its educational programs, is moving from five-year to six-year college degrees. For some fields, such as business and social work, curricular structure is looser and academic time slightly more flexible. Depending on the college or university policy, students may begin specialization in these fields at varying times, sometimes taking an introductory professional course as undergraduates but postponing formal professional study until graduate school.

The concerns of the collegiate career study programs for connections with their discourse communities, development of values such professional identity, connectedness with foundational disciplines, and methods of action inquiry are as inherent to their structure and educational planning as the characteristics of the disciplines that Phenix and others have astutely observed over the years.

Occupational Major Programs

Occupational majors, offered in two-year programs (or for shorter term certificates of competence) focus more on training for task performance and less on education for solving unstructured problems, than do the four-year programs we have labeled collegiate career studies. Many occupational programs are developed specifically to meet workforce needs of a local industry or business. Such academic plans may be tightly structured by the industrial needs, automatically achieving connectedness with the workplace, but leaving little autonomy for faculty to develop their own views about such program attributes as coherence or critical perspectives. Faculty may lack other aspects of planning autonomy as well; for example, many courses in automotive technology come prepackaged by instructional developers in the industry with manuals, videotapes, and practice exercises already prepared for the student to use. In some cases, too, the training may take place at the business site, rather than on the college campus. Instructors may be experts in the trade they teach but lack a college degree or other academic credentials considered typical for college teaching. There are many hundreds of such programs taught in the American community colleges.

Perhaps because of these circumstances, scholars have shown little interest in analyzing the attributes of academic plans in the occupational fields or in probing the views of faculty who teach them. The best we can do in our analysis is to speculate that influences on many occupational fields would resemble related professional fields in some respects. For example, programs to prepare library assistants, day care helpers, and dental assistants would likely share some of the emphases we have described for human service professional programs. Programs such as hospitality management and bakery management might share characteristics with other members of the enterprising group; commercial art and cosmetology with the professional creative artistic services. Beyond such obvious linkages, some occupational fields may not fit into our four-part classification of collegiate career study fields. Perhaps viewing them as guilds or trade associations would provide increased understanding of the structural dimensions that might be unique to occupational education fields.

Since occupational programs in community colleges continue to proliferate, preparing students for roles that they formerly learned through apprenticeships, researchers and policymakers need to study and understand this aspect of postsecondary curriculum more fully. The need for study is particularly urgent if educators judge it valuable to build linking relationships between occupational programs and such aspects of a students' program as basic skill development and general education. We now turn to such relationships informed by understanding of individual fields.

DESIGNING BALANCED COURSES AND PROGRAMS

We have observed that each academic field exerts strong influence on course and program planning, based on its structure, its value system, the types of problems it considers, its methods of inquiry, its symbols, and its scholarly or external practice community. Although we and others have grouped the disciplines and undergraduate professional fields in clusters based on similarities in these attributes, each field has unique and predominating patterns of academic planning. Most professors try to achieve coherence in their courses and programs by choosing and arranging subject matter in a way that seems logical to them and their close colleagues. They also try to make connections with students' lives and future lives. However, the choices instructors make may not seem as logical to students or even to colleagues from other fields. Similarly, connections may not be meaningful and therefore fail to encourage students' involvement and effort. The classifications of the fields we have discussed are useful in increasing awareness of these differences and the reasons for them. Once aware of the substantial variations by field, professors are often more receptive to sharing their ways of planning and teaching and welcome hearing how others plan. Faculty members, no less than their critics, can recognize the need to provide a

better balance between teaching the discipline and promoting other outcomes, such as students' intellectual growth or professional identity.

Using Influence Well: Achieving Balance

Despite their interest and good faith, the assumption that most faculty can move beyond casual interest in other disciplines and end their isolation without deliberate leadership is misguided. Influences on liberal arts fields, based in long tradition, tend to be relatively constant and internal; influences on collegiate career programs are external and more volatile, reflecting rapid changes in society's needs for competent professionals. In either case, separate fields pursue in relative isolation the patterns with which they are most familiar as they develop curriculum. The "connectedness" that may exist is not always put to deliberate use in academic planning.

In addition to negative rhetoric which provides little direction for improvement, there have been several substantive proposals to modify the isolation of the disciplines. In his 1987 book, *College: The Undergraduate Experience in America,* Ernest Boyer proposed that education should become a "seamless web" with integration between school and college levels, integration of liberal and professional studies, clearly articulated goals, and assessment that supports academic advising and curriculum development at all levels. Boyer claimed that colleges should become "learning communities" where discussion of varied points of view about all subjects, including education, would take place. *Integrity in the College Curriculum* also stressed that various aspects of knowledge should be integrated into a cumulative, coherent whole. These two reform reports did not fully develop specific recommendations for achieving the desired integration. They implied rather clearly, however, that faculty members themselves have integrated knowledge, know what needs to be done, and need only accept the responsibility of achieving this goal.

Dressel and Marcus (1982, p. 25) suggested that integration might be achieved by adapting the academic plan to the context in which the subsequent learning is to be used. They coined the term *contextual teaching* to represent a form of interdisciplinary teaching that could build on the disciplines. As Dressel and Marcus pointed out, the various organizing frameworks and characteristics of the disciplines are the familiar ground from which faculty develop courses and programs. Because these structures organize the disciplines as well as colleges and universities, curriculum improvements that advocate the wholesale overturn of these structures have been short lived. They therefore suggested that the disciplines must be used but in a "contextual" way. The context can be the application of a single discipline or several disciplines to a problem. In either case, teaching must focus on the ability to organize and apply knowledge rather than on the knowledge itself. Learning involves not only specific information but also thought, values, processes, materials, and structures for organizing the experiences and the environments in which the experiences will be provided. Thus, the teacher has the responsibility of understanding the context in which the learner is operating and the ways in which the learning is to be used.

Most suggestions for integration require dramatic changes in college organizational structure and relationships and thus are unlikely to be accepted. Dressel and Marcus, however, proposed that the strong influences of the fields can be viewed as assets rather than as liabilities. Acting on that assumption, we suggest that good course and program design are a matter of achieving balance in five interrelated areas:

1. The balances among the several key characteristics of an academic field (substance or service role, symbol systems, inquiry methods, values, and connections)

2. The balance between the broad educational purposes or rationales endorsed for learners and the specific goal of transmitting the content or substance of the field

3. The balance between coherence and critical perspectives

4. The balance between discourse with scholars within a specific field and those in related fields

5. The balance between connections with the world of scholarship and with its application in the world of work and life

Most professors will decide not to give equal weight to all possible factors within each of these types of balance, but most can profit from consciously reflecting on them with respect to planning courses and programs for majors.

For arts and sciences professors especially, the same balances are at issue (with potentially different decisions) when the academic plan is being created for general education. In a background paper prepared for the NIE Study Group that wrote *Involvement in Learning*, Zelda Gamson (1982) argued that undergraduates' education is "shaped by the interests and styles of the disciplines" (p. 4) and that this defeats its primary purpose of providing a liberal education. Gamson defined liberal education as "a reasoned discourse about questions that matter" (p. 29), and "a collective expression" about what the faculty believes important.

But which questions matter depends on which field you teach! If so, can there be such a thing as a "collective expression" of what is important? How do we create this reasoned discourse? Gamson and her colleagues (1984) described some principles of "generic learning" for general education on which to base such discussions: (1) life should set the agenda for the subjects to be considered; (2) the consideration of the chosen subjects should be comprehensive in scope; (3) the subjects should be treated in a critical and reflective way; and (4) the teaching strategies should aim toward integration. Paralleling closely the five balances we named, these four principles seem to provide a basis for discourse about general education that is relatively free of discipline cultures, if the discussants firmly resolve to keep their individual discipline cultures in check.

In the words of Dressel and Marcus (1982, p. xii), the primary problem in current college learning may not be with the disciplines but "rather that teachers, having become so immersed in the disciplines, no longer view(ed) themselves in relationship to the basic problems and concerns of mankind" (Dressel & Marcus, 1982, p. xii). Use of the disciplines as organizing frameworks either for knowledge or for programmatic structure does not, however, *inherently* result in narrowness or overspecialization. Rather, narrowness is a consequence of human choices.

Still, strong and effective plans for courses and programs within the both majors and general education require that instructors remain current with new advances in their fields, select sequences of material to help students learn progressively challenging material, and use instructional materials and resources that have proven successful. Conscientious curriculum designers will apply a variety of principles consistent with the traditions of their fields to develop effective plans that consider the learner, instructional processes, and evaluation. In the next sections we provide some alternatives that go beyond these basic activities of course and program planning and that focus on the five balances previously mentioned. These apply to a wide variety of fields but often escape professors' attention.

Balancing Attention to Characteristics of Academic Fields

Just as educators in collegiate career studies have been accused of focusing too intensely on the technical or substantive aspects of their fields, faculty in the liberal arts and science disciplines have been criticized for stressing the concepts and organization of the field and neglecting the development of enduring intellectual skills. The chief utility of reflecting on the typologies of disciplinary and career fields we have described is to focus faculty attention on aspects of their fields they tend to neglect in their planning. For example, instructors in the disciplines might ask if they are giving sufficient attention to the methods of inquiry of the field, thereby ensuring that students practice analytical skills. Are opportunities provided for students to go beyond learning the symbolic system of the field and actually use it in discourse with peers and other scholars? Do students understand the connections between their major and other fields? Are they asked to explore these connections deliberately? Can students identify and describe the value system that directs their attention to a problem in their major field and how it may differ from the perspective taken in a different field? In the undergraduate professional fields, the same questions apply but also include: Are students helped to make connections with the practice community? Are they helped to achieve a value orientation and code of ethics with regard to professional practice? Such questions require balanced attention in program planning to all of the five characteristics of an academic field, whether disciplinary or professional.

For instructors teaching introductory disciplinary courses in a general education program, reflecting on the characteristics of the field is similarly important and can prevent undue emphasis on discipline concepts with consequent neglect of other important purposes.

Balancing Purpose and Content

We have stressed broad underlying educational purposes as a beginning point in developing academic plans and noted that teaching students to think effectively is an important underlying rationale for many professors. Most faculty also endorse one or two other broad purposes, such as helping students to develop and enrich their lives as persons, to succeed as professional workers, or to implement social change. Because content and purpose are so closely related in developing academic plans, achieving balance in the major means constantly checking to see that content is not overshadowing broader purposes. For general education, this concern for balancing purpose and content has fostered experimentation with many interdisciplinary frameworks over the years. Some years ago, Bergquist compiled what he believed to be a comprehensive typology of innovative general education programs. The eight broad models he identified, defined in Figure 7-4 include heritage-based, thematic-based, competency-based, career-based, experience-based, student-based, values-based, and future-based. Bergquist arranged these possible frameworks in a conceptual circle along two axes, the poles of which are general–specific, and elective–prescriptive (Bergquist, Gould, & Greenberg, 1981, pp. 3–5).

Five of these eight themes are nearly identical to the various purposes or educational belief systems we have explored with faculty. (The "future-based" model may be a variant of the purpose we called "education for social change.") Notably missing, however, is a model based on effective thinking, which arguably undergirds all of the other models. Although faculty in collegiate career study programs were not typically included in these general education core programs based on the academic disciplines, we know that they, too, can relate to this list of models, at least when they are phrased as beliefs. An obvious question then arises: Is there potential for a core program or a set of distribution requirements that requires students to pursue some study in each of eight realms outlined by Bergquist, rather than choosing from the disciplines? Are these an alternative set to the experiences posed by the AAC, which are more closely driven by the disciplines? Is effective thinking a goal to be achieved by all of these models taken together as a total general education program, or by any one of them? Some colleges revising general education are selecting one of these domains to the exclusion of others. But including some experience in each domain would approach Gamson's criterion of comprehensiveness by encompassing most of the educational beliefs we have been identified among educators, both disciplinary and professional.

Interdisciplinary general education programs like those Bergquist examined may give lower division students a sense of the perspectives used by the academic community as a whole rather than attempting to initiate them into a specific disciplinary community of academics. Such an emphasis on multiple perspectives may be more popular with the humanities and social sciences faculties than with science faculties.

Balancing Coherence and Critical Perspectives

Coherence and critical perspectives are persistent themes of the recent era of curriculum reform. Although definitions differ, the public appears to view these as indicators that education has been successful. But we know

Each of the eight curricular models tends to be most closely associated with those models that are adjacent on the curricular circle and to differ profoundly from those models that appear on the opposite side of the circle. Though the curricular circle shows only a few of the numerous and complex dimensions that constitute the curriculum of a specific college, it provides a useful conceptual base for the categorization and description of curricular designs.

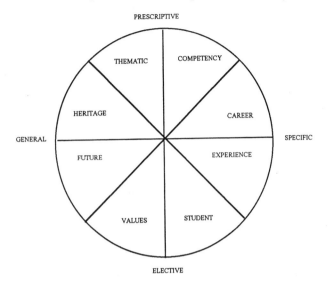

Key:

1. *Heritage-Based:* The curriculum is primarily designed to provide students with a clear and meaningful sense of their own cultural and historical background(s), thereby providing them with the knowledge and skills to deal with current and future problems associated with this heritage.
2. *Thematic-Based:* A specific, pressing problem or issue of our contemporary society is identified that encompasses a wide variety of academic disciplines; an educational program that will provide students with the resources needed to solve and/or cope with this problem or issue is then designed.
3. *Competency-Based:* A set of specific competencies which a student is to acquire and/or demonstrate prior to graduation is identified; educational resources (including course work) are developed, assembled or identified in order for the student to diagnose current levels and achieve desired levels of competence.
4. *Career-Based:* Programs are specifically designed to prepare students for a certain vocation, admissions to a professional training program, or a vocational decision-making process.
5. *Experienced-Based:* On-and-off campus experiences that are in some sense educational are created or provided; the college takes some responsibility for controlling the quality of the experiences, sequencing the experiences, and relating the learnings from these experiences to principles that have been conveyed through more traditional modes (lecture, discussions, seminars).
6. *Student-Based:* Students are allowed a significant role in determining: a) the nature of the formal educational experiences they are to receive, b) the ways in which these experiences are to be interpreted, and c) the criteria and means by which they are to be evaluated. Typically, some form of learning contract is developed between a student and mentor (teacher, advisor) or between several students (student-initiated and/or student-conducted courses).
7. Values-*Based:* Students are provided with the educational resources and experiences to clarify or expand on their current values or to acquire new values; these values are related to current social, political or religious issues or to the student's life and career plans.
8. *Future-Based:* Conditions are created for students to acquire knowledge, skills and attitudes that are appropriate to the creation of a desirable future or that are adaptive to a predictable future society.

FIGURE 7-4   A Typology of General Education Programs and Common Educational Beliefs, According to Bergquist.

Source: From *Designing Undergraduate Education: A Systematic Guide* by Bergquist, Gould, and Greenberg (1981), pp. 3–4. Jossey-Bass. Copyright 1977. Council of Independent Colleges (formerly Council for the Advancement of Small Colleges). Used with permission.

that it is difficult for faculty in some fields to achieve both of these goals. There appears to be a tradeoff between the two that is linked with the organizing structure of the field. Keeping the balance in mind, however, faculty members can deliberately stretch their thinking to search for ways to apply these concepts in their fields. They can be aware of their own strongly socialized views and accept the challenge of struggling to free themselves a bit from the discipline's predominating mode of thought. Science professors can make special efforts to develop critical challenges to some of the tenets of their field, for example, by questioning how the scientific methods might change in different world contexts and how scientific principles would operate under different sets of assumptions. Typically, such questions are posed only by graduate students in the sciences but they could be made meaningful to undergraduates. Social scientists who eschew coherence in favor of autonomy can deliberately seek coherence within the world of ideas by seeking commonalities among those with very different perspectives. The attempts to go beyond one's ordinary way of thinking can be shared with students. This changes the basis for the major from acceptance of the discipline to questioning and challenging its structure, values and methods.

Another type of proposal for coherence focuses on developing generic analytical abilities. An approach to develop such abilities might be grounded in theories of learning—specifically cognitive development (Hursh, Haas, & Moore, 1983). This approach would place problems society faces at the center of general education and encourage students to draw from various disciplines to attack the problems and to shift perspectives or frames of reference. In an experienced-based approach, students would need to act on information and construct it in new ways. Such an approach could be used in the freshman year or be integrated over the college course of study. The key point is that it changes the basis for a general education program plan from one of sampling disciplines to one based on how students learn. In this conception, as in others we have discussed, the frameworks used by the applied fields as well as those from the liberal arts disciplines could become part of the lower division students' perspectives.

Recently, Gerald Graff (1992) vigorously advocated another method of curriculum development that might help students develop critical perspectives as well as integration. Graff argued that students must be exposed to different perspectives to understand that the world may be viewed in different ways, and that the perspectives are often in conflict among well-respected scholars. He especially applied this to disciplines in which coherence is elusive because of ferment and emerging new paradigms. A parallel structure can be imagined for the collegiate career fields, which, like the disciplines, often conflict in value orientation. Like some other possibilities, this idea of learning multiple perspectives and the ability to critique one's own field may appeal more to faculty in humanities, artistic fields, and human service fields than to science or engineering faculty. Yet active collegial discussion of the ideas in the sciences might produce unexpected results. Scholars are talking more about how contact among faculty might be deliberately aimed at breaking barriers to curricular integration that separate the diverse fields. One way to learn respect for one another's disciplines is to probe intentionally how the other disciplines have to contribute to students' education.

Balancing Discourse Communities

Understanding the variations in the characteristics of disciplines and professional fields can open new discourse communities among scholars. Because researchers have emphasized the distinctions among academic cultures, it is easy to believe that professors are confined to a single definition of coherence by their discipline, based on how they themselves were taught and on the assumptions they hold about educational purposes and processes. It may be, however, that professors are more often confined by a failure to explicitly examine their assumptions and confront alternatives. In our experience, examining some alternative concepts of curricular integration allows faculty members to choose designs for courses and programs more deliberately and thereby benefit students, faculty, and the enterprise of higher education.

One way to understand potential benefits is to compare discourse about curriculum integration with discussions about multiculturalism. Both involve learning how to build mutual understanding, chose common or overlapping goals, and mesh the varying styles of disparate groups. Just as when adopting multicultural perspectives, educators must examine existing traditions and ask why they continue. Some believe that discipline boundaries no longer make sense and can be made permeable. Others believe that discipline differences do exist and that it is crucial to address them; they feel that differences should be studied to get varied perspectives on what we consider to be known and not known. Such collegial discussion centering on course objectives and instructional processes has potential to expand faculty members' horizons. In the Professional Preparation Project, which one of us directed, forty faculty members from both liberal arts and professional fields spent a day engaging in brief lessons taught from perspectives entirely different than their own. Participants acknowledged acquiring useful new views of teaching and learning.

Another example of expanding discourse communities was pursued extensively at Syracuse University, where a group of faculty from several disciplines met to share perspectives. Directing their thinking at students in an honors program whom they planned to engage in this discourse subsequently, they met for a year. They chose and read books and viewed works of art deliberately intended to provoke discussion reflecting the differences among their individual disciplines and professional fields. Their experiences are described very personally in *Contesting the Boundaries of Liberal and Professional Education: The Syracuse Experiment* (Marsh, 1988).

Reading and discussing preserves faculty autonomy, but pressing too hard for connections between faculty from very different academic cultures can lead to escalated conflict and renewed isolation. Faculty members whose orientations are already at the boundaries of their disciplines can best begin to bridge the cultures. Similarly, engagement with interdisciplinary problems incorporating both types of academic fields may be most effective for upper division students. At that level, students and professors can ask: What are the ways in which various types of learning can be brought to bear on real problems in need of solutions?

Balancing Scholarship and Its Application

Finally, we submit that faculty in all fields must examine the extent to which their academic plans balance learning the discipline with applying it. Those in professional fields look to outside practice settings more than to internal sources of references, while the reverse is true for the disciplines. Consequently, the professional faculty need constantly to remind themselves of important internal linkages, especially with fields that provide foundations and contextual study for their students, whereas disciplinary faculty need to be aware of the ways in which the external context might modify their their plans to make content, sequence and instructional process more more relevant.

General education core curricula past and present have focused on existing liberal arts disciplines, most typically humanities and social sciences. One might ask, however, as did Kaysen (1974), why the disciplines of knowledge must comprise core curricula. Could an equally meaningful core be structured around the linkages of professional service roles with society—the centers of society's activity such as human services, information services, production/enterprise services, and artistic services—with the liberal arts playing a crucial supporting role? Such a plan might engage students earlier and more fully by building on the strong motivating career interests they bring to college instead of, as some have charged, making the freshman year a general education purgatory (Arden, 1988).

Currently, the choices about what questions matter for general education are left largely to the liberal arts faculties who may or may not be directly concerned with application of the learning. If the collegiate career study faculty nominate some issues to help organize the core, on the basis of their relationship to useful contextual knowledge and generic abilities needed by students, the end result surely would include communication skills, critical thinking, interpersonal skills, and contextual knowledge. But new skills vital to today's society might receive greater emphasis such as ethics, values, leadership capabilities, and inquiry skills.

Negotiating Linkages among Academic Fields

To help faculty from several liberal studies disciplines and professional fields consider the possibilities for curricular coherence and integration, we developed a heuristic we called the PLUSS Collaboration/Integration Matrix (Stark, Lowther, Hagerty, & Lokken, 1988). The matrix, shown in Figure 7-5, helps faculty answer the question, "What are the most appropriate types of cross-discipline integration to help students achieve specific important outcomes?"

Use of the matrix as a template for discussion can lead to concrete and well-defined relations among disciplines. Although we developed it for integrating liberal and professional study, we have been told it was used at Northeastern University to guide discussions between groups of faculty members in two or more disciplines to link the majors and general education. It would work equally well to guide discussions for two or more career study fields.

The key to using the PLUSS system is to base discussion on common goals shared by the various fields. Initially, objectives and processes must be shared without criticism to establish an open climate for exchange. Usually, a brief discussion will reveal that the two groups of faculty are both developing academic plans and selecting instructional processes intended to achieve these goals. Once a common set of desired outcomes have been identified, discussion focuses on one objective at a time, defining the objective more fully and exploring the program linkages that might be used to achieve the goal most effectively. The possible types of program linkages are arranged in the nine-cell matrix.

The nine cells are defined by the intersection of three possible types of program structures and three possible types of teaching/learning emphases. The three program structures are: internal (courses planned and taught internally to a single department), external (courses delegated to another department to be planned and taught), and collaborative (courses planned and taught by the two

FIGURE 7-5   The PLUSS Matrix: A Conceptual Framework for Integrating Liberal and Professional Education

Teaching/Learning emphasis / Program Structure	Specialization	Contextual	Investigation
Internal	I-S	I-C	I-I
External	E-S	E-C	E-I
Collaborative	C-S	C-C	C-I

The rows in the matrix describe structures for coursework or activities established between fields as follows:

Internal: Coursework or activities that occur within the professional program.

External: Coursework or activities that occur in fields of study outside of the professional program, taught by faculty in other fields.

Collaborative: Coursework or activities (a) taken in other fields but taught by professional program faculty; (b) taken within the professional program but taught by faculty from other fields; or (c) taken within a merged or transformed program structure where two or more fields have united around common goals, themes, or concepts.

The columns in the matrix describe teaching and learning emphases within a field of study as follows:

Specialization: Emphasis on the specialized conceptual, technical, and integrative practice components of study in a particular field.

Contextual: Emphasis on knowledge of broad social, political, historical, and economic issues; values; contexts; and the arts.

Investigation: Emphasis on inquiry, analysis, and the search for innovative and creative solutions based on the active use of knowledge of broad social, political historical, and economic issues; values; contexts; and the arts

Source: From *PLUSS: Professional/Liberal Self-Study* by J. S. Stark, M. A. Lowther, B. M. K. Hagerty, and P. Lokken (1988). Ann Arbor: University of Michigan, Professional Preparation Network.

departments jointly). The three types of teaching/learning emphases include: (1) specialization (courses that are highly specialized or technical); (2) contextual (courses that may be specialized but which also consider the context in which the specialization takes place); and (3) investigation (courses that explore questions of mutual interest to one or more programs). The appropriate cell of the nine to foster desirable student outcomes would depend on the desired outcome; a different degree of collaboration might be appropriate to teach communication skills than to teach professional ethics.

One extreme position—but one that is probably typical in most current academic plans—insists that collegiate career study programs be both specialized and insular, teaching students technical skills without reference to other studies (Cell I-S in Figure 7-5). In contrast, the typical general education position, offering primarily contextual knowledge in the first two years of undergraduate study, is represented by Cell E-C. In Cell E-C, contextual knowledge, which may be extremely relevant for professional practice (as well as for citizenship and life) is taught by liberal arts faculty with little or no reference to its connection with the students' planned professions. More intentional integration of liberal and professional study would occur in any of the three cells in the row labeled "Collaborative." Whether collaborative specialization (Cell C-S), collaborative contextualization (Cell C-C), or collaborative investigation (Cell C-I) would be the most desirable strategy would depend on the specific educational objective being pursued.

BUILDING ON THE STRENGTH OF ACADEMIC FIELDS

Educational purposes broader than learning discipline concepts and methods should achieve a more prominent role in academic plans. To focus on such purposes in planning courses and programs professors will need to be secure in their disciplinary culture but capable of moving beyond its confines. These changes are difficult because they challenge familiar disciplinary tenets and require conversation that spans symbolic systems, value systems, and divergent methods of inquiry. Such conversations are unlikely to start spontaneously and require regular infusions of energy to keep them going. Persistence and strong leadership are important and success is most likely in a supportive educational environment.

From our discussions with faculty, we know that strong disciplinary models are modified for better balance and that modifications can help students achieve a more complete and satisfying education. When faculty take seriously the principle with which we began this chapter—that the purpose of structuring course content is to help the learner achieve order—they can improve and extend their notions of the place of the disciplines in the curriculum. We believe that conscious attention to several types of balance within an academic field and in its connections with others is necessary to create the most effective academic plans. Potential linkages within and among the disciplines leading to better coherence and integration in course and program plans might be achieved as deliberate designs.

CHAPTER 8

Influence of Learners

LEARNERS' INFLUENCES ON ACADEMIC PLANS

Learners' capabilities, preparation, motivation, effort, and goals may all influence faculty members as they plan courses and programs. In this chapter, we continue to draw on research to describe how faculty members consider learners when planning. We also examine recent advances in learning theories that may help faculty better understand how students learn and we suggest uses of these theories to design plans that meet needs of diverse groups of learners. We will return to these learning theories in Chapter 9, when we discuss how course and program plans might change if faculty more consciously used learning research to help them select instructional processes. In our discussion, we emphasize once more our understanding that discipline-related beliefs and curriculum patterns exert strong influence on faculty members. Accordingly, instructors in different fields will find different ideas about student learning useful.

When we discussed how disciplines influence faculty in selecting content for their academic plans, we linked purpose, content and sequence, reflecting our knowledge that faculty in an academic field tend to hold similar educational purposes and arrange content in similar ways. In this chapter, we point to another known relationship between elements of an academic plan—the link between learners and their individual educational purposes. This relationship is highlighted in Figure 8-1. By including student purposes in our discussion of learners, we acknowledge that student purposes and faculty purposes are not always the same. Even when faculty members construct plans with goals they feel are important, the purposes of students who experience the plan may differ.

Variations in student purposes reflect student diversity. As we show in Figure 8-1, learners are affected by influences external to the college or university, including their earlier preparation, their goals, and their future life and employment prospects and choices. These external influences differ in type and strength for students of different ages and backgrounds. For the 40% of students older than traditional college age and the 43% who attend part time, these external influences

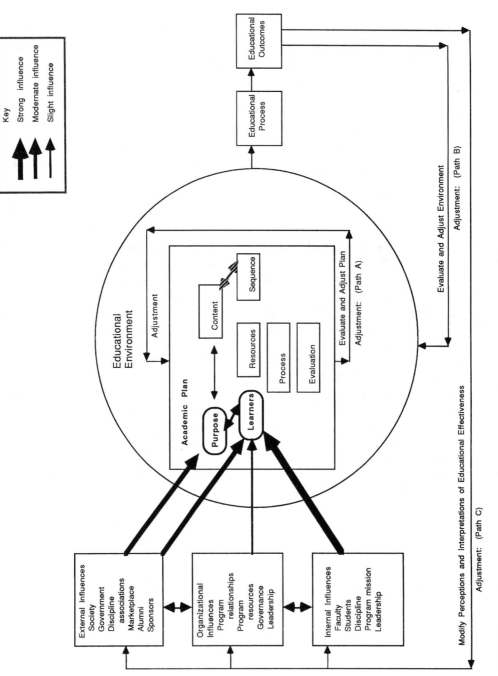

FIGURE 8-1   Academic Plans in Environmental Context: Focus on Learners and Their Purposes

may remain very strong. For traditional-age students who reside on campuses, influences from inside the college—faculty, other students, and missions of the programs in which they study—may be stronger than external influences during the college years. In either case, both the characteristics students bring to college and the nature of their involvement influence how they experience their education. More important, both their characteristics and their experiences may be substantially modified by attending college.

The emergence of remedial programs, multicultural curriculum options, and state-mandated articulation agreements between two- and four-year institutions are clear indicators of society's demand that collegewide planning accommodate learner diversity. At the course level, variations in individual student interests, preparation, and learning styles have long presented challenges to effective academic planning. At the program level, as well, faculty are increasingly called on to think in terms of such issues as cultural pluralism and students who have transferred from other colleges as they develop curricula. Yet learners are not always consciously considered at either level of academic planning; sometimes they are included in the plan only by default. Viewing the curriculum as an academic plan makes the learner's presence visible and may encourage educators to focus more systematic attention on learner needs and characteristics.

Learners' Influence on Course Planning

Faculty members in most fields report that several influences outweigh that of learners in course planning. These dominant influences include faculty members' beliefs about educational purpose (the knowledge, skills, and attitudes to be learned), content (the subject matter of learning), and sequence (the curricular arrangement of content to be learned). In interviews most faculty mentioned these other influences more frequently and elaborated them more fully than they did the influence of learners (Stark, Lowther, Ryan, et al., 1988). Although 69% of faculty in our survey said that they always considered students at some point when creating plans for introductory courses, only 15% said that they thought of students first (Stark, Lowther, Bentley, et al., 1990).

As instructors described the way they plan, they spoke of prototypic groups of learners that they kept in mind. Most based their notions about learners on their past classes; a few apparently based them on idealized assumptions about learner goals and characteristics. Instructors whose plans are based on idealized assumptions can receive rude shocks when their ideals are not met. We recall, for example, a history professor who told us that he taught for several years before he admitted that his students did not watch or listen to daily newscasts, rendering his use of current examples of history ineffective. Faculty members who assume that their classes are essentially similar from year to year might also be operating on shaky assumptions since the mix of students from varied backgrounds is changing rapidly on many campuses. In the next few sections, we will describe more fully what faculty members said about the influence of specific learner characteristics on their planning.

Learners' Backgrounds

When discussing the influence of students in course planning, only a few instructors mentioned considering such demographic characteristics as gender and ethnicity. Faculty members seemed wary of appearing to stereotype students based on fixed characteristics. The exceptions we encountered were faculty who believed that a neutral attitude toward gender, ethnicity, and culture ignored important differences among students and was, therefore, inappropriate. As society attempts to resolve issues of how to legitimate cultural, racial, ethnic, and gender differences, faculty members seem caught in a dilemma about making deliberate attempts to recognize these characteristics as they plan courses.

In contrast to ethnic or gender characteristics, faculty members frequently mentioned age as a student characteristic they considered when planning. Those teaching traditional-age college groups were often sensitive to students' lack of maturity in dealing with particular topics, while those teaching older groups described them as strongly motivated but often lacking in self-confidence and pressured by multiple family and work demands. In certain settings, instructors mentioned characteristics of students unique to that environment. In a college sponsored by a strict religious sect, for example, faculty members spoke of their attempts to expose students to a broader range of religious views than had been permitted in their homes. In the view of these instructors, broadened exposure would, in the end, lead to more firmly grounded religious commitment.

Learners' Preparation and Ability

Faculty stressed the influence of student preparation, often speaking as if it were synonymous with ability, but they usually avoided commenting on student "abilities" or "capabilities." Several told us that they preferred not to receive information about students' previous academic records that might influence their thinking. Among their reasons were possible cultural bias in traditional measures of intelligence or aptitude, or conclusions hastily drawn by previous teachers.

Faculty planning courses in different institutional settings and disciplines were influenced differently by the level of preparation students bring to the classroom, but all considered it important in their course planning. Those teaching in general education pro-

grams more often considered student characteristics and preparation influential than did those teaching in preprofessional courses, possibly because faculty in general education encounter a broader range of student preparation and ability.

Although fewer than 20% of faculty members we surveyed characterized their students in introductory courses as "not at all prepared" and 60% thought they they were "moderately well prepared," other researchers report more negative views based on reports from faculty and from students themselves. A nationwide study of over 5,400 faculty at 306 colleges and universities by the Carnegie Foundation for the Advancement of Teaching (1989) found that three-fourths of full-time faculty members (apparently teaching at all levels) felt that students were seriously underprepared in terms of basic skills. Information similar to the Carnegie data may be inferred from student self-reports such as those in the Cooperative Institutional Research Program's annual survey of college freshmen. For example, Dey, Astin, and Korn (1991) reported that students felt less prepared for college in the 1980s than in the 1960s and 1970s; more expected to seek help in reading and study skills. In corroborative data, between 1968 and 1990 the number of high school students who said they had checked out even one book or journal from their high school libraries had declined by 40%, and the number who had done unassigned work had declined by 24%. Goodman and Parochetti (1987) painted an even bleaker picture: many students in an open admission community college appeared to them to be "not only underprepared but 'undercapable'" (p. 49) of benefiting from remediation programs to improve basic skills because of cognitive or emotional underdevelopment.

There are considerable disciplinary and institutional differences in these impressions of student preparedness. Generally, we found that faculty teaching composition, mathematics, or literature in general education programs viewed their students as reasonably well prepared, even when the preparation was not as strong as they might wish. In contrast, instructors who taught fields typically not stressed in secondary school, such as fine arts, sociology, and business, more frequently judged their students to be underprepared.

Faculty members we interviewed believed they were sensitive to the limited preparation of students in such basic skills as writing, reading, listening, and numerical literacy. Instructors teaching the same field at different types of colleges differed, however, in their views of student preparedness. Those in both the most selective and the least selective institutions more often viewed their students as poorly prepared. These views of preparation may be based on different faculty expectations in very different types of institutions.

Most instructors did not feel confident about their ability to deal with underpreparation once they recognized it. This was especially true if learning skills were underdeveloped or students seemed poorly motivated. Few faculty members we interviewed or surveyed reported that they attempted to arrange material in their courses based on theoretical or empirical knowledge of how humans learn. However, while most reported little formal knowledge of learning theory, they felt that they had developed considerable intuitive sense over the years concerning what worked well and what did not work for different types of students. They used this "practical experience" in constructing academic plans aimed at students with average preparation. At the course level, most faculty created plans by establishing discipline goals first, then considered students' preparation, adjusted content, and made sequencing decisions.

The process of adjusting to student preparation after establishing content goals also varied by discipline. Faculty in fields that stress learning concepts and principles, particularly where concepts are hierarchical,

are strongly concerned with adequacy of student preparation. Yet, ironically, their tendency to arrange content sequentially may make them less likely to adjust to differences among students and more likely to lament that students do not keep the pace they set for the class to cover content. In contrast, faculty who see the personal and intellectual development of students as their primary teaching goal often teach in fields where material can be arranged more flexibly. Since student development is their goal, these instructors often focus on challenges in working with students at different levels of preparation; students who need help may be an interesting challenge rather than a burden requiring a change in plan. Frequently, these faculty noted satisfaction when students developed beyond what they had anticipated.

Learners' Goals

Faculty impressions of student preparedness to learn may be modified by differences in the goals they and their students hold for college and courses, as well as by the lack of importance faculty attach to some types of student goals. Instructors saw students' intellectual goals as important and believed they would become more like their teachers' goals with increased maturity. But only 35% of faculty teaching general education courses admitted that they were influenced by students' life or career goals. Faculty in arts and science fields saw career goals as minimally relevant to their course planning, but as might be expected, more than 80% of the preprofessional faculty surveyed reported that they were strongly influenced by students' career goals. The influence of student goals on course planning varied by type of institution as well as by academic field. Faculty in the most selective colleges were least influenced by students' life, career and educational goals, while faculty in the least selective colleges reported greater influence (Stark, Lowther,

Bentley, et al., 1990, p. 86). As we have discussed students' goals at diverse colleges and universities, many faculty members have expressed concern that students seem to lack intellectual goals but possess strong functional goals like "getting the course over with" and "getting a decent grade."

While developing the Student Goals Exploration (SGE), a survey used to stimulate discussion of goals in specific introductory courses, we found that even entering students reported intellectual goals for general education (Stark, Lowther, Shaw, & Sossen, 1991; Stark & Francis, 1995). In a few academic fields, however, we found substantial misunderstandings among entering college students about the purpose of college courses. Specifically, some beginning students thought studying psychology would help them solve personal problems or that studying sociology would provide social skills. Students who expected personally useful information from courses focusing on scientific principles and theories may have been surprised or disappointed when they encountered their instructor's plan. Similarly, faculty who fail to recognize that students are naive about the purposes of a course may interpret student behavior as inappropriate. This mutual disillusionment may be one source of faculty distress about what they perceive as students' lack of learning-directed goals.

The influence of "non-academic" characteristics such as students' goals can partially determine student success in a course. Since educators and students each may have distinct purposes, objectives, and preferred ways to reach these objectives, the success of an academic plan for students may require attempts to find common purposes on which to build. Some faculty members talked about how to find such commonalities and take them into account as they create academic plans. Others believed that discussing such differences with students and accommodating student goals was "coddling" and was, therefore, inappropriate for students at the college level.

Learners' Effort and Involvement

Most instructors say their plans are influenced by anticipated student effort. Just over 21% of faculty in the course planning survey thought their students expended a great deal of effort; nearly 12% thought they demonstrated very little or relatively little effort (Stark, Lowther, Bentley, et al., 1990, p. 82). Typically, then, faculty reported that students in their general education classes exhibited "a modest amount" of effort. The majority of faculty are concerned about lack of student effort when they are aware of it, and they regularly try to stimulate student involvement. More than 80% of the faculty we surveyed said that they tried to find ways to motivate or interest students to help them learn. The intensity and frequency of these attempts to motivate students and the form they take vary widely, ranging from holding extra review sessions to demanding that daily homework assignments be turned in. Some faculty members who strongly criticized students' lack of effort often indicated they were resigned to it as a "fact of life." They felt they could not afford to let lack of effort discourage them or deter them from getting on with the task of teaching the discipline. Yet Pace (1979) contends that students' quality of effort may be the single most influential variable in accounting for students' progress toward educational outcomes.

Many faculty members say they can recognize students who are disengaged even in large lecture classes, and they make various attempts to capture their attention. Some attempt to stimulate the inattentive or unprepared by calling on them unexpectedly in class. Most say they ask students who are not putting forth acceptable effort to visit them during office hours. Others motivate students by using collaborative approaches to learning that foster a sense of group responsibility. Some faculty make extensive efforts to connect course material to student interests. The most common strategies that faculty use to motivate students, however, are grades. Some faculty regularly remind students that grades will be calculated soon or discuss the weight of a particular exam in a student's grade; others devise elaborate systems of bonus points to stimulate students to work hard. Relatively few faculty we talked with believe that students would put forth maximum effort if extrinsic incentives such as grades were absent.

In contrast to the substantial need for extrinsic motivating strategies mentioned by faculty who teach in general education programs, professional program faculty felt it easier to capitalize on students' existing motivation by involving them in practical problems related to the career field. In interviews, faculty in fields like business, nursing, architecture, and engineering, for example, reported that visits with practicing professionals, field trips, observations in work settings, and discussions of current events in the field linked faculty members and students in common purposes. Scheduling such activities early in the program also helps students know whether they want to continue in a field of study. Students who persist in the major tend to be those who are strongly committed.

When we asked faculty members about connections between learner effort and course satisfaction, we found that most instructors formally assess student satisfaction only at term's end and delay adjustments based on student reaction until the next course offering. But we also found some faculty members who employed elaborate evaluation mechanisms as the course proceeded, using frequent "one-minute papers," journals, or student committees (usually in very large courses) to keep them informed of the status of student effort, motivation, and satisfaction. These were most often faculty members who were willing to make immediate adjustments in course plans.

Program Plans

We might expect that faculty who are responding to the current national emphasis on redesigning general education programs would make special attempts to discover more about learners' needs and preferences. In fact, reformers note that few such attempts are reported (Gaff, 1991). Groups of faculty who advocate required core courses for all students see little need to account for differences in students' goals. Those who are adjusting distribution requirements typically intend to reduce learners' freedom to follow their interests. Very little is mentioned in today's curriculum discussions about individualized or self-paced options. The current reform movement seems to focus more on purpose than on learners and to provide little opportunity for academic plans to reflect learners' needs or desires.

In program planning for major fields, decisions about educational objectives and choice of specific course sequences might be based on explicit consideration of student needs, abilities, prior preparation, and future plans. Most faculty program groups collect little formal data about these student characteristics to help them link program plans with students' goals and plans. For programs in both disciplines and professional fields, faculty seem to make decisions regarding the content and course sequence for majors based partly on images of ideal students and partly on daily contact with current students. To supplement these images and impressions, program faculty (or chairpersons) often monitor student enrollments in courses and program sequences. They interpret low enrollments as indicating student dissatisfaction and the need to change some element of the academic plan. In some colleges, teaching assignments are changed or program requirements restructured on the basis of student evaluations of individual instructors as well as on enrollment records.

During periodic but sporadic self-studies, program faculty in major fields may conduct surveys of student satisfaction. Such surveys may be more feasible and useful in medium-size institutions than in very small or very large colleges. The smallest colleges may have little need for formal inquiry since program faculty know their major students well and interact with them daily; in contrast, program faculty in the largest universities may have difficulty identifying the full range of students from whom they might appropriately solicit views. Usually, there are at least three groups of students from whom opinions might be sought: students majoring in the field to seek a related job after graduation or because of their intrinsic interest in the subject; students majoring in related fields who require a few intermediate or advanced courses; and students intending to pursue graduate study whom faculty members see as future scholars in their field.

As we interviewed faculty members about program plans, we found that plans frequently were aimed at the potential future scholars in the field, even when very few students had pursued such study recently. Because of the importance of this student group to faculty, the emphasis in many four-year colleges is on preparation for graduate study. Substantial efforts may be made to recruit students who will fit an existing plan based on preparation for graduate school rather than making adjustments in the program to fit current student characteristics. The parallel situation in two-year colleges may be that faculty aim programs at students who plan to transfer to an upper-division program, paying less attention to those who have career-directed or shorter term educational goals. In both cases, discussions of need for change based on students' goals, effort, and involvement often focus on creating longer lists of required courses, changing course sequences, or initiating capstone seminars and experiences. Thus, curricular change often focuses on the sequence and mechanics of the program rather than the basic purposes, content, or instructional process to serve learner needs.

One result of targeting academic programs at the most academically-oriented students is that programs may be more challenging, slightly more ambitious, and more oriented toward the scholarly aspects of the field than the majority of student majors believe they need. Even in professional fields these differences occur. Faculty may dwell on theoretical aspects of professional practice, while students are anxious to practice skills they anticipate needing on the job. Such incongruities in educational objectives may produce positive outcomes from a faculty viewpoint, since research shows that students come to think more like faculty and other students in the field of their major. From the student's viewpoint, however, there may be a negative outcome if the discrepancy between the need to prepare for postcollege employment and the program plan is too great.

The separation of learners from academic plans at the program level is undoubtedly also exacerbated by the historical and continuing physical and philosophical separation within colleges between academic programs and student service programs (see Garland & Grace, 1993). It is unusual for faculty in academic programs to collaborate with professional counseling staff in student services programs to gather information that could be important in developing academic plans. One of the obvious examples of this lack of collaboration is in career counseling. Career counselors have more contact with future employers than do most faculty members. The lack of contact between instructors and employers differs from field to field but may affect responsiveness of programs to both students and employment opportunities. The disjuncture is smallest in college career studies where students pursue field placements or internships; it is probably greatest in liberal arts fields where faculty do not directly address future careers of most students. The limited degree of contact between counselors and professors does not encourage the use of career data in constructing academic plans.

Collegewide Plans

At the collegewide level, students' influence on the total curriculum plan is usually indirect, except when matters of broad student concern cause unrest. Since the college mission is an *a priori* statement of what an institution believes is important for students to learn, achieve, and become, we would not expect it to be responsive to student goals. Rather, in most cases, students select an institution because its established mission is appropriate to their own goals. At least three types of colleges are especially inclined, however, to respond to students' characteristics and needs in collegewide planning. These include community colleges, colleges whose special mission is to serve nontraditional students (such as Empire State College in New York, and Thomas Edison College in New Jersey) and colleges in a poor market position that are working hard to maintain enrollments.

Rather surprisingly, however, systematic data collection about student backgrounds, goals, preparation, and effort may occur more often at the college level than at the program level. It is here that the authority, expertise, and resources needed to collect data, alone or in cooperation with state or private external agencies, are located. Executive officers can authorize voluntary data collection such as participation in the nationwide annual survey of entering students' preparation and goals conducted by the Cooperative Institutional Research Program (CIRP) of the Higher Education Research Institute at UCLA. Since the 1960s, these annual CIRP studies have tracked students' reasons for attending college, self-reported preparation and interests, and other information, and have gathered additional information after students have graduated. Despite the availability of a wide array

of information, colleges seem to use the data more frequently for estimating program enrollments and assessing the need for remedial services than to help plan other collegewide or program curricula. CIRP data, however, can be used to document gradual and sometimes little-noticed changes in college programs that result from shifting student populations and changing levels of preparation (Dey & Hurtado, 1994).

Other types of student data can also prove useful to academic planners. A number of colleges have begun to use the Student College Experiences Questionnaire (Pace, 1990a, 1990b, 1992; Kuh, Schuh, & Whitt, 1991) to collect self-reported data about the effort expended by enrolled students. Since this information can be linked directly to various elements of academic plans, it constitutes important outcome information with considerable promise for educational improvement among involved colleges.

CONTEMPORARY VIEWS OF LEARNING AND LEARNERS

In this section, we review recent thinking about learning and learners that might be used to make academic plans more effective. Since faculty members typically do not study learning theory, our goal is to review aspects of important theories that are specifically relevant to constructing academic plans. Based on such theories, educational programs and interventions can be intentionally designed to make a greater positive impact on students' intellectual development. Such deliberate design of educational programs, when adapted by faculty to suit their academic field and specific group of students, may improve academic plans.

Some faculty members are willing to address students' intellectual (cognitive) development but are uncomfortable when including students' emotional or attitudinal (affective) development in their academic plans. In our discussion, we emphasize the view that cognitive and affective learner development are inextricably linked. It is artificial to separate these two aspects of development because intellectual development requires active involvement by the learner. Involvement depends on positive attitudes and motivation as well as on an appropriately challenging educational environment. We have tried to simplify the psychological literature to make it more useful, so our first task in discussing these important relationships is to define some terms that may be new to many who construct academic plans. [For a more extensive but also simplified review, consult James R. Davis, *Better Teaching, More Learning* (1993). For technical treatments see the references by Pintrich (1988a, 1988b), McKeachie et al. (1990), Shuell (1986), and Sternberg (1985).]

What Is Cognition?

Cognition is a term psychologists use to describe the learning process—that is, how a person goes about acquiring information. Cognition includes people's general strategies for processing information, their prior knowledge about content, and their problem-solving and thinking skills. The regular patterns of cognition people tend to use are called *cognitive styles*. Psychologists believe that these cognitive styles or patterns link an individual's intellectual abilities and personality characteristics (Corno & Snow, 1986; Messick, 1984). Some educators believe that students' cognitive styles are closely related to their prior achievement, whereas others see them as more closely related to intelligence.

Cognitive skills are more specific than cognitive styles. They are acquired learning skills that may be crucial to future effectiveness in learning, problem solving, and critical thinking. The learner uses these skills when processing new information and storing it in memory (Pintrich et al., 1986). The ways

knowledge is organized when it is stored in memory are called *cognitive structures* (Ausubel, 1963, Ausubel, Novak, & Hanesian, 1978; Shavelson, 1974). Although theorists conceptualize these unobservable knowledge structures in different ways, all agree that the way new information is organized and linked to previous knowledge in one's memory is an important influence on meaningful learning.

While faculty commonly discuss student characteristics that they believe are important in learning, such as gender and content preparation, they are less likely to be familiar with cognitive variables such as "styles," "skills," and "structures" that cannot be observed directly. Yet psychologists believe these attributes are also very important in determining learning outcomes. Prior knowledge and general intellectual ability contribute to learning outcomes, but how they function to produce learning depends on cognitive processes used when encountering new information. More important, these cognitive processes (both skills and styles) can be learned, just as knowledge of content can be learned. Enhancing students' cognitive skills is therefore an important educational objective because it facilitates continued effective learning.

Cognitive Influences

To recognize the relation of the two important aspects of students' development—cognitive and affective—we discuss two sets of influences on student learning: (1) cognitive influences, which we have already described briefly—that is, the influence of students' ability (intelligence), cognitive styles, and cognitive skills or learning strategies—and (2) motivational influences, including motivation, student goals, and involvement. Utilizing both sets of influences and noting the interaction between them provides considerable opportunity to improve academic plans.

Intelligence/Ability

One view of learning popular among psychologists today—the information-processing approach—stresses the dynamic nature of intelligence. Compared to former "trait" theories of intelligence, the information-processing approach places less emphasis on learners' inherent capability and more emphasis on how learners can learn to perceive and process information and store it in memory for further use. For the instructor, this approach avoids the assumption that the student has some fixed capacity to learn and suggests less faculty attention to "filling the empty vessel" with content. Rather, the emphasis on processing suggests that the teacher give more attention to helping learners construct meaning as they try to relate new information to old. It also emphasizes helping students develop strategies needed to "learn to learn" so that they may continue learning in the future. Although psychologists have varied orientations to studying learning and intelligence, information-processing theories are currently well accepted and seem to be replacing older theories that view intelligence as static and possibly culturally biased. The new theories suggest potential ways of designing academic plans. We describe the dynamic approach to defining intelligence in some detail here.

Using an information-processing approach, Sternberg (1985) synthesized extensive research on intelligence to create a three-part model describing componential, contextual, and experiential forms of intelligence. (To relate it more closely to our usual ways of discussing college curriculum and learning outcomes, we will call componential intelligence *analytical intelligence*.) An overview of Sternberg's theory is shown in Figure 8-2.

A student's general analytical abilities can be thought of as cognitive abilities, but Sternberg called them "components" and has proposed three types: metacomponents, performance components, and knowledge acquisition components. Metacomponents are the higher order processes that are used to plan, monitor, and make decisions about more basic (lower level) cognitive processes, namely performance and knowledge-acquisition components. Some liken metacomponents to decisions made within a command or control center or at the executive level of an organization. Performance components are the cognitive processes used in executing specific tasks; knowledge-acquisition components are the cognitive processes used to learn new information. Using these three types of processes, individuals encounter new information and change their internal mental representations of objects or symbols. Thus, these general analytic abilities are closely related to the performance of academic tasks typically required of college students. Learning is about how people change concepts. Thus, it involves processes as well as content.

Sternberg asserted, however, that successful learning does not rely upon analytic intelligence (processing capability) alone; there are two other forms of intelligence—experiential and contextual intelligence. Experiential intelligence describes students' ability to be creative, going beyond the routine tasks to synthesize experiences in new and insightful ways. Contextual intelligence includes students' ability to adapt to, use, and manipulate the environment to serve their needs. This ability enables students to achieve better fits with their environments; it includes both problem-solving skills and social skills in relating to others in the environment. In sum, Sternberg's theory posits three basic types of intelligence: analytical, experiential, and contextual, each of which contributes to effective learning. The definitions of these three types of intelligence make it clear that all three are needed for success in

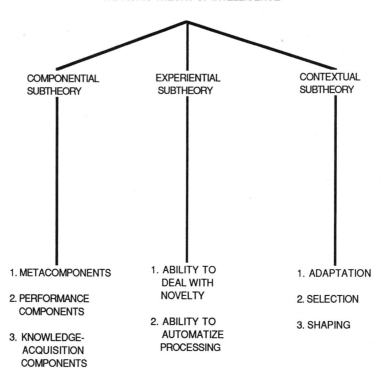

FIGURE 8-2   Sternberg's Triarchic Model of Intelligence, an Overview

Source: Beyond IQ: A Triarchic Theory of Human Intelligence by Robert J. Sternberg (1985),Cambridge University Press, p. 320. Reprinted by permission of Cambridge University Press.

college and should be enhanced by the college experience.

Cognitive Styles

Individuals seem to develop consistent and distinctive cognitive styles that remain somewhat stable from the early years to adulthood (Kagan & Kogan, 1970). These cognitive styles (or learning styles) apparently result from heredity, past experiences, and the demands of the present environment. Through cultural and socialization experiences in the family, at school, and at work, individuals learn to choose between certain styles in learning—for example, between acting quickly or reflecting on their proposed action, between using concrete experience or abstract analysis in solving problems (Kolb, 1981), between learning alone or with others (Canfield, 1988), between preferring complex material and preferring simple material, and between the tendency to focus on one solution versus considering a wide set of solutions. There are many definitions of cognitive styles and many instruments for assessing students' styles (for a nontechnical review, see Claxton & Murrell, 1987).

David Kolb measured differences in learning styles along two basic dimensions—abstract-concrete and active-reflective—and empirically identified four common learning styles: the converger, the diverger, the assimilator, and the accommodator (see Figure 8-3). Among the many typologies we might consider, we report his scheme here because it has been related to the disciplines as they typically are organized (Kolb, 1981). Students with a specific style may be most comfortable intellectually when studying in fields closely allied with their style. On the other hand, students may gain from the challenge of working in a field where the style differs from their preference. In nearly all general education programs, students must study a broad set of disciplines and are thus exposed to a variety of instructors' learning styles.

According to Kolb's theory, convergers characteristically apply ideas to practice. Individuals with a convergent learning style do best in situations where there is a single solution or right answer. Convergers tend to be unemotional, prefer to deal with things rather than people, tend to have focused interests, and often choose to specialize in the natural sciences and engineering.

Divergers, in contrast, are characteristically imaginative. They can readily view concrete situations from multiple perspectives and organize multiple relationships into a coherent and meaningful whole. Divergers excel in the generation of ideas, are interested in people, and tend to be emotional. Research indicates that the divergent style is characteristic of individuals who chose to study in humanities and liberal arts fields.

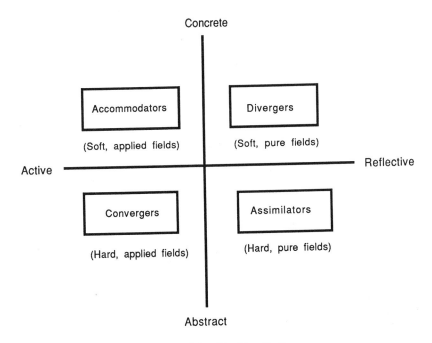

FIGURE 8-3 Learning Styles Identified by Kolb

Source: Adapted from "Learning Styles and Disciplinary Differences" by David Kolb in *The Modern American College* by Chickering and Associates (1981), pp. 232–255. Reprinted by permission of Jossey-Bass Publishers, Inc.

Assimilators typically have a strong ability to create theoretical models. They excel in inductive reasoning and in integrating disparate observations. Assimilators are more interested in abstract concepts than in people; they are also less concerned with the practical use of theories than with the soundness and precision of the theories. The assimilative learning style is characteristic of individuals in the basic sciences and mathematics.

Accommodators are good at carrying out plans and experiments; they often become involved in new experiences. Accommodators tend to be risk-takers and excel in situations that call for adaptation to specific, immediate circumstances. They tend to solve problems intuitively, relying heavily on others for information rather than their own analytical ability. Accommodators are often seen as impatient in interpersonal affairs, although they are not necessarily ill at ease with people. Accommodators are often found in technical or applied fields.

Faculty spoke only occasionally of student learning styles as they discussed course planning with us and usually assumed that students' styles were fixed and unyielding. Thus, they were skeptical about the instructional utility of knowing about learning styles and cited the difficulty of accommodating several fixed learning styles within large classes. But educational psychologists no longer believe that cognitive styles are fixed and unchanging personality characteristics. Instead, they believe that students can choose cognitive styles as preferred sets of strategies and approaches to learning. Furthermore, teachers can help students develop the ability to make these choices. Kolb clearly warns that the style patterns determined by his Learning Styles Inventory should not become stereotypes, since individuals can use different types of cognitive functioning in different content areas. For example, an individual may be concrete in a field requiring interac-tions with people but abstract in other work situations.

Learning Strategies

How one processes information (that is, how one learns) can be influenced by the use of learning strategies. Weinstein and Mayer (1986) identified four aspects of information processing that are within the learner's control: selection, acquisition, construction, and integration. In selection, the learners control the attention they give to stimuli or information in the environment; in acquisition, they transfer information from working (short-term) memory to long-term memory (permanent storage); in construction, learners actively build connections among ideas in working memory; and in integration, they connect new information with prior knowledge. Each of these steps in information processing is important for effective learning and retention.

Weinstein and Mayer also outlined four learning strategies—rehearsal, elaboration, organization, and monitoring—each of which can be basic or complex, depending on the task. These strategies can be used to control how information is processed and thus help to ensure that the essential four steps in effective learning take place. Table 8-1 shows some cognitive strategies and associated complex tasks.

Rehearsal strategies influence how information is encoded but do not generally help connect new information to prior knowledge. Rather, rehearsal strategies help to focus attention on the material to be learned. For example, a basic rehearsal strategy involves reciting names or items from a list; a more complex rehearsal strategy involves highlighting material in a text or copying it into a notebook.

Elaboration strategies help students transfer information to long-term memory by building internal connections among con-

TABLE 8-1   Complex Learning Strategies

Cognitive Strategies	Complex Tasks
A. Rehearsal strategies	Shadowing Copying material Verbatim note taking Underlining text
B. Elaboration strategies	Paraphrasing Summarizing Creating analogies Generative note taking Question answering

C. Organizational strategies	Selecting main idea:
	  Outlining
	  Networking
	  Diagramming

Source: Simplified from *Teaching and Learning in the College Classrooom: A Review of the Research Literature* by McKeachie, Pintrich, Lin, and Smith (1986), p. 26. Reprinted by permission of the National Center for Research to Improve Postsecondary Teaching and Learning, The University of Michigan.

cepts, facts, principles, etc. Examples of basic elaboration strategies are creating mental images or using mnemonic keywords; more complex strategies include paraphrasing, summarizing, creating analogies, and answering questions.

Organizational strategies help the learner select appropriate information and construct connections among the information to be learned. An example of a basic organizational strategy is clustering words into taxonomic categories. Students can select the main idea from a text or analyze the structure of the text through outlining or networking (linking ideas). Since selecting the main idea from a text is an important task for students, techniques that help students make connections can and should be developed.

Monitoring strategies are activities performed by students to deliberately regulate and control their learning and assist in its integration. Self-monitoring can take the form of self-testing to check comprehension or regulating the speed of reading to fit within a specific time frame. Such monitoring activities are all forms of *metacognition,* which, broadly defined, includes (1) having an awareness of and knowledge about one's learning processes, and (2) controlling and regulating one's learning (Brown, et al., 1983; Flavell, 1979). Weinstein and Mayer (1986) view all metacognitive activities, at least in part, as comprehension monitoring.

Motivational Influences

Recently, psychologists have phrased motivation theory in cognitive terms, which has helped them examine interactions among cognition, motivation, and instruction. For example, Pintrich and his associates (1986) demonstrated that motivation can influence students' performance by modifying the effects of the learning strategies they select and use. Students use different strategies as they approach learning tasks. Such approaches are akin to learning styles but more specific to the type of task. For example, students use two different approaches when reading textbooks: a "surface" processing style and a "deep" processing style (Marton & Saljo, 1976a, 1976b). Students who use surface processing simply plow through text and are satisfied that they have completed the reading task. In contrast, deep processors think about the meaning of the material and try to determine the author's aim and organizing scheme.

The value students attach to a specific task may determine whether they use a surface or a deep processing approach, which in turn affects learning, retention, and the integration of the materials learned. Whereas learning styles are somewhat consistent (though not fixed), learning strategies may vary according to the situation, especially with a student's motivation in that situation. Thus, researchers have begun to understand how motivation influences student outcomes as well as their choice of learning processes. In the following sections, we review the concepts of motivation, goals, and involvement, all of which are relevant as students experience academic plans.

Motivation

Motivation is a tendency to initiate and persist in a certain activity. Students' motivations may be changing and changeable, depending on the situation, and unquestionably influence their learning. Individuals may be encouraged to engage in an activity by their own inner (intrinsic) needs; in this case the strength of the need is an important, but fluctuating element of motivation. Alternatively, motivation may come from external (extrinsic) incentives; in this case, the source of the incentive and the length of time it has been offered are important because repeated external incentives can lose potency. The "value" of a task to an individual lies in its ability to fulfill the individual's intrinsic needs or to achieve desired extrinsic incentives.

In addition to the source (intrinsic or extrinsic) and the related value of the task, motivation depends on an individual's estimate of the potential result of engaging (or not engaging) in a behavior or activity. Projecting expectations of success can supply motivation, while expectations of failure can reduce it. From this rather rational perspective, students' motivation can be thought of as a function of the (1) value of a task in achieving incentives, and (2) estimated "expectancy" of success or failure. Knowing that motivation and expectancy are related is useful because it allows us to realize that motivation to learn can be influenced by the instructor's design for helping students to succeed as well as by the connections he makes to the needs that help them see value in a task.

These expectations of success or failure have affective (emotional) components that are inseparable from motivation. In forming expectations, students rely on perceptions of self-competence and estimates of task difficulty (McKeachie et al., 1990). The way students perceive their competence and the difficulty of a task influence their expectation of success, even when internal and external incentives exist.

Finally, in addition to estimating expectancies of success, students attribute their successes and failures to various causes. Some attribute successes to personal factors, such as their own ability and effort; others ascribe them to external (situational) causes. Albert Bandura (1977) referred to individuals' evaluation of their ability to do something as "self-efficacy." Self-efficacy, unlike self-concept or self-esteem, is situation-specific and therefore changes. Students may have one level of self-efficacy in a biology course and quite another estimate in English composition. Self-efficacy and expectancy are closely related, and both are related to learning effectiveness.

Whereas students estimate their self-efficacy in each setting by inferring the relative contribution of personal and situational factors to success or failure, their attributions to personal factors seem to be more consistent over time than those based on the situation. In other words, students who tend to attribute success to their own ability are likely to be stable over time. In contrast, students who attribute their successes or failures to situational causes (for example, the difficulty of the test or extra effort they put forth) may make less consistent estimates of self-efficacy because difficulty and effort change with the situation.

In summary, motivation is stimulated by a student's intrinsic or extrinsic need and the perceived value of an endeavor. The motivation is modified by the student's estimate of success, which, in turn, is affected by his self-efficacy in that situation and his perception of the difficulty of the task. He may, over time, consistently attribute success or failure to personal factors or to factors outside of his control. Weiner (1986) suggested that the two most important attributions in a context of academic achievement are ability (a personal factor) and effort (often a situational factor). Instructors, therefore, may be able to stimulate students' motivation by capitalizing on their intrinsic and extrinsic needs, by providing opportunities for them to succeed, and by helping them increase their self-efficacy in that educational setting by attributing success to their own ability and increased effort.

Recent research suggests that students' motivational patterns are also related to their cognitive strategies and to their ability to reflect on their own learning, a process psychologists call *metacognition*. Pintrich's work, for example, stresses the dynamic interplay of motivation, cognition, and metacognition in the college classroom. Encouraging students to reflect on their motivations, learning strategies, and attributions is an appropriate instructional strategy.

Goals

Goals are what students hope to achieve. Thus, they influence the value students place on a given endeavor or task and, consequently, they drive motivation and effort. Goals have a variety of attributes, including specificity, clarity, difficulty, temporality, importance, ownership, commitment, and stability (Stark, Shaw, & Lowther, 1989). Variations in these attributes determine the extent to which students "fit" instructors' academic plans. Ultimately, goals influence how students interact with the course or program in which they are enrolled.

The instructors we talked to about course planning seldom considered students' personal, social, and career goals. However, they often considered intellectual goals relevant. Intellectual goals include students' broad goals for attending college as well as their goals for completing specific courses, programs, and academic tasks, which may be situation-specific. In developing the SGE, we found that students' intellectual goals were related to, rather than distinct from, their personal and career goals. Despite the direct influence that student goals can have on the success of an academic plan, relatively little study of student goals has been conducted at the course and program level (Stark, Shaw, & Lowther, 1989).

Specifically relevant to our discussion of the learner are two types of goals students may adopt as they engage in any academic task: performance goals and learning goals (Dweck & Elliot, 1983; Nicholls, 1984). Students who adopt a performance goal focus on their own ability to do a task, rely on rigid standards, and tend to see errors as failures. Under these circumstances, attribution to personal factors can clearly be dysfunctional and decrease self-efficacy. Students who adopt a learning goal focus on the process of how to master the task. They view their performance on a flexible personal standard, are involved in the task rather than the outcome, and see errors as useful. Students may adopt a performance goal for one task or academic course and a learning goal for others.

Sometimes in academic settings, instructors view students' grade orientation as counteracting a learning goal orientation. Being oriented to pursue grades as opposed to learning for its own sake may have results similar to adopting performance goals. Obvious grade orientation may cause instructors to perceive that students lack intellectual goals. The LOGO inventory (Eison, 1981) quickly assesses these orientations by asking students to report their attitudes and typical behaviors. Students may be grade-oriented toward a specific course, toward a program, or toward college in general, or all three. It is not sufficient to examine students' broad goals for attending college and assume that these goals generalize to specific programs of study or specific courses. In planning academic programs at course and program levels, faculty members need to assess the specific goals and motivations of student groups they teach.

Interest and Involvement

Psychologists who are exploring interest theory are more committed to searching for intrinsic incentives for learning and take a less instrumental approach to motivation than do the advocates of the expectancy-value motivational theories we reviewed earlier. That is, they believe that factors somewhat more subjective than task value and expectations of success or failure stimulate motivation, at least in the intellectual and creative realms. Renninger (1992) defines *interest* as composed of knowledge and value, a more subjective view than the motivational scheme discussed by McKeachie and his colleagues (1990). Interest theory suggests that intrinsic interest can motivate individuals to pursue activities or objects that have no apparent instrumental value (Deci & Ryan, 1991). Although there are different conceptions of interest, researchers typically believe it emerges from an individual's interaction with the environment (Krapp, Hidi, & Renninger, 1992).

Interest may be individual or situational. Individual interests, as the name suggests, are specific to an individual, relatively stable, and usually associated with increased knowledge. Situational interests, in contrast, are generated by an environmental stimulus and tend to be shared among individuals. Situational interests may be short term and have a marginal influence on the individual's long-range thinking. Clearly, college instructors often hope to stimulate students' situational interests in hopes of producing longer range individual interests.

To us, interest seems to be related to *involvement*, a term Astin introduced to signify engagement with the academic environment. Involvement has not been fully defined but seems to build on the psychological constructs of motivation that we have just discussed. For example, involvement may be a function of motivation and expectancies, as well as of a student's estimate of the value of the task or activity. However, the expectancy models of motivation focus on the attitudes of students prior to engaging in a task and how those attitudes affect the energy devoted to it; involvement, in contrast, is a behavior, usually observed after it occurs. Motivation may stimulate involvement. If so, the relation of the two may be interactive; involvement may lead to greater motivation and thus to long-term development of new or strengthened individual involvement in a specific type of academic activity.

CONSIDERING LEARNERS IN COURSE AND PROGRAM DESIGN

Course planning and curricular revision need no longer be simply exercises in upgrading content. Cognitive psychologists have provided concepts of learning that suggest how curriculum planners may choose and arrange course material to facilitate its meaningful acquisition by students. Their ideas imply three primary tasks. One is to help students "create knowledge"—that is, to incorporate new information into existing knowledge structures in effective and efficient ways. This learner-created knowledge will be meaningful to students because it is connected with their previous understandings. A second and equally important task is to help students become more effective learners. A third task is to capitalize on students' existing interests, stimulate their motivation, and build more stable individual interests in the subject area and in learning for its own sake.

When the instructors' role is seen as aiding students in knowledge creation, rather than "transmitting" knowledge to them, instructors may be viewed as intermediaries between the conceptual structure of the discipline and the cognitive structures of the students (Novak, 1985). This should be a comfortable role for most college faculty because it does not require changing the disciplinary framework into which they have been socialized. Rather, it presents a new challenge in helping students enter that disciplinary culture more efficiently.

The second important task for faculty— and one in which they may be less confident—is to help students become more effective learners. Faculty members in every course can help students become aware of improved strategies for learning and problem solving. In most cases this will not require teaching very basic learning strategies such as rehearsal and elaboration (although some college students may need to develop very low level skills). More often, it will mean that instructors consciously attend to the relationship between discipline concepts and the learners' cognitive and motivational characteristics, guiding students in the use of more complex learning strategies that help them connect and integrate new knowledge. Effective instruction, in other words, is carefully planned instruction leading to integration.

Studies that have helped us understand how learners process information suggest three general questions for directing curriculum development:

1. How will students be motivated to achieve educational objectives?
2. How will the selection and arrangement of course content influence and be influenced by the learners' information-processing mechanisms?
3. What learning skills should students develop to help them integrate knowledge?

In short, students can be taught to learn effectively; they can be helped to integrate material coherently, and teachers can help them develop strategies that facilitate their own continued learning, construction of meaning, and enhanced motivation. In this view, learning is not simply a response. Rather, it results from the interaction of the educational situation's structure and the students' previously acquired ways of processing information. Learning success therefore results from a combination of effective cognitive skills, appropriate motivations, and carefully chosen educational experiences and activities.

In the sections that follow, we will discuss how faculty can construct academic plans that acknowledge the interaction of student characteristics and the learning process. We will provide additional, more specific, discussion of selecting instructional processes in Chapter 9.

Building on Student Goals and Enhancing Motivation

Knowing the motivational power of student goals, some faculty make deliberate and successful efforts to explore the goals students bring to classes and academic programs. These instructors acknowledge students' goals and discuss how a certain course may be useful to them in their lives and careers. They share why they have designed the course as they have. Such communication efforts are particularly useful in helping students recognize the value of general education requirements. For most general education students, communication about the value of the arts and sciences to their general education is too often neglected. Such messages can help all students develop appropriate learning goals that replace performance goals or grade-oriented goals. The key is to tap students' individual goals and plans, making explicit connections between course goals and students' intellectual and personal goals.

Deliberately addressing the goals of learner and teacher several times in an academic term can help motivate students to achieve course goals. To provide a basis for discussion of goals, we constructed the Student Goals Exploration (Stark, Lowther, Shaw, & Sossen, 1991). The SGE helps faculty members understand students' broader goals in relation to their course goals. Stark and her colleagues originally developed the inventory for general education courses in four-year colleges, but others have adapted it for community colleges and major fields. The SGE offers optional questions that allow an instructor to tailor it easily to his or her course or program. Such a goal inventory, administered by faculty in their classrooms, can benefit instructors and students. Through the inventory, which can reflect both the goals suggested by learning theories and those the instructor thinks are important, faculty and students can learn about goal patterns and initiate a dialogue to assess how students' behaviors contribute to or hinder goal achievement. The instructor may also use the SGE to measure at the beginning and end of the term how students feel about studying in this specific course, how they assess their study skills and expectations of success in the course, and what types of activities they are pursuing as they learn.

Some accommodations in course and program structures to meet learner goals are especially simple. Although every learning objective cannot be sufficiently individualized to motivate every student, a teacher may arrange flexible academic tasks so that students make progress toward their own goals. Periodic or term projects and some reading assignments in a course can be designed to allow students to pursue course topics close to their interests. For example, business majors taking a required philosophy course might write a term project on business ethics. Students in varied majors enrolled in a statistics course might work with data sets that utilize information from their own fields of study. In a political science course, nursing majors might explore the politics of health care reform proposals.

Knowledge of motivational theory can be useful too, particularly in choosing the sequence of course and program content and the types of instructional activities. It appears that tasks of moderate difficulty elicit the greatest persistence, whereas both easy and difficult tasks result in lower levels of persistence among students (Meyer, Folkes, & Weiner, 1976; Weiner, 1972, 1974). Making the tasks sufficiently challenging but not threatening requires that the professor gain some knowledge of students' feelings of self-efficacy in the specific course or program. The professor can then choose gradually more difficult levels and types of tasks that enhance students' expectancy of success, improve their self-efficacy, and increase the interest value of the specific field of study.

Psychologists have observed that students constantly assess their environment, making judgments about themselves, the tasks they face, and their incentives for tackling the tasks. These assessments affect student involvement in a given activity. Self-judgments are the "affective" component that cannot be ignored no matter how much faculty members may wish to do so. Stress occurs when students perceive an imbalance between what the environment requires of them and what they believe they can do to meet those demands. A modest amount of stress is challenging and encourages effort, but when students perceive that they cannot effectively cope with the demands being made by the environment, they withdraw from active participation. Thus, course goals and demands can be positive influences on students, but they can also be nonmotivating or even threatening, leading to anxiety, ineffective learning behaviors, or lack of incentives. Knowing students' abilities and perceptions of their abilities is important for understanding students' behaviors and feelings about a course. The attempts a few faculty make to motivate students by making courses extremely difficult in the first few weeks tend not to be consistent with what is now understood about student motivation and cognition.

Students' perceptions of self-competence may also vary according to the specific task; expectancy is complicated by the feelings students may have about a task as well as their perceptions of its difficulty, their instructors' expectations, and their classmates' attitudes about success and failure. Attention to students' learning styles, for example, can help the instructor develop alternative assignments for convergers and divergers. When the instructional process selected is collaborative learning, students with different learning styles can be joined in a group, each approaching the task in a different way and pooling their results. Alternately, students with similar learning styles can work together, later contrasting their efforts with those of other groups. But group work is not a panacea for everyone; learning style research tells us that some students learn best in groups, others alone.

The value an individual attaches to success or failure on a task is important to most tasks. Three aspects of task value are important influences on achievement: attainment value (the task's ability to provide challenge, to fulfill certain achievement needs, and to confirm a salient aspect of the self); intrinsic interest (the inherent enjoyment of the task); and utility value (how the task facilitates achievement of important goals) (Eccles, 1983). To ensure involvement and thus achievement, instructors developing course plans may want to systematically consider each aspect of task value.

Faculty members who have strong interest in their subject may erroneously assume

that students also possess intrinsic interest. Yet any student group shows substantial variations. Harter (1985) proposed five student-centered continua of intrinsic motivation along which a student may vary: challenge, curiosity, mastery, independent judgment, and internal evaluative criteria. Challenge involves a preference for easy or demanding tasks. Curiosity involves satisfying one's own interests in contrast to pleasing others. Mastery contrasts a preference for working alone with relying on others for assistance. Independent judgment reflects a belief that one is capable of making decisions rather than depending on others, such as the instructor. The final category, internal evaluative criteria, portrays the tendency to rely differentially on either internal or external criteria for judging performance. Some students credit successes to causes within themselves and failures to external factors. Faculty members developing courses or programs may wish to review their plans at least informally to see that they address student variations for each of these five elements.

Although the psychologists we have cited use varied and technological terms and may seem to be proposing different theories of motivation with divergent implications for instructional design, the key ideas are the same. Instructors should strive to discover, acknowledge, and build on students' goals and motivations, adjusting the pace of instruction to increase students' sense of self-confidence in the subject matter as well as their knowledge of facts and concepts.

Improving Learning through Involvement

Psychologists have helped us recognize that students should be active participants in the learning experience and active processors of information. Student involvement refers to the amount of physical and psychological energy that students devote to a specific academic experience. In assessing the extent of involvement, we can look at how much time students spend on an academic task or at the level of understanding that they achieved (Astin, 1984). Student involvement, as customarily discussed in higher education, emphasizes behavior which usually can be observed directly.

Achieving goals, according to Astin, is a direct function of student behavior, namely the amount and quality of time and effort they devote to goal-related activities. Astin argues that it is not so much what students believe or feel but what they do and how they behave that define and identify involvement. Because behaviors are more susceptible to direct observation than the attitudes that undergird them, most professors we interviewed could readily tell if their students were "involved" by informally observing their behavior in class. What seemed to baffle faculty, however, was how to plan courses to promote greater involvement and how to encourage more positive attitudes among students. Professors know they must compete with other forces and influences in students' lives for a share of finite time and energy. They are not always sure how to compete successfully.

Examining different conceptions of the teacher's role may provide some help. Like other more technical theories of motivation, Astin's ideas about involvement contrast sharply with the "content coverage" approach and with traditional views that the teacher's role is primarily (or merely) to expose students to the right subject matter. Involvement also contrasts with a "resources approach," which suggests that if adequate resources are brought together in one place, learning will occur. The concept of student involvement assigns an active, not passive, role to both students and professors. Consequently, the teacher is a facilitator but has a more extensive role than either lecturer or resource coordinator.

The challenge for instructors is to focus less on content and the teaching techniques

they themselves perform and more on what students are actually doing in and out of the classroom. How involved are students? How much time and energy are they devoting to the learning tasks? How can they be encouraged to devote more time and energy? Do the assigned tasks have value for students? If not, can students be helped to see the value? Can they expect to succeed? How can successful experiences be increased? Is interest growing rather than waning?

Passivity, in Astin's view, may reflect a lack of involvement; the instructor is therefore advised to pay attention to the passive, reticent, or unprepared student. This change is a difficult one for faculty members who teach large classes or who believe that there is insufficient time to "cover" the required content. The change may occur when faculty members recognize that although they are "covering" knowledge, many students are not "constructing" it. Student attribution of failure to someone or something in the situation other than their own effort is also a signal that change is needed.

As noted when we discussed the recent educational reform movement, the report *Involvement in Learning* (National Institute of Education, 1984) focused extensively on the process of curricular design and implementation. Following Astin, the report urged educators to design curriculum to foster involvement. In fact, it boldly asserted that the effectiveness of any educational policy or practice is directly related to the capacity of that policy or practice to increase student involvement. Apparently, the report writers thought these ideas were applicable at both the program level and the course level.

The suggestions about involvement merit more attention at the program level. Faculty in academic programs, such as majors, need to begin conversations about how to build on student goals and motivations and how to help students construct meaning from the set of courses they take in the field. Faculty who have thought about motivation and involvement when planning their own courses can readily translate their thinking to ask what changes might be recommended for programs. Of course, ideas will vary by field. One possible model involves undergraduate students in research projects that help them understand how inquiry leads to new knowledge (Weaver, 1991). For professional programs, internships and practica help to achieve integration. A parallel idea for the social sciences may be found in community involvement and service experiences.

Another helpful technique is a capstone course in which students reflect and write about connections between ideas from several program courses. Such activities apparently challenge some core curriculum proposals we have discussed because they urge that students discover and reconstruct knowledge rather than absorbing what others have discovered and written about. It may be useful to examine and utilize in greater detail types of involvement and socialization processes that characterize graduate programs, creating undergraduate counterparts that will benefit all students.

Encouraging Integration, Coherence, and Connectedness

Faculty usually have well-developed knowledge structures for the discipline they teach. The structure of the subject matter, also called *content structure*, is defined as "the web of concepts and their interrelationships in a body of instructional material" (Shavelson & Geeslin, 1975, p. 201). These structures used in classrooms are not accidental; faculty trained in a discipline tend to use the structure of the discipline to organize their courses. Although different faculty from the same discipline may structure disciplinary knowledge in somewhat different ways, the basic relationships among concepts are generally similar. Content structures, usually derived from textbooks and instructional materials, have been compared and classified.

To understand how students acquire knowledge, we must examine both the structure of the subject matter itself and the students' internal representations of the structure of that subject matter. Students' knowledge structures—that is, their individual representations and organizations of information—are therefore important to instructors who may use these understandings to improve course planning and instruction. Students' cognitive structures are related to their achievement in class, especially final course exams and course grades. Students' structures become more elaborate and similar to instructors' cognitive structures over a semester (Naveh-Benjamin, McKeachie, Lin, & Tucker, 1986). The superior student often organizes course concepts much as the instructor does.

It takes many years for a faculty member to master the natural content structure of a discipline, but fortunately it does not take as long to initiate students into that concept structure to improve their understanding and achievement. McKeachie et al. (1990) suggest that teachers regularly influence the development of students' knowledge structures when they (1) organize and present material in a meaningful way, (2) require students to actively organize the learning material, and (3) help students link instructional material to their own knowledge structures. Besides the traditional well-organized lecture, numerous techniques can be used to help students build appropriate cognitive structures.

Direct techniques ask students to arrange key concepts and propositions from a text, a lecture, or an experiment into spatial diagrams or hierarchical structures which indicate the relationships among them. Such spatial relationships may be trees and graphs, concept maps, or networks. Researchers also use indirect methods that are beyond the scope of our discussion here but can be modified by faculty to assess students' knowledge structures (see, e.g., Naveh-Benjamin & Lin, 1991). Having assessed students' existing knowledge structures and noted opportunities for building on prior knowledge and experience, instructors should be able to teach students the knowledge structures that should positively influence their learning outcomes.

To use this disciplinary approach, and because conceptual maps that relate ideas to each other depend on the relations within the subject matter (Posner & Rudnitsky, l994), faculty need to ask such questions as:

1. Is there a small set of fundamental concepts that underlie knowledge in the field?
2. How might these concepts and their relationships be represented?
3. How can these fundamental concepts and relationships be taught to the novice?
4. Is there a set of problems that students are expected to learn to solve? What is the problem-solving method?

Not all professors in all fields will find the same answer to these questions, nor will all be equally comfortable using concept maps to represent knowledge to students. The ideas of fostering integration and coherence through concept maps are likely to appeal to faculty in disciplines that teach concepts hierarchically, building linkages among them. For faculty in fields emphasizing students' personal development or those focusing on values, however, different but equally appropriate techniques would link concepts with social problems, career goals, or personal issues. Such deliberate linkages to practical concerns can also well serve students in vocational programs. For the humanities, ideas can be related to a central theme, such as expressiveness or aesthetic value, that relies on verbal representations or other forms of communication. In considering disciplinary structure, one must think not only about concepts and basic principles but also about modes of inquiry, problem-solving strategies, and organizing concepts that increase the meaningfulness of what is learned, thereby reducing the need for memorization.

We define curricular integration as resulting from the student's assimilation and reconstruction of the relations of concepts within an academic field and their connections with life and work. Thus, integration can be thought of as a process that occurs when students incorporate knowledge, behaviors, and attitudes included in the curricular plan into their own thoughts and lives. A "coherent" curricular plan can exist in a professor's mind or notebook, but curricular integration cannot take place until students interact with the plan and use it to develop meaning (Stark, 1986). Students' educational goals, as well as their cognitive and affective characteristics, will influence the degree to which they integrate the content of a plan. In some ways, integration resembles the concepts of coherence and connectedness used by the AAC task force in *Integrity in the College Curriculum.* Yet integration is a more complete concept because it requires interaction with the learner. Like the idea of involvement, it tells us that the plan should include consideration of the learner.

Fostering Intellectual Development

Psychology of learning is useful to curriculum planners because it helps professors to understand and modify the process of student intellectual development. In previous sections, we have considered how learners approach specific tasks and concepts at the lesson or course level, building their new knowledge into organized conceptual structures. We can also describe learning from a broader view, considering how the student relates to the educational process and to his world as a whole. This changing holistic relationship, which we will call intellectual development, may be viewed as the adoption of new learning styles, new patterns of learning, and new degrees of willingness to continue to learn. It will be reflected in the learner's approach to courses, to academic programs, and eventually to a chosen profession and lifestyle. It may include enhancement in all three of the types of intelligence outlined by Sternberg: analytical, contextual, and experiential.

A number of frameworks describe intellectual development. Some were developed prior to the new concepts of cognition we have discussed but are consistent with them. One of the most appealing and useful ways of describing development is generically referred to as *stage theory.* Such theories describe individuals as passing sequentially through life toward some optimum (or idealized) point of development. Progress through the stages is influenced by experiences the individuals encounter. Because nearly all faculty believe that learning to think effectively is an important goal of college, stage theories describing successive levels of intellectual development are appealing to most professors. However, just as different aspects of learning theory will be differentially useful to faculty in different academic fields as they construct academic plans, we know that not all faculty will find ways to capitalize on information provided by stage theories.

One stage theory of development that appeals to many faculty members is Perry's scheme of intellectual development, which helps us understand how students develop critical perspectives during college. On the basis of extensive interviews of male students at Harvard University over many years, Perry (1970) described how students gradually change their world views, developing from stereotypic thinking and reliance on moral and intellectual absolutes to more contextual, relative views of truth. Perry found that most of the men students began college in a *dualistic* stage; that is, they saw the world in ab-

solute, right/wrong terms, often based on what they had learned at home. In the college setting, dualists expect that courses will exhibit clear structures and that the instructor is the authority—that is, if not the source of complete truth, at least the source of the right answers in the discipline.

Following the dualism stage, students move into a stage characterized by *multiplicity.* They begin to see issues from multiple perspectives; they see the possibility that there is more than one right choice, and they begin to consult with others. Students now view instructors as individuals who, rather than providing truth, provide methods for getting answers. Students in this stage are more comfortable with less structure in the classroom and enjoy, or at least tolerate, more participatory course activities.

When students leave the multiplicity stage, they enter a stage in which they take responsibility for making choices in the face of multiple alternatives. Although they still consult with others, they realize that choices must be their own. During this stage of *relativism,* students accept the complexities of knowledge and observe that, although there may be many alternatives, some answers are better than others. Finally, a very few students move during the college years to *commitment,* choosing from among the various answers those they will espouse consistently.

Students report that the transition from dualism to multiplicity is most difficult. Some students are threatened by new ideas and may hold tightly to stereotypic beliefs. Perry notes that dualistic students often have difficulty making their own decisions and commitments in a relativistic and complex world. Sometimes the threats lead to psychological or even physical withdrawal from the source of the challenge. Thus, faculty who are aware of the varying developmental levels of students in their courses can help students manage feelings of inconsistency or threat in the early stages of development.

Development as described by the Perry scheme will be most relevant to faculty members in the social sciences and humanities who hope to help students develop critical perspectives on their world. Yet even science faculty members are finding that students must unlearn dualistic ways of thinking about such topics as evolution, human reproduction, and nuclear energy before they are open to developing new conceptions. Thus, knowledge about stages of intellectual development is useful to all instructors.

Perry collected his data through lengthy interviews over time, but other researchers have tried to develop shorter ways of assessing students' levels of intellectual development using inventories or short interviews that could be adapted for use in classrooms and programs. Assessing stages of student intellectual development is not easy. Interviews are time consuming but paper and pencil methods have often lacked reliability. One useful reliable paper and pencil instrument to measure Perry level of development, the Learning Context Questionnaire, was developed by Griffith and Chapman (1982). Other procedures can be obtained from a clearinghouse maintained by those interested in Perry's work (Moore, 1988).

Attempts to develop readily administered Perry-scheme instruments have been largely overshadowed by the modified developmental scheme and simplified interview protocol of the Reflective Judgment Inventory (King & Kitchener, 1994). Like Perry, King and Kitchener found a pattern of development progressing from absolute knowledge to relative knowledge and finally to an acceptance that some knowledge is more certain or truer than others for the individual student. In addition, they discovered that students in the lowest developmental stage (absolute knowledge) could not distinguish between well-structured problems (those that have answers) and ill-structured problems (those for which no clear answers exist).

They point out that many faculty members overestimate the intellectual maturity of their students as they choose content and instructional activities posing ill-structured problems. The unrealistic expectations that faculty may hold for students can cause low expectancy of success for students, lowered self-efficacy in the subject, and a generally downward spiral of decreased involvement. Like the Perry scheme, using the Kitchener and King Reflective Judgment Interview requires considerable training.

Baxter Magolda (1992) presented another scheme (see Table 8-2) and added the idea of "contextual knowing" as the ultimate step, stressing that only a few students achieve the stage of contextual knowing during the college years, if ever. According to data collected by Baxter Magolda, 70% of college freshmen are absolute knowers; the rest are "transitional knowers." Sophomores are about evenly divided between absolute and transitional knowers. A greater proportion of juniors and seniors show significant growth beyond this point, toward contextual knowing.

As educators have become more aware that students' learning and intellectual development depends on their background and other characteristics, they have gathered additional knowledge about gender differences in development. Perry's data were based on male students. More recently, Belenky and associates (1986) found that young women experienced patterns of intellectual development similar to those discovered by Perry for young men, with one significant difference. Belenky and her colleagues added "constructed knowledge," which uses both head and heart to see truth in a complex ambiguous world. These researchers distinguish between "separate knowing" and "connected knowing." Separate knowing (more typical of males) focuses on formal analysis of the object or topic under study, whereas "connected knowing" (more common among females)

TABLE 8-2 Baxter Magolda Model of Epistemological Reflection

Domains	Absolute Knowing	Transitional Knowing	Independent Knowing	Contextual Knowing
Role of learner	• Obtains knowledge from instructor	• Understands knowledge	• Thinks for self • Shares views with others • Creates own perspective	• Exchanges and compares perspectives • Thinks through problems • Integrates and applies knowledge
Role of peers	• Share materials • Explain what they have learned to each other	• Provide active exchanges	• Share views • Serve as a source of knowledge	• Enhance learning via quality contributions
Role of instructor	• Communicates knowledge appropriately • Ensures that students understand knowledge	• Uses methods aimed at understanding • Employs methods that help apply knowledge	• Promotes independent thinking • Promotes exchange of opinions	• Promotes application of knowledge in context • Promotes evaluative discussion of perspectives • Student and teacher critique each other
Evaluation	• Provides vehicle to show instructor what was learned	• Measures students' understanding of the material	• Rewards independent thinking	• Accurately measures competence • Student and teacher work toward goal and measure progress
Nature of knowledge	• Is certain or absolute	• Is partially certain and partially uncertain	• Is uncertain—everyone has own beliefs	• Is contextual; judge on basis of evidence in context

Source: From *Knowing and Reasoning in College: Gender-Related Patterns in Students' Intellectual Development* by Baxter Magolda (1992), p. 30. Reprinted by permission of Jossey-Bass Publishers, Inc.

focuses on a personal understanding of the object or topic. Separate learning emphasizes competition, logical reasoning, and other approaches that separate self from subject. Connected learning emphasizes cooperation, discussion, and clarification, approaches that involve learners with the subject and with one another. Adaptations in learning tasks may be used to accommodate these gender differences.

Academic Plans for Diverse Learners

As faculty plan courses and programs, a variety of special needs of learners (other than the separate learning styles of men and women and those of students at varying development stages) emerges as important. These include the needs of adult students, minority students, underprepared students, disabled students, and students who differ from others in some way such as sexual orientation, religious background, or cultural orientation. Gifted and talented students also have special needs. In terms of career development, students who are excessively career conscious, who are undecided about careers, or who return to college for specific retraining in their jobs all have very different needs. Specialized literatures deal with the needs of each of these special groups of students, so we mention them only briefly here to highlight how learning theory applies to constructing appropriate academic plans for them.

Adult Students. These students may have specific goals that require them to plan their own learning experiences. Their goals may be clearer and their motivation to succeed may be stronger than those of younger students. Because of their life obligations and various life transitions in which they are involved, they are often more interested in career advancement and less interested in developing social relationships on campus than

traditional-age students. They may require flexible time frames for learning and may necessarily have less involvement in college activities than younger students.

Adult students, particularly those who have struggled with formal education in the past, may also have low self-efficacy, and, in fact, their learning strategies may be underdeveloped. They may need help in setting standards that are appropriate for their own performance, rather than those relevant to their classmates of entirely different circumstances. They have life experiences that help them connect learning to things important to them, and instructors can capitalize on these connections to help improve success and thus self-confidence and improved learning skills. Typologies of learners abound and may be helpful in keeping diversity in mind. One lists five types of adult learners: (1) the confident, pragmatic, goal-oriented learner; (2) the affective learner; (3) the learner in transition; (4) the integrated learner; and (5) the risk-taker (Endorf & McNeff, 1990). Polson (1993) points out that many of the special plans and choices of instructional strategies that help faculty deal with adult students are also effective with traditional-age learners because they value the individual student. This valuing is a key point in designing academic plans to meet learner needs. [For other recent extensive reviews concerning adult learners, see Kasworm (1990) and Polson (1993).]

Minority Students. For minority students who are isolated from their own cultural communities, feelings may be as important as cognitive influences on learning. Tracey and Sedlacek (1987) listed a number of noncognitive factors that influence retention and academic success for minority students more decisively than cognitive factors. These factors include: (1) developing a positive self-concept and learning to bridge cultural gaps, (2) understanding and dealing with racism, (3) developing a realistic self-appraisal, (4) learning to formulate academic goals and to prefer long-range goals to short-range goals, (5) acquiring mentorship from a strong support person early in college, (6) gaining successful leadership experience within one's own cultural group, (7) experiencing community service, and (8) building on knowledge gained in non-traditional ways.

Other authors join Tracey and Sedlacek (1987) in asserting that, for minority students, attitude may be more important than pedagogy. A student's ethnic and cultural background must be considered in the academic plan because ethnic identity is a key factor in self-efficacy, and self-efficacy, in turn, is related to both motivation and effort. Some minority students have the feeling that they are bound to fail. Academic plans that reinforce this syndrome are unlikely to lead to success. Faculty in different disciplines can use this list to guide their choice of possible activities for minority students as they plan courses.

Underprepared Students. At the program level, four different approaches to structuring an academic plan for underprepared students have been common. These include (1) offering remedial skills courses, (2) providing learning assistance to individual students, (3) devising course-related supplementary learning activities for some objectives, and (4) connecting comprehensive learning assistance with regular academic courses. Those who direct special programs for underprepared students emphasize that comprehensive approaches usually work best. This observation is consistent with the learning theory we have reviewed. Isolated remedial skills courses are not as effective as comprehensive approaches to learning in regular courses where instructors develop learning strategies and use them to relate subject concepts into an organized view of the subject.

Students may have to start with basic learning strategies and move gradually to more complex strategies before they can proceed independently, but their self-efficacy with respect to the subject grows as they gradually acquire the ability to learn in regular courses. Embedding developmental efforts in regular courses also provides an opportunity to increase intrinsic interest in the subject matter by providing situational incentives. Roueche and Roueche (1993) have described successful efforts in community colleges to help underprepared students cope with college-level work.

Enhancing Students' Learning Strategies

When successfully utilized, the cognitive abilities of students can positively influence their success in a course or program. But students also come to their courses with differing levels of self-awareness and varying metacognitive skills—that is, with varying abilities to reflect on their own learning. By assessing students' abilities to use complex learning strategies, faculty may be able to diagnose problems and suggest ways of improving students' approaches to academic tasks. In one sense, it is possible to improve intelligence itself, if intelligence is viewed as a dynamic rather than static attribute.

One way to help students is to make them aware that they have the ability to map new concepts in relation to their prior knowledge. This recognition can increase their self-confidence in the subject matter. By paying explicit attention to learning strategies, instructors in all courses may help students make better use of the tools they already have for approaching and solving problems. Instructors can draw on students' experiential and contextual intelligence as well as their analytical intelligence. Tasks that require creative thinking and interpersonal relationships can supplement analytic tasks and challenge students in nontraditional academic ways. Although it appears daunting at first to the faculty member concerned with developing academic tasks in a course, the problem of differentiating among Sternberg's three types of student intelligence is not as intractable as it might appear. It merely means that professors cannot repeatedly use the same type of assignment but must tailor the assignments to the type of "intelligence" that they wish students to develop further.

These ideas are hardly new. One of the strongest advocates of meeting students' special needs and developing their learning skills has been K. Patricia Cross. Cross has considered adult learners, first-generation students, underprepared students, and minority students in her writing for many years. She has advanced the thesis that the curriculum must be reshaped to help such students master educational tasks and thus progress in both cognitive and affective domains. Cross also has asserted that traditional instruction must be modified to offer opportunities for mastery and for becoming excellent in work that society considers valuable.

A second thesis put forth by Cross more than thirty years ago was that learning should be individualized. She urged that teachers facilitate learning when they pay attention to these concepts:

1. The student must be active rather than passive.

2. The goals of learning must be clear and must be made explicit to the student.

3. Students will learn small lesson units dealing with a single concept faster than complex lessons.

4. Teachers must help students link concepts into networks.

5. Effective learning requires feedback and evaluation.

6. Individualized instruction features self-pacing and high levels of learner control.

Cross's ideas, which emphasize the importance of prior background and learning skills in college success, allow us to paraphrase cognitive theory as: "What you do may depend on who you are." Another educational psychologist, C. Robert Pace, who has developed ways to measure students' effort, may be characterized as saying "what counts is what you do" as a learner. Our consideration of learning theory helps us to see that these recommendations are closely related. We propose that "who you are may determine what you do, but what you do, in fact, changes who you are."

DEVELOPING INTENTIONAL LEARNERS

Many educators would agree that the primary goal of education is, in fact, to "change who you are." Educators hope to create learners who can learn effectively throughout their lifetimes, using learning skills, acquiring new knowledge, and organizing it for their life and career needs. This goal becomes increasingly more important as the rapid pace of technology makes both knowledge and the current ways of obtaining it obsolete almost daily.

While translating new knowledge about "learning to learn" for accounting educators revising their curricula, Francis, Mulder, and Stark (1995) thought of the optimal college graduate as an "intentional learner" (see Figure 8-4), defined this learner, and suggested roles for the instructor to promote the learner's attributes In their scheme, the process of "learning to learn" can be taught; in fact, a good teacher carefully orchestrates this process. Intentional learning develops the learner's conscious understanding of the learning process. An intentional learner learns "with self-directed purpose, intending and choosing *that* he will learn and *how* he will learn and *what* he will learn." (Francis, Mulder, & Stark, 1995, p. 13). The intentional learner is characterized by five attributes, arranged in a developmental hierarchy (pp. 13–15):

1. *Questioning:* Facts, theories, experiences; wanting to learn; asking independent questions about what is to be known

2. *Organizing:* Ideas, meaning, knowledge; developing understanding of what is learned

3. *Connecting:* New knowledge with old; integrating what is learned into a broader pattern of understanding

4. *Reflecting:* On what, how, and why one is learning; understanding one's learning needs and strategies

5. *Adapting:* To new situations and needs; using what is learned in a changing world or profession (p. 14)

Figure 8-4 depicts the process of becoming an intentional learner as cumulative and cyclical. The specific processes—attaining knowledge, developing intellectual skills, and learning intentionally—parallel Baxter Magolda's (1992) development stages of absolute, transitional, independent, and contextual knowing. The role of the teacher changes at each stage of development, a point we shall develop more fully.

Students naturally differ in their ability as intentional learners as they pursue different subject fields. Therefore, the instructor must select topics and strategies consistent with a student's current stage yet sufficiently challenging to move the student to the next stage. This model has been developed in detail for students in career fields, where learning to learn is an important professional attribute, but it has broader applicability to all students.

ESTABLISHING TWO-WAY COMMUNICATION WITH LEARNERS

To help learners link concepts and become intentional learners, instructors need to communicate the academic plan they have in mind. Instructors help students take responsibility for their learning by communicating a vision and purpose for the course or program. Effective communication about a course means that faculty share their purposes—the assumptions and principles of learning that direct how they select content and instructional activities, the concept map of the field that is the subject of the course, and the extent to which they tried to accommodate students' goals in the course plan. Similarly, program faculty must share their vision of the academic program with students who will commit time and energy to the study of a particular field. Such sharing requires self-confidence and openness on the part of faculty because students who are becoming intentional learners may question course and program plans as well as the value of particular subject matter contained within these plans.

Course syllabi and program descriptions therefore deserve more attention than they typically receive from faculty. Erikson and Strommer (1991) indicate that when they ask students at the end of their first year of college what might have helped them most, one of the three most frequent responses is "provide a better syllabus" (p. 81). A complete syllabus includes ideas about the instructor's thinking and course planning (Stark, Lowther, & Martens, 1984). We suggest that faculty discuss course goals and structure with students at the beginning of a course and periodically during it. Departmental advisors might follow this lead and periodically discuss program goals and structure as they meet with students throughout their academic careers.

The first step in improving communication with students about courses and programs is knowing who students are. To this end, colleges should begin to collect and store computerized information about individual students' learning styles, skills, and progress. They could then quickly prepare composite profiles of students for each class that is taught. These profiles would greatly assist faculty in course and program planning and might resemble the profiles that some

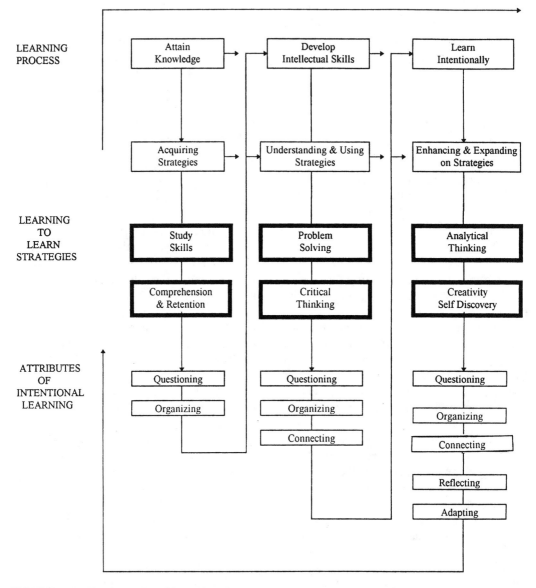

FIGURE 8-4   The Intentional Learning Process

Source: Intentional Learning: A Process of Learning to Learn in the Accounting Curriculum by M. C. Francis, T. Mulder, & J. S. Stark (1995), p. 17. Reprinted by permission of the American Accounting Association.

college and university development offices now construct on potential donors.

The class profile might include each student's's goals, previous preparation, basic skills levels, placement test information, preferred learning styles, and developed learning strategies. Of course, the data would be carefully chosen and developed; further, because students are constantly changing in both cognitive and motivational attributes, the information in each student's file would need to be updated frequently, probably each term. Advances in computer technology make the generation of course and program profiles feasible and advances in research on teaching and learning suggest their importance, even necessity. If thoughtfully prepared and explained, faculty can no longer legitimately insist that they don't need such information, might misinterpret it, or don't know how to use it.

Having a picture of the students in classes and programs will help faculty create academic plans that accommodate the needs of different learners. It will also enable faculty to better communicate to students why courses and programs are structured in particular ways. The more faculty and students know about each other's goals and plans and the more they understand what is happening in the classroom or program, the better the learning process will proceed.

The degree to which students integrate new knowledge may be significantly altered if instructors take seriously the ideas about learners and learning that we have discussed in this chapter. Instructors who increase their emphasis on learner integration in developing academic plans may need to develop new approaches to their work. Specifically, they must identify the possible obstacles to successful integration of knowledge and adjust their course and program plans to identify and meet specific student needs. They will also find ways to recognize when students have learned successfully and build on those experiences.

The role of college instructors in creating academic plans requires that they be versed in the central concepts of their discipline, consciously attend to the relationship among these concepts, and link them with tenets of learning psychology when selecting from a repertoire of pedagogical strategies.

CHAPTER 9

Selecting Instructional Processes

TRANSLATING CONTENT TO INSTRUCTIONAL FORM

In this chapter, we focus on how professors select instructional processes and on how other elements of the plan, such as educational purposes, discipline content, sequence, and perceptions of learners, affect their choices. Typically, a professor gradually acquires a repertoire of instructional activities to help students achieve specific educational objectives based on broad educational goals and the content of the academic field. If the instructor gives little conscious attention to either learning objectives or learner needs, the form in which students engage content may be primarily the lecture method. The faculty member's knowledge of how alternative instructional strategies might help learners achieve the objectives more successfully may expand his or her instructional choices.

The choice among instructional processes is also influenced by a variety of internal, organizational, and external factors, including college and program goals, existing organizational structures and traditions, and the availability of financial, technological,

and human resources. Influences within an academic program most strongly affect the instructional processes selected for courses, while organizational and external influences may be more potent for the instructional choices faculty make at the program level. Figure 9-1 gives a broad overview of these relationships among academic plan elements and the influences on instructional choices.

In the early part of this chapter we focus on what we know about how faculty choose instructional processes to carry out their objectives at the course, program, and college levels. We ask: How do faculty typically choose instructional strategies? What encourages them in a broad range of choices and what limits them? We will first describe course planning, then program and collegewide academic planning. At each level, we will describe not only the choices faculty most typically make when selecting instructional processes but also some common variations and recent innovations.

Subsequently, we attempt to expand the range of instructional choices that faculty may make by describing new considerations, based primarily on cognitive psychology, that

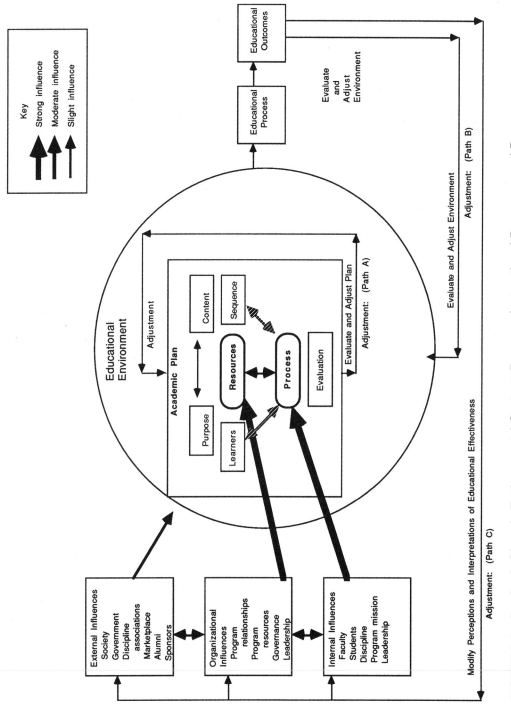

FIGURE 9-1 Academic Plans in Environmental Context: Focus on Instructional Processes and Resources

might encourage departures from long-standing instructional traditions. Since we intend to increase faculty awareness of alternative strategies for instruction, we ask such questions as: What choices might professors make if they were more aware of research on learner development? How can the educational environment better support the selection of appropriate processes? At the core of recent efforts to reshape curriculum are attempts to encourage faculty to establish clear expectations for learning, to evaluate the results of academic plans, and to use these evaluation results to improve courses and programs. Since we believe that these efforts will continue to be at the center of curriculum reform over the next few decades, we particularly stress here the importance of establishing and communicating clear expectations for learners. In Chapter 10, we will turn our attention to evaluating the results.

SELECTING INSTRUCTIONAL PROCESSES FOR COURSES

As instructors described their planning processes to us they translated their broad educational beliefs into more specific objectives for learning within the content area, thus building units of instruction. Their accustomed teaching style and a variety of contextual factors (such as college and program goals, learner goals, and available resources) influence how those units are actually taught. But they do not always fully articulate their objectives as they seek instructional processes the way they did in interviews.

One reason why the range of instructional plans faculty choose is somewhat narrow is that college-level research is lacking concerning which instructional processes are most effective for learning in particular disciplines and under varied circumstances. Without evidence of effectiveness, faculty members may and do choose from several types of instructional processes, including lectures

and discussions, often with little reason to prefer one over another. Lacking other rationales, choices may be based on preferred teaching style, the instructor's beliefs and inclination to interact with students, or simply on tradition.

Educational Objectives: Product of Purpose and Content

Disciplines and associated faculty beliefs about education are overwhelmingly the strongest influences as instructors plan courses and programs, affecting the purpose of education, the content selected, and how the content is sequenced. Faculty translate these into course objectives or, as we called them earlier following Posner, intended learning outcomes. Professors may or may not record these objectives in a syllabus, but most will share them in some form with students.

In our survey we asked faculty to state two actual objectives for their introductory course. Many faculty cited first some aspect of learning the concepts of the field. As we analyzed the remaining objectives, we were able to group them into broad categories that correspond fairly closely to the typology of educational purposes/beliefs we discussed earlier. In Table 9-1 we show the variation by academic field for the several broad goal themes we extracted from faculty responses. Clearly, different fields have different course objectives.

In stating objectives, instructors recognized that students have different levels of problem-solving ability, an important cognitive skill in all disciplines. Improving this ability often becomes a course objective. Especially in the sciences and mathematics, faculty members described to us how they tried to improve students' problem-solving abilities, usually by modeling and practice, as well as by helping students acquire the ability to retrieve information.

TABLE 9-1   Course Goals Contributed by Faculty Members in Selected Academic Fields

Type of Goal	Percent Responses by Academic Field[a]								
	Composition (n=415)	Literature (n=210)	History (n=263)	Sociology (n=141)	Psychology (n=180)	Biology (n=215)	Mathematics (n=304)	Nursing (n=68)	Business (n=91)
Concepts or knowledge in the field	23.4	47.1	52.7	53.6	56.3	55.2	36.8	55.8	54.4
Personal or social development	10.4	14.0	9.9	21.7	20.2	17.2	7.3	13.3	14.2
Intellectual development	20.4	15.8	22.0	18.4	10.4	11.9	19.6	6.2	5.9
Skill development	37.8	11.0	7.1	2.6	4.2	2.3	12.6	11.5	5.9
Value development	1.5	2.3	1.9	1.1	1.5	1.5	2.1	0.0	1.2
Great ideas	0.0	0.5	0.6	0.0	0.0	0.0	0.0	0.0	0.0
Preparation for the future	3.3	1.0	0.4	0.7	2.7	5.8	15.1	9.7	11.8
Aesthetics	1.0	7.8	2.6	0.4	0.9	2.8	1.2	0.0	1.8
Unclear	2.1	1.0	2.8	1.5	3.9	3.3	5.2	3.5	4.7
Total	99.9	100.5	100.0	100.0	100.1	100.0	99.9	100.0	99.9

Source: *Planning Introductory College Courses* by Stark, Lowther, Bentley et al. (1990), p. 114. Reprinted by permission of the National Center for Research to Improve Postsecondary Teaching and Learning, The University of Michigan.

[a]Each faculty member was asked to contribute two goals; a few contributed only one.

Instructors are also aware that students possess varying competencies with basic skills (such as reading, writing, speaking, listening, and mathematical reasoning). Along with their own course objectives, they take these factors into account when planning. Although faculty members in all fields noted substantial variation in students' basic skills, not all felt that improving them was a legitimate objective of their course. Most instructors felt a lack of training in what they, personally and pedagogically, could do about differences or how they might vary instructional processes to account for this student diversity. On campuses where a learning assistance center is available, faculty prefer to refer students for help than to struggle with this issue in the classroom.

Students also operate at different levels of intellectual development. Especially in the humanities and social science fields, instructors intend to help students move to higher levels of interpretation and critical analysis. Although they might not use educational or psychological terms to describe their instructional objectives, they deliberately try to design experiences that will help students make the types of intellectual transitions portrayed by the Perry Scheme or the Reflective Judgment Scheme. Specifically, they try to move students from dualistic positions that base notions of right and wrong on authority to relativistic positions that recognize differences of opinion as legitimate. Some may lead students toward the development of commitments and values. Particularly, at advanced course levels in college career studies, an instructional goal may be to encourage students to move from relativism to positions of moral and ethical commitment that signify professional identity.

Discussions about goals for students and some learner attributes tend to make faculty uncomfortable: these include motivation, anxiety, learning styles and making connections with students' lives. Faculty in our interviews worried about students who lacked motivation for their courses and often felt frustrated with their inability to increase it. Similarly, they felt helpless to deal with multiple learning styles and to create levels of anxiety to spur students on to greater effort but not cause too much stress. Finally, although over 50% of faculty in all fields desired to make connections between course content and students' lives, they felt that their efforts to do so were less than effective because of the diversity of students in their classes and the substantial number of students with lives quite different from their own.

Teaching Style: Product of Content and Faculty Background

Just as student learning styles are relatively enduring predispositions for dealing with new material, faculty teaching styles are adopted early and tend to persist. Academic field (particularly the extent to which field is structured hierarchically) and beliefs tend to interact with personal characteristics to produce in faculty specific preferences for teaching styles and instructional processes. Just as students' learning styles can be modified, however, faculty members' teaching preferences are not as immutable as is often believed; they may be altered by the context.

When studying teaching styles, Erdle and Murray (1986) reported that classroom teacher behavior varied along a single dimension; faculty used one of two styles—a task orientation or an interpersonal orientation. Natural science professors were more task oriented than faculty in other arts and science fields. A two-fold classification that uses a somewhat different basis contrasts the didactic teacher and the evocative teacher (Axelrod, 1973). The didactic teacher is inclined to tell students what is known, the evocative teacher to try to have them discover it for themselves. Subdividing this classification further, Dressel (1980), suggested that the evocative teacher may be oriented in one of four ways: toward the discipline, toward self, toward developing the students' minds, or toward developing the students as persons. He called these four styles: (1) discipline-centered teaching, (2) instructor-centered teaching, (3) student-centered cognitive teaching, and (4) student-centered affective teaching.

Dressel and Marcus (1982) conveyed the potentially strong association of these teaching styles with the disciplines by portraying Axelrod's typology in a chart that shows "typical" choices among course components (such as content, instructional method, classroom climate, and others) linked with each style (pp. 10–11). This chart, reproduced in Table 9-2, accords well with what we found in our interviews. In short, educational beliefs and discipline socialization are strongly associated with specific teaching styles and instructional practices.

Despite their detailed chart, Dressel and Marcus acknowledge that it is inappropriate to imply that faculty members who generally espouse a particular teaching style are restricted to the type of teaching typically associated with that style (p. l2). Discipline-based teaching philosophies are further modified by teachers' responses to other context factors as they are translated into selection of instructional processes. These philosophies also may be modified by exposure to new ideas over the course of a faculty member's career. Such changes are found in the reports of other observers.

Maryellen Weimer (1987) reported two categories of teaching style: the shaping theory (characteristic of developing teachers) and the transfer theory (characteristic of experienced instructors). Many new faculty believe they are molding the student whereas faculty who are more experienced view students as contributing partners. Axelrod (1973) provided a case study of a university teacher who gradually changed teaching style as he gained experience, moving toward a greater sharing of authority and responsibility with students. This research supports the gradual changes in teaching style (at least in the humanities) to a more student-centered approach as faculty members log more teaching years.

Kugel (1993) also asserts that faculty members pass through several stages in teaching. In this stage theory, they focus primarily on their own role in the classroom, then they shift to focus on the subject they teach, then to their students' abilities, and finally to helping the students becoming more active, applying the material and becoming independent learners.

In summary, while several researchers have proposed similar classifications of relatively enduring teaching styles, the classifications are not mutually exclusive and are especially sensitive to context. Old teaching styles may be modified through collegial contacts, especially with interdisciplinary teaching and new disciplinary paradigms. Similarly, as professors are exposed to new contexts and new ways of teaching, they may adapt their instructional choices and teaching behaviors to be more effective.

Choosing Forms for Implementation

Generally, decisions about instructional processes to be used in courses are made by instructors individually, thus teaching styles are relatively important. But there is wide variation. At one extreme, some literature and sociology programs give professors *carte blanche* to teach any topic in any way they believe desirable to achieve their personal concept of appropriate student development. At the other extreme, some college science departments tightly coordinate programs; several instructors teach the same lesson in introductory courses and give common examinations according to the same class schedule to ensure that students learn a basic foundation of concepts and principles.

TABLE 9-2 Characteristics of Course Components for Four Teaching Orientations

Components	Discipline-Centered Teaching	Instructor-Centered Teaching	Student-Centered Teaching (Cognitive Approach)	Student-Centered Teaching (Affective Approach)
Course content	Based on disciplinary concepts, principles, theories, and methods.	Based on teacher's preferences and perceptions.	Composed of materials interesting to students and productive of cognitive outcomes.	Secondary—used to help students in maturation.
Method of instruction	Lectures and standard text, with systematic coverage of the body of knowledge.	Lecture or teacher-dominated discussion highlighting teacher's personality.	Discussion, with special lectures to focus on important issues.	Emphasis on student involvement and interaction as a means of personal and social development.
Classroom setting	Emotion free, with emphasis on scholarly objectivity.	Teacher dominated and controlled.	Somewhat relaxed but intellectually stimulating.	Highly informal, encouraging free student expression of feelings and concerns.
Student–faculty interaction	Familiarity and intimacy with students discouraged.	Discussions with students focused on clarifying lecture points.	Interactions planned to be intellectually stimulating to students.	Interactions in groups, with instructors acting as moderators.
Assignments	All students in course given the same assignment.	Reflect the teacher's interests and views of the discipline.	Geared to cultivate the desire to move toward intellectual maturity.	No formal assignments—students encouraged to work toward self-expression.
Objectives and evaluation	Students judged and graded by comparison with mastery standards.	Students judged and graded on ability to imitate professorial approaches, perspectives, and formulations.	Students judged and graded on tasks that require new resources and strategies.	Students evaluated (perhaps by themselves and their peers) on participation and self-expression.

Category				
Professorial self-image	Identifies with the discipline rather than with teaching role.	Has strong ego and radiates self-confidence.	Developer of student's ability to analyze, reason, use language effectively, and solve problems.	Counselor and "resource person."
Students	Viewed as would-be majors and graduate school candidates.	Viewed as an audience or a source of acolytes.	Regarded as individuals who must become self-reliant in using their knowledge.	Viewed as individuals who must achieve self-insight and accept full responsibility for their own behavior and goals.
Adaptation to or in student groups	Course coverage standard for all sections.	Some adjustments made for different audiences.	Emphasis on the how and why of knowledge.	Group interaction used to motivate students to learn.
Originality or creativity	Students encouraged to use the standard way of solving pre-structured problems.	Originality in student responses acceptable if it does not clash with teacher's views.	Originality in thinking encouraged.	Each student expected to achieve self-realization.
Individualization	Assignments designed to help students master materials presented.	Students expected to adapt to teacher's interests rather than develop their own.	Students encouraged to develop their own analytic abilities.	Allows individuals to develop and acquire new resources and new ways of organizing ideas.
Source of standards	Standards of mastery set for each unit of learning by experts in the field.	Teacher standards based upon acceptance of his or her views.	Students expected to develop and use high standards in their own work.	Standards individually derived and self-imposed.
Objectivity	Expression of opinion in the classroom minimized.	Teacher's seeming objectivity actually highly subjective.	Analytical, objective, and logical instructional methods.	Understanding and acceptance more prized than objectivity.

Source: Teaching and Learning in College by Paul Dressel & Dora Marcus, copyright 1982 by Jossey-Bass Publishers, Inc., pp. 10–11. Reprinted by permission of Jossey-Bass Publishers, Inc.

Choices of instructional processes are related to decisions about sequencing content. The sequencing of ideas, which depends on the instructors' understanding of how ideas and concepts relate to one another in a course or program, is an important precursor of choosing instructional processes. Yet, more than one method of sequencing may be appropriate in most disciplines. Even in history, so frequently taught chronologically, alternative methods of sequencing can be effective.

Even when a specific sequence has been chosen for the content to be taught, instructional processes can be classified according to how much student involvement they entail. Weston and Cranton (1986) classified course-level instructional strategies into four general categories: instructor-centered, interactive, individualized, and experiential.

Instructor-centered strategies place the greatest responsibility on the instructor. The operational strategy is usually lecture but sometimes includes demonstration.

Interactive strategies use communication among students as well as communication between students and instructor. The discussion method is most common and is believed superior to the lecture for teaching high-level skills such as analysis, synthesis, and evaluation. Group project and peer teaching activities also belong in this category.

Individualized strategies are used to accommodate the different learning rates of students and to provide immediate feedback, intended to reinforce student effort. They emphasize the pacing of material and include programmed instruction, modularized instruction, and computer-assisted instruction (CAI).

Experiential instructional strategies often take place in settings other than the classroom. These types of instruction may be led by the instructor, they may be interactive, and they may also be individualized. Drill may be a form of experiential learning controlled by the instructor; laboratories may be either instructor controlled or student controlled, depending on the degree to which the students design their own experiments. Role playing, simulation, and games, where the student is distinctly more active and responsible than the instructor, may be used for a higher level of learning. In part, the choice among these groups of processes will depend upon conscious decisions and available resources.

Faculty members readily accept the responsibility of deciding which methods of instruction should be used under specific conditions to foster desired changes in students. They use trial and error to gain evidence that some instructional activities are more effective than others. Yet both our analysis of course syllabi and comments faculty made about how they taught confirmed that lecture remains the predominant mode of college teaching, particularly in introductory courses (see also Thielens, 1987). Today, lectures are often quite informal; faculty commonly reported some discussion between teacher and students.

In our studies of varied college career studies programs, we gathered considerable information about instructional strategies other than lectures. Frequently, faculty identified career-oriented educational objectives including attitudes such as professional identity and motivation to continue learning, and behaviors such as leadership. Often faculty members believed that these attitudes and behaviors were achieved in internship settings. The settings for these experiences, however, were often minimally supervised and on-site supervisors did not necessarily share the instructional goals. Although experiential education is very important in professional education, faculty spend relatively little time in designing it to achieve their objectives and they seldom authenticate their assumptions about what the students learn in the field.

Instructional Variations for Courses

Variations on the lecture method of teaching became common about the time of World War

II but, as we noted earlier, their use diminished when increased enrollments caused classes to expand in size. In the 1960s and 1970s scholars again recorded substantial movement toward experimentation with methods other than lectures. Most variations were stimulated by the need to increase student motivation or to deal with a broadening span of individual learning differences among students. Innovations included self-paced learning, mastery learning, programmed learning, competency-based education, and others (see Cole, 1978, for a good review of instructional experimentation in the 1970s).

Some variations directed at increasing motivation modify the traditional course structure or build on the lecture-discussion-laboratory choice within that structure. These include various types of in-class discussion techniques such as guided design—a problem-solving technique where students work in groups that systematically discuss problems related to the lecture. Laboratories can range from routinized programmed instruction to actual intellectual discovery.

The variations designed to accommodate individual differences often depart entirely from the lecture structure and may emphasize self-paced learning alternatives. Pacing is the rate at which information is presented to the learner. In the lecture, it is controlled by the instructor; in self-paced methods it is controlled by the learner. Examples of self-paced plans are the Keller plan, autotutorial methods, modular learning plans, and their technological cousin, computer-assisted instruction.

Individualized instruction became especially popular in the mid–1960s and 1970s. One form that provides considerable independence for the student to negotiate the topics and conditions of learning is contract learning. Contract learning allows students to set and clarify their own objectives for a course, to determine jointly with the professor the activities to achieve those objectives, and often to define the criteria for evaluation (Barlow, 1974). Although the contract method of teaching may sustain student motivation and increase student–teacher rapport, providing orientation, expertise, guidance and resources require a greater expenditure of teacher time than more traditional methods.

Mastery learning is a self-paced technique based on the assumption that all students can learn the material given sufficient time—a view well suited to an egalitarian approach to educational opportunity. In mastery learning, students know the criteria for success, take frequent quizzes or tests to check their performance on each instructional unit of material, and continue to study the material until they have the ability to answer a high percentage of the questions. The technique is best suited for teaching and learning materials that are hierarchically structured and sequential, with right and wrong answers and definite criteria for testing.

A specific form of mastery learning called programmed instruction was extensively explored in schools of education during the 1970s. Faculty members experimented with structured design models that required explicit specification of behavioral objectives, activities targeted to achieve the objects, self-paced learning, and evaluation to determine the extent to which students achieved (Gow & Yeager, 1975). Because the method required little synthesis on the part of the student, and promoted the recognition of facts and clues rather than the construction of meaning, it was never widely accepted in higher education.

Like programmed learning, competency-based education was based on the tenets of behavioral psychology and, at least for a short time, was popular in some colleges. It requires that instructors specify each desired learning outcome in behavioral or performance terms and establish an appropriate criterion level for achievement. Because the system emphasizes achievement instead of "time serving," it challenges the well-established credit hour system of measuring educational progress. In the 1970s, some colleges (e.g., Governor's State

University in Illinois, Mars Hill College in North Carolina, and Sterling College in Kansas) developed extensive competency-based programs. However, faculty in fields such as humanities found it difficult to phrase all learning in criterion-referenced terms subject to observation and measurement. Even in more hierarchical fields, measures were subject to instructors' judgments and lacked validity and reliability. In general, the movement could not sustain its momentum.

In the 1960s and 1970s, college instructors responded to the emerging recognition that students learned at different rates and saw different aspects of their education as relevant. During this period, adaptation to both students' motivational needs and their individual differences was accepted as a responsibility in college teaching. Instead of mass lecture courses, students in experimenting colleges and programs left the group to do individualized, self-paced work. Similarly, content was often separated into smaller and smaller chunks for easier learning and outcomes were described at the level of specific behavior. Although these instructional reforms are no longer in the spotlight and, in fact, some would now be contested on the basis of more recent developments in cognitive psychology, progress toward conscious choice of the instructional process was made during this era. Retrospectively, some educators believe that the movement toward individualized learning successfully promoted consciousness of learner needs in designing academic plans. Furthermore, the competency-based movement improved instruction by requiring faculty discussion to develop objectives and set the competency criteria.

These curricular ideas and innovations have been important precursors to today's emphasis on recognizing individual student variability and specifying criteria to meet demands for assessment of student learning. But questions remain: How can student needs be accommodated in courses without the elaborate testing and placement procedures that the structured models suggested? How can their achievement be measured without trivializing the learning desired in college?

Influence of Educational Context and Environment

In interviews and surveys, faculty shared with us several specific contextual factors that influenced them to varying degrees as they chose instructional processes. These included college and program goals and available resources, including time, incentive systems, textbooks, and organizational structures. Far less frequently, they cited learner goals, learning theory, and campus instructional assistance centers as important influences on planning. The way contextual influences operate to modify course objectives after they have already been developed from purpose and content led us to think of them as *filters* that accentuate or attenuate the influences of discipline. Figure 9-2 depicts the "filters" and "form" components of the contextual filters model of course planning we introduced earlier. Some filters may influence course planning positively, as when faculty take into account student goals or when laboratory assistants are available to help with preparation. In other cases, the filters may act as constraints, as when no suitable textbook can be found or class periods are the wrong length for effective teaching.

Of course, the educational environments within American colleges vary greatly, and so the influence of contextual factors varies too. Faculty teaching in a community college with many vocationally oriented programs will experience influences that differ in both nature and intensity from those on faculty teaching in a selective liberal arts college whose student body is drawn from several states. The community college may be subject to strong influences from local employers and job opportunities, whereas the liberal arts college may be most responsive to the requirements of distant graduate and professional schools. The influence of contextual factors varies by field as well. Not surpris-

Content and Background Considerations (Content)

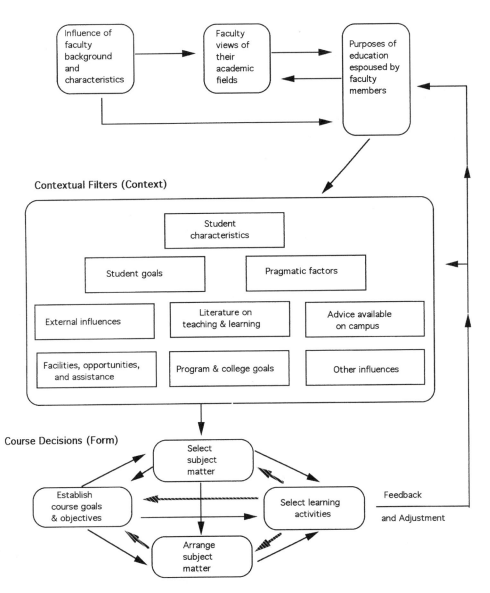

FIGURE 9-2   The Contextual Filters Model: Focus on Context and Form

Source: Planning College Courses: Influences on Faculty, by J. S. Stark, M. A. Lowther, R. J.
Bentley, et al. (1990), pp. 136–137. Reprinted by permission of The National Center for Research
to Improve Postsecondary Teaching and Learning, The University of Michigan.

ingly, biology professors are more concerned
about the adequacy of laboratory facilities
than are composition teachers. Some differences, however, are less obvious than college

type and field, and some filters may operate
very subtly.

  Internal and organizational influences
operate differently for instructors in different

fields. A great deal seems to depend on the relative strength of internal program (or department) forces compared to organizational forces outside the program. Organizational forces often vary depending on whether a program of study is largely insular or significantly influenced by its network of relationships within the institution and may also determine what level of resources is available. Contextual influences especially distinguish the traditional academic disciplines, affected more by internal influences, from those oriented toward career preparation, which typically respond to external pressures.

Contextual influences and resources modify how faculty construct academic plans, limit or expand the variety of plans they construct, and sometimes dictate the forms in which they implement their plans (instructional process) as well as the types of expectations they establish for students and for themselves. The contextual influences also modify teaching style, which is initially derived from disciplinary and educational beliefs. As we interviewed and surveyed faculty about contextual factors, we developed an understanding of some of the interactions of content and context that result in instructional form and, perhaps, limit the extent of deviation from lectures and discussions.

College and Program Goals

We found differences in how faculty perceived the effect of college and program goals on course goals. Most faculty told us that college goals had little direct influence on their course planning. They reported that college goals were somewhat vague and they simply accepted them without much reflection. College goals became important to faculty in their course planning when they dictated the level of student preparation (e.g., in an open-door community college or a highly selective liberal arts college) or when the goals were especially prominent, (e.g., in col-

leges with a strong religious orientation). In a few cases, mention of college goals brought negative reactions, as when they obliged a professor to teach general introductory subjects and foreclosed the opportunity to teach a specialty within the discipline. In other colleges, the same goals evoked positive response based on heightened faculty consciousness about the importance of general education reform. Some instructors were united in a common enterprise to raise the importance of their specific mission to accord with more general institutional purposes.

College goals may operate indirectly through their effect on program goals. The congruence between program goals and colleges goals often dictates the extent to which a program is eligible for scarce resources. When planning courses, faculty tend to attach strong influence to program goals. In fields where the content is viewed as hierarchically structured, program decisions strongly affect the way the courses are planned. For example, in mathematics, science, and nursing, faculty view courses and even study topics as important building blocks, not to be left to the whim of individual instructors. In fields where faculty autonomy and the goal of helping students develop multiple perspectives are viewed as more essential than sequential concept development, specific program goals are far less influential, but the orientation of the program toward autonomy is, itself, a strong influence. For example, faculty teaching in literature and sociology may consider the instructor's desire, expertise, and even current interests as essential to free intellectual development and creative teaching.

For career study fields, external forces encourage and strengthen specific program goals. Professional accreditation standards, state examination requirements, and the need to collaborate with professional personnel in practice sites strongly influence program goals and, thus, course goals. Table 9-3 compares the strength of influence reported by faculty in different fields for program and

TABLE 9-3   Emphasis on Contextual Influences Reported by Faculty Planning Courses

Influence	Percentage of Faculty[a]	
	General Education	**Professional Fields[b]**
Goals of my college	35	49
Goals of my program	65	83
Program's contribution to college	65	63
Student preparation	63	60
Student effort	53	50
Student ability	67	61
Student interests	58	59
Students' life goals	35	54
Students' career goals	35	78
Students' educational goals	51	73
Success of previous students	59	56
Accreditors	29	65
Employers	28	69
Professional associations	28	57
External examinations	14	54
Collegewide achievement tests	17	26
Other colleges' requirements	40	40
Available textbooks	54	60
Available facilities	34	46
Available opportunities (clinical, etc.)	22	48
Available teaching assistants	12	17
Available secretarial help	11	19
Available supplies	21	30
Class size	53	54
Class schedule	37	41
Assigned workload	37	43
Promotion or tenure pressure	9	11
Required instructional method	11	20
Advising office	7	13
Instructional development office	4	7
Student services office	4	7
Library services	38	49
Audiovisual services	35	50
Program chairperson	27	39
Colleagues	33	41
Articles/books on teaching/learning	31	55
Articles/books on my field	45	62

Source: Planning Introductory College Courses by J. S. Stark, M. A. Lowther, R. J. Bentley, et al. (1990), pp. 54, 56, 58, 59. Reprinted by permission of The National Center for Research to Improve Postsecondary Teaching and Learning, The University of Michigan.

[a]Percentage of faculty who rated the item as a "very strong" or "strong" influence on course planning.

[b]Professional fields included were nursing, business, and educational psychology.

college goals, as well as other contextual factors we will discuss shortly.

Even when reporting strong allegiance to program goals, faculty members identified much more closely with their own course goals. Time and again, when we inquired about program goals, the answer from faculty members was: "Well, I'm not sure how others in our program would feel about that, but in *my* course . . . "

Faculty Time and Incentives

When compared with program goals and teaching style, which direct and facilitate choices of instructional processes, some environmental context factors seem to exercise constraining influences, though not always the ones we might have predicted. For example, we expected faculty to attribute more influence to college incentive systems than they did.

Faculty almost always view time (or, more specifically, the lack of time) as influential in course planning. After exploring faculty activities, Gaff and Wilson (1971, pp. 479–480) listed thirteen types of faculty activities, including teaching, planning, preparing, housekeeping, meetings, counseling, keeping up to date, governance, administrative activities, research, and curriculum development. Numerous researchers have reported that these activities consume an average of 55 hours a week. Faculty frequently told us that they would plan their courses somewhat differently if administrative activities most peripheral to teaching were not so time consuming. However, in our studies of faculty members at liberal arts colleges, community colleges, comprehensive colleges, and doctoral universities, no faculty members complained that their research detracted from their course planning or vice versa.

Recently, a series of surveys of faculty at research universities (Gray, Froh, & Diamond, 1992) has shown that both faculty and administrators believe more emphasis should be placed on teaching, including planning. Yet these studies also report that faculty do not believe that good teaching will lead to advancement at their institution; instead, faculty perceive that they will jeopardize promotion and salary rewards if they concentrate on curriculum planning and teaching. Even in community colleges, faculty tend to believe that service, seniority, governance activities, and other characteristics, rather than good teaching, lead to advancement. Given these views, we were surprised that less than 10% of the faculty in our studies saw promotion and tenure pressures or other reward and incentive systems as influential in course planning. Faculty members were quick to point out that rewards did not necessarily follow participation in program curriculum development, but few said that this factor influenced their activities.

Learners' Goals

Faculty members attribute varying levels of importance to students' goals, depending on the level and type of course they are planning. Most instructors teaching general education courses felt that the material they taught would be useful regardless of students' directions or plans; thus, students' life and career goals influenced only about one-third of them. Still, they were sometimes in a quandary about whether they should aim an introductory course at the general education students or provide a foundation for future majors. They knew that designating a course as a prerequisite to other courses in the field often determines that foundational concepts and research methods take precedence over potential connections to the life and work of students planning other majors. Students who are simply "exploring" understandably get lost in the shuffle. Yet, particularly in more structured fields, faculty were reluctant to provide separate tracks for majors and non-majors, fearing that diluted course content could disadvantage students who might eventually be recruited as majors. These dilemmas exist primarily at the introductory level, student goals are far more influential in upper-division courses and in programs that prepare students for employment. Three-fourths of faculty in college career studies reported that they actively considered students' goals.

Available Resources

Teaching and learning resources can be helpful in selecting instructional processes when they are ample and can serve as constraints when they are scarce. Resources also may be viewed at two levels. The first level includes resources actually used in the classroom, such as instructional media or textbooks. The second and broader level includes a supportive environment, sufficient faculty members, and perhaps an instructional improvement program. We will discuss each of these levels in turn.

We asked faculty to rate the influence of various instructional teaching resources, including supplies, facilities, secretarial support, and various other categories, on their course planning. We found that the availability of an appropriate textbook was an important influence for more than 50% of the faculty surveyed. Physical facilities were also rated as very important in selected fields, such as biology and theater. Professional faculty rated the availability of practice opportunities, such as field trips or clinics, as very influential. In general, faculty indicated that other resources, such as supplies and secretarial assistance, were only weak influences (Stark, Lowther, Bentley, et al., 1990).

Textbooks.   Textbooks are among the strongest acknowledged influences on how faculty construct academic plans. In struc-

tured fields such as mathematics and science, faculty often followed the sequencing outlined in the textbook, thereby alleviating the need to make a decision on their own. Extensive dependence on textbooks was less frequent in fields such as literature and English composition, where instructors tend to choose materials from a wide variety of sources. One constraint faculty sometimes mentioned was lack of budget to purchase textbooks for examination; faculty must depend on free samples, which limits the range of choice. Instructors in many fields reported that commercial auxiliary materials that now accompany many textbooks tempted them not to develop their own instructional processes. This trend, of course, is related to the increased use of computer and media technology. The textbook and the computer can both facilitate and constrain effective curriculum planning.

Practical Matters.   An observer of daily activities among faculty in some colleges would attribute great influence to the plethora of pragmatic matters that structure the college instructor's day, week, and semester. Faculty arrange the material they teach to accommodate vacations, facility schedules, and even the time of the day. They generally believe that their classes are too large for optimal student learning, and they forego some active learning opportunities when seats are nonmovable. In some colleges, students work on assignments or tests that the professor has written out by hand on the blackboard or paper because no typist is available. Sometimes professors avoid giving written assignments because they lack time and help to read and comment on them for large classes. Even poor heating and lighting conditions can increase fatigue and reduce attentiveness for both students and faculty.

Despite these pragmatic constraints on instructional process, the faculty we interviewed seldom viewed their course or program planning as strongly influenced by any of these issues or situations. Exceptions occurred if resources recently had been sharply cut, or if useful new resources such as computers had raised professors' hopes but were insufficient in supply to fulfill their dreams of regular use. On the basis of these reports, we hypothesized that most college instructors are so accustomed to working with limited help and within constraining environmental situations that they overlook these situations unless the lack becomes extremely severe. Yet this dearth of assistance is surely, in some cases, related to the faculty complaint about lack of time and the limited importance given to the teaching role. It also limits innovation in selecting instructional processes.

Instructional Assistance. Many colleges now offer services that can be helpful to faculty members as they plan courses. These include student advising offices, curriculum and instructional development offices, student services offices, college library services, audiovisual services, computer centers, test-scoring centers, and libraries that include literature on teaching and learning. Overall, except for college libraries, faculty do not use these types of services very much. In all, we found that faculty at community colleges and nonselective liberal arts colleges, many of whom have backgrounds in education, were more likely to use a variety of services. Faculty in selective colleges found them less useful, often eschewing an emphasis on pedagogy in favor of disciplinary expertise and traditional teaching methods. Faculty in some fields use each service more than those in other fields. For example, faculty who give multiple-choice exams may use a test scoring center, whereas those who give essay exams may make more use of library resources.

The most useful sources of assistance in course planning cited by faculty were a departmental colleague at the institution (77.5%), a department or division chair (47.5%), course evaluations from students (47.5%), books or articles on instructional design (41%), a colleague from another institution (39.7%) or another department (23.2%), and one's disciplinary association (26.5%). These figures demonstrate faculty's strong dependence on disciplinary colleagues in course planning.

Offices providing services directly applicable to academic work, such as library and audiovisual services, were considered influential by at least 35% of the instructors surveyed. Only 15% of the faculty thought the services of a student assistance or tutoring center were useful; just over 11% thought the computing center services useful. Less than 10% of the faculty thought the services of an advising or student services office were influential in their course planning, although they willingly referred students to them for other assistance.

For most sources of assistance, we noted differences among fields. Instructors in professional courses rated virtually every source of assistance more influential than the general education instructors. In some cases professional field instructors thought some sources substantially more useful—for example, audiovisual centers, student course evaluations, and books or articles on instructional design. More intriguing than differences among fields is our finding that faculty who are influenced by one of these sources of assistance, whether it is an on-or off-campus source, may be influenced by other sources as well. Faculty who consult others during course planning tend to seek a wide variety of sources of assistance; those who do not consult work alone. In addition, our analyses indicated that some faculty members may more readily consult campus agencies, whereas others are more likely to consult colleagues more informally. Consultation may be a personal or professional style some faculty develop.

Of the faculty we surveyed, about 60% had the option of consulting an existing instructional development office because this service existed on their campuses. Yet a very small portion of the faculty—only 6.1% of those with such access—told us that the campus instructional development office was influential or likely to be helpful in their course planning. However, some had read handbooks like Wilbert McKeachie's *Teaching Tips* (now in its ninth edition) and Maryellen Weimer's *Improving College Teaching* (1990). Possibly reading is a more comfortable source for faculty than consultation.

Part-time faculty exhibited greater willingness than their full-time colleagues to seek assistance from colleagues and campus offices in planning their courses (Lowther, Stark, Genthon, & Bentley, 1991). We speculate that part-time faculty, who are employed for short terms, may recognize the need for more assistance in both teaching and orientation to college services. For most regular faculty, course planning seems to be a very solitary activity.

Organizational Structures and Traditions

Organizational structures may serve as strong influences on course planning. Many structures are so strongly embedded in the traditions of American higher education that faculty seldom question their existence. In fact, structural arrangements such as credits and degrees, advising systems, tests, grading practices, and the semester and quarter academic calendars are sometimes defined as synonymous with curriculum.

Some aspects of academic programming fall somewhere between structural mechanisms and instructional strategies. These include comprehensive examinations, laboratories, practica, internships, apprenticeships, cooperative education, credit by examination,

and credit for experience. If we view curriculum as an academic plan, then these existing structures and policies regarding the strategies clearly influence the plan's outcomes. Some arrangements such as separate summer sessions, continuing education programs with second-class status, and study skills centers, to name a few, can cast course planning into a specific model. Typically, however, faculty members planning individual courses have ceased to question the educational efficacy of these structures; they merely work within them.

In 1978, during a time of considerable discussion about how college terms and years were structured, Levine discussed the advantages and disadvantages of some common curriculum structures—for example, the course-credit system. The credit system offers flexibility by dividing the curriculum into small course-size units, allowing students to repeat these units and allowing variations in instructors and instructional plans for the different units. The system gives teachers a great deal of latitude in planning their own courses and provides blocks of work that help students transfer among colleges or among major specializations without starting over. It allows new ideas to be tried in selected courses.

The disadvantages of the course-credit system are that it may not help students integrate knowledge, it fails to place priorities on the most important courses and ideas, and it assumes that students learn well in course chunks and primarily in classroom settings. It also emphasizes certification by serving time in class over certification by learning, encourages students to be dependent on their teachers, can result in expensive redundancy, and makes it difficult to maintain uniform quality standards in multiple course sections. Today, most faculty seem unlikely to debate the well-entrenched course-credit system, much less champion major changes in it. This system, with its accompanying fifty-minute hour, structures course planning to a high degree. It is only one of many such structures to which faculty members seem to be oblivious.

SELECTING INSTRUCTIONAL PROCESSES FOR PROGRAMS AND COLLEGES

At the program level, groups of faculty develop views about instructional experiences they believe all students should have. Though developed by groups, these views are often implemented at the course level by specific instructors who design and supervise the specific experiences of students. Consequently, at the program level faculty members usually talk about instructional policies rather than instructional processes. Policies articulate and codify views about instructional process that faculty develop as a group for students as a group.

At the college level, instructional process may be thought of as the aggregation of program policies that may vary considerably within a single institution or even within distinct organizational units, such as colleges within a university or departments within a specialized college. Alternatively, we can think of collegewide processes as embodied in an environment that sets the stage for adopting instructional policies at the program level and instructional processes at the course level. The college environment influences program policies, which in turn influence the instructional processes professors develop and implement in courses. Each of these levels—educational environment, instructional policy, and instructional process—is linked with and influenced by other elements of academic plans at the relevant level. Such linkages are illustrated by the relationship of a college's provision of instructional resources to support those aspects of an educational environment it deems important to its purposes and to deny

resources to support programs not closely allied with its educational goals.

Elements of the academic plan are not fully distinct as we consider how content and context interact to become instructional form at the program and college level. Clearly college mission and program goals act directly to influence instructional decision making; at the same time, they are the internal and organizational influences that help to create the instructional environment.

At the program level, academic plans may be influenced by both external and internal sources. Faculty planning academic programs must supervise a collection of discrete and relatively autonomous courses and meld them into a coherent program that meets students' expectations and sometimes the expectations of external groups, such as employers. At the same time, professors must look to the college mission for broad guidance, to other organizational units for cooperation, and to the college instructional environment for resources that may influence their choices among instructional policies. The college environment, mission, and policies may encourage a supportive atmosphere for a specific type of general education program, a program with a regular internships like student teaching, or a special approach to the freshman year. In each case, the program needs to develop its own instructional policies in the context of this broader instructional environment.

Some dimensions of institutional and program mission that influence choice among instructional processes may be manifested by discrete differences in characteristics. For example, instructional process, policy, and environment will vary depending on whether the unit offers applied versus nonapplied study, provides graduate study or associate degree study, and provides transfer programs as well as shorter term or terminal educational programs. Other dimensions that establish the college- and program-level environments may be more aptly described as continua, with the ends representing extreme types. Examples are the extent of concern with student development versus discipline transmission; the degree of emphasis on service to community, region, or state; and the degree of religious orientation. These differences and others define the context that influences instructional policy. They are communicated to faculty and students, who are influenced by them to varying degrees in developing academic plans.

The applied–nonapplied dimension is the most obvious influence on decision making related to instructional processes. Clearly, faculty in professional or occupational fields are more likely than those in arts and sciences disciplines to select processes incorporating practical experiences or career-oriented skill development. At the other extreme of this continuum is the scholarly emphasis that may characterize selective liberal arts colleges and research universities that prepare students primarily for graduate school. These positions on the applied–nonapplied continuum can be identified in the instructional environment, policies, and processes at all levels of the academic plan.

Contextual Influences on General Education Programs

Collegewide contextual factors and organizational issues may interact with and attenuate the influence of college mission for general education programs. For example, colleges with general education distribution requirements have, de facto, made policy decisions about instructional process that default to the course level. Little program planning or faculty involvement is required for such a plan; policies consist mainly of lists of courses that satisfy the program requirements. The decision virtually assures classes of substantial

size, sometimes taught by faculty who would prefer other assignments and, too often, by faculty for whom there is no other available assignment. Some courses may serve dual purposes for general education and introduction to a major, effectively removing specific instructional decisions from the general education purview and leaving them to the program specialties or individual instructors by default. The importance of instructional resources is obvious here; general education programs typically do not have strong leadership or independent budgets that allow modification and customization of instructional policies and processes. There may be little motivation for faculty groups organized in their own discipline or professional specialties to contribute time or resources to the general education program. Most faculty members spend less time planning the general education program as a whole than their specialized major programs.

In contrast, general education programs with specific core requirements often require that faculty members from several disciplines devote considerable time to discussing decisions about instructional policies and processes. Such a group may have leadership and a budget and the authority to choose instructional processes—for example, small seminars over a large-group lecture with accompanying discussion groups to achieve certain goals. As they try to include multiple perspectives in the core, faculty planners may include prominent guest lecturers, field trips, or special library arrangements that require compromise among instructors representing varied disciplines. Where such collaborative conditions hold, general education programs make fairly deliberate choices about instructional process and related matters.

Although the impact of textbooks on general education programs is felt primarily in specific courses, instructors we interviewed also mentioned the importance of program-level decisions about texts. Textbooks, they explained, can set the stage for a program by conveying either a single perspective or multiple perspectives. When a group of instructors developing a general education program has diverse perspectives, the mix of views can make the determination of appropriate instructional materials a complex decision.

In many colleges and universities, enrollment in general education programs strongly influences the choice of instructional methods. If faculty attempt to depart from lecture methods with classes ranging from 100 to 500, they face logistical difficulties. Similarly, laboratory schedules for large groups of students may drive learning activities rather than the reverse, and lack of assistance in grading student work may strongly influence the type of examinations or assignments instructors use. If the learners attend part time, core requirements may be really impossible to develop and distribution requirements for general education may be the only possible means of ensuring breadth.

The preparation of learners also strongly influences policy formulation in general education instructional programs. Community colleges, two-year branch campuses of state universities, and nonselective liberal arts colleges must decide, for example, how to assist underprepared students. They may attempt to establish special diagnostic assessments of students' basic skills and provide remedial programs in conjunction with the core or distribution courses. Despite much discussion about change, the limited resources available for new types of instruction and the traditional structures colleges have developed preclude full consideration of the range of instructional program policies.

Contextual Influences on Major Fields

Major specializations are either applied (the career-oriented professional and occupa-

tional fields) or nonapplied (the academic disciplines). External influences on programs differ greatly for these two types, a fact that plays a role in the development of program instructional policy. Influences may come from associations, accreditors, employers, and government agencies.

Accreditors and Professional Associations

Faculty teaching in disciplines may attribute considerable influence in disseminating the discovery of new knowledge and changes in thinking within their fields to their disciplinary associations. Thus, scholarly associations may be influential in establishing program content due to changing paradigms or research agendas, yet have minor impact on instructional policies. Among many, one case of rather direct influence is the influence on English composition instruction by the Conference on College Composition and Communication (CCCC), which fostered writing across the curriculum. In another example, advocates for feminist history achieved changes in thinking about a traditional liberal arts discipline, causing programs to reorganize their requirements and course sequences. For structured fields, a prototype may be the influence of the American Chemical Society, which administers examinations and certifies chemistry programs that meet quality standards.

Although regional accreditors may influence instruction indirectly by assuring collegial governance structures and providing a resource base, they have little direct influence on how faculty plan liberal arts and science programs. In contrast, the choice of instructional policies and processes in many career studies fields is influenced quite directly by professional associations and accrediting groups. Both are often very powerful influences, setting standards for specific numbers of hours of clinical experience and ratios of students to faculty (e.g., in speech and hearing science) or prescribing detailed instructional objectives (e.g., in architecture). Arguably, accreditors both help to maintain high quality standards and improve instruction, or they may maintain very basic standards and limit the flexibility to adapt instruction.

Employers, Articulation, and Practical Matters

Instructors in many nonapplied disciplines do not relate to a specific group of job possibilities or employers, and they usually believe their academic plans should not be influenced by students' career considerations. In contrast, the influence of prospective employers is strong for some career programs. Many community colleges consult advisory board committees of employers in the community to assist them in planning occupational programs. Four-year college career studies, such as business, have similar boards, which not only provide input to planning but sometimes provide monetary resources for program development and enhancement. Some community college vocational programs and four-year college professional fields even develop school-to-work partnerships in which local business and industries help in the educational programs. Career-related fields are also more susceptible than academic disciplines to influence from other external examinations, including statewide certification and licensing exams.

Instructional processes and policies in some kinds of colleges are also affected by student transfer to other institutions. This influence has grown stronger over the last fifty years. For example, in Arizona, the accounting programs at several Mesa Community College campuses are strongly influenced by the receiving program in accounting at Arizona State University. Reciprocally, of course, upper-division programs in the receiving four-year state colleges and universities are af-

fected by the preparation of transfer students from community colleges. Even in the disciplinary fields, community college programs often adjust their instructional policies to articulate with four-year colleges and, conversely, four-year colleges adjust in anticipation of receiving transfer students whose initial preparation was provided elsewhere.

Resources and practical matters affecting programs are similar to those we mentioned for courses. In varied settings, choice of instructional processes may be especially constrained by lack of secretarial and technical assistance, by lack of research and development funds for instructional experimentation, by lack of leadership training for program chairs, and by excessive bureaucracy in the curriculum change process. Not all influences are due to lack of resources. Sometimes resources are available for services and activities that are underutilized by faculty. These include, among others, funds to travel to conferences specifically concerned with instruction, technology that is already installed but not fully used by faculty, and the services of instructional development centers.

Organizational Structures, Traditions, and Adaptations

Despite the diversity of American higher education, colleges have continued to rely on the lecture-discussion-laboratory process for instruction, and on the individual professor as both planner and director of learning activities. The organizational structures that have held curriculum innovation in check at the program and college level have included expectations that students would be of traditional college age and will travel to the campus, interact directly with faculty members in a peer group of learners, and attend for semester-long periods of time. The traditional division between general education and major fields has also shaped the instructional processes chosen for students.

The influx of new students or dissatisfaction with specific services sometimes has stimulated the creation of nontraditional curriculum structures at the program and college levels. Changes in structure, though rarer than innovations in course-level teaching processes, often attract greater attention among educators. Program faculty are often excited about their efforts and choose to publicize them at professional conferences and in written work. Because of the publicity gained by the college for educational innovation, administrators tend to support these dissemination efforts for program changes. Some of the new structures that are devised and advocated by innovative faculty members and students become institutionalized or are adopted elsewhere, while others simply disappear after a trial period.

Nontraditional study is of two types: first, learning that is not under the supervision of a formally recognized higher education institution, or, second, learning that is under such supervision but which differs significantly from the usual educational experiences offered there. In the 1960s and early 1970s, nontraditional processes included independent study (course level), student-designed curricula (program level), and external degrees (college level). In each case, the learning could be negotiated by contract. Although entire colleges adopted contract learning models, others allowed students to do some of their work as contract learning.

Two types of nontraditional programs that received a great deal of attention in the 1960s were designed to accommodate adult working students. The first type is the "college without walls" programs (such as Empire State College in New York, Thomas Edison College in New Jersey, and Minnesota Metropolitan College in Minneapolis) at which instructors are evaluators, counselors, and facilitators more than teachers, working with adult students to gain credit for previous work and study, design individualized programs, and obtain access to educational experiences. The second type is the various "experiential credit" arrangements which allow credit toward a college degree to students who have learned in ways other than in traditional college classrooms.

The move to assess and provide academic credit through formal evaluation of life experiences seems to have lost momentum, but gaining credit by examination remains a part of American higher education. For students who have taken advanced-level courses in high school, credit by examination is institutionalized in the Advanced Placement (AP) program of the College Board; for nontraditional students (and an increasing number of traditional ones) in the College Level Examination Proficiency (CLEP) tests administered periodically by Educational Testing Service. The purposes of these assessments of prior learning, according to Keeton (in Chickering and Associates, 1981) are:

1. To test the learner's qualifications to enter a program
2. To earn the learner an appropriate program placement
3. To help learner and teacher fit the program to the learner
4. To exempt the learner from the program and possibly award credentials
5. To guide educational planning (p. 633)

Another departure from traditional academic structure is cooperative education, an arrangement in which students combine study on campus with jobs in business or industry. A related plan includes cross-cultural experiences within the curriculum, as in the Kalamazoo College plan and others that emphasize a period of foreign study and other off-campus experiences. Most recently, a national emphasis on community service as an important part of the college experience has given a boost to education outside of the classroom, and recognition of the global economy has encouraged attention to international study. Such modifications in instructional process, usually requiring faculty and administrative decisions at program and college levels, may increase student motivation and integration of learning by presenting opportunities in which students can apply new knowledge. These practices that change the venue for learning are adopted by many colleges only after lengthy and heated debate about issues of quality.

Another example of an instructional modification at the college level is the one-month January term, introduced by some colleges in the 1960s. The January term was a response to the restlessness of students and to faculty desires for greater relevance and more individual choice. It provided a period where a single course, often innovative in content or instructional process, could be presented intensively in an abbreviated time frame. Extending the January term idea, a few colleges have experimented with other credit arrangements, such as a modular calendar that allows students to study one subject intensively. Extensive debate and major commitments of time and resources usually accompany such substantial variations from tradition. However, the innovations tend to be short-lived, partly because students often encounter difficulties when they present their nontraditional records for transfer or graduate school, and partly because new faculty, replacing those who made the commitment to nontraditional structure, often prefer to return to traditional forms.

In short, there have been numerous innovations in calendar, format, and program sequencing that can be classified as collegewide modifications in instructional process. Each curricular experiment, usually designed to respond to the continually increasing diversity of learners, academic fields, and society, has enjoyed temporary success. Although not necessarily enduring in their original forms, they have left their mark on more traditional academic plans. The trial and screening of such innovations, even for a relatively short time, provides a gradual means of change in instructional process toward flexibility to serve a wider variety of students

EXPANDING CHOICE AMONG INSTRUCTIONAL PROCESSES

A popular conference speaker has called good college teaching a "maddening mystery," claiming that because it is such a mystery faculty members either privatize it or recommend a technical "fix" (Palmer, 1990). Our purpose in this chapter is to discourage the use of either extreme. Rather, we assert that good teaching is the result of a good plan. It is not a mystery when faculty make conscious decisions about the way they select instructional processes and recognize how those decisions relate to decisions about other elements of academic plans.

Just as faculty don't talk much about improving instruction, they don't read about it much either. Few have been formally trained in how to teach. Furthermore, the differences among the disciplines and professional fields make conversation and formal instruction about teaching difficult; instructional alternatives that faculty in one field find successful are not always credible or applicable to those in a different field. All of these facts contribute to the aura of "mystery" that surrounds college teaching.

In contrast with previous periods of experimenting with instructional process, the reform period of the 1960s was a response to student demands for greater autonomy, more individualized learning, greater relevance, and fewer formal educational structures. Most of the new strategies at the course, program, and college levels were designed to cope with increased access—of adults and other nontraditional students. Grounded in behavioral psychology, the instructional variations introduced in this period tended to differentiate and separate both learners and units of subject content. Learners often worked at their own pace, attempting to master discrete bits of material before moving to other, sometimes unconnected, course topics.

In the 1980s and 1990s, the emphasis on instructional process relies on a quite different rationale; recommendations about instructional processes are based on new understandings of how humans learn that contrast with the behavioral psychology that prevailed earlier. The current emphasis is on reconnecting both knowledge and students. Knowledge is to be reunited by emphasizing the relationship among concepts, by exploring intersections among disciplines, and by consciously striving for coherence. Students are to be linked with each other in collaborative work groups in which they share learning processes, and with instructors in nonformal as well as formal interactions.

In behaviorally based instruction, faculty tried to (1) state clear expectations for learning outcomes, (2) organize instruction to achieve the outcomes, (3) gather evidence of outcome achievement; (4) modify teaching methods based on the degree of achievement, and (5) individualize instruction as much as possible. These individualized methods were particularly useful in sequential subjects that lent themselves to evaluation by systematic methods, especially in multiple-choice tests.

The emphasis in the 1990s has been on helping individual students construct meaning from what they learn, connecting it with what they already know, and urging them to articulate it in various ways. The emphasis is on collaborative learning as a social activity and on writing as a method of synthetic thinking. While achievement tests certainly have not been discarded, many instructors prefer to evaluate student learning on the students' own terms—using essay tests or portfolios of student work, as well as direct observation of problem-solving activities and group inter-

changes. These methods have been accepted most readily in the humanities, social sciences, and human service professional fields, although they can be useful in the pure and applied sciences as well.

Faculty are hearing about the new instructional alternatives from colleagues and at professional conferences, and some are trying these new methods. Yet most faculty still have limited exposure to instructional alternatives and to the educational theories on which such alternatives are based. Therefore, we have organized our discussion of alternatives in a way that relates to knowledge about the learner that we reviewed in Chapter 8. Many of the alternative instructional processes we mention here apply primarily to choices made at the course level. But we will provide a few examples of alternative program- and college-level plans as well. In many of the sections that follow, we state a postulate describing the assumption on which the discussion is based. Our intent is merely to request reflection on the stated premise. Specific instructors may or may not find a specific postulate true in their discipline or context.

Fostering Intellectual Development

Postulate: Learning depends on knowing how to learn.

The process of fostering intellectual development leads students from being amateur learners to being capable and independent learners—qualities we believe characterize the intentional learner. To help students acquire these qualities, the teacher must question the goal of every instructional task. One way to do this is to write down both broad course goals and more specific objectives, and to try to understand how each proposed instructional strategy would help students achieve the goal or objectives. What will be achieved by this term paper, laboratory exercise, field observation, small-group discussion, or demonstration? What meaning will the student make from this task? Is the task designed in such a way as to move the students along the path toward increased learning capability? The questions must be asked not only in terms of how the teacher views academic tasks but also in terms of how students may engage them. In the ideal scenario, the faculty member asks, for example, how an activity helps the students learn an important concept, how it will help students develop critical thinking skills, how it will help them identify with their future profession, how it will help them develop creativity, and most importantly, how it will help them become intentional learners.

In career studies, program faculty may collectively examine the professional role, questioning what aspects of professional development the various program educational activities, such as internships or capstone seminars, may foster. For nonapplied disciplines, faculty members may collectively discuss activities that might encourage students to recognize various scholarly paradigms and alternative points of view characterizing their field. In either case, an important program-level question is to ask which instructional processes ensure that students develop the inquiry and research skills needed to understand how the field developed and continues to develop. In interviewing faculty members, we found this goal to be strongly endorsed but seldom achieved.

Developing Study Skills and Learning Strategies

Postulate: Basic learning skills provide an essential foundation.

We have discussed the varied learning styles and personality factors that students bring to the classroom. We also noted that recent reform reports suggested helping students connect their learning to their lives and prior experiences. Today's diverse student population makes these individual steps more important than ever before. Some underprepared students lack basic study skills and learning strategies necessary for success in college work.

The most effective way to teach study skills is to embed them in the course material. Recall that there are two types of mechanisms at work in learning: cognitive strategies, which are the ways in which students process information, and metacognitive strategies, which help them understand which cognitive strategies to use and why. One way to teach study skills (which requires no special training) is to select reading assignments and devise questions that help students to achieve the deep-processing form of reading (e.g., actively questioning while reading, relating reading ideas to other parts of the course, relating evidence to conclusions, and developing intrinsic interest) rather than use surface processing strategies that encourage continued dependence on the instructor, fear of failure, and extrinsic motivation.

Using only slightly more complex means, Pintrich and his colleagues (Pintrich, 1988a, 1988b; Pintrich, McKeachie, & Lin, 1987) have found that they can successfully teach students to "learn how to learn" while teaching them about psychological principles behind the strategies. These researchers also have successfully used these ideas in courses other than psychology where the subject matter is less closely related to the learning tasks. The "learning to learn" course focuses on global strategies—processes such as comprehension monitoring, reviewing, and test-taking strategies. The topics in the course include learning from lectures, learning from reading, learning from discussions, learning from peers, cognitive models of memory and memory strategies, problem solving and creativity, writing, self-management and time management, motivation and anxiety, and test-taking strategies.

Knowing what strategies students already possess and assessing whether they are successful in expanding their available strategies is a bit more complex and requires initial diagnosis. Pintrich and others have found that diagnosis can be effectively combined with skill development. For example, when diagnosing and developing basic learning skills, an inventory called the Learning and Study Strategies Inventory (LASSI) is helpful (Weinstein, Palmer, & Schulte, 1987). The LASSI measures strengths and weaknesses in ten areas related to academic success, is administered in about thirty minutes, and is easily scored. The ten areas are attitude, motivation, time management, anxiety, concentration, information processing, selecting main ideas, study aids, self-testing, and test strategies.

At the program level, the faculty collectively can decide to devote attention to diagnosing study skills, as well as content knowledge, when they conduct placement tests. They can ensure that some basic-level courses include relevant aspects of study skill development. They can examine advising structures to be sure students are directed to special study skills centers where they exist on campus. Where help does not exist, programs can train peer tutors to help with the task. These program-level decisions involve conscious consideration of the elements of the program's academic plan that are often neglected.

Promoting Reflection and Metacognition

Postulate: No act of learning is complete unless the learner has reflected on its process and its results.

Reflecting on one's own learning style and strategies—a process psychologists call metacognition—is the step beyond merely achieving more efficient study skills. It involves conscious attention to what one is learning, why, and how. Students need to learn to think reflectively about their learning in order to be successful in college. Arons (1979) reminds us that most textbooks, assignments, and lectures encountered during college-level study of the natural and social sciences and humanities assume students have relatively sophisticated thinking and reasoning skills and linguistic processes. However, only about 25% of college students readily develop the skills necessary to cope with these materials. The others, Arons claims, may develop such intellectual capacities at a slower rate but usually are not afforded the opportunity to do so. Instead, pressured by volume and pace of content being introduced, these students attempt to memorize the material, losing sight of the intellectual processes that might help organize the chaos. Arons argues that the cultivation of intellectual capacities takes time; students must be allowed repeated practice in all subject-matter areas and be given explicit help and encouragement. They should also be urged to stand back and examine their reasoning processes and express them in their own words, even if this must be done at the expense of subject-matter coverage. Learning specialists agree that most instructors might question whether the hectic pace of covering increasingly more content encourages students to use surface processing and precludes reflection. Some advocate reducing the number of concepts taught, selecting only those that are crucial, while at the same time cultivating reflective learning. Through reflection, students can be led to move from rehearsal to more effective learning strategies such as elaboration merely by recognizing that this step is a necessary progression toward increased learning prowess.

Teaching the structure of the subject matter also greatly aids the learning process. Students are likely to forget specific ideas and skills without a framework that meaningfully ties them together. The more one has a sense of the structure of a field, the longer a learning session can continue without fatigue.

Learning outcomes can be improved by knowledge of discipline structure, and learning motivation can also be enhanced. We have mentioned concept mapping as a way that most instructors can supply structure in their courses. In effect, when a teacher constructs a lecture schedule, he or she is sketching a time-based concept map of the material to be presented in the course, although the map may never be recorded on paper in graphic form. Yet maps may be used explicitly to help students learn and interrelate ideas. A concept map is simply a two-dimensional diagram representing the conceptual structure of subject matter. It serves as a heuristic to guide understanding of the topics and concepts and their relation to each other. To construct a concept map for a structured field, one first identifies the concepts, principles, and so on to be taught, then arranges them in a hierarchical order from general to detailed, top to bottom. Finally, lines are drawn between each two related elements to show the linkages. A concept map of a course or program that is not hierarchically structured may be somewhat different; for example, one could arrange concepts as spokes around a central core of concepts. Figure 9-3 gives some examples of different types of concept maps. The academic plan theory around which this book is organized is a type of concept map that helps guide the reader and makes the major ideas easier to remember and relate to each other.

Instructors can present a concept map for an entire course; they can also present such a map at the beginning and end of each lecture as a way of directing students' attention to the topic of the day and later summarizing the session. Concept maps that students develop on their own may also be used as diagnostic tools to identify possible misconceptions about relationships and to assess the extent to which their conceptual knowledge in a course is becoming similar to that of the instructor.

The program faculty is an ideal body to discuss concept maps that portray the coherence intended by their program requirements and electives. This coherence is the most common focus of program curriculum discussion and involves which courses should be required and which elective; which should be taken first and which later. Concept maps constructed by the faculty could be used for improved communication with students. In Figure 9-4 we show a concept map that relates requirements and careers in the authors' professional doctoral program in higher education.

Cultivating Effective Thinking

Postulate: An important goal of education is learning to think effectively.

Effective thinking is the ultimate goal of instruction in all disciplines and fields and may be achieved at the same time that students learn content and learning skills. However, faculty in varied fields may disagree about what, precisely, constitutes effective thinking, and they may use different terms for it—for example, critical thinking, logical thinking, and analysis. Powers and Enright (1987) describe five dimensions of critical thinking and comment that their importance is different for different disciplines. They include (1) the analysis and evaluation of arguments, (2) the drawing of inferences and the developing of conclusions, (3) the definition and analysis of problems, (4) the ability to reason inductively, and (5) the generation of alternative explanations. To be inclusive, we will use these dimensions as synonyms in the discussion that follows but we will distinguish problem-solving as a specific type of critical or logical thinking.

In all fields, effective teaching actively involves students in a process of considering information, posing tentative hypotheses and answers, and then subjecting those propositions to analysis and evaluation. Ennis (1987), an acknowledged expert on critical thinking, defines it simply as "reasonable reflective

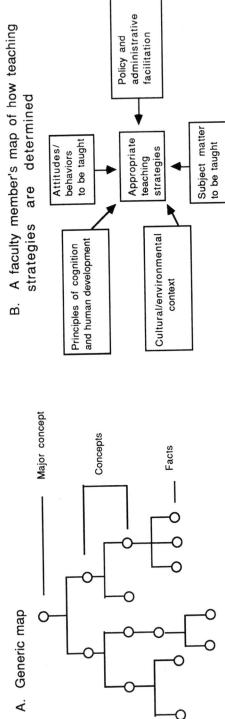

B. A faculty member's map of how teaching strategies are determined

Policy and administrative facilitation

Attitudes/ behaviors to be taught

Appropriate teaching strategies

Subject matter to be taught

Principles of cognition and human development

Cultural/environmental context

A. Generic map

Major concept

Concepts

Facts

C. A student's map of the social science and humanities fields

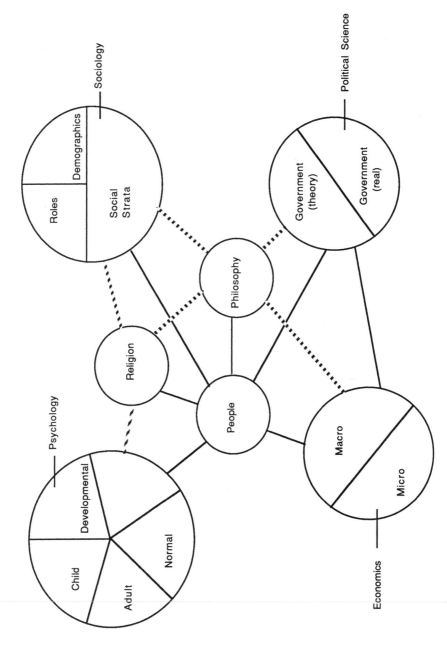

FIGURE 9-3 Concept Maps for Courses and Programs

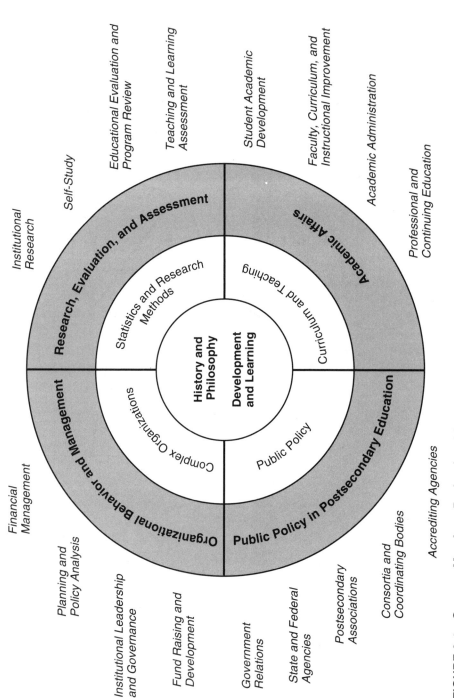

FIGURE 9-4 Concept Map for a Professional Program

Source: Graduate Programs in Higher and Continuing Education, Center for the Study of Higher Education, University of Michigan.

242

thinking focused on deciding what to believe or do." Not all students enter college with the analytical and evaluative skills needed for this reflective thinking. When instructors assume that they do, they may erroneously create assignments requiring skills that only the brightest students may have mastered (Arons, 1979). There are, however, specific techniques that appear to successfully cultivate effective thinking in students who lack them.

One method to motivate learners to develop and use their critical thinking abilities is to act as a role model for them, thinking through new problems and articulating the thinking process in front of the class. An expert thinker will, for example, quickly identify the essentials of the problem, recognize information that is irrelevant, note missing information that needs to be found, notice the similarity of a problem to one that has been solved before, and consciously weigh alternative arguments and solutions. The respected authors of two quite different books on critical thinking agree on the importance of modeling such thinking processes. John McPeck, author of *Teaching Critical Thinking* (1990), is illustrative of those who believe that one important task of instructors is to provide students with both the propensity and knowledge to engage in critical thinking. To do this, instructors must give up the pretense of omniscience and not only model behavior but encourage students to formulate and argue their own opinions. Stephen Brookfield, author of *Developing Critical Thinkers* (1988), contends that the instructor's task is to help students examine their beliefs through a variety of approaches, from listening to affirmation to direct confrontation. Because the ultimate decision to use critical thinking skills belongs to the students, instructors bear the responsibility to help students assess potential risks and also expectations that may result from changes in their thinking and behavior. This, Brookfield argues, is best achieved through personal modeling of ap-

propriate risk-taking behavior, analysis of assumptions, and open discussion of thinking processes.

There is considerable dispute about the transferability of thinking skills across subject domains and other situations. Some experts, such as McPeck, assert that critical thinking is subject-specific. The student must have the basic knowledge needed to analyze a situation or know where to find it in order to be an effective thinker. Such a position supports the idea of studying a wide range of college subjects. It does not, however, limit critical thinking instruction to the traditional disciplines. College career studies are also arenas in which thinking skills can be developed. Indeed, critical thinking about the subject is an integral part of the proper study of most subjects. Brookfield takes a different viewpoint, believing that the transfer of generic thinking skills is not only possible but essential because critical thinking is needed in many practical aspects of life after students leave the classroom. McKeachie (1988) takes a middle ground, believing that concrete examples are necessary to teach thinking but that explicit emphasis on problem-solving procedures and methods using varied examples, accompanied by verbalization of thinking processes, can promote transfer.

There are some obvious examples of how effective thinking is promoted by intentionally teaching students to transfer knowledge and skills to new situations. For example, the principles of writing sentences and paragraphs or those of computing and comparing percentages are not limited to the domains in which they originally were taught. Just as students are encouraged to use reading, writing, and arithmetic skills in many different types of situations, transfer of critical thinking skills probably can be encouraged by engaging the students in diverse uses of the skills likely to be encountered in life and work. Some suggestions for teaching critical thinking in a field include using examples of many types; being receptive to students' questions and creative solutions; insisting that students clarify, articulate, and defend their thinking about a issue; and encouraging students to challenge each others' thinking.

Problem solving is often viewed as a specific form of critical thinking. This terminology is most often used in structured fields, but problem-solving ability is an important cognitive skill in all areas of instruction. It usually includes the processes of retrieving information, weighing alternatives, and making decisions. The more expert the problem solver is, the more she is likely to know what information to seek and where to find it. Thus, to solve a problem, especially in the sciences, a student must know what skills to use, when to use them, and why. Thus, problem solving depends on a knowledge base, but knowledge is usually insufficient; the student must also practice applying it. There are two forms of problems to be solved: well-structured and ill-structured problems—that is, those that have answers and those that do not. Teaching students to solve well-structured problems is done differently for different discipline domains. Teaching ill-structured problems has no formula at all; in fact, creativity is the solution of ill-structured problems. Many educators believe that classroom instructors should ask students to solve ill-structured problems much more often than is typical.

Typically, it is left up to teachers in each specific course to introduce some principles of critical thinking and to find effective strategies; program faculty give this important goal little explicit attention. However, program faculty could work in groups to identify and formulate appropriate problems for students to evaluate and solve. Such a faculty exercise is particularly appropriate as the group designs a capstone course or a comprehensive examination for majors. Faculty

should expect students to recognize and use inductive and deductive reasoning; distinguish between fact and opinion; recognize fallacies in reasoning; draw reasonable conclusions from information found in various sources; defend their own conclusions rationally; comprehend, develop, and use concepts and generalizations; and synthesize materials from various sources.

Encouraging Research and Inquiry

Postulate: Students need to know how a field develops knowledge as well as what knowledge it has already developed.

Entering college students often believe that research is a process that occurs primarily in science fields (Shaw, Stark, Lowther, & Ryan, 1990). They fail to realize that all subjects, from humanities to career fields, are developing new knowledge and have characteristic research questions and methods of inquiry. In interviewing faculty members teaching introductory courses, we found that they devoted little time to increasing student awareness of research in their field; many believed it necessary for students first to have a command of vocabulary and basic facts, which meant postponing research to upper-division courses.

Yet undergraduate research programs where students work with a faculty member on specific projects, either individually or in small groups, have demonstrated success in introducing students to the world of ideas and research. Such projects also encourage students and faculty to interact outside of class, an activity amply demonstrated to be associated with students' intellectual development in college (Endo & Harpel, 1982). Weaver (1989) has compiled a set of examples of inquiry-oriented courses in varied disciplines from Hampshire College's program, which recognizes active learning and the centrality of inquiry. He intends to show by these examples how liberal education, which is deliberately designed to promote intellectual independence and initiative, may be distinct from education in the liberal arts. At Hampshire, the disciplines are considered tools rather than subjects for study and the conceptually based and cumulative curriculum undertakes "the cultivation of students' capacities for interpretation, discovery, creating, and the critical ability to recognize and understand the significance of competing theories and models" (p. 6).

Fostering Intentional Learning

Postulate: Intentional learners continue to learn and to improve their learning skills after college.

Students will not always be in a college classroom. They will need to learn in life—on the job, as parents, and as citizens. Faculty members who model the way they themselves learn, by exhibiting their thinking processes and sharing their research inquiries, can help students develop intentional learning skills. In Chapter 8, we mentioned the attributes of an intentional learner—questioning, organizing, connecting, reflecting, and adapting. For developing each attribute, instructors can consciously plan specific activities. The teaching roles that correspond to each attribute are emphasized in Figure 9-5.

In courses, the lower level intentional learning skills (questioning and organizing) can be developed by choosing instructional strategies that involve students in challenging what is taught and in understanding the structure of the field. One of the simplest mechanisms for reexamining instructional strategies in courses is to consider the level of questions asked in class and on examinations to be sure the more complex forms of thinking are being

used. Many instructors use Bloom's familiar hierarchy of learning levels—knowledge (lowest level), comprehension, application, analysis, synthesis, and evaluation (highest level)—as a guide for this regular self-examination of planning behavior.

The more advanced skills (connecting, reflecting, and adapting) will be fostered by choosing instructional activities that require students to use information resources outside of class. Traditionally, in many fields, this has meant doing library research and writing papers. Today's electronic information retrieval systems allow students to retrieve information rapidly and spend less time in laborious library work. Today's instructors have new and challenging opportunities to encourage students to spend the freed time reflecting on the information that is retrieved and connecting it with real problems. Specific intentional learning strategies will differ by field but must be consciously chosen and examined for their usefulness in promoting the desired outcomes.

At the program level, faculty members can examine the collection of courses students take to determine whether sufficient opportunities for becoming an intentional learner are provided. Though too often neglected, such an examination is usually the assumed goal of regular evaluation of general education programs. The faculty responsible for general education surely hope that the students will begin to develop these skills from questioning to adapting and be able to use them for several disciplines. To achieve this goal, it will often be necessary to provide strong leadership, an explicit articulation of the goal, and diligent program evaluation to establish program responsibility rather than leaving individual faculty members to promote these skills in specific classes. A spiral plan that engages students at higher levels of thinking during each year of their college education is suggested by the intentional

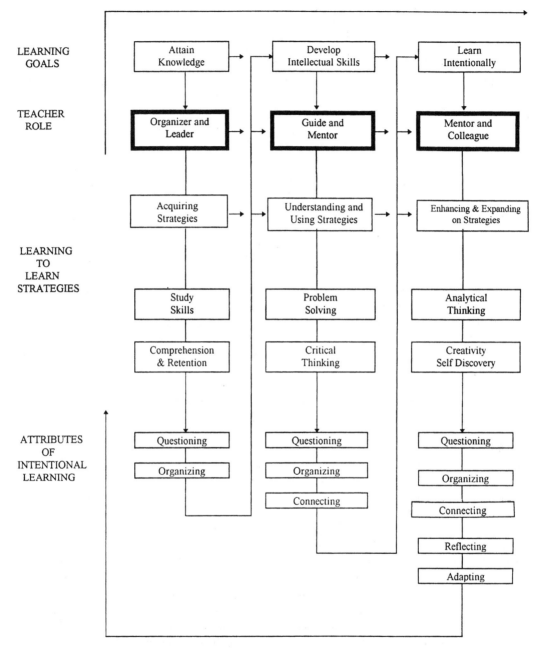

FIGURE 9-5   The Intentional Teaching/Learning Process

Source: Intentional Learning: A Process of Learning to Learn in the Accounting Curriculum by
Francis, Mulder, & Stark (1995), p. 49. Reprinted by permission of the American Accounting
Association.

learning process portrayed in Figure 9-5 but will require deliberate development.

In career specializations, program faculty often encourage intentional learning by giving explicit attention to the balance of theory and practice in a student's total course of study. How do the practical experiences help students adapt and connect principles and concepts? Should the two aspects be linked more closely? How do students apply reflective and adaptive behavior in professional practice settings? Faculty in career study fields may want to give similar attention to the linkages between the subjects that provide "contextual understanding" of professional practice. How, for example, does the learning in sociology for prospective nurses or teachers get linked with actual problems students will experience in the communities where they will later work?

For arts and sciences disciplines, the proper balance between abstract learning and the application of the learning in concrete ways is somewhat more difficult to describe but no less important. Often faculty can translate it into connections with related disciplines—for example, attempting to be sure that students reflect on relations between such fields as history, literature, and arts of a time period. For these outcomes to occur, it may be important to rethink the traditional single course lecture format of teaching in favor of some of the problem-solving groups, cluster course arrangements, and so on that we shall describe shortly. Another suitable translation of the balance between theory and practice is the development of critical perspective on a field. Instructional processes that ensure this type of program integration will require that the program make conscious decisions to expose students to alternate viewpoints, perhaps by team teaching or by requirements to study with professors espousing different views.

Collegewide decisions to encourage intentional learning could range from providing strong supporting resources for varied types of instruction to include creating a specific environment in which the teaching role is directed toward specific outcomes. Decisions about supporting resources include attention to such policy matters as library facilities and hours, computer availability and instruction, study rooms for both resident and commuter students, study skills centers, extracurricular academic event schedules, and a carefully planned and monitored advising and mentoring system. These create the environment for instructional processes to be carefully selected to promote student involvement and reflection on their intellectual development.

At the college level, some institutions have developed strong and distinctive programs that set high expectations and concepts of mastery for all students. At Alverno College in Wisconsin, for example, students receive no grades but must demonstrate achieved competence in eight abilities. Students are judged in relation to their own past performance, not normatively in relation to their peers. In such a system, faculty members have slightly less autonomy than is typical to design their own courses but considerably more guidance in choosing instructional processes and assignments that help students achieve the defined competences. The college-level position on what the instructional process should achieve has led to coherent programs and active student involvement.

Smaller colleges such as Alverno with a limited range of educational programs may devote more attention to considering college-level instructional process. At this level, instructional process/resources translates into college environment and the context for learning that pervades the institution. Recent activity at Philadelphia College of Textiles and Science demonstrates that such college-level attention to instructional process is not limited to liberal arts colleges. This relatively small career-oriented college has been recreating its curriculum to meld technical specializations with general education that places the major fields in context. Collaborative teams of faculty from liberal arts and professional fields are planning and teaching several professional courses. With college-wide support, and through participation in a regular series of workshops, these faculty teams have bridged disciplinary differences, developed concept maps of the new courses, and are testing collaboratively-developed instructional strategies.

As we mentioned in our discussion of educational purpose, the types of student outcomes toward which instructional processes aim become broader as one moves from course to program. At the course level, faculty members typically translate goals to objectives within the domain of the particular discipline. At the program level, broader goals such as career preparation, integration of various aspects of the major, and effective thinking take on increased importance. At the college level, the broadest goals are articulated—for example, that students should achieve independence, the capability to be intentional learners, citizenship skills, and self-esteem as well as specific academic and career competences. These broad goals may be indirectly fostered at the college level but researchers have found only small and inconsistent relationships between college characteristics and student achievement of such goals (Pascarella & Terenzini, 1991). Goals such as intentional learning are unlikely to be achieved unless there is a concerted collegewide effort to help faculty choose instructional processes with these goals in mind. A focus at the program level seems to hold the greatest potential for the reexamination of how instructional processes may best

be chosen to cultivate and shape student intellectual growth.

Increasing Motivation, Encouraging Involvement, and Achieving Integration

Postulate: Learning depends on wanting to learn.

Postulate: Students construct meaning from material uniquely and must be active learners to do so.

Motivation is required for active learning, but active learning and involvement can also increase motivation. Students' involvement in a task or activity is a function of their motivations and expectancies. It depends on their prior assessments of how the task will contribute to their personal goals. Yet students may not know how the task can contribute to their goals until they engage in it. This recursive relationship helps instructors choose processes that increase student motivation by capitalizing on their goals and interests; showing them how the learning can be valuable personally, intellectually, socially or occupationally; and establishing conditions that increase the chances of successful learning and increased self-confidence.

These important notions from cognitive science help to illuminate that it is the interaction between the learner and the learning experience that causes learning. Instructional processes in college that encourage students to be passive do not help students learn or prepare them well for continued learning in college or for becoming intentional lifelong learners. Students must be actively engaged with content—applying, testing, and reflecting on what they are learning. Increasing student engagement in college classrooms challenges centuries of practice in higher education, during which instructors have been more active than students.

Of course, students who are listening intently to a lecture and taking notes are active learners; they need not be moving or talking to learn. But faculty express great concern about the many students who seem not to be interested and attentive. The problem might be partly addressed by concerted efforts to accommodate their interests and establish situations in which passivity is not an option. Astin (1984, p. 305) argued that, in practice, this means that instructors should focus less on content and teaching techniques and more on what students are actually doing—that is, on how much time and energy they are devoting to the learning experience. We believe instructors should focus on how to select instructional processes that foster student engagement as well as content to be taught. Both content and student involvement are important. Posing challenges and making connections to demonstrate task value are essential ways of getting students' attention. Establishing a climate that fosters success and increases intrinsic motivation is a way of keeping it.

Earlier we mentioned Weston and Cranton's (1986) classification of instructional strategies based on extent of student activity: instructor-centered, interactive, individualized, and experiential. We believe this classification is incomplete. To accommodate all of the important cognitive development concepts, we believe that instructors may want to consider at least four additional dimensions besides student activity. We suggest examining task concreteness, degree of social interaction, level of learning strategies, and time frame.

1. *Task concreteness.* Instructional strategies may range from abstract to concrete. Al-

though most lectures are more abstract than experiential learning, some lectures can achieve a high degree of concreteness. Students with different learning styles may react well or poorly to concrete or abstract learning.

2. *Social interaction.* Another dimension of learning is the degree of social interaction among students. Within the category of experiential learning, for example, simulations may be done alone or in groups. Those whose social self-confidence is not strong may need to acquire more comfort in group project settings before learning well.

3. *Learning skill development.* A third dimension is the level of learning skill development required. Specific techniques within each of the activity classifications require different levels of learning skills. Students who are still learning to take notes may not succeed if asked to participate in information-seeking tasks and clinical experiences where advanced note-taking skills are required; those who are accustomed to surface processing when reading may fail at complex library assignments requiring synthesis.

4. *Task duration.* Finally, we suggest that time commitment or duration of a task is important. Students who are able to set only short-term learning goals and need feedback about their success may not do well in semester long projects.

Academic plans at the program level should attend to seeing that students gradually progress in their ability to do well in learning settings incorporating variations in all of these dimensions.

Modifying Lectures

Postulate: In a lecture, the instructor controls how information is paced and sequenced. Thus, he or she may increase coherence, yet not assure integration.

Postulate: Good lectures are character-ized by expressiveness, clarity, and organi-zation. They hold students' interest for rela-tively short periods.

Postulate: Any lecture can be improved by increasing the students' involvement in the ideas it shares.

Faculty members mention coherence as one reason why they lecture; they need to or-ganize materials for students. Similarly, fac-ulty members often write their own textbooks to introduce content in a sequence that seems coherent to them. In Chapter 8, we asserted that integration involves how students experi-ence the content they are learning. Depending on their prior learning and experience, they may or may not construct the same coherent meaning as their instructor. Our concern, then, is to select instructional processes that help achieve integration as well as coherence.

In addition to increasing coherence, the lecture method is appropriate for many teach-ing situations such as providing up-to-date information, summarizing widely scattered material, adapting material to student inter-ests and backgrounds, and building cognitive structures (Cameron, 1992). Lectures are less effective methods for developing students' thinking skills or promoting motivation. In-deed, when instructors' objectives go beyond the immediate acquisition of information, re-search indicates that nonlecture methods are preferable.

The traditional lecture period of fifty minutes is too long for the human attention span. So those who modify the lecture often seek to break up the length of time the in-structor speaks. Even in the context of a large lecture hall, a number of techniques can in-volve students in the lecture, incorporating discussion and encouraging higher order thinking skills within the traditional context.

Expert instructors also give an overview of their lecture at the beginning, perhaps in-troducing a concept network to help students understand the relationship of ideas. They in-clude a limited number of ideas in a lecture, no more than about five major chunks. They make lectures interesting and involve stu-dents by questioning, posing problems, using examples, and checking to see if students un-derstand key points. Occasionally they may stop and ask students to summarize, synthe-size, and reflect on what has been said. They provide opportunities to summarize at the end of class or, alternatively, leave students with a problem to solve for next time. They use writing exercises to help students articu-late their thoughts and integrate material. They ask pairs of students to question each other from time to time.

Activities such as one-minute papers and group discussions can be effectively incorpo-rated within lectures. In the one-minute paper, the instructor interrupts the lecture and asks the class to write their ideas or questions or to solve a problem. The questions can con-cern any element of the course that an in-structor wants to emphasize or examine (Cross & Angelo, 1988, p. 148). A variation is the one-sentence summary which requires students to answer a question represented by WDWWHWWW (Who Does/Did What to Whom, How, When, Where, and Why) about a given topic (Cross & Angelo, 1988, p. 62). Both techniques require students to synthe-size; both can also provide opportunities for students to use effective thinking skills. Nearly any of the numerous techniques for segmenting lectures can be adapted to suit the discipline taught.

Longer writing assignments are good ac-tive learning techniques as well. Students en-gaged in writing assignments must struggle with the information they have received, dis-cover their own methods for processing it, and organize their thinking so that it makes sense to another individual. The process of writing involves the student in invention, discovery of a purpose and focus, analysis, revision, and redrafting of work until it is acceptable. Writing can be used at the beginning, middle, or end of a lecture as well as for out-of-class assignments. A possible deliberately progressive sequence of assignments for a course begins with summary writing assignments, proceeds to synthesis and critique, and culminates in a research paper at the end of a course (Upham, 1989).

Like one-minute papers and other writing assignments, groups can be used to divide a lecture, focus attention on a key issue, and serve as a mechanism for active learning. Small groups of students, usually five to eight, discuss a concept or problem suggested by the lecturer. All or a few of the groups then present their ideas to the class. Such groups allow students to digest the information they have received, make their own sense of it, and provide the instructor with feedback regarding their understanding of the material. The feedback lecture incorporates several of these techniques: it involves a study guide, a pretest, and clear learning objectives. Students listen to a lecture, then small groups discuss issues. Guided design is an even more structured problem-solving technique designed by the teacher but done in small groups. It may be linked with lectures.

Marilla Svinicki, an instructional developer at the University of Texas at Austin, observes that one lament she hears repeatedly from instructors is: "I have too much content to cover!" (Svinicki, 1991, p. 1). This concern underlies most resistance to changing methods in college teaching. Svinicki points out that mere exposure to material does not constitute learning; it is not the lecture that produces learning, but the studying, summarizing, and organizing of lecture notes on which learning depends. In addition, the concern for coverage erroneously suggests that learning can occur only in the context of the class period or as a result of interaction with the instructor. Much learning, however, occurs outside of the classroom as students wrestle with content on their own. Instructional processes should assure that students are engaging in this struggle between class sessions.

Using Discussions as Active Processes

Postulate: Instruction should maximize meaning and reduce forgetting.

Postulate: Using discussion well requires careful planning of discussion questions.

The heavy reliance faculty place on the lecture method almost certainly comes at the expense of active learning that could promote student involvement. Consequently, students believe that faculty goals are to transmit facts or ideas rather than to teach effective thinking as faculty claim (Stark, Lowther, Ryan, et al., 1988). Discussions usually are more motivating to students than lectures, maintain their interest more fully, and are more effective means of developing thinking skills.

The key characteristic of a discussion that differentiates it from the lecture is that the instructor is not the only individual in the room who is assumed to know the answer to the questions asked. Students are encouraged to give their opinions, test their theories, and even offer guidance to others. In a discussion format close to the lecture, the instructor asks the class to identify the main points in a lecture and writes all the responses, good or bad, on the blackboard. She then elaborates on the students' points, restating them if necessary and adding detail. This method can be used to help students relate their own experiences to the course content and also provides the instructor with immediate feedback about the success of the lecture.

Most discussions are, however, slower and less efficient than lectures in presenting large bodies of information. They also may be minimally effective (or even threatening) for students who are reluctant to participate. Discussions are not effective with groups much larger than 30 students. Thus, whereas a variety of short discussions are useful in large classes, whole-group discussions cannot be sustained. One problem faculty face when leading discussions is their lack of training in posing the right kinds of questions for students. The type of question needs to be tailored to the students' level of understanding of the topic and the learning objective sought. The teacher may ask questions for clarification, to develop relationships, to summarize, and to challenge. Each of these is useful in specific situations, and a expert instructional planner develops a sense for which type is appropriate and how to choose a question of the needed type.

Different questions evoke specific responses and can be used to facilitate different stages of discussion. For example, to initiate a discussion, change the subject, or modify the direction of the discussion, instructors should ask students to think about their reactions to the information at hand, about how it makes them feel, about how other approaches might work, or about how the approach being discussed would work in other situations. To lead a student to a particular statement or to get students to progress through a set of logical steps to a conclusion, instructors can ask questions about the factors that might explain an occurrence or phenomenon, to propose next steps and to relate their comments to those of other students. It is also helpful to ask students to clarify or amplify what they have said and to rephrase answers.

Perhaps the most important type of question is one that probes for more information. Research indicates that questions involving memorization, comprehension, and application generated fewer statements from students than those demanding analysis, synthesis or evaluation. The single-correct-answer nature of some questions inhibits students from offering expanded responses that higher level questions elicit. Not only have investigators found that the higher level of students' responses tend to reflect the demands placed on them by instructors, but the amount of student participation also appears to be positively influenced (Dunkin & Barnes, 1986).

Choosing when to intervene in a discussion is one way of controlling the direction of a discussion and its outcomes. Fisch (1992) believes that "controlling" moves should be used judiciously and sparingly so that students are given as much freedom and responsibility as possible for their own learning. He suggests that the most useful questions for control and direction encourage further response from students without threatening, judging, or turning them off. Leading discussions that produce positive results is a demanding task.

Case Studies and Their Variations

Postulate: A touch of realism is often worth a heavy dose of abstraction.

Case studies provide a simulated real-life situation or problem to be solved, discussed, or extended. The other members of this group of interactive strategies are gaming, simulation, and role playing. All of these strategies attempt to link concepts being learned with some practical situation or with the interests of learners. Thus, they may foster motivation and encourage involvement.

Case teaching is a well-established strategy for interactive learning which originated in professional fields. Legal and medical education have used cases since the nineteenth century as a proxy for an apprenticeship or other real situation in which a decision or action is usually required. The method was popularized by the the Harvard Business School early in this century. The case is usually relatively short and focuses on a specific idea or dilemma to be grappled with. The case may demand a decision, or it may report an actual decision for critique and reflection (Boehrer & Linksy, 1990). Goals of case study instruction are several: to produce substantive knowledge, analytical skills, collaborative skills, self-confidence, and sometimes the ability to synthesize in writing and speech (Boehrer & Linksy, 1990). Well-developed case studies, properly used, can also encourage student responsibility, promote self-directed learning, and develop questioning skills.

A variation on the case study is the problem-based or project method of learning. Students work on a task that may be either structured or unstructured. They persist with the same group, get involved, develop pride in the group effort, and take responsibility for learning. Problem-based learning has been used in medical schools increasingly in the last few years to eliminate information overload in basic courses by replacing them with a problem drawn from real life. It represents a major philosophical change in the way medical instruction is designed; faculty members change from information dispensers to instructional guides and managers; students change from listeners to problem solvers. On the basis of research concerning this method, it appears that the faculty tutor must be first a content expert and, second, be trained in use of the process (W. Davis et al., 1992; Boud & Feletti, 1991).

Guided design, cases, role playing, and simulations are all forms of problem-centered instruction in which students must analyze complex problems together. The use of case studies that involve computer simulations can be very realistic, and the situations can be modified and manipulated in response to student input. Game simulations can be used in social sciences, in natural sciences, and in career fields. These processes are often enjoy-able and active as well as realistically valid, replicable, and convenient.

The content of the curriculum is being rethought in many fields because students can now use computers to simulate laboratory experiments as well as to learn through problem solving. In this case a new instructional method is breaking down traditional structures rather quickly without much advocacy from faculty. The confines of the laboratory are being expanded so that the three-hour desk lab session may disappear because the simulated experience can take place in the students' homes. Discussions within student problem-solving groups and tutorial sessions between students and faculty can also take place by electronic mail. Music studios, theaters, and concert halls can also be brought into students' living areas through CD-ROM and videotapes of extremely high quality. The exciting nature of these new opportunities could drive the selection and arrangement of content, wresting some autonomy from individual faculty members. As a result, students may lack some skills formerly acquired by traditional instruction but may acquire new and different ones as a result of the different modes of instruction.

Collaborative and Cooperative Learning

Postulate: Collaborative learning changes the traditional view of the teacher's authority.

Postulate: Students are most interested when there is a concrete problem to solve.

Postulate: Students who develop their own answers remember them.

Postulate: Many students, though not all, enjoy learning as a social activity.

Recently, a great deal of attention has been devoted to learning in groups. Strategies for group learning are founded on a solid base of knowledge about student learning and have proved successful in practice. Yet, these ideas are sufficiently far from the instructional knowledge of most college faculty members that their adoption is bound to be slow.

Many professors are reluctant to use groups because they fear that they will seem to be abandoning their teaching responsibilities or that students will be dissatisfied. Students who shared their feelings about group learning suggested ways instructors could make group work more positive (Common, 1989). Undergraduate students reported that their best group experiences were those in which the instructor formed the group. Perhaps this is because instructors can match student learning styles or join students with complementary talents. Effective groups are between four and seven students. Students who took group exams often reported that these provided positive experiences; the use of peer evaluations, however, got mixed reviews as some students viewed this assessment technique as destructive of peer trust.

One of the most important elements of a positive group learning experience is relevance; students need to know why the group work is important to them (Feichtner & Davis, cited in *The Teaching Professor,* 1991). Faculty can contribute to satisfying and effective learning by explaining the purposes of group learning, helping students set realistic expectations, creating diverse groups, providing multiple opportunities to make decisions, listening in on group discussions and offering advice, providing immediate feedback, and allowing groups to meet during regular class time.

Collaborative learning is a form of group inquiry in which teachers and students work together actively in the learning processes, with less status distance between teacher and student than is traditional. Research is often involved and knowledge is created in an atmosphere of community. Activities may take many forms such as projects, mentoring, or peer teaching, but all are based on the assumption that learners create knowledge in their minds. So that students become aware of learning as a process of discovery, they share responsibility for both shaping the course and teaching the subject. Collaborative learning may also stress developing interpersonal skills, team work, leadership skills, and communication skills.

Cooperative learning (not to be confused with cooperative education which involves work experiences) is a more structured type of collaborative learning in which students work in small groups to try to maximize each other's learning. For a learning experience to be cooperative, five basic elements must be included: positive interdependence, face-to-face interaction, individual accountability, social skills, and group processing (Johnson, Johnson, & Smith, 1991).

The desired interdependence is fostered in areas of goals, roles, resources, and rewards. Goal interdependence is achieved by requiring all group members to agree on the answer and strategies for solving each problem. The existence of a mutually shared group goal is the most important element in cooperative learning. Role interdependence requires that each group member be assigned a role—for example, the role of reader, facilitator, checker, and so on. The instructor creates positive resource interdependence by giving each group only one copy of the problem or assignment; all members work on the same problem sheet and share their insights with one another. Positive rewards for interdependence are structured by awarding points or credit based on each member's performance.

Face-to-face promotive interaction is the second element of cooperative learning; it exists when students encourage, assist, and support one another in the process of learning. Individual accountability exists when the instructor assesses each individual's performance and gives the results to the group. One way of structuring individual accountability is to test each student and then select one grade at random for the group.

If students do not have the social skills needed for successful cooperative group learning, these must be taught "as purposely and precisely as academic skills" (Johnson, Johnson, & Smith, 1991, p. 7). Finally, the instructor must assist the groups in processing information on how well they are achieving their goals and maintaining working relationships. Attention to processing helps maintain the group and also facilitates the learning of social skills because all members receive feedback on their participation.

Cooperative learning can be used to achieve a variety of purposes: teaching content, ensuring active information processing during a lecture, and providing long-term academic support. As implied by this list of aims, cooperative learning groups can be short-term one-class-period structures, or formations that last an entire term, year, or longer. The instructor's role in facilitating good group interaction is largely one of support and feedback. The instructor must specify the goals and objectives for the group; decide who will be in what group (heterogeneous groups work best); explain the task and goal structure to students; monitor the progress and effectiveness of the group, intervening when needed; and, finally, evaluate students' achievements and discuss the effectiveness of their cooperation and participation (Johnson, Johnson, & Smith, 1991).

Peer Teaching

Postulate: To teach is to learn twice (Whitman, 1988).

In peer teaching, one student learns the material and then teaches it to peers. A wide variety of arrangements may be used. For example, the student acting as teacher may be a tutor, the two students may write as a pair, or both may be involved in a mathematics workshop group. Whitman (1988) identifies five types of peers: near peers (other undergraduate students), undergraduate teaching assistants, tutors, counselors (with a general focus), and co-peers (partnerships and work groups). Johnson, Johnson, and Smith (1991) offer several ideas for structuring peer teaching using pairs of students: discussion pairs, explanation pairs, note-taking pairs, and feedback pairs.

Psychologists have found that the way students learn material in anticipation of peer teaching is different from the kind of learning that takes place when a student is required to take a test. When students explain to each other, they are required to test their knowledge; when they take notes together, they improve their synthesis skills. Just as articulation in a group learning situation resembles deep processing rather than surface processing of material, peer teaching requires elaboration rather than rehearsal or lower processes. A variation on cooperative learning, peer teaching is another vehicle for getting students actively and collaboratively involved in their learning. There are, of course, countless other permutations of student groupings and academic tasks. The key to their success as cooperative learning experiences lies in the ability and willingness of the instructor to structure, monitor, and evaluate the work of students in ways that are consistent with the cooperative learning emphasis on collaboration, rather than individual or competitive effort.

Learning Communities

Postulate: Learning communities foster social and intellectual involvement.

Learning communities are curriculum structures intended to provide opportunities for intellectual coherence and integration at the program level. When teacher and students work together in group peer learning, they create what has come to be known as a learning community. The simplest version is a set of coordinated studies in which a cohort of students and a team of faculty from different disciplines work on an intensive theme or interdisciplinary topic. Several disciplines may award the credits (Gabelnick, MacGregor, Matthews, & Smith, 1990). In some "federated learning communities," cohorts of students enroll in a group of courses or, sometimes, an integrated seminar with an unifying theme.

Several institutions have had success with interdisciplinary general education programs based on the learning community model (in one of its various forms). They find that student retention rates have increased as the communities create a unique environment based on social and intellectual membership. While extensive studies of student performance have not been done, preliminary data indicate that students in these settings achieve at higher levels than noninvolved students. For example, studies of cognitive development have found that freshman students enter learning communities at cognitive development levels typical of first-year students, experience unusual gains in intellectual development during their involvement in the learning community, and acquire cognitive developmental levels more like those of juniors and seniors than of college sophomores (Gabelnick et al., 1990).

While the empirical evidence on intellectual and cognitive gains may be sketchy at present, learning community models—whether they are structured as first-year interest groups or clusters of courses or linked courses—assuredly result in more intellectual interactions between students and faculty, increased student involvement in learning, and higher levels of student motivation. In addition to enhancing the student experience, however, learning communities are also viewed as vehicles for faculty development. Qualitative studies of faculty responses to participation have found that most instructors feel revitalized by the experience, especially after involvement in a model that demands extensive collaborative planning and teaching

with colleagues from different disciplines. The creative process of developing linked or team-taught courses is itself an important attention paid to instructional process.

Instructor receptivity to different learning community models, however, varies by discipline. Faculty in the sciences appear to be most attracted to cluster models, linked courses, and the federated communities model because they tend to use existing courses and sequences in the curriculum. Faculty in humanities and social sciences tend to prefer the integrated coordinated-study model based on stronger synthetic perspectives (Gabelnick et al., 1990). Tenured faculty in mid-career are the usual instructors involved in such approaches. Secure in their disciplines and institutions, they are often ready at this stage to take some risks and make the more extensive commitment to teaching that is required by the learning community model.

Extending Classrooms

Postulate: Students who listen sometimes learn; students who experience almost always learn.

Not all instructional processes need to be scheduled in classroom settings. Internships can help develop problem solving skills, interpersonal skills, ethics, career development, and personal maturity. Career decisions flow from engaging in a broad range of experiences. Whether on or off campus, students in fields such as the arts are usually involved extensively in theatre and musical performances that are influential. Most of the types of learning that take place off campus can be called experiential education. They may range from internships to cooperative education, and from study abroad to volunteer community service.

While much experiential education has been involved in the professional and career fields and is discussed in detail primarily in the journals of those fields, Sexton and Ungerer (1975) stress several themes as central to a conceptual framework for experiential education. One theme, regardless of field, is that experiential education helps students understand complex problems in their context and helps institutions respond to changes in the nature of work and the new demands of society. Experiential education also helps to prepare students for citizenship and can provide alternatives for students who are alienated from traditional forms of education or have been left out of the educational process.

Cooperative education (entirely different from cooperative learning) is a form of experiential learning that allows students to alternate or combine periods of academic study and employment. It provides students with opportunities to test career options before graduation while earning wages or salaries in the process. Northeastern University's program with full-time, semester-long internships is particularly well known.

Clearly, extensive use of experiential learning involves a program or college-level decision to adopt a specific instruction process as part of the set of options open to students—or even required of them. In making a decision of this type, which involves considerable superstructure to complete successfully, an instructional program is significantly influenced by its network of relationships within the college. It is also influenced by how much autonomy it has to make such decisions and how strongly it accepts program and college goals that may support or limit this type of innovation. For professional fields, an important influence is relationships with colleagues in practice settings where students can be placed for learning experiences and receive proper supervision. Theater experience requires a theater; student teaching requires a school in which the fledging teacher can teach. Perhaps most of all at the program level, the complexity of the decisions about instructional process illustrate the strong relationships between instructional process and instructional resources.

Creating Learner-Centered Academic Plans

Students with differing levels of preparation, aptitude, experience, motivation, and self-confidence frequently are in the same classrooms and academic programs. Many instructors manifest their concern and respect for these student differences and preferences and try to create opportunities for all students to achieve. Some of these required accommodations are fairly simple to implement; others are far more difficult. An important prerequisite is a supportive campus and program climate. The strategies we discuss here depart from the atomized self-paced instruction of an earlier era and focus on the new learning psychology.

Establishing Classroom and Program Environment

Postulate: If learning involves risk-taking, teaching involves trust-building (Svinicki, ca 1989, p. 1).

Psychologists tell us that students need a modest level of anxiety and a supportive climate to learn well. Stated another way, students will learn best when the classroom and program contain challenges but are places of trust and respect. Such a classroom climate views students as valued members of a learning group, respects students' answers, makes it safe to take risks, eliminates excessive anxiety, promotes links with students' goals, and considers students' learning stages and styles. Students can find stress challenging or threatening. Both too little and too much stress may lead to poor learning. According to Whitman et al. (1984), the key to reducing harmful stress is to help students understand what to expect, give feedback, and provide them with a sense of control over their own education.

In his most recent book, *New Life for the College Curriculum*, Gaff (1991) writes that "faculty members seldom talk about the emotional aspects of learning, but the good teacher knows about them, and she or he uses the student' interests, experiences, and perspectives to make the subject matter come to life" (p. 181). Students, Gaff continues, put their self-esteem "on the line" whenever they actively participate in a course. If their attempts at making contributions are met with empathy and understanding, the results will be increased trust, self-confidence, and self-esteem—even if the response to the student's overture is constructive criticism. In contrast, Gaff talks about instances of "learning abuse" which leave students constricted. Learning abuse occurs when students' comments are ignored, rejected out of hand, or met with derision. Such treatment bruises students' self-esteem and confidence and, if continued over time, turns learning into an anxiety-producing experience for students. The student's response to repeated learning abuse is to restrain his curiosity, to read only what is assigned, to answer questions only when they cannot be avoided, and to keep the instructor at a distance. When even these coping mechanisms are unsuccessful, a student may withdraw from a course or from an institution.

Today, many educators feel that the type of interaction that should occur in college is characterized by the joint responsibility of faculty and students for learning, an atmosphere of mutual respect, a common interest in inquiry, and a freedom from anxiety. Students should feel free to share ideas knowing they will be open to scrutiny but without threat. Because students have come from many years of education where the teacher's answer is usually considered correct and their answers often wrong, they may be unwilling to risk sharing their ideas at first. It can take a long time to establish the idea that the instructor really wants to know what students think and to help them connect what she or he thinks with what they think. The choice of instructional process may seem far removed from the establishment of climate, but many

instructional processes are feasible only if this type of climate exists.

While some educators do not espouse totally collegial relationships between instructors and students, few would choose to return to the threatening climate of strict discipline and rote recitation. Some, however, may inadvertently create such a climate. Consequently, one concrete step that all instructors can take as they develop academic plans is to assess the environment in their classrooms and, if needed, change instructional decisions to foster more collaborative conditions.

One concise but reasonably comprehensive set of guidelines for good classroom environment, is *Seven Principles for Good Practice in Undergraduate Education* (1987) developed by Arthur Chickering and Zelda Gamson. Briefly, the seven principles (and an accompanying Faculty Inventory for assessment of one's own classroom practice) encourage:

1. Frequent student–faculty interaction in and outside class which helps to motivate and involve students

2. Cooperation between students, rather than competitive and isolated study

3. Active learning through discussion, writing, and application of what is learned

4. Prompt feedback on student performance to help students assess their existing knowledge and competence.

5. Emphasis on time on task—that is, helping students to learn to use their time effectively

6. Communication of high expectations to all students, from the poorly prepared to the bright and motivated

7. Respect for the diverse talents and ways of learning that students bring to college

There is also an Institutional Inventory based on the *Seven Principles for Good Prac-*

tice that provides quick assessments of program or collegewide climate, academic practices, curriculum, faculty, support services, and facilities. The Faculty and Institutional Inventories can be used jointly or separately to assess institutional or program practices, norms, policies, and expectations; they provide a basis for discussion at program and college levels about creating more "educationally powerful environments" (Chickering, Gamson, & Barsi, 1989, p.3).

At the program level, the advising climate may be considered an important parallel to classroom climate. Nearly all faculty members perform advising, but some are better prepared than others. An advisor who takes an interest in students' problems other than those related to rules can establish a supportive climate. Even if the advisor does not have specific skills to handle the problem personally, he or she can help the student make an appointment with an counseling expert, thereby exhibiting an interest.

Reward and incentive systems, budgets for instruction, and allocations for personnel development exert potent collegewide influences on educational environments. These influences affect the selection of instructional processes indirectly. For collegewide influence to be important, support must be visible and vocal so that faculty know it is appropriate and even wise to take responsibility for exploring instructional alternatives. Alternatively, if no support is perceived, faculty may treat selection of instructional strategies casually or as a nonvalued activity.

Establishing and Communicating Expectations

Postulate: Students must know how good performance is to be judged if they are to perform well and judge themselves.

Postulate: The superior classroom develops students' intrinsic motivation for learning.

One of the most important and possibly most overlooked elements of good instruction is the communication of clear purposes, goals, and standards to students, both for a particular course and for specific learning units. Developing a community climate for learning means taking collective responsibility for a shared educational purpose based on clear and consistent understandings. In describing his course on "learning to learn," McKeachie (1987) cites his conviction that "much of my previous teaching was lacking because I failed to communicate to my students why fieldwork, discussions, essay questions, term papers, team research, lectures and textbooks were expected to contribute to their learning and to their ability to continue learning. I believe that all of us could do much more to help our students think about their own learning and become more active, strategic learners" (p. 138).

Identifying purposes and goals answers questions such as "What constitutes the subject matter to be learned in this course or unit?" "How does it relate to other parts of the curriculum?" "What are the objectives for student learning?"—in short, "What does the instructor expect, and what can the student expect?" It seems obvious that these questions can be addressed through a course syllabus that the instructor distributes and discusses on the first day of class. The answers are also embodied in other course mechanisms such as tests and grades which can be discussed with students in terms of their purposes in assisting learning.

The Syllabus.   In addition to acting as a mechanism for improving communication between student and instructor, a complete syllabus also helps students learn effectively by providing a guide to the instructor's thinking about the course purposes. An effective syllabus explains to students the rationale and purpose of the course as well as course content and procedures. It helps students answer basic questions such as "Why should I take this course?" "What am I going to learn from it?" and "How does it relate to my interests?" For instructors who carefully design their syllabus, it can be a manifestation of course design and may even portray the process of course development in which the instructor engaged.

Based on the ideas that emerged in interviews and a survey of course planning, Lowther, Stark, and Martens (1989) developed a short guidebook, *Preparing Course Syllabi for Improved Communication.* This guide serves as a checklist to help organize a course and to provide students with information about course content, the instructor's expectations, the methods of instruction and evaluation, and the overall course rationale. New instructors can use the guide as a checklist of what might be included, or it can be used by groups of faculty from different disciplines to stimulate discussion about improving communication with students. A number of the items included in the guide may seem obvious to the experienced instructor. We found, however, that they were often omitted in syllabi and that faculty seldom mentioned them in interviews. The effect of documenting the key planning assumptions for a course in the syllabus, and also of communicating them more fully to students is open to verification. We have encouraged faculty to experiment with longer and shorter syllabi and evaluate the effect on students.

While we offered a checklist of items, we did not suggest that all be included in every syllabus, although we do believe that more comprehensive information is preferable to a brief outline. The syllabi that faculty members shared with us during our studies of course planning reminded us of the types of essays reported by Marton, Hounsell, and Entwistle (1984). The researchers asked students to write an historical essay with certain specifications. They found three types of responses. First, some students wrote the essay with detail or opinion but with no organizational structure or point or view. (Similarly, some faculty members present a syllabus that is a list of assignments and requirements, often with no rationale.) Second, some students offered a viewpoint without organized support for it. (Some faculty members present a syllabus that has objectives but no explanation of the reasons that these objectives are important.) Third, some students developed an organized argument and supported it with data and reasoning. (Some faculty present a syllabus that is a comprehensive plan for the course, including well-developed organization and reasons.) The researchers judged essay responses that were less than comprehensive to be unsatisfactory. Similarly, sketchy syllabi are usually unsatisfactory, at least from the student's view.

The syllabus should be a flexible tool that can accommodate changes in plans and can be supplemented later in a course. Faculty should consider ten elements when preparing a syllabus:

1. *Basic information:* Information about the instructor, office hours, telephone numbers, and the like, and also basic course information such as title, number of credits, class meeting times and places, prerequisites, a catalog description, and identification of students for whom the course is intended.

2. *Course purpose, goals, and objectives:* A course rationale statement, general course goals, specific objectives and the relationship of the course to program goals, and/or general education requirements, and institutional mission.

3. *Educational beliefs:* Information regarding the instructor's beliefs about the purposes of education and the teaching role, as well as beliefs about students' capa-

bilities, their prior preparation, and the effort that is expected of them.

4. *Course outline:* A topic outline and rationale for this content, a definition of the discipline, including information about the modes of inquiry, assumptions, the language of the discipline, and the skills to be applied.

5. *Assignments and course calendar:* Readings, papers, required documentation style, if any; test and quizzes; projects; laboratories; field experiences; the relationship of the course goals to assignments and the objectives of assignments; and dates for major assignments, exams, quizzes, projects, and special activities.

6. *Textbooks:* Title, author, edition, publisher, where the textbook can be obtained and its availability, estimated price, and the reason for using the particular text(s).

7. *Supplementary readings:* Required readings, recommended readings, the location of supplementary readings, readings keyed to student abilities/interests, and whether books are available from the instructor's personal library.

8. *Methods of instruction:* Description of instructional techniques, the rationale for their use, a description of class form, and how techniques and the format achieve specified goals.

9. *Student feedback and grading procedures:* Information regarding the grading system and expectations for student learning, policies on assignments, tests, attendance, incomplete work and extra credit; also, information on how student learning will be assessed and monitored, such as quizzes and tests, papers, class participation, office visits and after-class discussions.

10. *Learning facilities and resources for students:* Library policies, learning-assistance policies, computer availability, and policies, and reasons for using resources.

At the program level, descriptions of the program's academic plan that parallel course syllabi are scarce indeed. We have found such documents primarily in such programs as nursing where professional accreditors typically have insisted on a total program framework and rationale. Construction of guides such as those used in nursing have the advantage of assuring that the faculty responsible for the program have discussed and articulated their plan. These guides inform students about how the program faculty conceptualize the field and intend to teach it to them. They define relationships between students and faculty within the educational program and emphasize such goals as helping students to become intentional learners or critical thinkers. They also can define how both students and the curricular plan itself will be evaluated. Such program guides might take as their outline the elements of the academic plan, developing each element as the faculty review and articulate their specific plan. The role of the advisor in communicating program goals is similar to that of a professor explaining a syllabus in an course. At the collegewide level, institutional catalogs and bulletins should similarly explain college goals and expectations.

Tests. Tests help to codify expectations in a course or program. If they are used in a supportive, nonthreatening manner, tests can help students assess what they know and help the teacher know what the students have successfully learned. Some consider tests to be excellent motivators; others believe they decrease motivation and learning. Some believe that final examinations are the worst types of tests because they are given at a time when there is no opportunity to improve. Finals may actually discourage true learning by implying that the material should be regurgitated, then forgotten since the course is over. In making this criticism, Schilling and Schilling (1994) propose a creative solution: entrance exams as prerequisites to the next courses in the sequence rather than final examinations as they now exist. Such a solution can involve students in preparing for the next success.

Several techniques exist to overcome the limitations of tests as currently used. For example, it is possible to build tests that build confidence rather than destroy it; a test can begin with easier items, thus helping the student get started with strong expectancy of success. Prompt feedback from tests can be arranged to help the student know what errors he or she made and what needs to be done to improve. The perceived fairness of the tester and his or her interest in using the results to help students learn is crucial. Ericksen (1984) argued that students are shortchanged when examinations are trivial, irrelevant, confusing, or tangential to the subject matter of a course.

One of the popular debates about tests is whether short answer or essay tests are better. Psychologists say it all depends on what types of skills are being assessed and in which discipline. Like other things, disciplines view this question differently. In either case, many faculty need to seek the help of professional testmakers to be sure their tests are reliable and valid.

In the *The Craft of Teaching* (1988), Kenneth Eble offered advice about creating, using, and scoring tests. Among his suggestions: Use a variety of testing methods, don't grade all tests, give prompt feedback, clarify test objectives before and after the test, let students contribute to test composition, and discuss tests both before and after they are given. Eble stressed that tests should be learning and motivational tools more than measurement tools; his advice on grading was therefore to be generous so as to reduce the threat that tests inevitably pose for students.

Grades. Fair and well-considered grading practices are another element of evaluation that can productively be tied to course goals and objectives. Not all students will meet course objectives easily or even accept them as valid. The credibility of the grading system depends on instructors' fair assessments of student performance in light of these objectives.

Like testing, grading has been strongly criticized and yet persists as part of the instructional scene. The best grading systems are those that help students know what they need to learn and how to improve their ability to learn it. In developing plans, instructors need to analyze whether the type of learning they want students to achieve is modeled by the tests and the grading system.

At the program level, comprehensive examinations and theses may be parallels to course level grades. Although these summative exercises often engender student anxiety, the program atmosphere can be one that encourages students to understand the goals of synthesis that they are being asked to undertake. At the college level, the overall environment may have more to do with specific pressure for learning than with the specific grading system used. Researchers have identified colleges with diverse grading systems that support strong intellectual climates where students' intrinsic motivation is high. Clarity of expectations may be the common reason. Carefully developed student orientation programs are a collegewide manifestation of concern for communicating expectations.

Individualizing Instructional Processes

Postulate: Every student learns in a unique way and at a unique pace.

Individualization and learning styles are not readily separated. We have mentioned that faculty find the idea of accommodating learning styles frustrating. How can they possibly accommodate the great diversity of learners in large classes? One way is to recognize that certain instructional processes work differently for students with different learning styles; that is, learning styles and teaching strategies jointly influence outcomes. Most research supports the thesis that students learn best in settings that accommodate their individual needs and styles. Psychologists call such differential effects trait–treatment interactions or aptitude–treatment interactions where the trait or aptitude characterizes the student and the "treatment" refers to the instructional strategy.

Quite a number of learner attributes can interact with instructional designs to produce different learning effects. In addition to learning styles, aptitude, anxiety, previous preparation, and whether a student attributes success to her own effort may all interact with instructional process to produce negative or positive achievement. One example comes from a study in which handing out a lecture outline helped students with a "dependent" learning style that relies on external cues but tended to confuse students with a "independent" learning style who organized information in their own ways (Ward & Clark, 1987). Similarly, students with interpersonally oriented learning styles gained more in a chemistry class from interactive learning opportunities such as peer-centered instruction, whereas those with other learning styles gained more from more impersonal media

such as textbooks (Andrews, 1981). The examples abound: contract learning is probably better for students who use good time management and have well-developed learning strategies; discussion is better for students who are outgoing enough to take an active part.

Clearly, the interaction between anxiety and instruction and between personality traits and instruction are complex. In establishing expectations, the instructor should consider at a minimum, the level of the instruction and the prior knowledge and special needs of students in a class. Depending on their skills and past experiences, nonthreatening exams may be better for anxious students and encourage them to improve their choice of learning strategies.

Clearly, allowing students to choose among supplementary readings or to develop their own term paper topics are two ways to provide opportunities for student involvement and to build choice into course content based on student goals and learning styles. In highly structured courses with few options for personalized assignments or readings, it may be possible to include examples from a variety of contexts in order to tap a greater number of student interests. For example, a biology lecture might include examples from medicine, environmental planning, genetics, or psychiatry. Building on Kolb's learning style model, Svinicki and Dixon (1987) suggested that concrete experience could include laboratories, observations, simulations and field work. Reflective observation could involve keeping journals, discussion, and brainstorming. Abstract conceptualization could use lectures, papers, projects and analogies. Active experimentation could build upon case studies, laboratories, simulations, and projects. Such a list makes clear that many instructors, who themselves have abstract learning styles, will need to consciously strive to accommodate students whose styles and experiences differ from their own. While every student interest cannot be accommodated in every class, conscious decisions help instructors to explore different contexts and address a variety of problems.

Instructional strategies are what the teacher selects and uses to promote learning. Academic tasks are the tasks that the students do that transform information and experiences into learning (Doyle, 1986). The instructors' choices of academic tasks can be based on knowledge about students' goals, motivation, and capabilities—that is, activities can be chosen to support learners' current levels of development. The new approaches to learning and instruction suggest that we can not only adapt the tasks to the learners but should also help learners become more suited to various tasks. But it will not always be clear even to the most experienced instructor how specific activities will contribute to instructional goals. What makes specific instructional activities work is a question for reflective teachers to think about and for researchers to pursue more systematically.

REFLECTING ON PLANNING AND TEACHING

Faculty members who construct careful academic plans can focus specifically on choosing instructional processes and reflect on how these choices are linked to the other elements of the academic plan. Variations in other plan elements may call for a change in instructional process; and reciprocally, trying new methods of instruction may prompt reconsiderations of beliefs and assumptions about education and learners and about one's discipline. However, the process of changing the way one constructs plans or teaches from the plan may be better undertaken in an evolutionary rather than a revolutionary way. Not all elements of an academic plan should be

varied simultaneously. As testimony, an accounting professor engaged in curriculum change told his colleagues he had learned that the product of complex topics and complex student thinking is a constant. "You can't move both upward at the same time, you must rachet up one then the other, seeking a new constant."

One commonly recognized aspect of good teaching reflected in student teaching evaluations is preparation for and organization of the course. Similarly, we have stressed that good teaching depends on good instructional designs. Such designs build motivation, promote learning skills along with subject learning, help students develop self-confidence, foster critical thinking and a spirit of inquiry, promote retention by making connections, help students to integrate knowledge, and increase students' proclivity to take responsibility for their own learning. In this sense, good teaching could be recognized as a potential outcome of good planning, although good planning does not ensure good teaching.

Some believe that college teachers who confront a severe discrepancy, an alternative situation, or a crisis become receptive to new methods of course planning and selection of a wider variety of instructional processes. However, just as teachers should encourage students to reflect on their goals and learning, teachers can be reflective about their teaching, and reflection can produce change. Peer consultations, classroom research, student evaluations, and case studies of teaching currently provide opportunities for reflection on teaching (see, respectively, Katz & Henry, 1988; Cross & Angelo, 1988). To extend current selection of instructional processes, we might develop principles for the professional development of teachers as planners to parallel principles we have suggested for students in the classroom: (1) use more collegial teamwork among faculty, (2) start with disciplinary groups that can build on common beliefs and styles, (3) move to groups of mixed disciplines that encourage exposure to new alternatives, (4) encourage self-confidence through more peer support and emphasis on teaching, and (5) improve motivation by raising the value of the teaching task in colleges and programs.

Which has greater potential to change and improve—the "teacher as planner" (the designer of the curriculum at the course, program, or college level) or "the teacher as actor" (the implementer of the chosen instructional process)? We have argued that changing the teacher as planner is likely to bring about positive change in the teacher as actor as well. Now we move to the teacher as evaluator.

CHAPTER 10

Evaluating and Adjusting Academic Plans

EVALUATING COURSES AND PROGRAMS

An emphasis on evaluating and adjusting courses and programs distinguishes our dynamic definition of curriculum as an academic plan from static definitions that merely list or describe courses, groups of courses, or learning experiences. The curriculum is constantly changing based on new needs and new information. The concept of an academic plan organizes thinking about evaluation because it helps to identify specific aspects of curriculum to change. Examining and adjusting each element of the plan guides curriculum analysis and leads to more systematic and deliberate change than when the specific elements of curriculum are not considered. In addition, evaluating the entire plan and its elements may be less threatening to the classroom instructor than evaluating only teaching behaviors; the elements of the academic plan point to essential steps in course planning that are essential precursors to good teaching but not identical with it.

In Figure 10-1 we illustrate how evaluation and adjustment operate in our proposed curriculum model in three ways. First, evaluations of specific course and program plans provide information which faculty members use to make adjustments (Path A). Second, evaluations of the overall college and university curriculum, often collaborative efforts by faculty and administrators (Path B), provide information to adjust both academic plans for an entire college and the educational environment in which course and program plans are created. In addition to these evaluation mechanisms that college personnel use directly to adjust academic plans, there is another evaluation and adjustment path outside the specific educational environment (Path C). This path suggests a process by which college outcomes are observed, aggregated, and interpreted by the public and policy makers, and perceived by these groups to be the "results of college." Whether well founded or not, these perceptions affect the nature and strength of the influences operating on colleges and universities, on their educational environments, and thus, indirectly, on academic plans.

In this chapter we focus on the two evaluation and adjustment processes typically used within an institution by faculty and

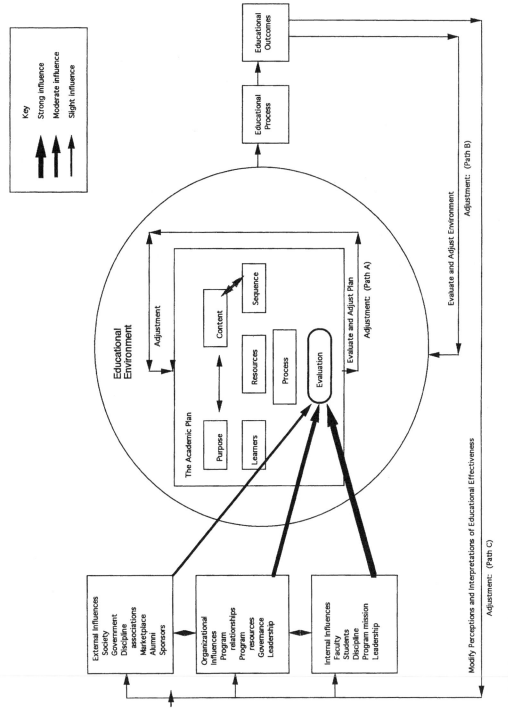

Key

Strong influence

Moderate influence

Slight influence

Educational Outcomes

Educational Process

Educational Environment

Adjustment

The Academic Plan

Content

Sequence

Resources

Process

Purpose

Learners

Evaluation

Evaluate and Adjust Plan

Adjustment: (Path A)

Evaluate and Adjust Environment

Adjustment: (Path B)

External Influences
Society
Government
Discipline
associations
Marketplace
Alumni
Sponsors

Organizational Influences
Program relationships
Program resources
Governance
Leadership

Internal Influences
Faculty
Students
Discipline
Program mission
Leadership

Modify Perceptions and Interpretations of Educational Effectiveness

Adjustment: (Path C)

FIGURE 10-1   Academic Plans in Environmental Context: Focus on Evaluation and Adjustment

administrators for courses and programs they have developed (Paths A and B). We will discuss administrative responsibilities for college-level aspects of Path B (such as program monitoring, accreditation, and externally mandated program reviews) and Path C in Chapter 11. Separating these three evaluation and adjustment processes is somewhat arbitrary. The three are linked but differ in form, in where they place primary responsibility, and in the degree to which they use formal processes. Path A is primarily a faculty activity and often informal. Path B requires effective administrative leadership to enhance and improve curriculum by providing a supportive environment. Finally, in the volatile context of higher education's increasing accountability, public perceptions and judgments developed through Path C have become increasingly important and may merit more systematic attention from both faculty and administrators.

Evaluations in Paths A and B that are aimed at improvement are often referred to by evaluators as *formative* evaluations. These may include measurement of student outcomes (assessment) and satisfaction (client evaluation) as well as estimates of how faculty themselves believe the plans work (professional judgment). Most frequently, and especially in general education programs and major fields, influences on these formative evaluation and adjustment processes are internal. In the case of occupational and professional programs, forces external to the unit such as employers or accreditors may help to define the evaluation of academic plans. Where collegewide review systems exist, organizational forces may also affect evaluation plans and adjustments.

Formal evaluation processes in Paths A and B that are aimed at making major decisions about program continuance are frequently called *summative* evaluation. They can lead to external judgments about a program's quality, staffing, and level of support as well as determining its existence. A college may initiate summative reviews for some of its programs, or state agencies may initiate such reviews for specific programs and colleges.

In contrast to the formal nature of most summative evaluations, formative evaluations by college faculty of their course and program plans traditionally have been casual and informal. In this chapter, we describe what we have learned about how faculty typically evaluate and adjust their academic plans. Then, as in previous chapters, we will describe alternatives and opportunities that may help faculty evaluate curricula more systematically and effectively.

In our discussion we will use the term *evaluation* in the broadest sense, connoting the process of examining an enterprise and making judgments about its effectiveness. In this usage, evaluation subsumes more specific processes such as assessment of student outcomes, self-study, and external program review. Evaluations may be conducted at any level of the academic plan.

HOW FACULTY EVALUATE AND ADJUST ACADEMIC PLANS

Much informal evaluation and adjustment of academic plans takes place at course and program levels. As academic units get larger, evaluations and adjustments are more difficult and thus less frequent. Even in a small college, differences of views about educational purposes and pedagogical processes among the disciplines can make evaluation and adjustment a highly political and unwieldy process. The larger the university, the less likely it is that institutionwide evaluations will occur regularly, unless summative reviews are initiated by outside agencies. Thus, the extent of direct faculty involvement in evaluation and adjustment also decreases from the course level to the collegewide level.

Course Plans

As we interviewed faculty about course and program planning, we learned that most faculty consciously make judgments about the way their academic plans are going. On the basis of these judgments, most make adjustments frequently, but some judge no changes to be necessary, and a few neglect to make changes even when the need is clear. Typically, faculty make several types of observations using three types of indicators: (1) how the instructor feels about the course (using professional judgment), (2) how students feel about the course (determining client satisfaction), and (3) how well students achieve course objectives as judged by examination results or similar indicators (assessing student achievement).

Professional Judgment

First and foremost, faculty rely on their own professional judgment when evaluating their courses. As experts in the fields they are teaching, they observe how much knowledge students acquire, how attentive they are, and how their written work and problem-solving skills are developing. In making these professional judgments, faculty frequently use informal observations, exchanges with students during class and office hours, and the types of questions students ask during help sessions.

In interviews and the course planning survey faculty described various indicators by which they monitored students' involvement in learning and the varying degrees of confidence they had in these indicators. Personal observation, the most frequent monitoring method, includes such activities as watching students' faces, observing discussions, and monitoring class attendance. Faculty used such observations daily and had modest confidence in them. Faculty also said that they observed how frequently students visited their offices, asked questions after class and completed assignments (Stark, Lowther, Ryan, et al., 1988; Stark, Lowther, Bentley, et al., 1990).

Faculty members also rely on formal measurements of student achievement and development—most often quizzes, tests, essays, projects, reports, and other assignments. Examinations and assignments are used weekly or monthly, less frequently than personal observations, but faculty have a higher degree of confidence in these indicators, perhaps because these measures specifically reflect the goals and objectives they have established for the course.

Faculty members who follow systematic course design models often have developed written course objectives and can describe quite clearly the extent to which the students have achieved each one. However, even professors who do not prepare written objectives for their courses have a strong sense of what they want students to know. They feel sure that they will recognize the obvious indicators of student intellectual growth. Yet most faculty members, whether or not they develop written objectives, tend to cast desired outcomes in terms of content acquisition rather than in terms of student outcomes. When asked how they wanted students to behave, think, or "be different" at the end of the course, professors typically answered indirectly by describing the content that they hoped to cover or convey to students. Some professors have considerable difficulty separating demonstrated student learning from their own intentions to cover material and their proficiency in doing so. Some may, in fact, believe that if they covered the material, the students should have learned it.

How faculty evaluate courses and examine whether students have achieved the course objectives differs substantially by discipline, paralleling the disciplinary variations in educational purposes and objectives. Faculty members in structured fields like sciences and mathematics more often believe that they can quantify student achievement based on demonstrated ability to supply information or solve problems on tests. To them, these methods seem appropriate in achieving their primary goals of learning systems of concepts and principles. Although there are variations within fields, these professors are more likely than instructors in other fields to conduct statistical analyses to determine which test items present the most difficulty for students and to calculate grades mathematically. They tend to emphasize acquisition of content rather than student development.

Faculty members in the humanities and many social science fields are more hesitant about the value of quantifying students' work and skeptical of the possibilities of doing so with precision. They often resist using multiple-choice tests and other measures that seem not to elicit the types of learning they try to cultivate in students, such as critical thinking and value awareness. These professors prefer essays, research papers, portfolios of student work, journal writing, and conversation as ways of judging student development rather than multiple choice tests. Professors in the social science fields often measure students' achievement by their ability to connect, compare, and contrast ideas and theories in organized essays. Those teaching in humanities fields may reward personal insight or a creative flair in students' work. They see student development as a more individualized process than do those in more structured fields. Thus, they may be quite resistant to judging students in any way that implies a single "correct" answer.

Different views of evaluation can also be illustrated among faculty in the varied professional and occupational fields. Programs preparing students for entrepreneurial professions often teach (and test for) specific concepts and problem solving skills, as well as behavioral skills such as accounting techniques or computer programming. Faculty members in these fields often evaluate students according to externally established standards—for example, the knowledge of principles tested by exams of the American Institute of Certified Public Accountants. In contrast, the skills taught in the artistic professions such as music, art, and dance are evaluated far more subjectively. In fact, as Schon (1987) pointed out, it may be easier for faculty members to model and recognize the desired artistic behavior than to verbalize criteria for it. Finally, the college career fields we have grouped as human services and information services are likely to have both clear-cut criteria for evaluating some student outcomes (such as how to give an injection in nursing, or how to conduct a bibliographic search in library science) and more subjective criteria for others (such as how to help clients deal with anxiety). Just as the traditional disciplines emphasize different types of effective thinking, the career studies programs emphasize different ways of "connecting" with the future occupation.

When we discussed with faculty how they evaluated the success of a course, the answers included informal modes of evaluation that are determined jointly by discipline, local context, and professional orientation. It would be difficult to write a single description of evaluation that would reflect the diversity of courses and academic plans in higher education. Even the way different groups of faculty define the common goal of cultivating "the ability to think effectively" differs, as do the ways they evaluate achievement of this goal.

Student Opinion

Evidence of student satisfaction with courses is gathered primarily through the evaluation forms that most colleges distribute each term. Research has shown that the standard course evaluations used by most colleges are reliable and valid; at least they consistently reveal common notions of "good teaching" among students (Cashin, 1988, 1995; Feldman, 1976; Marsh, 1984, 1987; Marsh & Bailey, 1993, Marsh & Dunkin, 1991). Extensive research has also documented that a few specific extraneous characteristics (such as class size and the student's initial interest in the course) influence these evaluations; standard forms therefore usually include questions that allow the effects of these variables to be examined and controlled. Student evaluation forms continue, however, to be controversial. Most are geared to a lecture and discussion style of teaching; thus some faculty complain that the forms are not well adapted to their particular disciplines and teaching styles or are not helpful for course revision. Despite this controversy, over 90% of faculty at all colleges in our nationally representative survey used the forms (willingly or unwillingly), and 48% of professors we surveyed said they use the results to make adjustments in their course the next time they plan it. In addition, we found instances where instructors also created mechanisms to solicit and use student feedback regularly during a course. For example, some professors established student committees (or "quality circles") to give them weekly reports about student progress and reaction. Such practices may be on the increase as colleges adapt business principles of "total quality management" to the classroom. For example, at Delaware Valley Community College faculty are developing an elaborate system of involving "student customers" in providing feedback within courses (Heverly, 1994).

It is important to distinguish evaluation of academic plans from the evaluation of teaching performance. Currently, student course evaluation forms focus primarily on the instructor's selection of instructional processes and on teacher behavior in the classroom—the two most visible aspects of a course. However, the selection of instructional processes is only one aspect of the academic plan about which instructors make decisions. Student views on other aspects, such as the usefulness of instructional materials, the appropriateness of sequencing of the content, and the effectiveness of the evaluation and adjustment processes are also important.

Other Opinions

Faculty in our studies reported that close colleagues were an important source of help in planning and adjusting their courses. In Table 10-1 we show the percentages of faculty who reported using each source of colleague help. Clearly, departmental colleagues are considered most helpful and colleagues in the same field at other colleges are seen as much more helpful than institutional colleagues in other fields. Department chairs and deans were moderately helpful; part-time faculty were more likely to turn to them as sources of opinion about course planning and adjustment than full-time faculty, perhaps because they have less contact with departmental colleagues (Lowther, Stark, Genthon, & Bentley, 1990).

Colleague help seldom extends to peer evaluation. Peer evaluation of courses is rare; but when faculty members team up with colleagues to help evaluate and improve each other's courses, they report the experience as satisfying and helpful. A detailed system of peer evaluation in which faculty observe a colleague's class and interview the students has been used in several New Jersey colleges and, though time consuming, is apparently useful to those who participate (Katz & Henry, 1988). This teamwork requires trust and clear ground rules.

The few faculty who have used instructional consultants find them helpful in adjusting course design—as, for example, in the instructional design center at Syracuse University described by Diamond. Based on talks with faculty, we speculate that once faculty members have obtained evaluative opinions

TABLE 10-1   Helpful Sources of Assistance or Feedback in Course Planning

Source	Helpfulness
Department colleague	71% (extremely helpful)
Department chair	48% (moderately helpful)
Colleague (same field) at another college	40% (moderately helpful)
Local colleague in another department	24% (not helpful)
Dean	20% (not helpful)
Family members	16% (not helpful)
Instructional Development Center	6% (not helpful)[a]

Souce: Planning Introductory College Courses by Stark, Lowther, Bentley, et al. (1990), p. 97. Reprinted by permission of The National Center for Research to Improve Postsecondary Teaching and Learning, The University of Michigan.
[a]Percentage based on campuses where such a center existed.

about their courses from varied sources and found these opinions useful, they tend to seek consultation again.

Current trends point to increasing use of evaluative opinions from outside the college organization. Based in the emphasis on accountability, the word *assessment* is now frequently used in education to mean the evaluation of student outcomes that may be more comprehensive, systematic, and neutral than the view of a single professor or group of professors. External assessments may be conducted to determine what outcomes students achieve from a single course, from a group of courses like those organized into a program plan, or from the entire college experience. Assessment may focus on short-range outcomes such as skills, knowledge, and behavior, as well as long-range outcomes such as attitudes and life success. Relevant outcomes are not limited to academic achievement but may include persistence in college, satisfaction with college, success in employment, and others. Although very few faculty members we interviewed between 1988 and 1990 said that such assessments were conducted at their college, many anticipated that externally driven assessments would become more common in the future. Faculty expressed concern about who would determine appropriate outcomes and indicators and whether outside judgments would be valid.

Making Adjustments

Faculty make small adjustments in their course plans frequently, both as they are teaching and in preparation for the next offering of the course. For example, a literature professor may decide to spend additional class time on a reading after the class discussion falters. Similarly, a biology instructor may make a time adjustment when students' unfamiliarity with laboratory equipment suggests that they will need extra time to finish the lab assignment. Although covering the content of the course is always a concern when an adjustment of this sort is made, the time spent thoroughly addressing a difficult topic can be time well spent if student learning is enhanced.

Simple classroom observations can lead to substantial course changes when faculty use classroom observations to adjust their academic plan in progress. One instructor examined assumptions about why some students were not fully engaged in the class and realized that he paced the instructional process based on eye contact he maintained with students who paid attention consistently. Daydreamers, with whom he never made any eye contact, never influenced his pacing. Once he realized this, the instructor began to select instructional processes and a sequence of the content that would make the class and future ones more productive for a larger proportion of the students (Katz & Henry, 1988, pp. 59–60).

Some elements of the course-level academic plan get adjusted far more frequently than others and we summarize our impressions about this in Table 10-2. The most common adjustments include incorporating advances in knowledge, trying new ways of sequencing material, or using newly available materials like textbooks and computer programs. These three types of adjustments (content, sequence, and resources) are often combined when refining a course. When instructors feel that a course is going very poorly, they may do a major overhaul. Typically, such an overhaul is planned for the succeeding term, but occasionally we heard about a professor totally restructuring a course in mid-term, usually changing the sequence or instructional process to relieve strong student dissatisfaction. We found little evidence of the stereotypical professor who teaches twenty years from the same course plans.

TABLE 10-2   Estimated Frequency of Adjusting Elements of Academic Plans

Element	Frequency of Adjustment
Purpose	Seldom
Content	Seldom
Resources	Often
Sequence	Often
Instructional process	Often and increasing
Evaluation	Seldom and increasing

We estimate that course purposes and objectives are quite stable and are least often adjusted but the specific discipline content used to achieve the objectives may be adjusted. Modest adjustments may be made in instructional processes but are limited by faculty preference for the lecture/discussion mode of teaching.

Instructional processes in colleges may change more often in the near future due to increased instructional awareness and accelerating change. Technology is now making strong inroads into traditional lectures; simulation is replacing "wet labs" in sciences; videotapes are replacing printed case studies in business and health sciences; and computers are replacing traditional drawing tools in art, architecture, and engineering design. Use of collaborative learning is increasing in varied disciplines and ranges from small groups that briefly discuss a concept in the middle of a traditional lecture to problem-solving teams that work a full semester on an interdisciplinary task. These changes are accompanied by an increase in classroom research, which allows immediate adjustment.

Classroom research often reveals that the professor has misjudged learners' preparedness for the level of material presented. Thus, many instructors use informal assessments such as student journals or other writing exercises to evaluate student preparedness and progress and also to turn students into active class participants. Steffens (1991) writes about changes he made in a large history survey course to better prepare the learners for the unfamiliar task of synthesizing historical material about the Middle Ages. His changes included asking students to write brief speculations, summaries, and explanations about a single event and share them with a neighbor. Deliberate changes by professors are often aimed at adjusting several elements of the academic plan simultaneously, in this case, purpose, content, learners and instructional process.

The "one-minute paper," one of the most widely used of the classroom assessment techniques recently popularized by Angelo and Cross (1993), is used by many faculty members to gather feedback about the success of several aspects of the academic plan. Near the conclusion of a class session, the instructor asks students to write responses on index cards to questions like these: (1) What was the most important thing you learned during this class? (2) What important question was left unanswered? By examining and summarizing the anonymous student responses, instructors can tell how well students are learning. Light (1990) concluded from his study of Harvard undergraduates that students appreciate these informal types of course evaluations and believe they have positive effects on their attitudes toward a course as well as their actual learning.

Most changes in courses that faculty make as they teach, or as they plan the next offering of the same course, are internally stimulated—that is, the course is the individual faculty member's possession and he or she adjusts it in individual ways. As we shall show, however, the new emphasis on assessment, on technology, and on helping students develop linkages among courses may be interacting now to reduce the solitary nature of course evaluation and adjustment.

Program Plans

As we interviewed faculty about how and why they evaluate and adjust their curriculum plans at the program level, we found few systematic processes for collecting information. Faculty tend to use very informal methods to gather data about how their program plans are working. Rather than set aside time periodically for regular review, faculty members said they dealt with specific problems when they seemed to need attention, as evidenced by major student dissatisfaction or by poor results on examinations. Sometimes in this in-

formal way, they evaluate only a specific component of a program or a selected instructional process, such as an internship, laboratory, or thesis requirement. Even colleges that maintain data on academic programs in departments or institutional research offices may limit this information to characteristics of students, faculty, budget, credit hours, and space allocations. Reviews that primarily collect input measures as proxies for educational quality are probably more correctly called program *audits* than evaluations. Little of this information typically collected is helpful in determining how well programs have met their educational goals.

We wondered whether faculty neglected program evaluation because they were concerned that self-study might lead to the demise or reassignment of their favorite courses, but faculty denied such turf concerns. Instead, they claimed that program evaluation efforts were neglected due to lack of leadership. Where strong program evaluation and regular adjustments exist, faculty always attributed them to a strong and sometimes visionary leader, usually a department chairperson. Faculty also reported that higher level administrators, such as deans, vice presidents, or presidents, set the stage by emphasizing the importance of the academic program and encouraging regular, nonthreatening self-study. When the impetus came from upper-level administrators, faculty responded eagerly if they felt the results would be used in a supportive way. It seems rare for faculty to initiate or maintain regular program review without this supportive leadership. The recent national emphasis on assessment and evaluation for all college programs is, however, causing such leadership to emerge in many colleges.

Evaluating Programs

There is no well-established parallel to the standard course evaluation at the program level. Student views about general education programs are perhaps least often gathered, and Gaff (1991) has documented and lamented this lack of student involvement. Possibly faculty feel that student opinions about these required programs are untrustworthy, that underclass students have limited perspectives, or that their comments would not be constructive.

Programs in major specializations are far more likely than general education programs to gather student opinions. In small colleges, faculty members know their major students well and often consult them when contemplating program adjustments. Even in large colleges and universities, departments may conduct opinion surveys of student majors, conduct student focus groups, or include student representatives on departmental committees. For example, in many large universities, student reactions to program plans and to teaching within the program can be obtained through electronic mail, a simple and immediate form of communication that allows faculty to pose questions for students to answer or solicit open-ended comments. Faculty using such techniques at many large campuses feel that students feel freer to speak their minds through the electronic media than they do in class. Graduating students also may be tracked as they pursue further study or employment to determine if they are satisfied with their preparation and have obtained needed career-related skills. Student opinion, gathered in these ways, is often used directly for adjustments.

Program evaluation is more likely than course evaluation to involve professional judgment from external experts. Program self-studies sometimes include visits by consultants (usually professors at a similar college and department) who are asked to comment on program strengths and weaknesses and suggest possible adjustments. A few colleges use a system of external faculty members who serve on senior thesis committees. Particularly in small colleges where faculty feel isolated from their discipline, both types of visits are valued as sources of information about how things are done in peer institutions.

Professional and occupational programs may also seek views on curriculum planning from colleagues who practice the profession or occupation outside of the college or university. For these programs, advisory boards are a common—and often a prestigious and powerful—catalyst for program adjustment.

A faculty group outside the program may also evaluate it to determine whether it should be discontinued, substantially altered, or merged with another unit. Most often, such a review is suggested or mandated at a higher administrative level, either periodically or at a time of crisis. In such evaluations, judgments are made about (1) whether the program is performing well at its task (merit), (2) whether the program is needed (worth), and (3) what actions should be taken to remedy discrepancies from "ideal" merit and worth. A judgment of "worth" concerns whether the college (or society) needs or chooses to have and support such an enterprise (Lincoln & Guba, 1980). Technically, decisions about merit and worth are independent of whether the evaluation process is formative or summative. Practically, however, a summative process will more often lead to a decision about worth, while a formative process to improve the program's merit will likely assert the worth of the program in advance.

As an example of the distinction between merit and worth, consider a program in social work located at a college that has refocused its mission primarily on technological fields. The social work program may provide excellent instruction and be judged highly meritorious. Yet because the college is changing its mission, an excellent human service program may be considered of little worth to the college. It might be discontinued or transferred to another nearby college focusing on human services, where its merit could continue to be supported.

Externally initiated program evaluations focus on either merit or worth, or both, and are usually called *program reviews*. We will use that term to distinguish an outside review from an program's internal self-study. In *Campus Trends 1992,* El-Khawas reports that 80% of colleges conduct program reviews, mostly periodically, with each program being reviewed every five years. Colleges we visit seem to have such reviews far less frequently, especially when state-level coordinating boards do not require them.

Program reviews within the college organization (as contrasted with internal self-study) are sometimes unpopular among faculty because their colleagues from other fields can be harsh critics. Often a program must defend itself when targeted for an organizational review, when a collegewide curriculum discussion threatens cutbacks, when another unit seeks service courses for nonmajors, or when the scope and number of its offerings are seen as too costly. At such times, faculty may simultaneously dispute data collected by the nonprogram reviewers and scurry to collect information they might have collected earlier and used more systematically for program self-study. Periodic reviews that are done regularly, whether or not crises exist, are less threatening and probably more productive.

Colleges responsible to their communities or regions, such as community colleges and state-funded colleges, probably have more regular evaluative curriculum mechanisms for programs than private institutions, particularly for career-directed programs. One rationale for these planned reviews is that taxpayers' dollars should be used to support only high-quality programs with an employment market. At some community colleges, for example, deans regularly target occupational programs for review and use information about employment opportunities and student job performance to make summative, as well as formative, decisions. Re-

views identify programs that fail to meet established criteria and, consequently, must be either improved or eliminated.

Making Adjustments

Unless external reviews dictate change, it is probably rare for faculty to initiate a new basic mission for an academic program. Rather, educational purpose typically remains stable, while subsidiary objectives and the particular content used to achieve them are gradually adjusted. Most major programs, both in disciplines and professional fields, regularly adapt disciplinary content gradually to respond to external influences such as advancing knowledge base and changing methods of inquiry.

Most program-level adjustments in elements of academic plans other than purpose and content are internally motivated. Like changes in courses, program-level changes are most frequently made in sequencing and selection of resource materials. Changes in program content are often accompanied by changes in the sequence in which students take courses or learn various topics within courses, especially when instructors believe students have inadequate foundations for courses as currently taught. Some fields, such as chemistry, accounting, and nursing, where faculty monitor the success of student majors on external examinations, may make changes frequently. Resources used in programs also change frequently. New textbooks, new tools such as computers, new databases or case studies, and especially the arrival of new faculty with recent training or field experience represent the types of changing resources to which programs must and do adjust.

Although program faculties do make group decisions to change instructional processes, a more typical first step is that one or two faculty members develop new instructional processes for their own reasons. After group acknowledgment, others may move a bit reluctantly to adjust their customary practices. Program leaders seldom make strong efforts to enforce change among those who move slowly. The ethos of a college, based in respect for faculty autonomy and creativity, simply does not lend itself to devoting large amounts of time or resources to insisting on systematic adjustment of instructional processes at the program level.

Like course changes, program-level curriculum adjustments often stem from informal observations by faculty that existing plans are not resulting in desired outcomes for students. For example, faculty in mathematics and science courses often view them as failing to achieve their purposes for many students and these courses have repeatedly been the object of program adjustments throughout the country (Steen, 1991). Hampshire College in Massachusetts recently changed the sequence and resources devoted to science and mathematics courses by using unified courses, without departments or disciplinary boundaries. At the University of California, Berkeley, Uri Treisman pioneered new instructional processes to enable underrepresented students to succeed with calculus; these adjustments have since been introduced at many colleges throughout the country.

Like mathematics educators, physics instructors have experimented frequently with changes to help connect their field with students' interests and preparation. For example, Dickinson College faculty recently altered instructional process in the introductory physics sequences by arranging the introductory course exclusively in workshop settings (Laws, 1991) where students learn at stations equipped with computers and collections of scientific apparatus. This adjustment in process must have required a concurrent significant increase in resources.

An illustrative adjustment in both purpose and process was made by the computer studies curriculum at Mohawk College of Applied Arts and Technology (Ontario). Faculty recognized that students in technical programs often needed to improve their writing and problem-solving skills as well as acquiring facts and principles (Hirshberg, 1992). Faculty therefore capitalized on learner interest by developing writing and problem-solving assignments related to students' future careers and taught problem-solving strategies within the computer programming course.

Adjustments also occur in general education, particularly when faculty perceive students as poorly prepared. The writing-across-the-curriculum movement, which asserts that students should be expected to write in every course, was initially advocated by English composition instructors and their disciplinary association, the Conference on College Composition and Communication (CCCC), but it now involves professors in fields outside of English. At Philadelphia College of Textiles and Science, for example, professors in business, textile design, fashion merchandising, and chemistry teach "writing-intensive" courses within the major fields.

Sometimes faculty engaged in internal change solicit external views to combine with their own perceptions. For example, Middlesex County Community College in New Jersey used surveys of the local business community about specific training needs when it revised its international business major (Edwards & Tonkin, 1990; Fersh, 1990). Similarly, Loop College (Illinois) not only integrated international perspectives into course content in business programs but developed strategies for the new purpose of promoting interaction between U.S.- and foreign-born Loop College students (Fifield & Sam, 1986).

Some changes in general education and discipline majors have been spurred by recent national reform reports, especially when associations like AAC have taken the lead in disseminating ideas and standards. It is easier, however, to find externally driven change in many elements of academic plans in career study fields where professional practice is changing. Using case studies, Boss and Lowther (1993) have documented such change in accounting, business, and pharmacy programs, and Stark, Lowther, and Hagerty (1986) compared curricular responses to several external stimuli for ten different professional programs. Nursing educators anticipate that national health care reform will require massive changes in program purpose and sequence to prepare nurses to work in preventive community health care settings, rather than in acute care settings like hospitals. Major changes to alter both fundamental purpose (and thus all other academic plan elements) are already well underway among accounting education programs, stimulated by over $4 million in grant funds contributed by a group of commercial accounting firms and administered by a professional association. Many of the program changes first developed for accounting have begun to affect other areas of business education, both in schools that received the grants and in those that did not. Dissemination occurs quickly today; new course syllabi and case studies to be used in accounting are available nationally through the Internet.

Program plans may be adjusted less frequently than course plans, but disciplinary and professional networks cause the changes to be of broader scope and often to be adopted in more than one institution, sometimes rather rapidly. The changes involve content, resource materials, instructional processes, and sometimes evaluation. Major adjustments in purpose, such as those predicted for nursing and those already underway in accounting, may require unusual crises or strong external stimuli.

Collegewide Plans

College missions, like program goals, tend to be stable and enduring. Yet adjustments can result from both systematic planning and crises. Systematic adjustments made in response to changes in society and its educational needs are usually gradual but may be broad in scope. For example, growing enrollments and diversified employment opportunities stimulated the conversion of many teachers' colleges in the 1940s and 1950s to universities offering liberal arts and a range of college career programs. Today, some states are again differentiating the missions of these public four-year colleges to serve specific clients more cost-effectively. During the course of their development, community colleges also have adjusted their missions to provide a wider variety of services. These institutions are especially susceptible to continued change as the needs of the populations they serve evolve. Typically, such adjustments in the missions of public colleges are externally stimulated and sometimes externally mandated. For example, the state of Ohio has adopted specific evaluation criteria that require its 46 two-year colleges to show that they prepare students for a wide range of careers, build partnerships with business and government agencies, and ensure student success in their remedial programs (Ways and Means, *Chronicle of Higher Education*, 1994, p. A21).

Changes in private college missions tend to occur gradually, as during 1950–1970 when many liberal arts colleges began to accept older students and develop career-oriented programs. Occasionally, unusual influences, such as the need to acquire financial stability based on a better market position or reputational rating, may cause an entire college to reexamine its curriculum (and even its mission) within more severe time constraints. Such influences can stimulate major change, particularly when college administrators are far-sighted and provide strong leadership. In *Academic Strategy* (1983), George Keller described change strategies that have "repositioned" colleges. Both drift and strategic repositioning are examples of cases where the impetus is external but the response is planned by the college.

With the exceptions of public planning, drift, and strategic response to crisis, most collegewide curriculum adjustments of educational purpose or content result from program-by-program reviews and evaluations. The frequency and nature of such reviews vary by state and type of control (public or private). Because of the influence of state governing and budgeting processes, public colleges are more likely than private schools to institute a policy of periodic review for all programs. Although private colleges and universities have sometimes developed systematic models of program review, in some states, a central board coordinates reviews and public colleges merely respond. In other states, a public college or university may take responsibility for leading each of its units in a self-study or external review, pruning or even eliminating programs that no longer seem to be closely linked to mission or worthy of scarce resources.

Internal Evaluations

Collegewide evaluations are most frequently undertaken in preparation for an external accreditation or program review. Institutions vary in their approach to self-studies. Some colleges take self-studies very seriously, creating large committees and producing comprehensive and useful reports. Others treat the process much more routinely. Sometimes self-studies are undertaken primarily for public relations or fund-raising purposes with the need to detect the areas for specific adjustments as a lesser priority.

College self-studies may assess collegewide services or practices and they may aggregate data from programs and courses. For example, student course evaluations, when used to develop an composite picture of instruction throughout a college, may help to identify needs for change. A Stanford University study of student transcripts aggregated information for several programs and integrated it with other data (Boli, Katchadourian, & Mahoney, 1988). Information converging from several programs could be used to strengthen an instructional development center, an audiovisual center, or a library. Such evaluations seem more likely to lead to adjustments in instructional processes and resources, however, than to changes in the content and mission elements of the academic plan.

Collegewide evaluations frequently use questionnaires to obtain the opinions of graduates or current students about their goal achievement in college. Harvard University recently completed a systematic study of its graduates of the classes of 1957, 1967, and 1977 (Light, 1990, 1992), and Pettit (1991) has described alumni studies conducted both by Georgetown University and by a consortium of Catholic colleges. Not surprisingly, colleges with institutional research offices capable of gathering and analyzing the data are more likely to carry out such evaluative studies. In very large universities with a variety of colleges, schools, or programs, it may be necessary to send customized surveys, geared to the specific college or program that students or alumni attended. The Association for Institutional Research provides member colleges with guidance in survey design and administration, models of the use of survey results, and professional development workshops related to collegewide studies. As in program change, colleges look to professional associations for leadership and for sharing of conceptual and technical ideas about various types of planning.

Sometimes changing times serve as an informal "needs assessment." For example, most colleges have added instruction in the use of computers and some recently have been discussing whether and how to give the entire curriculum a stronger multicultural or international focus. In other cases a formal needs assessment is undertaken to determine the importance or feasibility of adding new programs. At the extreme, a college may undertake a formal self-study to reposition itself in the marketplace, or to rethink its educational mission and academic plans to achieve a particular goal. Traditional rankings driven by reputations, resources, selectivity measures, and enrollment figures sometimes provide strong incentives. A well-known example, driven by both resource needs and adjusted purposes, is Kalamazoo College (Michigan). In the 1960s Kalamazoo developed the K-Plan, a unique curricular plan that eased the numbers of students on campus at any time through a twelve-month year by combining off-campus international and career experiences with on-campus liberal arts education. Less well known examples are also available. Clarkson University (New York) moved from a focus on engineering and business to a broader university curriculum in the 1980s. Mars Hill College (North Carolina) and Sterling College (Kansas) developed competency-based curricula in the 1970s (Levine, 1978, p. 231). Philadelphia College of Textiles and Science is currently carrying out a planned curricular change to integrate liberal and professional study more fully within the educational experiences of students in its historically technical programs. (Many more examples can be cited; see Townsend, Newell, & Wiese, 1992, and Cardozier, 1993.) A common element in nearly all of these colleges and others that have made major adjustments is the presence of leaders who have focused on curriculum plans and initiated adjustments, rather than devoting their energy to some other aspect of institutional planning.

Recently, a few institutions have developed model programs of collegewide assessment and have used the results to readjust major portions of the curriculum. Banta and Associates (1993) and Hutchings (ca. 1989) cite more than ten such programs that have become well known for systematic evaluation and adjustment procedures: Alverno College, Northeast Missouri State University, University of Tennessee–Knoxville, Miami-Dade Community College, Clayton State College, James Madison University, Kean College, Kings College, Rhode Island College, and State University of New York–College at Plattsburgh.

For administrators, as for faculty, professional meetings supply ideas about collegewide evaluation that may promote subsequent changes in curricula. Many collegewide evaluation mechanisms have been developed as administrators and faculty leaders have shared ideas about assessing student outcomes at annual conferences sponsored since 1985 by the American Association for Higher Education (AAHE). In 1993, AAHE added the emphasis of *continuous quality improvement* or CQI (better known in business settings as total quality management or TQM) to these conferences, encouraging colleges to use evaluation results more systematically in making adjustments to the curriculum as well as in functional areas of the institution. Such meetings have generated a strong rationale for colleges and universities to accept responsibility for assessment as internal activity. Some of the reasons are shown in Table 10-3.

External Evaluations

College curricula are frequently examined by outside groups, including accreditors, alumni visitors, and advisory boards. In some cases these evaluations are a fruitful source of new ideas and lead to actual change. In other cases, they serve primarily as a way of involving individuals who will support the college financially and politically. The usefulness of such groups in curriculum evaluation

TABLE 10-3 Reasons for Assessing Student Outcomes

1. To guide student progress
2. To improve course planning, program planning, and teaching
3. To provide a vehicle for faculty interchange
4. To help students understand the purpose of their educational activities
5. To demonstrate accountability
6. To enhance public relations
7. To reward (or not reward) teachers
8. To gain theoretical understanding about how students change and develop

and adjustment depends strongly on the intent and skill of college leaders.

External initiatives can increase the stakes for self-studies. For example, in the early 1980s, the state of Tennessee established a carrot-and-stick approach to evaluation called "performance funding"—awarding extra funds to colleges on the basis of program evaluations. As a result, the University of Tennessee and other public Tennessee institutions developed models of student assessment and program evaluation that others built on. Another example of external encouragement comes from the Fund for the Improvement of Postsecondary Education, which historically has provided financial support for innovative changes that colleges propose to develop, evaluate, and disseminate as models for others.

Voluntary regional accreditation has been a very powerful influence for collegewide review because, since 1945, it has been an eligibility criterion for many federal grant programs as well as a symbol of quality assurance to the public. In keeping with their emphasis on local mission and goals, however, accreditors have been very general about such standards. For example, the North Central Association of Colleges and Schools stated that a good evaluation plan links assessment to mission; addresses every aspect

of mission through some activity; provides evidence of campuswide participation in assessment planning, assesses general education, the major, and graduates; links the evaluation to a feedback and adjustment loop and monitors adjustments made; provides a reasonable timetable and clearly identifies responsibilities of participants and authority for oversight. (North Central Association, December 1992).

Perhaps because such standards are so general, questions about whether voluntary nongovernmental accreditation serves public purposes well have resulted in negative publicity to accreditors. During the late 1980s, federal officials demanded that accreditors provide assurance that student outcomes are measured, a role the agencies accepted somewhat reluctantly. In the 1990s federal legislation was enacted that supplements the accrediting role with new state review agencies and that mandates publication of specific data college leaders find minimally related to educational quality (the "Student Right to Know" Act). The tension is felt strongly by community college leaders who assert that community colleges have suffered as a result of this legislation, which focuses on low transfer and baccalaureate completion rates, regardless of students' goals and capabilities. As we approach the turn of the century, there is considerable public opinion that colleges need to do a better job with internal evaluation and communicate the results more adequately to the public, or risk more intensive scrutiny from external agencies (Newman, 1994; Hartle, 1994).

Making Adjustments

College missions generally undergo few adjustments. In times of financial stress, however, existing programs may be eliminated and new ones added in hopes of attracting new groups of students or serving new publics. Some of these adjustments in collegewide academic plans may be due to diffusion (we have called it the "bandwagon effect") and they may affect various aspects of the curriculum. Historically, one may point to many examples of institutions following the leader: the competency-based curriculum, as based on revised educational purpose and objectives, the 4-1-4 calendar as a way to adjust course sequences (Stark, 1972); and the Keller plan as a self-paced instructional process (Keller, 1968). These innovations and others like them during the same era caused many colleges to change calendars, faculty assignments, and ways of defining student achievement. The changes were undertaken partly because the testimony of proponents presented appealing ways to respond to student unrest in the 1970s.

More recent movements advocating changes in specific elements of collegewide plans include mandated multicultural requirements as an adjustment to purpose, developments of core curriculum as an adjustment to sequence in general education, cooperative (or collaborative) learning as a more active instructional process, and assessment of student outcomes as an adjustment to traditionally informal evaluation stragies. In large part, these developments respond to unrest about the value of college expressed by the public rather than by students.

Faculty members in social sciences and humanities may be more likely than those in sciences and professional fields to accept such collegewide changes, particularly if they respond to student demands or to promises of improved approaches to societal issues. Structured fields, like the sciences, and those with active external professional practitioner groups, may respond more slowly to student demands but more rapidly to professional influences such as those of employers. Particularly in community colleges, where the enduring mission is service to the community population, entirely new academic plans may be developed fairly rapidly for major seg-

ments of the institution when new needs arise, such as retraining for local business and industry.

Although the need for change may be as great, some bandwagon effects, such as those that change sequences or requirements for the entire college curriculum, are least likely to affect large universities, where governance and academic programs are decentralized (Ory & Parker, 1989). Other types of changes, particularly those depending on financial resources and those that directly incorporate new content developed from research activities, may be easier in large institutions.

At the collegewide level, adjustments in curriculum are infrequent, deliberated more intensively and formally than those for courses and programs (except in times of internal crisis) and more responsive to broad external influences in society. Such influences may include those affecting the educational environment for particular fields, such as health care reform or the globalization of business. Or the influences may affect the educational environment for higher education more broadly, such as a decline in public confidence about the quality of colleges and universities and consequent demands for accountability and responsiveness. Currently, considerable energy is being devoted in education to modify the process of collegewide evaluation and adjustment itself.

EVALUATION MODELS: AN OVERVIEW

Demands for assessment of student outcomes, an emphasis of recent reform reports, is spreading rapidly and appears to have high potential for changing higher education. Strong pressures on colleges to develop more elaborate evaluation procedures, particularly with respect to documenting student learning, have produced a barrage of demands with which many faculty members and administrators are trying to cope. Before describing selected alternative evaluation methods that might help in adjusting academic plans more systematically, we provide a brief contextual overview of the origins and evolution of educational evaluation. For a more complete history of evaluation and assessment and for a wider selection of models, see Worthen and Sanders (1987).

Accountability based on educational evaluation dates back at least forty years in elementary and secondary education. During the 1960s, as federal and state governments began to invest substantial funds in education and social programs at public school levels, government officials required that the success of the programs be ascertained before funding was continued or renewed. As a result, evaluation as a subfield of study in education and other social sciences grew and matured.

Most methods used in educational evaluation are derived from social science research methods. Modern evaluation methods in education are often traced to the work of educational psychologist Ralph Tyler (1969), who advocated a systematic model of establishing objectives for students, devising measures of these objectives, and then using the measures to determine if the objectives were achieved. This systematic process of curriculum evaluation was grounded in the empirical research tradition of education and psychology dominant during the 1940s and is widely accepted in elementary and secondary education. Thus, as one type of evaluation, assessment of student outcomes describes procedures well established in other realms of education by the 1980s but new to many colleges and universities. (In other contexts, the term *assessment* may mean testing students for placement purposes, evaluating employee performance, or evaluating a function or an office.)

Evaluators who view traditional procedures for measuring student learning as excessively mechanistic and limiting have developed alternative evaluation methods of data collection and interpretation. Some of these alternative models avoid quantifying student experiences in favor of gathering qualitative information such as student reports of educational experiences or course work portfolios, which serve as more "naturalistic" evaluation data. Other alternative models have grown from special philosophical assumptions about evaluation and education, and take the form of ideologies or "persuasions" (Nevo, 1983). For example, *illuminative* evaluators are persuaded that evaluators should take little or no responsibility for making interpretations or judgments; instead they should merely compile a full description of the activity and its results for action by decision makers. *Responsive* evaluators believe they should determine which program aspects are of specific interest to primary participants (usually referred to as *stakeholders*), evaluate those aspects, and then negotiate judgments and decisions with the stakeholders. *Goal-free* evaluators maintain that an evaluator must observe and describe consequences teachers and planners did not intend in education as well as those they did intend. Table 10-4 summarizes several types of evaluation and their purposes; Table 10-5 elaborates further by describing the typical components or steps in some well-known evaluation models.

Descriptive models (such as Models 1-4 in Table 10-5) are the most frequently used models in course, program, and collegewide curriculum review. We have mentioned these models in discussing faculty reports of their actual evaluation practices. Consciously or not, faculty and administrators use one or more of the models as they collect and describe information about how successful they and others feel academic plans have been. If student achievement is a focus of the evaluation, most descriptive materials focus on short-range outcome measures, seldom using long-range measures. If the academic plan as a whole is a focus, professional judgment may lead to descriptions that compare the program with that of other similar colleges.

TABLE 10-4   Types and Purposes of Evaluation

Type of Evaluation	Purposes
Formative evaluation	Decision making Improvement Planning
Summative evaluation	Accountability Selection Justification
Illuminative evaluation	Increase understanding Describe programs
Goal-free evaluation	Increase understanding Describe programs Improvement
Sociopolitical evaluation	Increase awareness Promote public relations Increase motivation
Authoritative evaluation	Exercise authority Administrative function Accountability
Responsive evaluation	Respond to varied stakeholders needs
Experimental evaluation	Basic research Accountability

Source: Based on discussions by Nevo (1983), Gardner (1977), and Worthen and Saunders (1987).

The methods used remain relatively informal and may depend on the interests and expertise of the specific faculty group involved.

Even when formal program self-studies are undertaken, such as those prepared for accreditation or periodic reviews, faculty and administrators continue to follow descriptive models. They might, for example, follow practices that evaluation experts would call "naturalistic evaluation" (Model 2) (Guba & Lincoln, 1985). In this model, evaluators (1) describe the program and its context, (2) report the description in terms that are understandable to the audience and responsive to their needs, and (3) suggest some program modifications and adjustments based on observed deficiencies and strengths, existing values, and implied standards of merit and worth (often comparisons with other programs).

With the new emphasis on assessment, however, some colleges have moved toward more formal evaluation models, often modifying the Tyler model. They have increased emphasis on defining learning objectives in terms of desired student outcomes, choosing various ways of describing how well students achieve outcomes corresponding to educational objectives, and attempting to attribute the outcomes to specific courses and programs. Educators who took these steps often believed that policymakers, accustomed to reviewing Model 5 data for elementary and secondary schools, would ultimately require similar data from colleges or mandate that accreditors require them. They recognized that state and federal officers find it useful to summarize and compare results of students' learning for different colleges and types of colleges succinctly, if possibly somewhat simplistically, based on Model 5 type data. As this trend gained momentum in the 1980s, opponents of Model 5 forms of evaluation protested that such simplistic indicators do not portray what students are learning very well and are not as helpful for formative purposes as other methods, both traditional and emerging. They cited negative side effects such as letting tests determine the content taught, limiting access of the educationally disadvantaged by setting rigid, unrealistic standards, decreasing students' motivation and increasing their anxiety by overtesting, and "locking in the curriculum" because of the expense of adjusting tests. Those who feared these outcomes countered the scientific evaluation movement by developing aspects of Model 2 for more natural evaluation of student learning and curricula.

Although public assessments and examinations have a long history, linking accountability processes for public colleges to student

TABLE 10-5   Five Selected Models of Evaluation

Model 1:   *Professional expert process (accreditation tradition)*
Propose standards.
Obtain agreement from relevant peer experts on standards.
Require self-study assessment against standards.
Have peer expert team examine self-study.
Report results of examination.
Have peer experts decide whether standards are met.

Model 2:   *Naturalistic evaluation (Guba and Lincoln)*
Gather descriptive information regarding the evaluation object, setting, and
　　surrounding conditions.
Determine the information desired by relevant audiences.
Gather information about relevant issues.
Gather information about values.
Gather information about standards for worth and merit.
Share with relevant audiences.
Negotiate decisions.

Model 3:   *Context, Inputs, Process, Products (CIPP) model (Stufflebeam)*
Describe:
　　program goals.
　　program design.
　　program implementation.
　　program outcomes.

Model 4:   *Countenance model (Stake)*
Describe:
　　prior conditions (antecedents).
　　implementation (transactions).
　　outcomes.

Model 5:   *Traditional evaluation (Tyler)*
State goals and objectives in behavioral terms.
Develop measurement instruments.
Measure achievement of goals and objectives.
Compare objectives with measured achievement.
Interpret findings; make recommendations.

Source: Adapted from *The Conceptualization of Educational Evaluation: An Analytical Review of the Literature* by David Nevo, *Review of Educational Research,* Vol. 53, No. 1, 1983. Copyright 1983 by the American Educational Research Association. Reprinted by permission of the publisher.

outcomes is new. Some educators view this link as intrusive and possibly threatening since national and state agendas may hold multiple goals for the assessment process, including some that are not related directly to improvement. Such goals include providing data for accountability and public relations, providing data to reward teachers, and providing data for research about the general condition of the educational system. Although we recognize that strong forces in the external environment are urging educators to adopt assessment in support of some of these goals, our discussion focuses on the two goals that lead most directly to adjustments in the academic plan: (1) guiding student progress and (2) improving course and program planning. Indeed, success in achieving these two goals may relieve some of the external pressures on colleges to achieve the others.

Since the current assessment movement began in higher education around 1984, many educators have abandoned their initial opposition because they have come to believe that the new emphasis on evaluation has a strong potential for improving education if leaders help colleges (and policymakers) keep focused on these two important educational purposes, guiding student progress and improving course and program planning. Curriculum leaders in colleges have, therefore, broadened their search for meaningful indicators and evaluation methods they view as less mechanistic than the scientific model. Their incorporation of qualitative research methods has found increased acceptance among faculty from various disciplines. Most experts now endorse collecting a variety of types of evidence—not only information about how well specific educational objectives were achieved but also evidence that both student and faculty goals were met without other undesirable consequences. The techniques used in assessment now may range from standardized examinations to student journals and portfolios.

Despite the influence of external forces urging the collection of evaluative data, faculty members are likely to remain the primary decision makers as well as the primary evaluators. Even if they state more formal goals and collect data in a more systematic way, professors will still reflect on and interpret the findings on the basis of disciplinary and professional understandings. Adjustments also will continue to be based on faculty perceptions of the available alternatives.

In colleges, the process of making curriculum adjustments differs from what policymakers may expect on the basis of experience in elementary and secondary education. For example, lengthy public debates and negotiations about change are often carried out by groups of faculty decision makers even after the evaluators (often a faculty committee) have made judgments and set forth recommendations. These debates about adjusting academic plans are held in collegewide governance forums, where campus politics and rhetoric are sometimes viewed as more influential than data. In addition, many stakeholders, including students and community interest groups, may join the debate. Reaching a decision in a context of competing interests can be a lengthy and contentious process. The widely publicized debates about core curriculum at Harvard and Stanford, for example, spanned several years during which many interested parties expressed their views.

Although the assessment of student outcomes is expanding the range of evaluation methods used in colleges and universities, increasing the faculty's propensity for change may come more slowly. Despite faculty members' proclivity to conduct empirical research in their own disciplines, they seldom initiate pilot studies or simulations to test curriculum innovations in context. Assessment results and techniques are only beginning to foster some experimentation with different curriculum designs that might improve teaching and learning.

There is evidence that the process of systematic evaluation can lead to positive adjustments in academic plans. For instance, the University of Tennessee has been using assessment in its general education program and eleven major fields since 1982. These eleven fields experimented with creating their own comprehensive examinations and have, as a result, pursued a wide variety of changes. Some of them have established core courses in the major, developed lists of expected student competences, increased emphasis on problem solving and application, involved students in self-assessment, improved advising, reviewed articulation agreements, written better program descriptions, and, on the basis of a clearer collective vision, stated expectations more clearly. Faculty have addressed additional means of evaluation as well, including analyzing prerequisites for courses, monitoring course-taking patterns, and improving test development (Banta & Schneider, 1988; Banta, 1994).

Experimentation with assessment may increase, as colleges are increasingly pressed by states and accreditors to state goals in terms of expected student behaviors, develop or adopt measurement instruments, collect data, interpret findings, and develop more systematic recommendations for changes. Academic plans may be improved by attention to a wider range of evaluation models and potential adjustments. In the next section, we will, therefore, focus on selected evaluation methods that have potential for facilitating improvements.

EXPANDING THE RANGE OF USEFUL EVALUATION MODELS

The four alternative evaluation models we will describe are applicable at each level of academic plan: course, program, and college. Each element of the academic plan (purpose, content, sequence, learner, resources and materials, instructional processes, evaluation, and adjustment) can be evaluated at each level, although some techniques are clearly more useful at some levels than others. Our discussion begins with those models most similar to current practice and moves to those least similar.

The four models are: (1) informal assessment, which enhances faculty members' ability to get direct feedback and make adjustments quickly; (2) student-centered evaluation that focuses on students' interpretations of their needs and behavior; (3) goal-free evaluation, in which evaluators look for unintended and undesirable consequences of the curriculum as well as intended ones; and (4) goal-focused evaluation using traditional methods to link intended learning outcomes and performance. The first two models focus primarily on educational process with some attention to outcomes. The third, goal-

free evaluation, gives about equal emphasis to process and outcomes; the fourth, goal-focused evaluation, attends largely to educational outcomes, with some attention to process. Most evaluators would assert that these models are rarely used in their pure forms and would recommend using combinations based on the evaluation problem at hand.

Informal Assessment

To suggest alternative evaluation processes that are most immediately useful to faculty, we begin our discussion with techniques that professors can select based on their chosen educational purposes, content, sequences, and instructional processes. These informal course-level evaluations require no special skills and can provide prompt feedback in the classroom. The ideas we suggest here supplement traditional processes of instructor-based evaluation rather than substitute for them.

Classroom/Course Assessment

All academic plans include evaluative mechanisms that can lead to potential adjustments in the plan. At the course level, a plan for evaluation focuses on gaining information directly useful to the professor, who is the course planner and usually the teacher. As with other elements of the academic plan, failure to explicitly make a decision to conduct evaluation represents an implicit decision that the evaluation would have been positive or that adjustments will be unnecessary.

Most teachers have a sense of how their courses are going and many record ideas for improvement immediately after teaching a course even if they did not consciously use other evaluation processes. Increasingly, however, faculty members are using a variety of techniques to evaluate their courses at an earlier stage and use them regularly through the term. Although many predate the current era, techniques called "classroom assessment" or "classroom research" were first formally proposed in 1985 (Cross & Angelo, 1988; Angelo & Cross, 1993; Angelo, 1993) and are now used in programs and collegewide studies as well as in courses (Light 1990, 1992). This method assumes teachers are most likely to make changes based on information they collect related to issues in their own classrooms. Some faculty report that using classroom assessment has fundamentally changed their thinking and has significantly improved students' learning.

Classroom assessment is based on an informal exchange between teacher and students. Grouped by purpose, there are three categories of classroom assessment techniques: (1) assessing course-related knowledge and skills; (2) assessing learner attitudes, values, and self-awareness; and (3) assessing learners' reactions to instruction. The techniques seek to evaluate students' prior knowledge, recall, and understanding; their analysis and critical thinking skills; their problem-solving skills; their creative thinking and synthesizing skills, and their skills in application and performance. Thus, they can be adapted to the educational purposes of a wide range of disciplines. Although the focus of some techniques is on learning outcomes for a specific class session or content unit, classroom processes can also be examined. The techniques are context-specific, designed to help students learn at the same time they help the teacher assess what and how well students are learning. Although the professor gathers information from students, the information sought is that which the professor believes will be helpful to him or her in changing those aspects of the academic plan that can be altered.

Angelo and Cross (1993) contend that it may be more useful to focus on how to improve students' learning (and help them make adjustments in learning) than on how to adjust an instructor's teaching. This focus on the learner is consistent with our intention of giving the learner an important place as an element in the academic plan, and it also contributes to the expansion of educational purpose. For example, if one goal of college is for students to become intentional learners and accept full responsibility for their learning, it is helpful to recognize that a necessary short-range goal may be to provide students with needed help in improving study habits.

When the focus is on student learning, classroom assessment is a mutually beneficial activity. By participating in a classroom assessment, students reinforce their understanding of course content and strengthen their self-assessment skills. Engaging students in assessment also helps to promote effective learning (MacGregor, 1993). They may gain self-confidence from realizing that faculty are interested in their success. Faculty learn to focus their teaching on the specific skills and knowledge they want to teach.

When an instructor uses one of the fifty classroom assessment techniques, the procedure includes planning, implementing, and responding phases. In the planning phase, the instructor develops a specific teaching goal or learning goal to focus on, selects a lesson to assess, and devises (or chooses) a classroom assessment technique to assess it. After using the technique and answering the "focus question," the instructor interprets the results and presents a summary to students in the class. The response includes any adjustments the instructor expects to make in the academic plan for the class as a result of the information gained.

Angelo and Cross stress that classroom assessment data should be used only to learn more about student learning and how to improve it. It should not affect student grades. The unit of evaluation is the class rather than the individual student; the class should be viewed as a learning community with whom the results of the assessment are shared. The process should engage students in reflection on their own learning.

The range of application of classroom assessment techniques is quite wide. A single technique can be adapted for use in a variety of classroom situations and disciplines. For example, a calculus professor adapted a classroom assessment technique called Documented Problem Solutions to help students become aware of their problem-solving strategies and then to improve them. He asked students to explain, step by step and in complete sentences, how they had solved a problem assigned for homework and then to compare their approaches in class. This strategy belongs to the first category of assessment techniques. It is designed to assess course-related knowledge and skills and is quite different from getting the correct answer using memorized formulas or cookbook techniques. It helped students recognize that their understanding and problem-solving skills could be improved. When responding to the same pool of examination questions used before the classroom assessment techniques, the students earned better grades.

The Course-Related Self-Confidence Survey is an example of a second type of classroom assessment—a technique used to assess learner attitudes and course-related study skills. It identifies factors that influence student confidence and, therefore, helps instructors develop sequences of material and instructional processes that build confidence. Angelo and Cross offer an example of a nursing instructor who used such a survey to better understand the self-confidence of student nurses in clinical practicum situations. In addition to a list of specific examples to be used in her teaching, she was able to help students create their own checklist of things they could do to monitor their behavior and improve their self-confidence. More formalized instruments such as the LASSI, which helps students assess their study strategies, and the Student Goals Exploration, which provides a basis for discussing student goals, may also be used in this way but involve more advance preparation and cost.

In the third category are techniques for assessing learner reactions to instruction. For example, the Group Instructional Feedback Technique (GIFT) is a method of focusing on students' reactions to teaching and to teachers. It uses student reports about what is helping or hindering their learning and solicits suggestions for improvement. To make the process easier and more comfortable for students, some faculty members ask a colleague to use this feedback technique with their students and then share the aggregated results with them.

Program Evaluation

The academic major program creates an environment that has received little attention, despite its importance to and impact on students (Pascarella, 1985). Many groups of faculty have little experience with systematic program evaluation other than professional judgment and external examinations. Increased use of other program-level evaluation strategies will require substantial coordination and sometimes training for faculty. Because program evaluation can determine the extent to which a particular curriculum design is effective and can encourage faculty to adjust those aspects that are least effective, the time and resources spent on coordination and training seem merited.

Perhaps it is possible to develop "program assessment techniques" that would be parallel to classroom assessment techniques. By definition, such techniques would engage groups of faculty in taking the "academic pulse" of students in their program in order to make changes promptly. To our knowledge, the time has been too short for such techniques to be extrapolated from Angelo and Cross's work on classroom research. At small colleges where faculty know their student majors well, see them almost daily, and can assess their progress informally, such program assessment techniques are congruent with procedures we called student-centered at the course level. In large universities and in general education programs in all institutions, where students are not known to as many professors, different procedures for gathering data would be needed.

Accurate description of the program's academic plan is a necessary first step. As we have mentioned earlier, detailed program plans with clear learning objectives are less common than detailed course syllabi. Here is a useful list of guidelines for stating program goals, adapted from one published by the American Dental Schools Association (Romberg, 1990, p. 12):

1. Goals should be relevant to the mission of the institution and should not conflict with its overall direction.

2. Goals should reflect the current philosophy and actions of the department, program or school within the institution. They should exhibit the consensus view and avoid statements reflecting the view of a few individuals.

3. Goals should not include aims that no one intends to carry out.

4. Goals should be written clearly and simply. Writers should avoid complex statements of multiple goals or outcomes, avoid jargon, and avoid complicated phrasing.

5. Whenever possible, goals should be stated in measurable terms. Writers should avoid goals that do not allow measurement but should allow goals that, though not measurable at present, may be measurable in the future.

Clearly these are general guidelines. Actual guidelines for describing program goals will vary according to the type of program: general education, discipline majors, professional majors, or occupational fields. But clear statements are necessary for the effective use of most evaluation strategies.

Some disciplines and collegiate career study fields may resist more formal efforts at evaluation but be willing to try informal means. An example is sociology, which, as we have already noted, lacks consensus as a field about specific educational outcomes and supports great latitude among faculty about the type of learning to take place. In this context, the American Sociological Association has provided leadership in sponsoring workshops for its members to develop faculty assessment skills (Wright, 1991).

The Association of American Colleges has developed a handbook called *Program Review and Quality in the Major* (1992). To be useful to a wide range of liberal arts disciplines, the guidelines are necessarily broad and range from informal to more formal evaluation strategies. After listing thirteen characteristics of a strong liberal arts major, the handbook provides a framework and series of questions for eight foci of program review focusing on (1) goals, (2) structure of the curriculum, (3) connections (within the major, with student needs, with scholarly inquiry, with other disciplines, with liberal learning), (4) teaching quality, (5) advising, (6) inclusiveness, (7) institutional support, and (8) outcomes assessment. Many of these categories can be most usefully evaluated by informal and student-centered strategies, while others lend themselves to goal-focused evaluation. The basic assumption of clear goals in this framework, however, leans away from goal-free evaluation, except as an auxiliary to the other methods.

Collegewide Evaluation

At the collegewide level, all of the types of evaluation are problematic because the diversity of students and programs limits generalizations about the college or university. There is an audience for collegewide evaluations among decision makers and the public but that audience is unlikely to make prompt use of the information to improve academic plans. Thus, at the college level, informal evaluation methods like classroom research that can be used at the program and course levels are not really applicable. Even when policymakers desire student outcome information for funding or comparisons among institutions, a descriptive, student-centered, or goal-free report about student outcomes in every program at a large state university would be voluminous and complex.

Most collegewide programs do not lend themselves readily to goal-focused evaluation, either, because overall college goals for students are broad and long-range, and thus difficult to measure. They may include such goals as acquiring wisdom, developing a sense of civic responsibility, or having a successful career. It is surprising, therefore, that researchers have spent considerable energy seeking evidence of the effects of various types of colleges on students, usually evaluating the impact of location, reputation, financial resources, and related issues, rather than elements of specific curricular plans on student development. Astin (1993) reported that the conditions usually found at small residential colleges seem to produce more learning but acknowledged that these conditions are difficult to reproduce in other settings. After an extensive analysis of this type of research, Pascarella and Terenzini (1991) reported little clear evidence that the type of college affects specific types of student learning.

Student-Centered Evaluation

We use the term *student-centered evaluation* to build on student opinions (now often gathered by faculty members) and to give student opinions a more central and formal place among course evaluation methods. Student-centered evaluation examines goal congruence between students and instructors, seeking to learn how students with varied goals fared in class or a program. It attempts to determine whether, from the students' perspective, an academic plan turns out to be useful, beneficial, and satisfying. Finally, it helps to illuminate the meanings that students are constructing from the material taught in the class or program, which may or may not be the meaning the instructors intend. In contrast to classroom assessment, which focuses on the learner but is directed by the teacher to satisfy her need for information, the focus of student-centered evaluation is on the students as information givers. Student-centered evaluations solicit information that students believe is important for assessing the educational context and process. By understanding students' expectations, professors can better help them understand the academic field and connect principles and theories they are teaching with personal dilemmas that people, in general, face during life and work.

Course Level

All methods used for student-centered evaluation involve listening to students' voices and hearing their perspectives. Sometimes professors who want to hear a variety of voices initially construct subgroups, based on goals, learning styles, or other characteristics. Beyond an initial classification, free and open-ended student responses are those obtained in reflective essays, focus groups, journals, or surveys that allow students to express themselves without being influenced by the instructor's perspective (e.g., through the wording of items on a survey). Asking students what they want from a course or program may seem like opening Pandora's box, but it can provide useful information for adjusting courses and programs. Students can be quite knowledgeable about their academic needs and often their comments can suggest simple but responsive changes.

In the second of two reports on the Harvard Assessment Seminars, Richard Light (1992) gave some good examples of how student-centered evaluation can work. Faculty members and researchers designed interviews with a random sample of Harvard students to collect student input about their learning needs. The students mentioned improving writing three times more often than any other need. Similarly interviews with graduating seniors helped to determine what efforts students had made personally to improve their writing during college and how they had benefited from course-related writing assignments. Three strong recommendations emerged. One suggestion concerned sequence: the overwhelming majority of seniors thought that writing should be emphasized in the upperclass years after students had adjusted to college and when writing instruction would be most appreciated. The second suggestion concerned content: seniors felt that writing instruction was most effective when organized around a substantive discipline, combining writing instruction with actual assignments. The third recommendation concerned instructional process. One of every five seniors reacted strongly against instructors who knowingly or unknowingly inserted their perspectives into a student's work, thus changing the "voice" of an essay or paper from the student's voice to the instructor's voice.

Faculty teaching in Harvard's Expository Writing Program gained additional information from meetings with first-year students. They discovered that learning was impeded when students misinterpreted instructors' comments on essays and were not given specific suggestions for revising the essays. Several concrete new strategies emerged for writing instructors as well as for students.

At Alverno College, which focuses on teaching students to become competent professional managers, student-centered evaluation is part of every program (Mentkowski, 1985; Mentkowski, O'Brien, McEachern, & Fowler, 1983). Alverno identified effective managers, interviewed them about what they do on the job, and developed a competence model with four clusters of abilities: socioemotional maturity, entrepreneurial abilities, intellectual abilities, and interpersonal abilities. The college also created a pool of more than five hundred behavior examples set in particular contexts. The model is student-centered because it focuses on what students need rather than on what instructors think they need, and because students are involved in their own evaluation and reassessment of their needs as they develop these abilities.

Harvard and Alverno asked students what they needed; another type of student-centered evaluation is to ask them what they are doing or have done. The concept of student "quality of effort," developed by C. Robert Pace, is useful for student-centered evaluation at all levels of the academic plan. Simply put, the more a student is meaningfully engaged in an academic task, the more he or she will learn. (Quality of effort is related to the concept of involvement identified with Astin but has a more fully developed operational meaning.) Pace argues that some educational processes are educationally and psychologically better ways of achieving learning goals than others. He uses the example of two students. The first has no particular interest in the subject matter of a course and gives it little attention until the last week of classes. She then devotes many hours to memorizing vocabulary and facts, highlighting generalizations in the text, and outlining topics that might be on the exam. In contrast, another student has been interested in the subject matter throughout the term, has often discussed it with friends, has read related materials that were not required, and has thought about how some of the ideas and facts relate to other subjects and the external world. Pace argues that although both students may get the same grade on the final exam, the second student has enjoyed a learning experience of a much higher quality because of her higher quality of effort. The difference in the learning the two have experienced can be identified by student self-reports of their activities.

Pace's College Student Experience Questionnaire (1987) comprises students' self-reports about fourteen categories of activities they perform in college. In practical terms, the more novels a student checks out from the library and reads, the more knowledge he will gain about literature. Involvement may be a precursor to high-quality effort; for example, having the opportunity to do hands-on work in the chemistry lab may encourage the student to put forth higher effort in the lab. Alternatively, prior successful learning about a subject may increase a student's tendency to get involved and to exert greater learning effort; the chemistry student may spend more time in the lab because of satisfaction and success in prior chemistry courses. These relationships are not yet fully understood, but whichever variable precedes the other, involvement seems a reasonable goal for higher education and one that can be assessed by student self-reports of their effort. One specific form of effort may result in lifelong learners. We defined the *intentional learner* as one who self-regulates learning and who not only chooses to expend effort but also chooses a type of effort appropriately fitted to the task and reflects on how well it succeeds.

The student-centered approach, then, can focus on evaluating the learner's quality of effort as determined through type, intensity, and frequency of activities, as well as the growth of positive attitudes, expectations, and metacognition in a specific course. The professor can then adjust the academic plan for that course in ways that encourage learners to pursue improved processes.

Program Level

The same types of open-ended, student-centered techniques can be used for programs as for courses except that considerable attention must be given to describing the scope of the program being evaluated. Students may not perceive a program's academic plan in the same way as the faculty who developed it. If a coherent program plan has not been published and discussed with students, they may particularly see a program—especially a general education program—as merely an isolated set of courses. An effort must also be made to get a good response. Mailed questionnaires may get a poor response or fail to produce the thoughtful responses desired.

The potential for low response and the difficulty of communicating the unity of programs under review call for creative techniques. Where an effective advising system is in place, students can be asked to respond in an open-ended reflective essay once or twice a year as they visit their advisor or register for courses. Alternatively, their opinions can be sought in required courses selected on a rotating basis. Courses can also be rotated as sources for portfolios of students' work. Student response will surely be improved if the program is careful to show students that adjustments have been made in the academic plan on the basis of previous student-centered evaluations.

Student-centered evaluation suggests collecting information about the meanings programs have for students. General education students might be queried about the connections between the general education program and their lives, or their major. Majors may be queried about connections between their courses of study and their future careers. An interesting example of a student-centered essay question to probe the type and nature of such connections students make is: "Suppose one of your professors in (general education core course) and one of your professors in (your major) were meeting for lunch to discuss important changes in the curriculum to improve your education. What are some topics you believe they should talk about?"

The College Student Experiences Questionnaire, mentioned earlier as a possible student self-report vehicle for courses, can also be used to provide reliable and valid evidence of the effort students put into and get out of their college programs. The CSEQ taps personal, social, and career matters as well as knowledge and intellectual skills. This instrument is ideal for getting first-hand student reports of the types of activities students have pursued in a program and for understanding what they think they have gained during a specified academic year.

The instrument's fourteen scales, which deal with a broad range of student experiences, can be grouped into three clusters. The cluster of questions measuring the students' quality of effort with respect to academic and intellectual experiences is most relevant to the academic plan and curricula. The questionnaire also asks students to report background information, their satisfaction with the college environment (including policies and procedures and relationships with faculty, administrative officials, and other students), and the relative emphases they feel that the institution (or program, if specified instead) has given to certain aspects of student development. Finally, students are asked to estimate the gains they feel they have made in areas such as career training, general education, writing ability, and analytical and logical thinking. All of these queries could be adjusted to the program level. A community college version, (CCSEQ) is also available (Friedlander, Pace, & Lehmann, 1990).

The assessment of student effort in a program is important because four types of general increases in student outcomes have been associated with high quality of effort: academic and intellectual growth, general growth, personal growth, and growth in scientific understanding. Students who have the highest scores on the academic/intellectual quality of effort scales typically spend forty hours or more per week on their schoolwork and perceive their own growth to be positively correlated with their effort.

College Level

At the college level, student-centered assessment designed to gauge reactions from current and past students is particularly useful because more direct methods of outcome measurement are logistically difficult. The CSEQ (and the CCSEQ for community colleges) include scales directly relevant to the collegewide level. These include student self-reports of quality of effort concerned with personal and interpersonal experiences, and the use of group facilities and opportunities.

Student effort may result in many types of outcomes that may also be measured more directly; specific outcomes to be examined must be carefully chosen, random samples of students must be used, and response rates should be maximized. For example, the outcomes of competence in ethical judgment and critical thinking in particular domains could be measured in a time series study, with pretests and posttests, over the entire college career. Aggregations of data from different programs on employment, life success, image, and public relations might also be assessed to paint a picture for the entire college.

Research has shown that knowing the quality of students' effort increases the ability to predict their college outcomes. Pace believes that increasing use of effort measures will change current research summaries that now emphasize relatively fixed student and institutional characteristics. If Pace is right, these will be revised so that what will count most will not be "who you are or where you are but what you do." The value of these student-centered evaluations at the college level is closely tied to their use. The results must be transmitted to offices with the power to adjust the total college environment.

Goal-Free Evaluation

Because goal-free evaluation focuses on what actually happened to students, and does not hold as a standard what the faculty intended should happen, the measures to be taken in a goal-free evaluation cannot be specified in advance. General questions to be posed for both students and professors may be: What was achieved? What happened in this course or program? How did you change during this educational experience? What things were positive for you? What was negative?

Because these questions are difficult to ask and answer in a neutral way, a good strategy in conducting goal-free evaluation is for an instructor to team with colleagues, each exploring the course taught by the other, or different aspects of a program.

Course Level

In doing goal-free course evaluations, faculty members must be alert to and willing to consider student responses about aspects of the classroom experience that are not specified in course objectives but occur nevertheless. Some of these outcomes may be positive but unexpected; others may be negative, indicating undesirable outcomes or procedures.

Negative outcomes might include: (1) students learning to dislike the course material although they are doing satisfactory academic work; (2) unintentional reinforcement of poor learning strategies or use of surface reading strategies by assigning too heavy a workload; (3) decreases in self-esteem or self-efficacy due to lack of opportunities for course success, and (4) feelings of discomfort by particular groups of students during course discussions.

Goal-free evaluations can also identify positive unintended outcomes: (1) students learning to model their own future teaching behavior after that of a successful instructor; (2) students learning to value viewpoints from persons of different cultural groups; (3)

students consciously developing their own independent learning skills, and (4) students acquiring metacognitive skills.

Program Level

Goal-free evaluation will provide important clues that help identify potential negative and positive unintended consequences of a program plan. The clues can help to structure open-ended essay questions and focus group topics among students for greater elaboration on these. Selected students can be important collaborators in conducting focus groups. Some colleges have successfully trained and used student focus group leaders for this task.

An often overlooked aspect of program design that lends itself to goal-free evaluation is linkages with other programs. Teaming up with other programs for mutual benefit is a reasonable strategy. An evaluation might include finding out what faculty in those related programs think is happening to students, as well as what students believe is happening to them in other programs. For example, a biology department might want to learn whether nursing students are being appropriately served by the foundation courses provided for them, and the nursing department may wish to know how it could facilitate the biology department's work. Both will want to know if students are experiencing conflicts or unusually positive experiences that were not fully anticipated.

College Level

Some goal-free evaluation techniques can be used at the college level, but they may seem unscientific to proponents of more systematic methods of evaluation. These types of data may also be time-consuming and expensive to collect and analyze. For example, in recent assessment studies, Harvard University asked students to keep logs of activities and reflect retroactively on their learning of the previous year. It asked graduates to describe the role language had in their lives after college.

At the college level, graduates who can report on their entire college experience are excellent sources for goal-free evaluation. Sometimes it takes several years after commencement for graduates to recognize positive and negative unintended consequences. This is particularly true when times change rapidly. Women graduates of the 1950s, for example, became conscious only belatedly that fewer options in sports, music, and careers were open to them than were open to males.

Special populations particularly should be sought out for their reflections on the college experience and its unintended consequences. This includes women, minorities, disabled students, and students studying in unusual types of majors. The goals of such students are sometimes sufficiently different from those of the average student that their interaction with specific education experiences will differ from the norm.

Another important group of students for whom consequences may be unintended are transfer students from community colleges or other institutions, and part-time students. Because four-year colleges and universities are so accustomed to thinking of college as a four-year package, the special outcomes of students who attend more than one college may be overlooked.

Goal-Focused Evaluation

Goal-focused evaluation is the traditional four-step empirical method of assessing the intended demonstrable outcomes of student learning. It includes: (1) establishing clear objectives; (2) developing measures; (3) measuring, and (4) interpreting the congruence of achievement scores with objectives.

Assessment of student learning that is focused on learning outcomes typically can take three forms: (1) description of the outcomes achieved; (2) description of change in the outcome measures from some previous measurement, and (3) attribution of change over time to the course or program being evaluated (Stark, 1990). The simplest of these three possibilities, most often used by faculty, is merely to describe the student outcomes. At the next level of complexity, changes in student outcomes are described by measuring student ability at a stage early in the course or program (pretest) and at a later date or series of dates (posttest(s)), and describing the gain. At the most complex level, the researcher adjusts the posttest measures to account for scoring differences on the pretests, and for other student characteristics known or suspected to affect either pretest or posttest. This method of adjusting gain scores provides evaluators with greater assurance that the change observed can really be "attributed" to the educational program and is a reasonable substitute for procedures that compare randomly assigned experimental and control classes. We will discuss each of these forms briefly; the first two methods may be more familiar to faculty members than the third.

A broad range of objectives may be evaluated with goal-focused evaluation methods. Acquisition of academic concepts and principles, broader outcomes such as multicultural sensitivity, and longer range outcomes such as career development may be assessed. This model also works well to evaluate cognitive, affective, and behavioral outcomes.

Course Level

Goal-focused evaluation at the course level is quite familiar to most faculty members. They are accustomed to measuring the achievement of course objectives with examinations, assignments, and papers. From these measures they often construct informal descriptions of student achievements such as grade distributions and profiles. Many faculty members may be surprised to learn that several areas of their home-grown tests and assignments need improvement to make the descriptions more meaningful. Some areas of deficiency in faculty-devised tests may be domain coverage, clarity, reliability, and validity. Banta and Schneider (1988) report, for example, that faculty in eleven fields who attempted to develop examinations for capstone senior seminars had difficulty constructing tests that required high levels of cognitive ability.

Describing Outcomes. Describing student outcomes requires that the outcome be clearly designated and that a measure be discovered or developed. The list of possible outcomes will differ for each college course. Some may be viewed as basic skills, some as general learned abilities acquired in college, and some as learning expected in particular academic courses. The items in Table 10-6

TABLE 10-6 Examples of Course-Level Objectives

1. *Basic skills:*
   Communication skills
   Problem-solving skills
   Numerical skills

2. *Course-related learning:*
   Vocabulary
   Facts
   Principles
   Concepts
   Methods of inquiry
   Methods of application
   Professional and occupational skills

3. *General abilities and attributes:*
   Cognitive characteristics such as
     conceptual flexibility
   Changes in orientation toward inquiry or
     toward the material encompassed in the
     course or program
   Evidence of become an independent
     thinker
   Evidence of becoming a continuing learner

suggest some examples in each of these broad categories within the domain of academic achievement.

Information to describe student performance on most of these objectives has traditionally been gathered with paper and pencil tests, performance tests, or observation by an expert observer. Tests and performance measures may be locally developed or faculty can use standardized tests that permit comparisons with a large population of students similar to those being tested. Other tests may be scored according to specific criteria for mastery (criterion-referenced tests) or in relation to scores for a group of students (norm-referenced tests). Many arguments, pro and con, may be made concerning the strengths and weaknesses of locally developed versus standardized tests. The strongest point in favor of locally developed tests is that they are most likely to measure course objectives the specific instructor actually planned to achieve. The strongest point against them is that they may not actually measure these outcomes validly and reliably if the professor is not skilled in test construction. Faculty members may find it valuable to work with a colleague to examine their tests carefully, checking for clarity, for coverage of important domains, and for assurance that the answers require appropriately high levels of effective thinking.

A class of students may be described in terms of the students' average scores on the outcome measure and the dispersion (spread) of those scores. Alternatively, the description could show what students can do or have learned in comparison with a preestablished criterion. A specific student's performance may be described in terms of the student's deviation from the class average or in terms of achieving the preset criteria. When course goals are clear, student-centered descriptions such as portfolios, anecdotal reports, and student journals may also be used.

General descriptions of student performance benefit both teachers and students.

They clarify objectives for teachers and students and identify areas in which congruence exists or is lacking. They make both teacher and student aware of multiple outcomes and objectives for a course or program (some intended, some not intended). They can also provide in-course feedback to a teacher about how the students are progressing toward objectives.

Describing Student Change. If description is the only form of evaluation used, students' gains during the course or program remain unknown. Analyses of how students change during a course are almost as simple to do as straight descriptions but have additional advantages. When appropriate, pretests can help the instructor understand what students know at the beginning of the course and adjust the instructional process accordingly. They may also help the instructor judge whether the plan needs adjustments for all students or just for specific subgroups. On the negative side, pretests must be used cautiously because they can also decrease motivation if the tests are so challenging that students feel inadequate to master the material. On the positive side, when shared with students, descriptions of change may give them a sense of achievement and renewed motivation.

Change can be described in a number of ways depending on the measure of student achievement used. Researchers can simply (and simplistically) subtract pretest scores from posttest scores and plot distributions of gain scores. They may display pretest and posttest scores as group profiles, as comparisons of percentage of students above a criterion point, or as correlated measures. All of these types of change scores must be interpreted carefully because students with greater initial proficiency have less opportunity to improve than those who are less proficient. Unless adjusted for pretest performance, a distribution of change scores is hard to interpret and may be misleading. [Professors who contemplate using change scores may wish to consult *Assessing for Excellence* by Astin (1991a) or the appendix of *How College Affects Students* by Pascarella and Terenzini (1991).]

Not all assessment requires change scores. In some cases the source of a change in students is obvious. A complex pretest in an unfamiliar foreign language, for example, will provide an exercise in guessing and frustration but little valuable information that the instructor could not attain by asking which students are familiar with the language from some other source. Pace (1985, p. 16) uses the interesting example that it would not be appropriate to push a beginning skier down the slope in order to measure his progress later.

Attributing Course-Level Outcomes. The most complete and sophisticated course-level evaluations attempt to attribute student change to the course plan or activities. Assessments of student learning will thus include evidence of change (or "value-added," to use Astin's original term) in a desired direction with respect to skills, attitudes, and behaviors that are the generally expected outcomes of a particular course or program. Attribution of change is not always complex. Suppose American students enrolled in a course in spoken Russian demonstrate considerable ability to speak Russian at the term's end. Although a few students might be sufficiently motivated to enhance their knowledge of Russian from other sources (say Berlitz tapes or tutoring from an international student), it would be most unusual if the majority of students gained their knowledge of Russian from sources other than the course. In another instance, it might be very difficult to demonstrate that particular learning occurred because the student was enrolled in a specific course. For example, students taking several courses that required essays probably could not attribute improvement in writing to any one of them. Similarly, those taking a course in American political systems during a national presidential election might acquire new knowledge of political systems from television coverage of the election as well as from the course. A third possibility is that the course had both a direct effect (class material) and an indirect effect (by encouraging them to watch TV coverage of the election). However, indirect effects of courses and programs are rarely examined.

The first step in attributing learning to a particular educational experience is to isolate and clearly specify the expected outcomes. The second step is to be sure the selected pretest reasonably measures students' capability before the course begins. A third step is to identify and measure other characteristics (mediating variables) related to the subject—for example, speaking Russian at home or a recent trip to Russia. Finally, the posttest scores are statistically regressed upon the pretest scores and appropriate mediating variables to determine the amount of change beyond that caused by these existing conditions; this result can reasonably be attributed to the course.

These steps represent a more complex procedure than most faculty members will use in evaluating their courses. The statistical techniques substitute for an actual experiment with two classes in which the students are randomly selected. Yet it is important to recognize that, in the absence of such procedures, one cannot attribute student change solely to the course. Traditional evaluation theorists believe that course outcomes can, with careful attention to competing hypotheses, be attributed to educational experiences through this value-added method, which substitutes for a true experimental design.

Pace (1985) adds an important perspective to this view, however, through his concept of quality of effort, which locates accountability for student outcomes with the student

as well as with the professor and the course. The current rhetoric about institutional accountability, Pace argues, makes instructors entirely accountable if students do not learn. It assumes that the students are buying a product when, in actuality, students themselves are eventually the product. Although Pace acknowledges that institutions are accountable for resources and facilities, programs and procedures, stimuli and standards, he argues that students are also accountable—for the amount, scope, and quality of effort they invest in their own learning and development and for the use they make of facilities and opportunities available from their college or university. Accountability for achievement and related student outcomes must consider both what institutions offer and what students do with those offerings.

To account for student effort when attempting to attribute learning to a course, an instructor needs to choose measures of student effort (and perhaps student motivation) as mediating variables that may relate directly to student success in the course. This viewpoint and related strategy is appealing to many faculty members who are willing to assess student learning in their courses and make adjustments to their academic plans but who realize that student effort is an important variable in the assessment equation which cannot easily be measured or statistically controlled.

Finally, even when student learning outcomes are the primary object of assessment, the basic purpose of evaluation is to adjust elements of the academic plan so that student learning will be improved. Thus, in evaluating a course, the teacher must assess both the plan and the specific student outcomes resulting from the plan. This fact requires documenting the plan, the intended learning outcomes, and the criteria for their successful achievement. It is helpful if each specified outcome is also associated with a measure that will help the professor know if it is achieved.

Program Level

As we have mentioned, goal-focused evaluation requires that an academic program develop clear goals and objectives as part of its academic plan. Establishing the goals and objectives provides an important opportunity for faculty members to explore the extent of agreement on the basic purposes of education undergirding the selection of specific content. Although faculty members in a specific discipline generally share common educational purposes, modest variation within the group means that even departments focusing strongly on learning concepts and principles will have some concern for students' personal and intellectual development and that departments primarily concerned with students' development will have some content goals. The mix of these educational purposes may depend on typical student career paths; the greater the proportion of students headed for graduate education, the greater the emphasis on content. Further-

more, faculty teaching students who are nearing the end of their formal education may place more emphasis on cultivating intentional learning attributes.

Several researchers have developed typologies of potential college outcomes which may be considered as frameworks within which faculty can phrase and evaluate important goals that they had not explicitly considered. Because most programs undergo periodic evaluation and revision, the typologies can be useful at each iteration in the cycle of refining academic plans.

The best-known comprehensive typology (by Astin, 1993, p. 45) has three dimensions: type of outcome (cognitive or affective), type of data to ascertain the outcome (behavioral or psychological), and time (long-term or short-term) (see Table 10-7). A recent variation used by other researchers, focusing more fully on the cognitive, motivational, and behavioral realms, is shown in Table 10-8 (Alexander & Stark, 1986). These general frameworks must be refined and

TABLE 10-7   Astin's Typology of Educational Outcomes

| Type of Data | Type of Outcome* | |
	Cognitive	Affective
Psychological	Subject-matter knowledge Academic ability Critical thinking ability Basic learning skills Special aptitudes Academic achievement	Values Interests Self-concepts Attitudes Beliefs Satisfaction with college
Behavioral	Degree attainment Vocational achievement Awards or special recognition	Leadership Citizenship Interpersonal relations Hobbies and avocations

Source: Reprinted from *Assessment for Excellence: The Philosophy and Practice of Assessment and Evaluation in Higher Education* by Alexander W. Astin, p. 45. Used by permission of The Oryx Press, 4041 N. Central at Indian School Road, Phoenix, AZ 85012, (800) 279-6799. All rights reserved. Reprinted by permission of Allyn and Bacon.

*A third dimension, time, is not shown.

TABLE 10-8   NCRIPTAL's Typology of Educational Outcomes

Form of Measurement	Academic Arena
Cognitive	Achievement (facts, principles, ideas, skills) Critical-thinking skills Problem-solving skills
Motivational	Satisfaction with college Involvement and effort Motivation Self-efficacy
Behavioral	Career and life goal exploration Exploration of diversity Persistence Relationships with faculty

Source: Focusing on Student Academic Outcomes: A Working Paper by Joanne Alexander and Joan S. Stark (1986), p. 14. Reprinted by permission of the National Center for Research to Improve Postsecondary Teaching and Learning, The University of Michigan.

made specific by faculty in each program at each institution. One suggested rule of thumb is that program objectives are clear when any two faculty members making up test items to evaluate their achievement would develop very similar items (Harris, 1985). We add that in programs using several critical perspectives or paradigms, the items might represent the several different schools of thought represented by the faculty.

For general education, the specific objectives to be evaluated will vary depending on how a college uses the term. The number of examinations that purport to measure general education outcomes is increasing. These now include the New Jersey Basic Skills Test, the College Outcome COMP Test (American College Testing Service), the Academic Profile (Educational Testing Service), and College BASE (University of Misssouri–Colum-

bia). Typically, program faculty evaluate some of these examinations for congruence with their goals and also consider developing their own examination (see Banta & Schneider, 1988). Depending on the measures used, students can be tested at the lowest levels of cognitive development, such as the acquisition of facts, or at higher levels, such as ability to synthesize, analyze, and evaluate. Some faculty groups have developed matrices with the specific types of knowledge and skills they expect students to acquire on one dimension and the various courses and program experiences expected to foster them, on the other. Such matrices help to pinpoint where specific types of outcomes are to be learned. Ewell (1991a) believes that, contrary to measuring only the easy outcomes of education, the recent assessment movement has caused faculty members to pay increased attention to noncognitive outcomes such as ethical development, attitudes, reflective judgment, critical thinking, and independent learning. Indeed, measures that try to capture student development in such areas have become more common in recent years.

Like their colleagues in general education programs, faculty in most major fields prefer to construct their own comprehensive examinations to measure students' development. This process of local construction fosters faculty ownership but also results in considerable duplication of effort and sometimes in poor test validity and reliability. Standard tests in major fields that faculty may wish to examine include those published by the Educational Testing Service, such as the College Academic Achievement Proficiency tests (CAAP), the Graduate Record Examination subject examinations, and the Professional Skills examinations for selected occupational fields.

The current attention to assessment, to establishing clear expectations for students, and to new knowledge about how students learn are encouraging specific occupational fields to devote more attention to outcomes and objectives. For example, Table 10-9 contains a list of desired outcomes now being valued in accounting education. Only a few years ago, accounting educators would have confined their attention to learning accounting principles and rules. Recently, they have explicitly included attention to how students integrate learning into coherent patterns, how they use learning in solving professional problems, and how they continue to expand

TABLE 10-9 Desired Student Outcomes for a Professional Program—Accounting

1. Working with people to achieve tasks
   Interpersonal skills
   Teamwork
   Leadership skills
   Understanding the work environment
   Communication skills
2. Solving problems (general)
   Critical and analytical thinking skills
   Unstructured and structured problem
      solving and decision making
3. Solving problems and making decisions in
      a business context
   Seeking and gathering information for
      business decisions
   Understanding the business context
   Understanding the societal/cultural context
   Seeing accounting as a coherent whole
   Using information in business decisions
4. Learning to be an independent learner
   Developing motivation
   Developing learning skills
   Developing information-seeking skills
5. Developing broad perspectives
   Global perspectives
   Ethical perspectives
   Entrepreneurial perspectives

Source: From proposals for change in accounting education submitted by more than fifty universities to the Accounting Education Change Commission, 1989 to 1994. Compiled by Stark.

their knowledge in a changing society. Furthermore, like dental educators, accounting educators have developed a comprehensive assessment handbook for their colleagues (Gainen & Locatelli, 1995).

The three levels of goal-focused evaluation we described for courses (description, description of change, attribution) are equally relevant at the program level. For determining attribution of outcomes at the program level, faculty might give more serious consideration to Astin's "input-environment-output" (I-E-O) model. This model, which can be adapted to any program, is useful for assessing the experiences of cohorts of students. It clarifies that entering students' characteristics important to program success must be defined and measured, the environment (instructional experiences) must be specified, and the outcomes must be measured. It calls attention to the "program environment" in which the academic plan is embedded and thus directs attention at the ultimate goal—to discover how to adjust the specific curriculum design to enhance desired student outcomes. The procedure requires that students' entering characteristics be statistically controlled, thus the design comes close to being able to infer causes and effects.

Although we suggest that faculty should try to control for entering student characteristics to determine whether learning is attributed to their programs, we believe student differences are too important to be disregarded as mere "statistical controls." One immediate example is the fact that large numbers of students at some four-year colleges are transfers; one cannot simply statistically eliminate the effects of education received at prior institutions. Also, different academic plans may produce different results for different students at different stages intellectual development. Students' knowledge bases must also be considered. One obvious example is that students from different racial and ethnic backgrounds may interact with content differently. Consider, for example, a course in business ethics enrolling students from many countries with different business cultures and practices. The ethics of American business might be more easily learned by American students who accept American business norms than by students from cultures where other norms are typical. It is as important to examine these interaction effects between student characteristics and curricular designs as it is to control student characteristics in examining aggregate patterns. In our example, a quite different type of academic plan might need to be constructed for the international students from different business cultures.

A comprehensive goal-focused evaluation plan will be linked with other types of evaluation we have described, particularly with student-centered evaluation, in order to fully account for these differences and make appropriate adjustments in the curriculum.

College Level

Goal-focused assessment at the college level may include standardized testing, including pretest and posttest comparisons using the input-environment-output (I-E-O) model. However, the difficulties in attribution are great since there are so many variations among students and so many alternative sources of learning to be controlled. Such studies will be best suited to small colleges or to carefully chosen and assiduously followed random samples of students in larger colleges. Other types of evaluation may be more useful. For example, transcript analysis and other "unobtrusive measures"—not involving the testing, interviewing, or survey of students directly—may be useful. Varied methods of transcript analyses recently have been developed to study the course sequences that students have taken (Zemsky, 1989), and to

relate them to other outcome characteristics (Boli, Katchdourian, & Mahoney, 1988; Ratcliff, 1992a). Given the evaluation and assessment challenge facing higher education, we might expect both faculty members and researchers to create many more new evaluation methods.

For large institutions, seeking attributes of the entire college that affect student learning may be a futile effort. But strong college-level leadership can help each college and department within the university move forward systematically toward goal-focused evaluation. Thus, the appropriate total college evaluation plan may be an aggregation of evaluations from specific programs, including not only the majors but general education and basic skills programs. Such a comprehensive plan must be flexible and adaptable to discipline differences but can focus on college-wide goals by using all of the types of evaluation we have described.

Among the many examples of colleges that have moved carefully and systematically toward collegewide processes by involving each department is South Dakota State University (SDSU). In 1985 the South Dakota Board of Regents implemented a seemingly inflexible assessment plan that faculty resisted. By 1988, however, SDSU had devised a substitute plan requiring every academic department to develop and use some assessment instrument or exit examination for graduating seniors as one part of the total program evaluation. Departments received a per-student subsidy and were eligible to compete in a small grant program to help develop assessment and evaluation instruments. The SDSU Assessment Program (South Dakota, July 1, 1988) locates goal-focused evaluation in the context of broader program review (see Figure 10-2). Recognizing that developing reliable and valid instruments would take time, the university administrators described the process as two overlapping cycles, including

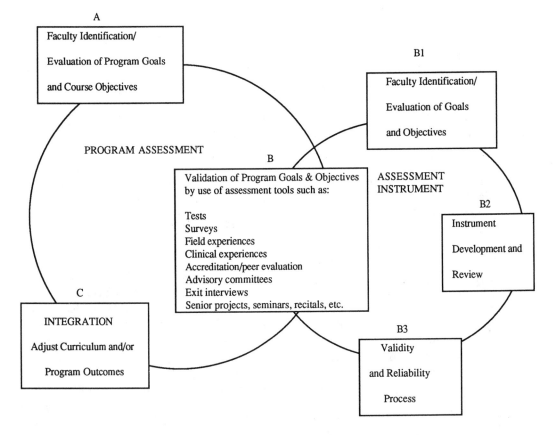

FIGURE 10-2   Assessment Process at South Dakota State University

Source: Developed by Kris M. Smith, Ph.D., for use in South Dakota State University assessment process. Found in *Assessment Plan, 1988,* South Dakota State University.

gradual improvement and meta-evaluation. Colleges in many states are at work on more systematic assessment plans.

Another model of a collegewide assessment program that includes goal-focused evaluation as well as other types of assessment is in place at the State University of New York at Albany (Burke & Volkwein, June 1992). Albany began assessing programs in the 1960s and launched a long-term assessment program in 1978 with a series of studies of student cohorts. The result is a comprehensive outcomes assessment model

(Figure 10-3), an extensive set of data bases about students (see Figure 10-4), and a set of individually chosen department assessment plans (Figure 10-5). In addition to a total plan for assessing the outcomes of general education, the SUNY-Albany plan offers each department a variety of options, ranging from senior essays to student portfolios. The program has resulted in a wide variety of adjustments and changes to the curriculum. The Albany program does not limit itself only to the measurement of easily measured academic outcomes but also assesses personal growth

Albany Outcomes Assessment Model

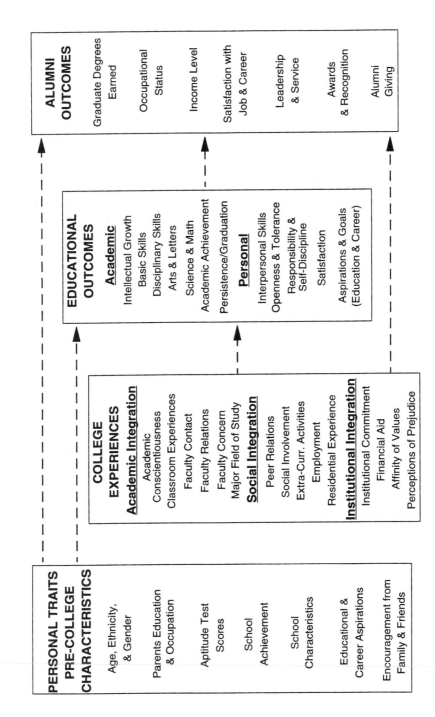

FIGURE 10-3   Outcomes Assessment Model from SUNY-Albany

Source: Outcomes Assessment at Albany by Joseph Burke and J. Fredericks Volkwein (1992), p. 3. Used by permission of the authors.

Albany Outcomes Databases

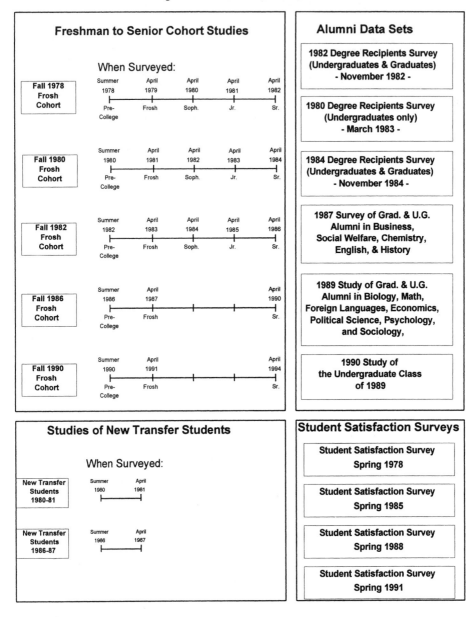

Freshman to Senior Cohort Studies

When Surveyed:

Fall 1978 Frosh Cohort

Summer 1978	April 1979	April 1980	April 1981	April 1982
Pre-College	Frosh	Soph.	Jr.	Sr.

Fall 1980 Frosh Cohort

Summer 1980	April 1981	April 1982	April 1983	April 1984
Pre-College	Frosh	Soph.	Jr.	Sr.

Fall 1982 Frosh Cohort

Summer 1982	April 1983	April 1984	April 1985	April 1986
Pre-College	Frosh	Soph.	Jr.	Sr.

Fall 1986 Frosh Cohort

Summer 1986	April 1987			April 1990
Pre-College	Frosh			Sr.

Fall 1990 Frosh Cohort

Summer 1990	April 1991			April 1994
Pre-College	Frosh			Sr.

Alumni Data Sets

1982 Degree Recipients Survey (Undergraduates & Graduates) - November 1982 -

1980 Degree Recipients Survey (Undergraduates only) - March 1983 -

1984 Degree Recipients Survey (Undergraduates & Graduates) - November 1984 -

1987 Survey of Grad. & U.G. Alumni in Business, Social Welfare, Chemistry, English, & History

1989 Study of Grad. & U.G. Alumni in Biology, Math, Foreign Languages, Economics, Political Science, Psychology, and Sociology,

1990 Study of the Undergraduate Class of 1989

Studies of New Transfer Students

When Surveyed:

New Transfer Students 1980-81

Summer 1980	April 1981

New Transfer Students 1986-87

Summer 1986	April 1987

Student Satisfaction Surveys

Student Satisfaction Survey Spring 1978

Student Satisfaction Survey Spring 1985

Student Satisfaction Survey Spring 1988

Student Satisfaction Survey Spring 1991

FIGURE 10-4   Databases at SUNY-Albany

Source: Outcomes Assessment at Albany by Joseph Burke and J. Fredericks Volkwein (1992), p. 2. Used by permission of the authors.

```
┌─────────────────────────────────────────────────────────┐
│                    University at Albany                   │
│            SUMMARY OF ASSESSMENT OPTIONS                  │
│                  IN THE DISCIPLINE                        │
└─────────────────────────────────────────────────────────┘
```

Senior Thesis or Research Project

Africana Studies (within senior seminar)
Latin American & Caribbean Studies
Women's Studies*
Music (Theory)
Political Science & Public Affairs*
French Studies (Honors)

Performance Experience

Theater (ACT Festival)
Music* (Performance)
Public Affairs (Internship)
Social Welfare (field internship with seminar)

Course Embedded & Capstone Experience

Africana Studies*
Biology
French Studies
Judaic Studies*
Linguistic & Cognitive Science*
Mathematics*
Philosophy
Religious Studies Program
Women's Studies*
Business Administration*
Social Welfare (seminar with internship)

Comprehensive Examination

Accounting* (CPA Exam)
Chemistry (ETS)
Computer Science (ETS)
German Language & Literature*
Hispanic & Italian*
Social Studies (NTE)
Music* (Theory Exam)
Physics (ETS)
Psychology* (ETS)
Slavic Languages & Literature*
Sociology* (ETS)

Student Portfolio of Learning Experiences

Art (portfolio of artistic works)
English (writing portfolio)

Senior Essay (or Survey) and Interview

Anthropology*
Atmospheric Science*
Classics (joint faculty-student review)
Communication
East Asian Studies (with faculty retreat)
Geological Science and Earth Sciences
German Language & Literature*
Hispanic & Italian*
History
Judaic Studies*
Psychology*
Slavic Languages & Literature*
Sociology*
Women's Studies*
Criminal Justice
Geography and Regional Planning

Alumni Studies and Use of Departmental and Placement Data

Anthropology*
Atmospheric Science*
Biology*
Economics
French Studies*
Geological Sciences*
Hispanic & Italian*
Linguistic & Cognitive Science*
Psychology*
Sociology*
Business Administration*
Accounting*

*Multi-Method Combination

FIGURE 10-5   Departmental Evaluation Options at SUNY-Albany

Source: Outcomes Assessment at Albany by Joseph Burke and J. Fredericks Volkwein (1992), p. 7. Used by permission of the authors.

of students and such supportive services as advising. It uses all of the types of evaluation we have discussed in this chapter.

EVALUATING EVALUATION

We have asserted that every element of the academic plan, including evaluation itself, should be evaluated and the results used to improve the next evaluation. Some evaluation experts refer to the process of examining the evaluation processes as *meta-evaluation.* This meta-evaluation can be viewed as a type of research and reflection on evaluation processes. Depending on the purpose of the evaluation, a variety of questions can be asked about any procedure. Key questions for formative evaluations include:

- Was the evaluation of appropriate scope and was it correctly targeted at learning outcomes?
- Did it involve both students and faculty?
- Was it a reasonable use of student and faculty energy?
- Was there open communication about the results?
- Did it change faculty and student behavior?
- Did it provide information for adjustments in academic plans?

- Did the adjustments promise improved education?

One conclusion that is readily drawn from observing current evaluation practice is that credibility and the use of evaluation data and assessment results for adjustments depends heavily on who conducts the assessments, chooses the measures, interprets the results, and is assigned responsibility for improvement. Imposing evaluation requirements and standard measures of learning on faculty violates their autonomy and creativity in planning academic courses and programs. According to one assessment expert, "academics are always inventive in finding ways to circumvent external initiatives for which they perceive little value" (Banta, 1994, p. 1). Under such circumstances, they are less likely to make effective interpretations and adjustments than if they develop assessment and evaluation procedures voluntarily. Yet strong and positive leadership is important since evaluation alone does not automatically produce curriculum change.

A second observation from meta-evaluation generally is that the level of academic plan being evaluated strongly affects the interpretation and usefulness of results for improving education. Table 10-10 shows how the characteristics of evaluation and adjustment vary on several dimensions over the

TABLE 10-10   Characteristics of Evaluation and Adjustment at Various Levels of Academic Plans

Level	Specificity of Outcomes	Formality of Procedures	Ease of Data Collection	Attributes of Learning	Promptness of Adjustment
Courses	Specific	Informal	Easy	Somewhat Uncertain	Rapid
Program	Both specific and general	Ranges: informal to formal	Ranges: easy to difficult	Uncertain	Slow
Collegewide	General	Formal	Difficult	Very uncertain	Very slow

three levels of academic plans. As we move from classroom to college level, the outcomes we seek to evaluate become less specific, the formality of procedures greater, the difficulty of collecting information about student knowledge, behavior, and opinion greater, the level of attribution less certain, and the promptness with which adjustments take place slower. Simply put, at the college level, evaluation Path A (shown in Figure 10-1) gives way to evaluation Path B, and the focus moves from learning outcomes to the environment in which academic plans are constructed. These observations imply that evaluations and adjustments to improve academic plans should occur at the lowest possible level—with leadership from above to help faculty in planning, implementing, and evaluating the plans. Assessment should be disaggregated to the program level to guide change and adjustment. College-level assess-

ment may be too broad and diffuse for all but the smallest colleges.

A third observation from reflecting on evaluation at any level is that diversity of students, programs, and colleges probably preclude either standard evaluation procedures or meaningful comparisons of learning outcomes for different institutions. Yet as college administrators play their role of interpreting college mission and achievements to the public (Path C in Figure 10-1), policymakers increasingly demand consistent collegewide measures. They fail to understand the diversity of missions and the extreme difficulty of attributing learning outcomes to college, especially to specific college experiences. This tension between public expectations that colleges can be ranked on simple measures and the realities of educational evaluation practice defines an important issue in curriculum assessment today.

CHAPTER 11

Administering Academic Plans and Guiding Change

WHO ADMINISTERS ACADEMIC PLANS?

Curriculum administration is the exercise of responsibility and authority to ensure the successful development, coordination, implementation, support, evaluation, and adjustment of academic plans. In most colleges and universities, faculty and administrators share responsibility for curriculum administration. The way in which this responsibility is distributed varies depending on the type of college and the level of the academic plan. Individual faculty may bear the full responsibility for planning the classes they teach, while faculty and administrators are jointly responsible for program plans and for the curriculum as a whole. Curriculum administration especially includes establishing and maintaining an educational environment in which academic plans can be carried out effectively and be adjusted and improved continuously. Our first focus in this chapter is the joint responsibility of faculty and administrators as they develop, implement, and foster adjustments of college courses and programs within their environment. Our second focus, on responsibility of

administrators for the environment in which academic plans are embedded, is highlighted in Figure 11-1. A third focus is on leadership needed for substantial and innovative curriculum change that responds to external influences—the path for change designated in Figure 11-1 by Path C. Here we highlight processes of change and propose three phases by which external influences are recognized, screened and included in the internal change agenda of colleges and universities.

Many academics believe that the best curriculum administration is the least possible administration. Professors, they believe, should be given carte blanche to develop courses and programs consistent with disciplinary tenets and individual interests. Yet uncoordinated programs may serve isolated interests and fail to achieve either a college's goals or students' goals. To balance the needs of faculty, students, the college, and society, good curriculum administration requires coordination of a most deliberate and sensitive sort. Research has shown that college leaders who establish a positive educational environment can provide coordination while fostering strong motivation for program leaders and

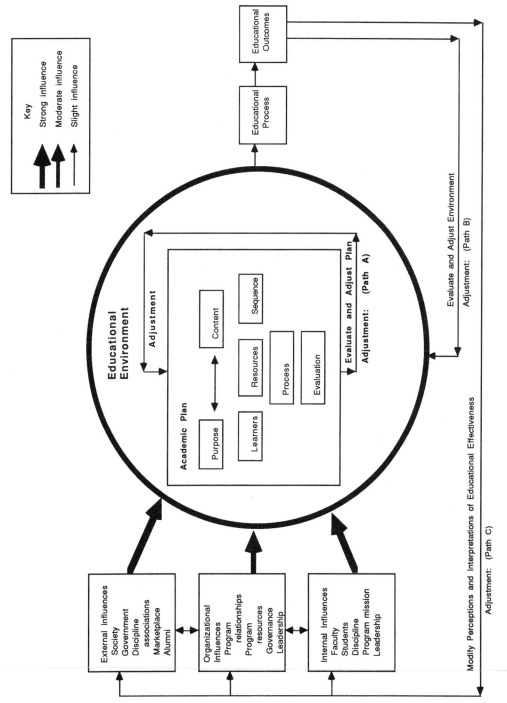

FIGURE 11-1 Academic Plans in Environmental Context: Focus on Administration

faculty to take curriculum planning seriously. The effective curriculum administrator must have the ability to establish dialogue about academic plans and the perseverance to attend to each element in the plans at all levels. Effective administration also requires an awareness of and concern for the internal, organiza- tional, and external forces that influence the curriculum. Viewed in its entirety, the academic plan framework can serve as a guide and checklist for administrators as well as for faculty who accept curriculum leadership.

In Figure 11-2, we have arrayed the elements of the academic plan in overlapping

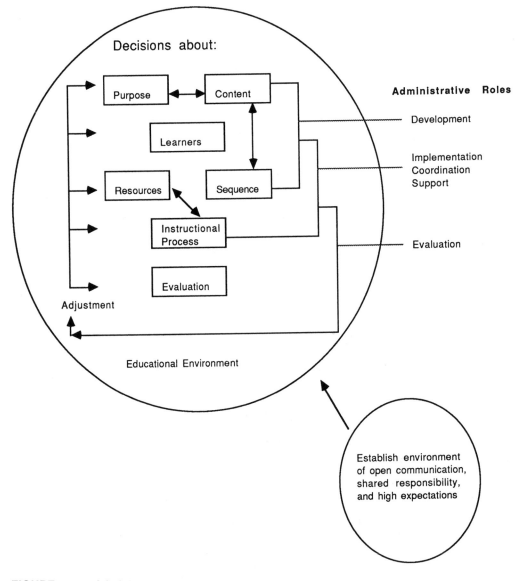

FIGURE 11-2   Administrative Roles and Academic Plans

groups, linking them to broad administrative functions: development, implementation, coordination, support, evaluation, and adjustment. All of these functions characterize an educational environment where college and program leaders give conscientious attention to curriculum.

Since colleges differ so greatly in mission and organization, our use of the term "ad-

ministrator" is necessarily general. We will speak of program chairs, deans, and vice-presidents as generic categories of administrators, recognizing that this scheme must be adapted for a specific setting. To clarify further the administrative roles that may be appropriate at each of these generic levels, we have developed Table 11-1, which provides a matrix of functions that are necessary if aca-

TABLE 11-1   A Matrix of Curriculum Administration Functions

	Development	Implementation	Evaluation
	Purpose, Content, Sequence	Learners, Resources, Process	Evaluation, Adjustment
Internal Matters (Program Chair)	(A) Keep abreast of trends in field. Design program plans and courses. Describe and communicate plans.	(B) Staff courses. Provide incentives for faculty. Understand learners. Support and budget. Select materials. Select processes.	(C) Monitor student progess. Monitor progress of plan. Determine merit and worth. Determine costs/benefits. Adjust plans. Report to dean.
Organizational Matters (Dean)	(D) Interrelate missions of programs. Relate program missions to college. Coordinate program sequences. Describe academic programs. Create collaborative climate.	(E) Staff programs. Gather data on learners. Allocate budget. Provide materials, services, instructional resources, other central services.	(F) Collect comparative data on: faculty. students. programs. budgets. planning. Encourage adjustment. Report to vice president.
External Matters (Vice-President)	(G) Review college mission. Relate programs to mission. Conduct collegewide planning for programs. Communicate mission. Establish expectations. Sense new markets.	(H) Staff college or departments. Allocate budget. Supervise public relations/student recruitment. Provide central services. Raise funds.	(I) Collect comparative data on departments and colleges. Support new programs. Adjust existing programs. Report to president and sponsors.

demic programs are to exist and thrive. The functions are grouped into nine categories, depending first on whether they deal with internal, organizational, or external relations, and second, on whether the broad phase of curriculum planning is development; implementation, coordination, and resource provision; or evaluation and improvement. The specific responsibilities appropriate for administrators at the institution (vice-president), college (dean), or program level (department chair) vary for each type of concern; responsibility is seldom focused at a single level.

Curriculum planning is usually specific to a discipline or professional field. Internal leadership in curriculum development is provided by a group of faculty with a program chair who acts as a coordinator. The overall goals are: (1) to develop high quality, coherent academic plans for the designated set of learners, (2) to coordinate the implementation of the plans within the program, including communication with faculty and students, and (3) to evaluate program effectiveness and encourage adjustments. The tasks of this coordinating role in overseeing development, implementation, and evaluation-adjustment are shown for the program level in Cells A, B, and C. Examples of specific tasks are illustrated in the cells; the evaluative functions in Cell C often are overseen by the individual in the post one administrative level above the responsible program chair, usually a dean.

Organizational leadership for curriculum planning involving several units (Cells D, E, F) is provided by program chairs and deans working together. The primary goals are: (1) to develop high quality academic plans for the designated set of learners, (2) to coordinate implementation of plans and policies, including communication with faculty members and students in the various units to ensure linkage and integration among programs, and (3) to work with the next higher level of administrative authority on evaluation and adjustment, often comparatively

with other units. A vice president for academic affairs is often the overall coordinator and evaluator.

At the external level (Cells G, H, I), leadership is provided by the deans and vice president for academic affairs working together with coordination by the college president. The overall goals are: (1) to ensure the development of programs faithful to the college mission, (2) to provide resources necessary for implementation, and (3) to monitor responsiveness, adaptability, quality, and accountability to societal and learner needs as well as to sponsor interests. The pattern of evaluation at the next highest level of authority, described in the previous two rows of the matrix, may be repeated if evaluation is coordinated by trustees or by a state-level agency above the president.

Leadership for curriculum development and day-to-day implementation can and should come from faculty members, while coordination should come from administrators (many of whom have been or remain faculty); evaluation and new vision should involve both groups. The intensity and nature of each group's involvement will vary depending on the setting and the curriculum task at hand. Faculty should hold some responsibility for curriculum development at all levels from course to collegewide programs. Similarly, administrators should show their joint ownership and responsibility by remaining informed about even the lowest levels of academic plans. Regardless of the formal structure, the primary goal should be the design of academic plans that are successful for students and society.

CURRICULUM LEADERSHIP AND ADMINISTRATIVE ROLES

From the many models available, (and despite its origin in business and its managerial focus), we have selected the "competing values" typology of management models

(Quinn, 1988; Quinn et al., 1990) as a useful framework in which to examine curriculum leadership and administration. We selected this model primarily because its dimensions are congruent with important elements of our theory of curriculum. One of its main dimensions—internal-external focus—parallels the internal and external influences on curriculum we have emphasized; the second dimension—flexibility-control—captures the tension between the autonomy faculty need for effective and creative curriculum planning and their accountability to sponsors and society. In addition, the model incorporates a wide range of administrative styles that might be used. Thus, consistent with our approach to describing alternatives to faculty members, it allows curriculum administrators at different levels and in different settings an opportunity to examine alternative roles relevant to their situation.

Quinn noted that four commonly accepted management models (rational goal, internal process, human relations, and open systems) appear to be based on very different values. For example, the human relations model stresses participation, openness, commitment, and morale in contrast to the rational goal model, which is defined by control and an external focus. The open systems model with its view toward environmental adaptiveness opposes the internal process model. Yet each model is similar to another in some respect. For example, the open systems model and human relations model share an emphasis on flexibility. The open systems and rational goal models both emphasize external focus; they may be viewed as complementary aspects of the larger construct of managerial leadership, each to be used in appropriate situations. Quinn (1988) therefore mapped the four models on two primary dimensions—internal-external and flexibility-control—as shown in Figure 11-3. Taken together, the four models occupy the four quadrants defined by these two axes. Quinn stressed that each requires a different set of leadership competencies. Thus the total model points to a range of potentially effective leadership roles which may be used at different times and different organizational levels of responsibility.

As we apply it to higher education, the competing values model supports the prevailing notion we developed in the curriculum administration matrix (Table 11-1), that the most effective and efficient curriculum administration occurs when those with the broadest responsibility provide balanced oversight of the internal, organizational, and external conditions that influence academic plans but reserve the major role in its development for those closest to implementation of the academic plan.

In the next sections, we discuss several aspects of curriculum administration by linking the managerial roles of Quinn's model with the educational environment and the elements of the academic plan. For each section, we also provide guidelines for administrators who are working toward enhancing curriculum development. These guidelines are necessarily broad and are intended to allow individuals to select those appropriate to their own role and setting.

Establishing the Educational Environment (Managerial Roles: Mentor; Facilitator)

To build effective academic plans at the college and program levels, the faculty must have expertise, flexibility to follow their creative talents, opportunities to consider alternatives, and resources to implement their plans. Most faculty feel that curriculum development is worthwhile and challenging but time-consuming and lacking in extrinsic rewards. Thus, they require strong and visible support to maintain a vital interest in it. According to one experienced college leader (Guskin, 1981, p. 2), an environment that motivates faculty is characterized by: shared

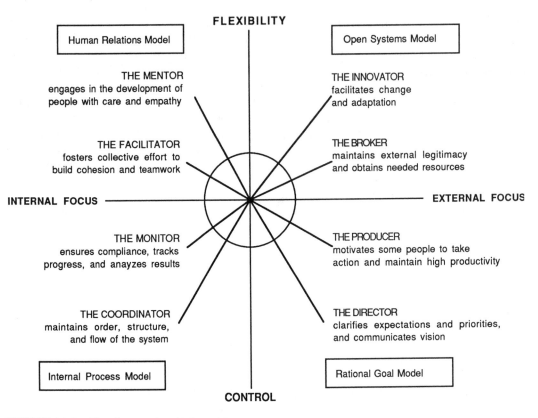

FIGURE 11-3   The Competing Values Model: Eight Managerial Roles

Source: Adapted from *Becoming a Master Manager: A Competency Framework* by Quinn, Raerman, Thompson, and McGrath (1990), pp. 11–15. From *Becoming a Master Manager* by Robert Quinn. Copyright 1990 by John Wiley & Sons, Inc. Reprinted by permission of John Wiley & Sons, Inc., and *Beyond Rational Management: Mastering the Paradoxes and Competing Demands of High Performance* by Robert Quinn. Copyright 1988 by Jossey-Bass, Inc. Used by permission of the publisher.

responsibility (a sense of ownership), freedom to experiment (a sense of security), public attention to curriculum (a sense of pride), and keeping pace with knowledge growth (a sense of intellectual vitality and high expectations for quality education). These conditions are minimal prerequisites for motivating individual faculty, meeting their professional needs, and fostering their sense of obligation to evaluate student learning and adjust academic plans accordingly.

Shared Responsibility and Freedom to Experiment

When curriculum is viewed as an academic plan, every member of a college or university staff holds some responsibility for it. A program coordinator or department chairperson has chief responsibility for leading departmental faculty in curriculum development and for coordinating the planned courses and experiences of enrolled students in a program. Program chairpersons (who may or may not have departmental budget authority) usually are accepted as curriculum leaders because they are experts in the subject field of the program. In units where diverse fields are grouped, the chairperson may be expert in only one of the programs offered. In this case, his or her leadership depends more on formal authority or persuasion than on subject matter expertise and colleagueship. The more diverse the units under an administrative umbrella, the more distant the leader is likely to be from the actual development of the academic plan.

The pair of inverted triangles shown in Figure 11-4 portray the typical arrangement. A top administrator's active role in planning is focused at the college level; his role at the course level is less active and he may play almost no role vis-à-vis the elements of the academic plan most closely linked to the learning process—that is, content, sequence, learners, and process. Yet his influence is felt with respect to resources, evaluation, and adjustment. Faculty members, in contrast, are most involved in creating, developing, and implementing academic plans at the course level, focusing on purpose, content, sequence, and choice of instructional process. At the college level, their roles become less active, although in some colleges they may assist both in gathering resources and in defining the college mission.

Considering the wide diversity of colleges and universities, Figure 11-4 represents a theme with many variations. At one end of the spectrum, the responsibility of college faculty for curriculum is virtually complete at many research universities and selective liberal arts colleges. In these settings, administrative decisions about curriculum are actually made by faculty committees, and administrators may be minimally involved at all levels. Faculty may directly recruit students to departments or programs and may help raise funds, in addition to planning the academic program. At the other end of the spectrum, where organized faculty unions bargain collectively with administrators, the roles of each group are often defined and distinguished by faculty contracts and "management rights." In such settings, faculty may feel no responsibility for helping the college establish the mission or raise funds; similarly, administrators may have limited participation and authority in decisions about courses and program content or sequence. Depending on local relationships, the codification of responsibilities may either minimize or exacerbate conflict in unionized colleges.

Even where strongly collegial models operate, the division of responsibility for curriculum can be a source of conflict. Faculty members who chair committees within programs, departments, and colleges become quasi-administrators, leading their colleagues

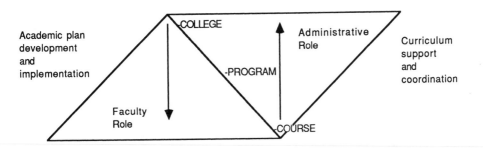

FIGURE 11-4   Faculty and Administrative Roles in Academic Planning

in the details of planning academic programs, but they often lack both authority for budget and accountability to ensure program success. Thus, some carefully formulated committee plans can fail because the necessary resources and staff do not accompany the assignment. Although it is philosophically and pedagogically sound for faculty and administrators to share administrative responsibility for curriculum, final accountability ultimately rests with the academic administrator in most colleges.

Even when the faculty play the primary role in curriculum development at the course and program level, administrators should not be passive players. They have an obligation to represent the college mission strongly. At one institution we visited, the administration's strong support created an environment in which faculty clearly felt motivated about curriculum change in general, and positive about planning for a new general education program specifically. Faculty members reported: "The president never gives a speech without emphasizing that the university mission is teaching the students of this region. We feel empowered in our work by the equal attention he gives to the educational program, not just budget and fund-raising."

Not only did the chief administrator in this state university regularly remind faculty of institutional mission, but he established expectations of careful attention to the curriculum by modeling that behavior himself. He did this by asking important questions that improved and focused the attention faculty gave to the design of academic plans; he encouraged curriculum committees to do the same, abandoning *pro forma* reviews in favor of collegial, but searching, discussions. Curriculum development is often considered hands off for administrators because they cannot be experts in every field. Yet administrators who accept the shared responsibility for program planning in a supportive, interested way at the can create a positive climate and thereby facilitate course planning.

Communication about the value of curriculum work is a key factor in fostering the freedom to experiment. Faculty in many colleges feel rewarded for research but believe that they will suffer in terms of promotion or salary rewards if they concentrate on curriculum planning and teaching. Yet recent studies show that, even in research universities, both faculty and administrators believe more emphasis should be placed on teaching (Gray, Froh, & Diamond, 1992; Cochran, 1989, p. 13). Administrators should examine the reward system and the promotions and tenure criteria to be sure that faculty who devote time to curriculum are likely to be rewarded, not discouraged. Early tenure reviews, as well as final decisions, should make clear that teaching and course planning are important criteria (along with research and service as fits the college mission) for long-term appointments.

The belief that faculty in research universities do not value teaching in the same way as faculty members in other types of colleges is only one example of misunderstanding that could be helped by open dialogue. The environment necessary for the effective creation of academic plans requires that such tensions between teaching and research be openly discussed to promote faculty security and vitality.

Open Communications and High Expectations

Academic vice-presidents typically think teaching and curriculum development need greater attention and visibility than they typically give it, yet feel that other demands on their time make such attention impossible (Cochran, 1989, p. 131). Faculty members and administrators often talk about curriculum and teaching, but discussions frequently are in the context of budgets and bureaucratic topics, while educational goals are neglected. For effective curriculum development, conversations need to be developed about educational purpose and about the conditions of teaching and its rewards. If the academic vice-president does no more than mention the importance of the curriculum at frequent intervals, communication will improve. For example, the academic vice-president's office might visibly help to develop all promotional and public relations materials to make sure they emphasize the educational mission and academic programs and highlight curriculum plans and successes as well as research facilities, athletics, or campus location.

Academic leaders can encourage programs to periodically and actively discuss their statements of purpose, their program objectives, and their ways of measuring them. To illustrate, the University of Utah David Eccles School of Business recently developed a matrix of its objectives for students and decided that every course must contribute to one or more objectives. In addition, they asked each faculty member to develop a short "teaching philosophy" for discussion. Administrators and faculty reported that these simple techniques opened many avenues for dialogue about curriculum change and evaluation and generated the feeling of being a learning community (Loebbecke, 1994). Communication about institutional mission and expectations for faculty and students are also critical. Key administrators should spend time engaging faculty in discussions of the college's mission if they expect it to be reflected in course-level and program-level plans.

Administrators might exhibit a sense of enthusiasm about the importance of good curriculum planning and teaching. They should be sure to acknowledge publicly faculty who exercise curriculum leadership. They might encourage faculty to develop peer support groups on curriculum development and teaching and give high importance to curriculum work at program and college levels during orientation for new faculty. Showing special attention to part-time faculty, whose role is primarily teaching, clearly signals the importance of the educational program.

Guidelines for Establishing a Supportive Environment for Curriculum Development: The Mentor and Facilitator Roles

- Establish a secure atmosphere. Spell out institutional priorities and the rewards for curricular experimentation. Publicly recognize that the process of curriculum development can be as valuable as the end result. Define failure as a valuable part of the learning process. Give ample time to test innovations and allow for revisions and adjustments. Be sure that ownership of the curriculum design and the credit for its success rest with the faculty.

- Foster a system of open communication. Good curriculum plans build on intellectually vital personnel and open processes. Open dialogue helps to establish collaborative relationships among and between faculty and administrators, and helps proponents and opponents to respect each others' views.

- Increase motivation and high expectations through frequent expressions of interest. Provide indications of interest, administrative support, and visibility for curriculum projects, as well as high expectations for quality process and product. Praise success. Give public credit to both those who have been successful and to those who were willing to try new ideas.

Developing Academic Plans (Managerial Roles: Producer; Director)

After an environment of shared responsibility, freedom to experiment, open dialogue, and high expectations has been established, developing strong academic plans within the college organization requires additional administrative actions. As we have already indicated, these actions are supported by several broad functions. The guidelines we offer are familiar to experienced academic administrators but are important enough to bear repeating with specific emphasis on their relation to developing academic plans.

Choosing Faculty Who Value Teaching

A key role for a program administrator (usually assisted by a faculty committee) is hiring faculty who are competent in their disciplines or fields. But discipline knowledge is insufficient; it is essential that faculty be competent as curriculum planners and teachers as well. Some universities where curriculum and instructional matters are discussed and valued are now including pedagogical skills and knowledge of how academic plans might be constructed in their doctoral programs, so we may predict that some new faculty members will have the requisite interest and skills. Other candidates will learn on the job either by their individual efforts or because their colleges and programs value teaching and create opportunities.

The importance of curriculum planning and teaching skills and interest should be stated in the advertisements for every faculty position. Candidates should be asked for position papers or statements of philosophy about curriculum development and, where possible, should submit actual course plans or syllabi they have constructed. The hiring process should include discussions of both course planning and teaching; this strategy safeguards against flashy seminar presentations without a solidly developed and clear academic plan. Finally, if feasible, a representative should observe the faculty candidate actually teaching on his or her current campus.

The leader of a faculty group in curriculum development also needs to provide ways for faculty to develop and maintain their competence in both subject matter and curriculum planning. Administrators send clear messages when they sponsor faculty travel to instructionally-related conferences as well as to discipline conferences, encourage exchange visits with other campuses to discuss curriculum development at the program level, or hold workshops on campus. A potent example of a positive change agent in our experience is an academic vice-president who not only organized curriculum development workshops but participated fully in every session.

Stressing the Centrality of Learners

An administrator who supports curriculum development will be careful to emphasize the centrality of students as learners. Because many administrative problems may deflect attention from student needs, such an emphasis may require conscious effort, particularly in colleges and universities where research or service are also important accepted missions. Alexander Astin (1979, 1991b) urged colleges and universities to take a moral stance about their enterprise by incorporating a philosophy of student development into their administrative actions. This philosophy should be multidimensional, encompassing students' cognitive skills, socialization, and career preparation. Based on the view that the teaching mission of colleges is central, Astin contended that college administrators should act on three assumptions: (1) that the principal function of educational administration is to enhance student development, (2) that the ultimate goal of acquiring resources is to use the resources in educational processes, and (3) that institutional quality should be measured in relation to student development goals (Astin, 1979, p. 4)

Adapting Astin's assumptions to administering academic plans, we note that the first assumption concerns developing the plan (and thus incorporates mission and purpose), the second concerns implementation of the plan, and the third concerns its evaluation. An administrator who tries to act on these assumptions will support curriculum decisions more effectively than one who sees administrative decisions as ends in themselves.

Administrators who believe learners are central will insist that profiles of student characteristics and achievement are routinely generated and supplied to faculty members and programs for discussion as they plan and adjust academic plans. These administrators will be directly involved in the improvement of all types of counseling services: academic, personal, and career. Recognizing that both academic departments and student services departments serve the cause of student learning, they will foster open dialogues between the two about curriculum development. In Astin's (1991b) words, "the values of an institution are reflected in the kinds of information that it collects about itself and pays attention to" (p. 27).

Promoting Goal Congruence

Periodic discussions about goals are valuable even if an institution is not planning extensive curriculum change. One important but often neglected task of the administrator is to ensure that program-level goals are congruent with the college mission. Often, congruency helps to determine the extent to which the program is eligible for limited or finite resources. Such external forces as accreditation, state examination requirements, and the need to collaborate with practice sites also require administrative attention to program goals in academic planning but college goals should be discussed in their own right, not simply when external influences urge their attention. Administrators must also examine the salience or compatibility of college goals, program goals, and student goals. All are important influences on curriculum planning and must be well understood and consciously addressed.

Guidelines for Assuring the Centrality of Teaching, Learning, and College Goals in Academic Plans: The Producer and Director Roles

- Ensure that newly hired faculty demonstrate skills in course planning and teaching. Seek new faculty with training in curriculum and instruction. Seek experienced faculty with a record of cooperative team membership in curriculum development. Give equal attention to enhancing the curriculum planning skills of current faculty.

- Be sure that faculty have the expertise and commitment necessary for the programs planned. If necessary, provide opportunity and incentives for expanding expertise. Resist creating programs based on vague promises of sufficient expertise.

- Provide information about students' characteristics and goals necessary for faculty to develop effective academic plans.

- Assess curriculum change proposals in light of both student characteristics and interests and also the potential impact of these changes on students.

- Link new and revised academic plans with known student goals and planned student outcomes. At the outset of the new curriculum, create a plan for assessing student learning and goal achievement.

- Be sure that curriculum proposals are consistent with college goals and with the college's public image. Invite participation from a wide spectrum of constituents during the early stages of curriculum development. But be sure it is clear that faculty and administrators are seeking advice, rather than making commitments to respond to special interest groups.

- Determine that academic plans at the program level link with college mission. Help faculty resist the temptation to offer programs that are beyond the scope of the institutional mission or that have been assigned to other institutional units.

- Be sure that faculty have an opportunity to associate with curriculum projects most in accord with their values and ideas. However, resist developing programs and sequences of courses that relate only to faculty interests but which ignore students' interests and demand.

Coordinating Academic Planning (Managerial Role: Coordinator)

Several types of academic programs require the coordinator role at the college level because they involve students and faculty from more than one academic planning unit. These include, for example, (1) general education programs, (2) developmental or remedial programs, (3) linkages among programs collaborating to prepare traditional majors, (4) interdisciplinary specializations, and (5) articulation with feeder schools (high schools or community colleges) or graduate schools. These organizational linkages may demand more administrative coordination than academic plans that are contained completely within the bounds of disciplines and professional majors where faculty commitment may be stronger. In fact, programs spanning organizational boundaries are so frequently neglected that they are sometimes called educational "orphans." When organizational units compete for limited resources, nurturing such programs may particularly require astute conflict resolution as well as protection and encouragement.

Providing Linkages and Encouraging Articulation

Earlier, we emphasized the importance of clearly designated administrative structure for programs that are not under the purview of specific disciplines and suggested some dialogues that might improve the integration of liberal and professional study. We return to these issues of linkage and coordination in both of these cases here.

General and Developmental Education. One of the reasons that general and developmental education seem to need frequent revamping is the traditional lack of administrative responsibility and concern for these areas. Lack of coordination contributes to the gradual attenuation of general education goals and to the proliferation of course options within core and distribution requirements. Many colleges now revising their general education programs recognize these trends and are, for the first time, establishing special associate dean positions for the continued coordination of this program. An appropriate next step is the assignment of a budget and a stable core faculty.

Developmental education programs now exist in most colleges and universities. Several important decisions concern whether students who need remedial work should be required to take them, whether the courses carry credit, how they articulate with nondevelopmental general education courses, and which faculty will be involved in planning and teaching them. Efficient administrative coordination requires strong leadership to achieve consensus about the philosophy of developmental education, to acquire resources, to implement the program, and to track results. Administrators at Miami-Dade Community Colleges provided this type of strong leadership to develop a system that guides students to courses of the proper level and tracks their progress by computer.

Interprogram Links. Many academic fields connect two or more related fields of study. One field may serve the other, as biology serves the needs of students in nursing, or they may be related, each reinforcing the other, as with biology courses for chemistry majors and chemistry courses for biology majors. Commonly, faculty designing plans at the program level overlook the need to coordinate these efforts with related departments. We recall two colleges where a professional field predicated its whole curriculum sequence on the assumed adoption of a new general education program. When the proposed general education program was defeated by the liberal arts faculty, the professional field was in serious trouble. Effective academic planning means not only that administrators must be alert to issues of smooth linkage but also that they develop efforts to promote multidisciplinary approaches involving more than one program. Administrators who have a broad view of several academic programs are in the best position to guide such efforts.

Interdisciplinary programs link academic plans so that students can structure specially-tailored curricula. An interdisciplinary program may depend on a fairly permanent link between two or more academic units or may be individualized for a specific student. Interdisciplinary programs are becoming increasingly important in educating students to tackle today's problems; yet they challenge faculty security because they require new organizational relationships. Because the relationship between faculty in different programs can be fragile, sensitive coordination is needed.

Articulation. In contrast to interdisciplinary programs, aggressive coordination is needed to develop articulation agreements. As students increasingly move among collegiate institutions and educational levels, coordination of their progress and advising is required. In institutions where many students transfer from lower division colleges (such as in the California State University system), administrators, counselors, and faculty members must help students choose an academic plan that builds on previous work. Administrators may have to insist that agreements about the transferability of courses be worked out despite faculty concerns about comparable content or quality.

Community colleges and nonselective liberal arts colleges are both influenced by the fact that their students often transfer to other institutions before completing a degree. Similarly, the receiving institutions, often four-year state colleges and universities, are influenced by the preparation of transfer students coming from other institutions. This influence has grown apace over the last fifty years and is now very strong. For example, in Arizona, all of the accounting programs at several Mesa Community College campuses teach a course strongly influenced by the receiving programs at Arizona State University. The successful effort to work out this articulation was a lengthy process.

Examining Administrative Functions, Structures, Policies, and Processes

People create the educational environment in which curriculum development takes place by developing policies and by creating structures and processes. In their role as leaders, administrators have the best opportunities to examine functions, structures, policies, and processes to be sure they support effective curriculum development. Although the demarcations are not always clear, administrative functions include tasks which support the academic programs either directly or indirectly; structures refer to enduring channels of communication, influence, or practice that influence how academic programs operate; policies refer to deliberate rules of operation that influence the academic program; and processes are the various ways that positions, structures, and policies actually interact to produce behavior.

Administrative Functions.   Most institutions need more dialogue about the roles and responsibilities of administrators and faculty with respect to curriculum. Particularly in large universities where top administration is far removed from the academic program, some faculty are disgruntled about substantial growth in the number of administrators who seem to have no positive impact on students' education. A healthy habit is to ask whether an administrative position fills the goal of freeing faculty to use their time and expertise for what they do best. This question should be asked publicly to reinforce the college mission and the high expectations held for quality educational programs.

Structures.   It is also important to publicly ask substantive questions about how administrative structures like budgets and facilities support the academic plan. In addition, all academically-related structures should be examined periodically for their impact on academic plans. Many structures—credits, degrees, grades, testing procedures, academic calendars, advising systems, and articulation practices—exist by tradition but affect and constrain the sequence of academic plans. Just as zero-based budgeting might cause us to examine expenditures, administrators might temporarily assume that these "curricular structures" do not exist and consider how they might therefore be alternatively conceived.

Policies.   Academic policies are codified rules and regulations which often are based on the assumption that current structures are appropriate. These include policies regarding comprehensive examinations, laboratories, practica, internships, apprenticeships, cooperative education, credit by examination, and credit for experience. To illustrate, the specific amount of academic credit students may gain through examination is a policy, but this policy depends on the existence of a credit structure. It would be a moot policy if credit as a coin of academic transaction were abolished. Like structures, policies should be reexamined regularly for their fit with educational mission and purpose, like instructional processes chosen at the course level, program level policies influence student outcomes. Policies on such issues as course enrollment, use of library reserves, faculty workload, course prerequisites, and registration procedures should therefore be reviewed and adjusted periodically.

Processes.   The process by which curriculum change takes place is also important. Some procedures may reinforce resistance to change, desired in some settings, but ill advised in others. For example, one university's written policy on changing course titles and descriptions or numbers requires that a course change must be originated at the department level (except in a set of approved interdisciplinary programs that allow other origins), and be approved by the (1) department, (2) college, (3) University Council (possibly the Graduate Council as well), (4) the University Senate, and (5) the University Governing Board. For more substantive changes that might be construed as affecting a program or changing a degree level, the State Coordinating Board must also approve. One can only imagine how stagnant business enterprises would become if relatively minor changes in operating procedure had to follow such a route for approval. Many more examples of similarly cumbersome processes could be given, all contributing to the inertia reputedly characteristic of curricular change in colleges and universities. Recently, under the umbrella of CQI (an adaptation of the Total Quality Management concept in business) college administrators have begun to examine structures, policies, and processes in light of the total educational purpose and service to students.

Guidelines for Coordinating Curriculum Plans and Planning Processes: The Coordinator Role

- Appoint strong leaders to see that the general education and remedial programs are well planned and institutionalized.
- Develop systematic methods to identify duplication or needed links in existing or proposed curriculum among departments. Seek economical solutions to duplication while safeguarding precious faculty autonomy and disciplinary identity.
- Encourage faculty to experiment with interdisciplinary relationships, recognizing and supporting the risks they take.
- Make articulation a priority; student needs, not administrative convenience, should take first place.
- Work with faculty to develop realistic expectations and a time line for discussing curriculum change and implementation. Allow sufficient time for the impact of proposals to be fully discussed but not belabored. Encourage, and if necessary insist, that decisions be made, not avoided. Streamline curriculum change processes.
- Require that new proposals have a clear time line for implementation that does not disadvantage enrolled students.
- Be sure counselors and students are informed well in advance of new requirements. Interpret changes and their rationale fully to students.

Implementing Academic Plans (Managerial Roles: Broker; Coordinator)

When faculty construct academic plans, they make two major choices about the means of implementation: selecting resources and selecting instructional processes. Often the two choices are linked, just as planning and teach-

ing are linked. The administrative role includes enlarging the set of alternatives from which faculty may choose, and reducing the constraints on their choices. In this sense the administrator may serve, not only as coordinator, but also as broker of new knowledge and practices.

Facilitating Instructional Choices

Faculty need considerable autonomy and flexibility to choose appropriate instructional processes. Increasingly professors work with other faculty members (and sometimes developers or media experts) as partners in curriculum development. It is important to hold equally high expectations for both individual and team development although the first is done in relative seclusion and the second is more open to scrutiny. It is also important to provide faculty with opportunities to try different processes freely.

Books, newsletters, and checklists are available to help faculty think about new alternatives as instructional choices. An administrator might, for example, supply copies of the Faculty Inventory of Good Practice in Undergraduate Education (Chickering, Gamson, & Barsi, 1989) which helps faculty rate themselves in six categories of good instructional practice: (1) encouraging student–faculty contact, (2) encouraging cooperation among students, (3) encouraging active learning, (4) giving prompt feedback, (5) emphasizing time on task, and (6) communicating high expectations. At the same time, administrators might assess the overall environment using the parallel Institutional Inventory which covers (1) classroom climate, (2) academic practices, (3) curriculum, (4) faculty, (5) academic support and student services, and (6) facilities.

Providing Resources

Some choices that faculty make as they design academic plans seem to be the results of contextual constraints; these include secretarial assistance, schedules, class sizes, rewards and incentives, and other working conditions. College teachers are so accustomed to accommodating constraints that they are not fully aware of them until the lack becomes acute or they become aware of an exciting foregone opportunity, but observers might attribute great influence to them if they visited some classrooms or departments and observed working conditions that are far inferior to those in business. Surely, the length of the scheduled class hour and fixed seats in lecture halls propel one toward the lecture, vacations influence the scheduling of tests and the sequencing of material, inadequate word-processing service contributes to infrequent or hastily done handouts, and class size often constrains active learning activities. One important role for the administrator, increasing budget problems notwithstanding, is to create discontent by making new and better alternatives more visible.

Providing Central Services and Facilities

Typically, a collegewide administrator is responsible for coordinating some central services and units that serve many or all programs in the college. Such service units include learning skills centers, libraries, audiovisual centers, computer centers, instructional development centers, career counseling centers, and bookstores. Supportive services also include test scoring and analysis, advising, and faculty workshops. The fact that faculty do not use these services extensively may argue that administrators should play a stronger brokering role that exposes additional faculty to more alternatives. In some colleges, where an unfortunate stigma has become attached to the use of instructional development centers, administrators may need to take a strong hand in changing the ethos. Another challenge is presented by the rapid increase in computer use for both planning and implementing academic plans. Ad-

ministrators need regularly to ascertain that all of these units and services support both the process of curriculum planning and the implementation of the plans.

Guidelines for Implementing Academic Planning: The Coordinator and Broker Roles

- Be sure financial resources are adequate to carry out academic plans and that the proposals demonstrate a reasonable cost per student. Do not encourage faculty to establish new programs first and plan to use them later to justify the need for additional funds.

- Be sure that needed facilities for new programs have been fully determined and that they exist or can be acquired. Be sure that facilities for existing programs are regularly and openly reviewed to be sure they support educational goals and processes.

- Use the Inventory of Good Practice in Undergraduate Education (Chickering, Gamson, & Barsi, 1987) to encourage professors to select active instructional processes. Increase awareness of the importance of teacher–student interaction.

- Develop opportunities for professors to learn about and select from a wide variety of instructional processes and to experiment with them in their academic plans.

- Identify opportunities for training in both subject matter and pedagogy that faculty will need. Suggest and provide resources for training opportunities.

Encouraging Evaluation (Managerial Role: Monitor)

Adjustments based on evaluation paths A and B in our model help to modify the college's academic plans directly; changes based on the external cycle (Path C) do so more indirectly by interpreting the views of society to the college, and interpreting the college's processes and outcomes to external constituents. Administrators often must move between the roles of mentor, facilitator, producer, moderator, and coordinator in the internal evaluation path, and the roles of innovator, broker, and monitor in the external evaluation path. Thus, academic administrators who work with curriculum evaluation actually use all of the managerial roles outlined in the competing values typology.

Establishing Evaluation Plans and Expectations

In public colleges, periodic evaluation cycles may be dictated by governmental agencies as well as accreditors; in independent colleges the leadership and accreditors have more leeway in determining the evaluation patterns. Numerous models of cyclical and collaborative evaluation processes are available to guide administrators at each type of college in evaluating curriculum.

Evaluation professionals agree that evaluating academic plans at any level requires a careful four-phase process: (1) planning, (2) information collection, (3) judgment, and (4) use of judgments. This is particularly true when many stakeholders are involved. Evaluation plans and procedures often must be acceptable to a wide variety of interested groups, including employers, graduate schools, transfer institutions, discipline associations, and state and federal officials. The definition of evaluation to be used should be deliberately chosen and the purpose clearly stated. Except in goal-free evaluation, criteria must be established to judge merit and worth. The plan should specify the decision makers, the specific object or target of the evaluation, the projected use of the information, and the clients who will gain. Faculty, especially, must understand the advantages of evaluation and have sufficient opportunity to weigh proposed adjustments before deciding to incorporate them into academic plans.

Developing Faculty Skills

Faculty members may need some new skills to strengthen their role in evaluating academic plans. Administrators who have supported teams of faculty in attending national assessment and evaluation conferences held since 1985 tell us that a productive interchange occurs among faculty members as evaluation strategies are devised and introduced. It may be important for administrators to initiate workshops on campus as well.

For informal methods such as classroom research, instructors need primarily a willingness to examine some of the appropriate techniques and courage to use them. For formal methods such as goal-focused evaluation, they need a knowledge of testing principles, and particularly an understanding of the limitations on test results and their attribution. To identify change through students' test scores and attribute it to classroom events, faculty will need some statistical capability. If departments need consultants, they may often be found among social science faculty or institutional researchers.

To help plan an expanded evaluation program, faculty need to gather information and use it well. Collaborative work is part of the planning process and faculty therefore also need good interpersonal skills, teamwork skills, and the willingness and ability to understand others' points of view. The traditional privacy of planning and teaching courses is reduced when a program group engages in a well-planned evaluation program; such collaboration requires new approaches.

Finally, if evaluation is to be a positive experience for faculty, rather than a burden, trained observers and helpers will be needed to collect and process data. If confidentiality is protected by coding records, student workers can assist with these tasks and gain from the experience. Ultimately, administrators have the responsibility for seeing that all of these conditions are possible.

Maintaining Evaluation Standards

Evaluation professionals have developed a set of standards—a sort of code of ethics for the appropriate conduct of evaluation and the use of results for improvement. These standards include statements about:

1. Utility standards: Ensuring that the evaluation provides practical information
2. Feasibility standards: Ensuring that the evaluation is realistic and prudent
3. Propriety standards: Ensuring that the evaluation is conducted legally and ethically
4. Accuracy standards: Ensuring that the evaluation reveals and conveys technically adequate information (Joint Committee, 1981, pp. 13–15)

Although administrators may delegate many of the details of the evaluation of academic plans to faculty, they should be sure that these standards are available, understood, and used. A set of similar guidelines, specifically for assessment of student learning outcomes, was recently developed by the American Association for Higher Education (1992) (see Table 11-2).

Using Evaluation Results Internally

One important role for the administrator is the interpretation and use of evaluation plans and results within the college. Administrators can encourage faculty members to evaluate and make their own interpretations of academic plans at the course level by encouraging the formative use of mid-semester student evaluations and classroom assessment techniques. Internal audiences for these evaluation results include faculty within a specific program, faculty in related programs who

TABLE 11-2   Principles of Good Practice for Assessing Student Learning

1. The assessment of student learning begins with educational values.
2. Assessment is most effective when it reflects an understanding of learning as multidimensional, integrated, and revealed in performance over time.
3. Assessment works best when the programs it seeks to improve have clear, explicitly stated purposes.
4. Assessment requires attention to outcomes but also and equally to the experiences that lead to those outcomes.
5. Assessment works best when it is ongoing, not episodic.
6. Assessment fosters wider improvement when representatives from across the educational community are involved.
7. Assessment makes a difference when it begins with issues of use and illuminates questions that people really care about.
8. Assessment is most likely to lead to improvement when it is part of a larger set of conditions that promote change.
9. Through assessment, educators meet responsibilities to students and to the public.

Source: Principles of Good Practice for Assessing Student Learning, AAHE Assessment Forum, American Association for Higher Education, 1992.

may learn from the efforts of others, and the students who participated in the evaluation. Externally, trustees, sponsors, employers, foundations, and state coordinating agencies may also be important. At the program level, the process of self-study is essential if gradual improvement is the intended result, but for administrators there is no escaping the responsibility for program review that moves beyond educational considerations to cost-effectiveness and considerations of worth and merit. Program review usually includes non-outcome measures about the program such as the number of graduates, enrollment, class size, course cost, workloads, cost per graduate, and national ratings of quality. Program review is often connected with budget allocations and efficiency dimensions, ideas most faculty find alien.

If evaluation or assessment results are to be used for administrative decisions such as program reduction or enhancement, administrators are wise to develop a flow chart and guidelines of the entire evaluation process in advance so that questions of fairness or appropriateness to the programs can be raised and dealt with early. The type of guidelines that are acceptable to faculty will vary with discipline. The process must be complete enough to be credible but not so cumbersome that an evaluation cycle will never be completed. A method should be included for evaluating the evaluation process itself, adjusting it make it more useful.

To maintain a supportive climate, indicators used for program evaluation should address important educational outcomes to the greatest possible extent, not merely outcomes that are easily measured. They should include reliable and valid indicators of the learning that are simple enough to be understood by faculty who are not professional evaluators and by the public. Even the best measures are unlikely to demonstrate clearly that the educational outcomes were produced only by the formal educational process, so such claims should be avoided. Evaluation methods can, however, statistically control for many differences in student knowledge or attitudes at the beginning of the educational program. Whenever possible, such controls should be implemented and standard educational research methods used to increase credibility of the evaluation.

Not all evaluation that deserves feedback and discussion involves educational research methods, however. Traditional methods such as peer reviews continue to be important and could be strengthened. Administrators can encourage effective reviews by providing

committees with clear charges, attending key meetings, setting the stage for committee reports, reading and commenting on reports, and publicizing them. But administrators can also cast peer review in a positive light and help faculty use these reviews to build better programs. Finally, administrators can sponsor open dialogue about a program's self-study or review results for institutional research purposes.

Meta-evaluation, the evaluation of an evaluation, leads us to improve not only procedures but knowledge about how procedures work. It should also help us improve the process of evaluating and adjusting. Administrators can use meta-evaluation to check for unintended consequences of evaluation. For example, students may experience negative effects of outcomes assessments, such as test anxiety or test fatigue. Similarly, anxious faculty may teach for the test or fear improper use of student assessments for faculty evaluation. Positive effects may include an increased sense of community among faculty, clarification of teaching goals and strategies, and increased sense of student responsibility for personal growth.

Interpreting Evaluation Results Externally

States and the federal government have increasingly initiated evaluative activities. By federal mandate, accrediting associations now require member institutions to evaluate student learning systematically by measuring appropriate outcomes of the educational process. Since they continue to see accreditors as ineffective quality monitors and instititution as lackadaisical in evaluation, government agencies have begun to develop standards and measurement indicators for skills to be learned in college (Edgerton, 1991; National Center for Education Statistics, 1992). In this context, it is unclear who will set standards for student learning in the future. Currently, the administrative task of developing cooperative relationships with state and federal officials and accreditors may also mean providing appropriate data about student outcomes to all three external agencies and resisting demands for data that may inappropriately represent an institution's educational program. Administrators need to keep abreast of the trends in this matter of external monitoring and they may wish to help develop stronger evaluation models or accrediting mechanisms rather than accept the federal government's interpretation of what constitutes appropriate general education outcomes. Because national standards might be used to make inappropriate comparisons of student outcomes among colleges and programs, administrators must establish models for use of evaluation results. Especially when the results of achievement examinations are discussed publicly, administrators must be particularly careful about making attributions where none are merited.

Because college enrollments are regulated by many states and linked with funding mechanisms, faculty and administrators must consider the advantages and disadvantages of making evaluation results for programs or divisions open to the public. Although there is a need to ensure mission achievement and to publicize the achievement to external audiences, declines in public faith in colleges have made it a tough act to balance candor with achieving external credibility.

Another important decision is whether to link student test results or peer reviews to program budgeting. While some applaud incentive funding others are convinced that this procedure presents artificial incentives and can lead to both misuse and abuse of evaluation data. Decisions about this matter depend heavily on the history and context at specific institutions.

Evaluating and Interpreting: Guidelines for the Monitor Role

- Establish a complete plan for evaluating both existing and new curricula, and follow up to see that it is undertaken. Anticipate well in advance the collection of data for future evaluations and accreditations.

- Devote at least as much time in public speeches and discussions to curriculum evaluation as to budget documents, financial planning, and building needs.

- Monitor evaluation processes carefully to be sure that attribution is not made where none is demonstrated.

- Develop careful feedback procedures for the internal use of evaluation information. Develop guidelines for the use of evaluation information to influence external constituencies. For example: (1) don't promise more than the institution can deliver; (2) get involved in developing state policies rather than reacting to them; (3) be positive in finding compromises with policymakers, not defensive; (4) supervise the college image that the public relations office is developing; (5) anticipate crises and develop contingency responses in advance; and (6) place personal meetings with important external figures high on the agenda.

Adjusting Academic Plans (Managerial Roles: Monitor; Facilitator)

Most adjustments faculty make in existing course and program plans tend to be routine and regular rather than substantial or dramatic. Similarly, when administrators and faculty foster changes in a college's educational environment, the changes tend to be gradual and of modest scope. Sometimes a change in the local environment sufficiently supports change or stimulates creativity to produce substantially new courses or programs. And sometimes creative academic leaders may encourage changes that can be classed as "innovations"—curriculum change based on a new concept, idea, or practice that departs radically from tradition in a specific college or program (Seymour, 1988).

While routine changes and new programs meeting specific needs derive mainly from internal influences, innovations typically stem from external influences acting on the educational environment and are usually guided by faculty and administration leaders who are attuned to these influences. We argue, therefore, that the two most common levels (routine adjustment and new program development) require administrators to act primarily as monitors and facilitators, roles characterized by internal processes and modest control. The third category, innovation, requires a much stronger external focus, a high degree of flexibility, and thus a different administrative role, that of innovator. We will discuss the monitoring role that administrators play in adjusting academic plans and creating substantially new programs in this section, and return to discussion of innovation as a separate issue.

Administering Curriculum Adjustments

The roles theorists describe for various internal change agents—the rational planner, the collaborator, the facilitator, and the linker or broker (see Lindquist 1974, pp. 148–149)—are congruent with some of the managerial/administrative roles we outlined earlier from Quinn's competing values model. Faculty leaders as well as administrators may play these roles. Much depends on what type of expertise is required in the specific change proposed and how credibility can be enhanced. Other studies also suggest that administrators interested in leading change will want to shift among Quinn's managerial roles as the change process progresses (Davis, Strand, Alexander, & Hussain, 1982).

Colleges traditionally have placed strong emphasis on achieving consensus and commitment to change at the lowest organizational level where curricular decisions are

often made. The collaborative, facilitative, and linking roles are most appropriate when the leader is less expert in the discipline or career field than the followers—surely the case when the leader/change agent is a collegewide administrator. When the leader possesses expertise—as is usually the case at the program chair level—these roles continue to be important, but the leader may also provide stronger leadership for curriculum change by taking a rational planner role.

We often assume that curriculum change is (or should be) the result of rational planning and this is the basis on which we have proposed adjustments based on evaluation. Yet we know that practice deviates from this model; models other than rationality are not only common but legitimate. Building on the earlier work of Havelock, Nordvall (1982) identified several change models used in higher education which vary in origin and use. In Table 11-3 we give the types of change and, in parentheses, their origins. All of the models may apply at the course, program, and college levels. We will elaborate here on the rational models, including the research and development model and the problem-solving model, since these are usually applicable to

---

TABLE 11-3   Models of Curriculum Change

1. Research, development, and diffusion models (based on logical/rational decision making)

2. Problem-solving models (based on identified need or action research)

3. Social interaction models (stimulated by opinion leaders)

4. Political or conflict models (stimulated by coalitions and pressure groups)

5. Linkage or adaptive development models (multiple sources, combines other models)

Source: Adapted from *The Process of Change in Higher Education Institutions* by R. C. Nordvall (1982). Used by permission of the American Association for Higher Education, Washington, D.C..

adjustments in the curriculum or the development of substantially new programs.

The research and development model of curriculum change depends on convincing arguments buttressed by research programs that identify a need for change and suggest a carefully-tested logical alternative. For example, an academic plan might be developed when research shows that embedding writing instruction in course material from the student's regular planned program is more effective than teaching writing separately from other studies. Such rational models may, in fact, be the least common for change in higher education curriculum, particularly since systematic goal-focused evaluation and research to identify and test alternatives are atypical for course and programs.

The problem-solving model originates in a felt need for change (based on either an internal or external diagnosis), a consequent willingness to change, and a deliberate search by organizational members for alternative solutions. Often solutions are found by examining what colleagues in similar settings are doing. This model, related to the well-accepted professional judgment approach to evaluation and adjustment, is fairly common in course and program planning. Earlier, we mentioned how professors can use classroom assessment techniques to improve their courses. At the program level, similar informal techniques help to gather information to diagnose the need for change. For example, faculty may rearrange the sequence of courses within a program because they sense that students who learn the concepts in a different sequence perform better in subsequent study.

Leadership always plays an important role in encouraging adjustments as well as in more substantial change that responds to both external and internal influences. Higher education has many change leaders but not all have the authority (or the persistence) to bring about the changes they propose. On any given issue, different perspectives on the proposed change and different power structures exist at each level and setting. Decentralization and diversity in higher education mean that many actors are involved in stimulating change. The potency of any particular agent or change strategy will differ with the issue at hand. When adjustments to courses and programs are pursued by rational or problem-solving modes, the steps taken parallel the major tasks in administering academic plans that we have already outlined: develop the purpose, implement the plan, and evaluate the results (see Figure 11-2). We turn now to some information about change strategies that may be useful to leaders who desire to use rational models to introduce substantial adjustments such as new programs.

Selecting and Using Effective Change Strategies

Major curriculum changes have frequently been achieved by creating new institutions or departments and by recruiting leaders with commitment to a given idea (Levine, 1978, p. 418). Since new funds for alternative programs and institutions are severely restricted today, substantial program adjustments may well depend on refining systematic change processes and giving more deliberate attention to opportunities. To us, these conditions highlight the need for colleges to select and train administrators and faculty leaders in using change strategies effectively.

Leaders of substantial change especially may need to be focused on mission, sensitive to opportunities in the external environment, communicative, willing to take risks, and prone to ask difficult questions (Seymour, 1988, pp. 14–17). They must be aware of four specific sets of characteristics known to affect the rate and success of change in college settings: (1) the characteristics of the proposed change; (2) the structure of the environment or situation; (3) the extent of involvement of those affected; and (4) the type of leadership (Rogers, 1968).

First, a proposed change has a better chance of adoption if it demonstrates relative advantage over the current situation, is compatible with current norms and expectations, is easy to understand and adopt, can readily be communicated and described, and is divisible so that it can be implemented in parts. These characteristics, of course, help to support curriculum adjustments made on a regular basis as well as more substantial changes such as new courses or programs.

The second set of characteristics includes the supportive educational environment we have already discussed including: (1) an open decision structure distinguished by free communication patterns, widespread involvement of faculty, effective group processes, and decentralized decision making, (2) consensus about institutional or program goals, coupled with a spirit of self-evaluation, (3) an accepted pattern for achieving change, (4) a clear expectation that change will occur when needs are identified, and (5) an appropriate reward system. Researchers remain ambiguous about whether financial instability or other strong environmental uncertainties promote or hinder change. Unstable conditions are believed to promote adaptive change in some settings, and hinder it in others. Possibly it depends on whether faculty and administrators perceive change as an opportunity rather than a threat.

The third generalization concerns involvement. Change seldom occurs in higher education curricula if faculty lack interest, motivation, or incentives to change. The way college faculty groups are organized tends to retard change and must be counterbalanced by strong interest. In addition to the organizational inertia typical in most settings, a special inertia develops in colleges when faculty become isolated into subgroups based on strong discipline identities, when departments and programs exercise their pluralistic power to

adopt or resist, when faculty tend to preserve traditional meritocratic college policies, and when educational outcomes are inadequately measured (Lindquist, 1974, 1978). Sometimes faculty are unwilling to be involved in change efforts because they find that the energy required is too great or their time too limited in comparison to the success or rewards expected. They also find it hard to admit that something they created at an earlier time really needs to be changed.

Finally, the fourth predictor of successful change is the type of leadership. As we have mentioned, leadership in colleges is expected to come from among those with expertise closest to the issue. Writing on change in general education, Gaff (1980) suggested that administrators should provide faculty task forces with support, encourage them to work visibly, and expect them to oversee the implementation of the change as well as recommend it. Although the difficulties of getting approval for curriculum changes in collegewide governance bodies are legendary, Gaff stressed that a single defeat for an important change proposal in an academic governance system should not cause the task force to abandon its work or the administration to take ownership. An initial defeat often achieves visibility and encourages other faculty to get involved and coalesce. Such strategies may be most effective in small colleges with a strong tradition of faculty leadership. Administrators may need to play a stronger coordinating and implementing role in larger institutions.

Recognizing Change Decisions

The type of leadership may particularly affect the type of change decisions, an important factor in whether change endures. Because of the autonomy enjoyed by faculty members, decisions to change academic plans are not always final or binding; they can be (1) optional for members, (2) contingent (i.e., rewards and incentives accrue to those who adopt the change), (3) collective (i.e., by agreement all should adopt), or (4) dictated by authority (Rogers, 1968). The extensive differences in educational purpose and pedagogical world views among disciplines and professional fields make it very likely that most curriculum change decisions in large colleges and universities will be optional or contingent. Small colleges or single-purpose colleges within a university may be more likely to reach collective agreements. In unionized colleges or occasionally in small denominational colleges, authority may rule. For example, Alfred and Linder (1990, p. 7) report that strategic decisions in community colleges are made 40% of the time by the president and board of trustees with little faculty involvement.

The type of decision for adoption may also vary with the level of the academic plan. The closer the level of the academic plan to the specific discipline expertise of faculty, the more fully faculty will be involved and, thus, potentially committed to, a specific curriculum change. Collective decisions are more likely at the program level than at the collegewide level where conflict models tend to favor optional or contingent decisions. The classic example of a contingent decision is probably the adoption of distribution requirements. The requirements provide flexibility and options for both students and faculty; but, in effect, they allow students the option of avoiding courses in certain subjects they perceive to be difficult, like mathematics and science. A related contingent decision is likely today as newly adopted general education core seminars focus on humanities, treating science and mathematics courses in the new required core as optional curricula because their content is "more structured" and may not lend itself to small-group discussion or problem-centered treatment. In part, a contingent adoption is used because the mathematics and science faculty are unwilling to create courses for nonscientists, and in part because many students will balk at studying this ma-terial in the core; in many colleges no one has full authority to force either group to join in a collective decision.

In a satirical essay, Cohen (1986), suggested that colleges avoid wasting time on debate and simply rotate among two versions of their curriculum every five years. This, he asserted, should satisfy those who desire change since curriculum changes seem to last no more than five years in any case. Some changes do persist but in other cases they revert because faculty and administrators cannot resist pressures from outside environments. (For example, in the face of graduate school demands for simple academic records, it is difficult to offer student profiles instead of traditional grades.) Also, in an open-decision environment, all decisions have opponents who may continue to work against them openly or covertly. Accordingly, many innovative curriculum changes in higher education have a tendency to revert to traditional forms, a process that may begin almost immediately after adoption. The death of a new program may be plotted by its enemies as carefully as its birth was attended by its friends.

Of course, this process of recurring patterns of change occurs on a macro level in higher education generally as well as on a micro level in courses, programs, and colleges. Examples abound of colleges that originated in the 1970s to focus on interdisciplinary study, independent learning, or nongraded study; many of these have now resumed more traditional practices of offering majors, minors, and grading systems (see Cardozier, 1993; Levine, 1978; and Townsend, Newell, & Weise, 1992, for discussions of some of these innovations). The recurring pattern is clearly illustrated in a 1986 proposal made by Frederick Starr, then president of Oberlin College for completion of the bachelor's degree in three years. Such a curriculum proposal was the subject of experiments popular in the 1940s, again in the 1970s (Stark, 1973), and yet again in the 1980s. In reflecting on these cycles of change, Fincher (1988) observed that higher education curriculum decisions take place by "provisional variation" and "selective retention" (p. 282). Like optional and contingent decisions, provisional variations are change decisions that are made consciously and tentatively, involving prolonged faculty debates and deliberation. Selective retention is the process of maintaining those variations that are subsequently seen as effective while allowing the rest to die an uncelebrated death. This process, according to Fincher, makes curricular change slow and indirect, rather than rapid and deliberate.

In this slow and indirect process, administrators play a small role in planning the content of the curriculum but a large role in establishing purpose, helping to set priorities, obtaining resources, and maintaining a supportive context. They play this role by fostering communication, supporting experimentation, and encouraging full consideration of decision alternatives in an atmosphere of trust. Just as the academic plan gives faculty members a guide to follow in developing curricula, it gives administrators a template to maintain a climate consistent with what is known about fostering change. We have incorporated some of the ideas from the change literature in the guidelines below.

Guidelines for Promoting Curriculum Adjustments (The Monitor and Facilitator Roles)

- All faculty members should have some involvement in decisions, although the involvement will differ by role.
- Communication should flow in all directions; all organizational members should be apprised of plans for change and of progress.
- Persons given responsibility for stimulating and implementing change should be knowledgeable, credible, and flexible.
- Goal consensus should be sought but leaders should be prepared to move forward with less than unanimity.
- All members of the organization should be encouraged to evaluate their own contributions and progress toward goals.
- The need for adjustments in reward systems should be foreseen and adjustments should be made at the beginning of a new program.
- New training needed for organizational members should be assured in advance.
- Administrative leaders should make public statements supporting the change and outlining their expectations for success.

EXTERNAL INFLUENCE, ADAPTIVE DEVELOPMENT, AND CHANGE

In a classic study, *Dynamics of Academic Reform* (1969), JB Lon Hefferlin tried to understand how curriculum changes occur. He generalized that change in higher education seldom occurs from the inside. Rather "outsiders initiate, insiders react." Based on his study, Hefferlin believed that the major problem in academic change is the difficulty of selecting among external ideas and using them to institute changes that will lead to improvement (p. 153). He noted, "Academic reform consists far more in the diffusion of educational ideas from one institution to another than in the creation of new ideas" (p. 156). Previously, we referred to this diffusion as "the bandwagon effect."

We know, however, that there are several models of curriculum change in addition to the bandwagon effect. We have discussed rational models used for internal adjustments: research and development, and problem solving. Other models respond more directly to external influences and may produce more dramatic change. In this section, we consider how external influences on the curriculum become part of the college's internal agenda, often leading to significant and responsive curriculum change, and sometimes resulting in innovations. This occurs through many change processes: social interaction, political conflict, and diffusion and adaptive development. These processes are not always distinct and they may operate simultaneously or in sequence.

Change that occurs through social interaction is not necessarily based on evidence or assessment of a need to change. Often exposure to an idea, persuasion from influential colleagues, the desire for social acceptability or prestige among peer colleges, or merely the sense that others are making the change is sufficient to initiate a pattern of rapid adoption that can be documented—the bandwagon approach. In some ways, this type of change could be viewed as goal-free because the objective for changing may be imprecisely formulated in the college that adopts it from another. An example is the 4-1-4 academic calendar adopted by a substantial number of small colleges during the 1970s. Motives ranged from improving financial stability to promoting learner development by making learning enjoyable, and (possibly) the mere appearance of responding to students. As a consequence of imprecise objectives, some colleges experienced unintended consequences such as accelerated programs of study leading to dormitory vacancies, obstacles for part-time students, and calendar rigidity that limited enrollment of mid-year transfer students (Stark, 1972). When change is based purely on social interaction and lacks clear goals, such unintended consequences may result in drift and help produce the recurring patterns of curriculum debate we have discussed.

Politically based change usually stems from social conflict or perceived social inequities. In some cases, because resulting changes are based disproportionately on the needs of interest groups who articulate them, change may be unstable or short-lived. However, in cases where the political conflict reflects changing societal norms or emerging

consensus, the change may be permanent. Increased access to higher education for underserved groups and incorporation of some of their culture into the curriculum is an example. Underserved groups struggled for many years to gain increased access to higher education and there were periods when opponents pitted concerns for quality against access. Today, it appears there is a strong commitment to access in most sectors of U.S. society; additional advances in access proceed according to other change models. Changes resulting from political conflict are often focused on real or perceived student needs.

Finally, change occurs through diffusion and adaptive development, a composite and complex process that exhibits characteristics of several change models. In diffusion models, opinion leaders or linking agents spread the word about change. A small number of individuals or institutions may be considered "early adopters," while other individuals or institutions take a wait-and-see attitude or are "laggards" (Lindquist, 1974). Diffusion is often slow, involving greater testing and adaptation in its new context than change based on social interaction. In these adaptive development processes colleges gradually adapt to turbulence in society, using a variety of processes and sources (Cameron, 1984). Since ideas are regularly diffusing and colleges are continually adapting, the composite diffusion and adaptive development model describes many externally driven curriculum changes rather well.

To illustrate how change may actually take place, we consider (from an outsider's perspective) a 1990s debate over changing the core of courses in Western Civilization at Stanford University. This highly publicized change appears to have followed a complex pattern involving several different change processes. A curriculum idea, originally introduced from outside the university by reform reports was consistent with an internal need (felt by at least some faculty and students) to adapt to changing times and a changing student body. These converging forces created increased awareness on campus including a diagnosis of the need to change. The solution devised involved modifying the core to include a greater range of cultural perspectives. Attempts to persuade faculty that (1) the diagnosis of a problem was correct and (2) that the solution offered was appropriate, subsequently led to political conflict as interest groups took positions on the new idea, engendering widespread campus or public debate even beyond the campus. Subsequently, even before the issue was resolved at Stanford, other colleges adopted ideas for changes being discussed there. These adoptions in other settings could be said to be stimulated by social interaction while Stanford was still in the adaptive development stage of testing the ideas and tailoring them to its own needs.

Because wide debate is so common on curriculum matters, many changes in academic plans that begin in a rational, problem-solving, or social interaction mode end up involving political conflict as well, as was apparently the case at Stanford. The extent of political conflict engendered may differ on each specific campus, but the process of change can be complex. Furthermore, the sequence in which different change processes occur may repeat. Curriculum changes that are introduced by opinion leaders or prestigious early adapters and that receive wide publicity are often assumed to be worthy of emulation by additional colleges before they actually demonstrate their worth.

The Influence Process and Stages of Internalization

A background of social or educational ferment often precedes major curriculum change and may affect nearly all aspects of an academic plan. Change usually results from multiple causes and has multiple effects, thus it is sometimes difficult to predict the form of adaptation and accommodations within a specific environment. For example, in the 1960s an influx of older students into higher education helped to bring about changes in degree time spans, credit by experience, and the development of nontraditional colleges. These changes occurred in a time of budget growth in higher education and emphasis on increasing access. It would be difficult to assign credit for development of "colleges without walls" to either one of these influences alone. Sometimes each college has a unique series of "critical events" leading to change (Finkelstein et al., 1984).

The relative strength of internal, organizational and external influences varies over time and specific forces within each of the influence categories change in potency. To illustrate, government policies always influence the educational environments of colleges and universities but government is more active at some times than at others. Its specific emphases also change periodically. During one period government funding might strongly support development of occupational programs in community colleges; during a subsequent period government agencies might criticize colleges for overspecialization and encourage them to deemphasize occupational programs and place more emphasis on basic communication skills or preparing students for transfer. Because curriculum reflects society, public opinion and external influences act powerfully over time to produce substantial curriculum change but, over the short term, the direction may be inconsistent.

The open boundaries between colleges and society foster interaction among internal, organizational and external influences and allow for transformation of one type of influence to others especially as it moves from society to campus. Notably, when specific external influences are sufficiently powerful (such as those supported by legal or fiscal authority), convincing (such as those that present strong ethical and moral obligations for colleges), or economically-sound (necessary for the nation's economic and civic welfare or defense) they may gradually come to become viewed by college personnel as internal, rather than external, forces. This evolutionary process takes place at different rates, depending on the influence and context. Other less powerful external influences are not internalized but fall by the wayside—for example, when political forces in power change, authorized funding is not forthcoming, or the nation turns its attention to other more immediate matters. The open boundary between colleges and society refutes the common stereotype of the university as an ivory tower, insulated from the society it serves. Rather the boundary is permeable as colleges accept and adapt to external influences and begin to see them as organizational and internal imperatives.

Further, our observations suggest that the movement of influences across boundaries can be linked to varied stages in the change process. Three stages of change accepted by all theorists (regardless of terms used and regardless of whether they are emphasizing rational change or diffusion and adaptation) are *initiation* (or awareness) *screening* (adaptation), and *adoption* (confirmation) (See Table 11-4). These stages or phases are related to the sources of influence urging the change, moving gradually from external to internal influences. During this transition, organizational influences (those influences within the institution but outside of a particular program unit) play a strong role in the screening process.

The first phase of response to a period of agitation or ferment in society is *initiation* or *awareness*. In this phase issues of new educational purposes and processes more appropriate to the nation's needs are raised, such as new content, a changing set of learners, new instructional processes, new materials and resources, more equitable treatment of special

TABLE 11-4   Stages in Curriculum Change Initiated by External Influences

1. *Initiation (Awareness) Stage:*
   Recognize need or opportunity (awareness, knowledge, assessment). Develop interest, suggest a plan, or formulate a solution.

2. *Screening (Adaptation) Stage:*
   Develop arguments for and against the change.
   Identify opinion leaders.
   Evaluate the plan or suggested solution.
   Explore similar programs elsewhere.
   Consider a small scale trial.
   Make tentative decision to adopt.
   Debate extensively.
   Make second tentative decision to adopt.

3. *Adoption (Confirmation) Stage:*
   Adopt the plan.
   Implement the plan.
   Establish future evaluation strategy.

groups, or the need for improved quality control. At this phase of problem recognition or initial public pressure, external influences are strong but colleges may resist curriculum change, either because the source is not perceived as legitimate or credible, because the need for change is not fully recognized, or simply because of organizational inertia.

The second phase of response is *screening* or *adaptation*. During this period, the college or program evaluates the possibilities for the proposed change and tentatively decides that a decision should be made to respond. During this time, political linkage agents may actively advocate the need for change or disseminate new models. This is a period when the colleges and universities typically accept the direction of society, cease active resistance, and gradually begin to incorporate new ideas into academic plans, adapting them to the local needs and setting. Decisions to accept the proposed change as an internal influence is still tentative at this point. If the events in society move on to other issues, the innovation may die a quiet death. External influences that do not survive the screening or adaptation process either fade away or continue to be external influences.

As a college becomes aware of a change possibility or is pressured to change by some external influence, the progress of adaptation often converts the external influence first into a set of organizational influences. This is true because much of the exploration of the feasibility or desirability of the change will proceed through discussions that involve program interrelationships, program financial allocations, governance patterns, and views of the fit of the suggested innovation with institutional or program mission. At this stage, with respect to strong external influence, college leaders may well ask about the consequence of not adopting a change and how to resolve the organizational tensions that seem to prevent adoption.

During the process of considering change, an idea may gradually gain acceptance and adherents. When the stage of *adoption* or *confirmation* is reached, the degree of acceptance is sufficiently great that the influence may no longer be viewed as external; it is now part of the college's internal agenda. The more completely a specific influence has been perceived as compatible with the college or program mission or values, the more likely it is to become an internal influence rather than an external one attributed to some external authority or pressure group. During this phase, some ideas become part of the fabric of colleges and universities and cease to be seen as innovations. An illustration of an external influence that was slowly internalized is the land-grant mission assigned to colleges by the Morrill Act in 1862. For fifty years or more prior to the passage of the legislation, advocates of education in science, agriculture, and mechanic arts argued that these studies would spur the nation's economic growth. Colleges, however, were not yet ready to recognize this need nor embrace new educational purposes or curriculum content. At this stage, the influence toward including these new subjects in the college curriculum was clearly external to colleges. As awareness rose and more professors began to teach practical studies, the need for change became part of the organizational context, creating internal tensions. Eventually, the change was fully adopted in the set of existing colleges designated as land-grants as well as in the newly created land-grant colleges, and became integrated with the existing mission.

Other illustrations of change that occurred through diffusion and became entrenched after reaching the adoption stage are the elective system, the distribution system, the academic major, and the pass/fail grading system. In contrast, examples of change that were tested briefly and propagated through social interaction but fell by the wayside were competency-based education and the 4–1–4 calendar in the 1970s. An example of a change that failed to achieve full adoption was the extensive push for improving science and mathematics education after Sputnik. Concern for this identified need for curriculum change dwindled in the face of other concerns aroused by the Vietnam War, student unrest, and student demands for relevance.

In today's environment, a confluence of several influences might spawn an innovative educational delivery system that is introduced and imitated in varied settings with minimal advance experimental trial. Imagine, for example, a fictional scenario: a state college is reacting to public criticisms of college curricula while simultaneously important educational opinion leaders are proposing ideas such as classroom research and active learning. Simultaneously economic forces are tightening college budgets and political conflict surrounds new state assessment requirements. Problem solvers who note these four simultaneous influences (public concern, declining budgets, assessment demands, and new pedagogical techniques) might suggest a planned change—

namely, to use peer teaching as a way of improving learning for both learner and tutor while reducing instructional costs. If the college is already in the process of adapting new technology, additional influence exists; planners may further modify the idea to include peer teaching by computer, rather than face-to-face interaction. In a next stage, the new computerized peer tutoring system could be adapted to allow a student's learning to be documented through a computer log, providing an innovative way of coping with assessment demands. Such a scenario for change proceeds in several ways, exhibiting organizational adaptation, planned change, and diffusion in response to external and internal pressures. In this case, possibly the internal value placed on instructional improvement would provide a way to make the external demands compatible with faculty norms.

Leadership for Adaptive Development

Cameron (1984, pp. 136–137) proposed that for colleges to be adaptive, college leaders need to use "Janusian thinking," looking both forward and backward (or, in organizational terms, outward and inward). We agree, but envision the Janus slowly pivoting so that one face can recognize and follow an external influence as it gradually becomes part of the college's internal agenda. A good leader, we believe, has the ability to recognize when this internalization has taken place and capitalize on the occasion. In Quinn's competing values model, the leader seeking innovation may need to move along the axis of external and internal concerns frequently.

To help leaders recognize the factors we have discussed here, we suggest a set of questions to guide thinking about influences and curriculum change. These questions are helpful in identifying the source and potency of influence and the stage of internalization by colleges and in guiding and predicting college response.

Guidelines for Thinking about Influences and Innovation

- What is the issue being addressed?
- What are the sources of influence—from origin of the issue to present?
- Who are the primary actors? the advocates? the opponents?
- What are the positions for and against the proposed change?
- How widespread is the influence/challenge? Does it affect all sectors of higher education? Does it affect all levels of academic plans: course, program, college?
- Which change processes are being followed?
- What is the current phase of the change process?
- What elements of the academic plan are likely to change?
- What level(s) of the plan are most likely to change (course, program, college)?
- Will the educational environment be changed?
- What are (1) impediments to and (2) enhancers of change?
- Does the proposed change meet criteria for success? Is it compatible with norms, divisible, credible, easy to understand, and so on?
- What type of leadership is needed?
- Which of the types of decisions is likely to ensue: optional, contingent, collective, or dictated?
- Is it likely that whole new structures (courses, programs, colleges) will need to be created?
- What new curricular resources may be needed?

- What may be the effects on students?
- What type of professional development for faculty and staff will be needed?
- What issues and questions remain to be resolved?
- What can be predicted about the success of the change?
- What type of evaluation plan makes sense?

Most influences and change processes can be usefully analyzed in this way, and one need not judge the value of the proposed change to ask these questions. College leaders with foresight will develop and use such checklists as the pressure for curriculum changes increases and incorporates a greater variety of voices from outside the institution.

Curriculum is an arena in which administrators can also stimulate change while upholding quality by asking carefully-targeted questions that encourage faculty to use rational planning and problem-solving modes as they adapt to a changing society. We adapted and expanded the work of Wood and Davis (1978) to develop the list of questions below that administrators should ask (and encourage faculty members to ask) about any curriculum proposal—new or old, adjustment or innovation. The questions establish the expectation that academic planning will be systematic and careful (if not entirely rational) and that, at the same time, it can be appropriately responsive to both external and internal agendas.

Guidelines for Questions to Ask about Curriculum Proposals

- Is the idea worth developing?
- Which elements of current academic plans will the idea affect?
- What will be the likely intended and unintended consequences at course, program, and college levels?

- Does the idea link with goals, values, and procedures already accepted in the college or university?
- Does the planned solution solve a problem? Are the advantages of the new idea over the status quo clear to those who must adapt, adopt, and implement?
- Is the current organizational environment supportive of this type of idea?
- Are knowledgeable, credible, and flexible opinion leaders committed to the idea and willing to work toward its adoption?
- Will new financial resources or staff be required? If so, what will be their role if the change does not endure?
- Is a trial of this idea feasible? Can needed adaptations be made as part of the trial? How long a trial period will provide a fair and consistent experiment? Can implementation proceed in feasible steps?
- When will the tentative decision be made? Is it a decision from which an orderly retreat can be made if needed? When is a final adoption likely? What are the expected criteria for final adoption?
- Is a continuous evaluation cycle built into the innovation for the long range future?

CURRICULUM CHANGE AND LEADERSHIP: PAST AND FUTURE

Curriculum change in American colleges has been extensive and responsive, not moribund or lacking in vigor as some claim, and has helped higher education to adapt to society's perceived needs. True, some change has failed to endure and some issues are debated repeatedly, but each iteration of the debate has included additional participants, more diverse students, and more complex academic programs and institutions. The variety of actors concerned about curriculum and the set of external pressures has expanded with each major period of change. For example, government agencies that were barely on the scene in the 1940s emerged as active participants in curriculum change in the 1980s, first as promoters of innovation, and then as regulators.

As colleges attempt to maintain a dynamic curriculum equilibrium with their societal environment, they recognize external influences, then attempt to internalize them to achieve stability. Once an influence is internalized, the college deals purposefully with each change influence. The process of internalization and diagnosis of the need for change is likely to promote, not reject, the proposed change. Change serves to modify the effectiveness of academic plans (the process we have called adjustment) and increases the effectiveness of the planning environment as it also enhances the responsiveness of colleges and universities to society. Currently, colleges are not viewed as very effective in the curriculum domain and face considerable pressure for curriculum reform. Reform in the last two decades of the twentieth century seems to have proceeded more rapidly than in previous reform eras.

Based on these observations, we submit that the process of college curriculum change cannot be understood in terms of change theory alone. Rather leaders must recognize three important factors that interact: (1) the nature of the influence pressing for change, (2) the change process that is operating, and (3) the extent to which external influence has been internalized by colleges and universities to become an organizational or internal influence. This proposition views the colleges as active adapters in the change process as they examine and internalize influences rather than as passive subjects of societal pressure. It views faculty members and administrators as sharing the responsibility for recognizing, screening and adapting new ideas.

Most academic adjustments are routine and concern content, sequence, instructional process, and resources but seldom alter educational purposes; programs and courses continue to be built on the foundation of old ones. But new models of communication may lead to more rapid change. Curriculum change in higher education has seldom been a "transformation" that changes the entire purpose of education (Toombs & Tierney, 1991), but transformations may indeed be imminent, spurred in numerous ways by societal and technological advances which link colleges to specific public concerns not only nationally but globally.

The pace of curricular change is increasing today partly because of rapid communication and partly because of the increase in interest groups who have a stake in higher education. Diffusion of new ideas and problem-solving activities now takes place rapidly among faculty—by electronic mail, the Internet, electronic journals, and FAX transmission. Views of external and internal constituencies about changes that society desires can be conveyed to college leaders immediately and forcefully. Increased communication may increase change based on conflict because it facilitates the organization and political effectiveness of interest groups in society who advocate new concerns.

In the next chapter, we will discuss several curriculum changes now in progress that illustrate recent influences on the college curriculum and their various stages of acceptance as part of colleges' internal agendas. Some seem to be in the final stage of internalization, namely adoption. Some seem to be at the screening stage, while other changes seem to stem from potent external forces that most colleges are just beginning to recognize.

Faculty and administrators, as well as trustees and policy makers, may profitably contemplate influences on the educational environment that will indirectly and directly shape future academic plans. Response to internal, organizational, and external influences will require varied change proposals, a range of strategies, and strong leadership.

CHAPTER 12

Curriculum Changes in Progress

CURRICULAR CHALLENGES COLLEGES FACE

When colleges make major curriculum changes in response to external influences, they extend and modify the historical patterns in which educators have adapted academic plans to society. In this chapter, we discuss three broad challenges to enhancing curriculum that were issued to colleges by external groups during the reform era of the 1980s and that continued to operate in the 1990s. The three challenges are (1) incorporating diverse perspectives, (2) increasing coherence, and (3) meeting conflicting expectations for quality and access. We first mentioned them as new approaches to old debates when we discussed the recent era of curriculum reform. We return to them now, considering them further in light of the academic plan theory we have developed.

The confluence of such recent changes in society as concern for the perspectives of different societal groups, competitive economic pressures in an increasingly global society, and rapid advances in information access through electronic technology have pressed

these changes on educators. Although colleges may differ in both the attention they give to each challenge and the actions they take, none is free to ignore them. The three challenges suggest specific curriculum changes which, in turn, imply changes in one or more elements of academic plans and at all levels: course, program, and college.

For each challenge, we have selected three specific related changes in progress, each of which can be traced to influences external to colleges and universities. Some of these influences, we argue, have now been partially or wholly accepted as internal agendas by some colleges; the extent of "internalization" predicts the "stage" of curricular change. Each of our choices of changes to discuss is intended to illustrate one of the three stages of curriculum change—awareness, screening, and adoption—that we have described.

In Table 12-1 we describe the three challenges and list the specific curriculum changes related to each that we have chosen to explore, one aspect representing each stage of progress. In the table we also identify the recurring curriculum debates to which each

TABLE 12-1   Characteristics of Curriculum Changes in Progress

Challenge	Related Historical Debate Pattern	Primary Recent Influences	Current Stage of Change Process		
			Adoption	Screening	Awareness
Incorporating diverse perspectives	Increased access	Government Pressure groups Economy Disciplines	Multicultural perspectives	Pluralist voices	Globalization
Increasing coherence	Prescription vs. choice General vs. specialized education	Government and association critiques Business Education	Core curricula	Inter-disciplinary studies	Connecting with life and work
Meeting expectations for quality and access	Accountability Instructional improvement Increased access	Government and national critiques Business Education	Effective thinking	Assessing learning	Instructional technology, distance learning

current issue is related and some sources of external influence. Colleges address these issues through a variety of change processes, including combinations of the processes we described earlier: conflict, social interaction, diffusion, adaptation, and rational planning.

Unlike systematic curriculum change processes that may lead to incremental adjustments in academic plans and educational environments, these broad challenges have strong potential to bring rapid change and alter basic educational purposes. Of course, neither the broad challenges nor the specific aspects of each we discuss are independent. For example, linkages exist between attempts to incorporate multicultural perspectives and decisions about what should be included in a core curriculum; between globalization and the increasing use of globe-spanning technology for instruction; between effective thinking and the problem-solving techniques often

used in interdisciplinary study. Because of their complex relationships, curriculum changes also influence each other as they progress. Due to extensive diversity in higher education, the picture of changes in progress represents a broad range of colleges with fair accuracy but probably be inaccurate for any specific college.

INCORPORATING DIVERSE PERSPECTIVES

We use *diverse perspectives* to include a wide variety of nontraditional views about education. First, under the rubric of multicultural study, we include programs like ethnic studies and women's studies that served as groundbreakers for a broader range of nontraditional views to be represented in the curriculum. These prepared the way for other programs such as gender studies, gay/lesbian studies, critical theory, and new research paradigms. Following Conrad and Haworth (1990), we will call all of these groups calling for change *pluralist voices*. Those calling for pluralism demand that the curriculum recognize and deal directly with the diverse nature of society; with multiple perspectives about lifestyles, learning, and the disciplines; and with the implications of these varying perspectives for meeting the needs of diverse learners. They insist that colleges create an educational environment that supports this diversity of thought. Colleges are only now becoming aware of some of these pluralist voices speaking from both outside and inside the colleges.

Multicultural studies (including ethnic and women's studies) have reached the *adoption* stage of change on most campuses. Nearly all colleges have accepted the need to respond to diverse learners and to teach content that reflects diversity. Now they are seeking the best ways to do so. We judge curricular response to the other pluralist voices, however, to be still at either the *screening* or the *awareness* stage of change in most institutions. Finally, we contend that a globally-oriented college curriculum is an inevitable extension of pluralism, but today this change remains at the *awareness* stage.

The screening of suggested changes focuses first on the pluralistic voices arising within the U.S.; consequently, globalization currently gets attention in only a few parts of some campuses. Typically, interested parties include business schools, foreign language programs, area studies, economic and political science programs, and, where they exist, professional schools such as medicine and public health. Large universities with multiple schools and colleges, leading scholars with international connections, and many international graduate students have moved farther toward developing global perspectives than most smaller undergraduate colleges or community colleges. However, few campuses

of any size or type have committed to developing academic plans that will acquaint all students intensively with what we might call the economic and cultural interfaces of the world's nations. Indeed, it is difficult to find a clear definition of what is meant by globalization and internationalization on campuses.

Discussion about these three specific aspects of incorporating diverse perspectives (multicultural studies, pluralist voices, and globalization) extend the historical pattern of debate about increasing access to higher education and about the expanding diversity of learners. Less directly, they are related to past debates about general versus specialized education and about student choice versus college prescription of content. Changes in the economic, political, ecological, and cultural aspects of society present challenges that are not new but that are continually being redefined by external circumstances.

When the nation's economic and industrial needs demanded it, modern languages and scientific studies replaced classical languages in U.S. colleges. Later, especially in periods of American nationalism, expectations for study in these fields were lowered and enrollments declined. In the future, when colleges debate the shape of academic plans it will be increasingly difficult to avoid requiring that students learn about modern interfaces between nations. To maintain competitiveness, the pendulum is already swinging back toward more language study and more technological study.

The broad category of curriculum change that we have called "incorporating diverse perspectives" has direct implications for curriculum purpose, sequence, and content, as well as the potential to further diversify learners, instructional resources, and selected instructional processes. Serious globalization of the college curriculum could transform academic plans and become a future standard for educational excellence for which colleges are held accountable. An ultimate result of increasing diversity and pluralism will be the recognition and incorporation in the curriculum all of the physical, cultural, gender, religious, critical, and economic perspectives of a world that is increasingly united by rapid transportation and information technology.

Multicultural Studies: Adoption Stage

The need to link learning with students' diverse backgrounds and goals provides a strong rationale for the diversity movement in curriculum; culturally-determined prior learning and motivations strongly affect achievement. Thus, one rationale some present for multicultural studies is that students with different backgrounds must have different instruction—that is, different content, sequence, and processes to help them succeed. Yet the challenge of incorporating diversity is more often defended on the grounds of educational purpose—namely, increasing understanding among groups in society.

Despite sometimes contentious debate, multiculturalism as a purpose of education has made significant progress in higher education. More than three-fourths of colleges and universities have integrated some multicultural work in their general education requirement; about one-third require specific courses focused on multicultural issues; and at least a third offer course work in gender and ethnic studies (El-Khawas, 1992). Two-year colleges are adopting multiculturalism less rapidly than four-year colleges, but research universities, often accused of neglecting the undergraduate curriculum and teaching, have made large strides in bringing multiculturalism to their academic programs.

Jerry Gaff (1992), describing recent changes in core programs, reported that campus leaders now see multiculturalism as a central and enduring feature of their general education programs. But Gaff reminds us that multiculturalism is not a monolithic construct. Depending on the participants in the discussion, it can variously represent the study of ethnicity, racial diversity, gender difference, the physically-challenged, sexual orientation, international issues, non-Western cultures, and cross-cultural issues. Still, when one speaks of multiculturalism on a college or university campus, the images that arise are usually connected to racial and ethnic issues. We will briefly trace the history of ethnic studies and women's studies, which have gained the strongest foothold. On some campuses, other programs, such as gay and lesbian studies, also fall in this category but are at an earlier stage of adoption and are more difficult to document.

Ethnic Studies

Ethnic studies programs were born of the social protest and political unrest of the 1960s and reflect demographic changes in both the U.S. population and higher education. New programs flourished during the 1970s as financial resources became available for program development, student aid, and the professional advancement of faculty of color. In the 1960s, the number of scholars of color in traditional departments was too small to build programs around departmentally based courses taught by faculty from traditional departments, so the first Black studies programs hired faculty for new and separate academic units (Butler & Schmitz, 1992). Today there are approximately 700 ethnic studies programs and departments on U.S. college and university campuses, including programs and departments in African American, Asian and Pacific Islander, American Indian/Alaskan Native, and Hispanic studies. Ethnic studies scholars have struggled to maintain programs covering all of these groups and add others such as Puerto Rican and Chicano studies (Butler, 1991).

Scholars and teachers in ethnic studies often use the insights of critical theory to help students understand the partiality of traditional studies, the effects of power and privilege, and the nature of difference and dominance (Butler & Schmitz, 1992). According to Butler (1991), ethnic studies emphasizes the need to know the full story of our shared pasts and presents. Part of this full story depends on (1) identifying the connections and interactions among the disciplines; (2) studying and defining the experiences of neglected people for their own sake; (3) correcting distortions of the majority and the minority due to exclusion; and (4) defining and structuring a curriculum that affirms the interconnectedness of human life, experience, and creativity. A recent article characterized multicultural studies as now in its "second generation" (*Chronicle of Higher Education*, June 15, 1994), but some advocates question whether its broad acceptance and its adaptation to all students have diluted these important purposes.

Women's Studies

The founders of women's studies courses and programs were the activists of the women's liberation movement of the late 1960s. The goal of fostering feminist consciousness inspired their attempts to recover the lost heritage of women's experiences and perceptions (Boxer, 1989). Although the first women's studies courses were offered in nonacademic settings or "free schools," faculty, staff, and students soon helped establish courses at colleges and universities that dealt with women's lives. During the 1970s, 300 campuses initiated women's studies programs. By 1985, there were 450 programs or departments across the country; by 1992, the number had grown to more than 620. In 1990, more than 5,200 faculty members were teaching courses in women's studies and 165 bachelor's degree programs had been developed (Carnegie Foundation, 1992). Such a rapid increase, especially during a period of tight higher ed-

ucation budgets, attests to the strength of the influence.

Scholars in women's studies come from many different disciplines but share a common goal: transforming what they perceive to be a male-centered curriculum. Most women's studies scholars today call for a total revision of the the curriculum, a complete transformation of methodology, and the adoption of a pedagogy in which the challenges of critical theory and feminist inquiry shape the questions being asked. Women and women's issues, they argue, can no longer remain on the margins of human inquiry, studied as objects rather than subjects and as an absence rather than a presence. The curriculum must change to meet this challenge.

Women's studies seeks to use knowledge to change women's lives and worlds. All teaching is viewed as a political act and the political transformation of the curriculum is seen as part of women's role in society. The purpose of academic plans is automatically called into question. As with ethnic studies, choice of content begins with the understanding that race, ethnicity, gender, and class form the basis of identity and culture. The content of women's studies must therefore confront these fundamental aspects of society. The process of transforming knowledge is complex, requiring both the recognition of women as agents in the creation of knowledge and the redefinition of knowledge through the act of making women's experience a primary subject for knowledge. Its goal, however, is to create a improved world for both genders.

In describing conceptual barriers to progress within the curriculum that parallel those in society, Minnich (1990) writes in *Transforming Knowledge*:

> As long as we do not engage in critique and correction of the curriculum, the framework of meaning behind particular questions of what to teach to whom will continue to prove inhospitable to all those who have been

excluded from knowledge and knowledge-making, and also from effective participation in understanding and exercising power on a basic cultural level. (pp. 11–12)

Minnich agrees with the vast majority of feminist and ethnic studies scholars who reject the mere addition of women and underrepresented groups to the present construction of knowledge ("mainstreaming") in favor of a true transformation of the curriculum.

Pluralist Voices and New Paradigms: Screening Stage

One result of a more ethnically and racially diverse college population has been the expansion of multicultural perspectives. The multiculturalists have applauded the increase in acceptable perspectives as a sign of a reinvigorated democracy. In contrast, conservative views, reflected in educational reform reports, have inspired a new group of reformers seeking to preserve tradition rather than promote change. These conservative forces link the view that there are multiple perspectives on what should be learned with predictions of the demise of intellectual life in colleges and universities and threats to the health of American democracy. These views, those of the traditionalists and those of the pluralists (Haworth & Conrad, 1990), are based on competing perspectives about curricular purpose. The debate has been in full swing since at least 1980; the adoption of a change representing the view of the pluralists is arguably at the *screening* stage.

The traditionalists believe that the purpose of undergraduate education is to expose students to the "enduring truths" of society and, thus, to preserve society's traditional intellectual and social values. They advocate a return to a curriculum which asserts the importance of reading "great books," believing that students must contemplate the knowledge of the past so that they will have a common

body of knowledge and language that enables them to live together as citizens. In this tradition, students must reflect on questions about the nature of life, religion, government, and other broad issues, not in terms of their own views but in terms of what great thinkers have thought and written. Contemplating the works of earlier intellectuals, conservatives assume, develops one's own critical thinking skills. The traditionalist influence is manifested in calls for increased general education requirements, more emphasis on the liberal arts prior to professional study, and strengthened skills of reading and writing in standard English. The traditionalists contend that a belief in the relativism of knowledge poses a great danger to a coherent curriculum and to the U.S. democratic system.

The pluralists, on the other hand, assert that the nature of personal experience affects learning. They believe that, when students from diverse cultural backgrounds read the works of the great thinkers, they interpret them differently. This is especially true if they accept norms from other cultures or do not believe themselves to be full members of American society. Such students, attending college in increasing numbers, may not find ways to connect the traditional intellectual and social values of Western culture to their own. The notion that knowledge is relative—that it is not neutral, not situated within the traditional disciplines, and not originated only by European thinkers—separates the pluralist voices from the traditionalist ones.

The debate between pluralists and traditionalists is waged in terms of the purpose of education, the content to be studied, and how experiences and perspectives of individual learners affect the way they construct meaning from content. But it also implies diversity in scholarly views of how knowledge is acquired and used. For example, Tierney (1991) points to the differences between the logical positivism of the traditionalists, who believe that knowledge is neutral and scholarship is objective, and views of the critical theorists who see the production of knowledge as socially and historically determined and research findings as provisional and tentative. In essence, the difference between the logical positivist scholar (the traditional voice) and the critical theorist (one of the pluralist voices) is in how knowledge is constructed and validated. By logical extension, the difference extends to how learners must engage knowledge—and hence, how teachers select instructional processes.

With respect to academic plans, curriculum traditionalists hope to understand the world in order to preserve and transmit accepted values; critical theorists seek to understand the world in order to teach students how to change it. The critical theorists focus on what is taught and the politics of who decides what is taught. One of the goals of critical theory, therefore, is to understand power as a process of enablement which can help individuals to understand their relationship to the world. Education is seen as an activity that helps to empower citizens by instilling a central concern for social justice and democracy.

While the traditionalists have turned to the past in seeking answers to today's educational ills, the pluralists look for new perspectives and modes of inquiry to create new ways of approaching old problems. Colleges and universities have proponents of both schools of thought among their faculty. What has now become an internal campus debate was, in fact, stimulated by societal structures and perceived inequities, including class and power struggles that have germinated for many years.

These educational purposes apply to many disciplines, especially in the humanities and social sciences. Thus, critical theorists have found homes in many programs; they claim no single academic territory. The actual influence on the disciplines of critical theory and of its offspring—deconstructionism, feminism, and Marxism and postmodernism—is

somewhat disputed. While some believe that such "isms" now dominate some fields, others argue that the changes are less extensive. It is clear, however, that general education programs, particularly in research universities, now include new approaches to the history of ideas whose roots are in critical theory (Franklin, Huber, & Laurence, 1992). The traditionalists no longer prevail and may be losing ground as the new ideas are screened.

Globalization: Awareness Stage

Until recently, humanities studies had roots primarily in the ideas of European thinkers; relatively few students studied ideas from the cultures of other (sometimes larger and more populous) portions of the world. The recent development of multicultural programs has helped to emphasize the importance of contemplating religion, history, philosophy, sociology, psychology, and political science as understood in non-Western nations.

During various periods in U.S. history, proponents of international education have argued in terms of economic competition, foreign diplomacy, and peace-keeping as well as cultural enrichment. Area studies programs in universities have often provided understanding of differences among various regions of the world, particularly developing countries that may be strategically important in defense. These programs were discrete and identifiable so that interested students and faculty could undertake them as study and research options. Deputy Secretary of State Clifton Wharton, Jr. (*Compass,* 1993), former president of Michigan State University, recently built a strong case for an more fully internationalized curriculum—one in which international aspects are infused throughout college study. Wharton stressed the importance of building a citizenry who understand foreign policy and how it is developed, the increasing interdependence of nations, the consequent need to provide leaders in business, industry, and government who appreciate global issues, and the importance of understanding the culture, history, and traditions of other nations in avoiding conflict and increasing the prospects for stability and peace. Such an infusion of international aspects into many courses and programs could be termed *internationalization. Globalization* of the curriculum is a still broader term, encompassing both multiculturalism and internationalization and espousing interdependence. Some view globalization as more focused on making the world a single community, stressing similarities and common problems rather than differences.

With the exception of some business programs that are already internationalized, a substantial change in the undergraduate curriculum would be needed to achieve internationalization and still more to achieve globalization. It is not yet possible to find more than a few examples of truly internationalized or globalized colleges. We therefore judge this change to be at the *awareness* stage. Colleges and universities have recognized the importance of global relationships but they have not yet begun to screen a set of potential responses, at least for undergraduate programs.

Whether one observes much international activity occurring depends, in part, on the definition one uses; in her 1992 summary Pickert lists "the study of relations among nations (international relations), particularly regions of the world (area studies), foreign languages and cultures, comparative and international approaches to particular disciplines, and the examination of issues affecting more than one country (environmental, global or peace studies)" (p. 1). She also reports that foreign language study is the most common curriculum manifestation of internationalization, often coupled with optional study abroad (p. 11). By using the first and broader definition, in 1987, 75% of U.S. colleges could claim that they were involved in international education. Using the second

definition, internationalization would look less common since less than 10% of college students studied a foreign language.

In a brief history of international education, Pickert (1992) indicates that, after nineteenth- and early twentieth-century support from private philanthropists, the U.S. government played the leading role in international educational exchange from World War I to World War II. Since that point, international education became nearly synonymous with educational activities funded by the U.S government (1992, pp. 3–5) which still provides a great deal of initiative. For example, the government funds several university Centers for International Business Education, language and area studies supported by Title VI of the Higher Education Act, and the National Security Education Program grants to colleges for incorporating more international education into U.S. higher education.

Advocacy for internationalizing relationships among colleges of the world, if not the undergraduate curriculum, has recently become an agenda item for several higher education associations. This supportive relationship was developed with government cooperation at a time when communism had collapsed in eastern Europe, apartheid had been officially abolished in South Africa, the North American Free Trade Agreement (NAFTA) was being established, and the new European Community had established agreements to promote student mobility within Europe. The time was clearly ripe for new emphasis. The need for leadership in the "internationalization" of the curriculum has been recognized.

Higher education associations are focusing on broad types of cooperation across national boundaries, such as technology transfer. While not directly curricular, these cooperative ventures may help to internalize the call for undergraduate curriculum development. A leading association, the American Council on Education, is actively promoting such cooperation. In 1993, ACE began *The Compass,* a newsletter on international matters. The initiatives described in its early issues include international efforts to define research agendas in various fields, train administrators in areas such as Total Quality Management and planning, exchange faculty and students, help underdeveloped countries strengthen faculty and college programs, and so on. Clearly, much is afoot and much is at stake. But the issues pursued are operational ones; it is hard to find concrete examples of academic plans that have been reshaped to have a strong international or global focus.

Several analysts who have examined the idea of infusing international issues into the undergraduate programs have asserted that working with the disciplines is essential (Groennings & Wiley, 1990). The seed for this approach, which could be called "internationalization across the curriculum" is in area studies, where faculty and students from several disciplines concentrate on a specific geographic region. A newer modification is to offer subspecialties for internationalization within major concentrations in both disciplines and professional fields. In some cases, such as at Oregon State University, students may elect to enhance their degrees by achieving an international certificate which may be an advantage in future careers (Pickert, 1992, p. 17). In a different analysis, Heginbotham (1994) claims that area studies must be supplanted by a problem-solving skills focused on issues important to groups of countries. Theme studies across cultures (e.g. the problems of pollution) that draw on the resources of one or more disciplines (economics, government, and sociology) may hold great potential and are consistent with other new emphases we will discuss—namely, interdisciplinary studies and active learning.

Internationalizing college curricula will call for new decisions about specific elements of academic plans, especially content, resources, and instructional processes. Among the best examples are those from Kalamazoo College and Lewis and Clark College, which have sent students on semesters abroad for many years as an integrated part of their programs. New possibilities include recent opportunities to use satellite broadcasts, electronic newspapers, video discs, CD-ROM, and worldwide computer conferences to help student build links. First, the teaching of foreign language can be made very efficient and economical by using technology to replace some in-class demonstration by professors. Second, new communication technology has removed one barrier to internationalization; one can now travel in virtual reality.

Several barriers hinder internationalization. First, many faculty members lack background in the international aspects of their disciplines, and present incentive systems are unlikely to encourage them to increase their attention to international work. Discipline structure is another barrier. For example, although scientists have actively cooperated at the scholarly level and universal mathematics terminology presents few language barriers, there are disincentives for undergraduate science students to study abroad. Part of this barrier, real or perceived, relates to the hierarchical sequencing of content in the sciences and the unwillingness of science faculty to vary this sequence. Another potential barrier involves career patterns and the need to meet certification standards in some fields. Accounting education, for example, has introduced international accounting concepts throughout its programs; yet a student who studied accounting in other countries might have severe difficulties meeting the course-specific requirements to take the CPA examination. In all disciplines, the crowding of too much content into the curriculum hinders taking on new missions.

Aside from logistical barriers, most American students have little motivation to go abroad or to devote intense attention to worldwide problems. Parochialism still pervades our colleges and universities, and many institutions lack counseling systems that would encourage students to think more broadly. The educational environment is not yet ready to be supportive of internationalization. Thus, we may anticipate that evolution of these programs may not be rapid. The idea of internationalization may need to include substantial research during the screening stage of change it has yet to enter, because there is scarcely any research on whether the existing international initiatives do increase students' awareness, cooperation, and commitment to international development, ecology, peace, or other important goals.

INCREASING COHERENCE

Coherence for the college curriculum has been stressed by opinion leaders in both government and higher education since at least 1828, when the authors of the Yale Report viewed coherence as threatened. It was a primary thesis of recent reform initiatives undertaken by the Association of American Colleges on behalf of its member institutions. Similar terms with slightly different shades of meaning, such as *connectedness, integrity,* and *integration,* have been used by others (Stark, 1986). Although the value of coherence, simply defined as studies that help students achieve a "meaningful whole," is well accepted in education, the definition of what constitutes such a program of study has gradually changed. Today's pluralistic society makes the struggle to define the coherent whole more difficult than ever before.

In the reform reports of the 1980s, government leaders and higher education leaders alike challenged colleges to demonstrate curriculum coherence in three distinct arenas. First, they demanded coherence within general education programs required of all students. This clarion call for coherence reflected a mistrust of both the basic preparation students receive in secondary

school and of the newer, more accessible forms of higher education such as the general education provided in some types of colleges. These issues, politely muted in most discussions, extend the historical debates about access and its perceived effect on quality academic standards, and about the value of general versus specialized education. Furthermore, they reflect another aspect of the political and social question we discussed with respect to multicultural and international issues: whether there is, in fact, a common culture to be learned.

Second, coherence implies that students can make conceptual linkages within traditional disciplines or can understand linkages among disciplines when they are jointly brought to bear on social or scientific problems. These disciplinary and interdisciplinary definitions are not easily applied today since the majority of undergraduate college students major in collegiate career studies rather than traditional disciplines. Thus, for traditionalists, many recent attempts to define coherence may fall short of the mark.

Third, those who take a more practical view of education expect coherence. They expect students' education to link with their professional or vocational goals, with their past lives, and with their general education, as well as with their future lives. This life-related coherence is sometimes called *connectedness.* Similar terms that have meaning in a career-related context are Boyer's (1987) discussion of "the enriched major" and Stark, Lowther, Hagerty, and Orczyk's (1986) definition of the "contextual competence" that characterizes integrated liberal and professional study.

In this section we examine three aspects of the challenge of coherence, each at a different stage in the change process. First, we discuss the call, voiced repeatedly throughout U.S. history, for the core curriculum to bring coherence to general education by assuring that all students have an equivalent foundation of studies. In the recent reform cycle, demand for a core curriculum is in the *adoption* stage. Many colleges have internalized this demand and are struggling to implement it.

Second, we deal with interdisciplinary approaches to education, both in general education and among undergraduate specializations. Interdisciplinary methods of achieving coherence also have been advocated in earlier times but are still being *screened* in the current cycle of reform.

Third, and finally, we discuss the coherence of making curricular connections to the workplace. The trend among students to choose college study related to their future careers continues unabated, despite protests from those who oppose undergraduate career specialization. Although this long-term trend has been recognized, we argue that it remains at the *awareness* stage of change because colleges and universities have not dealt with it directly. Until they do, the debate about the trend is stalemated and unlikely to result in reasonable balance or creative adaptations.

The Continuing Core Curriculum Debate: Adoption Stage

At one extreme in the continuing debate about coherence is the view that reading and analyzing a specified group of books provides coherence and should be undertaken by all students. Even many educators who do not insist on a specific list of books to be studied are convinced that there is some set of courses, readings, or experiences all college students should pursue to create the "floor" or "foundation" on which more specialized education should rest. In the public eye, the belief in a common floor is represented, however inadequately, by lists of things every literate person should know (such as that generated by E. D. Hirsch, 1988) and in the popularity of television quiz shows and party games that require the recollection of miscellaneous facts and figures. While not admiring

them quite as much as sports figures, musical performers, and movie personalities, the American public does respect persons who have acquired a body of knowledge.

The question of which body of knowledge should be studied plagues education today perhaps more acutely than in the past. Responding to advocates of achieving coherence through a core curriculum, Lauter (1991) expressed the dilemma this way: "The view of culture they offer begins from the assumption that it is something—a set of ideas, understandings, references, a "language"— that certain people in the past possessed and that most Americans of our 'mass society' no longer own" (p. 263). Even the casual observer of the quiz shows will recognize that Americans no longer own a common culture. Questions readily answered by teenage contestants stump the senior citizens, and vice versa. At the very least, there currently are diverging cultures for the two generations and perhaps a classical culture and a popular culture. Pluralists would argue that many more cultures exist; not only do traditional Western values emphasize one view of the world, but Western culture itself is changing. Whether or not one argues with his specific views, Lauter is certainly correct in his assessment that debating the college "canon" is a way of arguing other social changes and issues (for a fuller discussion, see Toma and Stark, 1995).

In its report, *A New Vitality in General Education,* the Association of American Colleges (1988), asserted that faculty at many institutions had side-stepped social arguments about what common knowledge should be required by establishing distribution requirements for general education. The AAC stated that general education had become "a minimal sampling of disciplines offered more or less willingly by departments." As one of the crucial changes in the future, these educators recommended that all students have eight general education experiences intended to develop good intellectual habits.

The experiences may be gained in many ways—from competency-based general education courses to learning communities that link several disciplines—and thus were couched in terms of process as well as content. In a sense, by using the term *experience,* which straddles the ideas of content and instructional process, AAC also side-stepped important curricular questions.

Many colleges, however, found the vagueness of the term experience acceptable and have internalized the responsibility to develop academic plans that achieve the set of experiences AAC described (Gaff, 1991). In part, the internalization of this external agenda occurred so quickly because faculty task forces generated the list of eight ideas and allowed flexibility for locally designed academic plans at the course, program, and college levels. Yet this very flexibility was denounced by critics on both sides of the debate who believe it dodges the primary social issues. Regarding the AAC's list of experiences, Lauter (1991) says, "That such an insipid list should be paraded as the goals of college education suggests how little the AAC group asked basic questions about the relationship of schooling to social priorities. The latter are never in fact considered, but only assumed" (p. 232).

However carefully planned, local versions of core curricula will not end the recurring debate about what educational experiences should be prescribed. Wide-scale adoptions of core curricula were undertaken in the 1920s and again in the 1940s, but each time these efforts reverted to more flexible arrangements and greater student choice. The repeated deterioration of core programs occurs not only because the content of the required portion of education is in question but, more basically, because opposing groups in society continue to argue the basic purposes of education. Is education a process of socialization into a dominant culture or is it the development of one's own value system or unique perspective? The issue of coherence in general education, therefore, is not separable from the issues of pluralism and relativism that have spawned new academic plans more responsive to diverse groups.

Just as society's view of what is coherent is not fixed for all time, faculty views of discipline boundaries and inquiry methods are regularly in flux. The separate disciplines have their own methods of achieving coherence. In many humanities and social science fields where paradigms are shifting, mechanisms to ensure that students develop critical perspectives are given high priority as a way of achieving coherence. In the natural and physical sciences, where the structure of knowledge and the paradigms for inquiry and truth validation are most concrete, coherence is emphasized through discipline structure and concept linkage. The real challenge, it appears, is for faculty representing the disciplines to accept the necessity of helping students develop all these dimensions of coherence, not simply the ones they find most palatable. This, of course, remains a viable argument for distribution requirements rather than a single core.

Recent trends to adopt core curricula and/or to tighten distribution requirements provide remedies for perceived excesses of student choice and assure greater commonality of study. But any permanent resolution of whether there should be a core curriculum is far in the future if possible at all. As the trend toward diversity of academic courses and programs continues, we may reasonably predict that ways to satisfy core or distribution requirements will again proliferate. With each recurrence of the debate, however, American higher education comes closer to an accommodation of multiple points of view on the one hand and, on the other, moves farther from a plan reinforcing a common cultural heritage. The challenge is to find the balance that will provide choice while preserving culture, one that will provide exposure to alternative perspectives while avoiding fragmentation.

Interdisciplinary Approaches: Screening Stage

One view of coherence focuses on acquiring the knowledge and thinking skills necessary to solve current political, cultural, economic, and public health problems. Such questions often require inquiry at the boundaries of traditional disciplines; this inquiry, in turn, leads to evolution in the questions that scholars believe are worth asking. The impetus for the evolution toward interdisciplinarity comes from society's demands for problem solutions and is internalized by scholars; thus it leads to changes in both methods of inquiry and academic plans. Throughout history, new disciplines have been created at the intersection of old ones as new problem-solving methods are needed. Interdisciplinary work is gaining increasing support among discipline-based faculty members who feel that most of today's complex problems cannot be solved by single discipline approaches.

Interdisciplinary approaches to problem solving occur most frequently at advanced levels of scholarship and research. Yet faculty members concerned with undergraduate curriculum have developed interdisciplinary courses and programs to achieve four goals: to decrease early specialization, to ensure some common learning, to appeal to student interests, and to engage students in research and problem solving. Most perplexing problems (for example, preserving the ecology of our planet) have a human dimension, a technological dimension, and an aesthetic dimension; thus, they cross the organizational boundaries within colleges and universities.

Recently, the call for increased interdisciplinarity as a way of achieving educational coherence has come from prestigious private foundations and college presidents as well as from scholars. Boyer (1987) observed that

undergraduates are enthusiastic about general education courses that link learning to contemporary issues. More such courses, Boyer argued, are needed to connect the general education program with the lives of students. To achieve this goal, he suggested an integrated general education core that introduces students not only to "essential knowledge" but also to "connections across the disciplines, and, in the end, to the application of knowledge to life beyond the campus" (p. 91).

Faculty members and students agree that content needs to be substantially reorganized for better coherence; some are experimenting with interdisciplinary organization. Although there is no mandate that interdisciplinary courses be taught by active methods, they may naturally lend themselves to problem-solving and collaborative instructional processes. Consequently, lacking a fixed instructional tradition, interdisciplinary courses may find fertile ground as active instructional processes become more prevalent.

Our own research indicated that connectedness, at least in theory, is a goal embraced by faculty from many different disciplines. In disciplines such as the natural sciences, where connectedness with other fields often seems a low priority when academic plans are constructed, faculty criticized neglect of this goal and appeared eager to encourage positive change. In the social sciences and humanities fields, faculty were more confident of the current success of their programs in making connections, but they still saw room for improvement. As might be expected, interdisciplinary fields such as women's studies and ethnic studies were most supportive of the goal of connecting learning, seeing it as a goal for the entire curriculum (Lattuca & Stark, 1994).

The full potential of integrating liberal and professional studies as a specific type of interdisciplinarity has not yet emerged. Collegiate career studies successfully link with the disciplines that provide their conceptual foundations. Examples are the relationship of engineering programs to calculus and of sociology to education programs. Among most undergraduate professional fields, faculty also make it very clear to students that their professional work takes place within a context that they can best understand through study of the traditional disciplines such as social sciences. This important concept of *situated knowledge*—that is, knowledge learned in connection with the context in which it will be used—is important to professional educators, but it might be more explicit. Professional educators often use a problem-solving strategy to link foundational studies with professional issues (Stark, Lowther, & Hagerty, 1986). Boyer's view that the career major should be enriched, AAC's view that professional education can be liberal, and Stark and Lowther's (1989) demonstration that professional education should be liberal suggest that these relationships might become both more deliberate and more interdisciplinary, each field drawing on others for meaning and building student interest based on career plans.

Women's studies supplies an example of more complete interdisciplinarity; it is interdisciplinary by nature and places great value on comparative ways of organizing knowledge and scholarship. Some argue that diffusion of women's studies has transformed the knowledge base of the humanities, the social sciences, and many of the natural sciences. Still, organizational debates may continue to hinder the growth of interdisciplinary studies, including women's studies.

There are many possible models for incorporating diverse perspectives as changes become adopted in colleges. New material may be infused into specified key courses or into all courses. The arrangements can be fully institutionalized, as when a department is established, or remain somewhat peripheral, as when a program is begun without separate departmental status. The most common organizational model for interdisciplinary programs involves a small coordinating committee of faculty who hold appointments and tenure in other academic departments (Boxer, 1989, p. 195). This peripheral structure impedes the development of a stable program both in terms of curriculum and administration. As is true for general education programs, the lack of authority for personnel decisions, class schedules and budget allocations, can negatively affect program offerings. These loose types of organizational structures may account for the failure of many interdisciplinary ideas to move from the screening stage to the adoption stage. Increased interest in building interdisciplinary departments, rather than promoting ambiguous program structures, will signal greater internalization of this curriculum change.

Yet organizational change may be slow to arrive. Some say the disciplines and their entrenched organizational fiefdoms are politically too strong; some believe the disciplines have a natural conceptual unity that keeps them intact as the organizers of knowledge; others blame the strong disciplinary socialization that most faculty members receive in graduate school. Whatever the mix of reasons, ferment arising from interdisciplinary discussions creates dissonance that pushes disciplines toward new possibilities. Interdisciplinary studies challenge the supremacy of the disciplines and thus have important implications for changing the curriculum. They foster communication and provide a locus for change and innovation. In addition, sometimes some interdisciplinary associations (such as the Association for Integrative Studies) now act as diffusion mechanisms. Such diffusion of interdisciplinary academic plans may represent an intermediate step in the process of change between screening and adoption. A key challenge in using interdisciplinary approaches is to modify the educational environment to equalize the power relationships between interdisciplinary programs and the traditional disciplines.

If educators are serious about seeking interdisciplinary solutions to the coherence problem, they must make other changes in educational environments. Interdisciplinary teaching requires that instructors view a topic through the perspective of other disciplines, perhaps one in which they have no formal training. To acquire mastery of significant scholarship outside one's area of specialization and to assimilate that knowledge into one's teaching requires a sense of professional security and a heavy commitment of time and energy. However, institutional or discipline incentive systems may not reward this commitment. An increase in interdisciplinarity may require adjustments in these systems.

Connecting with Life and Work: Awareness Stage

U.S. society is concerned about the development of human capital and how its investment in students' education will pay off in terms of productive employment, economic growth, and international competitiveness. This concern, and the related recurring debate about general versus specialized education, began prior to the passage of the Morrill Land Grant Act of 1862 and shows few signs of abating. The positions of various groups today are often polarized. To clarify the challenge, we will attempt here to summarize these positions, and to point out some inconsistencies in their arguments that hinder progress toward curriculum change. The fact that educators have allowed these arguments to remain ambiguous has kept this specific curriculum change at the *awareness* stage for many years.

As society and colleges have become more diverse, society has attached increasingly greater importance to education for work. Thus, undergraduate enrollments (and to a lesser extent numbers of faculty) have shifted to professional schools offering career

studies; the labor market is now the major determinant of what students study. The number of students majoring in specific liberal arts fields, especially humanities, has dropped compared to those majoring in business and other professional fields. Yet faculty rhetoric in many colleges ignores this shift and lends little legitimacy to the educational pursuits of this growing number of students. The challenge is to recognize this changing purpose of collegiate education and build it into academic planning.

In discussing these trends, Clark Kerr (1994a), former president of the University of California, concludes that higher education has served the American labor market very well. This specific service to society has complemented other educational functions. Kerr notes three great surges of activity that increased emphasis on service to the labor market: (1) the land grant movement, (2) the transformation of teachers' colleges into colleges offering many occupational programs and tied more closely to business, and (3) the rise of community colleges with their emphasis on vocational skills. He believes that higher education now supplies (even oversupplies) the labor market with educated workers; helps to sort out and distribute workers in a relatively effective way; provides a generally acceptable quality of education; and contributes to the economy indirectly through better health, job market mobility, acceptance of minority groups, greater political participation, higher levels of personal savings, more women in the labor market, and greater worker satisfaction.

Kerr believes that the success of higher education in contributing to the economy has caused legislators to provide more adequate funding than might otherwise be the case. The fact that political leaders argue their case for supporting higher education on the strength of its economic contributions and society's welfare challenges the view commonly advanced among educators that government leaders are opposed to career-oriented education. In fact, there may be little evidence that either political leaders or the public hold such a view. Instead, the State Higher Education Executive Officers (1992) report that state legislators ask more often whether students are getting jobs than whether they are reading the literary canon or developing values. Reports from state college groups like the American Association of State Colleges and Universities also stress the economic interdependence of colleges and the workplace. In some cases, communities depend directly on local colleges. For example, Miami-Dade Community College offers many two-year occupational programs that train firefighters, police, and medical support personnel. Its students are often new immigrants with limited verbal skills in English. Local and state citizens believe it is better, at least in the short run, to train competent technicians to serve community needs and be productive employees than to educate them in liberal arts fields.

In contrast to the view that colleges contribute to the labor market and the economy, some argue that society has failed to get an appropriate return on its investment or that higher education has ignored its obligations to society. According to one commentator, "In higher education we have tended to ignore indications of a substantial mismatch between what, when, and how we teach, on the one hand, and the requirements and expectations of the workplace on the other" (Lynton, 1984, p. 22). The possibility of a mismatch raises concerns about the nation's international competitiveness. New technology and increases in knowledge change the world of work and raise employer's hiring standards. Yet employers report that graduates lack basic skills and that the specific job skills they learn in school are rapidly outdated. As a result, employers invest heavily in educational programs for employees, often reteaching information or skills presumably learned earlier in school or college (Lynton,

1984). If the educational system is to retain a valued connection with the workplace, it must maintain currency and assure quality in a period of rapid change.

Yet the view that colleges have a responsibility to the workplace receives minimal circulation among many professors and college administrators. Some even deny it. In contrast to economic and political leaders, many educational spokespersons and a few government representatives (such as Lynne Cheney and William Bennett) have asserted that undergraduate study should focus primarily on the liberal arts while career education is postponed until graduate school. The argument is based on three assumptions that bear more careful analysis: (1) that liberal arts study is good preparation for work, especially over the long term; (2) that education designed to expand knowledge of the human condition is the sole property of the liberal arts; and (3) that all career-oriented education is narrow training. In particular, the claim that understanding human needs, values, and achievements can occur solely through the study of language, history, philosophy, religion, and art appreciation has been difficult to support or refute.

There is little research evidence to show that liberal arts courses or programs, as currently taught, provide the habits of mind and general skills deemed valuable. One problem is that it is difficult to separate these outcomes from students' backgrounds and prior preparation. Even if longitudinal studies were devised to document outcomes, the influences from other life experiences would allow few attributions to education. Yet few research attempts have been made because the answer has often preceded the question. A person is considered liberally educated if he or she has studied the liberal arts, and one who studies the liberal arts is becoming liberally educated. The fallacy in this circular argument is not hard to identify, but correcting it would be unpopular on most campuses.

Similarly, there is little evidence to show that all professional or occupational education at the undergraduate level is narrow skill training. At issue is the origin of the definitions of the words "narrow" and "broad." Early definitions of liberal education in the 1800s, encompassing reading and cultural studies, contrasted strongly with skill development in the manual trades then in use. Today, the contrast between liberal education and career study in the same university may be much less sharp. Some traditional academic disciplines are very narrow and professionalized, and some professional fields are very broad and interdisciplinary, drawing as they must from several parent disciplines and sources.

Instead of careful research on these definitional issues and claims, students, faculty, and society are treated to anecdotes that misconstrue the picture on both sides of the debate. Some writers try to illustrate the futility of majoring in the liberal arts disciplines by describing jobless graduates. Others try to illustrate narrowness of vocational courses by describing illiterate graduates. The rhetorical tricks played by both sides in this ongoing debate challenge even citizens with very strong critical thinking skills who are trying to sort out the arguments. Over the years, this general-versus-specialized-education debate has become polarized with each side—general studies and career studies—fighting for its share of students' time and loyalty. The liberal arts side is much more vocal, perhaps reflecting the fact that its enterprise has been contracting; the more successful collegiate career studies programs have made fewer public statements on these issues.

Some critics believe that "premature specialization" leads to a poor-quality college education regardless of whether the specialization is in career-studies or a discipline. Such an argument requires a definition of "premature." The traditional definition implies that students should concentrate on general studies in the undergraduate years, delaying any specialization whatsoever until graduate school. But today, increasing numbers of college students are older than the traditional 18- to -24 age group. They oppose this sequence, arguing that neither society nor individual families can afford to prolong the entrance of adults into the workplace. This group advocates the European system of permitting earlier specialization in college.

In the middle are those who propose various ways of achieving greater integration and, potentially, coherence between the general studies and the major field. Only a few institutions have undertaken such integration. Many of these have been historically technical colleges that "liberalized" their programs or, occasionally, liberal arts colleges that now offer career-oriented specialties.

Perhaps a better place to start than the tradition or history on a particular campus is to seek empirical (rather than rhetorical) answers to these questions:

- What type of education is needed by an individual to live and work in today's society?
- What preparation does he or she need to function in a society that will change often before the end of his or her lifetime?
- What types of knowledge, behaviors, values, and views characterize such a person?
- What types of purpose, content, and instructional processes will produce the desired knowledge, behaviors, and values?

These questions focus on purpose—the essential curriculum issue in general public discussions. It is insufficient, however, to ask these questions and then unquestioningly select one type of education as the ideal without supportive evidence. Educators who do so have, by default, chosen not to evaluate their academic plans.

Today's curriculum challenge is to develop a more careful approach to identifying and defining characteristics of an educated person for our society and connect the characteristics with specific content and instructional processes. Researchers need to pinpoint the effects of the liberal arts more precisely, separating them as clearly as possible from confounding issues such as student background and socioeconomic status. Similarly, researchers need to determine more completely what happens to graduates of various programs in the workplace over short-term and long-term periods.

Increased access to college means that students from lower economic strata see college as upward mobility; the high cost of education encourages students to earn a rapid return on their investment through prompt employment. Employers and taxpayers also want students to enter the work force promptly, rather than remain in college for lengthy periods, because a technological society demands specific preparation as well as general preparation.

Those who advocate stronger connections between education and careers feel that neither liberal learning nor professional learning is sufficient for today's society. Environmental disasters caused by technological accidents quickly reveal that contemplating values is insufficient to prevent harm; at the same time the threat of biological warfare shows us that technical expertise is insufficient without values.

MEETING CONFLICTING EXPECTATIONS FOR QUALITY EDUCATION

We have found only one definition of quality education on which nearly everyone agrees—that students should become "effective thinkers." All other purposes elicit some dis-

agreement among educators as well as among the public. Thus, quality education, however else defined, is related to effective thinking. The challenge of how this goal of high quality might be met was cogently described in the report *Involvement in Learning* (NIE, 1984), which urged that colleges establish high expectations, encourage student involvement, and assess outcomes. These three aspects of quality remain intricately linked as colleges and universities attempt to make these external demands part of their internal agenda.

We have asserted that the development of effective thinking can be assisted by developing a good academic plan (including selecting the best available instructional resources and processes for the plan), evaluating the results, and making adjustments systematically. Carefully developed academic plans do not, however, directly address the delicate balance between assuring quality and encouraging access for all students. This tension between quality and access continues to influence expectations for quality today as in the past. The result is conflicting expectations for colleges and universities that are simultaneously accountable for both access and quality. Addressing these expectations requires colleges to seek new and creative alternatives as they construct academic plans.

Colleges have gradually accepted and adopted some parts of the public mandates to improve quality. A substantial number of faculty members and administrators are taking seriously new knowledge about how students learn and are attempting to connect active learning and effective thinking. The pace of change in college instruction has increased somewhat as professors adopt new teaching strategies for courses and programs. Faculty are accepting new methods of educational evaluation and *adopting* them when they provide information directly useful for improving instruction.

Colleges continue to *screen* the demands of external agencies for summative assessment of student outcomes. Mandates from both states and accreditors now require that assessment be conducted and data be reported; sometimes state funding is contingent upon such assessments. Yet most campuses are still internalizing the assessment effort and are struggling with why, how, by whom, and for whom evaluation might be carried out. Colleges are especially wary of how assessment data will be used by external agencies to address the tension between quality and access. Assessment has not reached the adoption stage of change; quite possibly, it would disappear if the mandates were withdrawn.

Computer technology, still maturing rapidly, is a new partner with quality and access that can affect progress in both areas. It has strong potential to help ensure higher quality instruction, to develop new forms of instructional process, to extend access to new groups of students, and even to play a significant role in improving the assessment of educational quality. We have included instructional use of computing as part of the movement to meet expectations for quality because it seems likely that future definitions of quality education will assume that computer technology should have an important place in academic plans.

Awareness of the capabilities and possibilities of computers for enhancing learning and evaluation is high, but despite the heavy use of technology for noninstructional purposes, the screening process is not really underway for computer use in instruction. Are computers likely to end up in closets, then, as did earlier technologies with instructional promise? Probably not, because, in contrast to the passivity inflicted on learners by motion pictures and educational television, today's technology is interactive. Faculty who use computers can require that learners take an active part in their education. Thus, active learning, use of technology, and the

evaluation of academic plans are intricately linked with emerging demands for quality.

Learning to Think Effectively: Adoption Stage

In the 1980s, undergraduate education in colleges and universities began to receive increasing attention. In the wake of several critical reports, many faculty became aware of new instructional alternatives in planning and teaching their courses; thus, the potential for change was high. The reform reports specifically challenged faculty and institutions to consider how both general education and study in depth could be improved through students' active involvement in learning. This concern for student involvement also focused attention on the widely-accepted outcome of effective thinking.

Active learning has occurred for many years in laboratory courses, practica, discussion groups, and cooperative education. The concept of active learning was given a boost by the recent movement to infuse "writing across the curriculum" and by the development of computer conferencing, which allows extensive interaction among students and teachers even when they are not in the same place. Additional influence reached colleges and universities from opinion leaders in national higher education associations. These associations successfully sponsored materials designed to encourage faculty reflection on their own teaching and brought them to the attention of faculty members. Many college administrators supported planned change by ensuring that faculty committees and academic departments obtained the new materials. They also supported a social interaction model of change by sending teams of faculty members to conferences where the new ideas were analyzed and screened. These models were consistent with faculty decision processes in another way. That is, decisions were optional or contingent; faculty members were not forced to adopt any given new instructional practice. In the 1990s, the emphasis of the Clinton administration on community service for college students brought an active learning variation—experiential learning—clearly into the public eye.

What *is* especially important is increased recognition of the link between active learning and effective thinking. Educators have begun to accept the idea that achieving the goal of learning to think effectively involves some activity on the part of the student. The tendency to select instructional processes to ensure more student activity has progressed beyond the recognition stage. Yet the link between this goal and instructional process is still being analyzed and needs to be tested by developing more adequate and suitable means of evaluation.

Assessing and Adjusting Quality: Screening Stage

Society expects everyone who wishes to go to college to learn to think effectively. Yet some groups are concerned that academic standards are too flexible or too low and government agencies increasingly are mandating the collection of quality indicators for higher education. For example, the Southern Regional Education Board's Report, *Access to Quality* (1985), asserted that entering college students in the South are quite deficient in basic skills and must have remedial education. Additionally, the panel believed that much college-level work is not actually of collegiate quality. They urged states in the southern region to establish statewide standards for placement in collegiate courses creditable toward a college degree and to establish clear new standards for progress and for awarding the degree.

The SREB's stand is typical of the view, widely held since 1984, that improving higher education quality requires action by state leaders and cannot be left to those on campuses. Following the lead of officials in charge of precollege education, the Governors' Task Force and the Education Commission of the States added their voices to those of federal officials and educational reformers who support assessment. The six regional accrediting agencies, to which colleges and universities voluntarily belong, were beset from all sides with demands that they require institutions to present evidence of evaluation processes. Because federal agencies now supply financial assistance to students and use accrediting agencies as guarantors of educational quality, officials can persuade accreditors to adopt the new rules. Voluntary associations such as the American Association for Higher Education became opinion leaders in these efforts, helping colleges to convert these external demands to assessment strategies that seemed more consistent with educators' views. Seldom have so many forces outside colleges and universities joined to pressure them to undertake a specific activity.

Initially, the assessment movement met with strong resistance from colleges. Faculty and administrators opposed the direct entrance of government into quality determination, arguing that institutional diversity requires unique methods of assessment for each institution and program. They protested that the measures developed by governmental agencies were too simplistic or inappropriate for higher learning and, in fact, would actually obstruct the universally desired goal of helping students become effective thinkers. Yet, in the face of such strong influences, continued resistance to assessment was not an option for most colleges. Therefore, they began to develop creative ways to internalize these previously external demands and to use them to improve instruction.

One barrier to accepting assessment was the initial emphasis on standardized tests. Faculty in many fields considered these inappropriate measures of higher level effective thinking. Another barrier was critics' failure to recognize the substantial differences among the disciplines; a measure for student achievement in one field may be quite inappropriate in another. Still another difficulty was that many colleges lacked systematic data about learners' characteristics and abilities at entrance. This data deficiency made it impossible to attribute educational change to institutional or program effects. As educators have screened the demands for assessment, they have begun to develop measures adapted to the disciplines and to collect data they feel are suitable for measuring what students have gained. Despite considerable progress, these efforts are still at an early stage of development.

Still another barrier to accepting demands for assessment has been disputes about who makes evaluation judgments and how the judgments will be used. While some might argue that the threat of external intervention became sufficiently powerful to compel compliance with the assessment agenda, one can also make a convincing case that colleges have accepted assessment based on its potential for quality improvement, not on its use for accountability. The big unanswered question on campuses is not "Will assessment demonstrate quality to public sponsors?" but "Will assessment produce curricular improvement?" In any case, by the mid-1990s the focus on quality had shifted to screening strategies and techniques to be incorporated in assessing quality.

Using Technology Effectively: Awareness Stage

Some proposed changes require a lengthy period of awareness before faculty begin to analyze and screen them seriously. Then they move slowly into the next stage of innovation. The use of technology, both in the traditional classroom and for extending access to new learners, is one of the slow-moving changes on the horizon.

Use of technology for use in research, administration, routine communication, library searching, and word processing is well established in colleges. These uses developed rapidly as information technology pervaded the business world. In contrast, the influences pressing for the instructional use of technology are not especially strong. First, the need to develop students' computing skills for employment does not demand that computing be used as an instructional process. Second, there are no powerful external agencies threatening dire consequences if faculty do not use computer-based instruction.

According to experts, although 50% of faculty own a desktop computer, less than 10% of faculty actually use computers for instruction. Geoghegan (1994) attributes the lack of instructional use to the fact that early alliances between computer manufacturers and colleges involved faculty minimally and focused on technology while neglecting pedagogy and the disciplines. It is also possible that new advances in computers have come so fast that there has been little time for the typical contemplation and careful instructional planning faculty prefer before changing their instructional methods. Sometimes change requires a plateau—a period of accommodation and reflection. A variety of circumstances are creating awareness of instructional potential of computers, yet the rate of screening remains slow. External pressure may be increasing, however. In early 1994, the Clinton administration set the pace for the nation by announcing the National Information Infrastructure. In response, EDUCOM, a consortium of over 600 colleges and 122 technology companies, began a focus on instructional issues by launching the National Learning Infrastructure Initiative in November 1994. This group needs now to catch the attention of key college decision makers who are pressed by other issues.

Technology in Classrooms

Mainframe computers found their way onto the campuses less than fifty years ago. In some types of institutions, especially liberal arts colleges, their introduction brought heated debate about whether computer literacy, usually in the form of programming skills, was a legitimate course of study for credit. The debate never really was begun in earnest since successive definitions of computer literacy went out of date before faculty could agree on them. Rapid changes in technology are themselves an obstacle to adopting that technology.

Computers found their way to faculty desktops in the early 1980s and spread rapidly for about a decade. Word processing and calculating were among the first wide-scale uses, but communication is one of the most effective uses of computers on campus now. Electronic mail has changed the daily lives of most faculty members; they are accessible for rapid responses to student questions, as well as those from colleagues and administrators. There is a sense of closer communication with each of these groups. Another impetus for increased use arrived in the early 1990s, when the information highways were developed that allow faculty to retrieve infinite types of information. Still, instructional applications have lagged.

Given the recognized differences among disciplines in the construction of academic plans, there are good reasons to expect discipline differences in the rate of adoption of instructional technology. Although faculty in scientific and mathematical fields are more active in developing software, little is known about the specific effects of discipline. More will be learned as commercial materials become available and instructors who are not involved in developing software begin to use that developed by others, just as they might use textbooks.

Computers may be used for instruction at several levels. Computer-assisted learning for drill and practice is a technique that has been on campuses a long time. Well-established uses of computers on campuses include word processing, spreadsheets, graphic packages, information retrieval, and electronic mail, all of which can play a part in instruction and faculty–student communication. Although the personal computer has expanded some aspects of teaching and learning, particularly in writing and scientific computation, the greatest potential for change may be the use of multimedia education—the videotapes, videodiscs, and CD-ROMs—all of which can be linked with and controlled by computers.

Use of computers for direct instruction and for computer-supported cooperative learning is within reach. Much of the potential depends on two relatively recent developments—the Internet, a worldwide communication system, and the CD-ROM, a digitized system of compacting large amount of information on a small disk for retrieval on a inexpensive computer. Accessed through the Internet, the World Wide Web allows a seamless link of graphic images, sound, and text. Indeed, when one thinks of the potential for vicarious travel around the world, coupled with maps, photographs, and the voices of the speakers of each country that is possible with a CD-ROM, the distance that has been traveled is great, both toward instructional change and closer communication.

The possibilities of viewing things that have not been visible before range from three-dimensional models of crystals and molecules to videotape portrayals of ethical dilemmas that students can discuss. Music can be synthesized and different orchestral arrangement tried for their effect. Virtual reality is a system of making users feel like they are at a given place in three dimensions. Now, on CD-ROM, students can browse through encyclopedias, atlases, all of the holdings of the Library of Congress, museums, and newspaper archives, to name a few. Expensive laboratory slides in biology and medicine can be stored and retrieved without danger of deterioration or breakage. Economists can simulate varied economic conditions; chemists can simulate experiments without real chemicals, theater buffs can view real productions, and artists can generate computerized fabric designs, then control the looms that weave them.

Through LAN technology (Local Area Networks) many computers can be joined to transfer information, conduct demonstrations, or work on a problem jointly. On some campuses students bring small portable computers to class as "notebooks" and "download" the professor's notes from an electronic blackboard to their own files.

Interactive computing means that students' responses can determine what happens next. All of the images, graphics, and texts can be arranged so that they allow and even require that the learner be active. In computerized adaptive testing, for example, the test given varies with student preparation; the computer generates an easy or harder test item depending on how the student answered the previous question. One can imagine both test questions and lessons geared to the students' learning styles as well. The potential is enormous. There is no question that technology will change instruction. Children are starting to work with computers by age 3, and many will be prepared for these new instructional processes.

Why then, is movement toward change so slow? Why have computers not been fully adopted for instructional purposes? First, change is slow because faculty are slow to replace traditional lecture methods by any technology, including computers; most have not thought creatively about what instructional processes might supplant the lecture. Second, some of the early claims made about computers were negative; they raised the specter of impersonal education without student-instructor interaction. Third, instruction lags

because the educational environment is lukewarm. Faculty report that there are no clear rewards or peer review system for creating and evaluating instructional software (Kozma, Johnston, & Sossen, in progress). Furthermore, there is no defined system for helping faculty to learn how to use computers for instruction. In fact, the lack of learning opportunities for faculty in instructional technology casts in bold relief the fact that few teaching resources exist for faculty to develop new instructional skills of any sort.

In fact, by the mid-1990s, some of the negative expectations had been quashed. Although the interaction may be through electronic means rather than face to face, computers are now seen as fostering, rather than hindering, communication between professors and students. The professor can provide individualized attention and prompt tailored feedback. Interaction among students is also enhanced since computer networks can promote collaborative learning through conferencing and e-mail among individuals who never meet. Asynchronous arrangements give students automatic wait time to frame responses. Much of the responsibility for contributing ideas in a computer conference moves to the students. Electronic interactive communication methods may also encourage shy students to enter the discussion. All of these aspects of the new technology become advantages in efforts to use active means to encourage effective thinking.

The technology will not relieve faculty of the need to ask questions about the links between desired outcomes and instructional process in their academic plans. For example, we may ask how the computer will be used to move students from being novice problem solvers to expert problem solvers, novice learners to intentional learners, information seekers to information synthesizers, poor communicators to adept communicators, and aspiring professionals to competent professionals. We note, too, that many implications of the computer technology revolution are beyond the scope of our curriculum discussion but will occupy the attention of educators, administrators, and lawyers. These include copyright issues, technology transfer profits, royalties for software production, computer citizenship, privacy, and ethical use, data security, threats of loss of faculty jobs, and potential closing of institutions. Such a list portends a similarly lengthy set of problems when instruction using computers enters the adoption stage.

Distance Learning

Distance learning is defined by three characteristics: (1) it is interactive; (2) teacher and students are physically separated, and the students are at multiple locations; and (3) the time may be either synchronous or asynchronous (Cartwright, 1994). Clearly, telecommunications devices and the computer have now provided an effective technological means to facilitate distance learning. It is possible to limit the amount of traveling faculty members and students must do to interact on the material to be learned. The influences to use this technology are increasing in strength. Arguably, the first distance learning was the homework assignment. Later, independent study, contract learning, and self-paced work separated teacher and learner; correspondence courses and programmed instruction also had some elements of distance learning, but although the learner was autonomous, there was no dialogue or social interaction (Moore, 1973).

Distance learning as we think of it today has its historical roots in the "colleges without walls" of the 1970s; both these colleges and distance learning were developed to serve adult students whose responsibilities precluded travel to a traditional classroom. Both are part of the historical trend to increase access as well as the gradual movement toward increased student choice and re-

sponsibility for instructional involvement. The University of Mid-America, modeled on the British Open University, was an early attempt at distance learning using television as a delivery system. It reportedly served 20,000 students in seven midwestern states between 1974 and 1982 before closing due to funding problems. Although its life was short, the University of Mid-America was a catalyst for innovative thinking.

Today, 43% of college students attend part time and are potential distance learners. This expanding group has already established the need for alternatives to traditional classrooms. Obvious candidates are prisoners, the physically challenged, residents of geographically remote areas (e.g., the sparsely populated mountain states, Alaska, the widely separated Hawaiian Islands). In states with recognized needs, legislatures are providing funds to develop distance learning instead of constructing new campuses. The University of Alaska presents perhaps the most dramatic example with students hundreds of miles away linked to the campuses in Juneau and Fairbanks. Rural North Dakota serves over one thousand students by linking eleven campuses with interactive video. In 1995, the University of Maine began converting its education network into an official university without a campus. Utah linked its higher education institutions in a technology net; Maryland planned 300 distance learning sites by linking both public colleges and public high schools. Iowa linked colleges, offices, schools, and libraries so that people can take college courses from all of these places. The California State University DELTA project (Direct Enhancement of Learning through Technology Assistance & Alternatives) is being developed as an economical way to handle the crush of additional students expected in a few years without building new campuses. The *Chronicle of Higher Education* reported in 1994 that a group of young scholars were trying to establish a Virtual On-line University where students would take all classes live on computer networks (Jacobsen, 1994b). Associations called free-nets are linking members of local communities with information networks. Those without computers can sign on to the systems at some public libraries. Many predict that by 2010 most students will be able to take courses from universities all over the world, while the students enrolled in courses sponsored by a single university will be from many countries.

Not all education available at a distance comes from college classrooms. Libraries and museums also transmit books and journals by computer without ever being printed. The Micro Gallery of the National Gallery of Art gives details about its 2,500 pieces of art, providing a more comprehensive course in art appreciation and history than might be designed by a professor. The World Wide Web provides access to hundreds of databases on every conceivable topic.

Distance learning is a change that has been most advocated by those outside colleges—for example, state policymakers who have often been first to recognize the need to serve unserved populations. States are also willing to invest in distance learning as a way to serve a greater number of students at lower cost. Still, most of the influence that reaches faculty directly is the diffusion of information through media, journals, and newsletters. With specific exceptions in some of the low population areas, most faculty have not yet directly felt much pressure to be involved.

Several barriers hamper the widespread trial of distance learning. One, of course, is how slowly computerized instruction in general is being adopted. Another is the lack of faculty training for new roles. A third is the necessity for constructing academic plans far in advance, often without much knowledge of learner characteristics or responses. Beyond these issues, which concern faculty specifically, college and university administrators have sometimes resisted distance learning for

fear that their on-campus enrollments will decrease. Administrators have been particularly reluctant if they are asked to contribute substantial sums from already tight budgets to link with central network systems.

Since it is hard to monitor electronic transmissions, colleges in some states feel threatened by institutions from other states who beam electronic signals to prospective students, encouraging them to enroll. Within states, institutions also are beginning to battle over divisions of service territory. Distance learning may spawn a new kind turf battle over credit distribution and enrollment management. Clearly, distance learning has a high potential for forcing changes in educational environments as institutions necessarily cease to compete and begin to cooperate. The collegewide academic plan may be most strongly affected as various institutions agree to offer specific disciplines or programs while encouraging students seeking other specialities to get "on-line" with former competitors.

IMPLICATIONS OF CHANGES FOR ACADEMIC PLANNING

Purpose and Content

Diverse learners at U.S. colleges and universities bring new demands for curriculum change. Interest groups such as women and minorities combine their calls for change with those of critical theorists and internationalists who seek to promote a new vision of a global society. These pluralist perspectives lead to changes in educational purpose and content that would not occur if internal influences and adjustment processes were the sole determinants of academic plans. Analyzing the movement toward the inclusion of multicultural content in higher education, Levine and Cureton (1992) conclude that, despite "a quiet revolution of sorts," the activity has not been systematic; change has occurred more by accretion than design. The next question, they suggest, is what form the relationship between diverse perspectives and curriculum content should take. Answering such a question will require attention to educational purpose as well as to content.

In demanding change of educational purpose, pluralists seek to modify some of the traditional (and often discipline-bound) educational purposes faculty have espoused. Arguments are being advanced for new types of intellectual development, for greater emphasis on the clarification of values, and especially for education that prepares students to initiate transformative societal change. Both critical theory and ethnic studies challenge the notion that education is a value-free exploration of human history, activity, knowledge, and creativity. Thus, although teaching students to think effectively remains an important purpose, its definition is being broadened to move beyond the tradition of viewing knowledge as objective to a pluralistic view of knowledge as constructed by the student. According to Cole (1991), a profound chasm separates the claims of what is taught and the reality. The reality, she asserts, is that the curriculum in U.S. colleges and universities is based on a Eurocentric perspective of the world that reflects a racial, gender, and class bias distorting the experiences of those from other cultural traditions. The purpose of education, she continues, is not to help students gain an understanding of the world through the traditional disciplines. Rather, the student must study the world so that he or she may take a place in it, understand it, and actively participate in changing it.

Sequence

Faculty members who wish to achieve these new purposes must consciously make decisions about other elements of the academic plan. The struggle to include pluralistic views in the curriculum faces battles quite similar to

those faced in previous eras by disciplines as they emerged from parent fields such as natural philosophy. Pluralistic views must compete for scarce curricular space. The academic plan element we have called *sequence* encompasses many questions about how and when to include multicultural perspectives in the undergraduate course of study:

- Should a course on multiculturalism be required or encouraged? Is one course sufficient or is a sequence necessary?
- Should all courses be infused with multicultural perspectives?
- Is an entire program called for?
- What do we sacrifice by not reforming the curriculum?
- How can the new content be connected with students' past and future lives?
- What other content will be replaced as these connections are made?

According to Gaff (1991), the majority of recent change has come in the form of supplementing existing courses rather than in developing new courses. But the content and sequences of academic plans are reconfigured as new ideas are screened and adapted on each campus. Although the change to multiculturalism may be on the near horizon, the decisions about sequence needed to fully achieve a global curriculum may require totally new thinking about the content included in undergraduate education.

Concerns about sequence that stem from the effort to incorporate multiple perspectives link closely with the efforts to increase coherence. Although most educators and members of the public believe that they know what coherence means, attempts to share definitions and examples quickly reveal a wide variety of meanings. If the educational community admits multiple purposes, (that is, accepts pluralism), then decisions about variations in content, sequence, and choice of instructional process that must be made to achieve this elusive goal can be considered. On the other hand, if one does not admit that legitimate differences of opinion exist or that different forms of coherence are appropriate for different students, the discussion about constructing academic plans halts. Lack of recognition of these disparate views has caused educators to deal with the superficial aspects of coherence, like distribution requirements, rather than grapple with the more complex aspects of interdisciplinarity and integration of general and career education.

Coherence involves both content and sequence; it extends the recurring pattern of debate about general education versus specialized or utilitarian education. It also extends the long-standing debate about who should make curricular choices. Coherence and connectedness are not separate but linked with society's goals; new conceptions of what coherence means gradually replace old. Most of the general-versus-specialized-education conflict centers on the need for all students to acquire a breadth of study; the greatest threat to the liberal arts, however, may be a decrease in student majors. Some have accused the liberal arts fields of being as professionalized as collegiate career studies, arguing that they draw students into their own educational and disciplinary cultures, not the broader cultures of business, society, or other organizations. One radical remedy is to view majors in the arts and sciences as professional preparation for graduate school and the professorial or scholarly life. As such, they might be taught only in selected colleges and universities where clear linkages with graduate programs exist. Faculty in arts and sciences in other colleges could then devote their intellectual power to the general education program, supporting with contextual study those professional programs judged appropriate for the college mission. Such a proposal for distinctive missions seems especially feasible if,

through distance learning, many students begin to stay at home and enroll in the strongest programs from afar.

Resources

The question of instructional resources arises in academic plans in terms of the availability of both materials and instructors. Observers note only scattered commitment to the internationalization of the curriculum. Undoubtedly infusions of new resources for both travel and faculty development will be needed to achieve internationalization, along with stronger external influences to convince colleges to make this goal a program or college agenda.

Including readings by individuals of different cultures and theoretical perspectives involves a fairly simple change in resources. The need for different instructors is somewhat more controversial. Because of the personalized approaches to ethnic and women's studies, debate is sometimes intense about whether individuals who have not experienced minority or women's lives can teach about them adequately. For internationalization, the problem is one of faculty development; for ethnic and women's studies, some feel the problem is one of faculty recruitment.

Planning to use both active learning and instructional technology require infusions of three components: new funds, faculty development, and the recruitment of technical personnel, now only minimally represented in most colleges. Before using technology in the classroom, faculty must make more deliberate decisions about content, sequence, and process than is typical when planning for lecture and discussion methods. (In fact, some faculty plan quite casually for lectures and discussions in traditional classrooms; this may not be an option on the Internet or in a virtual classroom.) The success of distance learning may require a team approach to both planning and delivery that is unfamiliar to most faculty members. Although it will be important not to remove decisions about instructional process from the instructor's realm, new teams, including technical personnel and instructional design specialists, are a distinct possibility.

Instructional Process

Because the pluralistic voices call simultaneously for an end to the dominance of the traditional literary canon and an expansion of curricular boundaries to include other cultural and theoretical perspectives, they challenge colleges and universities to complement changes in curricular content with changes in instructional processes. Some urge a conceptualization of the teacher as helper rather than sage and the substitution of students' learning goals for teachers' course and program goals. They hope that students will be encouraged to examine conflicts rather than submerge them. In the new pedagogy, professors would empower students to recognize their own voices and abilities. Such a view of the learning process varies substantially from that underlying the traditional lecture. Are there best ways to help students take multiple perspectives? What methods work for what types of students?

The demand for new instructional process is, however, quite consistent with those of advocates for active learning and effective thinking. In fact, such changes are already in progress. The influences that encourage colleges to assure high-quality education affect the types of instructional experiences that are included in course and program plans most directly. These experiences seem likely to change rapidly as active learning increases, as technology-based instruction expands, and as better means of assessing the results are developed. Probably many of these changes could not have been fully implemented in earlier times. They awaited full acceptance of access to higher education for citizens regard-

less of background and location and the means of achieving it.

The emphasis on increasing coherence also implies new active instructional processes, notably problem solving. Life is a series of ill-structured problems to be solved, and students will need much practice. The subject domain of the problems is not as crucial as the adaptability needed to analyze the problem and consider alternative solutions. Both coherence and effective thinking transcend courses, disciplines, and current preparation for work. In this sense the liberal and utilitarian positions are congruent, and capitalizing on their respective strengths will require changes in instructional processes.

Learners

Both active learning processes and effective software designs must take into account the prior knowledge and abilities of students. Yet professors may have little face-to-face contact with distance learners. This will encourage instructional teams to develop software with options from which students can select, according to their backgrounds and learning styles. The ability to develop suitable options for technological teaching is likely to improve the ability to do so in the traditional classroom as well. The selection among options, however, raises important questions about how learners will be prepared to choose from a broader set of learning opportunities. For example: Will we have to develop learners' skills to make them intentional learners before they can handle distance learning? Will we need to modify some people's learning styles and strategies to allow them to be successful? What will provide motivation from afar? Will the technology change students' goals or expectations of succeeding at the task? Will students be inclined not to persist when the commitment to take a single course by distance learning is easily abandoned? Will computer knowledge become part of the required core of studies that every citizen should have? Will it be considered a new "basic skill" to be able to retrieve information from on-line sources? More questions than answers about learners and their preparation are available at this time.

An important question related to the connection between education and work concerns the degree to which colleges have a career counseling and job placement responsibility to their students. Nothing currently in the general education program leads to good decision making about majors or about future careers. In fact, students graduating from college receive little formal career direction. On the one hand, the majority of students change their majors during college, and educators wish to avoid tracking students into specialties too early. On the other hand, there is essentially no job exploration during the freshmen and sophomore years. The possibility of distant learners who have to make more and more of their academic and career choices independently may spur the development of improved materials, or it could simply reinforce the tendency of colleges to ignore counseling needs.

Evaluation and Adjustment

Evaluation and adjustment remain areas of the academic plan that are readily ignored, so good decisions are rare. Current measurement techniques may be of limited help in assessing whether new challenges have been addressed successfully. Educators who are just beginning to come to grips with assessing basic skills are far from capable of determining whether students have acquired attitudinal outcomes such as multiple perspectives.

Both active learning processes and technological instruction not only demand new methods of evaluation and adjustment but can help to provide them. For example, simulations and cases can provide active ways of evaluating student development; computers will increasingly be used for computer adaptive testing. Beyond these basic evaluation changes, however, external degrees and courses will pose many new questions about evaluation methods, testing strategies, coherence, and quality standards in new setting.

Yet the problem is more challenging than measurement alone. The traditional behaviorist psychology requires stating learning objectives and measuring their demonstration through goal-focused evaluation. In contrast, pluralist voices see knowledge as socially constructed. As such, it must be recognized as partial, incomplete, and distorted, differing for each learner, and preferably expressed in his or her own words. Measurement of learning, though never easy, may be more difficult to achieve if these two views of learning and evaluation lead to polarization of faculty groups. Without choosing one side or the other, we can see how complex questions become even more complex in the prevailing climate. It is hard to ask evaluation questions when the answers may be perceived to reflect adversely on specific groups or on the curricular solutions they have proposed and in which they have faith.

Educational Environments

One can imagine a wide variety of changes in educational environments as extended access through distance learning interacts with public demands for assessment and accountability. Computer-accessed communication will need to include electronic catalogs and advising services for students. At the program level, institutions will need to provide better guidance so students can find the opportunities available to them through technology in a convenient location and timeframe. Computers can enhance counseling by providing routine information and may free faculty and staff to deal more systematically with curriculum development.

As we noted, campuses may have to become more cooperative in offering distance learning. This could lead to the allocation of specific program specialities to different campuses, increasing specialization for both faculty and students. The potential for eliminating duplicate programs with small enrollments throughout a state holds the promise of economy that may free resources to develop new systems.

Calendars and credit systems may need to become much more flexible to accommodate students who accumulate credits from many colleges through distance learning and wish to apply them toward a degree. In contrast to current stress on coherent academic programs, the distance learner may, knowingly or unwittingly, pursue an extremely fragmented program. One can envision the need for a state-operated centralized record-keeping system linked with distance learning systems from all state-level institutions. Such a system could be programmed to block registration for course in the absence of pre-requisites or of correct fit with the students' program.

Distance learning also has the potential to redefine current concepts of equity in financial aid and increase the complexity of demands for accountability. Those students who can afford to buy a computer will have access; those who can't afford one will not. Conceivably, it will be necessary to provide computer access instead of tuition or as part of a tuition-based financial aid package. But when a distance student using an assigned computer drops out, who will be held accountable for loans and equipment return?

The pressures for quality education are strongly linked with other debates that are less directly related to academic plans. These include arguments to adjust the current balance of emphasis between research and teaching, to improve the training of college teachers, and to modify reward systems in research institutions. New norms for curriculum development and a new professional view of college teaching will develop to address fully the issues of quality assurance as access continues to broaden.

THE DYNAMIC CURRICULUM

Throughout our discussion, we have noted linkages among the three major challenges to achieve diverse perspectives, increase coherence, and meet conflicting expectations for quality and access. None of these changes in progress can be separated from the others, nor can they be separated from the societal context that presses them forward.

A great deal of rhetoric exhorts colleges to make curriculum changes. Usually such exhortations are based on beliefs that the existing academic plans are deficient or that change is not keeping pace with society. Some curriculum changes result from internal review and related decisions. Internally initiated changes are usually slow and deliberate, and, at the same time, they may be either rational or political. Other changes respond to societal influences; we have suggested that these external influences often become internalized before colleges respond to them. In the process they are recognized, screened, and finally adopted. Despite the three stages, this process can be rapid when the influence is strong and the source powerful.

The curriculum changes we selected for discussion demonstrate several models of change: problem-solving models, diffusion models, rational models, and power-coercion models. A problem-solving model resulted as some colleges self-identified with external diagnoses of curricular deficiencies made in national reports and critiques, leading faculty to seek correctives. Associations encouraged change through social interaction models when they published reports showing that others were pursuing change. In fostering social interaction and diffusion, the higher education associations accepted the role of linkage agents and opinion leaders. Several "early adopter" campuses that measured student educational outcomes and used the knowledge gained in curricular revisions also illustrate the diffusion model. Various associations showcased the work of these institutions for others to follow. Finally, elements of a power–coercion model of change have been mentioned, specifically, when states and accreditors have mandated skills and achievement testing to ensure quality or specified that distance learning will replace campus construction.

While the college curriculum may appear static to some, it is actually quite dynamic because the influences toward change wax and wane. Among them are the evolving social relationships in society reflected in the emergence of multicultural perspectives, the evolving paradigms and knowledge bases in the disciplines noted in the emergence of new academic voices, the new ways of learning based on evolving psychological knowledge and technological capability, and the changing demographics of learners as access has increased. Quality standards are not fixed; their changes are reflected in the emerging relativism that some loathe and others applaud. Even national boundaries vary, causing changing definitions of what internationalization and globalization of education might mean in the future.

Earlier we maintained that educational purpose does not typically change as a result of systematic evaluation and adjustment processes. Rather the enduring curriculum debates that lead to changes in purpose are those that result from shifts in society. Often these changes occur over long periods and are hardly noticed. The slow process of translating influences from society to the curriculum and the lengthy debates about specific changes have usually insulated the curriculum from direct political intervention. Academic change has moved in a slow and deliberate manner to adapt to society rather than to reform it.

A relatively common way to open a discussion about colleges reflects their position as target of reform movements from many external groups. One author began by saying that "higher education needs more flexibility and responsiveness than in the past" because of "today's conditions" (Seymour, 1988, p. 31). From a historical standpoint this statement could have begun a speech in any era of U.S. history. Certainly the rapid growth of disciplines and colleges in the 1920s and 1930s required flexibility and responsiveness. Major adaptations were made in university structure to undertake crucial war-related research in the 1940s, followed promptly by the return of a new type of adult student, the war veteran. Surely, higher education demonstrated its resiliency during the forties. Substantial flexibility and responsiveness again characterized the 1960s and 1970s when student protests caused loosening of curricular structures. One could argue that responsiveness and flexibility are required today just as they have always been required. Alternatively, one could argue that a fundamental change in society—namely, the rapidity with which information is now exchanged—creates a greater need for flexibility. One reason for faculty and administrators to recognize increasing the potency of the influences on curriculum, the stages of progress toward change, and the specific aspects of academic plans that are likely to be affected is to help mold external issues before they become fully internalized in colleges.

CHAPTER 13

Shaping Curriculum Research and Practice

THE ACADEMIC PLAN THEORY AS A GUIDE FOR RESEARCH

We have defined *curriculum* as an academic plan that is developed in a historical, social, and political context. Using this definition, we outlined a theory of college curriculum that provides an organizing framework for considering curricular issues, serves as a guide for curriculum research, and helps faculty and administrators design academic plans more effectively. The core of the academic plan theory includes eight elements or decision categories and the relationships among them. The theory also links the evaluation of educational outcomes with adjustments in both academic plans and the environment in which they are developed. A final part of the theory focuses on how factors internal and external to colleges and academic programs influence the educational environment and thus, directly or indirectly, affect the elements of the plan.

Using this theoretical framework to organize our discussion we devoted chapters to one or several of the eight elements essential to developing an academic plan, focusing on

decisions that college professors make as curriculum planners. In each case we first outlined what we know about how professors currently plan courses and programs, then described alternative ideas about planning that might make their plans more effective. We referred to the professors' current informal practices as *planning,* reserving *design* for processes that include more systematic and deliberate attention to each element. We concluded our discussion by elaborating on the evaluation element, which can lead to adjustment and thus to a new cycle of planning.

Then we turned our attention to the educational environment in which academic plans are developed. We acknowledged the joint role of faculty and administrators as key decision makers about curricular plans, but focused on the role of administrators in establishing a supportive environment for planning internally and organizationally. We also examined more fully the interface between society and the college environment, noting that the curriculum changes through both routine adjustment and innovation. We hypothesized that, once colleges become aware of a new demand from society and have examined and screened it, they may accept and adapt it in their local contexts. This multistage change process of awareness, screening, and adoption both guides and slows the curriculum's response to changes in society. From this perspective, we examined three broad areas of curriculum change now in progress, estimating their current stage of "internalization" by colleges and universities. Now we return to our theory of curriculum, elaborating more fully on its advantages and suggesting that it can be tested and extended.

Others have constructed models and frameworks for examining curriculum but the task is challenging and most models have remained incomplete. In an important synthesis of literature on college curriculum planning, Conrad and Pratt (1983, pp. 16–17) described several existing models of curriculum planning and asserted that diverse models led to confusion and were not useful to planners. They described five deficiencies of these models:

1. Insufficient attention to relations with the internal and external environments of the college or university

2. Too little interaction between various components of curriculum, compared to the emphasis on individual components

3. Prescriptive models, rather than descriptive or explanatory models

4. Models that do not encourage the integration of nontraditional curricula

5. Models too abstract to be actually applicable to curriculum planning

The descriptive and explanatory theory of curriculum that we have presented addresses the deficiencies Conrad and Pratt described. In this chapter, we explore the relationships within the theory that need to be developed and tested, summarize the utility of our theory for guiding curriculum decisions, and pose some challenges for the future.

What Is Curriculum Theory?

The traditional function of curriculum theory and research is to guide the development, implementation, and evaluation of plans for learning. Discussions of curriculum theory for elementary and secondary schools are often devoted primarily to the examination of the *decisions* that determine what is taught and why. This implies that reasonably consistent and coherent principles about how decisions are made can constitute a curriculum theory. In higher education also, professors espouse principles that form the basis for decisions and actions, although such principles are shared infrequently. Thus a basis for theory exists if the theory can capture in a consistent framework the variety of decisions professors make.

In addition to making decisions about academic plans, another seldom-acknowledged similarity exists between college and precollege education. Educational theorists point out that at the elementary and secondary school level, decisions about curriculum are negotiated in society. This is also true for colleges but in higher education, course-level academic plans often do not *appear* to be directly negotiated with society. Rather, societal issues may be filtered through an individual instructor's perspectives. At the program level, the process of negotiation with society begins to become more obvious, but faculty view academic programs as chiefly products of influences within the university. Finally, at the institutional level, academics may reluctantly admit that missions are often directly negotiated, if not with society as a whole, then with special sectors of society. In truth, as historical examples make clear, society's influence affects every level of academic plan. A viable theory must incorporate these influences to correctly describe decisions about change.

For elementary and secondary school curriculum, writers have developed many theories and even typologies to classify them. One common typology includes structure-oriented theories, value-oriented theories, content-oriented theories, and process-oriented theories. The theoretical frame that is operating—structure, value, content, or process—is the one that focuses the debate about curriculum decisions. It is obvious that this range of possible theories exists in higher education as well.

We return, therefore, to a question we posed earlier: Why has a theory (or at least a model) of curriculum decisions in higher education been lacking? Quite possibly no theory has been developed because the task was too large as envisioned. In an early analysis, Toombs (1977–78) believed that the vast scope of the topic would likely prevent the creation of a general theory:

> The theory would have to encompass the range at [sic] individual behaviors, attitudes and values among young adults and other potential students. It would have to link the psychologies of learning, personality, and development into the formal and informal curriculum. On the faculty side, the relationship of a professor to his or her field of knowledge as institutionalized in the university would have to be accounted for, a feat which amounts to constructing a unified theory of knowledge and another for organizational behavior. Finally, such a theory would need to explain the relationship between institutions and society. (p. 21)

In a sense, Toombs was right. Only the broadest theory can be generalized to fit diverse and relatively autonomous settings. The variety of academic programs available to diverse students in very different types of U.S. colleges implies numerous dimensions of a theory. To show the comprehensive set of literatures related to curriculum, Stark and Lowther (1986) published a graphic depiction similar to that shown in Figure 13-1. When academic plans become the central

focus, the diagram demonstrates that almost any topic in higher education can be viewed as relevant to the curriculum, creating the possibility of very complex theories.

It appears that Toombs's early work envisioned a theory that simultaneously belonged to all the classifications developed by curriculum theorists, as well as all the topics portrayed in Figure 13-1. He called for a theory that would be at once driven by structure, content, values, and process. For example, his theory would not only include learners as a major element but would require a complete listing of all of their possible variations.

We believe that a useful theory must be more focused and parsimonious than the one Toombs envisioned, or all hopes of testing it and using it to shape practice would be dashed. In our view, a useful theory can encompass all of the possible perspectives by emphasizing one and subsuming the others within it. Therefore, when we emphasized decisions about important academic plan elements, we subsumed the content-driven, value-driven, and process-driven theories within what curriculum analysts have called a structural theory. A structural theory assumes that teaching and learning activities can be identified, designed, and directed. In a structural theory, the content (disciplines) and values (purposes) to be learned, as well as the instructional processes to be used, become elements of the theory that may be varied to achieve different designs rather than prescribing a single design. Because the elements remain generic, rather than assuming normative identities, the permissible variations include those which currently exist and those which may emerge in the future.

In colleges, however, we will be misunderstood if we use the term *structural* theory of curriculum because the term *curriculum structure* usually connotes the counting of course credits, the approval of prerequisite courses, and similar aspects of managing academic programs. A focus on these manage-

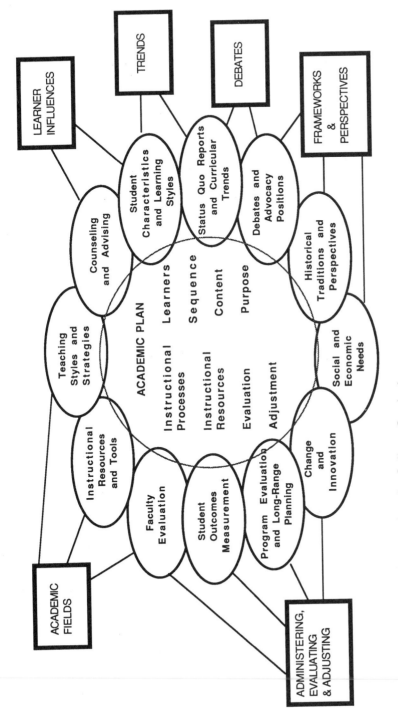

FIGURE 13-1 **Literature Related to the College Curriculum**

Source: Adapted from *Designs for Learning* by Stark & Lowther (1986), p. 7. Reprinted by permission of the National Center for Research to Improve Postsecondary Teaching and Learning, The University of Michigan.

ment structures would imply that a structural theory would be static, dealing mostly with "things" such as space, workload, enrollment, costs, library volumes, salaries, and organizational infrastructures. We think the important theorizing that college faculty have neglected about their own curriculum enterprise concerns instead "dynamic issues," especially those that involve the interactions of people and the processes that concern people. The teacher–student, teacher–teacher, and student–student relationships, and the processes of teaching/learning, evaluating, and adjusting are dynamic and changing. Thus, while our theory fits the structural classification as defined by other curriculum theorists, we prefer to call it a dynamic structural theory to emphasize that a carefully designed and flexible academic plan should be continuously shaping the institutional scaffolding, not the reverse.

We have linked the elements in our theory in ways that seem appropriate to us and that represent the reality we have observed. The truth of these propositions and the nature of the linkages are tentative; they present a scheme to be explored and to be questioned. If a predicted relationship fails to be confirmed, then some component of the theory must be mistaken and we must rethink it. Because a tested theory has been lacking, there have been many speculations and expressions of curricular preferences but few studies about curriculum that can be compared and few replicable tests of relationships.

Testing and Extending the Theory

Testing a theory is akin to meta-evaluation, which we stressed when discussing the evaluation of academic plans. Meta-evaluation, or evaluating the evaluation process for academic plans, can lead us to improve our evaluation procedures. In the same way, theory

testing may help us modify the way we define the elements of an academic plan and extend our theory in the future. Meta-evaluation reminds us of the need to evaluate our own work as curriculum theorists and planners, partly because as researchers we are curious about the activity of curriculum development, and partly because we believe that examining our own ways of constructing meaning will make the theory more useful for others.

Evaluators and researchers have different motives. Research is undertaken because an investigator is curious about the world and hopes to find generalizations that will fit many similar settings; in applied fields such as education, he or she frequently believes that research will lead to frameworks that guide evaluation and, thus, better decisions (Worthen & Sanders, 1987). Decision makers undertake evaluation because they must make decisions and wish to make the best ones possible. They often evaluate without guidance from theory and limit the evaluation to the specific context of the necessary decision. These two differently focused processes of evaluation and research may be connected more closely with respect to curriculum planning than for some other issues. We have proposed the need for a theory of curriculum because, by understanding the nature of curriculum plans and the context in which they are made (whether or not we theorize about them), we can contribute to the process of evaluation throughout our research. In education and the social sciences, where naturally occurring phenomena are under study and human lives are at stake, it is often difficult to demonstrate relationships within a theory. Nevertheless, making the theory more solid can improve our understanding and ability to guide curriculum practice.

We introduced the idea that the academic plan could be viewed as a theory of curriculum because this allowed us to specify elements that occur in any academic plan and about which decisions must be made. The second step is to show how one decision affects another. Both of these types of knowledge are of interest to decision makers and researchers.

Exploring Relationships among the Plan's Elements

We have identified a reasonably parsimonious set of or elements in curriculum planning, identified some tentative relationships among them, and built on our observations to derive some hypotheses. In Figure 13-2 we have arranged the elements of the academic plan spatially to be more assertive than we have been earlier about some of the known and unknown relationships. In the figure, we have grouped the elements of the academic plan into three sets: (1) those concerned with curricular intent and its development (purpose

and content); (2) those concerned with implementation (learners, sequences, resources), and with instructional process; and (3) those concerned with evaluation. Not surprisingly, when the elements are grouped in this way, the similarity with Astin's input-environment-output model is striking—as it should be, for both are systems models. The problem that characterizes college curriculum thinking is that only the first set—the concern with intent—has been fully acknowledged as the grist of typical discussions of curriculum. All relationships within the sets and among the sets have not been systematically explored. We have used heavy, solid arrows to show the relationships that we believe are well substantiated and shaded arrows to indicate those that are more speculative.

A key element in our framework, as in all curriculum discussions, is the purpose of

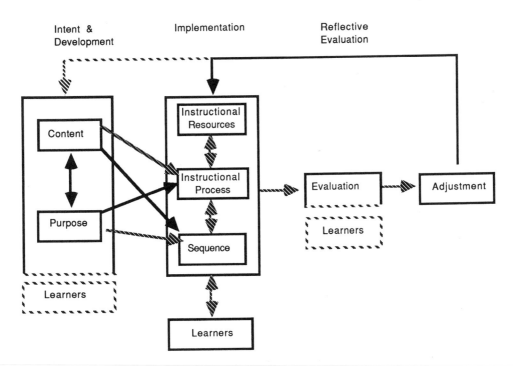

FIGURE 13-2   A Proposed Set of Relationships among Academic Plan Elements

education. Instead of viewing this element as the only important one, however, we have recognized its links with other elements. What are the natures of these links? At this point, we are on solid ground to assert, for example, that, based on the characteristics of their field, faculty members in different academic fields may choose different purposes and related instructional sequences and processes. In fact, we are frequently able to predict purpose, content, and sequence based on discipline and to recognize special conditions when the specific context in which curriculum decisions are made may make such predictions inaccurate.

We have documented also that, while most faculty aim to teach effective thinking, they have different ways of defining it based on their field and the other purposes of education they espouse. Consequently, we are convinced that, *content* (broadly defined as the characteristics of the academic field and the professor's view of it) is the second most important predictor of how academic plans are shaped. Content is always important—for career-oriented programs as well as for the traditional liberal arts disciplines. Furthermore, the interaction of content and purpose translates to instructional process and sequence in ways often independent of learner influence. Thus, in the intent stage of developing academic plans, we include learners in a disconnected broken box to show them as potentially, but not currently, influential. Apparently, the needs of learners become most concrete for faculty at the implementation stage, an observation we portray with a solid box.

Recently, the assessment movement has drawn increased attention to the links between the elements of evaluation and learners. So we show the learner as a "potential" consideration in the evaluation part of the plan as well. Despite recent research that re-lates course-taking patterns to general outcomes (Ratcliff, 1992a), we continue to have relatively little information on the relation of academic plans to student outcomes other than discipline concepts and skills.

Finally, we tentatively label the evaluation and adjustment stage of curriculum planning as *reflective evaluation* to indicate that evaluation does not produce adjustment automatically and use a dotted line to show that it infrequently affects intent. Rather, professional interpretation and reflection accompanies evaluation. Too little is known about how adjustment decisions are shaped by evaluation decisions to omit professional judgment. Perhaps *reflection* should be an additional element in the academic plan theory.

It is also important to note what we have not included in the academic plan. First, we have not considered the personal characteristics of professors as a separate element since our investigations found these typically subsumed under their educational beliefs and their disciplinary socialization. Second, we have not included institutional characteristics as an element of the plan because these are largely encompassed by educational purpose, learners, and, to a lesser extent, content. Third, because it seldom enters curriculum decisions we have largely ignored the guidance and advising function that may determine how learners enter and experience the academic plan. These issues are incorporated in both the influence of learners and the external influences that operate distinctively in each college or university. Depending on their perspectives, other researchers may identify key elements they feel are missing from our academic plan.

What relationships do we need to know more about? We have much folklore but little empirical evidence about the relationships between discipline content and general learned abilities. That is, what precisely can be known about the capabilities that result from studying specific content? As Figure 13-2 implies, the relation may depend on several intervening matters, namely (1) the instructor's view of the student as learner, (2) the type of instructional processes chosen, or (3) the way the student constructs meaning in the instructional setting. The encompassing question relating the elements of academic plans remains: What combination of content, sequencing, instructional resources, and processes will achieve a specified educational purpose for a given learner?

Exploring Environmental Influences on Academic Plans

Throughout the book, we have speculated on the strength of the external, organizational, and internal influences on each element of the academic plan we have discussed. Our speculations are based on common sense, casual encounter, and limited systematic observation; they need additional development. To keep the theory general, we have usually avoided isolating and discussing specific influences because the mix of agents within each of the three categories changes over time. We encourage researchers to continue probing these relationships.

A wealth of existing studies adapted from the broad literature on organizational theory and administrative practice in education and other settings provided us a firmer basis for understanding internal and organizational influences than for external ones. On the basis of our own research, we also know more about course-level and program-level influences on curriculum than about those that operate at the institutional level. Even so, we have not attempted to explore all of the organizational or internal variables that might affect the educational environment or how the influence process occurs. Many of these in-

fluences may operate quite indirectly on the curriculum. The key questions in this set of relationships that merit the joint attention of organizational and curricular researchers are: What types of influence operate most intensely on specific elements of the academic plan? What is the mediating influence of the educational environment on each? What types of attention to influences from within and outside of a college lead to carefully considered and responsive curriculum change—that is, to change characterized by explicit attention to each element of the academic plan?

Connecting with Emerging Curriculum Research

Conrad and Haworth (1990) provided a cogent statement about why it is important to study curriculum:

> The curriculum forms the nucleus of colleges and universities. As the vehicle for organizing teaching and learning, the curriculum provides the major domain for academic decision-making, expresses institutional purposes and values, and serves as the primary touchstone in the professional lives of students, faculty, and administrators. Given its importance, the curriculum has historically served as an arena for discussion and debate about the ends and means of learning in higher education. (p. 2)

Despite its importance, relatively little systematic curriculum research has been done in higher education. Conrad and Pratt (1983) attempted to isolate and describe the major threads of research on academic programs. From 200 general examinations of curriculum (as opposed to discipline-specific studies or studies testing specific instructional processes), they identified six major lines of inquiry about curriculum: (1) case studies of curricular "incidents," (2) traditional and revisionist histories, (3) multiple-site studies of academic change or conceptions of the change process, (4) descriptive studies, including frequency distributions of specific practices, (5) outcome studies, and (6) conceptual frameworks that refine terminology or suggest potential avenues for organizing research. Conrad and Pratt failed to find any group of significant studies that related academic programs to educational outcomes or to the actual learning processes that students experience.

Studies connecting outcomes and academic plans have become far more common since the mid-1980s primarily as a result of the assessment movement. Since it is now clear that grades often indicate how well students complied with college policies and practices rather than being reliable and valid measures of what they learned in college (Pascarella & Terenzini, 1991, p. 62), the development of new measures and methods has been required. While descriptive research about curriculum planning and change has increased, correlational, predictive, and evaluation research remain underdeveloped. This state of affairs has been summarized by those who have thoroughly reviewed existing literature. There is considerable research support for the idea that college, in general, increases students' verbal reasoning, verbal comprehension, and mathematical ability even after variations in their prior ability and preparation have been taken into account (Pascarella, 1985). However, most of the studies showing positive effects have studied the college experience as a whole. But, according to an extensive review by Pascarella and Terenzini (1991), studies of students' gains in thinking and reasoning are notably missing and few experimental studies have compared these gains with those of control groups of students or noncollege individuals who did not experience the specific program being examined. Pascarella (1985, pp. 40–44) suggests that we need studies focusing more directly on the specific departmental or program environment in which the students are studying. These studies should consider not only the planned academic experiences but also how students self-select themselves into programs and how they interact with other students and faculty in the program environment.

Studies attempting to document student growth in classrooms, in general education, or in particular fields of research have been approached from inconsistent perspectives. In some cases the student is the unit of analysis (demonstrating substantial change), and in others the institution is the unit of analysis (demonstrating small effects); but studies using the academic program (or clusters of courses) as the unit of analysis have been sorely missing. We believe it is important to analyze the connections between outcomes and academic plans at the course and program levels as well as at the institutional level. It appears that support for this type of research is growing.

We have found a range of studies that examine outcomes; from those that only imply or infer connections between curriculum and student outcomes to those that attempt to demonstrate that academic programs are likely responsible for student change. We have observed the following types: (1) student self-reports about their academic behavior and learning progress (Astin, 1978, 1988, 1993; Dey, Astin, & Korn, 1991; Pace, 1987; Terenzini, Theophilides, & Lorang, 1984; Volkwein & Carbone, 1994); (2) studies that count what courses college offer (catalog studies) or those students select within the choices they are allowed (transcript studies) (Blackburn et al., 1976; Dressel & DeLisle, 1970; Toombs, Amey, & Fairweather, 1989); (3) studies that not only count what courses students take but also examine patterns and sequences of courses typical of specific colleges, programs, or student groups (Adelman, 1990; Zemsky, 1989); (4) studies that count courses, examine patterns and sequences, and ultimately try to relate the patterns to measures of academic achievement (Ratcliff, 1992a, 1992b).

Student self-report data are simple to obtain so these types of studies are increasingly used on campuses. Colleges that participate in the Cooperative Institutional Research Program or other large-scale studies can obtain early student profiles on which to build a database. Transcript studies are also now easy to conduct from both local computerized records and large longitudinal databases gathered on national samples like the National Longitudinal Study of the Class of 1972. When replicated locally, these types of studies can provide suitable information to help colleges judge and potentially adjust academic plans. Especially the model developed by Zemsky (1989) (based on tracking courses 25,465 students actually took for the bachelor's degree at twenty-eight institutions) can help colleges develop a portrait of the choices students are actually making. Using the model faculty can assess the "depth," "breadth," and "temporality" of current student programs and can weigh this against their own missions and normative standards. Finally, while it requires statistically sophisticated procedures, the Coursework Cluster Analysis Model (also called the "differential coursework technique") developed by Ratcliff (1992b) identifies clusters of students who took similar course patterns in general education and determines whether students in the clusters change differentially from freshman to senior year on measures of general learned abilities. Ratcliff claims that once a specific college obtains this information using outcome measures of their choice, it can identify course patterns taken by students with the greatest gains in learned abili-

ties and restructure the curriculum to emulate them.

In planning curriculum research for the future, we need to distinguish clearly between (1) repetitive data collection favored by policy makers to compare educational programs or support policy initiatives, (2) evaluation research to judge a specific curriculum's effectiveness (Paths A and B in our theory), and (3) basic research to understand the curriculum decision processes implied in the theory itself. All are needed. Basic research can help to pave the way for new applied research methods that will be useful to specific institutions. Our contribution of the academic plan theory should expand this emerging base of curriculum research. It can help researchers formulate questions more carefully and productively.

Our experience suggests, however, that it will be necessary to extend both basic and applied research beyond statistical models that seek correlations and cause and effect relationships. Varied approaches will be needed to encourage faculty to reflect on academic planning at the program level as well as for their own courses. We have found that the fourfold classification we used for evaluation studies (informal, client-centered, goal-free, or goal-focused) presents a fruitful array of methods. All of these types of evaluation research are important to relate outcomes to various elements or combinations of elements of the academic plan.

In Table 13-1, we use this varied set of research methods as an organizational scheme to suggest only a few of the many challenging questions that could be asked to extend our knowledge of relationships within the academic plan theory. Additional studies should focus on the relations among elements of the academic plan as well as on how the environment and the plan elements are directly and indirectly affected by the internal, organiza-

TABLE 13-1   Curriculum Research Studies That Present Challenges

Informal Studies

- What are the experiences of faculty teams that work together to construct academic plans for courses? When they include only faculty members? When they include instructional design specialists?
- How do learners develop "learning to learn" skills, and how can instructors arrange content sequences to promote this development?
- What can be learned from faculty reports and reflections on the process of program planning? What important variables enter into planning?
- How and why do faculty select alternatives to the lecture and discussion as instructional processes in courses?

Student-Centered Studies

- In the view of students, are colleges focusing on basic general education that should have been taught in high schools or on liberal education that promotes higher levels of cultural knowledge and critical thinking?
- How do students change the ways they articulate and integrate knowledge content as they cross the boundary from high school to college?
- What do various groups of students believe is the optimum mix of (1) learning what is known, (2) learning to find new knowledge, and (3) learning to construe old knowledge in new ways?

Goal-Free Studies

- How do students make connections between life and work, between courses, and between ideas? What, if anything, in an academic plan assists them in making these connections? What hinders them?
- How do students experience transitions from college to work?
- What unique outcomes, if any, occur when faculty discuss advances in learning psychology?
- What experiences do students report who believe they have successfully integrated general and specialized education?

Goal-Focused Studies

Some of the practical goal-focused research questions to be asked are those that focus on more than one element of the academic plan (The relevant plan elements are in parentheses).

- What is the average level of (and variation in) basic, general, or liberal skills (such as communication and critical thinking skills) that students receiving college degrees actually demonstrate? (purpose and content)
- What evidence is there that a required core curriculum promotes a sense of community? (process and outcomes)
- What are the effects of studying a Eurocentric core for students from varied backgrounds? (learners, content, and outcomes)
- Are interdisciplinary studies more likely to prepare students for citizenship than disciplinary studies? If so, what appears to produce this effect and under what circumstances? (sequence, content, learners, outcomes)
- Is achievement in interdisciplinary study more dependent on what is taught or how it is taught? (content, process)
- Do specific types of content or specific types of instructional processes promote especially broad or especially narrow thinking among students? (purpose, content, outcomes)
- What evidence is there to indicate the balance between humanistic and scientific studies that a citizen needs to function well in a technological society?

tional, and external influences we have discussed. By providing varied approaches, faculty can be important collaborators.

THE ACADEMIC PLAN THEORY AS A GUIDE FOR SHAPING PRACTICE

We have defined curriculum development as the process by which a professor or group of professors solve the complex problem of constructing a learning plan by making a series of decisions. Clearly, the way a problem is defined is important in limiting or expanding the range of solutions. Our way of defining curriculum development as a decision-making process leads us to a systematic mode of problem solving. It helps us convert an unstructured problem to one that is more structured and, thus, potentially more easily solved because it focuses on a specific and identifiable set of variables. The theory also helps us reconceptualize other problems. For example, in defining curriculum as a set of dynamic interrelated decisions, instead of as a set of unrelated decisions or a static set of course listings, we have been able to see curriculum change not only as remarkable innovation but as a continuing process of adjustment and renewal. This analysis allows us to consider each decision carefully and recognize its relation to the entire plan, making adjustments as needed.

Assumptions and Advantages

Every theory is based on some assumptions; ours is no exception. We mention some assumptions here. In American colleges and universities, many individuals are typically involved in the problem-solving activity we call curriculum development, and the mix of actors changes at different levels of academic planning. In developing a theory concerning academic planning, we have assumed that faculty and administrators in a particular col-

lege have some authority to create, change, and adjust academic plans. In such an environment, decision making is nearly continuous: course and program planning usually occur before the educational process begins, continue interactively as the plan is underway, and occur more intensively again before the next iteration. Yet our consideration of the influences on curriculum reminds us that the power to plan and to change plans may be limited by specific settings. In the United States, governmental agencies, religious sponsors, state-wide system agreements, professional field entrance requirements, and even system-wide textbook choices can limit the local decisions in academic planning. In countries with a nationally established curriculum, decisions may be made for each element of the academic plan in national ministries rather than on campuses. Our theory may not represent reality in settings where our assumption of faculty responsibility does not hold.

Many writers who have urged the improvement of teaching have given a mere nod to curriculum development (usually course planning) as one relatively minor teaching task. Our definition of curriculum as an academic plan relies upon a different assumption. We reverse the usual hierarchy to view the development of the plan in its specific context as the broader task; the choice of instructional processes is one aspect of the plan's development. Planning is independent of future implementation. We think this specific approach may lead professors to select new ways of implementing instruction since the instruction is chosen deliberately to carry out the purpose; the purpose is not modified to suit the mode of instruction.

Based on our experience and research, we have also assumed that, since academic plans define much of professors' daily activity, faculty are interested in improving them. Faculty perspectives on academic planning generally have been limited rather than expansive; this may account for the disinterest often attributed to them. We have observed that faculty, like other professionals, are self-motivated and self-reflective in their work. They privately reflect on their behavior using varied frames of reference as a basis for decisions. Exposure to more ideas about academic plans and more alternatives associated with each element can increase professors' awareness of the context in which their decisions occur and improve their decisions.

Expanding how faculty think about curriculum problems is important because, at least in the United States, the responsibility and final initiative for curriculum change rests with the faculty. Yet we recognize that many of the forces that propel curriculum change come initially from outside the university. We have assumed that these influences come through multiple channels because faculty, administrators, and students are regularly in contact with external constituencies. We have noted that many of the same influences have waxed and waned through American history, and we believe the general theory allows analysis at any point in time. We do not, however, presume that our theory elucidates the many complex ways in which the influence process actually takes place.

Building on these several assumptions, we initially described five very general advantages of defining curriculum as an academic plan. Such a definition can (1) promote clarity about curriculum influences, (2) be applicable at lesson, course, program and college levels, (3) encourage explicit attention to student learning, (4) encourage faculty to share views as they plan, and (5) encourage a dynamic view of curriculum development. Now, having developed the options for each element of the academic plan more fully, we can be more specific about benefits to faculty

members in their work. Using the organizational scheme we used to discuss curriculum administration, we group these benefits in three sets as in Figure 13-2: intent and its development; implementation; and reflective evaluation of curriculum.

Intent and Its Development

Using the eight elements of the academic plan can help faculty groups to focus their discussions about purpose and proceed with their deliberations in an orderly way. The elements of the academic plan can provide a framework or checklist for faculty to organize thinking and decision making. The plan's focus on content promotes recognition that faculty in different academic fields may disagree on some decisions and agree on others. This can help identify common ground for productive discourse especially at program and college levels.

The list of elements also provides a way to describe varied academic plans more completely than is customary. In fact, the elements can become the frame for a syllabus and a vehicle for helping students to understand and participate in a plan for their education. This aspect of the plan is particularly important when it helps faculty and students to jointly discuss course purposes and how the content and instructional processes are intended to achieve them. Finally, the obvious linkages among the elements of the academic plan can help anticipate the effect of decisions about one element on another element. For example, we know that purpose, content, and sequence are often linked and also associated with a discipline. Yet temporarily separating these three for discussion and planning can raise faculty awareness, helping them to distinguish tinkering with the academic plan from making substantive decisions about its key elements.

Implementation

Faculty members can use the theoretical framework of the academic plan to guide them in the choice of appropriate strategies for improvement. Choices of instructional sequence, resources, and processes lead to specific ways of implementing the plan and may be aimed at particular groups of learners. The theory may help in improving the selection of instructional processes by focusing on this task developmentally, as a planning decision that can be improved, rather than as a personal success or failure of individual professors. The theory can also help in budgeting by encouraging attention to the instructional resources and facilities needed for a particular plan. Since budgets may seem to be constraining rather than enabling forces, they are better recognized and coped with early, particularly when decision makers plan to make substantial curriculum changes. Exploring the extent to which the environment supports decisions about each specific plan element may help to pinpoint sources of tension between faculty and administration that can be easily remedied. Use of the theory may suggest that certain support services should be provided or others evaluated to better implement specific plans. This analysis allows faculty to identify what is needed and make appropriate recommendations for change.

Reflective Evaluation and Adjustment

The academic plan theory helps us determine what evidence to gather and examine in order to evaluate and improve curriculum. For example, we might look specifically at the relation of student course outcomes to the purposes professors intended, or at the relation between program sequencing and instructional processes. The theory helps us identify

important connections that might otherwise be overlooked. The theory also helps us propose alternative explanations for observed outcomes, particularly those that are unexpected or were not intended. For example, if students fail to learn basic skills, use of the plan may suggest exploring a specific problem—perhaps teachers have failed to link content and purpose to learner interests. Such specific explanations encourage more productive solutions than broad criticisms, for example, that faculty are not teaching their students well or that the length of the academic term is too short. In brief, the theory can help us sort through possible causes, even if it is impossible to demonstrate cause and effect. When evaluative data are available and change is warranted, the theory helps us recognize that alternative decisions should be suggested. It does not prescribe which alternatives should be chosen or hold out any specific academic plan as a panacea to correct curriculum deficiencies.

Research and theory change policy and practice by raising new questions and helping to restructure debate. Since all faculty members are already curriculum planners, the theory can help them to become curriculum designers, more conscious of their own assumptions and decisions and aware of alternative routes to desired outcomes.

THE ACADEMIC PLAN THEORY AS A GUIDE FOR LEADERS IN ENHANCING CURRICULUM

Frequently, tensions spring up between faculty and administrators about the coordination of academic plans. The second part of our theory, which focuses on the educational environment in which academic plans are constructed, provides a framework to outline possible leadership roles. The academic plan theory cannot automatically change people's behavior nor ease tensions, but it can help the two groups to delineate the respective roles each should play. The actual roles chosen will vary with specific institutions and positions; the considerations are sufficiently general to encompass diverse settings.

In defining the educational environment in which academic plans are developed, the theory includes two levels of evaluation and adjustment. These two levels suggest one basis for negotiating the division of responsibility between faculty members and administrators. If both groups recognize that faculty have the expertise necessary to construct specific academic plans at course and program levels, and administrators have the authority and responsibility to foster supportive environmental conditions, both groups can play important and complementary roles in enhancing quality.

This two-level theory helped us to examine policies and structures by connecting each component of the plan with potentially useful managerial roles, responsibilities, and styles in the planning process. The administrator becomes a broker between internal and organizational influences in the planning process. She needs to be aware of such internal influences as faculty expertise and learner characteristics that affect decision making. Within the organization, she needs to understand networks, conflicts, and dependencies among programs as well as occasions when collaboration and competition are likely to influence decisions.

Asking the Right Questions

The eight elements of the plan also help to suggest specific questions that leaders may ask. The type of questions may be varied slightly for each level of academic plan, for different stages in planning, and for colleges with different missions. The theory simply reminds us that an important role for administrators who are not experts in the specific disciplines engaged in planning is to ask appropriate questions, such as these:

A Checklist for Assessing New Curriculum Ideas

- What purposes, assumptions, learning theories, and changing societal conditions stimulate and justify this curricular change?

- What assessments of students' needs justify this change? What will the typical student be like before, during, and after exposure to this curriculum in intellectual development, attitudes, satisfaction with program, skill development, or career development?

- What will students at the extremes in ability or preparation be like before, during, and after exposure to this curriculum? If substantially different effects are foreseen for different types of students, what special resources are needed?

- What content (key concepts, core courses, themes, related electives, requirements, and modes of inquiry) will be taught? Are these reasonable for students to learn and faculty to teach? Are they connected with other aspects of the educational program?

- How much time will faculty and students need to devote to this program? Is this time commitment realistic in terms of other obligations? How is the program sequenced and linked with other programs for students and faculty?

- Is expertise available—faculty, teaching assistants, or outside lectures? Are retraining opportunities needed? Can peer institutions share useful experience?

- What instructional processes will be selected and used? Will these require special facilities or arrangements? What provisions have been made for students to be active learners?

- What evaluation plan has been put into place? Who will be responsible for its implementation? How will the results be used to revise or refine the new program?

Asking the Questions in the Right Way

The principles of curriculum administration that we have discussed balance administrative and faculty responsibilities for the academic plan at each stage and level of planning. These principles and balances strongly resemble concepts now being discussed by higher education administrators under the rubric of Continuous Quality Improvement (CQI), or Total Quality Management (TQM) (Marchese, 1991, 1992). Advocates claim that TQM principles have radically changed U.S. industry by producing a clearer definition of market, by focusing squarely on customer satisfaction, and by instituting processes of continuous improvement in the delivery of products and services. Since 1990, a spate of books, conferences, and newsletters designed for administrators in higher education have urged colleges and universities to adopt these principles both for general administration and instructional development (see, for example, Chaffee & Sherr, 1992; *Change,* special issue, May–June 1993; Seymour, 1993; Sherr & Teeter, 1991).

Although some argue that the principles espoused by proponents of CQI are nothing more than good management, and a set of tools, others believe that CQI incorporates leadership and human behavior theories with systems thinking and statistical process control to produce new organizational cultures. These cultures are customer-oriented and quality-driven; they build on teamwork and the pursuit of excellence. CQI also requires

continual improvement of processes, the use of data for decision making, the reduction of complexity and waste, and the granting of appropriate authority to individuals within the organization. Based on the development of capable employees who understand the principles of Continuous Quality Improvement, who know how to work in teams, and who have well-developed problem-solving skills, CQI stresses human resource development in the form of training and recognition.

Although people in higher education, particularly faculty, often object to the ideas and language of CQI—for example, the tendency to think of and refer to students as "customers"—the incorporation of continuous quality improvement principles in higher education can be appropriate. The theory of the academic plan, which stresses the existence and use of three evaluation paths, is consistent with CQI principles. This theory also represents a kind of systems thinking in which inputs to the academic plan, processes, and outputs are considered within a particular educational context. Thus, improvement can occur at various points in the flow and at various levels of authority. Here we develop some of these parallels between our conceptualization of curriculum development and administration and what the advocates of "quality" propose.

"Satisfying the customer" in CQI parlance requires knowing the customer. While one primary customer in higher education institutions and in our discussion of the academic plan is the student, other clienteles must also be considered. Our framework, which postulates internal, organizational, and external influences within an educational environment or context, suggests that we think of a variety of constituencies—employers, parents, alumni, governmental agencies, etc. —as customers as well. These groups help to create the educational environment in which the plan is constructed and implemented and in which the student experiences the plan. Furthermore, as the recent emphasis on assessment and accountability attests, these groups have their own sets of demands and expectations for the academic plan. The concept of a single type of customer simply does not mesh with our diverse system of higher education.

To satisfy their constituencies, educational institutions, their administrations, and faculties must have a clearly defined sense of the market(s) for their educational services. Being customer-driven means explicitly identifying customers, and their needs, which, in turn, means gathering information about customer's needs. As we have mentioned earlier, the data gathering done in higher education institutions is often haphazard. We have suggested more systematic approaches to data collection that are consistent with the CQI principles of management. We discussed student and classroom assessment, knowledge of student characteristics and demographics, identification of learning styles, and evaluation to develop a greater understanding of who students are, what they need, and what they want from courses, programs, and colleges. We have also emphasized that information must be collected at various points in the process—before a course or program begins, during its progress, and after its completion—and by various sets of individuals.

In general, faculty are most immediately concerned with the academic plan they devise for the students in their classes; curriculum leaders and administrators are typically concerned with the larger picture—for example, the students in a department or program, or the entire population of a college or university. The educational environment, however, is not simply an aggregation of experiences in individual classes; it must be more consciously structured and coordinated. Faculty, administrators and students must work as a team to create the desired ethos; faculty and students should be involved in the typically

administrative task of interpreting the academic plan and its outcomes to external constituencies.

Still another resemblance can be noted between CQI and our views on the academic plan: the reliance on human resource development to improve the process. We discussed the need for instructional development programs to aid in the improvement of academic plans at the course and program level. CQI advocates point to the danger of assuming that all employees have the problem-solving and teamwork skills needed for a continuous improvement environment. Accordingly, TQM firms invest heavily in training and development to bring employees up to speed. Similarly, we have stressed the importance of faculty development to improve the quality of individual academic plans and the curriculum as a whole. Faculty, we have argued, must be given opportunities to develop their skills and knowledge bases and to try new ideas, and they must believe that the institution values such initiatives.

Reformers who have addressed curriculum and instruction in higher education have urged colleges and universities to set high standards and establish clearer expectations. To do so, many colleges and universities follow pace-setter institutions, adapting these school's most successful ideas to their own settings. We called this influence the "bandwagon effect" but in CQI, the same phenomenon is called benchmarking—that is, the process of finding organizations with superior practices and unabashedly adapting them. Often, colleges and universities identify ideas or practices in their external environments that they adapt for their own use. Although the social interaction and diffusion processes of change may not be as deliberate as benchmarking, or may be the result of a mandate to respond (as in the case of assessment in some states), the end result is very similar: successful practices are adopted wholly or in part, and educational processes are thereby altered. Of course, the diversity of educational institutions in the United States requires that benchmarks at the course, program, and collegewide levels be carefully considered before being implemented. Although standardization may be a goal for manufacturing companies, the production of cookie-cutter students should not be the intention of colleges and universities.

Chaffee and Sherr (1992) contend that some fundamental points of view characterize administrators of CQI-oriented institutions. These include (1) believing that the primary job of the administrator is to remove barriers that prevent people from doing quality work; (2) improving processes when something goes wrong, instead of blaming individuals; (3) creating a supportive environment marked by cooperation and teamwork rather than competition; (4) valuing education and training; (5) providing authority to improve processes down the line; and (6) aligning personnel and performance systems with the values of cooperation, initiative, teamwork, and continuous improvement. We have argued that a primary role for administrators with respect to curriculum is to create a supportive environment in which effective academic plans can be created. This supportive environment necessarily involves faculty employees, who hold the expertise in the disciplines and fields taught; administrators cannot run the business of higher education alone. Our discussion of creating an appropriate environment included all or most of the specific principles that CQI theorists now discuss: reducing fear in the employment setting, allowing for variability, building intrinsic reward systems, encouraging risk-taking, developing trust, and assigning responsibility and authority appropriately.

Despite long traditions of faculty involvement and faculty responsibility for the curriculum, the proponents of CQI encounter resistance from faculty who oppose the creation of additional administrative infrastruc-

tures to supervise their work and monitor quality. Many faculty insist that quality can not be "managed." In fact, they are likely to feel that administrators who actively discuss management systems are "overadministering" and thereby reducing trust and discouraging risk taking—precisely the opposite of what CQI advocates intend. CQI proponents counter that workers (in this case, faculty) cannot outperform the limits of the system; inefficiencies that hinder their best work must be identified and removed. Because of the interaction of these two views, the challenge to CQI in curriculum development is to find ways to increase sensitive coordination and administrative teamwork among faculty, administrators, and experts in instructional development while avoiding the violation of faculty autonomy or creativity. The task for the administrator is to make the system supportive of the best faculty efforts. Sometimes new concepts, such as instructional development, will need to be tried. These new initiatives may appear at first to violate faculty autonomy but may eventually enhance faculty creativity.

Our concept of the academic plan differs in one very identifiable way from TQM or CQI. Specifically, our theory incorporates meta-evaluation, the process of determining whether an evaluation has been useful and productive. Many versions and interpretations of TQM have been adopted by colleges and universities, and this proliferation has caused considerable confusion. Some of this confusion might have been averted by a systematic meta-evaluation principle that would ensure monitoring of the CQI processes themselves. Many believe that CQI concepts are a panacea for higher education; proponents assume that they will work and promote improvement. We believe that the theory of the academic plan with its three evaluative paths is a more stable type of systems analysis to apply to curriculum. Moreover, it can be tested and evaluated for its own utility precisely because it does not avoid evaluating its own utility.

GUIDING RESPONSIVENESS TO SOCIETY

Academic plans are adjusted, in part, in response to the broader context of the society in which the educational organization exists. Looking outside the institution, leaders recognize new trends and mandates. Administrators have a special obligation to help faculty become aware of such demands and begin to screen them for suitability. Currently, new college constituencies, rapid technological advances, and demands for new types of coherence from society present substantial challenges. In U.S. society, these challenges are overlaid on the historical precedents of recurring debates that balance quality and access, choice and prescription, and general and specialized study. The academic plan theory cannot, of course, change the course of history, nor can it predict those external influences to which a specific college or program should attend. The theory can, however, help faculty and administrators recognize that a college must anticipate the influences on its academic plans and that advocacy in curriculum debates must be distinguished from evidence. In short, including influences in the same theoretical framework as the academic plan helps to balance external pressures and decisions with a college's internal purposes and values.

Anticipating Important Influences

We have suggested that the process of change in college curriculum depends on the interaction of three primary factors: (1) the nature of the influence pressing for change, (2) the change processes that are operating, and (3) the extent to which external influence has been internalized by colleges and universities to become an organizational or internal influ-

ence. Our theory suggests that faculty and administrators might identify impending pressures to change. It can help them to recognize the source of the pressure and screen (or reject) a particular influence as appropriate (or inappropriate) to the college's mission. Recognizing the source and rate of progress of a major influence also allows administrators to estimate the amount of time needed for to prepare for action.

Wars, depressions, or unanticipated technological advances may alter the higher education curriculum as drastically in the future as they have done in the past. Inventions such as television, jet airplanes, birth-control pills, and electronic mail are good examples of scientific advances that have changed society and even restructured power relationships, resulting in a changed student body and a different curriculum. Research and theory never can predict or control these major influences on curriculum. But some changes, like those in a increasingly multicultural, technologically-linked society, can be more readily anticipated, interpreted, and perhaps adapted.

A college that regularly weighs new ideas and their demands against its mission and estimates the influences on its programs is more likely to invest its energies in long-range planning than to divert them to fight short-term brush fires. For example, today's college leaders might examine how their curriculum might be changed if students were to take most of their courses by electronic means from their homes. One need only examine the changes that technology has wrought in university libraries in recent decades to realize that the increased pace of external change demands that colleges be proactive rather than resist new thinking about such issues.

Basing Decisions on Analysis

Recent critiques of the curriculum have tended to assign blame and prescribe global remedies rather than apply analytical skills to examining academic plans and their outcomes. Debaters get into heated discussions with little possibility of changing strongly-held, opposing views about the purpose of education. It has become fashionable to issue accusations that the wrong content is being taught, that students are not learning, that teachers are not devoting enough time to teaching, that particular cultural groups are being ignored, that sufficient resources are not provided, and that administrators do not support curriculum development. All such lamentations are too imprecise to be useful. Policymakers should not shout "fire" so often about education that the public abandons the enterprise, assuming that it is too charred to salvage.

Since our task in curriculum development is problem solving, we have tried to build a comprehensive theory based on analytical approaches useful for faculty and administrators. More specifically, we have tried to move the debate from advocacy and speculation about what will work to approaches that help us consciously select alternatives, test our decisions, and adjust them based on results. Thus, we have insisted that a wide variety of evaluation strategies should be applied to academic plans of all types, including those that some educators believe are eternally exempt from scrutiny.

Our theory is process oriented rather than normative or prescriptive. It directs our attention to the process of planning rather than prescribing content or proposing a linear sequence of planning steps. It does not prescribe specific decisions, yet it helps planners make their decisions more explicit. We recognize, however, that any specific curriculum necessarily incorporates the values and purposes of its creators. Furthermore, academic plans, when implemented, incorporate the values of the learners who experience them. The process-oriented approach allows educators to identify the values of each set of participants,

to concentrate on elements of curriculum, and to discuss them more effectively.

As we have described, however, there are many frames of reference for viewing curriculum. These include the critical frame, the feminist frame, the multicultural frame, and the frames of specific disciplines to name a few. A theory constructed under the assumptions of one frame of reference may or may not hold up under an alternative set of assumptions. Some groups of "alternative theorists" focus on "what is taught" or the politics of "who decides what is taught." Our theory tries to accommodate all of these perspectives but not to be directed solely by any one of them.

Critical theorists, especially, might argue that our frame simply assumes that the purpose of education is that of U.S. society. They view this society and, hence, its educational purpose, as inequitable. Although the decision elements are based on our experience and our discussions with a wide range of college teachers, critical theorists may judge our choices about dividing academic plans into specific elements as biased, because they are based on existing tradition. Conceivably, in a transformed society some of these decisions would be moot while others, not currently in our framework, would become important. Because of the development of these new perspectives, the challenges and discussions about curriculum are different than they might have been at the time of the Yale report of 1828 or even between the two world wars.

Anticipating these challenges to the foundational aspects of our theory brings us full circle to show how the theory itself reflects current tensions in society and is subject to change as society changes. Just as the critical perspective challenges what is taught in the curriculum, some curriculum theorists would challenge our way of viewing it and constructing it. It should be so because all theories should be examined as the reality they purport to represent changes.

SHAPING ACADEMIC PLANS FOR THE FUTURE

College curricula are products of many forces, values, and perspectives within our society. There is no single curriculum; rather there are many curricula—different for students, colleges, programs, and subject fields. The forces that drive these curricula are not always the same ones nor do they always push in the same direction; in fact, academic plans are often characterized by compromise. It has long been acknowledged that both administrators and faculty need to be realistic analysts of the *politics* of curriculum development. As communication in our society has become more rapid and government has begun to play an increasingly larger role in setting policy for colleges and universities, it is becoming apparent that more than campus politics will challenge curriculum planners. Often policymakers experiment first and schedule the research later. A new way of thinking about the curriculum might go far in convincing policymakers that educators are indeed developing expertise in their profession of college teaching as well as in their research areas.

Administrators, too, may need to have new ways of thinking to focus their attention on curriculum. The newsletter, *Pew Policy Roundtables,* lists several forces or influences that key college administrators believe are important: funding rescissions, enrollment declines, an increasingly diverse student body, student preparation or its lack, student consumerism, the fragmentation of content, competition from noncollege educational agen-

cies, government regulation, and criticism. With such concerns before them, it may be continue to be difficult to get college presidents thinking systematically about curriculum. But we hope they will be sufficiently intrigued by our development of how the academic plan is shaped to ask some key questions.

The greatest challenges for the future are (1) how to bring greater reflection and balance to debates about the college curriculum, (2) how to foster more deliberate and well-conceived research and experimentation with the curriculum by faculty groups, and (3) how to translate research findings and theory about curriculum into forms that college professors, administrators, and policymakers can use. Our view of curriculum as an academic plan is itself an innovation for higher education. We judge that analytical thinking about the curriculum is at the "awareness" stage of change. We have tried to move it to the "screening" stage by suggesting some new conceptualizations.

We have shown that a general theoretical model of curriculum development in higher education can have practical value for others by advancing basic knowledge about how academic plans are constructed and implemented. Since we have attempted to inform practice as well as develop theory, we hope that some of the ideas we have shared in this book will be useful to faculty and administrators. This book will be successful to the extent that it challenges current thinking about curriculum, providing more useful ways of problem solving.

Bibliography

1992 ACT scores remain stable. (1993). *ACTIV-ITY*, Newsletter of the American College Testing Program, *30*(3), 2.

AAC. *See* Association of American Colleges.

AASCU. *See* American Association of State Colleges and Universities.

AAHE. *See* American Association for Higher Education.

ACE. *See* American Council on Education.

ACT. *See* American College Testing Program

Adams, M. (Ed.). (1992). *Promoting diversity in college classrooms: Innovative responses for the curriculum, faculty, and institutions* (New Directions for Teaching and Learning No. 52). San Francisco: Jossey-Bass.

Adelman, C. (1984, December). *Starting with students: Promising approaches in American higher education.* Report prepared for the Study Group on the Conditions of Excellence in American Higher Education. Washington, DC: National Institute of Education.

Adelman, C. (Ed.). (1989, September). *Signs and traces: Model indicators of college student learning in the disciplines.* Washington, DC: U.S. Department of Education, Office of Research.

Adelman, C. (1990). *A college course map: Taxonomy and transcript data.* Washington, DC: U.S. Department of Education, Office of Educational Research and Improvement.

Adelman, C. (1991, June). *Women at thirtysomething: Paradoxes of attainment.* U.S. Department of Education, Office of Educational Research and Improvement.

Adelman, C. (1992a, February). *The way we are: The community colleges as American thermometer.* U.S. Department of Education, Office of Educational Research and Improvement.

Adelman, C. (1992b, October). *Tourists in our own land: Cultural literacies and the college curriculum,* U.S. Department of Education, Office of Educational Research and Improvement.

Ahlgren, A., & Boyer, C. (1981). Visceral priorities: Roots of confusion in liberal education. *Journal of Higher Education, 52*(2), 173–181.

Ahrendt, K. M. (Ed.). (1987). *Teaching the developmental student.* (New Directions for Community Colleges, No. 57). San Francisco, Jossey-Bass.

Albright, M. J., & Graf, D. L. (Eds.) (1992). *Teaching in the information age: The role of educational technology* (New Directions for Teaching and Learning No. 51). San Francisco: Jossey-Bass.

Alexander, J. C. (1993, December 1). The irrational disciplinarity of undergraduate education. *The Chronicle of Higher Education, 40*(15), B–3.

Alexander, J. & Stark, J. S. (1986). *Focusing on student academic outcomes: A working paper.* Ann Arbor: The University of Michigan, National Center for Research to Improve Postsecondary Teaching and Learning.

Alfred, R. L., & Linder, V. P. (1990). *Rhetoric to reality: Effectiveness in community colleges.* Ann Arbor: University of Michigan: Center for the Study of Higher and Postsecondary Education, Community College Consortium.

Altman, H. B., & Cashin, W. E. (1992, September). *Writing a syllabus* (IDEA Paper No. 27). Manhattan, KS: Kansas State University, Center for Faculty Evaluation and Development.

American Association for Higher Education (AAHE). (1985). *Contexts for learning: The major sectors of American higher education.* Washington, DC: Author. (Reprinted from the U.S. Government Printing Office.)

American Association for Higher Education. (1992). *Principles of good practice for assessing student learning.* Washington, DC: The AAHE Assessment Forum, Author.

American Association of State Colleges and Universities (AASCU). (1985). *Guidelines: Incorporating an international dimension in colleges and universities.* Washington, DC: Author.

American Association of State Colleges and Universities. (1986, November). *To secure the blessings of liberty* (Report of the National Commission on the Role and Future of State Colleges and Universities). Washington, DC: Author.

American Institute of Certified Public Accountants. (1993, March). *Accounting Educators: FYI.* 4(4).

Anderson, A. A. (1991). Three kinds of goodness: Clustering courses as a model for contemporary higher education. *Studies in Higher Education, 16*(3), 309–318.

Anderson, G. L. (1974). *Trends in education for the professions* (ERIC/AAHE Research Report No. 7). Washington, DC: American Association for Higher Education.

Andrews, J. D. W. (1981). Teaching format and student style: Their interactive effects on learning. *Research in Higher Education, 14*(2), 161–178.

Angelo, T. A. (Ed.). (1991). *Classroom research: Early lessons from success.* (New Directions for Teaching and Learning, No. 46). San Francisco: Jossey-Bass.

Angelo, T. A., & Cross, K. P. (1993). *Classroom assessment techniques: A handbook for faculty* (2nd ed.). San Francisco: Jossey-Bass.

Arden, E. (1988, July 13). There's no reason why our core curriculum should make freshman year a purgatory. *The Chronicle of Higher Education, 34*(14), B2

Armour, R., & Fuhrmann, B. (Eds.). (1989). *Integrating liberal learning and professional study* (New Directions for Teaching and Learning, No. 40). San Francisco: Jossey-Bass.

Arns, K. F. (Ed.) (1981). *Occupational education today* (New Directions for Community Colleges, No. 31). San Francisco: Jossey-Bass.

Arons, A. B. (1979). Some thoughts on reasoning capacities implicitly expected of college students. In J. Lockhead & J. Cements (Eds.), *Cognitive process instruction—Research on teaching thinking skills* (pp. 209–215). Philadelphia: The Franklin Institute Press,

Association of American Colleges (AAC). (1985). *Integrity in the college curriculum: A report to the academic community.* Washington, DC: Author.

Association of American Colleges, Task Group on General Education. (1988). *A new vitality in general education.* Washington, DC: Author.

Association of American Colleges, Project on Liberal Learning, Study-in-Depth, and the Arts and Sciences Major. (1991a). *The challenge of connecting learning.* Washington, DC: Author.

Association of American Colleges, Project on Liberal Learning, Study-in-Depth, and the Arts and Sciences Major. (1991b). *Reports from the fields.* Washington, DC: Author.

Association of American Colleges, Project on Liberal Learning, Study-in-Depth, and the Arts and Sciences Major. (1992). *Program review and educational quality in the major: A faculty handbook.* Washington, DC: Author.

Association of American Colleges, Project on Strong Foundations for General Education. (1994, January). *Strong foundations.* Washington, DC: Author.

Astin, A. W. (1978). *Four critical years: Effects of college on beliefs, attitudes and knowledge.* San Francisco: Jossey-Bass.

Astin, A. W. (1979). Student-oriented management: A proposal for change. In A. W. Astin, H. R. Bowen, & C. M. Chambers. *Evaluating educational quality: A conference summary.* Washington, DC: Council on Postsecondary Accreditation.

Astin, A. W. (1984). Student involvement: A developmental theory for higher education. *Journal of College Student Personnel, 25,* 297–308.

Astin, A. W. (1985, April). The value-added debate . . . Continued. (Reply to Jonathan Warren). *AAHE Bulletin.* Washington, DC: American Association for Higher Education. *37*(8), 11–12.

Astin, A. W. (1988). *Achieving educational excellence.* San Francisco: Jossey-Bass. (Original work published 1985)

Astin, A. W. (1989, Spring). Moral messages of the university. *Educational Record, 70*(2), 22–25.

Astin, A. W. (1991a). *Assessment for excellence: The philosophy and practice of assessment and evaluation in higher education.* New York: Macmillan.

Astin, A. W. (1991b). *The unrealized potential of American higher education* (The Louise McBee Lecture). Athens: University of Georgia, Institute of Higher Education.

Astin, A. W. (1993). *What matters in college? Four critical years revisited.* San Francisco: Jossey-Bass.

Astin, A. W. Green, K. C., & Korn, W. S. (1987). *The American freshman: Twenty-year trends, 1966–1985.* Los Angeles: UCLA, Cooperative Institutional Research Program.

Astin, A. W., Panos, R. J., & Creager, J. A. (1967). *National norms of entering college freshmen—Fall 1966.* Washington, DC: American Council on Education.

Ausubel, D. P. (1963). *The psychology of meaningful learning.* New York: Grune & Stratton.

Ausubel, D. P., Novak, J. D., & Hanesian, H. (1978). *Educational psychology: A cognitive view* (2nd ed.). New York: Holt, Rinehart & Winston.

Axelrod, J. (1973). *The university teacher as artist.* San Francisco: Jossey-Bass.

Baer, E. R. (1994, March–April). Muddling through educational improvement: Deans & technology. *Change: The Magazine of Higher Learning. 26*(2), 31–33.

Baird, L. L. (1988). A map of postsecondary assessment. *Research in Higher Education. 28*(2), 99–115.

Bandura, A. (1977). *Social learning theory.* Englewood Cliffs, NJ: Prentice Hall.

Banta, T. W. (Ed.). (1988). *Implementing outcomes assessment: Promise and perils* (New Directions for Institutional Research, No. 59). San Francisco: Jossey-Bass.

Banta, T. W. (1994). Using outcomes assessment to improve educational programs. In M. Weimer & R. Menges (Eds.), *Better teaching and learning in college: Toward more scholarly practice.* San Francisco: Jossey-Bass.

Banta, T. W., & Associates. (1993). *Making a difference: Outcomes of a decade of assessment in higher education.* San Francisco: Jossey-Bass.

Banta, T. W., & Schneider, J. A. (1988). Using faculty-developed exit examinations to evaluate academic programs. *Journal of Higher Education, 59*(1), 69–83.

Barak, R. J., & Breier, B. E. (1990). *Successful program review.* San Francisco: Jossey-Bass.

Barlow, R. M. (1974). An experiment with learning contracts. *Journal of Higher Education, 45*(6), 441–449.

Baxter Magolda, M. B. (1992). *Knowing and reasoning in college: Gender-related patterns in students' intellectual development.* San Francisco: Jossey-Bass.

Beauchamp, G. A. (1982). Curriculum theory: Meaning, development, and use. *Theory into Practice, 21*(1), 23–27.

Becher, T. (1989). *Academic tribes and territories: Intellectual enquiry and the cultures of disciplines.* Bristol, PA: Society for Research into Higher Education and the Open University Press.

Behr, A. L. (1988). Exploring the lecture method: an empirical study. *Studies in Higher Education,* 13(2), 189–200.

Belenky, M., Clinchy, B., Goldberger, N., & Tarule, J. (1986). *Women's ways of knowing: The development of self, voice, and mind.* New York: Basic Books.

Bell, D. (1966). *The reforming of general education: The Columbia College experience in its national setting.* Garden City, NY: Anchor, Doubleday.

Benderson, A. (1990). Critical thinking: Critical issues. *Focus.* Princeton, NJ: Educational Testing Service.

Bennett, W. (1984). *To reclaim a legacy: A report on the humanities in higher education.* Washington, DC: National Endowment for the Humanities.

Bergquist, W. H., Gould, R. H., & Greenberg, E. M. (1981). *Designing undergraduate education: A systematic guide.* San Francisco: Jossey-Bass.

Bigge, M. L., & Shermis, S. S. (1992). *Learning theories for teachers* (5th ed.), New York: HarperCollins.

Biglan, A. (1973a, June). The characteristics of subject matter in different academic areas. *Journal of Applied Psychology, 57,* 195–203.

Biglan, A. (1973b, June). Relationships between subject matter characteristics and the structure and output of university departments. *Journal of Applied Psychology, 57,* 204–213.

Birnbaum, R. (1985). State colleges: An unsettled quality, In *Contexts for learning: The major sectors of American higher education* (pp. 17–32). Washington, DC: U.S. Government Printing Office, 1985. (Reprinted by American Association for Higher Education.)

Blackburn, R. T., Armstrong, E., Conrad, C., Didham, J., & McKune, T. (1976). *Changing practices in undergraduate education: A report prepared for the Carnegie Council on Policy Studies.* Berkeley, CA: Carnegie Foundation for the Advancement of Teaching.

Blanchard, R. O., & Christ, W. G. (1993). *Media education and the liberal arts: A blueprint for the new professionalism.* Hillsdale, NJ: Erlbaum.

Bloom, A. (1987). *The closing of the American mind: How higher education has failed democracy and impoverished the souls of today's students.* New York: Simon and Schuster.

Bloom, B. S. (Ed.). (1956). *Taxonomy of educational objectives: Cognitive domain.* New York: McKay.

Boehrer, J., & Linsky, M. (1990). Teaching with cases: Learning to question. In M. Svinicki (Ed.), *The changing face of college teaching* (New Directions for Teaching and Learning No. 42, pp. 41–57). San Francisco: Jossey-Bass.

Bok, D. (1974). On the purposes of undergraduate education. *Daedalus, 103*(4), 159–172.

Bok, D. (1986, November–December). Toward higher learning: The importance of assessing outcomes. *Change: The Magazine of Higher Learning, 18*(6), 18–27.

Boli, J., Katchadourian, H., & Mahoney, S. (1988). Analyzing academic records for informed administration. *Journal of Higher Education, 59*(1), 54–68.

Bonwell, C. C., & Eison, J. A. (1991). *Active learning: Creating excitement in the classroom* (ASHE/ERIC Higher Education Report No. 1). Washington, DC: The George Washington University, School of Education and Human Development.

Border, L. L. B., & Chism, N. V. (Eds.). (1992). *Teaching for diversity* (New Directions for Teaching and Learning No. 49). San Francisco: Jossey-Bass.

Borko, H., & Livingston, C. (1989). Cognition and improvisation: Differences in mathematics instruction by expert and novice teachers. *American Educational Research Journal, 26*(4), 473–498.

Boss, M. A., & Lowther, M. A. (1993, November). *Factors influencing curriculum change in professional programs.* Paper presented at the Association for the Study of Higher Education, Pittsburgh, PA.

Boud, D., & Feletti, G. (1991). *The challenge of problem-based learning.* London: Kogan Page.

Bouton, C., & Garth, R. Y. (1983). *Learning in groups.* San Francisco: Jossey-Bass.

Bowen, H. R. (1977). *Investment in learning: The individual and social value of American higher education.* San Francisco: Jossey-Bass.

Boxer, M. J. (1989) Women's studies, feminist goals, and the science of women. In C. S. Pearson, J. G. Touchton, & D. L. Shavlik (Eds.), *Educating the majority: Women challenge tradition in higher education.* New York: American Council on Education.

Boyer, E. L. (1987). *College: The undergraduate experience in America.* Princeton, NJ: Carnegie Foundation for the Advancement of Teaching.

Boyer, E. L. (1990). *Scholarship reconsidered: Priorities of the professoriate.* Princeton, NJ: Carnegie Foundation for the Advancement of Teaching.

Breivik, P. S. (Ed.). (1986). *Managing programs for learning outside the classroom* (New Directions for Higher Education No. 56). San Francisco: Jossey-Bass.

Brint, S., & Karabel, J. (1989). American education, meritocratic ideology, and the legitimization of inequity: The community college and the problem of American exceptionalism. *Higher Education, 18*(6), 725–735.

Brookfield, S. D. (1988). *Developing critical thinkers: Challenging adults to explore alternative ways of thinking and acting.* San Francisco: Jossey-Bass.

Brown, A. L., Bransford, J. D., Ferrara, R. A., & Campione, J. C. (1983). Learning, remembering and understanding. In P. H. Mussen (Ed.), *Handbook of child psychology* (pp. 77–166). New York: Wiley.

Brown, J. H. U., & Comola, J. (1991). Education for the workplace. In J. H. U. Brown & J. Comola (Eds.) *Educating for excellence: Improving quality and productivity in the 90's* (pp. 44–58) New York: Auburn House.

Brubacher, J. S., & Rudy, W. (1976). *Higher education in transition: A history of the American colleges and universities, 1636–1976* (3rd ed., rev. and enl.). New York: Harper & Row.

Bruffee, K. A. (1987, March–April). The art of collaborative learning: Making the most of knowledgeable peers. *Change: The Magazine of Higher Learning, 19*(2), 42–47.

Bruner, J. (1966). *The process of education.* New York: Atheneum.

Bucher, R., & Stelling, J. G. (1977). *Becoming professional.* Beverly Hills, CA: Sage.

Burke, J. C., & Volkwein, J. F. (1992, June). *Outcomes assessment at Albany.* Report to the State University of New York. Albany, NY: State University of New York.

Butler, J. (1991). *Liberal learning and the women's studies major.* College Park, MD: National Women's Studies Association.

Butler, J., & Schmitz, B. (1992). Ethnic studies, women's studies and multiculturalism. *Change: The Magazine of Higher Learning. 24*(1), 37–41.

Cameron, B. J. (1992, September). What's good and not so good about lectures. *UTS Newsletter* (Winnipeg: University of Manitoba, Centre for Higher Education, Research and Development). *1*, 1.

Cameron, B. J. (1993, January). Effective teaching: What is it? *UTS Newsletter* (Winnipeg: University of Manitoba, Centre for Higher Education, Research and Development). *1*(2), 1, 3

Cameron, K. S. (1984). Organizational adaptation and higher education. *Journal of Higher Education, 55*(2), 122–144.

Canfield, A. A. (1988). *Learning styles inventory manual.* Los Angeles: Western Psychological Services.

Cardozier, V. R. (Ed.). (1993). *Important lessons from innovative colleges and universities* (New Directions for Higher Education No. 82). San Francisco: Jossey-Bass.

Carnegie Foundation for the Advancement of Teaching. (1977). *Missions of the college curriculum: A contemporary review with suggestions.* San Francisco: Jossey-Bass.

Carnegie Foundation for the Advancement of Teaching. (1989). *The condition of the professoriate: Attitudes and trends, 1989.* Princeton, NJ: Author.

Carnegie Foundation for the Advancement of Teaching. (1992) Change trendlines: Signs of a changing curriculum. *Change: The Magazine of Higher Learning, 24*(1), 49–52.

Carnochan, W. B. (1993). *The battleground of the curriculum: Liberal education and the American experience.* Stanford, CA: Stanford University Press.

Carter, H. (1992). The convergence of international and multicultural education: Schism or coalition? *International Education Forum 12*(1), 32–41.

Cartwright, G. P. (1994, July/August). Distance learning: A different time, a different place. *Change: The Magazine of Higher Learning, 26*(4), 30–31.

Cashin, W. (1988, September). *Student ratings of teaching: A summary of the research.* (IDEA

Paper No. 20). Manhattan, KS: Kansas State University, Center for Faculty Evaluation and Development.

Cashin, W. E. (1989, September). *Defining and evaluating college teaching* (IDEA Paper No. 21). Manhattan, KS: Kansas State University, Center for Faculty Evaluation and Development.

Cashin, W. E. (September, 1995). *Student ratings of teaching: The research revisited* (IDEA Paper No. 32). Manhattan, KS: Kansas State University, Center for Faculty Evaluation and Development.

Cashin, W., & McKnight, P. C. (1986, January). *Improving discussions* (IDEA Paper No. 15). Manhattan, KS: Kansas State University, Center for Faculty Evaluation and Development.

Chaffee, E. E., & Sherr, L. A. (1992). *Quality: Transforming postsecondary education* (ASHE-ERIC Higher Education Reports No. 3). Washington, DC: George Washington University.

Change: The Magazine of Higher Learning. (1993, May–June). Special Issue on Continuous Quality Improvement Principles for Higher Education Administrators.

Characteristics of the nation's postsecondary institutions: Academic year: 1992–93. (December 1993). Washington, DC: U.S. Department of Education, Office of Educational Research and Improvement. (NCES 93-476).

Cheit, E. (1975). *The useful arts and the liberal tradition.* New York: McGraw-Hill.

Cheney, L. V. (1986, September 1) Students of success. *Newsweek, 108*, 7.

Cheney, L. V. (1988). *Humanities in America: A report to the president, the Congress, and the American people.* Washington, DC: National Endowment for the Humanities.

Cheney, L. V. (1989). *50 Hours: A core curriculum for college students.* Washington, DC: National Endowment for the Humanities.

Cheney, L. V. (1993, January–February). Multiculturalism done right: Taking steps to build support for change. *Change: The Magazine of Higher Learning, 25*(1), 8–10.

Chickering, A. W. (1969). *Education and identity.* San Francisco: Jossey-Bass.

Chickering, A. W., & Associates (1981). *The mod-ern American college: Responding to the new realities of diverse students and a changing society.* San Francisco: Jossey-Bass.

Chickering, A. W., & Gamson, Z. F. (1987, March). Seven principles of good practice in undergraduate education. *AAHE Bulletin, 39*(7), 3–7.

Chickering, A. W., & Gamson, Z. F. (Eds.). (1991, Fall) *Applying the seven principles of good practice in undergraduate education.* (New Directions for Teaching and Learning No. 47). San Francisco: Jossey-Bass.

Chickering, A. W., Gamson, Z. F., & Barsi, L. M. (1989). *Inventories of good practice in undergraduate education* (Faculty Inventory and Institutional Inventory). *The Wingspread Journal, 9*(2), 1–4. Racine, WI: Johnson Foundation.

Chickering, A. W., & Reisser, L. (1993). *Education and identity* (2nd ed.). San Francisco, Jossey-Bass.

Chronicle of Higher Education. (1994, September 1). *1994 Almanac, 41*(1), Whole issue.

Chronicle of Higher Education. (1995, September 1). 1995 *Almanac, 42*(1), Whole issue.

Clark, C. M., & Peterson, P. (1986). Teachers' thought processes. In M. C. Wittrock (Ed.), *Handbook of research on teaching.* (3rd ed, pp. 874–905). New York: Macmillan.

Clark, M. E., & Wawrytko, S. (Eds.) (1990). *Rethinking the curriculum: Toward an integrated, interdisciplinary college education.* Westport, CT: Greenwood Press.

Claxton, C. S., & Murrell, P. (1987). *Learning styles: Implications for improving educational practices* (ERIC-ASHE Higher Education Report No. 4). Washington, DC: George Washington University.

Clinchy, B., Belenky, M., Goldberger, N., & Tarule, J. (1985) Connected education for women. *Journal of Education, 167*(3), 28–45.

Cochran, L. H. (1989). *Administrative commitment to teaching.* Cape Girardeau, MO: Step-up, Inc.

Cohen, A. M. (Ed.). (1979). *Shaping the curriculum* (New Directions for Community Colleges No. 25). San Francisco: Jossey-Bass.

Cohen, A. M. (1985). The community college in the American educational system. In *Contexts for learning: The major sectors of American higher education* (pp. 1–16). Washington, DC: U.S. Government Printing Office. (Reprinted by the American Association for Higher Education.)

Cohen, A. M. (Ed.). (1994). *Relating curriculum and transfer* (New Directions for Community Colleges No. 86). San Francisco: Jossey-Bass.

Cohen, A. M., & Brawer, F. B. (1982). *The American community college.* San Francisco: Jossey-Bass.

Cohen, S. (1986, June 11). Ant wars, three-headed dogs, and curriculum changes, (Point of View) *Chronicle of Higher Education, 32*(15), 88.

Cole, C. C., Jr. (1978). *To improve instruction* (ERIC/ASHE Higher Education Research Report No. 2). Washington, DC: Association for the Study of Higher Education.

Cole, J. B. (1991). Black studies in liberal arts education. In J. E. Butler & J. C. Walter (Eds.), *Transforming the curriculum: Ethnic studies and women's studies.* (pp. 131–147). Albany: State University of New York Press.

College Board. (1983). *Academic preparation for college: What students need to know and be able to do.* New York: Author.

College graduates in the labor market: Today and the future. (1990). *ACE Research Briefs 1*(5).

College-level remedial education in the fall of 1989 (NCES 91-191). Washington, DC: National Center for Education Statistics.

Common, D. (1989). Master teachers in higher education: A matter of settings. *Review of Higher Education, 12*(4), 375–386.

Community and junior colleges: A recent profile. (1990). *ACE Research Briefs, 1*(4).

Compass, The (Newsletter of the American Council on Education. 1(1), May 1993, and *2*(2), May 1994.

Cones, J., Noonan, J., & Janha, D. (Eds). (1983). *Teaching minority students.* (New Directions for Teaching and Learning No. 16), San Francisco: Jossey-Bass.

Connelly, F. M., & Lantz, O. (1994). Definitions of curriculum. In T. Husen & T. N. Postlethwaite (Eds.), *The international encyclopedia of education* (pp. 1160–1163). New York: Pergamon Press.

Conrad, C. F. (1978). A grounded theory of academic change. *Sociology of Education, 51,* 110–112.

Conrad, C. F., & Haworth, J. G. (Eds.). (1990). *Curriculum in transition.* Needham Heights, MA: Ginn Press.

Conrad, C. F., & Haworth, J. G. (1990, February 5). Draft paper. Madison: University of Wisconsin.

Conrad, C. F., & Pratt, A. M. (1983). Making decisions about the curriculum: From metaphor to model. *Journal of Higher Education, 54*(1), 16–30.

Conrad, C. F., & Pratt, A. M. (1986). Research on academic programs: An inquiry into an emerging field. In J. C. Smart (Ed.). *Higher education: Handbook of theory and research* (Vol. 2, pp. 235–273). New York: Agathon Press.

Conrad, C. F., & Wyer, J. C. (1980). *Liberal education in transition* (AAHE-ERIC Higher Education Research Report No. 3). Washington, DC: American Association for Higher Education.

Corno, L., & Snow, R. (1986). Adapting teaching to individual differences among learners. In M. Wittrock (Ed.), *Handbook of Research on Teaching.* (3rd ed., pp. 605–629). New York: Macmillan.

Creswell, J. W., & Roskens, R. W. (1981). The Biglan studies of differences among academic areas. *The Review of Higher Education, 4*(3), 1–16.

Cross, K. P. (1976a). *Accent on learning: Improving instruction and reshaping the curriculum.* San Francisco: Jossey-Bass.

Cross, K. P. (1976b). *Beyond the open door: New students to higher education.* San Francisco: Jossey-Bass.

Cross, K. P. (1981). *Adults as learners: Increasing participation and facilitating learning.* San Francisco: Jossey-Bass.

Cross, K. P. (1987, March 2). *Teaching for learning.* Speech presented at the National Conference on Higher Education, American Association for Higher Education, Chicago.

Cross, K. P. (1989). *Feedback in the classroom: Making assessment matter.* Washington, DC: American Association for Higher Education, Assessment Forum.

Cross, K. P. (1992, April). Remarks made in panel discussion at American Educational Research Association, San Francisco.

Cross, K. P., & Angelo, T. A. (1988). *Classroom assessment techniques: A handbook for faculty.* Ann Arbor: University of Michigan, National Center for Research to Improve Postsecondary Teaching and Learning.

Cuban, L. (1990, January). Reforming again, again, and again. *Educational Researcher, 19*(1), 3–13.

Curriculum content of bachelor's degrees (1986, November). *OERI Bulletin.* CS 86-317b. Washington, DC: U.S. Department of Education, Office of Educational Research and Improvement.

Curry, L., Wergin, J. F., & Associates. (1993). *Educating professionals.* San Francisco: Jossey-Bass.

Curtis, M. H. (1985) Confronting an ancient dichotomy: A proposal for integrating liberal and professional education. *Phi Kappa Phi Journal, 65*(3), 10–12.

Darby, J., Kjollerstrom, B., & Martin, J. (Eds). (1994). *Higher education 1998 transformed by learning technology.* Oxford: CTISS Publications.

Davis, J. R. (1993). *Better teaching; More learning.* Phoenix, AZ: Oryx Press.

Davis, R. H., Strand, R., Alexander, L. T., & Hussain, M. N. (1982). The impact of organizational and innovator variables on instructional innovation in higher education. *Journal of Higher Education, 53*(5), 568–586.

Davis, T. M., & Murrell, P. H. (1993). *Turning teaching into learning: The role of student responsibility in the collegiate experience* (ASHE-ERIC Higher Education Report No. 8). Washington, DC: George Washington University.

Davis, W. K., Nairn, R., Paine, M. E., Anderson, R. M., & Oh, M. S. (1992). Effects of expert and non-expert facilitators on the small-group process and on student performance. *Academic Medicine, 67*(7), 470–474.

Deci, E. L., & Ryan, R. M. (1991). A motivational approach to self: Integration in personality. In R. Dienstbier (Ed.), *Perspectives on motivation: Nebraska Symposium on Motivation*, Lincoln: University of Nebraska Press.

DeNeve, H. M. F. (1991). University teachers' thinking about lecturing: Student evaluation of lecturing as an improvement perspective for the teacher. *Higher Education, 22*, 63–91.

Dey, E. L., Astin, A. W., & Korn, W. S. (1991). *The American freshman: Twenty-five year trends, 1966–1990.* Washington, DC: American Council on Education and UCLA Higher Education Research Institute.

Dey, E. L., & Hurtado, S. (1994). *College impact, student impact: A reconsideration of the role of students within American higher education.* Paper presented at the 34th Annual Forum of the Association for Institutional Research, New Orleans.

Diamond, R. M. (1989). *Designing and improving courses and curricula in higher education.* San Francisco: Jossey-Bass.

Dill, D. C., & Friedman, C. P. (1979). An analysis of frameworks for research on innovation and change in higher education. *Review of Educational Research, 49,* 411–435.

Donald, J. G. (1983). Knowledge structures: Methods for exploring course content. *Journal of Higher Education, 54,* 31–41.

Donald, J. G. (1990). University professors' views of knowledge and validation processes. *Journal of Educational Psychology, 82*(2), 242–249.

Donald, J. G. (1992). The development of thinking processes in postsecondary education: Application of a working model. *Higher Education, 24,* 413–430.

Donald, J. G., & Sullivan, A. (Eds.). (1985). *Using research to improve teaching* (New Directions for Teaching and Learning No. 23). San Francisco: Jossey-Bass.

Doyle, W. (1986). Content representation in teachers' definitions of academic work. *Journal of Curriculum Studies, 18,* 365–367.

Dressel, P. L. (1971). *College and university curriculum.* (2nd ed.). Berkeley: McCutchan. (Original work published in 1968).

Dressel, P. L. (1979a, Fall). Liberal education: Developing the characteristics of a liberally educated person. *Liberal Education*, 313–322.

Dressel, P. L. (1979b). A look at new curriculum models for undergraduate education. *Journal of Higher Education, 50*(4), 389–397. (Originally published February 1965, *36*(2), 89–96).

Dressel, P. L. (1980). *Improving degree programs: A guide to curriculum development, adminis-*

tration and review. San Francisco: Jossey-Bass.

Dressel, P. L., & DeLisle, F. H. (1970). *Undergraduate curriculum trends.* Washington, DC: American Council on Education.

Dressel, P. L. & Marcus, D. (1982). *On teaching and learning in college.* San Francisco: Jossey-Bass.

Duncan, W. J. (1977, October). Professional education and the liberating tradition: An action alternative. *Liberal Education, 63*(3), 453–461.

Dunkin, M. J., & Barnes, J. (1986). Research on teaching in higher education. In M. Wittrock (Ed.), *Handbook of research on teaching* (3rd ed., pp. 754–777). New York: Macmillan.

Dweck, C. S., & Elliott, E. S. (1983). Achievement motivation. In P. Mussen (Ed.), *Handbook of child psychology* (Vol. 4, pp. 643–691). New York: Wiley.

Eaton, J. (Ed.). (1988). *Colleges of choice: The enabling impact of the community college.* New York: Macmillan.

Eble, K. E. (1988). *The craft of teaching* (2nd ed.). San Francisco: Jossey-Bass.

Eccles, J. (1983). Expectancies, values and academic behaviors. In J. T. Spence (Ed.), *Achievement and achievement motives.* (pp. 75–146). San Francisco: Freedman.

ECS. *See* Education Commission of the States.

Edgerton, R. (1991, December). National standards are coming! . . . National standards are coming! *AAHE Bulletin, 44*(4), 8–12.

Edgerton, R. (1992, September–October). Editorial: Textbooks and faculty rewards. *Change: The Magazine of Higher Learning, 24*(5), 4

Education Commission of the States (ECS). (1986, July). *Transforming the state role in higher education.* Denver, CO: Author.

Edwards, J., & Tonkin, H. R. (1990). Internationalizing the community college: Strategies for the classroom. In R. K. Greenfield (Ed.) *Developing international education programs* (New Directions for Community Colleges No. 70, pp. 17–26). San Francisco: Jossey-Bass.

Ehrmann, S. C. (1994, March–April). Making sense of technology: A dean's progress. *Change: The Magazine of Higher Learning, 26*(2), 34–53.

Eisner, E. W. (1979) *The educational imagination:*

On the design and evaluation of school programs. New York: Macmillan.

Eisner, E. W., & Vallance, E. (Eds.). (1974). *Conflicting conceptions of the curriculum.* (National Society for the Study of Education, Series on Contemporary Educational Issues) Berkeley, CA: McCutchan.

Eison, J. (1981). A new instrument for assessing students' orientations towards grades and learning. *Psychological Reports, 48,* 919–924.

Eldred, M. D., & Marienau, C. (1979). *Adult baccalaureate programs* (ERIC/AAHE Higher Education Research Reports No. 9). Washington, DC: American Association for Higher Education.

Eliot, C. W. (1989). Liberty in education. In Lester F. Goodchild & Harold S. Wechsler (Eds.). *The ASHE reader on the history of higher education* (pp. 373–380). Needham Heights, MA: Ginn Press. (Original work published 1898).

El-Khawas, E. (1986). *Campus trends, 1986.* Washington, DC: American Council on Education.

El-Khawas, E. (1987a). Colleges reclaim the assessment initiative. *Educational Record. 68*(2), 54–58.

El-Khawas, E. (1987b), *Campus trends, 1987.* Washington, DC: American Council on Education.

El-Khawas, E. (1988), *Campus trends, 1988.* Washington, DC: American Council on Education.

El-Khawas, E. (1989), *Campus trends, 1989.* Washington, DC: American Council on Education.

El-Khawas, E. (1990), *Campus trends, 1990.* Washington, DC: American Council on Education.

El-Khawas, E. (1991), *Campus trends, 1991.* Washington, DC: American Council on Education.

El-Khawas, E. (1992), *Campus trends, 1992.* Washington, DC: American Council on Education.

El-Khawas, E. (1993). *Campus trends, 1993.* Washington, DC: American Council on Education.

El-Khawas, E., Carter, D. J., & Ottinger, C. (1988).

Community college fact book. New York: Collier Macmillan.

Endo, J. J., & Harpel, R. L. (1982). The effect of student–faculty interaction on students' educational outcomes. *Research in Higher Education, 16*(2), 115–138.

Endorf, M., & McNeff, M. (1990, Winter). The adult learner—Five types. *Journal of Staff, Program & Organization Development, 8*(4), 209–215.

English, S. (1994). *Student outcomes of internationalization.* Ann Arbor: University of Michigan, Center for the Study of Higher and Postsecondary Education. Unpublished paper in our possession.

Ennis, R. H. (1987). A taxonomy of critical thinking dispositions and abilities. In J. B. Baron & R. J. Sternberg (Eds.), *Teaching for thinking* (pp. 9–26). New York: Freeman.

Erdle, S., & Murray, H. G. (1986). Interfaculty differences in classroom teaching behaviors and their relationship to student instructional ratings. *Research in Higher Education, 24*(2), 115–127.

Ericksen, S. (1984). *The essence of good teaching: Helping students learn and remember what they learn.* San Francisco: Jossey-Bass.

Erickson, G. R., & Erickson, B. L. (1979). Improving college teaching: An evaluation of a teaching consultation procedure. *Journal of Higher Education, 50*(5), 670–683.

Erikson, B. L, & Strommer, D. W. (1991). *Teaching college freshmen.* San Francisco: Jossey-Bass.

Erwin, T. D. (1991). *Assessing student learning and development.* San Francisco: Jossey-Bass.

ETS. *See* Educational Testing Service

Ewell, P. T. (1985, April). The value-added debate . . . Continued. (Reply to Jonathan Warren). *AAHE Bulletin.* Washington, DC: American Association for Higher Education. *37*(8), 12–13.

Ewell, P. T. (1989). *Assessment, accountability, and improvement: Managing the contradiction.* Washington, DC: American Association for Higher Education, Assessment Forum.

Ewell, P. T. (1991a). Assessment and public accountability: Back to the future. *Change: The Magazine of Higher Learning, 23*(6), 12–17.

Ewell, P. T. (1991b). To capture the ineffable: New forms of assessment in higher education. In G. Grant (Ed.), *Review of research in education* (Vol. 17, pp. 75–125). Washington, DC: American Educational Research Association.

Feasley, C. E. (1978). *Serving learners at a distance: A guide to program practices* (ASHE-ERIC Higher Education Research Reports No. 5). Washington, DC: Association for the Study of Higher Education.

Featherstone, J. (1989). Playing Marco Polo: A response to Harry Judge. *Comparative Education, 25*(3), 339–344.

Feichtner, S. B., & Davis, E. Why some groups fail: A survey of students' experiences with learning groups. Cited in *The Teaching Professor* (1991, November) 5 (9).

Feldman, K. A. (1976). The superior college teacher from the student's view. *Research in Higher Education, 5*(3), 243–288.

Fersh, S. (1990). Adding an international dimension to the community college: Examples and implications. In R. K. Greenfield (Ed.), *Developing international education programs* (New Directions for Community Colleges No. 70, pp 67–75). San Francisco: Jossey-Bass.

Fetters, M. L., Hoopes, J., & Tropp, M. (1989). Integrating concepts from accounting, American history, and English literature: A cluster course approach. *Journal of Accounting Education, 7,* 69–82.

Fifield, M. L., & Sam, D. F. (1986). Loop College Business and International Education Project. Chicago: Chicago City Colleges (ED 269 056). Cited in R. I. Cape and A. Y. Colby (1990) Sources and information: Internationalizing in the community college. In R. K. Greenfield, (Ed.) *Developing international education programs* (New Directions for Community Colleges No. 70, pp. 17–26). San Francisco: Jossey-Bass.

Fincher, C. (1988). Provisional variation and selective retention in curricular change. *Research in Higher Education, 28*(3), 281–285.

Finkelstein, M. J., Farrar, D., & Pfnister, A. O. (1984). The adaptation of liberal arts colleges to the 1970s: An analysis of critical events. *Journal of Higher Education, 55*(2), 242–268.

Fisch, L. (1992, November). Using responsive

questions to facilitate discussion. *The Teaching Professor, 6*(9), 5

Flavell, J. H. (1979). Metacognition and cognitive monitoring: A new area of cognitive developmental inquiry. *American Psychologist, 34*(9), 906–911.

Fleming, J. (1984). *Blacks in college.* San Francisco: Jossey-Bass.

Ford, G. W., & Pugno, L. (1964). *The structure of knowledge and the curriculum.* Chicago: Rand McNally.

Fraley, L. E., & Vargas, E. A. (1975). Academic tradition and instructional technology. *Journal of Higher Education, 46*(1), 1–15.

Francis, M. C., Mulder, T., & Stark, J. S. (1995). *Intentional learning: A process of learning to learn in the accounting curriculum.* Sarasota, FL: Accounting Education Change Commission and the American Accounting Association.

Franklin, P., Huber, B. J., & Laurence, D. (1992, January–February). Continuity and change in the study of literature. *Change: The Magazine of Higher Learning, 24*(1) 42–48.

Friedlander, J., Pace, C. R., & Lehmann, P. W. (1990). *Community colleges student experiences questionnaire.* Los Angeles: University of California Los Angeles: Center for the Study of Evaluation.

Friedmann, J. (1967). A conceptual model for the analysis of planning behavior. *Administrative Science Quarterly, 12*, 225–252.

Fund for the Improvement of Postsecondary Education. (1990). *Lessons learned from FIPSE projects.* Washington, DC: Author.

Furukawa, J. M., Cohen, N., & Sumpter, K. (1982). Improving student achievement. *Research in Higher Education, 16*(3), 245–253.

Gabelnick, F., MacGregor, J., Matthews, R. S., & Smith, B. L. (Eds.). (1990, Spring). *Learning communities: Creating connections among students, faculty, and disciplines* (New Directions for Teaching and Learning No. 41). San Francisco: Jossey-Bass.

Gaff, J. G. (1980). Avoiding the potholes: Strategies for reforming general education. *Educational Record, 61*(4), 50–59.

Gaff, J. G. (1991). *New life for the college curriculum: Assessing achievements and further progress in the reform of general education.* San Francisco: Jossey-Bass.

Gaff, J. G. (1992). Beyond politics: The educational issues inherent in multicultural education. *Change: The Magazine of Higher Learning, 24*(1), 31–35.

Gaff, J. G., & Wilson, R. (1971). The teaching environment. *AAUP Bulletin, 57*(4). 475–493.

Gainen, J., & Locatelli, P. (1995). *Assessment for the new curriculum: A guide for professional accounting programs.* Sarasota, FL: Accounting Education Change Commission and the American Accounting Association.

Gamson, Z. F. (1982). *A little light on the subject: Keeping general and liberal education alive.* Paper presented to the National Commission on Excellence in Education, Washington, DC.

Gamson, Z. F., & Associates. (1984). *Liberating education.* San Francisco: Jossey-Bass.

Gardner, D. E. (1977). Five evaluation frameworks: Implications for decision making in higher education. *Journal of Higher Education, 48*(5), 571–593.

Garland, P. H., & Grace, T. W. (1993). *New perspectives for student affairs professionals: Evolving realities, responsibilities and roles* (ASHE-ERIC Higher Education Reports No. 7). Washington, DC: The George Washington University.

Gay, G. (1980). Conceptual models of the curriculum-planning process. In A. W. Foshay (Ed), *Considered Action for Curriculum Improvement* (pp. 120–143). Alexandria, VA: Association for Supervision and Curriculum Development.

Geiger, R. L. (1985). Research universities: Their role in undergraduate education. *In Contexts for learning: The major sectors of American higher education* (pp. 49–65). Washington DC: U.S. Government Printing Office. (Reprinted by American Association for Higher Education.)

Geiger, R. L. (1986). *To advance knowledge: The growth of American research universities, 1900–1940.* New York: Oxford University Press.

Geoghegan, W. (1994, September). Stuck at the barricades: Can information technology really enter the mainstream of teaching and learning? *AAHE Bulletin, 47*(1), 13–16.

Gilligan, C. (1982). *In a different voice: Psychological theory and women's development.* Cambridge, MA: Harvard University Press.

Golin, S. (1990, December). Four arguments for peer collaboration and student interviewing. *AAHE Bulletin, 43*(4), 9–10.

Goodman, G., & Parochetti, J. A. (1987). Curriculum crisis: The challenge of the '80s. *Innovative Higher Education, 12*(1), 47–50.

Gow, D. T., & Yeager, J. L. (1975). The design and development of individualized curriculum materials for higher education. *Journal of Higher Education, 46*(1), 41–54.

Graff, G. (1988, February 17). Conflicts over the curriculum are here to stay: They should be made educationally productive. *The Chronicle of Higher Education. 34*(23), A48.

Graff, G. (1992). *Beyond the culture wars: How teaching the conflicts can revitalize American education.* New York: Norton.

Grant, G., & Riesmann, D. (Eds.). (1978). *The perpetual dream: Reform and experiment in the American college.* Chicago: University of Chicago Press.

Grasha, A. F. (1972). Observations on relating teaching goals to student response styles and classroom methods. *American Psychologist, 27*, 144–147.

Gray, P. J. (Ed.). (1989). *Achieving assessment goals using evaluation techniques* (New Directions for Higher Education No. 67). San Francisco: Jossey-Bass.

Gray, P. J., Froh, R. C, & Diamond, R. M. (1992, March). *A national study of research universities: On the balance between research and undergraduate teaching.* Syracuse, NY: Syracuse University, Center for Instructional Development.

Green, T. F. (1981). Acquisition of purpose. In Arthur W. Chickering & Associates, *The modern American college* (pp. 543–555). San Francisco: Jossey-Bass.

Greene, M. (1993, January–February). The passions of pluralism: Multiculturalism and the expanding community. *Educational Researcher, 22*(1), 13–18.

Greenfield, R. K. (Ed.). (1990). *Developing international education programs.* (New Directions for Community Colleges No. 70, pp. 17–26.) San Francisco: Jossey-Bass.

Griffin, C. W. (Ed.). (1982). *Teaching writing in all disciplines.* (New Directions for Teaching and Learning No. 12). San Francisco: Jossey-Bass.

Griffith, J. V., & Chapman, D. W. (1982). *Learning context questionnaire.* Davidson, NC: Davidson College.

Groennings, S., & Wiley, D. S. (1990). *Group portrait: Internationalizing the disciplines.* New York: American Forum for Global Education.

Guba, E. G., & Lincoln, Y. S. (1985). *Effective evaluation: Improving the usefulness of evaluation through responsive and naturalistic approaches.* San Francisco: Jossey-Bass.

Gumport, P. (1988). Curricula as signposts of cultural change. *Review of Higher Education, 12*(1), 49–61.

Guskey, T. R., & Easton, J. Q. (1988). *Improving student learning in college classrooms.* Springfield, IL: Charles C. Thomas.

Guskin, A. E. (Ed.). (1981). *The administrator's role in effective teaching* (New Directions for Teaching and Learning No. 5), San Francisco: Jossey-Bass.

Guyon, J. C., & Klasek, C. B. (1991). Toward the year 2,000: Preparing for the international dimension in higher education. *International Education Forum, 11*(2), 70–78.

Haber, S. (1991). *The quest for authority and honor in the American professions, 1750–1900.* Chicago: University of Chicago Press.

Hagerty, B. M. K., & Stark, J. S. (1989). Comparing educational accreditation standards in selected professional fields. *Journal of Higher Education, 60*(1), 1–20.

Hallett, J. J. (1988, Winter). The changing face of work. *Journal of Career Planning and Employment, 48*(2), 52–55.

Halliburton, D. (1977a). Perspectives on the curriculum. In A. W. Chickering, D. Halliburton, W. H. Bergquist, & J. Lindquist (Eds.), *Developing the college curriculum* (pp. 37–50). Washington, DC: Council for the Advancement of Small Colleges,

Halliburton, D. (1977b). Designing curriculum. In A. W. Chickering, D. Halliburton, W. H. Bergquist, & J. Lindquist (Eds.), *Developing the college curriculum* (pp. 51–74). Washington, DC: Council for the Advancement of Small Colleges.

Halpern, D. F. (1994). *Changing college classrooms: New teaching and learning strategies for an increasingly complex world.* San Francisco: Jossey-Bass.

Hansen, W. L., & Stampen, J. 0. (1993). Higher education: No better access without better quality. *Higher Education Extension Service Review, 4*(2).

Harris, J. (1985, June). *Assessing outcomes in higher education: Practical suggestions for getting started.* Paper given at the National Conference on Assessment in Higher Education, University of South Carolina, Columbia, SC.

Harter, S. (1985). Competence as a dimension of self-evaluation: Toward a comprehensive model of self-worth. In R. Leahy (Ed.) *The development of the self.* New York: Academic.

Hartle, T. W. (1994). Will increased regulation threaten the academy's independence? *Educational Record, 75*(1), 53–56.

Harvard Committee. (1945). *General education in a free society.* Cambridge, MA: Harvard University Press.

Haworth, J. G., & Conrad, C. F. (1990). Curricular transformations: Traditional and emerging voices. In C. F. Conrad & J. G. Haworth (Eds.). *Curriculum in transition: Perspectives on the undergraduate experience.* Needham Heights, MA: Ginn Press.

Hefferlin, JB L. (1969). *Dynamics of academic reform.* San Francisco: Jossey-Bass.

Heginbotham, S. J. (1994, October 19). Shifting the focus of international programs. *Point of View: The Chronicle of Higher Education,* p. A68.

Henry, D. (1975). *Challenges past, challenges present: An analysis of American higher education since 1930.* San Francisco: Jossey-Bass.

Heverly, M. A. (1994, May). *Applying total quality to the teaching/learning process.* Media, PA: Delaware Valley Community College. Paper given at the Association for Institutional Research Forum, New Orleans.

Hewson, P. W., & Posner, G. J. (1984). The use of schema theory in the design of instructional materials: A physics example. *Instructional Science, 13,* 119–139.

Hexter, H., & Lippincott, J. (1990). Campuses and student assessment. *Research Briefs, 1*(8).

Washington, DC: American Council on Education.

Hiemstra, R., & Sisco, B. (1990). *Individualizing instruction: Making learning personal, empowering, and successful.* San Francisco: Jossey-Bass.

Hirsch, E. D., Jr. (1988). *Cultural literacy: What every American needs to know.* New York: Vintage Books.

Hirst, P. H. (1974). *Knowledge and the curriculum: A collection of philosophical papers.* Boston: Routledge & Kegan Paul.

Hodgkinson, H. (1971). *Institutions in transition.* Carnegie Council on Policy Studies. San Francisco: Jossey-Bass.

Holleman, M. (Ed.). (1990). *The role of the learning resources center in instruction.* (New Directions for Community Colleges No. 71). San Francisco: Jossey-Bass.

Hook, S., Kurtz, P., & Todorovich, M. (1975). *The philosophy of the curriculum.* Buffalo, NY: Prometheus.

Huenecke, D. (1982, January). What is curriculum theorizing? What are its implications for practice? *Educational Leadership, 39*(4), 290–294.

Hursh, B., Haas, P., & Moore, M. (1983). An interdisciplinary model to implement general education. *Journal of Higher Education, 54*(1), 42–59.

Hutchings, P. (ca. 1989). *Six stories: Implementing successful assessment.* Washington, DC: American Association for Higher Education.

Jackson, P. W. (1992). Conceptions of curriculum and curriculum specialists. In P. W. Jackson (Ed.), *Handbook of research on curriculum* (pp. 3–40). New York: Macmillan.

Jacobson, R. L. (1994a, July 6). Extending the reach of "virtual" classrooms. *Chronicle of Higher Education,* A19–A23.

Jacobson, R. L. (1994b, November 16). Scholars plan a "virtual university," offering courses exclusively on the internet. *Chronicle of Higher Education,* A20–A21.

Johnson, D. W., Johnson, R. T. & Smith, K. A. (1991). *Cooperative learning: Increasing college faculty instructional productivity* (ASHE ERIC Higher Education Reports No. 4). Washington, DC: The George Washington University.

Johnson, G. R., Fink, L. D., Eubanks, I. D., Lewis, K. G., & Whitcomb, D. B. (1987). The higher education curriculum crisis. *Community/Junior College Quarterly, 11*, 253–265.

Johnson, M., Jr. (1967, April). Definitions and models in curriculum theory, *Educational Theory, 17*(2), 127–140.

Johnston, J., & Kozma, R. B. (Eds.). (1993). *When lectures fail: Educational computing in the humanities.* Ann Arbor: The University of Michigan, National Center for Research to Improve Postsecondary Teaching and Learning.

Johnston, J. S., Jr., & Associates. (1987). *Educating managers: Executive effectiveness through liberal learning.* San Francisco: Jossey-Bass.

Johnston, J. S., Jr., & Associates. (1989). *Those who can: Undergraduate programs to prepare arts and sciences majors for teaching.* Washington, DC: Association of American Colleges.

Johnston, J. S., Jr., & Edelstein, R. J. (1993). *Beyond borders: Profiles in international education.* Washington, DC: Association of American Colleges and American Assembly of Collegiate Schools of Business.

Johnston, J. S. Jr., Shaman, S., & Zemsky, R. (1988). *Unfinished design: The humanities and social sciences in undergraduate engineering education.* Washington, DC: Association of American Colleges.

Johnston, W. B., & Arnold, A. P. (1987). *Workforce 2000: Work and workers for the twenty-first century.* New York: Dutton.

Johnstone, S. M. (1991). Research on telecommunicated learning: Past, present and future. In *Electronic links for learning: Annals of the American Academic of Political and Social Science* (special edition). Newbury Park, CA: Sage.

Joint Committee on Standards for Educational Evaluation. (1981). *Standards for evaluation of education programs, projects, and materials.* New York: McGraw-Hill.

Jones, D. J., & Watson, B. C. (1990). *High risk students in higher education: Future trends* (ASHE-ERIC Higher Education Report No. 3). Washington, DC: George Washington University.

Kagan, J., & Kogan, N. (1970). Individual variation in cognitive process. In P. Mussen (Ed.), *Carmichael's manual of child psychology* (Vol. 1, pp. 1273–1365). New York: Wiley.

Kanter, S. (1991). *Academic Workplace Newsletter*, p. 6. Boston: New England Resource Center for Higher Education.

Kanter, S., London, H., & Gamson, Z. F. (1990). *The implementation of general education: Some early findings* (Working Paper No. 5). Boston: New England Resource Center for Higher Education.

Kasworm, C. E. (1990). Adult undergraduates in higher education: A review of past research perspectives. *Review of Educational Research, 60*(3), 345–372.

Katz, J., & Henry, M. (1988). *Turning professors into teachers: A new approach to faculty development and student learning.* New York: Macmillan.

Kaysen, C. (Ed.) (1973). *Content and context: Essays on college education.* New York: McGraw-Hill.

Kaysen, C. (1974). What should undergraduate education do? *Daedalus, 103*(4), 180–185.

Keeton, M. (1981). Assessing and credentialling prior experience. In A. W. Chickering & Associates. *The modern American college.* (pp. 631–641). San Francisco: Jossey-Bass.

Keller, F. S. (1968). Goodbye teacher . . . *Journal of Applied Behavior Analysis, 1*, 76–89.

Keller, G. (1983). *Academic strategy.* Baltimore: The Johns Hopkins University Press.

Keller, P. (1982). *Getting at the core: Curricular reform at Harvard.* Cambridge, MA: Harvard University Press.

Kennedy, D. (1991, March 3). *The improvement of teaching: An essay to the Stanford community.* Palo Alto, CA: Stanford University.

Kerlinger, F. (1973). *Foundations of behavioral research.* (2nd ed.). New York: Holt, Rinehart and Winston.

Kerr, C. (1977). Foreword. In F. Rudolph. *Curriculum: A history of the American undergraduate course of study since 1936.* San Francisco: Jossey-Bass.

Kerr, C. (1994a). How well has higher education in the United States met the test of service to the labor market? In C. Kerr (Ed.), *Troubled times for American higher education: The*

1990s and beyond (Chapter 4) Albany, NY: SUNY Press.

Kerr, C. (1994b). Restoring quality to undergraduate education. In C. Kerr (Ed.), *Troubled times for American higher education: The 1990s and beyond* (Chapter 9). Albany, NY: SUNY Press.

Kimball, B. (1986). *Orators and philosophers: A history of the idea of liberal education.* New York: Teachers College Press.

Kimball, B. (1988, May). The historical and cultural dimensions of the recent reports on undergraduate education. *American Journal of Education, 96*(3), 293–322.

King, A. R., Jr., & Brownell, J. A. (1966). *The curriculum and the disciplines of knowledge: A theory of curriculum practice.* New York: Wiley.

King, P. M., & Kitchener, K. S. (1994). *Developing reflective judgment: Understanding and promoting intellectual growth and critical thinking in adolescents and adults.* San Francisco: Jossey-Bass.

Klein, J. T. (1990). *Interdisciplinarity: History, theory and practice.* Detroit: Wayne State University Press.

Kolb, D. (1981). Learning styles and disciplinary differences. In A. W. Chickering & Associates. *The modern American college* (pp. 232–255). San Francisco: Jossey-Bass.

Kolb, D. (1984). *Experiential learning: Experience as the source of learning and development.* Englewood Cliffs, NJ: Prentice-Hall.

Kozma, R. B. (1978). Faculty development and the adoption and diffusion of classroom innovations. *Journal of Higher Education, 49*(5), 438–449.

Kozma, R. B. (1979). Communication, rewards, and the use of classroom innovations. *Journal of Higher Education, 50*(6), 761–771.

Kozma, R. B. (1985). A grounded theory of instructional innovation in higher education. *Journal of Higher Education, 56*(3), 300–319.

Kozma, R. B. (1991). Learning with media. *Review of Educational Research, 61*(2), 179–211.

Kozma, R. B., Belle, L. W., & Williams, G. (1978). *Instructional techniques in higher education.* Englewood Cliffs, NJ: Educational Technology Publications.

Kozma, R. B., & Johnston, J. (1991). The technological revolution comes to the classroom. *Change: The Magazine of Higher Learning, 23*(1), 10–23.

Kozma, R. B., Johnston, J., & Sossen, P. *Survey of academic software developers in progress.* University of Michigan. Personal knowledge.

Kramer, M., & Weiner, S. S. (1994). *Dialogues for diversity: Community and ethnicity on campus.* Phoenix, AZ: Oryx Press.

Krapp, A., Hidi, S., & Renninger, K. A. (1992). Interest, learning and development. In K. A. Renninger, S. Hidi, & A. Krapp (Eds.), *The role of interest in learning and development.* (pp. 3–25). Hillsdale, NJ: Lawrence Erlbaum Associates.

Kugel, P. (1993). How professors develop as teachers. *Studies in Higher Education, 18*(3), 315–328.

Kuh, G. D., Schuh, J. H., Whitt, E. & Associates. (1991). *Involving colleges.* San Francisco: Jossey-Bass.

Kuhn, T. S. (1970). *The structure of scientific revolutions* (2nd ed., enl.). Chicago: University of Chicago Press.

Kurfiss, J. G. (1988). *Critical thinking: Theory, research, practice, and possibilities* (ASHE-ERIC Higher Education Report No. 2). Washington, DC: George Washington University.

Lambert, R. (1989). *International studies and the undergraduate.* Washington, DC: American Council on Education.

Lambert, R. (1990). Foreign language use among international business graduates. *Annals of the American Academy of Political and Social Science, 511*, 47–59.

Larson, M. S. (1977). *The rise of professionalism: A sociological analysis.* Berkeley: University of California Press.

Lattuca, L. R., & Stark, J. S. (1994). Will disciplinary perspectives impede curriculum reform? *Journal of Higher Education, 65*(4), 401–426.

Lattuca, L. R., & Stark, J. S. (1995). Modifying the major: Discretionary thoughts from ten disciplines. *The Review of Higher Education, 18*(3), 315–344.

Lattuca, L. R. (1993, Summer). *Influences on interdisciplinary scholarship in research universities.* Ann Arbor: University of Michigan, Center for the Study of Higher and Postsecondary Education. Unpublished paper in our possession.

Lauter, P. (1991). *Canons and contexts.* New York: Oxford University Press.

Laws, P. (1991). Workshop physics: Learning introductory physics by doing it. *Change: The Magazine of Higher Learning, 23,* 20–27.

Lee, W. A., & Gilmour, J. E., Jr. (1977). A procedure for the development of new programs in postsecondary education. *Journal of Higher Education, 48*(3), 304–320.

Leinwand, G. (1983, November). *Without a nickel: The challenge of internationalizing the curriculum and the campus.* Washington, DC: American Association of State Colleges and Universities.

Leithwood, K. A. (1985). Curriculum diffusion. In T. Husen & T. N. Postlethwaite (Eds.). *The international encyclopedia of education* (pp. 1181–1183). New York: Pergamon Press.

Leslie, L. L., & Brinkman, P. T. (1988). *The economic value of higher education.* New York: Macmillan.

Levine, A. (1980). *When dreams and heroes died: A portrait of today's college student.* San Francisco: Jossey-Bass.

Levine, A. (1986). De'ja vu: Reviewing educational reports from the past. *Change: The Magazine of Higher Learning, 18*(1), 50–52.

Levine, A. (1978). *Handbook on undergraduate curriculum.* San Francisco: Jossey-Bass.

Levine, A., & Cureton, J. (1992). The quiet revolution: Eleven facts about multiculturalism and the curriculum. *Change: The Magazine of Higher Learning, 24*(1), 24–35.

Lewis, C. W. (1994). An education for the global marketplace . . . *College Board Review, 171,* 12–17.

Lichtenberg, J. (1992, September–October). The new paradox of the college textbook. *Change: The Magazine of Higher Learning, 24*(5), 11–17.

Light, R. J. (1990). *The Harvard assessment seminars: Explorations with students and faculty about teaching, learning, and student life.* (First Report). Cambridge, MA: Harvard University.

Light, R. J. (1992). *The Harvard assessment seminars: Explorations with students and faculty about teaching, learning, and student life.*

(Second Report). Cambridge, MA: Harvard University.

Lincoln, Y. S., & Guba, E. G. (1980). The distinction between merit and worth in evaluation. *Educational Evaluation and Policy Analysis, 2*(4), 61–71.

Lindquist, J. (1974). Political linkage: The academic innovation process. *Journal of Higher Education, 45*(5), 323–343.

Lindquist, J. (1978). *Strategies for Change.* Berkeley, CA: Pacific Soundings Press.

Lisensky, R. P., Pfnister, A. O., & Sweet, S. D. (1985). *The new liberal learning: Technology and the liberal arts.* Washington, DC: Council of Independent Colleges.

Livengood, J. M. (1992). Students' motivational goals and beliefs about effort and ability as they relate to college academic success. *Research in Higher Education, 33*(2), 247–261.

Loacker, G. (1988). Faculty as a force to improve instruction through assessment. In J. McMillan (Ed.), *Assessing students' learning* (New Directions for Teaching and Learning No. 34) (pp. 19–32). San Francisco: Jossey-Bass.

Locke, L. (1989, July/August). General education: In search of facts. *Change: The Magazine of Higher Learning, 21*(4), 20–23.

Loebbecke, J. (1994). Presentation to the Accounting Education Change Commission. Salt Lake City, UT. (Photocopy in our possession.)

Lowman, J. (1984). *Mastering the techniques of teaching.* San Francisco: Jossey-Bass.

Lowther, M. A., & Stark, J. S. (1990, April). *Course planning patterns of college teachers.* Paper presented at the meeting of the American Educational Research Association, Boston.

Lowther, M. A., Stark, J. S., Genthon, M. L., & Bentley, R. J. (1990). Comparing introductory course planning among full-time and part-time faculty. *Research in Higher Education, 31*(6), 495–517.

Lowther, M. A., Stark, J. S., & Martens, G. G. (1989). *Preparing course syllabi for improved communication.* Ann Arbor: The University of Michigan, National Center for Research to Improve Postsecondary Teaching and Learning.

Lucas, A. F. (1990). Using psychological models to understand student motivation. In M. D.

Svinicki (Ed.), *The changing face of college teaching* (New Directions for Teaching and Learning No. 42, pp. 103–114). San Francisco: Jossey-Bass.

Lucas, A. F. (Ed). (1989). *The department chairperson's role in enhancing college teaching* (New Directions for Teaching and Learning No. 37). San Francisco: Jossey-Bass.

Lynton, E. A. (1984). *The missing connection between business and the universities.* New York: Macmillan.

Machlup, F. (1975). *Education and economic growth.* New York: New York University Press.

Madaus, G. F., & Stufflebeam, D. (Eds.) (1989). *Educational evaluation: Classic works of Ralph W. Tyler.* Boston: Kluwer.

Marchese, T. (1972). Re-examining the undergraduate sequence of studies. *Journal of Higher Education, 43*(2), 110–122.

Marchese, T. (1991, November). TQM teaches the academy, *AAHE Bulletin, 44*(3), 3–9.

Marchese, T. (1992, November). AAHE and TQM (. . . Make that "CQI"), *AAHE Bulletin, 45*(3), 11.

Marsh, H. W. (1984). Students' evaluation of university teaching: Dimensionality, reliability, validity, potential biases, and utility. *Journal of Educational Psychology, 76*(5), 707–754.

Marsh, H. W. (1987). *Students' evaluation of university teaching: Research findings, methodological issues, and directions for future research.* Elmsford, NY: Pergamon Press.

Marsh, H. W., & Bailey, M. (1993). Multidimensional students' evaluations of teaching effectiveness: A profile analysis. *Journal of Higher Education, 64*(1), 1–18.

Marsh, H. W., & Dunkin, M. J. (1991). Students' evaluations of university teaching: A multidimensional perspective. In J. Smart (Ed), *Higher education: Handbook of theory and research* (Vol. 8, pp.143–233). New York: Agathon Press.

Marsh, P. T. (Ed.). (1988). *Contesting the boundaries of liberal and professional education: The Syracuse experiment.* Syracuse, NY: Syracuse University Press.

Marshall, R., & Tucker, M. (1992). *Thinking for a living: Work, skills, and the future of the American economy.* New York: Basic Books.

Marton, F., Hounsell, D., & Entwhistle, N. (1984) *The experience of learning.* Edinburgh: Scottish Academic Press.

Marton, F., & Saljo, R. (1976a). On qualitative differences in learning, I: Outcome and process. *British Journal of Educational Psychology, 46,* 4–11.

Marton, F., & Saljo, R. (1976b). On qualitative differences in learning, II: Outcomes as a function of the learner's conception of the task. *British Journal of Educational Psychology, 46,* 115–127.

Mayhew, L., & Ford, P. J. (1979). *Changing the curriculum.* San Francisco: Jossey-Bass.

Mayville, W. V. (1978). *Interdisciplinary: The mutable paradigm* (AAHE-ERIC Higher Education Research Reports No. 9). Washington, DC: American Association for Higher Education.

McCabe, R. (1984). *The reform of the educational program at Miami-Dade community college.* Miami: Miami-Dade Community College.

McCabe, R. (ca. 1984). *A status report on the comprehensive educational reform of Miami-Dade Community College.* Miami: Miami-Dade Community College.

McCabe, R. (1988). The educational program of the American community college: A transition. In J. Eaton (Ed.), *Colleges of choice: The enabling impact of the community college* (pp. 93–115). New York: Macmillan.

McClain, C. (1987, Winter). Assessment produces degrees with integrity. *Educational Record, 68*(1), 47–52.

McKeachie, W. J. (1987). Teaching, teaching teaching, and research on teaching. *Teaching of Psychology, 14*(3), 135–138.

McKeachie, W. J. (1988) Teaching thinking. ACCENTS, *2*(1),1. (Publication of the National Center for Research to Improve Postsecondary Teaching and Learning, Ann Arbor, MI).

McKeachie, W. J. (1990). Research on college teaching: The historical background. *Journal of Educational Psychology, 82*(2) 189–200.

McKeachie, W. J. (1994). *Teaching tips: A guidebook for the beginning college teacher.* (9th ed.). Lexington, MA: D. C. Heath and Company.

McKeachie, W. J., Pintrich, P. R., and Lin, Y.

(1985). Teaching learning strategies. *Educational Psychologist, 20*(3), 153–160.

McKeachie, W. J., Pintrich, P. R., Lin, Y., & Smith, D. A. F. (1986). *Teaching and learning in the college classroom: A review of the research literature.* Ann Arbor: University of Michigan, National Center for Research to Improve Postsecondary Teaching and Learning.

McKeachie, W. J., Pintrich, P. R., Lin, Y., Smith, D. A. F., & Sharma, R. (1990). *Teaching and learning in the college classroom: A review of the research literature* (2nd ed.). Ann Arbor: University of Michigan, National Center for Research to Improve Postsecondary Teaching and Learning.

McLaughlin, M. W., & Phillips, D. C. (Eds). (1991). *Evaluation and education: At quarter century.* Chicago: University of Chicago Press.

McLeod, S. H. (Ed.) (1988). *Strengthening programs for writing across the curriculum* (New Directions for Teaching and Learning No. 36). San Francisco: Jossey-Bass.

McMillan, J. H. (1987). Enhancing college students' critical thinking: A review of studies. *Research in Higher Education, 26*(1), 3–28.

McMillan, J. H. (Ed.) (1988a). *Assessing students' learning* (New Directions for Teaching and Learning No. 34). San Francisco: Jossey-Bass.

McMillan, J. H. (1988b). Beyond value-added education: Improvement is not enough. *Journal of Higher Education, 59*(5), 564–579.

McPeck, J., E. (1990). Teaching critical thinking. New York: Routledge, Chapman & Hall, Inc.

Menges, R. J., & Svinicki, M. D. (Eds.) (1991). *College teaching: From theory to practice* (New Directions for Teaching and Learning No. 45). San Francisco: Jossey-Bass.

Mentkowksi, M. (1985, March). *Developing lifelong abilities in the professional school student: The context, the questions, and the evidence for ability-based learning.* Paper presented at the Annual Meeting of the American Association of Dental Schools, Las Vegas, NV.

Mentkowski, M., Astin, A. W., Ewell, P. T., & Moran, E. T. (1991). *Catching theory up with practice: Conceptual frameworks for assessment.* Washington, DC: American Association for Higher Education, AAHE Assessment Forum.

Mentkowski, M., & Doherty, A. (1984, February). Abilities that last a lifetime: Outcomes of the Alverno experience. *AAHE Bulletin, 36*(6), 5–14.

Mentkowski, M., & Loacker, G. (1985). Assessing and validating the outcomes of college. In P. T. Ewell (Ed.), *Assessing educational outcomes* (New Directions for Institutional Research No. 47). San Francisco: Jossey-Bass.

Mentkowksi, M., O'Brien, K., McEachern, W., & Fowler, D. (1983). *Developing a professional competence model for management education.* Milwaukee, WI: Alverno College, Office of Research and Evaluation/Department of Business and Management.

Mentkowski, M., & Rogers, G. (1993, Summer). Connecting education, work, and citizenship: How assessment can help. *Metropolitan universities: An international forum, 4*(1).

Messick, S. (1984, Spring). The nature of cognitive styles: Problem and promise in educational practice. *Educational Psychologist, 19*(2), 59–74.

Meyer, P. (1975). *Awarding college credit for non-college learning.* San Francisco: Jossey-Bass.

Meyer, W. V., Folkes, V. S., & Weiner, B. (1976). The perceived informational value and affective consequences of choice behavior and intermediate difficulty task selection. *Journal of Research in Personality, 10*, 410–423.

Meyerson, M. (1974). Civilizing education: Uniting liberal and professional learning. *Daedelus.* (Special Issue, pp. 173–179).

Millard, R. (1992). *Today's myths and tomorrow's realities.* San Francisco: Jossey-Bass.

Miller, M. A., & McCartan, A. M. (1990, May–June). Making the case for new interdisciplinary programs. *Change: The Magazine of Higher Learning, 22*(3), 28–35.

Minnich, E. (1990). *Transforming knowledge.* Philadelphia: Temple University Press.

Monaghan, P. (1994, March 2). "Sensoriums" and "virtual textbooks." *Chronicle of Higher Education,* A27, A29

Mooney, C. J. (1989, November 8). Professors are upbeat about profession but uneasy about students, standards. *Chronicle of Higher Education, 36*(10), 1, A–18.

Mooney, C. J. (1991, March 13). Stanford unveils plan designed to elevate status of teaching. *Chronicle of Higher Education, 36*(10), A–15.

Moore, M. G. (1973). Toward a theory of independent learning and teaching. *Journal of Higher Education, 44*(12), 661–679.

Moore, W. S. (1988). Perry network cumulative bibliography and copy service catalog. Athens, GA: Center for the Study of Intellectual Development.

Moos, R. H. (1979). *Evaluating educational environments.* San Francisco: Jossey-Bass.

Mortimer, K. P., & Tierney, M. L. (1979). *The three "Rs" of the eighties: Reduction, reallocation, and retrenchment* (AAHE-ERIC Higher Education Research Report No. 4). Washington, DC: American Association for Higher Education.

Moulakis, A. (1994). *Beyond utility: Liberal education for the technological age.* Columbia: University of Missouri Press.

Murray, H. G. (1991). Effective teaching behaviors in the college classroom. In J. C. Smart (Ed.), *Higher education: Handbook of theory and research* (Vol. 7, pp. 135–172). New York: Agathon Press.

Naisbitt, J. (1982). *Megatrends: Ten new directions transforming our lives.* New York: Warner Books.

Naisbitt, J. (1990). *Megatrends 2000: Ten new directions for the 1990s.* New York: Morrow.

National Center for Educational Statistics. (1992). *The national assessment of college student learning: Identification of skills to be taught, learned, and assessed.* Washington, DC: U.S. Department of Education, Office of Educational Research and Improvement.

National Center for Education Statistics. (1993, June). *Adult education: Main reasons for participating* (Statistics in Brief, NCES 93-451). Washington, DC: U.S. Department of Education, Office of Educational Research and Improvement.

National Center for Education Statistics. (1994a, November). The structure of education in the United States. In *Mini-digest of education statistics* (NCES 94-131). Washington DC: U.S. Department of Education, Office of Educational Research and Improvement.

National Center for Education Statistics. (1994b). *The condition of education, 1994* (NCES 94-149). Washington, DC: U.S. Department of Education, Office of Educational Research and Improvement.

National Center for Education Statistics. (1994c). *The national assessment of college student learning: Identification of skills to be taught, learned and assessed. (A report on a study design workshop)* (NCES 94-286). Washington, DC: U.S. Department of Education.

National Commission on Excellence. (1983, April). *A nation at risk: The imperative for education reform.* Washington, DC: U.S. Department of Education.

National Governors' Association. (1986, August). *Time for results: The governors' 1991 report on education.* Washington, DC: Center for Policy Research and Analysis.

National Institute of Education. (1984, October). *Involvement in learning: Realizing the potential of American higher education* (Report of the NIE Study Group on the Condition of Excellence in American Higher Education). Washington, DC: U.S. Government Printing Office.

National Institute of Education and American Association for Higher Education. (1985). *Contexts for learning: The major sectors of American higher education.* Washington DC: U.S. Government Printing Office. (Reprinted by American Association for Higher Education.)

Naveh-Benjamin, M. & Lin, Y. (1991). *Assessing students' organization of concepts: A manual for measuring course specific knowledge structures.* Ann Arbor: University of Michigan, National Center for Research to Improve Postsecondary Teaching and Learning.

Naveh-Benjamin, M., McKeachie, W. J., & Lin, Y. (1989). Use of the ordered-tree technique to assess students' initial knowledge and conceptual learning. *Teaching of Psychology, 16*, 182–187.

Naveh-Benjamin, M., McKeachie, W. J., Lin, Y., & Tucker, D. (1986). Inferring students' cognitive structure and their development using the "ordered-tree" technique. *Journal of Educational Psychology, 78*(2), 130–140.

Nevo, D. (1983). The conceptualization of educational evaluation: An analytical review of the literature. *Review of Educational Research, 53*(1), 117–128.

Newell, W. H. (1988, April). Interdisciplinary studies are alive and well: A status report. *AAHE Bulletin, 40*(8), 10–12.

Newman, F. (1994, May 29). *Information architects: A vision for the new century.* Address given at the Association of Institutional Research Forum, New Orleans.

Newman, J. H. (1959). *The idea of a university.* New York: Image Books.

Nicholls, J. G. (1984). Achievement motivation: Conceptions of ability, subjective experience, task choice and performance. *Psychological Review, 91*, 328–346.

Nordvall, R. C. (1982). *The process of change in higher education institutions* (ERIC/AAHE Research Reports No.7). Washington, DC: American Association for Higher Education.

North Central Association of Colleges and Schools. (1992, December). *Briefing, 10*(3), 8. Chicago: Author.

Novak, J. D. (1985). Metalearning and metaknowledge strategies to help students learn how to learn. In L. West & A. Pines (Eds.), *Cognitive structure and conceptual change* (pp. 189–209). New York: Academic.

Ory, J. C., & Parker, S. A. (1989). Assessment activities at large research universities. *Research in Higher Education, 30*(4), 375–385.

Ottinger, C. (Ed.). (1989). *Higher education today: Facts in brief.* Washington, DC: American Council on Education.

Pace, C. R. (1979). *Measuring the outcomes of college.* San Francisco: Jossey-Bass.

Pace, C. R. (1984). *Measuring the quality of college student experiences.* Los Angeles: University of California, Higher Education Research Institute.

Pace, C. R. (1985). Perspectives and problems in student outcomes research. In P. T. Ewell (Ed.). *Assessing educational outcomes* (New Directions for Institutional Research No. 47, pp. 7–18). San Francisco: Jossey-Bass.

Pace, C. R. (1987). *CSEQ: Test manual and norms: College student experiences questionnaire.* Los Angeles: University of California, Center for the Study of Evaluation.

Pace, C. R. (1990a). *College student experiences questionnaire* (3rd ed.). Los Angeles: University of California, Center for the Study of Evaluation.

Pace, C. R. (1990b). *The undergraduates.* Los Angeles: University of California, Center for the Study of Evaluation.

Pace, C. R. (1992). *College student experiences questionnaire: Norms for the third edition, 1990.* Los Angeles: University of California, Center for the Study of Evaluation.

Palmer, P. J. (1990, January–February). Good teaching: A matter of living the mystery. *Change: The Magazine of Higher Learning, 22*(1), 11–16.

Participation in GED programs remains high, (1994, June 27). *Higher Education and National Affairs, 43*(12), 3.

Pascarella, E. T. (1985). College environmental influences on learning and cognitive development: A critical review and synthesis. In J. C. Smart (Ed.), *Higher education: Handbook of theory and research* (Vol. 1, pp. 1–62). New York: Agathon Press.

Pascarella, E. T., & Terenzini, P. T. (1991). *How college affects students.* San Francisco: Jossey-Bass.

Perry, R. P. (1990). Introduction. [To the special section on instruction in higher education.] *Journal of Educational Psychology, 82*(2), 183–188.

Perry, W. G., Jr. (1970). *Forms of intellectual and ethical development in the college years: A scheme.* New York: Holt, Rinehart and Winston.

Perry, W. G., Jr. (1981). Cognitive and ethical growth: The making of meaning. In A. W. Chickering & Associates, *The modern American college* (pp. 76–116). San Francisco: Jossey-Bass.

Petrie, H. G. (1992). Interdisciplinary education: Are we faced with insurmountable opportunities? In G. Grant (Ed.), *Review of research in education* (Vol. 18). Washington, DC: American Educational Research Association.

Pettit, J. (1991, Summer). Listening to your alumni: One way to assess academic outcomes. *AIR Professional File 41*, 1–10.

Pew Higher Education Roundtable. (1993, November). *Policy Perspectives 5*(2), Philadelphia, PA: Pew Charitable Trusts & University of Pennsylvania, Institute for Research on Higher Education.

Phenix, P. H. (1986/1964). *Realms of meaning: A philosophy of the curriculum for general education.* New York: McGraw Hill. (Original work published in 1964).

Pickert, S. M. (1992). *Preparing for a global community: Achieving an international perspective in higher education* (ASHE-ERIC Higher Education Reports No. 2). Washington, DC: George Washington University.

Pickert, S. M., & Turlington, B. (1992). *Internationalizing the undergraduate curriculum: A handbook for campus leaders.* Washington, DC: American Council on Education.

Pintrich, P. R. (1988a). A process-oriented view of student motivation and cognition. In J. S. Stark & L. A. Mets (Eds.), *Improving teaching and learning through research* (New Directions for Institutional Research No. 57, pp. 65–79). San Francisco: Jossey-Bass.

Pintrich, P. R. (1988b). Student learning and college teaching. In R. E. Young and K. E. Eble (Eds.). *College teaching and learning: Preparing for new commitments* (New Directions for Teaching and Learning No. 33, pp. 71–86). San Francisco: Jossey-Bass.

Pintrich, P. R., Cross, D. R., Kozma, R. B., & McKeachie, W. J. (1986). Instructional psychology. *Annual Review of Psychology,* 37, 611–651.

Pintrich, P. R., McKeachie, W. J., & Lin, Y. (1987). Teaching a course in learning to learn. *Teaching of Psychology, 14*(2), 81–86.

Polson, C. J. (1993). *Teaching adult students* (IDEA Paper No. 29). Manhattan, KS: Kansas State University, Center for Faculty Evaluation and Development.

Posner, G. J. (1974). The extensiveness of curriculum structure: A conceptual scheme. *Review of Educational Research, 44*(4), 401–407.

Posner, G. J. (1978). Tools for curriculum research and development: Potential contributions from cognitive science. *Curriculum Inquiry, 8*(4), 311–340.

Posner, G. J. (1980, October 23). *New developments in curricular research: It's the thought that counts.* Invited address to the Northeast-ern Educational Research Association, Ellenville, NY. (Copy in our possession)

Posner, G. J. (1981, April). *Promising directions in curriculum knowledge: A cognitive psychology perspective.* Paper presented at the annual meeting of the American Educational Research Association, Los Angeles.

Posner, G. J. (1985). Curriculum knowledge. In T. Husen & T. N. Postlethwaite (Eds.), *The international encyclopedia of education* (pp. 1223–1227). New York: Pergamon Press.

Posner, G. J. (1988). Models of curriculum planning. In L. E. Beyer & M. W. Apple (Eds.), *The curriculum: Problems, politics and possibilities* (pp. 77–97). Albany: State University of New York Press.

Posner, G. J. (1992). *Analyzing the curriculum.* New York: McGraw-Hill.

Posner, G. J., & Rudnitsky, Alan N. (1994). *Course design: A guide to curriculum development for teachers* (4th ed.). White Plains, NY: Longman Press.

Posner, G. J. & Strike, K. A. (1976). A categorization scheme for principles of sequencing content. *Review of Educational Research, 46*(4), 665–689.

Powell J. P., & Shanker, V. S. (1982). The course planning and monitoring activities of a university teacher. *Higher Education, 11,* 289–301.

Powers, D., & Enright, M. (1987). Analytical reasoning skills in graduate study. *Journal of Higher Education, 58*(6), 658–682.

Quinn, R. E. (1988). *Beyond rational management: Mastering the paradoxes and competing demands of high performance.* San Francisco: Jossey-Bass.

Quinn, R. E., Raerman, S. R., Thompson, M. P., & McGrath, M. R. (1990). *Becoming a master manager: A competency framework.* New York: Wiley.

Ratcliff, J. (Ed.) (1992a). *Assessment and curriculum reform* (New Directions for Higher Education No. 80). San Francisco: Jossey-Bass.

Ratcliff, J. L. (1992b). What we can learn from coursework patterns about improving the undergraduate curriculum. In J. L. Ratcliff (Ed.). *Assessment and curriculum reform* (New Directions for Higher Education No. 80, pp. 5–22). San Francisco: Jossey-Bass.

Reed, J. W. (1990, May/June). Against the core: The Cheney report and the environment for learning. *Change: The Magazine of Higher Learning, 22*(3), 6–8.

Reeves, Jane, & McGovern, Thomas V. (1990, April 24). The school of social work. *VCU Voice* (Newsletter of Virginia Commonwealth University, Richmond).

Rehnke, M. F. (Ed.). (1982–1983). *Liberal learning and career preparation* (Current Issues in Higher Education No. 2). Washington, DC: American Association for Higher Education.

Rehnke, M. F. (Ed.). (1987). *Creating career programs in a liberal arts context* (New Directions for Higher Education No. 57). San Francisco: Jossey-Bass.

Reich, R. (1991). *The work of nations: Preparing ourselves for 21st-century capitalism.* New York: Knopf.

Reichmann, S. W., & Grasha, A. F. (1974). A rational approach to developing and assessing the construct validity of a student learning style scales instrument. *Journal of Psychology, 87*, 213–223.

Renninger, K. A. (1992). Individual interest and development: Implications for theory and practice. In K. A. Renninger, S. Hidi, & A. Krapp (Eds.), *The role of interest in learning and development.* Hillsdale, NJ: Lawrence Erlbaum Associates.

Rhoades, G. (1991). Professional education: Stratifying curricula and perpetuating privilege in higher education. In J. C. Smart (Ed.), *Higher education: Handbook of theory and research* (Vol. 7, pp. 334–375). New York: Agathon Press.

Richardson, R. (1987). *Fostering minority access and achievement.* San Francisco: Jossey-Bass.

Rogers, E. M. (1968). The communication of innovations in a complex institution. *Educational Record, 49*(1), 67–77.

Rogers, E. M. (1983). *Diffusion of innovations.* (3rd ed.). New York: Free Press.

Rogers, E. M., & Shoemaker, F. F. (1971). *Communication of innovations: A cross cultural approach.* New York: Free Press.

Romberg, E. (Ed.). (1990). *Outcomes assessment: A resource book.* Washington, DC: American Association of Dental Schools.

Rossides, D. (1987). Knee-jerk formalism: The higher education reports. *Journal of Higher Education, 58*(4), 404–429.

Roueche, J. E. (Ed.). (1977). *Increasing basic skills by developmental studies* (New Directions for Higher Education No. 20). San Francisco: Jossey-Bass.

Roueche, J. E., & Baker, G. A., III (1987). *Access to excellence: The open-door college.* Washington, DC: Community College Press.

Roueche, J., & Roueche, S. (1993, Spring). Has the friendship cooled and the love affair ended? Responding to realities of at-risk students. *The College Board Review, 167*, 12–17, 26.

Rudolph, F. (1962). *The American college and university: A history.* New York: Vintage Books.

Rudolph, F. (1977). *Curriculum: A history of the American undergraduate course of study since 1636.* San Francisco: Jossey-Bass.

Ruskin, R. S. (1974). *The personalized system of instruction: An educational alternative* (AAHE-ERIC Research Report No. 5). Washington, DC: American Association for Higher Education.

Ryan, G. A. (1974). *PSI, Keller's personalized system of instruction: An appraisal.* Washington, DC: American Psychological Association.

Ryan, G. (1993). Student perceptions about self-directed learning in a professional course implementing problem-based learning. *Studies in Higher Education, 18*(1), 53–63.

Ryan, M. P., & Martens, G. G. (1989). *Planning a college course: A guidebook for the graduate teaching assistant.* Ann Arbor: University of Michigan, National Center for Research to Improve Postsecondary Teaching and Learning.

Schecter, M. G. (1990). Internationalizing the undergraduate curriculum. *International Education Forum, 10*(1), 14–20.

Scheetz, L. P. (1991). *Recruiting trends 1991–92: A study of businesses, industries, and governmental agencies employing new college graduates.* (ERIC Document Research Service: ED 340 306).

Schilling, K. L., & Schilling, K. M. (1994, February 2). Final exams discourage learning. Point of View. *The Chronicle of Higher Education, 40*(22), A–52.

Schmitz, B. (1992). *Core curriculum and cultural*

pluralism. Washington, DC: Association of American Colleges.

Schneider, C. G, & Green, W. S. (Eds.) (1993). *Strengthening the college major* (New Directions for Higher Education No. 84). San Francisco: Jossey-Bass.

Schon, D. A. (1987). *Educating the reflective practitioner.* San Francisco: Jossey-Bass.

Schratz, M. (1992). Researching while teaching: An action research approach in higher education. *Studies in Higher Education, 17*(1), 81–95.

Schubert, W. H. (1986). *Curriculum: Perspective, paradigm, and possibility.* New York: Macmillan.

Scott, R. A. (1990). *Strategies for internationalizing campus and curriculum.* Washington, DC: American Association of State Colleges and Universities.

Sears, J. T., & Marshall, J. D. (Eds.). (1990). *Teaching and thinking about curriculum: Critical inquiries.* New York: Teachers College Press.

Seeley, J. (n.d.). Draft paper in our possession.

Seldin, P., & Associates. (1990). *How administrators can improve teaching.* San Francisco: Jossey-Bass.

Sexton, R. F., & Ungerer, R. A. (1975). *Rationales for experiential education* (ERIC-AAHE Research Report No. 3). Washington, DC: American Association for Higher Education.

Seymour, D. T. (1988). *Developing academic programs: The climate for innovation* (ASHE-ERIC Higher Education Report No. 3). Washington, DC: The ERIC Clearinghouse on Higher Education and the Association for the Study of Higher Education.

Seymour, D. T. (1991, November). TQM on campus: What the pioneers are finding. *AAHE Bulletin, 44*(3), 11–13.

Seymour, D. T. (1993). *On Q: Causing quality in higher education.* Phoenix, AZ: Oryx Press.

Shapiro, J. Z. (1986). Evaluation research and educational decision making: A review of the literature. In J. C. Smart (Ed.), *Higher education: Handbook of theory and research* (Vol 2, pp. 163–206). New York: Agathon.

Shavelson, R. J. (1974). Methods for examining representations of a subject matter structure in students' memory. *Journal of Research in Science Teaching, 11*, 231–250.

Shavelson, R. J., & Geeslin, W. E. (1975). A method for examining subject-matter structure in instructional material. *Journal of Structural Learning, 4*, 199–218.

Shaw, K. M., Stark, J. S., Lowther, M. A., & Ryan, M. P. (1990, April). *Students' goal changes as an indicator of academic socialization in college subjects.* Paper presented at the American Educational Research Association, Boston.

Shaw, K. M., Stark, J. S., Lowther, M. A., & Sossen, P. (1990, May). *Predicting students' college and course goals from their background characteristics.* Paper presented at the Association for Institutional Research Forum, Louisville, KY.

SHEEO. See State Higher Education Executive Officers

Sherman, T. M., Armistead, L. P., Fowler, F., Barksdale, M. A., & Reif, G. (1987). The quest for excellence in university teaching. *Journal of Higher Education, 48*(1), 66–84.

Sherr, L. A., & Teeter, D. J. (Eds.). (1991). *Total quality management in higher education.* (New Directions for Institutional Research No. 71). San Francisco: Jossey-Bass.

Sherr, L. A., & Lozier, G. G. (1991). Total quality management in higher education. In L. A. Sherr & D. J. Teeter (Eds.), *Total quality management in higher education* (New Directions for Institutional Research No. 71, pp. 3–11). San Francisco: Jossey-Bass.

Short, E. C. (1983). The forms and use of alternative curriculum development strategies. *Curriculum Inquiry, 13*(1), 43–64.

Shuell, T. J. (1986). Cognitive conceptions of learning. *Review of Educational Research, 56*(4), 411–436.

Sjoquist, D. P. (1993). Globalizing general education: Changing world; changing needs. In N. A. Raismann (Ed.), *Directing general education outcomes* (New Directions for Community Colleges No 81, pp. 51–58). San Francisco: Jossey-Bass.

Sloan, D. (1971). Harmony, chaos, and consensus: The American college curriculum. *Teachers College Record, 73*, 221–251.

Smart, J. C. (1985). Holland environments as

reinforcement systems. *Research in Higher Education, 23*(5), 279–292.

Smith, B. L., & MacGregor, J. T. (1993, Spring). What is collaborative learning? *Washington Center News, 7*(3), 3–11.

Smith, R. M. (1982). *Learning how to learn.* New York: Cambridge Press.

Smith, R. M., & Associates. (1990). *Learning to learn across the life span.* San Francisco: Jossey-Bass.

Smith, T. R., & Drabenstolt, M. (1992). The role of universities in regional economic development. In W. E. Becker & D. R. Lewis (Eds.), *The economy of American higher education* (pp. 199–221). Boston: Kluwer Academic Publishers.

Snow, C. P. (1959). *The two cultures and the scientific revolution.* Cambridge: Cambridge University Press.

Snyder, T. (Ed.). (1993). *120 years of American education: A statistical portrait.* Washington, D.C.: Department of Education, National Center for Education Statistics.

South Dakota State University (1988, July 1). *Assessment plan.*

Southern Regional Education Board. (1979). The search for general education: The pendulum swings back. *Issues in Higher Education* No. 15. Newsletter of the Southern Regional Education Board, Atlanta, GA.

Southern Regional Education Board. (1985). *Access to quality undergraduate education: A report to the Southern Regional Education Board by its Commission for Educational Quality.* Atlanta, GA: Author.

Spear, K. I. (Ed.). (1984). *Rejuvenating introductory courses* (New Directions for Teaching and Learning No. 20). San Francisco: Jossey-Bass.

SREB. *See* Southern Regional Education Board.

Stanley, L. C., & Ambron, J. (Eds.). (1991). *Writing across the curriculum in community colleges* (New Directions for Community Colleges No. 73). San Francisco: Jossey-Bass.

Stanton, C. M. (1976, March). Reflections on `vocationalized' liberal education. *The Educational Forum, 40*(3), 297–302.

Stanton, C. M. (1978). A perception-based model for the evolution of career and value education within the liberal arts. *Journal of Higher Education, 49*(1), 70–81.

Stark, J. S. (1972). The 4-1-4 bandwagon. *Journal of Higher Education, 43*(5), 381–390.

Stark, J. S. (1973). The three-year B.A: Who will choose it? Who will benefit? *Journal of Higher Education, 44*(9), 703–715.

Stark, J. S. (1978). *Inside information: A handbook on better information for student choice.* Washington, DC: American Association for Higher Education.

Stark, J. S. (1986). On defining coherence and integrity in the curriculum. *Research in Higher Education, 24*(4), 433–436.

Stark, J. S. (1987, Spring). Liberal education and professional programs: Conflict, coexistence or compatibility? In M. A. F. Rehnke (Ed.), *Creating career programs in a liberal arts context* (New Directions for Higher Education No. 57, pp. 91–102). San Francisco: Jossey-Bass.

Stark, J. S. (1989, Summer). Seeking coherence in the curriculum. In C. H. Pazandak (Ed.), *Improving undergraduate education in large universities* (New Directions for Higher Education, No. 66, pp. 65–76). San Francisco: Jossey-Bass.

Stark, J. S. (1990). Approaches to assessing educational outcomes. *Journal of Health Administration Education, 8*(2), 210–226.

Stark, J. S., & Associates. (1977). *The many faces of educational consumerism.* Lexington, MA: D. C. Heath.

Stark, J. S., & Francis, M. C. (in progress). Exploring students' goals in general education. Ann Arbor: University of Michigan. Draft paper.

Stark, J. S., & Lattuca, L. R. (1993). Diversity among disciplines: The same goal for all?. In C. G. Schneider & W. S. Green (Eds.), *Strengthening the college major* (New Directions for Higher Education No. 84, pp. 71–86). San Francisco: Jossey-Bass.

Stark, J. S., & Lowther, M. A. (n.d.) *Executive summary. The University of Michigan professional preparation study.* Ann Arbor: University of Michigan, Center for the Study of Higher and Postsecondary Education.

Stark, J. S., & Lowther, M. A. (1986). *Designing the learning plan: A review of research and theory related to college curricula.* Ann Arbor: University of Michigan, National Center for Research to Improve Postsecondary Teaching and Learning.

Stark, J. S. & Lowther, M. A. (1988a). Perspectives on course and program planning. In J. S. Stark & L. Mets (Eds.), *Improving teaching and learning through research* (New Directions for Institutional Research No. 57, pp. 39–52). San Francisco: Jossey-Bass.

Stark, J. S., & Lowther, M. A. (1988b). *Strengthening the ties that bind: Integrating undergraduate liberal and professional study.* Ann Arbor: University of Michigan, Professional Preparation Network.

Stark, J. S., & Lowther, M. A. (1989). Exploring common ground in liberal and professional education. In R. A. Armour & B. Fuhrmann (Eds.), *Integrating liberal learning and professional education* (New Directions for Teaching and Learning No. 40, pp. 7–10.) San Francisco: Jossey-Bass.

Stark, J. S., Lowther, M. A., Bentley, R. J., Ryan, M. P., Martens, G. G., Genthon, M. L., Wren, P. A., & Shaw, K. M. (1990a). *Planning introductory college courses: Influences on faculty.* Ann Arbor: University of Michigan, National Center for Research to Improve Postsecondary Teaching and Learning

Stark, J. S., Lowther, M. A., Bentley, R. J., & Martens, G. G. (1990b). Disciplinary differences in course planning. *Review of Higher Education, 13*(2), 141–165.

Stark, J. S., Lowther, M. A., & Hagerty, B. M. K. (1986). *Responsive professional education: Balancing outcomes and opportunities* (ASHE/ERIC Higher Education Report No. 3). Washington, DC: George Washington University and Association for The Study of Higher Education.

Stark, J. S., Lowther, M. A., & Hagerty, B. M. K. (1987a). Faculty perceptions of professional preparation environments. *Journal of Higher Education, 58*(5), 530–561.

Stark, J. S., Lowther, M. A., & Hagerty, B. M. K. (1987b). Faculty and administrator views of influences on professional programs. *Research in Higher Education, 27*(1), 63–83.

Stark, J. S., Lowther, M. A., Hagerty, B. M. K., & Lokken, P. (1988). *PLUSS: Professional/lib-eral undergraduate self-study.* Ann Arbor: University of Michigan, Professional Preparation Network.

Stark, J. S., Lowther, M. A., Hagerty, B. M. K., & Orczyk, C. (1986). A conceptual framework for the study of preservice professional programs in colleges and universities. *Journal of Higher Education, 57*(3), 231–258.

Stark, J. S., Lowther, M. A., Ryan, M. P., Bomotti, S. Smith, Genthon, M. L., Haven, C. L., & Martens, G. G. (1988). *Reflections on course planning: Faculty and students consider influences and goals.* Ann Arbor: University of Michigan, National Center for Research to Improve Postsecondary Teaching and Learning.

Stark, J. S., Lowther, M. A., & Shaw, K. M. Faculty perspectives on program planning. (Draft paper, 1995).

Stark, J. S., Lowther, M. A., Shaw, K. M., & Sossen, P. L. (1991). *Student goals exploration: User's manual* (Institutional Research Guide; Classroom Research Guide). Ann Arbor: University of Michigan, National Center for Research to Improve Postsecondary Teaching and Learning.

Stark, J. S., Lowther, M. A., Sossen, P. L., & Shaw, K. M. (1991). *Course planning exploration for program self-study.* Ann Arbor: University of Michigan, National Center for Research to Improve Postsecondary Teaching and Learning.

Stark, J. S., & Marchese, T. J. (1979). Auditing college publications for prospective students. *Journal of Higher Education, 49*(1), 82–92.

Stark, J. S., & Morstain, B. R. (1978). Educational orientations of faculty in liberal arts colleges. *Journal of Higher Education, 49*(5), 420–437.

Stark, J. S., & Shaw, K. M. (ca. 1990). *Do college faculty report different influences when planning introductory and advanced courses?* Ann Arbor: University of Michigan. National Center for Research to Improve Postsecondary Teaching and Learning.

Stark, J. S., Shaw, K. M., & Lowther, M. A. (1989). *Student goals in college and courses: A missing link in assessing student achievement* (ASHE-ERIC Higher Education Report No. 6). Washington, DC: George Washington

University and Association for the Study of Higher Education.

Stark, J. S., & Thomas, A. M. (Eds.). (1994). *Assessment and program evaluation.* Needham Heights, MA: Simon and Schuster Custom Publishing.

Stark, J. S., Zaruba, K., Lattuca, L. R., & Francis, M. C. (1994). Recurring debates in the college curriculum. Ann Arbor: University of Michigan. Unpublished paper.

Starr, J. F. (1986, December 1). Carnegie report neglects importance of science, research, and intellectual pluralism. *Higher Education and National Affairs, 35*(23), 7–8.

State Higher Education Executive Officers. (1992, September). *Building a quality workforce: An agenda for postsecondary education.* Denver: Author.

Steen, L. A. (1991). Reading for science literacy. *Change: The Magazine of Higher Learning, 23*(4), 11–19.

Steeples, D. W. (Ed.). (1990). *Managing change in higher education* (New Directions for Higher Education No 71). San Francisco: Jossey-Bass.

Steffens, H. (1991). Using informal writing to find interest and meaning in history. *Social Studies, 82,* 107–109.

Steinberg, E. R. (1991). *Computer-assisted instruction: A synthesis of theory, practice and technology.* Hillsdale, NJ: Lawrence Erlbaum Associates.

Sternberg, R. J. (1985). *Beyond IQ: A triarchic theory of human intelligence.* Cambridge: Cambridge University Press.

Stevens, E. (1988). Tinkering with teaching. *Review of Higher Education, 12*(1), 63–78.

Stice, J. E. (Ed.). (1987). *Developing critical thinking and problem solving abilities* (New Directions for Teaching and Learning No. 30). San Francisco: Jossey-Bass.

Stimpson, C. R. (1988, March–April). Is there a core in this curriculum? (And is it really necessary?). *Change: The Magazine of Higher Learning, 20*(2), 26–31.

Stonewater, J. K., & Stonewater, B. B. (1984, February). Teaching problem-solving: Implications from cognitive development research. *AAHE Bulletin: Research Currents, 36*(6), 7–10.

Students of the '90s: What do they want from college? (1993, September–October). *Change: The Magazine of Higher Learning, 25*(4), Whole Issue.

Study Group on the Condition of Excellence in American Higher Education. (1984). *Involvement in learning: Realizing the potential of American higher education.* Washington, DC: National Institute of Education.

Study Group on the Condition of Excellence in American Higher Education. (1985). *Contexts for learning: The major sectors of American higher education.* Washington, DC: U.S. Government Printing Office. (Reprinted by the American Association for Higher Education).

Svinicki, M., D. (ca. 1989). If learning involves risk-taking; teaching involves trust-building. *Teaching excellence: Toward the best in the academy* (Newsletter of the Professional and Organizational Development Network, sample issue).

Svinicki, M. D. (Ed.). (1990). *The changing face of college teaching* (New Directions for Teaching and Learning No. 42). San Francisco: Jossey-Bass.

Svinicki, M. D. (1991, December). So much content, so little time. *UC Ideas: A Forum for the Exchange of Information, 6*(1), 1–2.

Svnicki, M., & Dixon, N. M. (1987). Kolb model modified for classroom activities. *College Teaching, 35*(4), 141-146.

Taba, H. (1962). *Curriculum development: Theory and practice.* New York: Harcourt, Brace and World.

Terenzini, P. T. (1989). Assessment with open eyes. *Journal of Higher Education, 60*(6), 644–664.

Terenzini, P. T., Theophilides, C., & Lorang, W. G. (1984). Influences on students' perceptions of their academic skills development during college. *Journal of Higher Education, 55*(5), 621–636.

Terenzini, P. T., Pascarella, E. T., & Lorang, W. G. (1982 An assessment of the academic and social influences on freshman year educational outcomes. *The Review of Higher Education, 5*(2), 86–109.

Terenzini, P. T., & Wright, T. W. (1987). Influences on students' academic growth during four years of college. *Research in Higher Education, 26*(2), 161–179.

Thelin, J. R. (1992, January–February). The curriculum crusades and the conservative backlash. *Change: The Magazine of Higher Learning, 24*(1), 17–23.

Thielens, W. (1987, April). *The disciplines and undergraduate lecturing.* Paper presented at the meeting of the American Educational Research Association, Washington, DC.

Tierney, W. G. (1989). *Curricular landscapes, democratic values: Transformative leadership in higher education.* New York: Praeger.

Tierney, W. G. (Ed.). (1991). *Culture and ideology in higher education: A critical agenda.* New York: Praeger.

Toma, J. D., & Stark, J. S. (1995, winter). Pluralism in the curriculum: Understanding its foundations and evolution. *Review of Higher Education, 18*(2), 217–232.

Tomlinson, L. (1989). *Postsecondary developmental programs: A traditional agenda with new imperatives* (ASHE-ERIC Higher Education Report No. 3). Washington, DC: George Washington University.

Toombs, W. (1977-1978). The application of design-based curriculum analysis to general education. *Review of Higher Education, 1,* 18–29.

Toombs, W., Amey, M., & Fairweather, J. (1989, January 7). *Open to view: A catalog analysis of general education.* Paper given at the Association of American Colleges, Washington, DC.

Toombs, W., & Tierney, W. G. (1991). *Meeting the mandate: Renewing the college and departmental curriculum* (ASHE-ERIC Higher Education Report No. 6). Washington, DC: George Washington University, School of Education and Human Development.

Toombs, W., & Tierney, W. G. (1993). Curriculum definitions and reference points. *Journal of Curriculum and Supervision, 8*(3), 175–195.

Toulmin, S. (1972). *Human understanding* (Vol. 1). Oxford: Clarendon Press.

Townsend, B. K., Newell, L. J., & Wiese, M. D. (1992). *Creating distinctiveness: Lessons from uncommon colleges and universities* (ASHE-ERIC Higher Education Reports No. 6). Washington, DC: George Washington

University, School of Education and Human Development.

TQM: Will it work on campus? (1993, May–June, Special issue). *Change: The Magazine of Higher Learning, 25*(3), Whole Issue.

Tracey, T. J., & Sedlacek, W. E. (1987, January). Prediction of college graduation using noncognitive variables by race. *Measurement and Evaluation in Counseling and Development, 19*(4), 177–184.

Tripe, R. L. K. (1990). *Problem solving and writing: A teaching/learning model for computer studies.* Paper presented at the 12th International Conference on Teaching Excellence and Conference of Administrators, Austin, Texas. (ERIC Document Reproduction Service: ED 324 039).

Trivett, D. A. (1975). *Competency programs in higher education* (ERIC/AAHE Research Report No. 7), Washington, DC: American Association for Higher Education.

Tucker, M. (1991, June 5). Many U.S. colleges are really inefficient high-priced secondary schools. *Chronicle of Higher Education, 37*(38), A36.

Tyler, R. W. (1969). *Basic principles of curriculum and instruction.* Chicago: University of Chicago Press.

Underwood, D. G. (1991). Taking inventory: Identifying assessment activities. *Research in Higher Education, 32*(1), 59–69.

U.S. Department of Education, Office of Educational Research and Improvement. (June 1992). *National assessment of college student learning: Issues and concerns, a report on a study design workshop.* (NCES Bulletin 92-068). Washington, DC. U.S. Dept. of Education National Center for Education Statistics.

Upcraft, M. L., Gardner, J. N., & Associates. (1989). *The freshman year experience.* San Francisco: Jossey-Bass.

Upham, C. (1989, March). Writing tips: Process instruction in the teaching of writing. *Network Newsletter on College Teaching. 7,* 7.

Useem, M. (1989). *Liberal education and the corporation: The hiring and advancement of college graduates.* Hawthorne, NY: Walter de-Gruyter.

Van Doren, M. (1959). *Liberal education.* Boston:

Beacon Press. (Original work published in 1943).

Van Patten, J., Chao, C. I., & Reigeluth, C. M. (1986). A review of strategies for sequencing and synthesizing instruction. *Review of Educational Research, 56*(4), 437–471.

Vander Meer, A. W., & Lyons, M. D. (1979). Professional fields and the liberal arts: 1958–78. *Educational Record, 60,* 197–201.

Vars, G. F. (1982). Designs for general education. *Journal of Higher Education, 53*(1), 216–226.

Veysey, L. (1973). Stability and experiment in the American undergraduate curriculum. In C. Kaysen (Ed.), *Content and context* (pp. 1–63). New York: McGraw-Hill.

Volkwein, J. F., & Carbone, D. A. (1994). The impact of departmental research and teaching climates on undergraduate growth and satisfaction. *Journal of Higher Education, 65*(2), 147–167.

Vollmer, H. M., & Mills, D. L. (1966). *Professionalization.* Englewood Cliffs, NJ: Prentice-Hall

Walker, D. F. (1980). A barnstorming tour of writing on curriculum. In A. W. Foshay (Ed.), *Considered action for curriculum improvement,* pp.71–81. Alexandria, VA: Association for Supervision and Curriculum Development.

Walker, D. (1990). *Fundamentals of curriculum.* New York: Harcourt Brace Jovanovich.

Ward, T. J., Jr. & Clark, H. T., III. (1987). The effect of field-dependence and outline condition on learning high- and low-structure information from a lecture. *Research in Higher Education, 27*(3), 259–272.

Warren, J. (1984, September). The blind alley of value added. *AAHE Bulletin, 37*(1), 10–13.

Warren, J. (1992). Learning as an indicator of educational quality. *Studies in Higher Education, 17*(3), 337–348.

Warren, J. (1985). The changing characteristics of community college students. In W. Deegan, D. Tillery & Associates, *Renewing the American community college.* San Francisco: Jossey-Bass.

Ways and means. (1994, January 19). *Chronicle of Higher Education, 40*(20), A21.

Weaver, F. S. (1991). *Liberal education: Critical essays on professions, pedagogy, and structure.* New York: Teachers College Press.

Weaver, F. S. (Ed.). (1989). *Promoting inquiry in undergraduate learning* (New Directions for Teaching and Learning No. 38). San Francisco: Jossey-Bass.

Wechsler, H. S. (1977). *The qualifying student: A history of selective college admissions in America.* New York: Wiley.

Weimer, M. G. (Ed.). (1987). *Teaching large classes well* (New Directions for Teaching and Learning No. 32). San Francisco: Jossey-Bass.

Weimer, M. G. (1990). *Improving college teaching.* San Francisco: Jossey-Bass.

Weiner, B. (1972). *Theories of motivation: From mechanisms to cognition.* Chicago: Markham.

Weiner, B. (1974). *Achievement motivation and attribution theory.* Morristown, NJ: General Learning Press.

Weiner, B. (1986). *An attributional theory of motivation and motion.* New York: Springer-Varlag.

Weingartner, R. (1993). *Undergraduate curriculum: Goals and means.* Washington, DC: American Council on Education/Oryx Press.

Weinstein, C., Palmer D., & Schulte, A. (1987). *LASSI: The Learning and Study Strategies Inventory.* Clearwater, FL: H&H Publishing.

Weinstein, C. E., & Mayer, R. E. (1986). The teaching of learning strategies. In M. Wittrock (Ed.), *Handbook of research on teaching* (pp. 315–327). New York: Macmillan.

Welty, W. M. (1989, July–August). Discussion method teaching: How to make it work. *Change: The Magazine of Higher Learning, 21*(4), 40–49.

West, L. H. T., & Pines, A. L. (1985). *Cognitive structure and conceptual change.* New York: Academic Press.

Weston, C., & Cranton, P. A. (1986, May–June). Selecting instructional strategies. *Journal of Higher Education, 57*(3), 259–288.

Whipple, W. (1987, October). Collaborative learning: Recognizing it when we see it. *AAHE Bulletin, 40*(2), 3–7.

White, A. M. (Ed.). (1981). *Interdisciplinary teaching* (New Directions for Teaching and Learning No. 8). San Francisco: Jossey-Bass.

Whitman, N. A. (1986). *Increasing students' learning: A faculty guide to reducing stress among students* (ASHE-ERIC Higher Education Report No. 4). Washington, DC: Association for the Study of Higher Education.

Whitman, N. A. (1988). *Peer teaching: To teach is to learn twice* (ASHE-ERIC Higher Education Reports No. 4). Washington, DC: George Washington University.

Whitman, N. A., Spendlove, D. C., & Clark, C. H. (1984). *Student stress: effects and solutions* (ASHE-ERIC Higher Education Report No. 2). Washington, D.C: Association for the Study of Higher Education.

Wilkinson, T. W., & Sherman, T. M. (1991, November). Telecommunications-based distance education: Who's doing what? *Educational Technology, 31*(11), 54–59.

Williams, D. Z. (1991, Spring). The challenge of change in accounting education. *Issues in Accounting Education, 6*(1), 126–133.

Willis, D. (1993). Academic involvement at university. *Higher Education, 25*, 133–150.

Wilson, R., Gaff, J., Dienst, E., Wood, L., & Bavry, J. (1975). *College professors and their impact on students.* New York: Wiley.

Wingspread Group on Higher Education. (1993, December). *An American imperative: Higher expectations for higher education.* Racine, WI: The Johnson Foundation and others.

Winter, D. G., McClelland, D. C., & Stewart, A. J. (1982). *A new case for the liberal arts: Assessing institutional goals and student development.* San Francisco: Jossey-Bass.

Wirth, A. G. (1992). *Education and work for the year 2000.* San Francisco: Jossey-Bass.

Witt, A. A., Wattenbarger, J. L., Gollattscheck, J. F., & Suppiger, J. E. (1994). *America's community colleges: The first century.* Washington, DC: American Association of Community Colleges.

Wood, L., & Davis, B. G. (1978). *Designing and evaluating higher education curricula* (AAHE/ERIC Higher Education Research Report No. 8). Washington, DC: American Association for Higher Education.

Wood, D. (1990, March 23). College telecourses reach remote learners. *Christian Science Monitor,* p. 13.

Wood, D. (1990, March 19). Video options go to the head of the class. *Christian Science Monitor,* p. 13.

Worthen B. R., & Sanders, J. R. (1987). *Educational evaluation: Alternative approaches and practical guidelines.* White Plains, NY: Longman Press.

Wright, B. D. (1991, November). Discipline-based assessment: The case of sociology. *AAHE Bulletin, 44*(3), 14–16.

Wyer, J. C. (1993, January/February). Change where you might least expect it: Accounting education. *Change: The Magazine of Higher Learning, 25*(1), 12–17.

Yale Report of 1828. (1989). In L. F. Goodchild & H. S. Wechsler (Eds.), *The ASHE reader on the history of higher education* (pp. 171–178). Needham Heights, MA: Ginn Press. (Original work published 1828).

Yarbrough, L. (1992). Three questions for the multiculturalism debate. *Change: The Magazine of Higher Learning, 24*(1), 64–69.

Yinger, R. J. (1979). Routine in teacher planning. *Theory into Practice, 18*, 163–169.

Zaltman, G., & Duncan, R. (1977). *Strategies for planned change.* New York: Wiley.

Zemsky, R. (1989). *Structure and coherence: Measuring the undergraduate curriculum.* Washington, DC: Association of American Colleges.

Zikopoulos, M. (Ed.). (1989). *Open doors, 1988/1989: Report on international educational exchange.* New York: Institute of International Education.

Zook, G. (Chairman). (1948). *Higher education for democracy: A report of the President's Commission on Higher Education.* New York: Harper & Row.

Zuniga, R. E., & Johnston, S. M. (1994). *New pathways to a degree: An assessment of the use of instructional technologies at seven institutions.* Paper presented at the Association for Institutional Research Forum, New Orleans, LA.

APPENDIX

Timeline of Trends in United States Curriculum: 1600s to 1994

1600s

1636   The first college of the American colonies, Harvard, is founded.

1642   Harvard awards the first bachelor's degrees in America.

1652   Harvard expands original three-year course of study to four years.

1692   William and Mary is founded; places greater emphasis on mathematics, history, and science than Harvard.

1700s

1701   Yale chartered as the Collegiate School in Connecticut.

1711   William and Mary establishes first scientific professorship in an American college.

1714   Yale acquires several hundred academic books; adds mathematics to its curriculum as a result.

1720   Yale adds astronomy to its curriculum.

1728   Harvard establishes first professorship in mathematics and natural philosophy (physics).

1740   Yale curriculum moves from medieval scholasticism to "new learning."

1743   Yale's president tells students that aim of education is knowledge of God.

1745   Yale offers geometry; adds mathematics to junior year curriculum; requires arithmetic for admission.

Sources: Brubacher and Rudy (1976), Jencks and Riesman (1968), Levine (1978), and Rudolph (1977, 1990).

1750s

1750   Forensic debate appears at Yale in 1750s.

1754   Kings College (New York) opens with courses in husbandry and commerce.
        English language debates held at previously all-Latin Harvard commencement.
        William Smith becomes provost at College of Philadelphia and begins to design a curriculum without a specific religious mission.

1755   Harvard makes Hebrew an elective rather than required course.
        Yale appoints its first professor, rather than relying on president and young tutors, for instruction.

1756   College of Philadelphia introduces a more utilitarian, three-year curriculum that includes new subjects of political science, agriculture, mechanics, history, and chemistry.
        Undergraduate exhibitions in English language oratory begin at Harvard.

1759   Colonial colleges graduate more than 100 men.

1760s

1765   First English language textbook in ethics published.
        College of Philadelphia establishes first chair in medicine in colonies.

1766   Harvard builds its first classroom.

1767   Yale adds English grammar and oratory to sophomore-year curriculum
        Harvard tutors begin to specialize in teaching a single subject rather than teach all subjects.

1768   Princeton adds study of belles lettres to its curriculum.

1770s

1770   Non-degree-seeking students admitted to colleges.
        Princeton students form two extracurricular literary societies to provide intellectual stimulation outside the formal curriculum.

1771   Belles lettres enters curriculum at Yale.

1776   Six of eight American colleges have professorships in mathematics and natural philosophy (physics).
        William and Mary College establishes Phi Beta Kappa.

1777   Yale's Ezra Stiles proposes professorships in medicine, law, ecclesiastical history, civil history, Hebrew, oratory, oriental languages, and belles lettres.

1779   Political controversies enliven Yale commencement debates.
        Thomas Jefferson abolishes professorships of divinity and Asian languages at College of William and Mary; adds professorships in public administration, modern languages, medical sciences, natural history,

international law and fine arts to the curriculum; shifts curriculum from religious to secular purpose; allows students a small number of electives.

Columbia adds French to the formal curriculum; William and Mary follows.

1780s

1781   Yale president delivers commencement address in Hebrew; students deliver debates and disputes in English.

1782   Harvard students permitted to choose French as language requirement; study of Hebrew language no longer required.

1783   Yale rejects otherwise qualified female applicant.

1784   Plans for four faculties, arts, law, divinity, and medicine, made at Columbia.

1785   Yale uses first English literature textbook.
First state college, University of Georgia, chartered.

1788   All American colleges now have chairs in mathematics and natural philosophy.

1789   Philadelphia College establishes first professorship of botany and natural history.
Harvard endows first chair in moral philosophy.
Yale eliminates syllogistic debate from the curriculum.

1790s

1792   Princeton adds mathematics oratory to commencement.

1793   Princeton adds belles lettres oratory to commencement.

1793   William and Mary requires French for admission until 1799.

1795   Williams College establishes its first professorship, for the study of French language.
Union College allows four years of French language study to substitute for four years of Greek.

1796   Princeton appoints first American professor of chemistry in arts college without a medical program.
Moral philosophy textbooks begin to include sections on physiology.
Princeton trustees turn down plans to eliminate Greek and Latin after freshman year and to expand science instruction.

1800s

1800   Almost every American college has a science professor.

1802   Union College allows nondegree courses.

Bowdoin president attacks elective system; decries "light reading."

Benjamin Silliman revolutionizes study of chemistry, geology, and mineralogy at Yale.

West Point, the first technical college in America, is established; offers first formal instruction in engineering.

1804   Union College establishes senior-year moral philosophy course.

1807   Yale makes chemistry a senior requirement.

Harvard adds geography as admissions requirement.

1810s

1810   Harvard abandons syllogistic debate.

Columbia adopts four-year curriculum.

1815   Union College adds parallel courses; allows seniors to devote last year to science; awards bachelor of arts degree for scientific program.

1816   University of Pennsylvania establishes four-man faculty of physical science and rural economy.

Harvard founds professorship in modern languages.

1819   Harvard begins instruction in modern languages.

1820s

1820s   The blackboard makes its first appearance in the classroom at Bowdoin College.

1820   Many colleges add algebra to college admissions requirements.

1824   Rensselaer Polytechnic founded; becomes center of applied science in United States; uses first systematic field work, chemistry and physics labs, and makes engineering a course of study.

University of Virginia opens: no universitywide degree awarded; degrees awarded based on general examinations within field of study.

1825   Yale tutors record quality of performance of students in recitations.

Yale begins to offer noncredit curricular options.

Harvard adopts electives, syllabi, tutorials, student ability groupings, and admission of nondegree candidates; first departments to put faculty in control of curriculum.

1826   Beginning in 1826, James Marsh, president of the University of Vermont, introduces a number of innovations, including the partial course plan and electives to support the prescribed curriculum, the Socratic method of teaching, course sections, term exams and annual comprehensive exams, a modern language requirement for degree candidates, the division of the faculty into four departments, and the elimination of class-year divisions.

Union College offers parallel (nondegree) course in sciences as an alternative to classical program.

1827   Amherst plans for curriculum without Latin or Greek; it fails due to lack of support and money.

1828   Yale Report defends classical education.
Kenyon College introduces one-on-one faculty advising.

1829   West Point cadets form American Association for Promotion of Science, Literature and the Arts (forerunner of the American Association for the Advancement of Science).

1830s

1830s   Written biennial exams (sophomore and senior years) begin to replace oral exams; provide comparative standards on which to measure student progress.

1830   Columbia adds science and literacy curriculum certificate program (no Greek or Latin required).
Henry Wadsworth Longfellow becomes first professor of modern languages at Bowdoin.
Tutors at Yale begin to specialize.

1831   Yale begins to build first American college art museum.
Ohio University establishes program to prepare public school teachers.

1835   (also 1840, 1841) Harvard begins to reduce requirements in mathematics, Latin, Greek and English; optional after freshman year.
Oberlin adds music professorship.
Rensselaer awards first engineering degree.

1836   Columbia adds architecture, engineering, and business to curriculum.
Wesleyan Female College of Georgia becomes first degree-granting women's college.

1838   Harvard adopts elective programs in mathematics to meet students' career goals.
Connecticut Wesleyan awards bachelor of science degree for science course.

1839   First normal school for preparation of teachers established in Massachusetts.

1840s

1840   Mark Hopkins of Williams College uses skeleton and manikin in teaching ethics.

1841   Oberlin awards first bachelor of arts degree for women graduates.
Yale offers modern language instruction at student's expense; German offered as curricular option (noncredit).

1842   Harvard offers a professorship with promise of limited classroom obligations.

1843   Virtually all courses at Harvard offered on elective basis after freshman year; faculty opinion divided.

Williams College adds junior course in American history.

Columbia scientific parallel course program terminated.

1844   American colleges add geometry to admissions requirements.

1845   President of Jacksonville, Illinois, college argues for appropriateness of common education for the minority.

Union becomes first liberal arts college to have engineering program.

1846   Williams College adds German as option; removed from inclusion in other courses.

Princeton professor resigns after being rebuked for interspersing Greek literature in Greek language classes.

1847   Yale creates school of applied chemistry as section of new department of philosophy and the arts; moves toward creation of graduate school.

Harvard adds undergraduate program in science; creates Lawrence Scientific School with less stringent admissions standards.

Harvard and University of Michigan add ancient history to admissions requirements.

Tuition-free Academy of New York chartered by New York legislature (now City College of New York).

1849   Avery College for Black students founded in Pennsylvania.

1850s

1850   Popularity of college attendance declines while American population increases (through 1880).

Brown University adopts variable student loads, more science courses, modified extension program and free electives.

University of Rochester founded; offers both Bachelor of Arts and Bachelor of Science degrees.

Science schools begin to multiply.

Engineering programs move into curriculum.

Moral philosophy courses used as capstones; parallel courses (three-year, nondegree programs without Latin and Greek requirements) catch on.

1851   Dartmouth College adds French courses.

Brown University awards first bachelor of philosophy (nondegree, partial, nonclassical course); program dies four years later.

Harvard grants bachelor of science degree to science school graduates.

University of Louisiana establishes business school.

1852   Yale adds engineering to course of study; grants bachelor of philosophy to science school graduates.

1853   University of Michigan awards first earned master's degree (for specific program, not number of years of study).

1854   American Missionary Society formed to bring higher education to black population; founds six colleges in six years.

1855   Michigan State University becomes the first state agricultural college.

1856   Lehigh University founded as scientific and technical college.

1857   Harvard introduces the blue book; instructors grade examinations.

1858   Williams College students organize art society; lay foundation for art library.

          Harvard students work in laboratory rather than observing experiments in a lecture hall.

1860s

1860s   At least 25 institutions adopt three-year parallel scientific bachelor's degree.

1861   Yale awards first Ph.D.s in United States.

1862   Morrill Act establishes land-grant institutions.

1865   Utilitarian reforms take hold in post–Civil War era.

1866   Two-thirds of Catholic colleges offer commercial courses of study.

1868   Cornell University opens; first institution in United States to use a selective admissions policy.

          University of Missouri creates a school of education.

1869   Charles William Eliot becomes president of Harvard; moves college toward an elective system.

          Harvard removes students' disciplinary records from grade calculation.

          Yale offers first university program in fine arts.

1870s

1870s   72,000 students enrolled in approximately 1,000 high schools; public high schools curriculum and standards influence college curriculum; rationalization of state systems of education.

          Colleges begin to abandon their college preparatory departments and rely on high school certificates for admission.

          College population begins to grow.

          Land-grant colleges award bachelor of home economics to women.

          United States history, physical geography, and English composition appear as admissions requirements.

          Iowa professor requires laboratory work in chemistry.

1870	University of Michigan faculty periodically visit and inspect local high schools to ensure quality of programs and applicants; add United States history and physical geography to admissions requirements.
	Harvard lists courses by subject, not class year, in catalog.
	Princeton adds English composition and grammar to its admissions requirements.
1871	Yale president defends traditional curriculum against newer programs.
1872	Harvard eliminates all senior year requirements; does same for junior year (1873), sophomore year (1884) and freshman year, except English composition.
	Syracuse University opens school of fine arts offering bachelor's degrees in architecture and painting.
1873	Princeton adds three-year science course; adds engineering in 1874.
	Wheaton College awards "sister of arts" to women.
1875	The first women's colleges, Smith and Wellesley Colleges, founded.
1876	Johns Hopkins, America's first research university, opens.
1877	Harvard adopts numerical scale of 100 for grading; replaced with five letter grades in 1883.
1878	Johns Hopkins catalog makes first known reference to major and minor.
	New York State Regents establish statewide high school exams.
1879	New England colleges get together to discuss uniform English admissions requirements; followed by conferences on admissions requirements in classics and mathematics during 1880s.

1880s

1880s	Seminar approach appears in undergraduate courses at Harvard, Cornell, and The University of Michigan.
	Harvard undergraduates begin using library in significant numbers to prepare research papers for seminars; junior faculty become more professional than senior faculty. Harvard seduces faculty from other institutions with promise of exclusively graduate course focus.
	Professors of history begin to appear in significant numbers.
	Rise of academic departments and disciplines.
	Professional academic associations begin to appear.
	Harvard becomes a university.
1881	Cornell offers first course in electrical engineering and creates first department of American history.
1883	American boys' boarding schools for wealthy urbanites begin to proliferate (through early 1900s).

Phi Beta Kappa speaker decries classical education as inadequate for 19th century life.

Modern Language Association founded.

1884   Classical education debate in popular and academic press; University of Wisconsin's president defends classical languages as antidote to materialism.

University of California system adopts system of accrediting high schools.

American Historical Association founded.

1885   Northeast Association of Colleges and Secondary Schools formed.

Idea of major developed.

Princeton greatly opens electives for juniors and seniors.

American Economics Association founded.

1886   Harvard accepts physics and advanced mathematics as admission requirements in place of Greek; possible to get bachelor of arts through science program.

Yale begins to reduce requirements in ancient language, mathematics; increases requirements in English and modern language.

St. Louis University is among first Catholic colleges to adopt standard organization of American colleges.

Professors of psychology begin to appear.

1888   Clark University opens with focus on graduate education; president is graduate of Johns Hopkins.

1889   American Bankers' Association encourages colleges and universities to found business schools.

1890s

1890   A separate-but-equal extension of the Morrill Act creates funding for Black land grant colleges.

Harvard eliminates distinction between undergraduate and graduate faculty.

1892   National Education Association's Committee of Ten defines college preparatory course of study and recommends a high school curriculum.

1895   Harvard replaces letter grades with new scale of merit—passed with distinction, passed, failed.

1896   National Association of State Universities created.

1897   Columbia eliminates Greek as an entrance and graduation requirement.

1899   Yale students can include a year of medical training or five hours of law in their bachelor's degree programs.

Association of Catholic Colleges founded.

1900s

1900   Association of American Universities, Association of Land Grant Colleges founded.
        College Entrance Examination Board organized.
        Columbia eliminates Latin as entrance requirement but requires courses in college Latin.

1901   First College Entrance Examination Board tests administered.
        More and more colleges add electives to their curricula.
        American Philosophical Association founded.

1902   Harvard eliminates four-year residency requirement for bachelor of arts.
        Two-year junior college opened as experiment in Joliet, Illinois.
        Dartmouth and New York University eliminate Greek as an entrance requirement; Yale follows in 1904.

1904   Wisconsin Idea proposed (University of Wisconsin offers extension and correspondence courses on popular topics and technical subjects; faculty experts work on state problems).
        Harvard urges every department to offer at least one course for nonspecializing students.
        American Political Science Association established.

1905   Columbia University allows students to enroll jointly in undergraduate college and professional school programs to shorten time needed to earn both degrees; Universities of Michigan and Wisconsin and other large private and state universities adopt professional option plans.
        Cornell replaces free elective system with distribution system.
        American Sociological Association founded.

1906   First cooperative education program offered by University of Cincinnati School of Engineering.
        Carnegie Foundation for the Advancement of Teaching founded.
        Harvard creates a department of social ethics in response to student interest in problem of urban poverty.
        State of California authorizes cities to develop junior colleges as extensions of existing high schools.

1909   City College of New York offers first night-school bachelor's degree program.
        Harvard introduces major and general education system.

1910s

1910   Harvard introduces comprehensive examination in the major and honors distinction for exceptional performance on the examination.
        Harvard adopts concentration and distribution requirements.

1911   Training School in Public Service founded at Syracuse University.
Carnegie Corporation is founded.

1913   Rockefeller Foundation established.

1914   University of North Dakota adds special drill courses in mathematics and
English when high schools force them to reduce entrance require-
ments.
Association of American Colleges founded.

1915   Catholic Education Association adopts new set of standards to propel
Catholic colleges into higher education mainstream.
Association of American Universities dictates minimum requirements for
libraries and science laboratories.
Association of American University Professors founded after faculty dis-
missals at several institutions.

1920s

1920   National Defense Act establishes Reserve Officer Training Corps (ROTC).

1921   Swarthmore College introduces an honors program.

1927   University of Wisconsin Experimental College established; lasts five years.

1928   Harvard introduces residential academic units.
University of Oregon reorganizes faculty into four divisions: exact sciences, biological sciences, social sciences, and arts and letters, each
with required freshman year general course.

1929   Sarah Lawrence College, one of the first schools to adopt a progressive philosophy of education and curriculum, is founded.

1930s

1932   University of Minnesota creates a two-year general education division.

1933   Black Mountain, an experimental college, is founded.
Yale accommodates scientists who dislike distribution requirements; re-
duces distribution requirements in science to one year.

1935   Framingham Teachers' College, a normal school, adds bachelor of science
and arts degrees to its offerings.

1937   Great Books curriculum introduced at St. John's College in Maryland.

1940s

1944   Congress passes the G.I. Bill which provides direct financial assistance to
veterans; college enrollments soar and student body profiles change
dramatically, but curricula are minimally altered.

1945   The Committee on the Objectives of a General Education in a Free Society publishes the Harvard Redbook in support of general education curricula.

1947   President's Commission on Higher Education for Democracy issues a report calling for tuition-free education for all youth for the first two years of college, lower tuition for upper division, graduate and professional schooling, expansion of adult education opportunities, development of community colleges, equal access to a college education for all Americans, and a renewed emphasis on general education.

1950s

1951   Ford Foundation supports advanced placement courses and early admissions programs at twelve colleges and secondary schools.

1954   Decision in *Brown* v. *Board of Education* desegregation case launches a new era of increased access to higher education.

1957   The United States responds to the Soviet Union's launch of Sputnik by creating accelerated science and language instruction programs.

1958   The National Defense Education Act offers undergraduate loans, graduate fellowships, institutional aid for teacher education and broad support for education in the sciences, mathematics and foreign language.

1958   Hampshire College Plan proposes study on a 4-1-4 calendar, with credit-bearing winter term mini-courses; adopted by Eckerd College (Florida) in 1960 and others shortly thereafter.

1960s

1964   Student unrest at the University of California, Berkeley, focuses national attention on college campuses; Berkeley students create a student-run Free University.
        Civil Rights Act of 1964 furthers access to college for members of minority groups.

1965   Carnegie Corporation and the Office of Economic Opportunity create Upward Bound, a program to assist underprepared and unmotivated students with academic potential.

1965   The Experimental College at Berkeley, modeled on Meiklejohn College at Wisconsin, opens; operates for four years.
        University of California, Santa Cruz, a new campus based on the British concept of collegiate education, opens; consists of small residential colleges and emphasizes small classes and interdisciplinary nonlecture instruction.

The Higher Education Act of 1965 provides financial aid to individual students as well as institutional aid for research, libraries, recruitment, educational facilities, and improvement of undergraduate education to public and private colleges.

1966   The Keller plan for self-paced learning is developed.

1967   The College Level Examination Program (CLEP) introduces tests to measure subject matter proficiency at college level; allows many adult students to earn college credits without coursework.

Federal regulations extend opportunities to older Americans.

1968   The Higher Education Amendments of 1968 establish a program of Special Services for Disadvantaged Students, which includes remedial instruction, counseling, and support services.

New College in Florida abandons senior interdisciplinary seminars because seniors are too specialized for interdisciplinary work.

1968   Simon's Rock, an "early college" offering a college education to 16- to 20-year-old students, is founded in Massachusetts.

1969   New York State founds Empire State College for adult learners.

Students demand and win radical revision of Brown University curriculum.

1970s

1970   New York State creates the Regents' External Degree which is awarded on the basis of examinations and college-equivalent credit alone.

San Diego State and Cornell Universities establish first women's studies programs.

1971   Amherst College faculty eliminates all general education requirements.

Minnesota legislature establishes Metropolitan State University, an external degree institution.

1972   Education Amendments of 1972 establish the Fund for the Improvement of Postsecondary Education (FIPSE), the National Institute of Education (NIE), and massive student financial aid programs.

Sterling College introduces a competency-based undergraduate curriculum; Mars Hill College and others follow.

Title IX of the federal Higher Education Act expands opportunities for women.

1973   Rehabilitation Act extends access to disabled Americans.

1980s

1984   William Bennett writes *To Reclaim a Legacy,* published by National Endowment for the Humanities.

National Institute of Education issues *Involvement in Learning: Realizing the Potential of American Higher Education.*

1985   Association of American Colleges publishes *Integrity in the College Curriculum.*

First Assessment Conference co-sponsored by the American Association for Higher Education and the University of South Carolina.

K. Patricia Cross develops idea of classroom research.

1986   American Association of State Colleges and Universities publishes *To Secure the Blessings of Liberty: Report of the National Commission on the Role and Future of State Colleges and Universities.*

National Institute of Education awards grant to University of Michigan for a five-year National Center for Research to Improve Postsecondary Teaching and Learning.

1987   President of Carnegie Foundation for the Advancement of Teaching, Ernest Boyer, independently publishes *College: The Undergraduate Experience in America.*

1988   Association of American Colleges publishes *A New Vitality in General Education.*

1989   Lynne Cheney and National Endowment for the Humanities issue *50 Hours: A Core Curriculum for College Students.*

Stanford debate over the transition from Western Civilization requirement to Culture, Ideas, and Values, a required course with a broader conceptualization of cultural heritage, attracts national attention.

1990s

1991   Association of American Colleges publishes *The Challenge of Connecting Learning* and *Reports from the Fields.*

Office of Educational Research and Improvement awards grant for five-year National Center for Teaching, Learning, and Assessment to The Pennsylvania State University.

1993   Wingspread Group on Higher Education publishes *An American Imperative: Higher Expectations for Higher Education*

Accrediting function being rethought.

1994   Association of American Colleges publishes *Sustaining Vitality in General Education.*

The Internet allows faculty across the United States to communicate by computer and access large sets of information.

Stanford recommends some revision in its required course in Culture, Ideas, and Values and establishes additional required courses in science, mathematics, language, and writing.

Index

Note: Specific disciplines and fields of study are listed under *Academic fields, listed.* Items in the "Timeline of Trends in United States Curriculum," pp. 424–437, are not indexed.

AAC (*see* Association of American Colleges)
AAHE (*see* American Association for Higher Education)
AASCU (*see* American Association of State Colleges and Universities)
Abilities-based curriculum, 131
"Absolute knowing," 205, 209
Absolutism, as intellectual stage, 203–204
Abstract-concrete learning styles, 191, 263
Academic calendar (*see* Structure, organizational)
Academic fields, 141–178 (*see also* Disciplines, Collegiate career study, Occupational programs), *listed:*
  accounting, 66, 106, 126, 131, 149, 165, 166, 208, 270, 276, 277, 302, 323, 351
  African American studies, 126–127, 346
  agriculture, 46, 47, 51, 57, 70, 74, 143, 339
  anthropology, 68, 147
  architecture, 51, 149, 163, 164, 166–168
  area studies 27, 51, 68, 307, 345, 349–350, 351
  art, 30, 68, 146, 149, 150, 164, 165, 166–167, 174, 176, 270, 273, 364, 367
  Asian studies, 346
  auto mechanics, 150
  bakery management programs, 168
  biology, 146, 154–155, 160, 215, 272, 295, 306, 323, 356, 365
  Black studies, 346
  business, 46, 54, 65, 70, 83, 138, 143, 148, 154, 156, 164, 185, 215, 273, 277, 280, 306, 314
  calculus, 277, 289
  chemistry, 65, 66, 127, 166, 276, 277, 293, 306, 323
  Chicano studies, 346
  commercial art, 168
  communication, 51
  computer and information science, 51, 68, 270, 273, 277
  cosmetology, 168
  criminal justice, 307
  dance, 146, 164, 166, 270
  day care helpers, 168
  dental assistants, 168
  dentistry, 48, 54, 302
  drama, 164, 365
  economics, 68, 160–163, 241, 306, 351, 365
  education, 51, 66, 149, 163. 166, 378
  elementary education, 70, 115, 134, 283, 286
  engineering, 46, 51, 53–54, 67–68, 83, 130, 148–149, 150, 153, 163, 164, 166–167, 174, 185, 191, 273, 280, 356
  English language/literature, 27, 53, 68, 84, 144, 146, 153–157, 182, 215, 217, 219, 224, 227, 247, 272, 277, 306 (*see also* Writing skills)
  ethnic studies, 27, 51, 68, 72, 344, 346–347, 355, 368–369
  fine/applied arts, 51, 53, 154
  foreign languages, 26, 65, 51, 68, 84, 298, 306–307, 345, 350–351
  general duties, 158
  genetic engineering, 126
  genetics, 263
  geography, 68, 307
  geology, 307
  history, 27, 65, 68, 92, 120, 128, 143–146, 154, 156–158, 160–163, 173, 181, 215, 220, 247, 260, 273, 306

Academic fields, *(cont.)*
  home economics, 51
  hospitality management programs, 168
  humanities, 65, 91, 105, 126, 150, 217, 222, 236,
    238, 241, 244, 256, 334
  human client services, 149, 156, 164–166, 174,
    176, 270, 275
  human resource development, 163, 389–390
  human relations management, 315
  human services, 236
  journalism, 54, 106, 149, 163–167
  law, 48, 51, 54, 143, 149, 158, 252
  liberal arts/studies, 4, 21, 47, 51, 54, 56, 82, 85,
    87, 91, 94, 99–100, 104–105, 131, 138,
    143–144, 153, 158–163, 169–171, 176, 186,
    191, 280, 290, 322, 348, 352, 355–359, 369,
    380, 384
  library assistants, 168
  library science, 51, 54, 149, 156, 164, 270
  linguistics, 307
  mathematics, 26, 51, 54, 145–146, 148, 155,
    160–163, 166, 182, 192, 215, 270, 351
  mechanic arts, 47, 74, 339
  medicine, 48, 54, 66, 143, 158, 252, 253, 263,
    345, 365
  military science, 51
  molecular biology, 155
  music, 164, 166, 270, 296, 364
  natural sciences, 238, 253
  Near Eastern studies, 54, 124
  nursing, 46, 54, 121, 128, 130, 139, 143,
    148–150, 156–158, 163–167, 185, 198, 215,
    224–225, 261, 270, 276, 277, 289, 295, 323,
    356
  performing arts, 156, 297
  pharmacy, 53–54, 149–150, 163, 165–168, 277
  philosophy, 26–27, 65, 68, 72, 84, 144–146,
    160–163, 241
  physical sciences, 51, 68, 146, 354
  physical therapy, 54
  physics, 143, 147, 148, 153, 160–163, 166, 277
  political science, 68, 160–163, 198, 241, 299,
    306, 307, 345
  psychiatry, 263
  psychology, 48, 51, 65, 68, 133, 144, 146, 153,
    155, 160–163, 184, 215, 241, 306, 356
  public administration, 54
  public affairs and services, 51
  public health programs, 345
  Puerto Rican studies, 346

  religion, 51, 162, 145–146, 160–163, 241
  social sciences, 65–66, 126, 129, 144–146, 150,
    152, 154, 160–162, 172, 174, 176, 201, 204,
    217, 236, 238, 241, 253, 255–256, 270,
    282–283, 349, 354–356, 378
  social work, 46, 51, 54, 106, 130, 149, 163–164,
    166, 168, 275
  sociology, 65, 68, 127, 128, 143, 144, 150, 155,
    160–163, 166, 182, 184, 215, 217, 224, 241,
    290, 306, 307, 351
  teacher education, 46, 47, 67, 83, 156, 163, 167,
    168, 357
  textile design, 277
  theater, 227, 257, 307
  women's studies, 27, 99, 124, 307, 344,
    347–349, 355–356, 369
Academic plan *(see also* Faculty, Students):
  adjustment of, 10–11, 14, 30–31, 96–97, 121,
    266–309, 343–373
  administering, 310–342
  assumptions of, 1–6, 385–386
  coherence of, 159–160, 163, 172–173, 352–360
  college-level, 139–140, 230–235, 294–296 *(see
    also* College-level)
  collegiate career studies, 147–178 *(see also* Col-
    legiate career studies)
  communication of, 121, 128–129, 209, 328–
    330
  content of, 10–13, 26–27, 63–70, 84–87,
    116–120, 126–130, 151–158, 172, 212–217,
    367–368 *(see also* Content)
  context of, 118–119, 170, 222–224, 231–232,
    310–342
  Continuous Quality Improvement, 389–392
  coordination of, 322–325
  course level, 114–124, 133–136, 150–158,
    181–185, 214–230, 266–274, 291–293,
    295–299 *(see also* Course-level)
  definition of, 7–22
  design of, 37–40, 113–140
  environment of, 19–21, 42–44, 222–224,
    310–373 *(see also* Environment)
  evaluation of, 9, 10, 11, 14, 30–31, 73–79,
    96–97, 107–109, 111, 121, 266–309,
    326–330, 360–367, 371 *(see also* Access,
    Evaluation, Quality)
  faculty and, 113–140, 268–282
  implementation of, 217–220, 325, 387
  influences on, 15–19, 42–44, 97–112, 115–117,
    130–132, 141–178, 196–208, 212–214,

229–230, 233–235 (*see* External influences, Internal influences)

instructional processes in, 9, 10–11, 13–14, 30–31, 70–73, 94–95, 107, 120–121, 128, 212–265, 370 (*see also* Instructional activities)

instructional resources in, 10–11, 14, 95–96, 369–370

learners, 10–11, 13, 27–29, 56–63, 91–93, 179–211, 370–371 (*see also* Students)

occupational programs, 148–178, 357

program level, 124–139, 158–178, 185–187, 230–235, 266–268, 274–278, 293–295, 300–303 (*see also* Program-level)

purpose, 9, 10–12, 24–26, 44–56, 84–87, 172, 214–216, 367–368 (*see also* Purpose)

reforms of, 80–112

relationship among elements of, 10–11, 379–381

research on, 23, 187–211, 287, 374–394

sequence of, 10, 11, 13, 29–30, 87–90, 368–369

specialized education and, 105–106

strengths of, 7–24, 169–178, 264–265, 386

structure in, 87–90

theory of, 40–41, 374–394

types of, 152–153, 257–264

Academic Profile (test), 301

Academic Strategy, 131, 277

Access (*see also* Quality):
as educational and social value, 72, 79, 82, 83, 92, 93, 98, 107–108, 110, 344, 345, 352, 360, 373, 392

vs. quality, 56–63, 73–79, 107–109, 284, 336–337, 344, 360–367

Access to Quality, 362

Accommodators, learning style of, 191

Accountability:
and assessment, 281, 283–285, 363

history of, 74–75, 283

and outcomes, 79, 254, 299

public pressures for, 98, 268, 272, 281, 282, 344, 373

as purpose of evaluation, 284

Accreditation:
agencies of, 33, 75, 96, 99, 108, 126, 362

and educational environment, 18, 33, 44, 56, 77, 224, 268, 304, 321, 361

and evaluation, 133, 268, 279–281, 284, 285, 327, 329–330

influence of, 85–86, 125, 141, 225, 232–233, 261, 373

ACE (*see* American Council on Education)

Achievement:
and accountability, 299, 330

and adjustment, 225, 236, 282

of students, 192, 199, 269, 285, 300, 301, 305, 383

Active adaptation, 342

Active learning:
as educational goal, 5, 34, 71, 94, 99, 107, 131, 135, 138, 199–200, 208, 245, 248–252, 255, 258, 282, 325, 326, 344, 351, 361, 362, 369, 388

and instructional processes, 14, 94, 188, 326, 355, 361, 370

Active-reflective learning styles, 191

Activism (*see* Students, activism of)

Adaptive development:
and curriculum, 209–210, 245–246, 331, 335–341

and intentional learning, 209–210

as stage of change, 336–331, 344

Adjustment:
influenced by, 1–6, 96–97, 186, 275–309, 335–341, 370

as part of academic plan, 14, 15, 16, 30–31, 96–97, 121, 266–309, 330–342, 371, 374, 379–380, 387, 342, 374

role of administrators in, 313, 330–342

role of faculty in, 268–282

screening stage of, 362–363

at various levels, 121, 133, 272, 281–282, 308

Administrative practices, 325, 381

Administrators:
and academic planning, 129, 169, 176, 178, 225, 228, 271, 272, 275, 310–342, 350, 356, 387, 394

and assessment/evaluation, 268, 275–276, 280–281, 308–309, 330, 332

and change, 89, 131, 275, 331–333, 339, 341–342

and constituencies, 103, 294, 390, 394

and curriculum planning, 5, 102, 125, 127, 136, 140, 226, 280, 288, 312–335, 374, 387–392

and environment, 99, 277, 305, 310–312, 314–331, 349–350, 361

and faculty, 95, 315, 324, 387–390

and institutional mission, 25, 230, 277, 313, 332

and students, 207, 300, 302

roles of, 314–335

Admission scores, 58, 75, 98, 108

Adoption:
  as stage of change, 338–339, 343–373, 375
  of core curriculum, 353–355
  of multicultural studies, 346–348
  of thinking skills, 361–362
Adults:
  education program for, 49, 92
  as learners, 28, 60–61, 92, 121, 206, 208, 337,
    366, 373
Advanced Placement tests, 76, 234
Advisement (*see also* Counseling):
  influence of, 225, 228, 247, 250, 290, 293, 377
  of students, 91, 92, 103, 128, 169, 228, 229, 238,
    286, 323, 324, 326, 380
Advisory boards, use of, 233, 275, 280, 304
Advocacy positions, and adjustment, 377, 392
Aesthetic disciplines, 146, 150, 154–155, 164, 215
Affirmative action policies, 63
Alexander, J. C., 147
Alfred, Richard L., 334
Alumni, 163, 279, 280, 305–307
Alverno College, 131, 139–40, 247, 280, 292
American Association for Higher Education, 99,
    100, 102, 280, 328, 362
American Association of State Colleges and Uni-
    versities, 81, 83, 84, 92, 93, 358
American Chemical Society, 232
American College Testing program (ACT), 78, 301
American Council on Education, 53, 67, 98–99,
    102, 103, 350–351
American Dental Schools Association, 290
*American Imperative: Higher Expectations for
    Higher Education, An,* 81, 104
American Institute of Certified Public Accountants,
    270
Amherst College, 66
Analysis, 4, 38, 204, 210, 294, 301, 302, 392–393
Analytical intelligence, 174, 189–190, 203, 208
Anderson, G. Lester, 149
Angelo, Thomas A., 31, 153, 275, 288, 289
Applied studies, 143, 147–148, 153–154, 192,
    230–232 (*see also* Academic fields,
    Pure/Applied, Collegiate career studies, Oc-
    cupational programs)
Arizona State University, 323
Articulation agreements, 58, 66, 75, 104, 108, 120,
    286, 322–323, 325
Arts and sciences, 53, 158–163, 247, 256 (*see also*
    Academic fields, *listed*)
Assessing for Excellence, 298

Assessment (*see also* Evaluation):
  and accountability, 108–109, 281, 285–286,
    361–363
  in classroom, 31, 133, 153, 258, 272, 287–289,
    291, 328, 332, 390
  at college level, 82, 91, 133, 272, 280, 290–291,
    307
  and curriculum development, 153, 169, 201–202,
    272, 285–286, 307
  development of, 83, 100, 108, 201–202, 208,
    272, 283, 285–286, 304, 362–362, 373, 382
  history of, 283, 285, 304, 361–363, 382
  instruments for, 287, 296, 297, 304
  of learning, 96, 99, 102–104, 108–109, 131, 208,
    238, 261–262, 268, 269, 328, 344, 362–363
  of outcomes, 97, 283, 360, 362–363, 370
  at program level, 272, 275, 289–290, 304–305
Assimilation, as learning style, 191–192
Associate degrees, 51, 61, 230
Association for Institutional Research, 279
Association for Integrative Studies, 356
Association of American Colleges, 76, 81, 82, 84,
    87, 90, 92–94, 102, 106–108, 158, 167, 172,
    202, 277, 290, 352–353
  Liberal Learning in the Arts and Science Project,
    159
  Project Task Force on Liberal Learning in the
    Major, 147–148
  Task Group on General Education, 81, 84, 87,
    90, 92–94, 102, 106, 107, 108, 172, 202,
    277, 354, 355
Assumptions:
  about curriculum, 23, 220, 260–261, 264, 388
  about education, 7–9, 15, 32–33, 38–39, 175,
    236–264, 272, 283
  influence of, 150–151, 209, 393
  and purpose, 175
Astin, Alexander W., 28, 31, 81, 85, 100, 182, 196,
    200, 249, 291, 292, 298, 320, 321
  typology (input-environment-output) of educa-
    tional outcomes, 300, 302, 379
Atlanta College of Art, 106
Attainment value, 199
Attitudes of learners, 188, 207, 238, 289, 293, 300,
    388
Attribution, of change, 248, 296, 298–299, 330,
    363, 382
Audiovisual centers, 228, 279, 326
Audits (*see* Assessment)
Authoritative evaluation, 284

Awareness:
  as stage of change, 338, 343–373, 375
  of globalization, 349–352
  of technology, 363–367
Axelrod's typology of teaching styles, 217

Babson College, 138
Baccalaureate colleges, 50, 51, 57, 61, 67, 68
Balance, planning for, 169–178, 315, 394
Bandura, Albert, 194
Bandwagon effect (*see* Diffusion)
Banta, Trudy W., 280, 297
Behavioral objectives, 70, 221, 236, 283, 285
Behavioral outcomes, 296, 300–301
Behavioral psychology, 221, 236
Belenky, M., 204
Bell, Terrell H., 98, 144
Benchmarking, 390–391 (*see also* Bandwagon effect)
Bennett, William, 81, 83, 86, 90, 92, 94, 98, 99,
  101, 102, 106, 358
Bergquist, W. H., 29, 172, 173
Better Teaching, More Learning, 188
Biglan, Anthony, 146–148, 161
Black colleges, 78
Bloom, Allan, 106
Bloom, Benjamin, 133, 245
Bok, Derek, 25
Boss, Michelle, 277
Bowen, Howard, 25
Boyer, Ernest L., 81, 83, 86, 91–95, 97, 169, 352,
  356, 355
British Open University, 366
Broker, administrative role of, 325–326, 327, 331,
  387
Brookfield, Stephen, 243
Budget, allocation of, 101, 227, 275, 322, 324, 330,
  387
Business:
  educational values of, 149, 166–168, 350
  ethics of, 166–167, 303
  faculty of, 156, 167, 182, 307, 325, 326, 345
  influence of, 163, 165, 215, 225, 233, 344, 357
  and management, 51, 53, 68
  students in, 66, 144, 198

California Community College system, 66
California State University system, 66, 323
  DELTA Project of, 366
Cameron, Kim S., 340

Campus Trends, 99, 102, 276
Canon (*see* Great works)
Carnegie Classification of Colleges, 49–51
Carnegie Commission, 25
Carnegie Foundation for the Advancement of
  Teaching, 16, 81, 83, 182
Career counseling, 186, 215, 244, 321, 326, 370
Career studies (*see* Collegiate career studies, Occupational programs)
Catalog, 132, 382–383
Center for Instructional Development, 136
Center for Policy Research and Analysis, 81
Centers for International Business Education, 350
Certification requirements, 165, 229, 233, 351 (*see also* External influences)
Chaffee, Ellen, 390
Chapman, David, W., 204
Challenge of Connecting Learning: Liberal Learning in the Arts and Science Major, The, 81,
  90, 93, 94–95, 107
Change (*see also* Adjustment, Administrators, Attribution, External influences, Internal influences, Leadership, Reforms):
  and academic planning, 114, 310–373
  by diffusion, 37, 131, 281–282, 331, 335–339,
    342, 344, 373, 390
  examples of, 277, 334, 339–340
  implications of, 367–372
  influenced by, 1–6, 332–333, 335–341
  processes of, 5–6, 331, 335–340, 342, 344, 361
  rate of, 330, 342, 373
  resistance to, 333, 334, 338–340, 390
  rewards for, 333–334
  strategies for, 278–279, 332–333, 332
  unintended consequences of, 329, 336, 341, 387
Change: The Magazine of Higher Learning, 102
Cheney, Lynne V., 81, 83, 86, 91, 93, 94, 99, 106,
  358
Chickering, Arthur W., 28, 33, 35, 258
Choice, of students in coursework, 63–70, 106–107,
  172, 235, 263, 344, 345, 392 (*see also* Prescription, Electives)
Chronicle of Higher Education, The, 108, 366
Citizenship, as educational goal, 83–87, 248, 257,
  291, 300, 384
Civil rights movement, 99
Civil War, 42, 57, 65, 70
Clarkson University, 280
Class size, influence of, 225, 227, 232–233, 252,
  271, 326, 329

Classical education, 47, 48, 70
Clayton State College, 280
Client-centered research, 268, 269, 383–384
Clinton policies, 95–96, 362–363
Closed discourse systems, 164
Closing of the American Mind, The, 106
Cognitive:
 definition of, 188
 development, 28, 34, 174, 187–188, 208, 301
  (*see also* Intellectual development)
 frameworks, and disciplines, 146, 248–249
 outcomes, 296, 300–301
 psychology, 135, 208, 212–213
 skills and styles, 183–184, 188, 190–197, 201,
  206–208, 237, 256, 288, 297, 300, 302,
  320
Cohen, Arthur M., 55
Cohen, S., 334
Coherence:
 in academic fields, 90–91, 159–160, 163, 167,
  175, 352, 359
 in academic plan, 6, 47, 65, 70, 110–111, 136,
  137, 160, 169, 176, 255, 352–360, 368
 and critical perspectives, 170, 172–174
 definition of, 352
 as educational value, 110–111, 126, 167, 169,
  249, 344
 need for, 174, 201–202, 236, 247, 392
 problems in incorporating, 137, 344, 352–360
Cole, Johnetta B., 368
Collaboration:
 and academic plan, 141, 295, 327, 386
 with administrators, 266, 313, 319
 in curriculum development, 123–124, 125, 133,
  136, 140, 178, 295, 355, 388
 influences on, 141
Collaboration/Integration Matrix, 176–177
Collaborative learning, 14, 107, 135, 184, 199, 236,
  253–256, 258, 273, 282
 program structures for, 176–178, 365
Collaborator, administrative role of, 331
Colleagues:
 and assessment/evaluation, 289, 295, 301, 328
 influence of, 110, 336
 and planning, 122–123, 129, 271, 272, 297
Collective decisions, 334, 340
"College, The," 70
College Academic Achievement Proficiency
  (CAAP), 301
College BASE, 301
College Board, 76, 234

College level:
 and academic planning, 131, 139–140, 187,
  230–235, 247–248, 315, 343–373, 375
 adjustment at, 133, 281–282, 331, 340, 343, 344,
  375
 and administrators, 310–342
 assessment/evaluation, 133, 268, 272, 278–282,
  287, 290–291, 295, 296, 303–309, 390 (*see
  also* Self-study)
 curriculum planning for, 120, 125, 126, 129–133,
  136–139, 212–213, 247, 354
 goals for, 120, 222–226, 321
 and institutional mission, 139–140
College Level Examination Proficiency, 234
College Outcomes COMP Test, 301
College Student Experiences Questionnaire, 293,
  294
Colleges and universities (*see* Institutional)
"Colleges without walls," 234, 337, 366
*College: The Undergraduate Experience in Amer-
  ica,* 81, 83, 86, 91, 93, 94, 95, 105–106, 169
College type, importance of, 153, 187, 291, 310
Collegia, as alternative to disciplines, 147
Collegiate career studies (*see also* Academic fields,
  listed; Occupational studies; Professional
  programs):
 and academic planning, 127, 141, 149, 158, 231,
  232, 247, 253, 256, 264, 290, 385
 characteristics of, 148, 149–150, 163–164, 243,
  352
 definitions, 143, 148–150, 237
 and disciplines/related studies, 126, 148–150,
  163, 164, 176, 322, 355, 356, 357
 evaluation/adjustment, 268, 270, 275–276, 282
 as field, 4, 21, 48, 54–55, 83, 100, 104, 120, 124,
  126, 128, 130–132, 138, 163–168, 171, 175,
  178, 185, 201, 232–233
 influenced by, 158, 163–169, 224, 225, 227, 357
 and practice settings, 163, 175
 teaching in, 220, 227–228, 252, 256–257
 values of, 164, 174
Columbia University, 70
Commitment, as intellectual stage, 203, 217
Commonality, in curriculum structure, 137–38
Communication:
 and planning, 209, 250, 254, 260, 319, 335
 trends in, 333, 342, 365, 394
Communism, 48, 350
Community, as educational value, 148–149, 329
Community College Student Experience Questionnaire (CCSEQ), 294

Community colleges, 25, 46, 47, 59, 60, 74, 75, 92, 120, 151, 168, 187, 226, 233, 296, 322, 323, 337, 443
   and academic fields, 146, 150, 357
   and assessment/evaluation, 276, 281
   history of, 49, 64
   influences on, 222, 282
   mission of, 67, 153, 201, 277
   students of, 61, 63, 66, 108, 182, 198, 207 (*see also* transfer students)
   transfer from, 56, 230, 281, 327
Community groups (*see* Stakeholders)
Compass, The, 351
Compensatory coursework (*see* Remedial education)
Competence (*see* Students):
   as educational goal, 28, 158, 165–167
   and faculty, 320
   in students, 76, 221–222, 248, 286, 294
Competency-based curriculum, 70, 131, 172, 173, 221–222, 247, 280, 282, 339, 353
Competency certification, 168
Competition:
   and educational environment, 191, 206, 390
   among institutions, 367, 394
Componential intelligence, 189–190
Comprehension skills, 210, 237, 245–246, 252
Comprehensive colleges, 49, 53, 67, 103, 226
Computers, 228, 247, 326 (*see also* Technology):
   CD-ROM and, 253, 351, 364
   conferencing with, 351, 361, 365
   electronic mail/publications on, 275, 342, 351, 364
   faculty use of, 71, 253, 322, 363–365, 373
   instructional use of, 62, 74, 211, 220–221, 253, 261, 273, 276, 277, 279, 326, 361, 364–365, 369, 370, 373
   literacy and, 100, 363, 364, 366
   problems of, 363, 365, 366
Concept learning (*see* Content)
Concept mapping, 115–117, 135, 151, 197, 201–202, 208–209, 239–242, 249
Conference on College Composition and Communication, 232, 277
Confirmation, as stage of change, 338–339
Conjunctive components, of disciplines, 145
   of collegiate career studies, 150, 164, 165
Connected knowing/learning, 159, 162–163, 204, 206, 236
Connectedness (*see also* Coherence, Interdisciplinarity):

as educational value, 86, 90, 110–111, 152, 192, 201–202, 208–210, 290, 352, 360
   among fields of study, 159–168, 170–171, 176–178, 197, 226, 245–246, 250, 264, 293–294, 323, 347, 353, 355, 357–360, 384
   among work/life, and learning, 140, 143, 160–163, 206, 217, 280, 348, 357–360
Conrad, Clifton F., 35–37, 39, 65, 375, 381–382
Constituencies (*see* Public opinion, Stakeholders)
"Constructed knowledge," of women students, 204
Content (*see also* Student development, Knowledge):
   debate over, 63–70
   diversity of perspectives on, 345, 368
   educational values of, 338, 351, 354, 355, 369
   as element of academic plan, 10–13, 15–16, 44, 63–70, 84–87, 114, 116–120, 126–130, 134, 151–158, 172, 181, 202, 212–217, 230, 272, 273, 287, 348, 367–368, 388
   influences on, 26, 116–120, 126, 138, 141, 148, 151, 156, 201, 269, 376, 380
   and other parts of academic plan, 212–213, 368, 379–380, 386
   and planning, 114, 127–128, 134, 181
   and purpose, 172, 270, 300, 368, 380
   research on, 376, 377, 384
   student involvement with, 224, 230, 248, 317
Content-oriented theories, of curriculum, 376
Contesting the Boundaries of Liberal and Professional Education: The Syracuse Experiment, 175
Context (*see* Environment)
"Contextual competence," 167, 352
Contextual emphasis, in PLUSS system, 177–178
Contextual filters, 115–117, 151, 222
Contextual intelligence, 189–190, 203, 208
Contextual knowing, 176, 178, 204, 205, 209
Contextual teaching, 170
Contingent decisions, 333, 335, 340
Continuous learning, 26, 89, 220, 297 (*see also* Intentional learning)
Continuous Quality Improvement (CQI), 280, 324, 389–392
Contract learning, 221, 234, 263, 366
Convergent disciplines, 147
Convergers, as learning style, 191, 199
Cooperative Institutional Research Program (CIRP), 182, 187, 383
Cooperative learning, 124, 138, 206, 229, 234, 253–258, 282, 324–325, 361, 364, 390

Coordination, as administrative responsibility, 310, 313–314, 323, 325

Coordinator, administrative role of, 322–327

Core curriculum (*see also* Choice, Prescription):
  and academic plan, 47, 54, 56, 64, 65, 67, 91, 93, 94, 103, 106, 131, 231–232, 286, 322, 334, 337, 344, 354
  adoption stage of, 353–355
  and disciplines, 159, 172, 176
  and educational values, 282, 353–354, 384
  proposals and reforms for, 86, 185, 201, 286, 346, 352–354

Correlational research, 382

Council on Postsecondary Accreditation, 99

Counseling, of students, 186, 226, 255, 321, 325, 373, 377, 380

Course Design: A Guide to Curriculum Development for Teachers, 134

Course level (*see also* Curriculum):
  assessment/evaluation of, 269, 272, 287–289, 295–299, 315, 390
  changes in, 37, 285–286, 331, 334, 340, 343–344, 385
  curriculum at, 113–139, 147, 150–158, 169–170, 175, 183, 196–197, 199, 212–230, 260, 266–274, 320, 332, 354
  influenced by, 5, 181–185, 286–287, 324, 376
  research on, 382–383, 390

Course Planning Exploration, 139

Course-Related Self-Confidence Survey, 289

Coursework Cluster Analysis Model, 383

Craft of Teaching, The, 262

Creativity, 149, 189, 208, 210, 219, 224, 237, 244, 246, 270, 277

Credit units, 8, 13, 29, 53, 56, 72, 132, 168, 221, 229, 275, 322, 324, 376
  by examination, 229, 234, 324
  for experience, 72, 324, 337

Criterion-referenced tests (*see* Mastery)

Critical perspectives, 159–161, 162, 167–168, 172–174, 203–204, 301

Critical theory, 345, 348–349, 368, 370, 393

Critical thinking, as educational goal, 12, 26, 27, 76, 88, 117, 120, 132, 138, 148, 176, 188, 210, 226–227, 239, 243–244, 246–247, 261, 264, 270, 294, 300–302, 348, 359, 384 (*see also* Thinking skills, Intentional learning)

Cross, K. Patricia, 28, 31, 133, 153, 208, 275, 288–289

Cultural literacy, 26, 27, 107, 353 (*see also* Multiculturalism)

Culture, academic, 144, 162, 171, 181, 189, 197, 206, 389

Curriculum:
  change in, 186, 292, 330–373
  definitions of, 1–2, 7–21, 84, 374–376, 385 (*see also* Academic plan)
  design, 5, 15–19, 29–30, 37–40, 113, 133–140, 159, 167, 169, 221, 251, 253, 265, 286, 374, 385–387
  as dynamic process, 372–373, 386
  enhancing, 228, 349–350, 377, 387–392
  influenced by, 15–19, 79, 212–213, 374–394
  planning, 4, 16–19, 129–133, 202, 320, 341, 388–389

Curriculum: A History of the American Course of Study since 1636, 44

Davis, Barbara G., 341

Davis, James R., 188

Decision making, 26, 135, 284, 302, 333–335, 375, 378, 385, 387, 389, 393

Degrees, 229, 300, 324, 334, 337
  numbers of, 57, 60, 61
  types of, 49–51

Delaware Valley Community College, 271

Denominational colleges, 25, 47, 49, 153, 182, 224, 231, 279, 334

Departments, functioning of, 47–48, 62, 82, 124, 146–147, 300

Descriptive evaluation, 283–285, 291

Descriptive research, 382

Developing Critical Thinkers, 243

Dewey, John, 70

Dey, Eric, 182

Diamond, Robert, 38, 136–137, 139, 271

Dickinson College, 277

"Differential coursework technique," 383

Director, administrative role of, 319–322

Disciplined-centered academic planning, 152

Disciplines (*see also* Majors, Academic fields):
  assessment/evaluation in, 269–270, 307, 329
  characteristics of, 12, 34, 143, 145, 169, 175, 178, 191, 169–171, 175, 224, 237, 351, 354, 356
  classifications of, 144–148
  emergence of, 355, 368
  influence of on academic plans, 4, 7, 26, 32, 38–39, 51, 114, 116–117, 119–120, 122,

125, 127, 132, 134–135, 140–178, 183, 201, 212–214, 217, 223–225, 228, 232–233, 245, 261, 264–265, 273, 276, 334, 380, 386

influence of on faculty, 28, 148–149, 160–161, 170, 179, 218–219, 231, 264–265, 320, 325, 331, 333, 384

and students, 54, 147, 156, 204, 185, 271, 277, 290

and teaching, 133, 175, 214, 217–219, 243, 247, 250, 262, 305, 350, 364

types of, 146–147, 164, 356

Discourse communities, 149, 159, 164–166, 170, 174–175

Discovery activities, 74, 210

Distance education, 59, 63, 344, 366–367, 373

management of, 372–373, 366–367, 369

and students, 366, 370, 392

Distribution requirements (*see* Core curriculum)

Divergers, learning style of, 191, 199

Diversity:

and academic planning, 21, 56, 206–209, 309, 376

as educational value, 27, 110–111, 332, 344–352

in higher education, 9, 24, 26, 44, 42, 49, 82, 166, 309, 362, 390

perspectives on, 6, 161, 174, 268, 291, 343–352

in students, 28, 45–46, 56–57, 76, 78, 93, 206–207, 217, 221–222, 237, 257–258, 263, 301–303, 309, 320, 329, 345, 346, 348, 394, 110–111, 206–209, 345–346

Doctorate-granting universities, 46, 47, 50, 53, 103

Donald, Janet, 153–154, 160–161

Dressel, Paul, 33–35, 40, 143, 145–147, 149–150, 160, 164, 170–171, 217

Dynamic structural theory, 378

Dynamics of Academic Reform, The, 335

"Early adopters," 336–337, 373

Eaton, Judith, 25

Eble, Kenneth, 262

Education Commission of the States, 81–82, 93, 96, 362

Educational psychology, 156, 157, 192, 225, 250, 283

Educational Testing Service, 139, 234, 301

EDUCOM, 363

Effective thinking (*see* Thinking skills)

Elaboration, as stage, 238, 255

Elective courses, 53, 63–67, 82, 339

Electronics and education (*see* Computers)

Elementary schools, 31–32, 83, 98, 284, 375

Eliot, Charles William, 65, 102

Elitism, in higher education, 56, 59, 63, 74, 143, 148, 163

El-Khawas, Elaine, 108, 276

Empire State College, 187, 234

Empiric disciplines, 146, 150, 154–155

Empirical evidence, 153, 161–162, 164

Employee performance, 49, 283

Employers (*see* Job market)

Enrollment, higher education, 60, 378

as feedback, 130, 185, 187, 277, 280, 328, 330

history and trends in, 50, 58, 60, 62, 70, 74, 324, 367, 394

Entrepreneurial perspectives, 270, 292, 302

Environment:

administrators and, 310–342, 374

and change, 161, 282, 310–342, 374

of classroom, 217–218, 240, 257–258

and evaluation, 266, 294, 295, 371–372, 388

impact of, 6, 42–44, 126–127, 136, 188–189, 190, 192, 196, 222–224, 230–235, 294, 319, 325, 330, 351, 382, 387, 389–390

influence of on academic plan, 2, 19, 35, 39, 114–119, 151, 153, 214, 222–230, 240, 247, 257, 262, 263, 270, 318–319, 374

supportiveness of, 161, 227, 230, 250, 257, 268, 313–343, 371–372

Erikson, S., 209

Essentialism, 25, 26

Ethics, 32, 89, 146, 256, 302, 328, 366

Ethnic (*see also* Diversity, Students):

issues, and curriculum, 303, 346–347

students, 26, 61, 68, 92–93, 181, 305, 346

European influences, 47, 348–350, 368, 384

Evaluation (*see also* Assessment):

and academic planning, 5, 15–16, 28, 30–31, 35–36, 73–79, 82, 107–109, 134–136, 205, 266–309, 371, 374, 379–380

and adjustment, 44, 139, 273, 281, 299, 321

administrative role in, 139, 268, 308–309, 313–314, 326–330

at college level, 133, 266, 278–282, 287, 303, 308, 326–330

at course level, 121, 266, 269–274, 283–285, 287, 308

and curriculum, 3, 14, 31, 214, 261, 266, 388

faculty involvement in, 236, 263, 268–282, 298, 327

improvement of, 220, 268, 287–308

Evaluation *(cont.)*
   process of, 327–329, 340–341
   at program level, 139, 266, 274–278, 285, 287, 308
   purposes of, 111–112, 283–285
   reforms/trends in, 77, 96–97, 108–109, 281, 283–284, 329–330, 370
   research and models in, 268, 282–308, 303, 328, 377–378, 382
   and students, 30, 208, 245, 265, 271, 287, 301, 325, 362
   types of, 5, 57, 218, 252, 269, 279, 283–285, 287, 290–308, 320
Evergreen State College, 131, 138
Ewell, Peter T., 301
Examinations *(see* Instructional activities)
Expectancy-value motivational theories, 196
Expectations *(see* Motivation)
Experiential intelligence, 189–190, 203, 208
Experiential learning, 172–174, 220, 256, 257, 362
Experimental colleges, 70–71
Experimental College, The, 70
Experimentation, in higher education, 70, 192, 284, 286–287, 326, 334–335, 394
Expository Writing Program, Harvard, 292
Extension programs, 46, 70
External degrees, 59–60, 234
External influences, 98–101, 142, 162–163, 179–180, 321, 374, 375
   on academic planning, 1–6, 16–20, 26, 33, 79–112, 120, 125–131, 151, 157, 163, 166, 169, 176–177, 212–213, 223, 230, 232–233, 327, 335–342, 386
   on adjustment, 267, 277, 287, 310, 334–342, 363, 367, 373, 392–394
   and administrators, 312–314, 335–342
   on assessment/evaluation, 267–268, 270, 272, 275–276, 280, 285–286, 328, 330
   internalization of, 42–44, 337–339, 342, 370, 374–375, 386, 392
Externships, 165

Facilitator, as administrative role, 223, 315–319, 327, 330–335
Facilities, and academic planning, 119, 130, 223, 225, 227, 261, 299, 326, 330, 387–388
Faculty:
   and academic planning, 2, 8–9, 15, 25–26, 37, 82, 85, 101, 105, 113–140, 147, 181, 215, 233, 268–282, 317–318, 322, 375, 385–387

   and administrators, 226, 310–343, 374, 387–388, 390, 392
   characteristics of, 30, 32–33, 122–125, 130, 135, 136, 151, 175, 183, 223, 277, 308, 325, 333, 346, 380, 386, 390
   classroom performance/teaching style of, 2, 5, 14, 30, 82, 94, 133–134, 151, 153–154, 166, 171, 176–178, 197, 209, 216–220, 224, 226, 240, 243, 246, 247, 251–253, 257–258, 261, 288, 304, 320, 324–326, 329, 351, 360, 376–378
   and computers *(see* Computers, instructional use of)
   development of, 16, 99, 105, 117, 133, 138, 144, 151, 154–158, 211, 217, 228–229, 233, 235, 250, 264, 277, 279, 304, 320–321, 326–328, 335, 341, 357, 367, 369–370, 373, 390
   and evaluation/adjustment, 102, 105, 268–282, 286, 289, 327, 332, 377
   hiring of, 319–321, 369
   influenced by, 115–117, 141–178, 217, 223, 319, 373 *(see also* Disciplines)
   and other faculty, 8–9, 15, 24, 122–126, 146–147, 175, 217, 225, 228, 247, 255–257, 264, 265, 317, 322, 331, 344, 357, 394
   part-time, 229, 271, 319
   ratings of by students, 95, 121, 129, 185, 228, 230, 257, 264, 270–271, 279, 290, 328–329
   rewards/incentives for, 103, 110–111, 222, 225–226, 250, 365, 378
   roles of, 46–48, 138, 148, 205, 227, 234, 243, 253, 276, 320, 370
   security of, in teaching environment, 316, 319, 323
   strategies and skills of *(see* Instructional activities)
   and students, 121–122, 179–211, 227, 246, 258, 261, 289, 325–326, 381
   support staff and, 70, 94, 123, 225, 227, 233, 325–326
   team teaching by, 123, 138, 247, 256, 302, 321, 369, 384, 389, 390
   workload of, 225, 324, 329, 378
Faculty Inventory of Good Practice in Undergraduate Education, 325, 326
Failure, of students, 194–200, 319
Feedback *(see* Evaluation)
50 Hours: A Core Curriculum for College Students, 81, 83, 86, 91, 93, 94, 96
Financial aid *(see* Funding)

Fincher, Cameron, 335
Finn, Chester, 100
Formative evaluation, 268, 275–276, 284
4-1-4 academic calendar, 235, 282, 336, 339
Four-year colleges, 75, 148, 153, 233, 277, 296, 302, 323
 students at, 51, 198, 346
Francis, Marlene C., 208, 210
Free schools, 347
"Free-nets," 367
Fund for the Improvement of Postsecondary Education (FIPSE), 87, 99–100, 106, 132, 281
Funding (*see also* Government):
 for academic planning, 56, 75, 130, 233, 250, 291, 316–318, 326, 329
 and change/innovation, 130–131, 279, 281–282, 330, 332, 338–339, 369, 373
 cuts in, 101, 281
 influence of on academic planning, 73–79, 330, 357
 sources of, 44, 74, 163, 305, 328, 337, 341
 for students (*see* Students, financial aid)
Fund raising, 279, 313
Future-based general education, 172, 173

Gaff, Jerry G., 105, 226, 257–258, 275, 333, 346, 368
Gamson, Zelda, 85, 99–100, 170–172, 258
Gay, Geneva, 31–32, 33, 37
Gay/lesbian studies, 344, 346
Gender:
 influence of, 153, 156, 163, 204–206, 346, 370
 of students, 181, 188, 305 (*see also* Students)
 studies, 344, 346
General education, 79, 82, 99, 120, 124, 128, 131–132, 384, 392 (*see also* Disciplines, Liberal education):
 and academic planning, 228, 268, 277, 282, 290
 administration of, 171, 230, 322, 325
 assessment of, 224, 281, 286, 293, 301, 303
 change in, 53–54, 86–87, 104–106, 333–334, 344–346, 357, 369
 coherence in, 137, 352–353, 359, 369
 goals for, 144, 170–171, 178, 183, 349, 355
 and other academic fields, 91, 169, 171–172, 225, 231–233, 348, 353
 requirements for, 55–56, 65, 67, 74
 and students, 182, 184, 191, 197, 198, 226, 232, 274–275, 277, 294, 359
General Education in a Free Society, 49

General Equivalent Diploma (GED), 78
Geoghegan, W., 363
Georgetown University, 279
G.I. Bill (1945), 58–59, 75, 77
Gifted/talented students, 206
Globalization, 235, 237, 342–352, 368, 373
Goal-focused evaluation, 283–284, 287, 290–291, 295–308, 327, 332, 336 (*see also* Assessment)
Goal-focused research, 383–384
Goal-free evaluation, 295–296
Goals:
 in academic fields, 1, 5, 160–161
 and academic planning, 198, 212–214, 216, 224–226, 230, 236–237, 248, 255, 257, 264, 290
 of faculty, 117, 208, 218, 246
 and mission, 169, 281, 290, 321
 selection criteria for, 31, 195, 198, 215, 290, 293, 321, 333, 329
 of students, 27–29, 179–180, 183, 186, 195–198, 200, 202, 207, 215, 219, 226–227, 250, 254, 257, 263–264, 291
Goodman, G., 182
Gould, R. H., 29
Governance, and adjustment, 18, 131, 232, 279, 282, 286, 324, 333, 334, 339
Government agencies, 42, 281, 324
 and accreditation, 99, 281, 362
 evaluation of, 77, 314, 327–330, 362
 funding and, 33, 59, 67, 74–75, 77–78, 83, 95, 98, 99, 276, 283, 330
 history of role of, 74–75, 283, 342, 394
 influence of, 60, 75, 98, 100, 103, 124, 287, 291, 321, 342, 344, 361, 337, 362, 367, 373, 377, 385, 394
 and occupational programs, 55–56, 357
 student loans and (*see* Students, financial aid)
Governor's State University, 221–222
Governors' Task Force, 362
Grades, 72, 229, 247, 260, 262, 296, 324, 334, 339
 and learning, 195–196, 201, 382
 as motivation, 185, 197–198
Graduate education, 46, 48, 51, 72, 168, 219, 230–231, 235, 300, 327, 334
Graduate Record Examination, 301
Graduate/teaching assistants, 70, 94, 123, 232, 255
Graduates, 57, 60, 129, 275, 279, 281, 329, 359, 384 (*see also* Students)
Graff, Gerald, 174

Grant, Gerald, 99, 106
"Great works," 26, 34, 84, 92, 102, 215, 307, 348, 353, 358
Green, Thomas F., 28
Greenberg, E. M., 29
Griffith, John V., 204
Group Instructional Feedback Technique (GIFT), 289
Guidance (*see* Counseling)

Hagerty, B. M. K., 2, 16, 138–139,158, 163, 166, 177, 277, 352
Halliburton, David, 38–39
Hampshire College, 66, 277
Hard/soft disciplines, 147, 148, 161
Harter. S., 199
Harvard Assessment Seminars, 291–292
Harvard Business School, 252–253
Harvard Committee on General Education, 144
Harvard Law School, 48
"Harvard Redbook," 49
Harvard University, 25, 28, 48, 49, 56, 65, 102, 131, 203, 279, 295–296
Hatch Act, 75
Haworth, Jennifer G., 381
Health professions, 51, 53, 56, 66, 106, 165, 273, 277
Hefferlin, JB Lon, 335
Heginbotham, S. J., 351
Hewson, P.W., 140
High schools (*see* Secondary education)
Higher Education Acts (1965, 1968, 1972), 60, 75, 77
Higher Education and the American Resurgence, 81
Higher Education for Democracy, 58, 60
Higher Education Research Institute, 187
Hirsch, E. D., 18, 353
Honors program, 93, 175
Hopkins, Mark, 428
How College Affects Students, 298
Humanities:
    and academic planning, 154, 176, 202, 270
    change in, 106, 160, 282, 354
    characteristics of, 144–145, 162, 174, 349, 357
    faculty of, 129, 146, 152, 160–161
    and interdisciplinarity, 172, 355–356, 384
    students in, 66, 191, 204
Humanities in America: A Report to the President,

the Congress, and the American People, 81, 83
Hutchins, Robert Maynard, 70, 280

Illuminative evaluation, 283–284
Image, of institution, 294, 330
Improving College Teaching, 229
Improving Degree Programs, 34–35
Incentive funding, 330
Inclusiveness, as educational value, 159–161, 290, 347
Independent colleges, 46, 52, 60, 62, 277
Independent judgment, 199
Independent knowing, 205, 209
Independent learning, 55, 205, 295, 297, 301, 302, 334
Independent study, 72, 234, 366
Indiana University, 65
Individualized instruction, 208, 219–222, 234–236, 249, 263–264, 323
Information-processing skills, 176, 189–190, 192–193, 197, 210, 229, 237–238, 249, 255, 289, 295, 302, 365
Information service fields, 149, 156, 164, 166, 176, 270
Initiation, as stage of change, 338
Innovation (*see also* Change):
    in academic planning, 23, 37, 70–73, 99, 124, 212–213, 228, 233–235, 257, 282, 286, 330–331, 363, 374, 385
    influences on, 131–132, 281, 337–342, 356, 366, 394
    literature about, 377
Innovator, administrative role, 330–342
Input-environment-output (I-E-O) model, of A. Astin, 302–303, 379
Inquiry, methods of, 149, 154, 155, 164, 166, 169, 170–171, 176, 178, 202, 244–245, 261, 297, 388
Institutional (*see also* Mission):
    characteristics, 2, 183, 290–291, 317, 319–320, 380
    selectivity, 183, 224, 228, 231, 280, 291, 323
    size, as factor, 129–132, 186, 282, 289–290, 334
    research offices, 129, 279
Institutional Goals Inventory, 139
Institutional Inventory of Good Practice in Under-graduate Education, 325
Instructional activities, 13–14, 28, 114–115,

120–121, 128, 132, 140, 154–156, 212–213, 220, 261, 264, 302, 344, 376, 390

Instructional activities, *listed:*

analogies, 193

apprenticeships, 165, 169, 229, 252, 324

assignments, 269, 296

capstone experiences, 106, 128, 161, 165, 186, 201, 297, 307

case studies, 253, 273, 276–277, 370

diagramming, 193 (*see also* Concept maps)

discussion, 70, 120, 123, 214, 218, 221, 224, 231, 233, 237, 250–253, 255, 258, 263, 270–273, 295, 361, 369, 384

feedback, 220, 251, 254–255, 258, 261

field experiences, 70, 95, 165, 186, 227, 231, 237, 261, 263, 304, 307

focus groups, 275, 291, 295

games, as teacher strategy, 220

group learning, 219, 249–255, 257

guest lecturers, 231

homework, 184, 366

journals, 185, 263, 270, 273, 286, 291, 297

laboratories, 65, 70, 76, 120, 128, 220, 221, 229, 232, 233, 236–237, 253, 261, 263, 272, 275, 293, 324, 361, 365

lectures, 14, 30, 70, 74, 107, 114, 120, 184, 201, 220–221, 214, 218, 224, 231–233, 237–238, 247, 249–252, 263, 271, 273, 326, 365, 369, 384, 384

memorization, 238, 252

note taking, 249, 255

one-minute papers, 185, 250, 273

one-sentence summary, 250

papers, 263, 283

performance, 189–190, 195, 197, 307

portfolios, 236, 270, 286, 293, 297, 307

practica, 201, 225, 229, 289, 304, 324, 361

projects, 220, 253, 254, 261, 263

questioning, 245, 246, 250–253

quizzes, 221, 261

readings, 28, 261, 263, 353

reviewing, 237

role playing, 220, 253

seminars, 30, 71, 94, 128, 231, 304, 307, 320

senior projects, 106, 304, 307

simulation, 220, 252–253, 263, 286, 370

summarizing, 193, 250, 273

syllabus, 5, 28, 30, 66, 95, 115, 121, 128, 209, 214, 220, 259–261, 277, 290, 320, 386

teamwork, 254, 264

testing:

and course objectives, 201, 262, 297

development/analysis of, 284, 287, 301, 305, 326, 329

instructional use of, 28, 30, 72, 103, 121, 122, 201, 221, 229, 236–237, 248, 254, 260–262, 269, 270, 286, 296–297, 326, 304, 324

pre-/posttests, 296, 298–299, 303

standardized, 297, 301, 303, 362–363

textbooks, 123, 218, 222, 225, 227, 231–232, 238, 250, 261, 263, 273, 276, 325, 364, 385

tutoring, 207, 228, 238, 253, 255, 298

underlining text, 193

Instructional design/development:

activity of, 38, 136, 325, 227–229, 251, 264, 390

centers of, 125–126, 133, 136, 222–223, 225, 227, 228–229, 233, 272, 279, 326

consultants in, 271–272, 325, 384

materials for, 33, 114–115, 171, 201, 271, 313

Instructional media, 125, 227, 325

Instructional processes:

in academic planning, 13–14, 16, 30–31, 32, 34, 44, 70, 94–95, 135, 212–265, 271, 325–326, 377–378, 381–382, 385, 387–380, 386

change in, 70–73, 79, 94–95, 107, 110–111, 227, 273, 276–277, 279, 338, 388

educational values of, 193, 345–346, 349, 351, 354, 360, 369–370, 384

and students, 93, 217, 289, 362

Instructional resources, 14, 16, 29, 44, 95–96, 245–248, 257, 313, 338, 345–346, 360, 365, 369, 377, 379 (*see also* Computers)

Instructor-centered teaching, 217–219, 220, 249

Integrated Postsecondary Education Data System (IPEDS), 51

Integration (*see also* Coherence, Connectedness):

in academic fields, 158, 169, 201, 280, 322, 375, 384

as educational value, 110–111, 165, 176, 193, 249, 264, 304

of knowledge, 126, 138, 161, 192, 196–197, 201–202, 205–206, 211, 229, 235, 250, 302, 305, 352, 384

social, of students, 255, 305

Integrity in the College Curriculum: A Report to the Academic Community, 80, 84–85, 87, 90, 92, 94, 96, 101, 102, 105–106, 169, 202

Intentional learning, 208–210, 236, 245–248, 261, 288, 293, 300, 370, 365

Interactive learning, 220, 249, 252, 263

Interdisciplinarity: (*see also* Area studies)
    and academic planning, 126, 170, 217, 256, 356
    development of, 175, 332, 334, 355–357
    as educational value, 27, 47, 110–111, 175, 273, 323, 325, 369
    goals of, 353, 351
    programs of, 14, 51, 54, 72, 124, 138, 152, 158, 159, 162, 163, 172, 176, 344, 355–357, 384
Interest (*see* Motivation; Students, interests of)
Internal influences, 16–20, 26, 33, 79–112, 179–180, 312–314, 374–375
    on academic planning, 1–6, 126–130, 142, 146, 157, 163, 176–177, 212–213, 223–224, 230, 232, 267, 276, 386
    and change, 101–102, 337–338, 342
    and evaluation, 199, 279–280, 287, 328, 337–340
International competition, 97, 357–358
International education, 54, 103, 108, 235, 277, 279–280, 349–352, 369, 373, 385 (*see also* Globalization)
Internet (*see* Computers)
Internships, 128, 168, 186, 201, 220, 229, 230, 237, 256, 257, 275, 307, 324
Interpretation, as administrative function, 328–330, 380, 390, 394
Involvement, and learning, 196, 199–201, 204, 248–249, 256, 269, 293, 333, 335, 360
Involvement in Learning: Realizing the Potential of American Higher Education, 80, 85, 91, 92, 94–96, 99–100, 102, 108, 170, 200, 360

James Madison University, 280
January term (*see* 4-1-4 calendar)
Job market:
    education for, 12, 55, 230, 357, 360, 370
    influence of, 18, 141, 156, 163, 168, 222, 225, 230, 233, 268, 276, 277, 282, 294, 305, 327–328, 357–358, 360, 366
Johnson Foundation, 81
Johnston, Joseph S., Jr., 81
Junior colleges (*see* Community colleges)

Kalamazoo College, 234, 280, 351
Kaysen, Carl, 176
Kean College, 280
Keller, George, 131
Keller Plan, 70, 131, 221, 277, 282
Kennedy, Donald, 25
Kerr, Clark, 44–45, 56, 357
King, Patricia, 204

Kings College, 280
Kitchener, Karen, 204
Knowledge:
    and discipline, 153, 201–202, 205, 353
    as educational goal, 147, 170, 189–190, 197, 349, 376, 384
    "essential," 32, 151, 158, 170–171, 201, 209–210, 215, 244, 300, 353; (*see also* Content; Core curriculum; Great works)
Kolb, David, and model, 133, 145, 147, 191, 192, 263

Labor market (*see* Job market)
LAN (*see* Local Area Networks), 365
Land Grant Act (1862), 357
    and colleges, 70, 71, 74, 339, 357
Lauter, Paul, 353, 354
Leadership, 220, 231, 233, 254, 279, 310–342, 389
    (*see also* Administrators)
Learners (*see* Goals, Intentional learning, Outcomes, Students)
Learning activities (*see* Instructional activities)
Learning and Study Strategies Inventory (LASSI), 238, 289
Learning assistance (*see* Remedial education)
Learning communities, 91, 94, 138, 169, 255–256, 288, 344
Learning Context Questionnaire, 204
Learning strategies (*see* Cognitive skills)
Learning Styles Inventory, 192
Learning styles/skills (*see also* Students):
    influence of discipline on, 145, 147, 191
    information about, 191, 217, 237–238, 246, 249, 254, 257, 263, 377, 390
    and teaching styles, 145, 147, 191–192, 199, 263 (*see also* Faculty, classroom performance)
Learning theory, 117, 125, 174, 183, 187–196, 222, 223, 225, 228, 236, 388
Learning to learn (*see* Metacognition)
Levine, Arthur, 25–27, 72–73, 367
Lewis and Clark College, 351
Liberal arts colleges, 46, 48, 130, 143, 224, 226, 228, 232, 245, 277, 323, 359, 364 (*see also* Baccalaureate colleges)
Liberal Learning in the Arts and Sciences Major: The Challenge of Connecting Learning, 159–160
Liberating Education, 99
Library facilities, 120, 225, 228, 247, 279, 324, 326, 364, 367, 378

Library of Congress, 364
Life/nonlife disciplines, classification of, 147
Lifetime learners, 208, 293
Light, Richard J., 275, 291–292
Linder, Vincent, 334
Local Area Networks (LAN), 365
Locke, Lawrence, 54
Logical positivism, 348
LOGO inventory, 195–196
Loop College, 277
Lowther, Malcolm A., 2, 12, 16, 28, 39, 81, 87–89,
93, 113–114, 122, 131, 138–139, 152, 158,
163, 166, 177, 181, 184, 195, 198, 225–229,
260–261

McCabe, Robert, 25
McKeachie, Wilbert J., 133–135, 196, 201, 229,
243, 250
McPeck, John, 243
Majors (*see also* Collegiate career studies):
  and academic fields, 51, 53–55, 64, 66, 124, 126,
  144, 148, 150, 158, 163–178, 232–233, 244,
  301, 334, 339
  assessment/evaluation of, 268, 275–276, 281,
  286, 289–291
  coordination of, 322, 370
  and general education, 176, 226, 359
  history of, 48, 53, 65
  influences on, 66, 158–163
  reforms in, 86, 90, 106–108
  students in, 53, 185, 198, 219, 227, 296,
  305
Marcus, Dora, 34, 143, 145–147, 149–150, 160,
164, 170, 171, 217
Mars Hill College, 131, 222, 280
Mastery learning, 70, 199, 218, 221, 297
Mathematics skills, 67, 68, 86, 108, 120, 121, 124,
138, 156–158, 183, 214–215, 224, 227, 243,
255, 297, 305–307, 334, 339, 356
Mayer, R. E., 192
Meaning, construction of, 192, 200–202, 221, 291,
236, 248, 378, 381
Measurement (*see* Assessment)
Meiklejohn, Alexander, 70
Memory, 188–189, 192–193, 202, 237, 251–252,
264
Mentoring:
  administrative role of, 315–319, 327
  and learning, 246–247, 254

Merit (*see also* Worth), 275–276, 284–285, 313,
327, 328
Mesa Community College, 233, 323
Metacognition, 193, 195, 208, 237–239, 246, 250,
293, 295, 384
Metacomponents, of cognitive abilities, 189–190
Meta-evaluation, 268, 308–309, 329, 378, 391–392
Miami-Dade Community College, 67, 280, 322, 358
Michigan State University, 349
Middlesex County Community College, 277
Military academies, 47
Minnesota Metropolitan College, 234
Minnich, E., 347–348
Minor fields, 64–65, 334
Mission, of college or program:
  and administration, 25, 230, 277, 313, 332
  and change, 63, 131, 276, 281, 339, 392
  communication of, 30, 132, 330
  drift in, 278–279, 336
  influence on, 7, 26, 44, 46, 78, 126–127, 139,
  144, 163, 181, 231, 277, 280, 281, 290, 318,
  324, 392
  influenced by, 75, 281, 375
  and institutional type, 18, 26, 48, 56, 101, 130,
  187
  students, 132–133, 250
Models:
  academic-rational, 32, 33
  of change, 331–332, 372–373
  of collegiate career studies (by Stark), 164–168
  competing values in, 4, 327, 331, 340
  contextual filters in, 115–117
  of curriculum, 31–40 (by Conrad and Pratt, Dressel, Gay), 103, 114–117, 133–140, 136–137
  (by Diamond), 138, 302–303; European,
  46–47
  of disciplines, 145–150, 154, 160–162, 164, 168
  (by Biglan, Phenix)
  of evaluation, 31–32 (by Tyler, Astin), 268,
  282–308, 285 (CIIP), 303–304, 330, 375
  of general education, 172–173
  of intellectual development, 203–206 (by Baxter-
  Magolda, Kitchener and King, Perry)
  of leadership, 292, 314–316
  of professional/liberal education competencies,
  89–91, 106
  of student coursework, 148, 383
  of talent development (by Astin), 28
  types of, 31–35, 85, 138, 205, 283, 285, 315,
  331, 373, 379, 383

Modern Language Association, 18

Mohawk College of Applied Arts and Technology, 277

Monitor, as administrative role, 326–335

Monitoring, and learning, 192–193, 269, 330

"Moral Messages of the University," 81

Moral positions, 146, 320, 338, (*see also* Ethics)

Morrill Land-Grant Act:
  of 1862, 46–47, 57, 63, 64, 75, 339
  of 1890, 58, 75, 77

Motivation (*see also* Students):
  and administrators, 312–313
  definition of, 194, 196, 199
  and learning, 6, 193–197, 214, 220, 221, 230, 236, 239, 248–250, 256, 262, 264–265, 284, 293, 298–299, 302, 318–319, 325, 333
  outcomes and, 235, 250, 257, 300–330
  strategies for, 120, 183–185, 198, 217, 277, 286, 315–316
  theory of, 194, 196, 198, 200

Mulder, Timothy, 208

Multiculturalism (*see also* Globalization):
  and curriculum, 234, 279, 282, 344–348, 368, 393
  as educational value, 47, 92, 103, 175, 181, 206, 295–296, 346, 350, 352, 369, 392
  perspectives reflecting, 336–337, 344, 346, 373

Multiplicity, as intellectual stage, 191, 203, 204, 224

"Multiversities," 56

Museums, 364, 367

National Center for Research to Improve Postsecondary Teaching and Learning (NCRIPTAL), 100, 115, 120

National Center for Teaching, Learning, and Assessment (NCTLA), 100

National Center on Education and the Economy, 108

National Defense Education Act (1958), 75

National Endowment for the Humanities, 81–83, 98, 101, 103

National Gallery of Art, 367

National Governors' Association, 81, 83, 85, 96

National Information Infrastructure, 363

National Institute of Education, 82, 85–86, 92, 94, 99–100, 102, 170

National Longitudinal Study of the Class of 1972, 100, 383

National Security Education Program, 350

Nation at Risk, A, 98

Naturalistic evaluation, 283–285

NCRIPTAL (*see* National Center for Research to Improve Postsecondary Teaching and Learning)

Networking, 193, 201, 208, 257

New England Resource Center for Higher Education, 103

New Jersey Basic Skills Test, 301

New Life for the College Curriculum, A, 257–258

Newman, Frank, 81

New Vitality in General Education, A, 81, 83, 87, 90, 93, 94, 97, 105, 353

NIE (*see* National Institute of Education)

Nonapplied study, 230–232

Nontraditional colleges/curriculum, 234, 296, 337, 344, 375

Non-Western culture, 84, 346, 349

Nordvall, Robert C., 331

Norm-referenced tests, 297

North American Free Trade Agreement, 350

North Central Association of Colleges and Schools, 281

Northeastern University, 176, 257

Northeast Missouri State University, 280

Oberlin College, 105, 334

Objectives (*see* Goals)

Observations (*see* Evaluation)

Occupational programs 12, 25, 46, 54, 56, 143, 148–178, 222, 227, 233, 337, 357–358 (*see also* Academic fields, *listed*)
  and academic fields, 53, 148–150, 163, 168–169, 172–173, 176, 232, 358
  and academic planning, 154, 202, 276, 380
  criticisms of, 358–359
  definition of, 143
  as educational goal, 46, 118, 120, 126, 143, 144, 172, 195, 277, 290, 291, 294, 296, 301, 302, 320, 353, 358, 369
  evaluation of, 209, 268, 270, 275–276, 352, 369
  and institutions, 55, 150, 277, 359
  and other fields, 172, 173, 176
  as student goal, 53, 179–180, 186, 206, 227, 294, 300, 305, 388

Office of Educational Research and Improvement (OERI), 66, 100

Open symbol systems, 149, 166

Opinion leaders, 331, 336–338, 341, 373

Optional decision, 333, 335, 340

Orczyk, Cynthia, 1, 16, 158, 352
Oregon State University, 351
Organizational influences:
    on academic fields, 145, 150, 163
    on academic planning, 16–20, 79–101, 136,
        140–144, 146, 151, 229, 267, 268, 341, 339,
        378, 381, 392
    and change, 101, 337–38
    and students, 179–180
Organization, as learning strategy, 192–193, 201
Outcomes (*see also* Assessment; Students):
    and academic field, 88–90, 239, 358
    assessment of, 97, 282, 290, 295–299, 300–309,
        328
    Astin's typology of, 300
    intended and unintended, 135, 139, 283, 295,
        298
    learning, 15, 25, 29, 32, 84, 87, 214, 247, 269,
        297, 300–309, 374, 384, 387
    research needed on, 35, 300, 382, 384
    types of, 218, 221–222, 283, 299–301, 329
Outcomes-centered instruction, 236

Pace, C. Robert, 184, 208, 292–293, 298–299
Paradigms:
    of academic fields, 29, 129, 147, 163, 217, 232,
        301, 373
    educational qualities of, 174, 348–349
    new, 237, 345, 348–349
Parochetti, J. A., 182
Pascarella, Ernest T., 291, 298, 382
Passivity in learning, 71, 135, 200, 208, 248–249,
    342, 361, 365
Pedagogy (*see* Faculty, Instructional activities, In-
    structional processes)
Peer review, 153, 161–162, 164, 285, 329–330
Peers:
    and faculty, 220, 254–255, 265, 319
    and learners, 205, 218, 233, 237, 255, 263, 271,
        304–305 (*see also* Instructional activities,
        listed)
Pennsylvania State University, The, 100
Perennialism, educational philosophy of, 25, 27
Performance funding, 281
Perry, William G., and scheme, 28, 29, 133,
    203–204, 217
Persistence:
    and difficulty of task, 198–199
    and graduation, 256, 272, 301, 305
    as leadership quality, 332

Personal development, as educational goal, 156,
    172, 195, 202, 294, 300
Perspectives, curricular, 22–42, 344–352, 377
Pew Policy Roundtables, 394
Phenix, P. H., classification, 145–150, 154, 160,
    162, 164, 168
Philadelphia College of Textiles and Science, 106,
    139, 247–248, 277, 280
Philosophy of education, 32, 72, 320
Pickert, S. M., 350
Pintrich, Paul R., 193, 195
Placement testing, 222, 234, 238, 283, 307
Planning (*see* Academic planning, Curriculum)
Pluralism:
    and coherence, 352, 368
    and curriculum, 32, 102, 348–349, 354, 368, 370
    as educational value, 64, 65, 106, 107, 353
    in higher education, 47–48, 344–345
PLUSS Guide (*see* Professional/Liberal Undergrad-
    uate Self–Study)
Policies, definition of, 323–324
Policymakers (*see also* Administrators)
    and academic plans, 139, 169
    and evaluation, 284, 286, 290, 309, 330, 383
Political:
    conflict models, 331, 336–337, 342
    correctness, 107, 370
    influences, on higher education, 37, 79, 83, 338
        (*see also* Social pressures)
Politics, internal, 37, 125, 131, 268, 280, 286, 349,
    352, 370
Polson, C. J., 206
Posner, George J., 38, 120, 134–135, 137–140, 214
Practice:
    academic plan as guide for, 214, 247, 385–387
    communities, 166–167, 169, 171
    sites, 150, 164–168, 224, 257, 321
Practitioners, influence of, 143–149, 163, 275, 282
Pragmatic inquiry methods, 164
Pratt, Anne, 35–37, 39, 375
Predictive research, need for, 382
*Preparing Course Syllabi for Improved Communi-
    cation,* 260
Preprofessional courses (*see* Collegiate career stud-
    ies)
Prescription, in coursework: 63–70, 72, 82, 90,
    97–98, 102, 106–107, 172, 185, 344–345,
    354, 375, 392
President's Commission on Higher Education for
    Democracy, 49, 50

Princeton University, 56
"Principles of Good Practice for Undergraduate Education," 107
Private colleges (*see Indpendent colleges*)
Problem solving:
    and academic field, 147, 149–150, 164, 169, 244,
    and academic plans, 197, 394
    as educational goal, 126, 155, 246, 257, 286, 301–302
    and instructional process, 214, 221, 243, 251, 253, 355, 370, 394
    and students, 185, 189, 205, 221, 247, 253
    skills of, 168, 188, 210, 214, 236–237, 239, 244, 253, 256, 269, 270, 277, 289, 297, 351, 389–390
    types/structure of, 150, 202, 204, 219, 244, 273, 331–332, 335, 337, 373, 385
Processes (*see* Instructional processes)
Process-oriented theories, of curriculum, 376
Producer, administrative role of, 319–322, 327
Production/enterprise services, 149, 156, 163, 164, 176
Professional:
    associations and publications, 33, 47, 48, 126, 141, 169, 225, 228, 232–233, 279, 280, 320, 327, 350–351, 361, 373
    programs, 148–178 (*see also* Academic fields, Collegiate career studies)
    qualities:
        competencies, 89–91
        commitment, 156, 163–165
        ethics, 150, 156, 164, 166, 172, 178
        identity, 156, 164, 166, 169, 217, 220, 237
Professional/Liberal Undergraduate Self-Study (PLUSS), 138–139, 176–177
Professional Preparation Network, 81, 87, 91, 106
Program level (*see also* Academic plan, Course-level, College-level):
    and academic plan, 2, 5, 124–139, 158–178, 185–187, 196–197, 212–213, 255–257, 262, 285–286, 315, 322, 329
    and administrators, 268, 313, 329, 331, 385
    assessment at, 272, 266–268, 274–278, 289–291, 300–303, 390
    change at, 276–278, 331, 334, 340, 344
    characteristics of, 44, 51, 128, 209, 232, 354
    evaluation at, 281, 285, 287, 294–296, 300–303, 377
    and faculty, 332, 384
    goals at, 223–226, 257–258, 290

influences on, 147–148, 181, 279, 299, 302
research needed on, 383
review of, 276, 328–329
students at, needs of, 181, 185–187
Programmed instruction, 366
Program Review and Educational Quality in the Major, 81, 83, 290
Progressivism, 25
Project on Liberal Learning, Study-in-Depth, and the Arts and Sciences Major/Project on Liberal Learning in the Major, 81, 147–148
Project on Strong Foundations for General Education, 81
Psychology of learning, 32, 34, 70, 140, 146, 211, 283, 292, 376, 384
Public colleges, 50, 60, 62
Public opinion (*see also* Social pressures):
    and assessment/evaluation, 290, 309, 324, 328, 330
    and constituencies, 9, 32, 344, 392
    and educational purpose, 7–8, 144
    satisfaction, with higher education, 282, 324, 337, 387
Public relations, management of, 279, 284–285, 294, 313, 319, 329–330
Pure/applied fields, 147–148, 153–154
Purpose:
    and adjustment, 273, 276–277, 280
    assessment/evaluation of, 229, 268, 328, 373
    of education, 15–16, 44–56, 104, 170, 208, 359
    faculty views on, 12, 151, 153
    influenced by, 100, 141, 335, 367–368, 373, 380
    influence of on academic plan, 32, 44, 84, 116–117, 134–136, 151, 172, 212–214, 223, 287, 300, 367–368, 379–380, 385, 388
    perspectives on, 24–25, 44–56, 345, 348, 367–368, 377
    research needed on, 235, 384
    statements of, 132, 250, 319

Qualitative research, 166, 283, 286 (*see also* Assessment, Evaluation)
Quality (*see also* Access):
    vs. access, 56–64, 70–79, 107–109, 282, 336, 338, 341, 344, 360–367
    adjustments in, 329, 362–367
    assessment of, 268, 271, 329, 362–367
    as educational purpose, 77–78, 82, 92, 97, 100, 108–109, 360, 367, 373, 390, 392
    expectations for, 324, 360–367

indicators of, 352, 362–367
"quality of effort" evaluation, 292–294, 299
Quantitative research, 166, 263
Quinn, Robert, 315, 331, 340

Ratcliff, J. L., 383
Rational change, 331–332, 335, 337, 338, 373
Rational planning, 315, 331, 344
Reading skills, 217, 237, 263
"Realms of meaning" classification, 145, 147, 164
Reconstructionism, educational philosophy, 25
Reed, James W., 107
Reflection:
    by faculty, 248, 250, 264–265, 301, 380, 384,
        386–387, 394
    by students, 209–210, 238–239, 245, 246, 288,
        293
Reflective Judgment Inventory, 204, 217
Reforms, 80–112, 343–373 (see also Assessment,
        Change, Social pressures):
    and coherence, 172, 174, 352
    and critical perspectives, 172, 174
    critiques of, 103–112
    of curriculum, 4, 37, 42, 47, 64, 79–112, 237,
        337, 368, 393
    examples of, 336–337
    history of, 80–112, 373
        in 1900–1960s, 48, 235–236, 337, 354
        in 1960s–1980s, 72–73, 75, 81, 131, 147, 336,
            343, 361
        in 1990s, 54, 80–84, 236, 343, 362
    influences on, 83–84, 97–102, 373, 390
    and integration, 169–170
    pace of, 80, 102–103
    structural, 103, 132, 332, 340
    and student assessments, 282
Rehearsal, as learning strategy, 192, 197, 238, 255
Relativism, 106, 203, 217, 354 (see also Pluralism)
Relevance (see also Coherence):
    as educational goal, 70, 72, 222, 235, 328, 344,
        352
    as student demand, 26, 235, 339, 346 (see also
        Students)
Religion (see also Denominational colleges):
    and faculty beliefs, 117, 156–157
    influence of on education, 77, 385
    and student beliefs, 206
Remedial education, 67, 74, 76, 77, 92, 207, 217,
        225, 228–229, 232, 247, 261, 277, 322,
        325–326, 362

Renninger, K. A., 196
*Reports from the Fields: Liberal Learning in the
        Arts and Sciences Major,* 81, 83
Research:
    and administration, 282, 308, 319, 390, 394
    in classroom, 131, 264, 273, 327
    and evaluation, 282, 308, 378
    on learning, 22–40, 105, 179, 187–211, 214, 226,
        232, 254, 283–285, 374–394
    methods, types of, 244–245, 286, 303–304,
        383–384, 293
    and mission, 56, 320
    need for, 6, 187, 276, 284, 351, 374–394
    by students, 75, 201, 244, 270
    vs. teaching, 94, 373
Research universities, 46, 47, 50, 53, 107, 163, 226,
        318, 346, 349
Resources (see also Instructional resources):
    administration of, 103, 224, 227–228, 233,
        279–280, 313–314, 322, 335, 340, 351,
        369–370
    and learning activities, 116–117, 200, 212–213,
        222, 230, 233, 247, 261, 273, 276–277,
        320–321, 325, 387–388
    and motivation, 232, 235, 299, 325, 338
Responsive evaluation, 283–284
Rewards and incentives, for faculty, 163, 281, 285,
        326, 333, 335, 357, 373, 390
Rhode Island College, 280
Riesmann, David, 99, 106
Risk-taking, 243, 257–258
Rossides, Daniel, 105
Roueche, John E., 78, 207
Roueche, Suanne, 207
Rudnitsky, A. N., 134–135
Rudolph, Frederick, 44, 79
"Rural" disciplines, 147
Rutgers University, 107

Sanders, J. R., 283
Schneider, C., 297
Scholarly associations (see Professional associa-
        tions)
*Scholarship Reconsidered: Priorities of the Profes-
        soriate,* 81
Scholastic Aptitude Test, 75
Schön, Donald, 270
Scientific evaluation movement, 284
Screening, as stage of change, 338–339, 343–373,
        375, 392

Secondary education, 31–32, 38, 58, 70, 78, 83, 98, 192, 352, 375
  and curriculum, 59, 76, 93, 115, 134, 283–284, 322, 352, 366, 384
Sciences, 191, 214, 217, 224, 227, 236, 244, 256, 354–356 (*see also* Academic fields, *listed*, Disciplines)
Self-paced instruction, 14, 71, 72, 246, 253, 282, 366
Self-studies, 268, 275–276, 279, 284–285, 328
  influences on, 275, 280, 281, 329
Sequence:
  adjustments in, 273, 276, 277, 368–369
  as aspect of academic planning, 13, 15–16, 29, 44, 115, 120, 126–128, 134, 136–137, 138, 160–161, 171, 181, 212–213, 220, 287, 332, 379, 386–387
  influenced by, 148, 303, 323, 326, 345, 380
  influences on, 282, 287, 289, 292, 351, 368–369, 388
  outcomes of, 273, 303, 384
  proposed reforms in, 87, 90–91, 337, 368
  research about, 271, 368, 377, 384
Service component, of higher education, 149–150, 156, 164, 170
Servicemen's Readjustment Act of 1944 (*see* G.I. Bill)
Settings, for instruction, 220, 229, 256–257
Seven Principles for Good Practice in Undergraduate Education, 258–259
SGE (*see* Student Goals Exploration)
Shaman, Susan, 81
Shaw, Kathleen M., 28, 113, 184, 195, 198
Skills mastery, as educational goal, 55, 118, 151, 153, 155, 157, 169, 221, 358, 388
Snow, C. P., 162
Social change as educational goal, 12, 72, 152–153, 172–173, 349
Social interactions, and education, 146–147, 249, 253–255, 336, 337, 339, 344, 373, 390 (*see also* Students)
Social interaction model of change, 331, 337
Social pressures for educational changes, 24, 25, 27, 32, 70, 97–98, 150, 154, 155, 162, 177, 202, 232, 257, 282, 293, 323, 327, 331, 336–337, 342, 344, 355, 357, 358, 369, 373–375, 377, 388, 392–393
  current examples of, 344–345, 349–352, 377
  historical examples of, 48–49, 56, 58, 64–65, 70,

  75, 102, 350, 393 (*see also* G.I. Bill, Sputnik)
Society for College and University Planning, 129
Sociopolitical evaluation, 284
Sossen, Paula, 184, 198
South Dakota State University, 303–304
Southern Regional Education Board (SREB), 362
Specialized education, 46–49, 53–56, 65, 74, 79, 82, 86, 93, 105–106, 144, 171, 344, 345, 357, 359, 392
Sputnik (October 1957), 47, 49, 64, 65, 97, 339
Stake, Robert, 285
Stakeholders, influence of, 16, 18, 24, 32, 283–284, 286, 327, 342
Stanford University, 25, 106, 131, 279, 286, 336
Starr, J. Frederick, 105, 334
State agencies, influence of on education (*see* Government)
State colleges, 46–47, 83, 124, 243
State Higher Education Executive Officers, 358
State University of New York at Albany, 280, 304–308
Sterling College, 222, 280
Sternberg, Robert J., 189–190, 203, 208
Stimpson, Catherine, 107
Strengthening the Ties That Bind: Integrating Undergraduate Liberal and Professional Study, 81, 87, 93
Strike, Kenneth, 120
Strommer, D., 209
Strong Foundations: Twelve Principles for Effective General Education Programs, 83
Structure:
  in academic fields, 144–148, 150, 168, 169
  and change/reforms, 87, 90–91, 103, 132, 234–235, 332, 340
  and curriculum, 8, 24, 72, 114, 116–117, 136–138, 143, 158, 238–239, 290, 323, 385
  importance of, 29–30, 72, 143, 145, 209
  organizational, 69, 145, 212–213, 222–225, 227, 229–230, 233–235, 323–324
  theories of, 145, 376
Student-based general education, 172, 173
Student-centered evaluation, 287, 291–294, 303
Student-centered teaching, 217–219
Student-created majors, 72
Student Goals Exploration (SGE), 184, 195, 198, 289
"Student Right to Know" Act, 281

Students (*see also* Enrollment, Faculty):
  abilities of, 13, 16, 30, 32, 100, 185, 188–190,
      194, 195, 205, 225, 283, 298, 300, 348,
      370–371, 383
  activism of, 70, 80, 82, 97, 282, 339
  affective development of, 187–188, 198–199,
      206, 208, 292–294, 296, 300
  Alaskan Native, 61, 346
  American Indian, 61, 346
  Asian, 61, 68
  assessment/self-assessment of, 100, 286, 288,
      291–295, 390
  backgrounds of, 12, 62, 105, 181–182, 187, 305,
      324, 349, 358–359
  Black, 56, 58, 59, 61, 65, 68
  characteristics of, 28, 33, 45, 118–119, 127, 140,
      156, 182, 185, 235–264, 273, 275, 305, 313,
      320–321, 363, 370, 373, 377, 379–380, 390
  community service of, 49, 95, 186, 207, 231,
      234–235, 256, 247, 362
  commuter, 58, 62, 92
  disabled, 206, 296, 346, 366
  diversity in, 44, 92–93, 179–180
  efforts of, 195, 207–208, 225, 294, 299, 301
  in Europe, 350
  as factor in academic planning, 15, 44, 56–63,
      90–93, 114, 116–117, 127, 179–211,
      378–380
  feedback from, 25–26, 129, 185, 198–199, 217,
      221, 250–251, 255, 264, 270, 271, 275, 283,
      291–295, 329, 382–383
  female, 46, 56, 57–59, 61, 65, 68, 99, 296, 357
  financial aid to, 60, 62–63, 75, 305, 362
  gay/lesbian, 26, 206
  goals/motivation of, 63–70, 156, 179–181,
      183–184, 188, 193–197, 209, 222, 223,
      225–227, 237, 248, 258, 279, 321, 357,
      370
  Hispanic, 61, 68, 346
  influences of, 136, 181
  influences on, 91–93, 179–180, 221, 321
  intellectual development of, 12, 28, 30, 33–34,
      100, 118, 133, 145, 152–154, 156–158, 169,
      183–184, 187–190, 195, 202–206, 209–210,
      215, 217–219, 224, 231, 236, 246, 256, 269,
      270, 281, 285–286, 294, 301–303, 305, 320,
      336, 338, 376, 382, 388 (*see also* Thinking
      skills, Writing skills)
  intelligence of, 189–190, 207–208
  international, 61–62, 303, 351
  interpersonal skills of, 61, 189, 206, 256, 294,
      303, 351
  learning skills/styles, 70–74, 133, 135, 138, 166,
      174, 181, 183–185, 190–192, 196, 199, 203,
      209–210, 217, 238, 249, 264, 269, 272–273,
      291, 305–306, 329, 334, 373, 386, 394 (*see
      also* Remedial education)
  male, 46, 57, 68, 204
  minority, 61, 92–93, 206–208, 296, 357
  motivation of, 100, 102, 107–108, 183–184, 188,
      193–199, 206–207, 252, 264, 277, 291, 293,
      300, 301, 325, 360, 387
  Native American, 68
  needs of, 125, 147, 151, 287, 325, 336, 388
  nontraditional, 28, 56, 59, 62, 72, 74–75, 92, 93,
      102, 159, 179–180, 182, 187, 206–208,
      234–235, 257, 277, 336, 348, 359, 366
  organizations for, 104, 125
  outcomes for, 12, 30, 96, 104, 129, 132–134,
      176, 178, 184, 266, 268, 270, 272, 280–282,
      284, 286, 288, 290–291, 296, 305–306, 321,
      377
  Pacific Islander, 61, 346
  part-time, 61–62, 179, 181, 232, 296, 319, 336
  preparation of, 74, 76, 102, 118, 120, 179–183,
      187, 188, 207, 232, 237, 257, 263, 273,
      276–277, 394
  profiles of, 320–321
  research about, 179, 182, 187, 244, 321, 377,
      384, 390
  residential, 58, 62, 181, 233, 247, 305
  retention of, 92, 93, 107, 193, 210
  satisfaction with college, 186, 268–269, 272,
      300, 301, 305–306, 388, 389
  self-efficacy of, 146, 194–195, 198–199, 204,
      206–208, 245–246, 248, 255–258, 264, 295,
      300, 301
  socialization of, 190, 201, 218, 320
  stress of, 198–199, 217, 237–238, 257–258, 262
  success for, 194–199, 201, 204, 206–207, 237,
      262, 263, 272, 294, 335, 341
  transfer, 66, 181, 186, 233, 296, 302, 306, 323,
      336, 337
Study abroad programs, 124, 234, 350–351
Study Group on the Condition of Excellence in
      American Higher Education, 81
Stufflebeam, Daniel, 285
Substantive:
  disciplines, 145–146, 170
  structure, 145, 149, 164–165

Summative evaluation, 268, 275–276, 284

Surveys (*see* Assessment, Evaluation)

Sustaining Vitality in General Education, 81

Svinicki, Marilla, 251, 263

Symbol systems, 145, 149, 150, 154, 155–156, 164, 165–166, 169, 170, 178, 261

Synoptic disciplines, 145, 146, 154–55, 162

Syntactical structure, 145, 149, 150, 154, 164, 166

Syracuse University, 136, 175, 271

Taba, Hilda, 10

Task performance, 150, 168, 292

Task Group on General Education (*see* Association of American Colleges)

Teaching (*see* Faculty, Instructional processes)

Teaching Critical Thinking, 243

Teaching Goals Inventory, 153

Teaching Tips, 134, 229

Technical fields/schools, 46, 53, 149, 164–165, 192, 369

Technology (*see also* Computers, Distance education):
    awareness stage of acceptance of, 363–367
    developments in, 14, 47, 74, 358, 392
    electronic forms of, 5, 94–95, 253, 343–344, 361, 364
    implications of, 208, 350, 360, 366, 384
    instructional use of, 110–111, 131, 273, 351, 363–364, 370
    Internet, 364–367
    World Wide Web, 364, 367

Temporality, in curriculum structure, 137–138

Terenzini, Patrick T., 298, 382

Tests (*see* Instructional activities)

Textbooks (*see* Instructional activities)

Thematic-based general education, 172, 173

Thielens, Wagner, 114

Thinking skills:
    as educational goal, 12–13, 74, 147–148, 151–153, 155, 172, 203, 206, 219–220, 238, 239, 244, 245–246, 249, 250, 252–253, 255, 256, 264, 270, 288, 294, 297, 331, 344, 360–368, 380
    and learning, 209–210, 239, 243–244, 251, 294, 382, 384

Theory:
    of academic plan, 24, 40–41, 165, 374–394
    and practice, 150, 165, 187, 217, 247, 385–392

Thomas Edison College, 187

Thorndike, Robert, 70

Tierney, William, 18, 38, 348

Time for Results: The Governors' 1991 Report on Education, 81, 83, 86, 96

Timeline, historical, 1600s–1994, 424–437

Time/time management, 221–222, 226, 229, 237–238, 258, 263

Title VI of the Higher Education Act, 350

Toombs, William, 18, 24, 35, 37–38, 115, 139, 376

To Reclaim a Legacy: A Report on the Humanities in Higher Education, 80, 84, 90, 92, 94, 96, 101

To Secure the Blessings of Liberty: Report of the National Commission on the Role and Future of State Colleges and Universities, 81, 84, 92, 93, 95, 96–96

Total Quality Management (TQM), 271, 280, 324, 351, 389–392 (*see also* Continuous Quality Improvement)

Toulmin, S., 144, 146, 147

Traditionalists, 144, 348–349, 352–353, 370, 377

Transcripts, studies of, 100, 279, 303, 382–383

Transfer students (*see* Students, transfer)

Transforming Knowledge, 347–348

Transforming the State Role in Higher Education, 81–82, 93, 96

"Transitional knowers," 204–206, 209

Treisman, Uri, 277

Trends:
    and academic planning, 6, 272, 282, 329–330, 343–373, 377, 394
    and administrators, 281, 341–342, 392

Truman Commission, 59

Trust, in teaching environment, 271, 335, 390

Tucker, Marc, 108

Two-year colleges, 53, 55, 60, 61, 72, 93, 143, 168, 346

Tyler, Ralph, 31–32, 284, 383

Undergraduate education, 46, 48, 82, 94, 99, 133, 353, 357 (*see also* Students):
    and academic field, 141, 163
    and assessment, 108, 275
    and internationalism, 350–351
    numbers of, 51, 60
    reforms proposed in, 85–86

Unfinished Design: The Humanities and Social Sciences in Undergraduate Engineering Education, 81

Unions, 33, 317, 334

"Universities without walls," 60

University of Alaska, 366
University of California, Berkeley, 277
University of California, Los Angeles, 75–76, 100, 187
University of California, Santa Cruz, 131
University of California system, 66, 357
University of Maine, 366
University of Michigan, 58, 81, 100
University of Mid-America, 366
University of Missouri-Columbia, 301
University of Pennsylvania, 74
University of Tennessee, 100, 286, 280, 281
University of Texas, Austin, 251
University of Utah, 319
University of Virginia, 48
University of Wisconsin, 70
"Urban disciplines", 147
Utilitarian mission of, 46, 56

Vallance, E., 32
Validation processes, 153–154, 161
Value-added assessment, 31, 85, 298–299
Value-oriented curriculum, 172–173, 376
Values:
    clarification of, 12, 25, 118, 104, 152–155, 171, 368, 376
    and conceptual maps, 202
    in education, 23, 176, 200, 215, 270, 360
    and evaluation, 285, 328
    structure of, in academic fields, 145, 149–150, 164, 166–167, 169, 174, 178
    of students, 300, 305

Veterinary medicine, 54
Videodiscs/tapes, 273, 351, 364
Vietnam War, 65, 339
Virtual On-line University, 366–367
Vocational education (*see* Occupational programs)

Weimer, Maryellen, 217, 229
Weiner, B., 195
Weinstein, Claire E., 192, 193
Western civilization, in curriculum, 53, 65, 84, 106–107, 131, 336–337, 353
Wharton, Clifton, Jr., 349–350
Wingspread Group on Higher Education, 81, 104
Women (*see* Students, Academic fields, *listed*)
Wood, Lynn, 341
Work (*see* Connectedness)
Workforce (*see* Job market)
Work–study programs, 233–234
Worth, as program criterion, 275–276, 284, 285, 313, 327, 328 (*see also* Merit)
Worthen, B. R., 283
Writing skills, 53, 107, 120, 166, 182, 183, 215, 217, 227, 232, 236–237, 243, 245, 250–251, 255, 258, 269–270, 273, 277, 291, 292, 294–296, 298–299, 307, 332, 348, 361
Wyer, Jean C., 65

Yale Report of 1828, 47, 64, 102, 352, 393

Zemsky, Robert, 81, 383
Zero-based budgeting, 324